READER'S DIGEST

—

You and the Law

—

The Reader's Digest Association, Inc.
Pleasantville, New York   Montreal

ACKNOWLEDGMENTS

The editors of Reader's Digest gratefully acknowledge
the contributions to this book of Advisory Editor

Henry V. Poor
Associate Dean, Yale University Law School, 1967-1972

Mr. Poor's extensive and untiring help in the writing and editing of the manuscript and his conviction that legal principles can and should be made clear and easy to understand are in large part responsible for the usefulness and success of YOU AND THE LAW.

The editors wish to express their thanks to the New Jersey State Bar Association, New York University School of Law, Northeastern University School of Law and more than 200 state and federal offices and agencies for their assistance in updating the charts in this Second Revised Edition.

CONTENTS

IV. Your Protection Against Crime and Criminal Charges

V. Your Personal Property, Contracts and Purchases

YOUR RIGHT TO OWN, ENJOY AND DISPOSE OF PERSONAL PROPERTY

PATENTS, TRADE SECRETS, COPYRIGHTS AND TRADEMARKS

CONTRACTS

SALE AND PURCHASE OF GOODS

USE AND PROTECTION OF PROPERTY YOU ENTRUST TO OTHERS

VI. Your Automobile

OWNING AN AUTOMOBILE

OPERATING YOUR AUTOMOBILE

VII. Your Home, Apartment and Real Estate
RENTING YOUR HOME OR APARTMENT; RELATIONS BETWEEN LANDLORD AND TENANT

IX. Your Job, Profession or Business; Your Social Security

X. Your Money, Credit and Investments

YOUR MONEY, BANK ACCOUNTS AND CHECKS

YOUR CREDIT AND PERSONAL LOANS

WHEN YOU CAN'T PAY: INSOLVENCY AND BANKRUPTCY

IF YOU INVEST YOUR MONEY

INSURANCE AGAINST SICKNESS AND ACCIDENT

XII. Your Estate, Will and Death

MAKING YOUR WILL

IF YOU DIE WITHOUT MAKING A WILL

INTRODUCTION

Law is the set of rules that we have established to make it easier for us to live with one another. It has grown out of thousands of years of experience, and it is still growing and changing as our society grows and changes. The law affects all of us every day in almost everything we do, whether we are aware of it or not.

People think of law as a complicated field, and in a sense they are right. The law must encompass all the complex elements of human society. But everyone can understand its fundamental principles—and it is important enough to us so that we should be familiar with them.

YOU AND THE LAW will give you just this kind of basic but essential legal knowledge: information that will save you needless worry, trouble and possible expense. It will help you to understand the legal principles that underlie even ordinary transactions—buying a house or a television set, writing a check, getting married, taking out an insurance policy, joining a union, lending a car to a friend, signing a lease—and hundreds of other everyday activities.

This book is *not* intended as a substitute for a lawyer, however, nor as a do-it-yourself kit. It does suggest when you may or may not require a lawyer's services. But in any serious situation or when you are in doubt, there is no substitute for competent professional advice. Trying to act as your own lawyer can be costly and—in some instances—dangerous.

YOU AND THE LAW will help you to be a better-informed client when you do seek professional counsel, and in this way it will help your lawyer to serve you better when you need his advice. It will also enable you to understand the lawyer's role and the problems he must consider in handling the legal matter you have taken to him, so that the two of you can cooperate more effectively to further your own best interests.

It will lead you to understand the lawyer's value to the community and to your own family, not only in helping you in times of trouble, but in handling routine affairs in such a way that problems are less likely to arise in the future. You will see the desirability of having a family lawyer as a friend and counselor like your doctor and your clergyman.

As you read through the book, you will also get a better idea of what "the law" is—that it is not a rigidly fixed body of rules, but a complex interweaving of court decisions, state and federal statutes, regulations and procedures. You will see how interpretations of the different state laws by different courts—or small variations in the circumstances of a case—may lead to very different conclusions in two seemingly similar situations. You will discover that there are no final answers. The law lives, grows and changes. No book or set of books, however large, can tell you with complete assurance what is "right," what is "wrong" or what the final outcome of any case will be.

One reason that people are sometimes reluctant to consult a lawyer or to inform themselves on legal topics is their feeling that the language lawyers use is intentionally mysterious, designed to baffle the layman. In YOU AND THE LAW we have attempted to discuss common legal problems in language that is clear and simple, but still accurate. Wherever possible, we have presented legal subjects as though you, the reader, were personally involved. We have invented situations in which you are the imaginary buyer or seller, plaintiff or defendant, so that you can see more easily how the theory of law applies in human situations.

A book of this size cannot cover all legal subjects. For example, YOU AND THE LAW does not discuss admiralty or international law so it can give more coverage to legal matters that confront us in our daily lives. It does not deal with the huge field of income taxation, both because the law changes so often and because its problems are as much financial as legal. Similarly, it devotes little attention to complex business problems, since anyone involved in them would most likely already have his own lawyer. In many of the areas that we do discuss, the law changes surprisingly fast. Enormous developments have taken place in a short time in two areas that now receive much publicity: civil rights and liberties, and criminal law and procedure. Our treatment of these subjects tries to point up trends rather than to give you clear-cut statements of "the law."

YOU AND THE LAW devotes a chapter to each major area of the law that is likely to affect you. The treatment of each area is deliberately general, because no two of our fifty states have exactly the same constitution, statutes, courts or case decisions. For details you are referred to a chart showing the law of your state on a specific subject of importance. Topics are also cross-referenced back and forth among the chapters, so that you can easily find the information you need. In the back of the book there is a glossary of legal terms, a law dictionary to help you with words that may be unfamiliar to you.

The part your lawyer plays in our legal system is discussed fully in chapter 14, with suggestions as to how you can find legal help when you need it and how you can work most effectively with your lawyer.

Remember the importance of seeking advice when you need it. No book can give you the final word on any legal subject. So keep in mind our first and only "final word": when in doubt, see your lawyer.

HOW TO USE THIS BOOK

YOU AND THE LAW is divided into fourteen chapters and 651 consecutively numbered topical sections, each of which discusses a specific aspect of the law as it affects you and the members of your family in your everyday lives. The descriptive titles of the chapters and sections are listed in the complete table of contents, which begins on page 3.

We suggest that you skim the table of contents now in order to get a general idea of the organization of YOU AND THE LAW and to see how the various areas of the law it covers are related to one another.

Using the Table of Contents

The table of contents is your first step in looking for the information you want. Let's say that you need to know what points should be covered in a contract for the sale of a house. As you look through the contents, you will see that chapter 7 is entitled "Your Home, Apartment and Real Estate" and that the second part of the chapter is called "Buying Your Home." Immediately under this heading, you will see several numbered topical headings, including **"281. The Contract."** By turning to section 281 you will find what you want to know.

Using the Cross-reference System

Within the topical section that discusses your particular interest, you will often find cross-references to other sections that deal with related subjects or supply more information on the same topic. For example, in section 281 on the contract for the sale of a house you will find cross-references to section 180, which discusses when contracts must be in writing; section 283, which gives information about deeds; section 291, which describes kinds of mortgages; and many others. By turning to these sections, you will find more information on these subjects.

Using the Index

You can also find the information you want by consulting the complete and comprehensive index at the back of the book. The index refers you to topics by page number. In the example we have been discussing, either *sale, real property* or *property, real: sales contract* refers you to page 317 where the information appears.

Using the Glossary

An alphabetical glossary of over 1,000 legal terms appears on pages 749–821. Many entries include cross-references to topical sections in the text that help to explain the definition given.

Using the Charts

Throughout the book are charts that summarize some of the important laws of the fifty states and the District of Columbia. Cross-references in the text will direct you to those charts that give detailed information about the subject you are interested in. The charts are also indexed.

These charts are based on the most up-to-date law digests available and have been carefully researched and checked. Do not act in reliance on information in them, however, without confirming its accuracy with a lawyer or with the appropriate state agency. This important reservation is necessary because:

State laws frequently change.

The laws on which the charts are based may have been revised since this book went to press.

Statutes are complicated.

The brief summaries suitable for chart presentation are necessarily simplified and cannot take into account all the complications or possible interpretations of a law that may fill many printed pages.

CHAPTER ONE

What Is the Law?

The law is the witness and external deposit
of our moral life. Its history is the history
of the moral development of the race.

—OLIVER WENDELL HOLMES, JR.

1

What Is the Law?

WHERE OUR LAW COMES FROM

No one has neatly defined law in all its aspects. It is the sum total of the rules men and women live by if there is to be any order. No society can last long without some kind of legal system. Even dictators claim to follow legal rules. Under our Anglo-American system laws are a restraint on both government and people. Law reflects society. A simple rural community needs relatively few laws. A complex industrial society such as ours needs a complicated legal framework, which in turn creates a need for persons specially trained to the law. These people are judges and lawyers. What they do is not mysterious. Every citizen owes it to himself to have some knowledge of the essentials of law and our legal system.

1. The Early Background of Our Legal System • Suppose you want to draw a family tree of our American laws and procedures for enforcing them. To find the roots, you would have to go very far back into history. Perhaps the earliest root you could find would be in 1900 B.C. It was in approximately that year that the Code of Hammurabi was set forth for the ancient Sumerians who lived in civilization's cradle along the Tigris and Euphrates rivers. That code contains the first known system of law. It describes various offenses and indicates the penalties for each. Our phrase for such a system is "criminal law" (see chapter 4, "Your Protection Against Crime and Criminal Charges," page 133). The next famous codification of laws was the Ten Commandments, given to the Jewish people by Moses around 1200 B.C. These commandments are woven into the fabric of Western society. We find their precepts written into many of our laws, such as those against murder, adultery, perjury.

You would find another important root in ancient Greece, which went far to develop the philosophy, often expressed in the United States today, that a country should be ruled by law, not by men. The Greeks had well-understood laws of property, contracts and commerce generally. They also started to try legal cases before citizens whom we call jurors.

As the Greek culture gave way to the Roman, these basic but simple early roots merged gradually into a much more complete and carefully spelled-out body of law. The Twelve Tables published in Rome in 450 B.C. were a set of moral principles and practices for use by Romans alone. A thousand years later all laws were brought together and codified, or put into a code—Corpus Juris Civilis ("Body of Civil Laws")—under the

Emperor Justinian I about 560 A.D. The Corpus Juris was the most complete collection of laws up to that time and had enormous influence on the development of law in the countries that were part of or controlled by the Roman Empire. As the Roman Empire gradually fell apart, much of Roman law became the canon law of the Roman Catholic church. These several strands were tied together under Napoleon in 1804. The Napoleonic Code is the basis of civil law in Louisiana, which was settled by the French and did not come into the United States until 1812.

2. The Common Law • Your search for all the roots of modern American law is not ended, however, until you locate another one that is harder both to find and to describe or explain. This root is loosely called common law. Its beginnings are lost in the mists of the history of northern Europe and Scandinavia, which were scarcely touched by the influence of the Roman Empire and from which England was frequently invaded by peoples who remained, intermarried with the local citizens and greatly affected their customs and habits. These local customs became well established. Although the Romans ruled Britain for almost 400 years, the development of the Justinian code and of Roman law was still 100 years away when they left England. Canon law did not come to England until 600 A.D., when the English were converted to Christianity. This law of the church has been a significant factor in English legal history and has acquired a name all its own—equity. For a great many years two parallel courts existed in England, courts of equity, which were free to apply principles of conscience, and common-law courts. The common law is so called because it was commonly applied throughout the kingdom of England.

The last successful invasion of England was by the Normans in 1066. From then on, the English were able to develop their own legal system. They did so in a typically English manner. They avoided the method of trying to write all known laws down on paper. They won basic rights from their rulers, such as Magna Charta from King John in 1215. For the rest, they contented themselves with the developing courts and with trials by jury for contests between individual citizens over property, personal injuries and contracts. From time to time acts of Parliament were relied on to define specific crimes and to prescribe penalties. Judges and members of Parliament made British law by bits and pieces. This, then, is the common law: custom, tradition, decisions by judges in specific cases and acts of Parliament.

This system had been well established in the 400 years between 1215 and 1620, when the Pilgrims landed on Plymouth Rock. In the early years of the American colonies, the legal experience differed considerably according to the background of the settlers. Lawyers were few; important cases were decided in London. Nevertheless, it is fair to say that the common law became the most important single root of the American legal system.

The important thing to remember about the common law as it affects us today is that in talking about "the law" we are really talking about two different kinds of law: case law and statutory law. *Case law* is based on the earlier decisions reached by courts in similar situations. It comes down to us in the form of written court decisions. The principles set forth in these decisions must be applied anew to the particular facts in every individual case that comes before a court. The earlier decisions that embody these principles are called *precedents*. On the other hand, *statutory law* comes to us in the form of written laws, or *acts*, whose exact words have been drafted and approved by a federal, state or local legislature. We refer to these statutes when we talk about the "laws" of a nation, state or city.

3. Our Federal System • The end of the colonial period in 1776 meant the end of the only governmental system the colonists had known: colonial legislatures with limited powers, a British governor in each colony, with final authority existing 3,000 miles away in the British monarchy in London. An entirely new governmental system had to be developed after the Declaration of Independence in 1776. That it took time to do so is understandable. But in 1789 the United States Constitution was formally adopted, and it created the governmental framework for our new and unique legal system.

Our system is unique because it is federal. The United States government exists alongside the governments of the different states. We have two overlapping governmental systems, each of which has authority in some areas but not in others. The states have no authority in foreign affairs; the U.S. government has no right to tax real property. In most of the states the people elect senior officials: (a) of the executive branches of the federal and state governments (President, Vice-President, governor, lieutenant governor and so on); (b) of the legislative branches (senators, members of the House of Representatives, state senators and state assemblymen); and (c) of part of the judicial branches (judges of the state and local courts). Judges of the various federal courts are appointed for life by the President, with the consent of the U.S. Senate.

Our American sysem of government seems to some unwieldy or top-heavy. As we have said, our system is really two systems: national, on the one hand, and state and local, on the other. Moreover, each of the two systems has the three branches, supposed to be equal in power: the executive, the legislative and the judicial. The whole apparatus seems cumbersome at times.

But we should remember that it was planned that way, not with the thought of being cumbersome, but with the thought that there was no other way to avoid or prevent what was feared most in 1789: an all-powerful executive in an all-powerful national government. The years that have passed since 1789 have seen a gradual growth in the power of the national government at the expense of the state governments. Governmental experts for many years have predicted, some with enthusiasm and others with dismay, that sooner or later the states will have little power left. The states are still flourishing, however, and there are those who believe they see signs that the states' powers may be revived as some people become disillusioned with the inability of the national government to handle many of today's and tomorrow's problems.

How Our Laws Are Made and Enforced

4. Our Constitutions: Basic Laws • The basic laws of the land are contained in our constitutions: the U.S. Constitution and the constitutions of our fifty states. The U.S. Constitution can be amended—theoretically, abolished—in one of two ways: (a) two thirds of the members of both houses of Congress (the Senate and the House of Representatives) may propose amendments, or (b) on the application of the legislatures of two thirds of the states, Congress calls a convention for proposing amendments. Whichever method for considering amendments is chosen, the amendments become part of the Constitution only when ratified either by the legislatures of three fourths of the states or by special conventions in three fourths of the states. Congress determines which of the two ratification procedures is to be followed. In fact, the only method yet used for adopting any of the present twenty-six amendments to the U.S. Constitution has been the proposal of the amendment by Congress and later the ratification by state legislatures.

Constitutions of the various states vary widely as to provisions for their amendment. Some states require a constitutional convention every so often. Other states seldom change their constitutions. Some state constitutions are as short as that of the United States, while others occupy hundreds of pages.

All our constitutions, whether briefly or at length, set out the basic governmental structure of executive, legislative and judicial branches. The judicial is the one that most concerns us in this book. It is the branch that has to do with the courts and their powers and responsibilities and with the licensing of lawyers, generally regarded as officers of the courts.

5. The Executive • The executive branch of our federal, state and local governments is most familiar to us as it is personified in a chief executive: the President of the United States, the governor of a state, the mayor of a city. The chief executive is usually an elected official who holds office for a term of years specified in the constitution or charter. It is the responsibility of the executive branch to propose new laws to the legislature, to approve or disapprove laws that have been passed and to enforce the statutes that are on the books. In other words, it is the job of the executive to see that the government runs as it is supposed to. While the executive branch has no power to pass laws, it does set up regulatory and administrative agencies—ranging in scope from the U.S. Department of Agriculture and the Veterans Administration to a county roads bureau —that have a certain discretionary power to make and enforce regulations in their areas of administration (see section 9).

6. The Legislature • Legislatures are the law-making branches of federal, state and local governments. The Congress of the United States, a state assembly and a city board of aldermen or a city council are all legislatures. Many legislatures are divided into two parts or houses (often called a senate and a house of representatives, as in the U.S. Congress), whose members are elected for terms of varying lengths. Each house must vote in favor of a bill before it is sent on to the executive to be signed into law. The U.S. Constitution and the constitutions of most of the states provide for the passage of a bill into law despite the objection of the executive branch if a sufficiently large majority of the legislators vote in favor of the bill. This process is known as overriding a veto. Laws passed by state legislatures are called statutes; those by municipal legislatures, ordinances.

Any law passed by the legislative branch may be reviewed by the judicial branch of the government if someone affected by the law argues that it is contrary to the state or federal constitution. If a court with proper jurisdiction finds that a law is unconstitutional, it becomes inoperative. This power of the courts to examine the constitutionality of laws passed by the legislature is called the *right of judicial review*. It is one of the strongest weapons a citizen has in protecting his constitutional rights.

7. Federal Courts · The federal judicial system is simple. There is at least one U.S. district court in each of the fifty states. Heavily populated states have more than one district court. These U.S. district courts are what lawyers call *courts of general jurisdiction:* they have the power to hear and pass judgment on both civil and criminal cases, that is, cases involving claimed violations of your personal civil rights and cases involving violations of federal criminal laws. In civil cases, however, there are two restrictions on persons suing in the federal district courts: the plaintiff and the defendant must be residents of different states, and the amount involved in the lawsuit must be $10,000 or more. If you as a resident of Utah have a claim against a fellow resident of Utah for $11,000 for breach of contract (see section 184), you may not sue in the U.S. district court system. But you could if you were a resident of Arizona. As lawyers put it, there must be "diversity of citizenship" in most cases in order to enable you to sue in the U.S. district court. Moreover, even though there is diversity of citizenship, if the amount of the claim is only $9,000, the U.S. court is not open to you.

There are some kinds of lawsuits, however, that do not depend on diversity of citizenship or on the "jurisdictional amount" of $10,000. These cases belong exclusively in the U.S. district courts either because the Constitution says so or because Congress has said so. Among these cases are lawsuits in bankruptcy, patents, trademarks and copyrights, and in admiralty (disputes involving maritime matters or matters pertaining to or arising from the use of navigational waters).

Alongside the U.S. district courts are several U.S. courts of limited jurisdiction, which handle only certain kinds of cases: the United States Court of Claims, to handle lawsuits against the U.S. government; the United States Customs Court, to handle cases arising under the tariff laws; and the United States Tax Court, which handles cases arising under the Internal Revenue Code.

There are also several U.S. courts that are concerned only with *appeals,* or pleas for the reversal of decisions by lower courts. In each of ten districts around the United States, and in the District of Columbia, there is a U.S. court of appeals to handle appeals from decisions by the

OUR FEDERAL COURT SYSTEM

UNITED STATES SUPREME COURT
Washington, D.C.

Tries lawsuits between the states. May review decisions of federal appellate courts and specialized federal courts. May review decisions of the highest court of appeals in a state if a constitutional question or federal law is involved.

CHART
1

Decisions of highest
state courts for review

U.S. COURTS OF APPEALS

Eleven courts, often called circuit courts, sitting in each of 10 judicial circuits and the District of Columbia. Hear appeals from U.S. district courts and review decisions of federal administrative agencies.

U.S. COURT OF CUSTOMS AND PATENT APPEALS
Washington, D.C.

U.S. COURT OF CLAIMS

Hears suits against the U.S. government. Evidence may be given before court commissioners at various locations throughout the country.

U.S. DISTRICT COURTS

Approximately 90 courts sitting in all parts of the United States and in Puerto Rico and the Virgin Islands. Try both civil and criminal cases, as explained in section 7, and sit as bankruptcy and admiralty courts as well. May review decisions of federal administrative agencies.

TAX COURT OF THE UNITED STATES
Washington, D.C.

Hears cases arising under federal tax laws.

U.S. CUSTOMS COURT
New York, N.Y.

Hears cases arising under federal tariff laws.

U.S. COURT OF MILITARY APPEALS
Washington, D.C.

Hears appeals from court-martial convictions. There is no further appeal from the decisions of this court.

Appeals from
military tribunals

31

U.S. district courts within those ten districts and the District of Columbia. In Washington, D.C., are the United States Court of Customs and Patent Appeals and the United States Court of Military Appeals, which is the final appellate court in court-martial cases.

Sitting majestically atop this whole structure of federal courts is the United States Supreme Court. Of course, it has power to entertain appeals from all federal appellate courts. In some cases it is also authorized to take an appeal directly from a U.S. district court. Wherever the highest court in one of the states decides a question interpreting the U.S. Constitution, the Supreme Court has jurisdiction to review that decision. An unsuccessful plaintiff or defendant in such a case may request a review by the U.S. Supreme Court by filing a *writ of certiorari*. The Court may then decide whether or not the legal questions presented by the case justify review. Finally, the U.S. Supreme Court is the only court with the power to handle a lawsuit between two states.

8. State and Local Courts • The judiciary, or judicial systems, of the various states varies widely, but the same general pattern prevails as in the federal judiciary. At the lowest level is a series of courts with very limited jurisdiction or power. Their names differ, the name usually conveying a good idea of the specific function of the court.

In metropolitan areas there are *small claims courts,* for handling cases where the amount involved is small, usually between $100 and $500: a plaintiff is suing for nondelivery of an upholstered chair he bought from the defendant, a department store; a plaintiff corner grocer is suing to collect overdue bills in the total amount of $250; a plaintiff is suing the city for $400 damages caused to his home by the carelessness of the water meter inspector. (For more details, see section 620.) As you will find in chapter 8, the more heavily populated states have *family courts,* which deal exclusively with minors and juvenile delinquents; the less populated states give special jurisdiction in juvenile cases to judges of the regular court system who handle cases involving juveniles. *Traffic courts* have jurisdiction only over minor traffic violations. In the more rural parts of the country traffic cases may be handled by *police court judges,* who have jurisdiction over minor offenses and misdemeanors. Many states have special *probate courts* for handling the probate, or proving, of wills and of claims against estates of persons who die with or without wills (see section 585). Appeals can be taken from the decision of all such courts of limited jurisdiction to one—and sometimes more than one —higher court designated by state statute.

OUR STATE AND LOCAL COURTS

No two states have identical court systems, but all are similar in their general outlines. This diagram shows the profile of an imaginary but typical system of state and local courts.

STATE SUPREME COURT

Hears appeals from all inferior courts of record. Court of last resort except for constitutional matters, which may be appealed to U.S. Supreme Court.

INTERMEDIATE APPELLATE COURTS

(In some states only)
Hear appeals from the decisions of courts of general and special jurisdiction and from criminal courts.

TRIAL COURTS

DISTRICT, COUNTY OR MUNICIPAL COURT
Has general jurisdiction: hears civil suits and criminal cases.

JUVENILE OR FAMILY COURT
Hears domestic, juvenile delinquency and youthful offender cases.

PROBATE COURT
Probates wills and hears claims against estates.

CRIMINAL COURT
Hears criminal cases.

LOCAL COURTS

(Cases heard in these courts frequently cannot be appealed. Names may vary according to locality.)

Traffic Court
Police Court
Small Claims Court
Justice of the Peace

Immediately above these "special purpose" courts are state *courts of general jurisdiction,* that is, courts that are empowered to entertain any case where the amount involved exceeds a certain sum, say $3,000. Such courts of general jurisdiction handle criminal as well as civil cases. By and large, the civil cases coming before these courts involve violation of contracts; the commission of torts (see chapter 3, "Your Protection Against Wrongs," page 81), including a huge number of personal injury and negligence cases arising out of automobile accidents, and libel and slander actions; divorce, annulment and other matrimonial actions; plus a variety of cases involving the use of property, such as zoning and condemnation by the state for highway or other public construction.

The size of a state determines whether it has one or more levels of *appellate courts,* courts that entertain only appeals from lower courts. The respective roles of the trial and the appellate courts are important.

Trial courts have the responsibility of finding the facts in a particular case: Did the landlord overcharge the tenant? Did the defendant drive fifty miles in a thirty-mile-an-hour zone? Did the city building inspector say he wouldn't certify the building as fit for occupancy unless he was paid $100? Did the shipping company fail to deliver 1,000 gallons of oil as it had promised? Such facts as these are determined in a trial, sometimes by a jury, sometimes by a judge without a jury. The judge then applies the law to the facts as the jury finds them.

The *appellate court,* at least in theory, does not review the trial court's findings of fact; its only function is to decide whether the trial judge correctly applied the law. If the appellate court believes he did, his decision is upheld. But if it finds that the trial judge did make a mistake in applying the law to the facts—or in procedure—it will reverse or modify the decision. When an appellate court reverses a lower court's decision, it has the alternative of letting the matter stand or of returning the case to the lower court for a new trial or for any further proceedings that seem appropriate. If the subject matter of the lawsuit in the state court involves a right under the U.S. Constitution—if, for example, the plaintiff charges that under a state statute his property has been taken without full court review (violating his Constitutional right to due process of law)—and the highest state court decides the constitution is *not* violated, an appeal may be taken to the U.S. Supreme Court. That Court always has the last word on matters involving the U.S. Constitution.

9. Administrative Agencies • One other source of laws—apart from constitutions, judicial decisions and the statutes or ordinances passed by

34

federal, state and local legislatures—is the decisions and rulings of administrative agencies. By *administrative agencies* we mean the whole range from old-line governmental departments like the departments of State, Treasury and Labor, through the newer federal regulatory agencies like the Federal Communications Commission, the Atomic Energy Commission and the Food and Drug Administration, to the state departments of education and motor vehicles, and the purely local offices such as the city health department and police department.

In general, the courts are reluctant to interfere with the operations and rulings of these governmental departments. As an example, despite all the hue and cry over the U.S. Department of State's refusal to validate U.S. passports for travel in certain countries, the courts have refused to order the department to do so. The courts will not intervene unless there is convincing evidence that a governmental agency is acting arbitrarily or unreasonably. In decision after decision in cases involving administrative action or inaction, the courts express the opinion that they don't know the reasons for what the agency is doing or not doing, and therefore they decline to force an administrator's hand.

A classic legal remedy called a *writ of mandamus* (from the Latin word meaning "we command") was used long ago to compel administrative action. Usually, however, American courts issue a writ of mandamus to compel routine action where there seems to be no good reason for its not being taken. The public election official who, from sheer spite, declines to issue a certificate of election to the obvious winner might be compelled to do so by the courts in response to a plea for a writ of mandamus. But it is extremely doubtful that the Securities and Exchange Commission would be ordered, by a writ of mandamus, to approve a particular issue of common stock by a corporation. The court would probably say that the approval or disapproval of stock issues is exactly what the Securities and Exchange Commission was created to do and that the courts have no business substituting their uninformed judgment for the expert knowledge and experience of the members and staff of the commission.

Some of these governmental departments and agencies, particularly the regulatory agencies, do make what amount to laws or issue instructions that have the effect of laws. The Securities and Exchange Commission regulates the securities markets, such as the stock exchanges, by issuing rules that can result in heavy penalties if they are violated. The Food and Drug Administration can require drug manufacturers to put labels on their products warning the public against their misuse or even their use.

35

The Department of Agriculture tightly controls how much of what farm products may be sold. State highway departments have wide authority for the control of speed on the highways and the licensing of operators of motor vehicles. State public utility commissions set the rates that may be charged by telephone companies and by power and light companies.

Because all these agencies and departments are run by human beings, occasions are bound to arise when their orders, rules or instructions are unlawful, unjustified or unclear. They can be tested in the courts. Regulations that seem carefully designed to achieve a purpose for which the agency was created will not lightly be reversed. To protest such a regulation effectively, you must be able to establish that it is vague or discriminatory, or that it doesn't achieve a public purpose, or that it is beyond the powers of the agency, or that the agency in trying to fine or otherwise penalize you didn't give you adequate notice of your wrongdoing or an opportunity to have your alleged wrongdoing judicially reviewed. The courts are too busy to interfere with the day-to-day operations of government departments and will not do so unless their attention is caught by charges of improper behavior resulting in the threatened loss of your recognized legal rights.

WRITTEN LAWS AND RECORDS

10. Statutes, Regulations and Decisions • All the laws under which you live and work exist somewhere, in black and white. We have already noted what they are: the U.S. Constitution, the constitution of your state, the acts or statutes adopted by the U.S. Congress and by the legislature of your state and the local ordinances of your community's legislature (called by a variety of names, such as city council, board of aldermen, town or village board). These are, altogether, the constitutional and the legislative laws that affect you. The administrative laws or regulations are the ones we have discussed in the previous section, such as the rules of the motor vehicle bureau of your state or the regulations of the Internal Revenue Service. Finally, there are the decisions by the courts of the United States and of your own state. These decisions have the full force of the law behind them, meaning that what they say you must abide by, and the government will force you to, under penalty of fine or imprisonment or both.

You may ask where and how you can find all these laws and regulations. To find them all, you would have to go to a large public library. You should have no trouble finding the constitutions of the United States and of your state. And the librarian would help you locate acts of Congress, your state legislature and your local governing body and the regulations of major government departments and regulatory agencies. But to find the court cases that are meaningful to you, to interpret and understand them, you must go to a lawyer. The books that line the walls of a law library contain records of court decisions in all kinds of cases that go back hundreds of years to the English common law.

11. Personal and Business Records • Basic personal documents or records are easy to find. Birth and death records are kept and certificates issued by different authorities around the country, usually by your local health department, occasionally by a state agency. Marriage licenses and certificates are issued either by the county clerk's office or by a municipal licensing office, and sometimes by a justice of the peace. Deeds to real estate are usually recorded in the county clerk's office, as are real estate and chattel mortgages and loans, leasing security agreements and conditional sales agreements. You would be wise to consult your lawyer, your local banker or a public accountant for information about what reports you may be required to file regarding any business you may operate.

Sources for birth, death, marriage and divorce records in the 50 states and the District of Columbia are shown on chart 3, page 40.

THE LAWYERS AND THE COURTS

12. Where Lawyers Fit In • Lawyers are to the courts what doctors are to hospitals: the trained professional men and women who use the services offered for the benefit of their clients, the legal equivalent of patients. But the lawyer is by no means simply a figure in a courtroom drama. He has an even more important role in advising his client in such a way that he need never go to court in the first place. Many successful lawyers have never entered a courtroom in their lives.

Among the various tasks that lawyers perform, the most important from the point of view of the average person is that of counseling individuals about the many transactions that come up in their daily lives which may not require the services of a courtroom specialist but do require legal advice. Even here some trial experience will enable a lawyer better to judge what may happen if a case should reach the courtroom. But in most situations you need not a fiery orator but a sensible adviser who will help you buy a house, draft a will or interpret a contract.

Nonetheless, if you are the object of a serious lawsuit, it is imperative that you have a trained trial lawyer to represent you in court. And if you are prosecuted for a major crime, it is your right to have one.

Many people do not fully understand or even accept the right of the accused to a lawyer's help, and because they don't, they find it somehow improper or immoral that lawyers should be available for the defense of all accused persons.

To the lawyer who knows our legal system and its heritage, the attitude of these people is equally hard to understand. To him, a legal contest is a substitute for a duel—an "adversary proceeding" in which the lawyer's duty is to do anything he can to advance his client's interest. He may not violate the canons of professional ethics, and unless he treats the judge with a minimum of respect he may be held in contempt of court. Within these limits the lawyer is a warrior for his client, using skills of expression and argumentation and drawing upon his knowledge of the law and of human nature so that his client's case will appear stronger than that of his opponent, whether the opponent is John Doe in a civil case or the people in a criminal case.

For a complete discussion of the lawyer's role, see chapter 14, "Your Lawyer," page 719.

13. The Adversary Proceeding—Cornerstone of Our System • The fact that a trial is a fair contest—called by lawyers an *adversary proceeding* —makes it the cornerstone of justice under our system of law. In chapter 3, "Your Protection Against Wrongs," page 81, and chapter 4, "Your Protection Against Crime and Criminal Charges," page 133, the role of the lawyer in handling civil and criminal cases is set out more fully. All we are emphasizing here is the great value to the people of the adversary nature of legal proceedings under our American legal system. The lawyer's first and only responsibility is to his client. The judge, not the lawyer, is there to see to it that the public's interest is protected. The judge knows the rules—that is, the laws and the procedures that may be followed in court—and it's up to him to decide when a lawyer is trying to bend or twist them in his client's interest. Our system is an effort to make a trial a true adversary proceeding, a contest between two parties theoretically on a similar footing because each is represented by a lawyer thoroughly familiar with the law and how to make maximum use of it.

This idea is particularly important in criminal cases, where the whole power of the state may be turned against a single individual. In some countries the method of handling criminal proceedings is essentially different, with the judge acting as both judge and prosecutor. The accused is presumed guilty until his innocence can be proved. The judge is not an impartial arbiter between two opponents; his interest is in convicting the accused unless he can be convinced that the accusation is false or faulty under the law. In Anglo-American criminal procedure the judge is supposed to start off with an open mind. On the one hand, the public prosecutor—the state's, district or U.S. attorney—has the burden of establishing beyond a reasonable doubt that the accused actually committed an offense that is punishable by fine or imprisonment. On the other hand, the lawyer for the accused, in order to win an acquittal, need only raise doubts in the mind of the judge (and jury, if there is one) that the accused could have or did commit the offense as charged.

Is our Anglo-American legal system perfect? Of course not. But it is the only one in the world that tries to give evenhanded justice to all persons and to protect them from illegal prosecution by the government.

Are all our judges wise and free from prejudice? Of course not. But they are the only judges in the world who have real freedom to act as they think the law dictates and who can resist governmental pressures brought to bear on judges elsewhere.

Does the government have an advantage over the accused? Of course. It is scarcely the function of the judiciary to rule against the interests of government, to permit the creation of a condition of anarchy that would certainly mean the end of the rule of law. Yet many accused persons are found innocent, where the facts do not establish guilt beyond a reasonable doubt.

Does everyone accused of a crime in this country receive expert legal counsel? No, for a variety of reasons we shall discuss. But by rulings of the U.S. Supreme Court, the government in every state is now required to make a lawyer available to every person charged with the commission of a *felony,* or major offense. The U.S. government itself has adopted a statute making public funds available to pay lawyers for all persons accused of federal offenses. There is perhaps no other country in the world so careful to protect the legal rights of persons accused of crimes of any kind.

WHERE RECORDS ARE KEPT

CHART 3

Birth & Death Records	Marriage Records	Divorce Records
ALABAMA Since 1908: Division of Vital Statistics, State Department of Health, Montgomery 36130	Since August 1936: Division of Vital Statistics, State Department of Health, Montgomery 36130 Before August 1936: Probate judge, county where license issued	Since 1950: Division of Vital Statistics, State Department of Health, Montgomery 36130 Before 1950: Court of equity clerk or registrar, county where divorce granted
ALASKA Since 1913: Bureau of Vital Statistics, Department of Health and Social Services, Pouch H-02G, Juneau 99811	Bureau of Vital Statistics, Department of Health and Social Services, Pouch H-02G, Juneau 99811	Since 1950: Bureau of Vital Statistics, Department of Health and Social Services, Pouch H-02G, Juneau 99811 Before 1950: Superior court clerk, judicial district where divorce granted: Juneau & Ketchikan (1st district), Nome (2nd), Anchorage (3rd), Fairbanks (4th)
ARIZONA Vital Records Section, Department of Health Services, P.O. Box 3887, Phoenix 85030	Superior court clerk, county where license issued	Superior court clerk, county where divorce granted
ARKANSAS Since February 1914: Division of Vital Records, Arkansas Department of Health, Little Rock 72201	Since 1917: Division of Vital Records, Arkansas Department of Health, Little Rock 72201 Before 1917: County clerk, county where license issued	Since 1923: Division of Vital Records, Arkansas Department of Health, Little Rock 72201 Before 1923: County or chancery court clerk, county where divorce granted
CALIFORNIA Since July 1905: Vital Statistics Section, State Department of Health, 410 N Street, Sacramento 95814 Before July 1905: County recorder or city health office in county or city where event occurred	Vital Statistics Section, State Department of Health, 410 N Street, Sacramento 95814	Since 1962: Vital Statistics, Department of Health, 410 N Street, Sacramento 95814 Before 1962: Superior court clerk, county where divorce granted

Many occasions may arise when you need copies of birth, death, marriage or divorce records. This chart shows where to write in your state for information or copies of these records. The fee for a certified copy of a record (usually two dollars) must be paid in advance.

Birth & Death Records	Marriage Records	Divorce Records
COLORADO Records and Statistics Section, Department of Health, 4210 East 11th Avenue, Denver 80220	County clerk, county where license issued For statewide index of marriages: Records and Statistics Section, Department of Health, 4210 East 11th Avenue, Denver 80220	1940–1967: District or county court clerk, county where divorce granted Before 1940 and after 1967: Records and Statistics Section, Department of Health, 4210 East 11th Avenue, Denver 80220
CONNECTICUT Since July 1897: Public Health Statistics Section, State Department of Health, 79 Elm Street, Hartford 06115 Before July 1897: Registrar of vital statistics, town where event occurred	Since July 1897: Public Health Statistics Section, State Department of Health, 79 Elm Street, Hartford 06115 Before July 1897: Registrar of vital statistics, town where license issued	Since June 1947: Public Health Statistics Section, State Department of Health, 79 Elm Street, Hartford 06115 Before June 1947: Superior court clerk, county where divorce granted
DELAWARE Bureau of Vital Statistics, Division of Public Health, Dept. of Health & Social Services, Jesse S. Cooper Memorial Bldg., Dover 19901	Same	Certified copies: Prothonotary, county where divorce granted For statewide index of divorces since 1932: Bureau of Vital Statistics, Division of Public Health, Dept. of Health & Social Services, Dover 19901
DISTRICT OF COLUMBIA Vital Records Section, Room 1028, 300 Indiana Avenue N.W., Washington 20001	Clerk, Superior Court of the District of Columbia, Washington 20004	Since September 16, 1956: Clerk, Superior Court for the District of Columbia, Family Division, 451 Indiana, Washington 20001 Before September 16, 1956: Clerk, U.S. District Court for the District of Columbia, Washington 20001
FLORIDA Dept. of Health & Rehabilitative Services, Division of Health, Bureau of Vital Statistics, P.O. Box 210, Jacksonville 32201	Since June 6, 1927: Bureau of Vital Statistics, State Division of Health, P.O. Box 210, Jacksonville 32201 Before June 6, 1927: Circuit court clerk, county where license issued	Since June 6, 1927: Bureau of Vital Statistics, State Division of Health, P.O. Box 210, Jacksonville 32201 Before June 6, 1927: Circuit court clerk, county where divorce granted

CHART *3* (cont.)

Birth & Death Records	Marriage Records	Divorce Records

GEORGIA

Vital Records Service, State Department of Human Resources, 47 Trinity Avenue S.W., Atlanta 30334

Since June 9, 1952: Vital Records Service, State Department of Human Resources, 47 Trinity Avenue S.W., Atlanta 30334
Before June 9, 1952: County ordinary, county where license issued

Since 1952: Vital Records Service, State Department of Human Resources, 47 Trinity Avenue S.W., Atlanta 30334
Before 1952: Superior court clerk, county where divorce granted

HAWAII

Research and Statistics Office, State Department of Health, P.O. Box 3378, Honolulu 96801

Same

Since July 1951: Research and Statistics Office, State Department of Health, P.O. Box 3378, Honolulu 96801
Before July 1951: Circuit court, county where divorce granted

IDAHO

Bureau of Vital Statistics, State Department of Health and Welfare, Statehouse, Boise 83720

Since 1947: Bureau of Vital Statistics, State Department of Health and Welfare, Statehouse, Boise 83720
Before 1947: County recorder, county where license issued

Since 1947: Bureau of Vital Statistics, State Department of Health and Welfare, Statehouse, Boise 83720
Before 1947: County recorder, county where divorce granted

ILLINOIS

Since 1916: Office of Vital Records, State Department of Public Health, 535 W. Jefferson St., Springfield 62706
Before 1916: County clerk, county where event occurred

Since 1962: Bureau of Vital Statistics, State Department of Public Health, Springfield 62706
Before 1962: County clerk, county where license issued

Since 1962: Office of Vital Records, State Department of Public Health, Springfield 62706
Before 1962: Circuit court clerk, county where divorce granted

INDIANA

Births since October 1907 & deaths since 1900: Division of Vital Records, State Board of Health, 1330 West Michigan Street, Indianapolis 46202
Before those dates: Health officer, city or county where event occurred

Since 1958: Division of Vital Records, State Board of Health, 1330 West Michigan Street, Indianapolis 46202
Before 1958: Circuit or superior court clerk, county where license issued

County clerk, county where divorce granted

IOWA

Division of Records and Statistics, State Department of Health, Des Moines 50319

Same

Since 1906: Division of Records and Statistics, State Department of Health, Des Moines 50319
Before 1906: County clerk, county where divorce granted

Birth & Death Records	Marriage Records	Divorce Records

KANSAS

Since July 1911: Bureau of Registration & Health Statistics, 6700 S. Topeka Avenue, Topeka 66620
Before July 1911: County clerk, county where event occurred

Since May 1913: Bureau of Registration & Health Statistics, 6700 S. Topeka Avenue, Topeka 66620
Before May 1913: Probate judge, county where license issued

Since July 1951: Bureau of Registration & Health Statistics, 6700 S. Topeka Avenue, Topeka 66620
Before July 1951: Clerk of district court where divorce granted

KENTUCKY

Office of Vital Statistics, 275 East Main Street, Frankfort 40601

Since July 1958: Office of Vital Statistics, 275 East Main Street, Frankfort 40601
Before July 1958: County court clerk, county where license issued

Since July 1958: Office of Vital Statistics, 275 East Main Street, Frankfort 40601
Before July 1958: Circuit court clerk, county where divorce granted

LOUISIANA

Since July 1914: Office of Vital Records, P.O. Box 60630, New Orleans 70160
Before July 1914: Parish clerk, parish where event occurred

Court clerk, parish where license issued
For statewide index of marriages since 1946: Division of Public Health Statistics, State Board of Health, P.O. Box 60630, New Orleans 70160

Court clerk, parish where divorce granted
For statewide index of divorces since 1946: Division of Public Health Statistics, State Board of Health, P.O. Box 60630, New Orleans 70160

New Orleans

Since 1790: Office of Vital Records, P.O. Box 60630, New Orleans 70160

Since 1831: Same

Same

MAINE

Since 1892: Office of Vital Statistics, State Department of Human Services, State House, Augusta 04333
Before 1892: Town clerk, town where event occurred

Office of Vital Statistics, State Department of Human Services, State House, Augusta 04333; or local office where intentions were filed

Since 1892: Office of Vital Statistics, State Department of Human Services, State House, Augusta 04333
Before 1892: Superior court clerk, county where divorce granted or district court clerk, judicial division where divorce granted

MARYLAND

Division of Vital Records, Department of Health and Mental Hygiene, Herbert R. O'Conor Building, 201 West Preston Street, Baltimore 21201

Same

Same

CHART *3* (cont.)

Birth & Death Records	Marriage Records	Divorce Records
MASSACHUSETTS Since 1841: Registrar of Vital Statistics, McCormack Building, 1 Ashburton Place, Boston 02108 Before 1841: Clerk, city or town where event occurred **Boston** City Registrar, Registry Division, Health Department, Room 705, City Hall Annex, Boston 02133	Registrar of Vital Statistics, McCormack Building, 1 Ashburton Place, Boston 02108 Same	Superior court clerk or registrar of probate in county where divorce granted Same
MICHIGAN Office of Vital and Health Statistics, Department of Public Health, P.O. Box 30035, 3500 North Logan Street, Lansing 48909; or county clerk, county where event occurred	Office of Vital and Health Statistics, Department of Public Health, P.O. Box 30035, 3500 North Logan Street, Lansing 48909; or county clerk, county where license issued	Office of Vital and Health Statistics, Department of Public Health, P.O. Box 30035, 3500 North Logan Street, Lansing 48909; or county clerk, county where divorce granted
MINNESOTA Since 1908: Minn. Dept. of Health, Section of Vital Statistics, 717 Delaware St., SE. Minneapolis 55440 Before 1908: District court clerk, county where event occurred **Minneapolis, St. Paul** City Health Department	District court clerk, county where license issued For statewide index of marriages since 1958: Minn. Dept. of Health, Section of Vital Statistics, 717 Delaware St., SE Minneapolis 55440	District court clerk, county where divorce granted For statewide index of divorces since 1970: Minn. Dept. of Health, Section of Vital Statistics, 717 Delaware St., SE Minneapolis 55440
MISSISSIPPI Vital Records Registration Unit, State Board of Health, P.O. Box 1700, Jackson 39205	Since 1926 (excluding period July 1, 1938–Dec. 31, 1941): Vital Records Registration Unit, State Board of Health, P.O. Box 1700, Jackson 39205 Before 1926 (and for period given above): Circuit clerk, county where license issued	Chancery clerk, county where divorce granted
MISSOURI Vital Records, Division of Health, P.O. Box 570, Jefferson City 65101	Since July 1948: Vital Records, Division of Health, P.O. Box 570, Jefferson City 65101 Before July 1948: Recorder of Deeds, county where license issued	Since July 1948: Vital Records, Division of Health, P.O. Box 570, Jefferson City 65101 Before July 1948: Circuit court clerk, county where divorce granted
MONTANA Bureau of Records and Statistics, State Department of Health and Environmental Sciences, Helena 59601	District court clerk, county where license issued For statewide index of marriages since July 1943: Bureau of Records and Statistics, State Department of Health and Environmental Services, Helena 59601	District court clerk, county where divorce granted For statewide index of divorces since 1943: Bureau of Records and Statistics, State Department of Health and Environmental Services, Helena 59601

Birth & Death Records	Marriage Records	Divorce Records
NEBRASKA Bureau of Vital Statistics, State Department of Health, 301 Centennial Mall South, Lincoln 68509	Since 1909: Bureau of Vital Statistics, State Department of Health, 301 Centennial Mall South, Lincoln 68509 Before 1909: County court, county where license issued	Since 1909: Bureau of Vital Statistics, State Department of Health, 301 Centennial Mall South, Lincoln 68509 Before 1909: Clerk of district court where divorce granted
NEVADA Since July 1911: Department of Human Resources, Division of Health, Section of Vital Statistics, Capitol Complex, Carson City 89710 Before July 1911: County recorder, county where event occurred	County recorder, county where license issued For statewide index of marriages since Jan. 1968: Department of Human Resources, Division of Health, Section of Vital Statistics, Capitol Complex, Carson City 89710	County clerk, county where divorce granted For statewide index of divorces since 1968: Department of Human Resources, Division of Health, Section of Vital Statistics, Capitol Complex, Carson City 89710
NEW HAMPSHIRE Department of Health and Welfare, Division of Public Health, Bureau of Vital Statistics, 61 South Spring Street, Concord 03301	Same	Department of Health and Welfare, Division of Public Health, Bureau of Vital Statistics, 61 South Spring Street, Concord 03301; or clerk of superior court which issued decree
NEW JERSEY State Department of Health, Bureau of Vital Statistics, Box 1540, Trenton 08625	Same	Superior Court, Chancery Division, State House, Room 320, Trenton 08625
NEW MEXICO Vital Records, Health and Social Services Department, PERA Building, Room 118, P.O. Box 2348, Santa Fe 87503	County clerk, county where marriage performed	District court clerk, county where divorce granted
NEW YORK Bureau of Vital Records, State Department of Health, Albany 12237 **New York City** Bureau of Records and Statistics, borough where event occurred	For 1880–1907 & since May 1915: Bureau of Vital Records, State Department of Health, Albany 12237 For 1908–April 1915: County clerk, county where license issued Since May 13, 1943: City clerk's office, where license obtained. For 1908–May 12, 1943: City clerk's office in borough of bride; nonresidents, city clerk's office where license obtained	Since 1963: Bureau of Vital Records, State Department of Health, Albany 12237 Before 1963: County clerk, county where divorce granted Borough of court where divorce granted

CHART *3* (cont.)

Birth & Death Records	Marriage Records	Divorce Records
NORTH CAROLINA Vital Records Branch, Division of Health Services, P.O. Box 2091, Raleigh 27602	Since 1962: Vital Records Branch, Division of Health Services, P.O. Box 2091, Raleigh 27602 Before 1962: Register of deeds, county where marriage performed	Since 1958: Vital Records Branch, Division of Health Services, P.O. Box 2091, Raleigh 27602 Before 1958: Superior court clerk, county where divorce granted
NORTH DAKOTA Division of Vital Records, State Department of Health, State Capitol, Bismarck 58505	Since July 1925: Division of Vital Records, State Department of Health, State Capitol, Bismarck 58505 Before July 1925: county judge, county where license issued	District court clerk, county where divorce granted For statewide index of divorces since July 1949: Division of Vital Records, State Department of Health, State Capitol, Bismarck 58505
OHIO Since December 20, 1908: Division of Vital Statistics, State Department of Health, G-20 State Departments Building, Columbus 43215 Before December 20, 1908: Probate court, county where event occurred	Since 1948: Division of Vital Statistics, State Department of Health, G-20 State Departments Building, Columbus 43215 Before 1948: Probate judge, county where license issued	Since 1948: Division of Vital Statistics, State Department of Health, G-20 State Departments Building, Columbus 43215 Before 1948: Court of common pleas clerk, county where divorce granted
OKLAHOMA Vital Records Section, Oklahoma State Department of Health, Northeast 10th and Stonewall, P.O. Box 53551, Oklahoma City 73105	Court clerk, county where license issued	Court clerk, county where divorce granted
OREGON Vital Statistics Section, Oregon State Health Division, P.O. Box 231, Portland 97207	Since 1907: Vital Statistics Section, Oregon State Health Division, P.O. Box 231, Portland 97207 Before 1907: County clerk, county where license issued	Since 1925: Vital Statistics Section, Oregon State Health Division, P.O. Box 231, Portland 97207 Before 1925: County clerk, county where divorce granted
PENNSYLVANIA Since 1906: Division of Vital Statistics, P.O. Box 1528, New Castle 16103 Before 1906: Register of wills, orphans court, county where event occurred	Marriage license clerk, county court house, county seat where license issued	Prothonotary, court house, county seat where divorce granted

Birth & Death Records	Marriage Records	Divorce Records
RHODE ISLAND Since 1853: Division of Vital Statistics, State Department of Health, Room 101, Health Bldg., Davis St., Providence 02908 Before 1853: Town clerk, town where event occurred	Same	Family Court of Rhode Island, 22 Hayes Street, Providence 02903; or Family court clerk, county where divorce granted
SOUTH CAROLINA Bureau of Vital Statistics, State Board of Health, Sims Building, Columbia 29201 Before 1915: for birth records, County Health Department in county of birth	Since July 1950: Bureau of Vital Statistics, State Board of Health, Sims Building, Columbia 29201 For July 1911–June 1950: Probate judge, county where license issued	Since July 1962: Bureau of Vital Statistics, State Board of Health, Sims Building, Columbia 29201 For April 1949–June 1962: County clerk, county where petition filed
SOUTH DAKOTA Public Health Statistics, State Department of Health, Joe Foss Building, Pierre 57501	Since 1905: Public Health Statistics, State Department of Health, Joe Foss Building, Pierre 57501 Before 1905: County treasurer, county where license issued	Since 1905: Public Health Statistics, State Department of Health, Joe Foss Building, Pierre 57501 Before 1905: Court clerk, county where divorce granted
TENNESSEE Vital Records, State Department of Public Health, Hull Building, Nashville 37219	Since July 1945: Vital Records, State Department of Public Health, Hull Building, Nashville 37219 Before July 1945: County court clerk, county where license issued	Since July 1945: Vital Records, State Department of Public Health, Hull Building, Nashville 37219 Before July 1945: Clerk of court where divorce granted
TEXAS Bureau of Vital Statistics, Texas Department of Health Resources, 1100 West 49th Street, Austin 78756	County clerk, county where license issued For statewide index of marriage license applications since Jan. 1966: Bureau of Vital Statistics in Austin (address at left)	District court clerk, county where divorce granted For statewide index of divorces since Jan. 1968: Bureau of Vital Statistics in Austin (address at left)
UTAH Since 1905: Bureau of Health Statistics, Utah State Division of Health, 44 Medical Drive, Salt Lake City 84113 Before 1905: County clerk, county where event occurred (in Salt Lake City and Ogden, city boards of health)	County clerk, county where license issued	District court clerk, county where divorce granted

CHART 3 (cont.)

Birth & Death Records	Marriage Records	Divorce Records
VERMONT Secretary of State, Vital Records Department, State House, Montpelier 05602	Since 1857: Secretary of State, Vital Records Department, State House, Montpelier 05602 Before 1857: Town clerk, town where license issued	Since 1860: Secretary of State, Vital Records Department, State House, Montpelier 05602 Before 1860: County court clerk, county where divorce granted
VIRGINIA Bureau of Vital Records & Health Statistics, State Department of Health, Madison Building, Box 1000, Richmond 23208	Since 1853: Bureau of Vital Records and Health Statistics, State Department of Health, Madison Building, Box 1000, Richmond 23208 Before 1853: Court clerk, county or city where license issued	Since 1918: Bureau of Vital Records and Health Statistics, State Department of Health, Madison Building, Box 1000, Richmond 23208 Before 1918: Court clerk, county or city where divorce granted
WASHINGTON Since July 1907: Bureau of Vital Statistics, State Department of Health, P.O. Box 9709, Olympia 98504 Before July 1907: Auditor, county where event occurred	Since 1968: Bureau of Vital Statistics, Division of Health, State Dept. of Social & Health Services, P.O. Box 9709, Olympia 98504 Before 1968: County auditor, county where license issued	Since 1968: Bureau of Vital Statistics, Division of Health, State Dept. of Social & Health Services, P.O. Box 9709, Olympia 98504 Before 1968: County clerk, county where divorce granted
WEST VIRGINIA Since 1917: Division of Vital Statistics, State Department of Health, State Office Building No. 3, Charleston 25305 Before 1917: County court clerk, county where event occurred	Since 1921: Division of Vital Statistics, State Department of Health, State Office Building No. 3, Charleston 25305 Before 1921: County clerk, county where license issued	Circuit court clerk, chancery side, county where divorce granted
WISCONSIN Section of Vital Records, Division of Health, P.O. Box 309, Madison 53701	Same	Same
WYOMING Since 1909: Vital Records Services, Division of Health & Medical Services, Hathaway Building, Cheyenne 82002	Since May 1941: Vital Records Services, Division of Health & Medical Services, Hathaway Building, Cheyenne 82002 Before May 1941: County clerk, county where license issued	Since May 1941: Vital Records Services, Division of Health & Medical Services, Hathaway Building, Cheyenne 82002 Before May 1941: District court clerk, county where divorce granted

CHAPTER TWO

Your Personal Rights and Obligations

We hold these truths to be self-evident, that all men are created equal, that they are endowed by their Creator with certain unalienable Rights, that among these are Life, Liberty and the pursuit of Happiness.

—DECLARATION OF INDEPENDENCE

2

Your Personal Rights and Obligations

Some Key Points in This Chapter—
Consult these sections for information on:

Charts in This Chapter

Your Rights as a Citizen

This chapter describes your basic rights as a citizen of the United States. These rights are defined by the Constitution of the United States and by the first ten amendments to it, commonly called the Bill of Rights. Many of them are outgrowths of the old English common law. Because the framers of the Constitution regarded the possession of these rights as the natural state of all mankind, they referred to them as "unalienable Rights," rights that cannot be given or taken away. In fact, however, your rights under the Constitution can legally be suspended in some circumstances, which are discussed in this chapter. Wrongful violations of rights are discussed in chapter 3, "Your Protection Against Wrongs," page 81, and chapter 4, "Your Protection Against Crime and Criminal Charges," page 133.

14. What Makes You a United States Citizen • To get the full protection of the laws of any country, you must be a citizen of that country or a legally accepted permanent resident alien. You may become a citizen of the United States either by birth or by naturalization. There are no other methods of obtaining United States citizenship.

Anyone born in the United States or its territories is a U.S. citizen. You are also a citizen if you were born outside the country but one of your parents was a U.S. citizen at the time of your birth and your birth was registered with the U.S. consulate.

Naturalization is a path to full citizenship that millions of Americans have followed. In most instances, to qualify for naturalization, a person must first enter the United States as a permanent resident. He does this by obtaining a passport or other travel document, stamped by a U.S. consular official in his own country, plus an *immigrant visa,* a permit to enter the United States permanently. If he is already in this country and changing from a nonimmigrant to an immigrant visa, he deals with the Immigration and Naturalization Service. At the end of five years after his permanent entry (unless he has been out of country for more than one year without Immigration Service permission), the immigrant may file a petition for naturalization with the clerk of a U.S. district court or a state court of general jurisdiction (see section 8). He may file at the end of three years if he is married to a U.S. citizen.

Between the time one's naturalization petition is filed and the time when one may be sworn as a United States citizen by the judge of a U.S. district court, one should pay careful attention to the regulations about traveling and living outside the United States, and consult the clerk of the court where the petition was filed or the immigration officials of the U.S. Department of Justice if one has any doubts. Special naturalization procedures are provided for persons who have completed three years of honorable military service.

No one should take the oath to become an American citizen unless he means what he says or swears to. A person who takes the oath falsely or with serious mental reservations may later be prosecuted for having obtained his naturalization fraudulently. If found guilty, he may be denaturalized and deported to the country from which he emigrated.

15. Sources of Your Rights as a Citizen of the United States • The principal sources of your rights as an American citizen are two documents: the constitution of your state and the Constitution of the United States. Certain other basic rights that you enjoy but that are not explicitly spelled out in any document derive from the old English common law on which our own legal system is based (see section 2).

You will remember from the American history courses you took in school that the United States was legally established by action of over two-thirds of the original thirteen states in 1788, when they ratified the constitution that delegates from the thirteen states had written at the Constitutional Convention in Philadelphia. After these delegates had agreed upon a constitution, it was submitted to a constitutional convention in each state for approval before it became law.

The governments of the thirteen states preceded the United States government, just as the constitutions of those states preceded the United States Constitution. Necessarily, therefore, the powers of the United States government, as set forth in the U.S. Constitution, are powers given up by the states. A good example is the power to coin money. That power previously resided in the states. The states gave it up because they realized that a national government could not function financially if there were thirteen different kinds of currency in existence.

Most important, perhaps, is the fact that the states gave up these powers grudgingly. Why? Because the citizens of the various states were determined not to surrender basic liberties to an all-powerful central government, having just gone through seven years of agonizing war to seize those liberties from the British monarchy.

No discussion of your rights as an American citizen makes much sense unless you keep clearly in mind the dual nature of the American system, which we call *federalism*. On one side are the governments of the fifty states; on the other is the national, or federal, government. Each side has powers of its own. Each must respect the powers of the other. Too heavy a reliance on states' rights is likely to result in a weak and ineffectual national government. Too heavy a reliance on the federal government is likely to result in just the situation our forefathers tried to avoid, an all-powerful central government that would only repeat the evils of the British monarchy.

This was the danger that most Americans feared in 1790: the tyranny of the national government, not of the state governments. The residents of the thirteen colonies, stretching from Massachusetts to Georgia, had few fears of their own governments, which they knew and which they believed they could control. But they truly feared the new and unknown government they had created by ratifying the United States Constitution. Accordingly, some insisted on the adoption of ten amendments to the U.S. Constitution as a condition of approving its ratification. Together these ten amendments, the first ten, are called the *Bill of Rights,* which is discussed below. They were designed to limit the powers of the federal government, not of the states.

For the next seventy-five years the American people looked to their state governments to protect and preserve their basic civil liberties under their several state constitutions. Little happened during those years to diminish the authority of the state governments, and little happened to bring about any significant increase in the power of the federal government. Only a handful of cases was brought into court during those years by citizens of the United States seeking the help of the federal government in enforcing the basic rights guaranteed by the Bill of Rights.

With the end of the Civil War, however, a wholly new situation developed. Northerners were convinced that the institution of slavery must be clearly and absolutely outlawed throughout the United States—and it was, by the adoption, in December 1865, of the Thirteenth Amendment to the Constitution. Almost three years later, in July 1868, the Fourteenth Amendment was adopted, to make more meaningful the rights and privileges of all American citizens, of whatever kind and wherever born.

Together with the first ten amendments, as we shall see, the Fourteenth Amendment has been used by the courts to bring about the enormous changes in the American legal structure that have taken place since the end of the Civil War. The language of the first section of this amendment is interesting, directed as it is against the states, whereas the first ten amendments are directed against the federal government.

> Section 1. All persons born or naturalized in the United States, and subject to the jurisdiction thereof, are citizens of the United States and of the State wherein they reside. No State shall make or enforce any law which shall abridge the privileges or immunities of citizens of the United States; nor shall any State deprive any person of life, liberty, or property, without due process of law; nor deny to any person within its jurisdiction the equal protection of the laws.

The two phrases "due process of law" and "equal protection of the laws" are the ones the courts have used to strike down state censorship statutes, state statutes requiring licenses for parading and state statutes banning picketing in labor disputes. The "due process of law" phrase has also been used to require all states to ensure that every person accused of a crime has the right to consult or engage legal counsel and that no one can be imprisoned for an unreasonable period of time without a hearing.

The courts have reasoned that the many civil rights and liberties protected by the Bill of Rights from violation by the federal government were incorporated by the Fourteenth Amendment into the rights of the citizens of the United States and hence protected from violation by the government of any state.

As a citizen, therefore, you have two principal sources of protection against any violation of your basic individual rights. One is the constitution and laws of your own state. The other is the Constitution and laws of the United States. Over the years the U.S. Constitution and laws have been the most meaningful, because local conditions in one or another state create prejudices that may conflict with the full enforcement of the rights guaranteed by the U.S. Constitution. In all the years since the adoption of the Bill of Rights, designed to control the activities of the national government, those ten amendments, plus the Fourteenth, have been used to control the actions of the state governments. The federal government, whose power was once so feared, has become the government of last resort for persons asserting their civil rights and liberties.

Now let us take a look at each of these basic liberties and see what each of them means in practice.

16. Your Right to Freedom of Speech and Freedom of the Press · The First Amendment to the United States Constitution, the first of the Bill of Rights, says that "Congress shall make no law . . . abridging [limiting] the freedom of speech, or of the press; or the right of the people peaceably to assemble, and to petition the Government for a redress of grievances." A similar provision is found in the constitutions of many states. Many of us believe freedom of speech and the press is the one fundamental personal right or liberty. We could do without the right to carry weapons or the right to a grand jury in a federal case or several other rights. But inability to speak and write and publish freely is, we think, simply inconsistent with a democracy.

And so the courts have held, but with exception or within limits, because in a world crowded with people with conflicting interests, no freedom is absolute.

Freedom of speech does not exist in the abstract. You as an individual, despite the words quoted above from the First Amendment, are not free to stand up on a street corner and urge your listeners to follow you now and kill the President of the United States or the governor of your state or the mayor of your city, or anyone else, for that matter.

You may discuss—from the street corner or in the columns of a newspaper (above or underground) or in pamphlets distributed by hand or through the mail—the beauties you see in a monarchy or in a society where all persons have two or more wives or husbands. But if you urge the commission of a crime, you will very likely be charged with a crime yourself: inciting to riot, bringing about or seeking to bring about murder or arson (see sections 91, 112, 121, 129). And it's one thing to urge people to have several wives, but to actually have more than one is to commit the crime of bigamy (see section 116).

Governmental interference with freedom of speech takes several forms. On the one hand are laws that attempt to control speech or publication before the event. On the other are laws that impose penalties after the event. The courts will declare unconstitutional both controls and penalties unless they are generally applicable, are specific enough for all to understand and can be justified as an exercise of the police power, which includes the public's right to protect itself from harmful writings. A few examples may be helpful.

A law requiring the preliminary showing of motion pictures to a state (or municipal) licensing board is constitutional if its purpose is only to protect the public from films that are offensive to public morals or accepted standards of decency, but the courts do not hesitate to substitute their judgment for that of the licensing board if they disagree with it.

United States customs officials have the right to challenge the importation into the United States of books and magazines they regard as obscene or subversive, but they must obtain judicial support of their opinion by going to court first.

The postmaster general, using his power to grant magazines a second-class mailing privilege, has unsuccessfully tried to deny permits to magazines he found objectionable, but he has successfully denied the use of the mails to people trying to promote schemes that defraud the public.

Activists recently indicted for various crimes against the flag of the United States have defended their actions as a form of symbolic speech, and the reaction of the courts to this assertion is by no means clear.

A particular challenge to the concept of freedom of the press has arisen with the recent increase in the amount of printed matter on our newsstands that would certainly have been classified as obscene and pornographic only a few years ago. In trying to strike a balance between the public's right to read what it chooses and its right to protect itself against material that is offensive by the standards of the community, the courts have been forced to walk a narrow line. Unable to lay down a satisfactory general rule as to what is and what is not obscene, they have found it necessary to examine each case on its merits. The result is that unscrupulous publishers can print and distribute material that is clearly prurient with the knowledge that, practically speaking, they run only a moderate risk of prosecution and conviction for their violation of obscenity statutes. More or less the same situation exists in regard to films.

Control of material broadcast by radio or television has not been seriously challenged in the courts. The number of radio frequencies and television channels is limited, and Congress has given the Federal Communications Commission broad powers to supervise what is transmitted by the limited number of broadcasters and telecasters it licenses. Here is an instance in which controls are imposed over what kind of material may be broadcast by the media and in which stiff penalties will be assessed if the controls are violated.

The radio and television media have much less practical freedom than do publishers of newspapers, magazines and books. Because the renewal of its license to broadcast depends on the approval of a federal regulatory agency, a radio or television station will normally exercise a very considerable degree of self-censorship simply to protect its economic interests. The result may be a bland diet for the public, but, on the other hand, the threat of outside censorship is unlikely to materialize.

Any legal challenge to the controls over radio and television would most likely come about as the result of objection to specific censorship of a particular program on the ground that it was obscene or subversive.

If such a case should ever arise, the Supreme Court would probably follow the procedure adopted in censorship cases involving books and motion pictures, which is not to question the public's right to protect itself against obscenity or subversion but to decide in the individual case before it whether the challenged radio or television program is, by any reasonable standard, obscene or subversive.

The most troublesome cases involving freedom of speech and press, and of assembly, have arisen from efforts by the national and state governments to protect themselves against frankly revolutionary individuals and groups. Until recently the Communist party and its sympathizers have caused most trouble in this area, ever since the Communist takeover in Russia in 1917. In the past few years other openly revolutionary groups have come forth, particularly among blacks and students, calling for violent change or overthrow of our governmental system.

What occupies the attention of the courts in all cases of this kind is the problem of whether the speech in which these groups indulge is likely to lead to illegal action. When do valid dissent and debate aimed at influencing people's beliefs influence their conduct instead and cause them to do something the law forbids?

So far the courts have taken a lenient view, reflecting the philosophy about their role expressed by the eminent former federal jurist Learned Hand when he said:

> The most important issues [as concerns free speech] arise when a majority of the voters are hostile, often bitterly hostile, to the dissidents against whom the statute is directed; and legislatures are more likely than courts to repress what ought to be free. It is true that the periods of passion or panic are ordinarily not very long, and that they are usually succeeded by a serener and more tolerant temper; but, as I have just said, serious damage may have been done that cannot be undone, and no restitution is ordinarily possible for the individuals who have suffered.

17. Your Right to Freedom of Assembly • As we have already indicated, freedom of assembly is a right guaranteed against unreasonable federal and state interference. Municipalities may properly require that large rallies and parades be held only after the police department has been notified.

They may also require permits, as long as the requirement is a general one that all organizations must meet. A law authorizing the police to issue permits for parades would be unconstitutional if the police were given any discretion in issuing such permits except in the interest of keeping traffic moving. A city ordinance requiring permits for all parades down the middle of a shopping center would be supported in the courts. But the courts would strike down as too vague an ordinance that required permits for parades by members of "subversive" organizations.

The same is true for mass rallies. The police may properly be given the right to issue or deny permits under certain prescribed conditions. But those conditions must be clear and must apply to all applicants. The role of the police is to keep the peace; they may not constitutionally be given the right to pick and choose among different groups applying for permission to hold a rally.

Similarly, now that picketing is regarded as a form of self-expression, it is controlled by the same rules as freedom of speech, press and assembly. You have a right to picket so long as the picketing is peaceful (see sections 386, 388). The police have no right to interfere with peaceful picketing or to arrest peaceful picketers. But if the picketing becomes violent, the police have the right and duty to stop it and to arrest persons inciting the picketers to interfere with the freedoms of others.

18. Your Right to Freedom of Religion • The very first part of the First Amendment to the Constitution reads: "Congress shall make no law respecting an establishment of religion, or prohibiting the free exercise thereof. . . ." You will note again that this amendment is directed at Congress, not at the state legislatures. The language seems simple enough, but thousands of hours of judges' and lawyers' time have been spent interpreting it, and more are certain to be spent in the future.

There is little doubt that the states in 1790 were determined to prevent the creation by the national government of the kind of established church that existed and still exists in many countries. Today the Church of England is the officially established church in the United Kingdom: Parliament approves the bishops and other clergy designated by the queen; even the Book of Common Prayer cannot be altered without parliamentary approval. France disestablished the Roman Catholic Church during the French Revolution—that is, severed the state's ties with the church. In Italy the Church of Rome is still the "official" church.

In some states in the Union, particularly in New England, it was long after 1790 that public support for the Congregational Church came to an end. But from the early 1800s until the end of World War II most Americans agreed that church and state should be kept separate from each other. Then trouble arose—from economic problems, not from any desire to bring the two closer together. A question asked in the mid-1940s was whether public funds could be constitutionally used to pay the

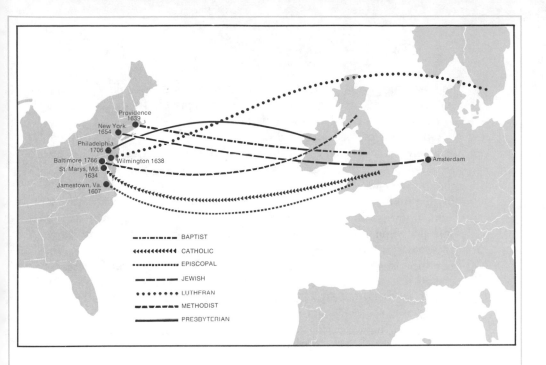

AMERICA'S DIVERSE RELIGIONS:
FROM THE BEGINNING TO THE PRESENT DAY

Members of many different religious groups came from Europe and established their first settlements along the Eastern seaboard, as shown above. The provisions of our Constitution that guarantee religious freedom reflect this tradition of diversity. Later settlers often made their homes far from the original colonies. As a result, our religious distribution today differs markedly from that of pre-Revolutionary War days.

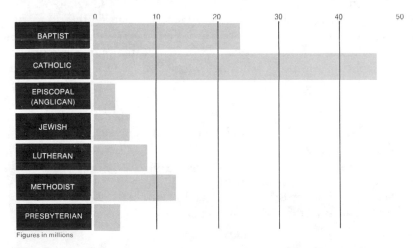

Membership in each major religion has grown with our population. The chart above shows membership by religious group in 1970.

cost of transporting children to and from schools, including parochial schools. Several of the state legislatures appropriated funds for this kind of transportation, and the battle was on.

Opponents of this use of public funds claimed it was unconstitutional as a "law respecting an establishment of religion." Nonsense, said others, the statutes say nothing about one or another church; they merely permit the expenses of transporting children to all kinds of schools to be paid by the public. The courts in several states that had passed such statutes agreed, and so did the United States Supreme Court; payment of such transportation expenses does not violate the United States Constitution. In some states, however, the courts have held that payment for transportation to parochial schools does violate state constitutional provisions similar to that of the First Amendment.

The problem first raised by the school transportation cases is far from settled. What is involved is the use of public funds for private or sectarian educational purposes. As the expenses of education have risen, the finances of private institutions have become gravely endangered, and many private schools are seeking public funds to survive. Some courts are willing to help if the public funds are made available to all, with no discrimination. Thus, books may be purchased by the state and made available to all school and college students, and it seems likely that state funds may legally be made available to all schools and colleges to finance construction of educational buildings. But these and related problems are still unresolved.

The "released time" question has proved less difficult. Does the First Amendment to the U.S. Constitution permit public school students to be released during the hours they are supposed to be in school so that they can be given religious instruction by teachers outside the school system? The Supreme Court has replied that the First Amendment is violated if the religious instruction is carried on within the public school itself, on public school property, but is not if the religious instruction is given elsewhere, off school property.

In an effort to expand the scope of the First Amendment ban on the establishment of religion, some parents have challenged the practice in public schools of Bible reading and a daily prayer. Although this practice was once fairly general throughout the United States, and had been upheld by the courts of a clear majority of the states where it had been challenged as a violation of state constitutions, the U.S. Supreme Court held in 1963 that Bible reading and classroom prayer violate the First Amendment to the U.S. Constitution and must be stopped.

The second clause of the First Amendment that is concerned with religious liberty is the one prohibiting the Congress from passing any law prohibiting the "free exercise thereof." This clause should be read carefully, because it doesn't mean what it seems to say—as the Mormons found out in 1879 when one of them was prosecuted for the crime of bigamy. Bigamy (see section 116) is the act of marrying one wife or husband while still married to another. Polygyny, or the state of having several wives at the same time, was a practice approved by Mormon church doctrine, and the early leaders of that church practiced it faithfully. Being polygynous, said the Mormons, was engaging in the "free exercise" of their religion.

Not so, said the U.S. Supreme Court. Polygyny is a practice almost universally condemned in the Western world. It is inconceivable that anyone intended to permit, much less make legal, its practice in the United States. The First Amendment, the Court decided, sets up no absolute right to a course of conduct just because it is permitted by one's religion. Religious freedom must give way to reasonable restrictions that have been adopted to protect the health, safety and convenience of the entire community.

The principle in the Mormon case is simple and would unquestionably be followed if a new church arose that permitted marriage between persons closely related to each other by blood, a marriage now forbidden by all states (see sections 118, 311). In the same vein, federal courts have held that the "free exercise" clause does not permit parents who are members of a particular religious sect to withold medical care from a sick child because such care is contrary to the sect's doctrine.

Exemption from taxation of property owned by religious and educational institutions is another aspect of the First Amendment's reach that is very much an issue today—again for economic reasons. Most states and municipalities are prevented by state constitutions from imposing real estate taxes on property owned by churches and schools and operated for church and school purposes. Similarly, the Internal Revenue Code of the U.S. government and the tax laws of those states that have income taxes exempt the income of churches from income tax and also give donors of money to churches a tax deduction for such gifts. These tax deductions have recently been upheld after challenge in the U.S. Supreme Court.

However, trouble may be ahead for some religious and educational institutions that take advantage of their tax exemptions and use part of their real property or income for commercial purposes. Some churches and universities own a considerable amount of real estate, especially in urban areas, which they rent out to businesses. They may then try to avoid paying income taxes on the rent by claiming that the property is owned by a church or an educational institution. Some churches have more capital or income than they need, and invest the excess in a variety of money-making activities. Sooner or later these commercial uses of church and university property are likely to be taxed, even if the courts continue to exempt from taxation property that is exclusively devoted to church or school use.

19. Your Right to Vote • The power to regulate elections and determine voter qualification has for most of our history been regarded as resting in the states, not in the national government. All that the United States Constitution prescribes is that "the electors in each State shall have the qualifications requisite for electors of the most numerous branch of the State legislature" (Article I, Section 2; Seventeenth Amendment, Clause 1). Because the qualifications for electors of the lower house of the state legislature clearly are the concern of the state government, it seemed logical that Congress had no responsibility for deciding the qualifications of persons entitled to vote within the state.

On three occasions, however, the American people have intervened to make declarations covering the right to vote. The Fifteenth Amendment, adopted in 1870, prohibits the United States or any state from denying or abridging the right of U.S. citizens to vote "on account of race, color, or previous condition of servitude." That amendment was necessary because even after the Civil War some southern states refused to permit Negroes to vote. The Nineteenth Amendment, adopted in 1920, prohibits the United States or any state from denying or abridging the right of United States citizens to vote "on account of sex."

Neither the Fifteenth nor the Nineteenth Amendment, however, nor even Section 2 of Article I, says that the United States government has the right to determine the age at which you may vote, or how the people's votes in any state are to be apportioned. As a result, different voting ages were set in different states, with the most common age being 21. But in the late 1960s the trend toward a lower voting age was clearly under way, and with the ratification of the Twenty-Sixth Amendment in July 1971 it became the law of the land that "the right of citizens of the United States, who are eighteen years of age or older, to vote shall not be denied or abridged by the United States or by any state on account of age." And Congress was duly empowered to enforce the article.

From the Civil War on, various states, especially in the South, have

HOW YOU QUALIFY TO VOTE

This chart shows the qualifications required for voting in state and local elections. The 1970 federal Voting Rights Amendments abolished residence requirements of over 30 days for federal elections, and local qualifications are being liberalized.

CHART 4	Residence Requirements			Registration		Where to Register
	State	County	Precinct	In Person	By Mail[1]	
ALABAMA	30 days	None	None	Yes	Yes	County Board of Registrars
ALASKA	30 days	30 days in election district	30 days	Yes	Yes[1]	State Election Office, city or borough clerk or precinct registrar
ARIZONA	50 days	30 days	30 days	Yes	Yes	County recorder
ARKANSAS	1 year	6 months	30 days	Yes	No	Permanent registrar or his deputy
CALIFORNIA	None	None	29 days[2]	Yes	Yes	County clerk[3]
COLORADO	32 days	None	32 days	Yes	Yes	County or city clerk (in Denver, Election Commission)
CONNECTICUT	None	None	None[4]	Yes	No	Town clerk or registrar of voters
DELAWARE	None	None	21 days[2]	Yes	Yes	County Department of Elections
D.C.	30 days	None	None	Yes	Yes	District Board of Elections, public libraries or other designated places
FLORIDA	30 days	30 days	None[4]	Yes	No[5]	County supervisor of elections
GEORGIA	30 days	30 days	30 days	Yes	No[6]	County Board of Registrars
HAWAII	None	None	30 days[2]	Yes	Yes	County clerk (in Honolulu, city clerk)
IDAHO	None	5 days[3]	10 days[2]	Yes	Yes	County auditor
ILLINOIS	30 days	30 days	30 days	Yes	No[7]	County clerk[8]
INDIANA	30 days	30 days (township)	30 days	Yes	Yes	County clerk or Board of Registration
IOWA	None	None	10 days[2]	Yes	Yes	City or town clerk, commissioner of registration or mobile registrar
KANSAS	None	None	20 days[2]	Yes	Yes	County clerk[9]
KENTUCKY	30 days	30 days	30 days	Yes	Yes	County clerk (in Louisville, Board of Registration Commissioners)
LOUISIANA	30 days	30 days	30 days	Yes	No[10]	Registrar of parish
MAINE	None	None	None[4]	Yes	Yes	Registrar of voters in towns; Board of Registration in cities
MARYLAND	29 days	29 days	None	Yes	Yes	Board of Supervisors of Election
MASSACHUSETTS	None	None	20 days[2]	Yes	No	Town or city clerk
MICHIGAN	30 days	30 days	30 days	Yes	Yes	City or township clerk[11]
MINNESOTA	20 days	None	None	Yes	Yes	City clerk, county auditor or at polls election day
MISSISSIPPI	30 days	30 days	30 days	Yes	No	City clerk or county registrar
MISSOURI	30 days	30 days	30 days	Yes[12]	Yes[13]	County clerk[14]
MONTANA	1 year	30 days	None	Yes	Yes	County clerk & recorder
NEBRASKA	None	None	None[4]	Yes	Yes	County clerk[15]
NEVADA	30 days	30 days	10 days	Yes	Yes	County clerk

CHART 4 (cont.)	Residence Requirements			Registration		Where to Register
	State	County	Precinct	In Person	By Mail	
NEW HAMPSHIRE	None	None	10 days[2]	Yes[16]	Yes[17]	Board of Supervisors of Checklist of town or city
NEW JERSEY	30 days	30 days	29 days[2]	Yes	Yes	County Board of Elections or municipal clerk
NEW MEXICO	None	None	42 days[2]	Yes	No	County clerk
NEW YORK	30 days	30 days	10 days	Yes	Yes	County Board of Elections (in N.Y borough boards of elections)
NORTH CAROLINA	30 days	None	30 days	Yes	No	County chairman of Board of Elections or local registrar
NORTH DAKOTA	30 days	30 days	30 days	[18]	[18]	
OHIO	30 days	30 days	30 days	Yes	No	County Election Board or other designated place
OKLAHOMA	None	None	None[4]	Yes	No	County Election Board or deputy registrar
OREGON	30 days	None	None	Yes	Yes	County clerk or registrar of elections
PENNSYLVANIA	30 days	None	30 days	Yes	Yes	County Board of Elections (in Philadelphia, Registration Division)
RHODE ISLAND	30 days	30 days	None	Yes	No	Local Board of Canvassers and Registration
SOUTH CAROLINA	None	None	None[4]	Yes	No	County Registration Board
SOUTH DAKOTA	None	None	None[4]	Yes	Yes	County or city auditor, town clerk or municipal finance officer
TENNESSEE	20 days	None	None	Yes	Yes	County Election Commission
TEXAS	None	None	None[4]	Yes	Yes	County tax assessor-collector
UTAH	30 days	None	10 days[2]	Yes	Yes	County clerk
VERMONT	None	None	None[4]	[16]	[16]	Board of Civil Authority of town or city
VIRGINIA	None	None	30 days	Yes	No	General registrar of county or city
WASHINGTON	30 days	30 days	30 days	Yes	No	County auditor or city clerk
WEST VIRGINIA	30 days	30 days	None	Yes	Yes	Clerk of county commission
WISCONSIN	10 days	10 days	10 days	Yes[12]	Yes	City, town or village clerk[19]
WYOMING	30 days	30 days	10 days	Yes	Yes	County clerk

(1) Register by mail with Lieutenant Governor, Pouch AA, Juneau 99811.
(2) A registration requirement, not a residence requirement.
(3) Registrar of voters in Los Angeles, Monterey, Orange, San Bernardino, San Diego, San Francisco and Santa Clara counties.
(4) Bona fide residence is required.
(5) Federal employes may reregister by mail.
(6) Qualified residents abroad and federal employes outside state may register by mail.
(7) Military personnel may register by mail.
(8) Board of Election Commissioners in Aurora, Bloomington, Cairo, Chicago, Danville, East St. Louis, Galesburg, Peoria, Rockford and Springfield.
(9) Election commissioner in Johnson, Sedgwick, Shawnee and Wyandotte counties.
(10) Students, federal employes and persons in interstate commerce may register by mail.
(11) Any branch office of Secretary of State that issues driver licenses.
(12) Registration is not required in rural areas.
(13) Registration by mail is allowed except in counties or cities with Board of Election Commissioners.
(14) Board of Election Commissioners in Kansas City, St. Louis city and county and Jackson County.
(15) Election commissioner in Buffalo, Douglas, Lancaster, Platte and Sarpy counties.
(16) Checklist system of registration is used.
(17) For absentee registration, apply to the city or town clerk.
(18) No registration is required.
(19) Milwaukee Board of Election Commissioners.

tried to prevent blacks from voting, despite the Fifteenth Amendment. The establishment of all-white primary elections, the imposition of poll taxes, the requirement of literacy tests—these were some of the devices tried. The Supreme Court knocked them all down on the ground that they were made unconstitutional both by the Fifteenth Amendment and by the clause in the Fourteenth Amendment prohibiting any state from denying to any person within its jurisdiction "equal protection of the laws." In the Voting Rights Act of 1965, Congress gave the federal government and the federal courts additional powers to make the voting privileges in the Fourteenth and Fifteenth amendments meaningful.

20. Your Right to Hold Public Office • Any adult United States citizen who has not been convicted of a felony (see section 90) is entitled to hold public office. Age limitations are few. The President of the United States must be thirty-five years of age, a "natural-born" citizen and a resident of the United States for fourteen years. A U.S. senator must be at least thirty years old and a citizen for nine years; a representative must be twenty-five years old and a citizen for seven years. Qualifications for state elective offices, both executive and legislative, will be found in the various state constitutions.

21. Your Right to Keep and Bear Arms • Although this right is apparently guaranteed by the Constitution, in practice it is subject to widespread regulation by state laws (check chart 5, page 66 to see what your state statute provides). The provision, in the Second Amendment to the U.S. Constitution, that "the right of the people to keep and bear arms, shall not be infringed" has been held not to limit the states' rights to legislate in this area. The United States is the only nation whose citizens are permitted such an unlimited right, which is partly a holdover from our frontier traditions and partly a reflection of the states' fear of a too-powerful central government in the period following the Revolution. This right has cost us dearly in lives of persons killed by the disaffected, the unstable and the emotionally ill, and it seems likely that it will gradually be more and more restricted.

22. Your Right to Individual Privacy • This basic right, which includes the prohibition in the Fourth Amendment against unreasonable search and seizure, will clearly be increasingly difficult to maintain in a highly complex society and with the growth of electronic listening devices. Many responsible persons who are experts on such devices are deeply

YOUR RIGHT TO OWN AND CARRY FIREARMS

NSP=No statutory provision

CHART 5	Is a License Required to Buy a Handgun?	Is There a Waiting Period Between Purchase & Delivery?	Are Handgun Sales Reported to Police?	Who May Not Buy a Handgun?
ALABAMA	No	Yes: 48 hours	Yes	Persons under 18; persons convicted of a crime of violence; drug addicts; alcoholics; former mental patients
ALASKA	No	No	No	NSP
ARIZONA	No	No	No	Persons under 18 without consent of parent or guardian
ARKANSAS	No	No	No	NSP
CALIFORNIA	No	Yes: 15 days	Yes[3]	Persons under 18 without parental consent; persons under 16
COLORADO	No	No	No	NSP
CONNECTICUT	Yes	Yes: 2 weeks (if buyer is not licensed to carry)	Yes	Persons under 18; convicted felons; aliens
DELAWARE	No	No	No	Minors; convicted felons; former mental patients; intoxicated persons
DISTRICT OF COLUMBIA	No	Yes: 48 hours	Yes	Persons under 21; same as who may not possess
FLORIDA	No	No (but 72 hours in Miami Beach)	Only in Miami and Miami Beach	Persons under 18 without parental consent[7]; convicted felons; alcoholics; drug addicts; former mental patients
GEORGIA	No	No	Reported to Ordinary	Persons under 21
HAWAII	Yes	No	Yes	Persons under 20; persons convicted of violent crimes or illegal drug use
IDAHO	No	No	No	Persons under 16 without written parental consent
ILLINOIS	No[12]	Yes: 72 hours	No	Minors under 18; persons under 21 convicted of misdemeanor or of delinquency; footnote 12 except age limitation
INDIANA	No	Yes: 7 days	No	Persons under 18; persons convicted of a crime of violence; drug addicts; alcoholics; persons of unsound mind
IOWA	No	No	Yes	Persons under 18
KANSAS	No	No	No	Minors; alcoholics; addicts; convicted felons

(1) No license or permit is required to carry a handgun in a person's home or place of business or on his own property.

(2) But a license is required to carry a handgun openly or concealed in a vehicle.

(3) Sales reported to Department of Justice at Sacramento, but mail-order sales must be reported to police 5 days prior to ordering.

(4) But law prohibits possession or carrying of a firearm, concealed or openly, with the intent to use it against another person.

(5) But law prohibits anyone from carrying loaded rifle or shotgun in any vehicle.

(6) Five character witnesses must swear that

Despite the apparent Constitutional guarantee of the citizen's right to keep and bear arms (see section 21), the use and ownership of firearms are in fact strictly regulated by state laws, as shown below. See also section 114.

Is a License Required to Carry a Handgun?		Who May Not Possess or Use a Handgun?	Is a License Required to Carry or Possess a Rifle or Shotgun?	Is a License Required to Buy Ammunition?	Is a License Required to Sell Firearms (Retail)?
Openly	Concealed				
No[1,2]	Yes[1,2]	Persons under 18; convicted felons; drug addicts; alcoholics; mental patients	No	No	No, except handguns
No	Illegal to carry	Persons convicted of a felony or misdemeanor involving weapons or assault	No	No	No
No	Illegal to carry	Persons convicted of crime of violence; convicted felon; adjudicated mental incompetent; person involuntarily committed to a mental institution; person under 18	No	No	No
Illegal to carry	Illegal to carry		No	No	No
No	Yes	Drug addicts; convicted felons; persons under 18 not accompanied by parent or guardian or without written permission; mental patients	No	No	No, except handguns
No	No	Persons convicted of crime of violence within 10 year of conviction or 10 years after incarceration, whichever is greater; alcoholics; drug addicts	No	No	No
Yes	Yes	Persons under 18; convicted felons; aliens	No[5]	No	No, except handguns
No	Yes[6]	Aliens	No[5]	No	No, except handguns
Yes[1]	Yes[1]	Drug addicts; felons; insane persons; persons convicted of violation of firearm, prostitution or vagrancy laws	NSP	NSP	Yes
Yes[8]	Yes[8]	Convicted felons; persons under 16 unless accompanied by adult	No	No	No
Yes[9,10]	Illegal to carry	Persons who do not meet conditions of footnote 9	No	No	Yes
Yes	Yes	Fugitives from justice; persons convicted of crime of violence or narcotics abuse	No[11]	No	Yes
No	Yes	Persons under 12 while in forest camping or in a vehicle	No	No	No
Yes	Illegal to carry	[12]	No[12]	No[12]	No
Yes[1]	Yes[1]	Same as who may not buy a handgun	No	No	No, except handguns
No[2]	Yes[1]	NSP	NSP	No	No, except handguns
No	Illegal to carry	Minors; convicted felons; drug addicts; alcoholics	No	No	No

the applicant needs a firearm to protect his person or property.

(7) In Miami no one under 21 may buy a handgun unless parent signs the purchase application. In Miami Beach no minor may buy or otherwise acquire a handgun.

(8) Person must be over 21 and of good moral character and must post a bond of $100–$1,000, depending on the county.

(9) Applicant must be 21 and mentally competent, must not have been convicted of a felony in the last 10 years or a misdemeanor in the last 2 years and must post a bond of $300.

CHART 5 (cont.)	Is a License Required to Buy a Handgun?	Is There a Waiting Period Between Purchase & Delivery?	Are Handgun Sales Reported to Police?	Who May Not Buy a Handgun?
KENTUCKY	No	No	NSP	NSP
LOUISIANA	NSP	NSP	NSP	Persons under 18
MAINE	No	No	No	Persons under 16
MARYLAND	No	Yes: 1 week	Yes	Persons under 21; persons convicted of a crime of violence; fugitives from justice; alcoholics; drug addicts; persons of unsound mind
MASSACHUSETTS	Yes	No	Yes	Minors under 21 (except for minors 18–21 with license to carry); felons; incompetents; drug addicts; aliens
MICHIGAN	Yes	No	Yes	Persons under 18; aliens; persons who have not resided in state 6 months; insane persons; persons convicted within past 8 years
MINNESOTA	No	No	No	NSP
MISSISSIPPI	No	No	No	Minors; persons who are intoxicated
MISSOURI	Yes[17]	No	No	Persons without permits[17]
MONTANA	No	No	No	NSP
NEBRASKA	No	No	No	NSP
NEVADA	No	No	No	Minors under 18
NEW HAMPSHIRE	No[19]	No	No	Minors
NEW JERSEY	Yes	Yes: 1 week	Yes	Persons convicted of felony while armed; persons convicted of drug offenses[18]
NEW MEXICO	No	No	No	NSP
NEW YORK	Yes	No	Yes	Persons under 16 and persons without valid license to possess firearms
NORTH CAROLINA	Yes	No	No	Persons without permit (Sheriff issues a permit only to persons of good character who require a handgun for self-defense or protection of the home)

(10) No license is required to carry a handgun in a car.

(11) All firearms must be registered.

(12) All residents must obtain a firearm owner's identification card in order to acquire or possess any firearm or ammunition. Identification cards are not issued to persons under 21 without written parental consent, to persons convicted of a felony or imprisoned within the last 5 years, to drug addicts or to persons who are mentally retarded or who have been in a mental institution within the last 5 years.

(13) But all rifles and shotguns with barrels less than 20 inches long must be registered with the Department of Public Safety.

(14) But every dealer, upon first engaging in business, must register with the Department of Public Safety.

(15) But a person must obtain an identification card from the local police to acquire, possess or own a rifle or shotgun. The follow-

| Is a License Required to Carry a Handgun? | | Who May Not Possess or Use a Handgun? | Is a License Required to Carry or Possess a Rifle or Shotgun? | Is a License Required to Buy Ammunition? | Is a License Required to Sell Firearms (Retail)? |
Openly	Concealed				
No	Illegal to carry	Convicted felon	No	No	NSP
No[4]	Illegal to carry	Enemy aliens; persons convicted of violent felonies within past 10 years	No[13]	No	No[14]
No	Yes	Convicted felons released from jail within the last 5 years	No[5]	No	No
Yes	Yes	Persons under 21; persons convicted of a crime of violence; fugitives from justice; alcoholics; drug addicts; persons of unsound mind	No[5]	No	No, except handguns
Yes	Yes	Minors under 18 without written parental consent; felons; incompetents; addicts; aliens	No[5,15]	Yes	Yes
Yes[1]	Yes	Same as those who may not buy handguns	Yes[20]	No	No
Yes[1]	Yes[1]	[21]	Yes[1]	No	No
No	Illegal to carry	Persons under 16; convicted felons	No[16]	No	No
No	Illegal to carry	NSP	No	No	No
No	Yes[18]	Children under 14 unless accompanied by parent or qualified instructor	No	No	No
No	Illegal to carry[24]	Persons under 18; fugitives from justice; convicted felons	NSP	No	No
No	Yes	Children under 14 unless accompanied by adult; aliens; convicted felons	No	No	No
Yes[26]	Yes[1,26]	Convicted felons without permit	No[5]	No	No, except handguns
Yes[1]	Yes	Persons under 10 unless accompanied by licensed adult	Yes; identification card[5,22]	No	Yes
No	No	Persons under the influence of alcohol or narcotics; prisoners	No	No	No
Yes[29]	Yes	Persons under 16; persons without license to possess; aliens; former convicts	No[5,23,25]	No[25]	Yes
No	Illegal to carry	Convicted felons	No	No	No, except handguns

ing may not receive a card: (a) persons convicted of a felony in the last 5 years; (b) persons who have been confined to a mental institution; (c) drug addicts, alcoholics or persons who have violated state or federal drug laws; (d) persons under 15 and persons between 15 and 18 without parental consent.

(16) But all firearms with a muzzle velocity of more than 2,000 feet per second must be registered with the county sheriff.

(17) Permits are issued only to persons of lawful age, good moral character and who sheriff feels will not endanger the public safety.

(18) Only U.S. citizens and residents of the state for 6 months may apply for a permit.

(19) But license is required for convicted felons.

(20) Pistol defined to include firearms up to 30 inches in length.

(21) Minors under 18 not under supervision of

69

CHART 5 (cont.)	Is a License Required to Buy a Handgun?	Is There a Waiting Period Between Purchase & Delivery?	Are Hand-gun Sales Reported to Police?	Who May Not Buy a Handgun?
NORTH DAKOTA	Yes	Yes	Yes	Persons without a license to carry; persons under 17; persons convicted of violent crime in the last 10 years; drug addicts; alcoholics; emotionally unstable persons
OHIO	No	No	No	30
OKLAHOMA	No	No	No	Minors; convicted felons; mental incompetents
OREGON	No	5 days	Yes	Persons under 18; convicted felons
PENNSYLVANIA	No[27]	Yes: 48 hours	Yes	Persons under 17
RHODE ISLAND	No	Yes: 72 hours	Yes	Same as who may not possess a handgun
SOUTH CAROLINA	No	No	No	Persons convicted of crime of violence; persons under 21; members of subversive organizations; persons judicially adjudged unfit to possess or carry a handgun
SOUTH DAKOTA	No	Yes: 48 hours	Yes	NSP
TENNESSEE	No	15 days	Yes	Minors; aliens; persons convicted of crime of violence; fugitives from justice; mental incompetents; alcoholics; drug addicts; persons convicted of illegal sale of liquor
TEXAS	No	No	No	Minors without parental consent
UTAH	No	No	Yes	Convicts; addicts; incompetents; aliens; minors without parental consent; under 14 must be accompanied by parent
VERMONT	No	No	No	Persons under 16
VIRGINIA	Only in counties with population density over 1,000 persons a square mile	No	In some counties to clerk of county circuit court	Persons under 18
WASHINGTON	No[32]	Yes: 72 hours	Yes	Persons convicted of crime of violence; drug addicts; alcoholics; former confined mental patients
WEST VIRGINIA	No	No	No	NSP
WISCONSIN	No	Yes: 48 hours	No	Minors
WYOMING	No	No	No	NSP

parent or guardian; persons convicted of crime of violence in the past 10 years; persons committed as mentally ill or for alcoholism; convicted drug offenders.

(22) Permits or identification cards are not issued to persons under 18; persons with physical defect or illness making use of firearms unsafe; persons who were committed to a mental institution; convicted criminals; alcoholics; drug addicts; members of subversive organizations; persons who would endanger public welfare.

(23) In New York City a permit is required for the possession and purchase of rifles and shotguns. Permits are not issued to persons under 18; convicted criminals; persons who have been committed to a mental institution; drug addicts; alcoholics; mental incompetents; persons dishonorably discharged from armed services for felonious offense. Rifles and shotguns must be registered with city Firearms Control Board.

(24) Except if carrying while engaged in lawful employment.

Is a License Required to Carry a Handgun?		Who May Not Possess or Use a Handgun?	Is a License Required to Carry or Possess a Rifle or Shotgun?	Is a License Required to Buy Ammunition?	Is a License Required to Sell Firearms (Retail)?
Openly	Concealed				
Yes[1]	Yes[1]	Persons under 15 unless accompanied by parent; persons convicted of a crime; drug addicts	No	No	No, except handguns in some cities
No	No	Same as footnote 30, but minimum age is 18, not 21	No	No	No
Illegal to carry	Illegal to carry	Same as who may not buy a handgun	No	No	Yes
No	Yes[1]	Convicted felons; minors under 14; imprisoned persons	No	No	No, except handguns
No	Yes[1]	Persons under 17	No[27]	No	No, except handguns
Yes[1]	Yes[1]	Persons convicted of crime of violence; incompetents; alcoholics; addicts; fugitives from justice; aliens in U.S. less than 10 years; persons under 21	Yes[5,31]	No	Yes
Illegal to carry	Illegal to carry	Persons convicted of crime of violence; persons under 21; members of subversive organizations; persons judicially adjudged unfit to possess or carry handgun	No	No	No, except handguns
No[2]	Yes	Persons under 15 without parental consent; convicted felons	No	No	No, except handguns
No[28]	No[28]	NSP[28]	No	No	Yes
Illegal to carry	Illegal to carry	Felon convicted of act of violence, but he may possess handgun on premises where he lives	No	No	No, except handguns
No	Yes	Incompetents; minors without parental consent; under 14 must be accompanied by parent; aliens	No	No	No
No[4]	No[4]	Persons under 16 without parental consent; vagrants	No[5]	No	No
No	Yes	NSP	No[5]	No	No, except handguns
No	Yes[1,32]	Persons convicted of a crime of violence; minors under 14 without supervision by parent, person approved by parent or certified safety instructor	No[5,32]	No	No, except handguns
Yes	Yes	Persons under 18; aliens; persons who have not resided in the state for 1 year; addicts; alcoholics	Yes[5]	No	No, except handguns
No	Illegal to carry	Persons under 16 unless accompanied by an adult	No[5]	No	No
No	Illegal to carry	Aliens	No	No	No, except rifles or shotguns

(25) In New York City no rifle or shotgun ammunition may be sold to anyone not possessing a rifle or shotgun permit and certificate of registration.

(26) License required to carry loaded handgun.

(27) In Philadelphia a license is required to buy any firearms. Licenses are not issued to persons under 18; persons convicted of crimes of violence or violating Pennsylvania firearms law; persons convicted of selling, using or possessing drugs; alcoholics.

(28) But state law prohibits the carrying of a handgun "with the intent to go armed."

(29) In addition to state permit, must obtain permit from New York City.

(30) Fugitives; persons indicted for violent felonies; adjudicated juvenile delinquents; drug addicts; alcoholics; mental incompetents; persons under 21.

(31) If length is less than 26 inches.

(32) But aliens must obtain license to possess handgun, rifle or shotgun.

concerned over the threat that they represent to the privacy of all of us.

The role of the police can to some extent be controlled by the courts. With few exceptions, your home or office may not legally be searched by the police without a warrant. A search warrant is a legal document signed by a judge on the basis of information, supplied by a district attorney or a police official, that supports the belief that a crime has been committed and that evidence may be found at the scene of the search. The number of warrants issued at the present time is not regarded by experts as excessive.

Warrants are also required for legal wiretapping, a form of listening in on your telephone line. There is nothing to prevent the police from tapping your wire without a warrant, but evidence obtained by illegal wiretapping is not admissible in the federal courts or in many state courts.

Unfortunately, your privacy can be invaded in many ways other than physical search or listening devices. The burgeoning use of charge accounts of all kinds, especially of credit cards (see section 455), plus the equally rapid growth in the use of life and casualty insurance, has given a vast amount of information about you to many people you have never met or heard of. Members of the International Consumer Credit Association have files on millions of American citizens. These files contain information on your salary, your outside income, your debts and how you pay them and your reputation in your community. Life and casualty insurance companies have their own associations or bureaus which gather and keep similar information, as well as information on your health and even on your habits and any brushes you may have had with the law.

The reliability of this information depends on the persons who supplied and collected it. Some of it may be inaccurate, and you may suffer from a company's reliance on wrong information with no knowledge of what the true facts are. If you have been denied an insurance policy for which you have applied, you should stand your ground and demand to know why. Insurance is an industry that is closely regulated by the states, and you have a right to be told the reason for an insurance company's action that seems unreasonable to you.

Furthermore, of course, the federal and state governments have at least as much information about you as the retail merchant or the insurance company. The federal Internal Revenue Service and the Social Security Administration have to keep up with the most recent facts about your finances. Officials of these and other governmental bureaus are obliged to keep those facts confidential, and you should not hesitate to protest loudly if you have any reason to believe that information about you is being improperly disclosed. The price of liberty remains, as it has always been, eternal vigilance.

A number of states have recently passed laws authorizing police to stop and "frisk" people whose behavior seems suspicious, to determine whether they are carrying weapons, contraband, or the like. Despite the objections of civil liberties groups, courts appear increasingly likely to uphold this kind of action by the police.

Conditions in the community at the time may be an important factor in determining whether such police action is justifiable. If conditions were calm and the individual whom the police stopped merely seemed peculiar, the courts would probably not sanction his being stopped and frisked. But if a series of burglaries had been committed in the neighborhood and the police were conducting an intensive search for the burglars, the judge would probably uphold the policeman who was perhaps a bit too zealous in stopping someone he saw hurrying along the street late at night with a bag that might well have contained burglar tools.

23. Your Right to the Full Enjoyment of Your Property • Your property rights are protected by both federal and state constitutional and statutory provisions and by the precedents of common law. Most meaningful of these protections is the constitutional language prohibiting the taking of property without "due process of law." Although that phrase is hard to define exactly, it means at the least that your property may not constitutionally be taken from you without a judicial hearing by a court that has jurisdiction over you and the property. It also means that you must have received sufficient notice of the purpose of the hearing to prepare your defense.

This protection covers a variety of ways in which government may try to "take" your property. If you believe that your real estate is being assessed at too high a figure or that your tax rate is too high or was improperly set by the local taxing authorities, you are entitled to a trial before the authorities can fine you or sell your property for nonpayment of taxes. If a new road is planned to go through your property, you are entitled to payment for the fair value of the property—and to a hearing to settle what the fair value is. If your property is condemned for any public purpose, "due process of law" means a judicial hearing and notice to you so that you can prepare your case. It also means that your property can be taken only for a public purpose; many lawsuits are brought every year to determine whether the declared purpose is public.

In addition to these rights that fall under the "due process" clause of the Constitution, every citizen enjoys the old common-law right to the full use and quiet enjoyment of his property, whether it is personal property or real estate. There are both civil and criminal remedies for violations of this right (see sections 45, 46, 113).

24. Your Right to Equal Protection of the Laws • You will remember that the first section of the Fourteenth Amendment to the U.S. Constitution (see section 15) provides that no state shall "deny to any person within its jurisdiction the equal protection of the laws." Perhaps more than any other language in the Constitution, this "equal protection" clause has been used to strengthen and broaden civil rights.

The clause has been used to strike down a San Francisco city ordinance so administered as to deny licenses to Chinese laundries; to overturn the conviction of Jehovah's Witnesses who held Bible talks in a public park in Maryland despite the park commissioner's refusal of a permit because he disapproved of the sect; to declare unconstitutional an Oklahoma statute providing for the sterilization of criminals, because there was no reasonable classification of the criminals to be sterilized; and to strike down a variety of statutes, rules, regulations and ordinances which the Court has found to discriminate against blacks.

One of the most famous cases in which "equal protection of the laws" was found lacking was the Supreme Court decision involving school systems that were designed to provide "separate but equal" facilities for white and black students. The Court said that such school systems were separate but unequal, and that they therefore deprived the black students of the equal protection of the laws.

"Equal protection" clauses are currently being used in some states to attack the system of supporting public schools with property taxes, the case being made that communities with high property values can provide better educational facilities for their children.

In another area, Congress and many state and city legislatures have passed statutes and ordinances barring Communists from federal, state and municipal employment. The reasoning is that a true Communist is loyal only to something different from the federal, state or municipal government; why should he have equal protection under our laws? Many of these employment statutes have been upheld in the courts, along with the statutes requiring employment applicants to reveal their connection with subversive organizations. Whether the Supreme Court will uphold a particular statute depends a great deal on its wording and on the circumstances under which it was passed.

The Court's philosophy in applying the "equal protection" and "due process" clauses found forceful expression by Congress in the Civil Rights Act of 1964, which squarely bans discrimination in employment on the ground of color or sex. The act also bars discrimination in the use of public accommodations, such as hotels, motels and transportation facilities, as well as in labor organizations and employment agencies.

The act's most controversial application concerns the prohibition against the use of federal funds to support any educational institution or system that discriminates on the basis of race, color or national origin.

25. Your Right or Privilege Against Self-Incrimination • This right is spelled out in the Fifth Amendment to the United States Constitution (and in the constitutions of all states except Iowa and New Jersey): "No person . . . shall be compelled in any criminal case to be a witness against himself . . ." The privilege may be exercised in several ways. In a criminal trial its use is simple enough: the accused simply refuses to take the stand or to testify in his own defense, and the trial judge must instruct the jury not to draw unfavorable conclusions from this silence.

The privilege against self-incrimination represented a revolt against hundreds of years of legal procedure in which accused persons were examined under oath not only to obtain evidence but to get confessions as well. Today the privilege can be claimed by a witness summoned to appear before and testify in a congressional investigation or an investigation conducted by a state legislative committee.

It is true that in recent years there have been notorious abuses of the privilege against self-incrimination by alleged racketeers called before such committees. But the right is an important one, and society is prepared to uphold it even though it is sometimes misused.

The privilege is personal only, and cannot be claimed to protect others. Nor can it be claimed by a corporation or an institution; it can be invoked only by a natural person. Moreover, the person claiming the privilege must have some reason for doing so: he must have a plausible reason to fear that the answer he gives to a question may in fact result in his being charged with the commission of a crime. If you were summoned to appear before a state legislative committee investigating the need for traffic lights at important intersections, and you were asked how many times you had failed to obey a stop sign at a major intersection near your home, you could not properly decline to answer on the ground that you might be incriminated—that is, subject to criminal prosecution.

Also, there are times when your fear of being incriminated by your own statements is meaningless because you have already been guaranteed immunity from prosecution. Such guarantees are frequently made by public prosecutors or district attorneys in criminal proceedings they want to start with grand jury indictments. If the guarantee of immunity is broad, you have nothing to lose by testifying. If, having received such a guarantee of immunity, you still refuse to testify, you may be found guilty of contempt of court, fined and even sent to jail.

These are shifting legal sands, and to walk on them with any confidence you should first see your lawyer if you receive a summons either to appear or to testify.

26. Your Right to Due Process of Law · Your right to due process of law is even more important in protecting your personal freedom than it is in protecting your property rights. The courts have interpreted the Fifth Amendment guarantee that you shall not "be deprived of life, liberty, or property, without due process of law," in combination with the Fourteenth Amendment guarantee of equal protection, to give every American citizen a clear-cut and powerful group of rights if he should be accused of a crime.

If you are arrested, the police must inform you of your rights and give you a chance to exercise them by placing a phone call to a friend, a lawyer or a member of your family. You cannot be held incommunicado.

You have the right to a lawyer's services from the very moment of your arrest, and you are not required to say anything to anyone until you have had the chance to consult a lawyer. If you have no lawyer of your own or cannot afford one, the court will appoint one to handle your case.

You have a right to know what charges are made against you and to have a hearing before a magistrate within a reasonable amount of time after your arrest.

If you are held for trial you have a right to have reasonable bail set as security for your release.

You have the right to a prompt jury trial.

You have the right to confront and cross-examine your accusers and the witnesses against you and to call witnesses on your behalf.

You cannot be tried twice for the same offense.

If you are convicted, you cannot be subjected to cruel or unusual punishment.

These, briefly, are the rights of an accused person under due process of law. They are described in detail in the sections below and in chapter 4, "Your Protection Against Crime and Criminal Charges," page 133.

27. Your Right to Habeas Corpus • Habeas corpus is an old common-law writ, or legal order, which commands the release of a person who is being detained illegally. *Habeas corpus* is Latin for "you have the body." Your right to the writ of habeas corpus is guaranteed in Article I, Section 9, of the United States Constitution with these words: "The privilege of the writ of *habeas corpus* shall not be suspended, unless when in cases of rebellion or invasion the public safety may require it."

A person who has been arrested and held too long without a hearing or who has been arrested on the basis of evidence illegally obtained (see sections 22, 154, 303) or has not been granted one of his rights under due process of law (see section 26) may be freed on a writ of habeas corpus obtained by his lawyer or by a friend. To obtain a writ it is necessary to appear before the court and set forth reasons why the detention is illegal. If the judge agrees, the detained person will be released.

28. Your Right Against Double Jeopardy • This is simply your right not to be tried twice for the same offense. Before you can invoke this right, however, the first trial must actually have begun, which usually means that the jury has been impaneled and sworn. But the protection against double jeopardy does not bar a trial in a state court after a trial in a federal court for the same offense, or vice versa. The right against double jeopardy bars the government not only from starting a new criminal trial after it has failed to get a conviction the first time but also from appealing a verdict of acquittal. Of course, the accused may appeal a verdict against him.

29. Your Right to a Jury Trial • The Sixth Amendment to the United States Constitution assures everyone "the right to a speedy and public trial, by an impartial jury. . . ." Do what they will, in many parts of the country today the courts are unable to provide a speedy trial. In cities especially, the number of cases coming before courts exceeds their ability to keep up. Delays of months are not uncommon in criminal cases; and some civil cases, particularly in automobile negligence or accident matters, are held up for years. No court has yet determined what is a speedy trial, nor is one likely to for quite a while.

The right to trial in all criminal cases "by an impartial jury" is guaranteed by the Sixth Amendment to the Constitution. This is one of several rights that for many years were regarded as applying to federal matters only, not to state cases. In 1970, however, the Supreme Court took a large step forward and cleared up a good deal of confusion as to what

77

constitutes a criminal case and whether a state court might constitutionally limit the right to trial by jury. The Court said that a jury trial must be provided where the penalty for the crime charged would be imprisonment for longer than six months. An accused may not waive the right to a jury trial in a case that might result in a death sentence.

The Supreme Court has held that there is no magic to the number twelve that is used in all federal cases. In other words, states may constitutionally provide for juries of less than twelve persons.

As regards impartiality of jurors, no class of persons in a community may be excluded: women and members of minority groups are fully entitled to serve on juries. In fact, where a member of a minority group is charged with a crime, the indications are strong that other minority members must be given an opportunity to serve as jurors as long as they meet the usual technical qualifications therefor in a particular case.

LIMITATION AND SUSPENSION OF YOUR RIGHTS

30. Curfew · All the rights that we've discussed earlier in this chapter can be fully enjoyed only in times of relative peace and tranquility. The American people have been fortunate in the small number of occasions on which one or more of these rights have been suspended. But such situations have occurred and may occur again. The mildest form of suspension of your rights is a *curfew,* a status or condition of uncertain ancestry and legitimacy under which, by order of a mayor or the selectmen of a city or town, all business establishments are closed down and all citizens must stay off the streets between the hours mentioned in the order. Curfews were commonly ordered in our cities during the riots and civil disorders of the 1960s and early 1970s.

The curfew is limited to the terms of the order. It does not take the place of or in any way modify existing laws or regulations. Violation of a curfew order is a minor offense and does not constitute a crime.

31. Martial Law · The most familiar form of suspension of civil liberties is a declaration of a state of martial law. It is really no law at all, but rather the supplanting of existing law by the orders of a military commander. Martial law may be declared in a situation in which the regular legal system has broken down and the enforcement officials, the police, have become unable to keep order. There is no body of martial law—no book of doctrines or procedures. In situations such as civil war, wherein military forces must remain in control for a prolonged period, the commanding officer will usually try to work through the existing legal machinery or issue new orders called Martial Law Regulations.

Martial law should not be confused with military law. Military law is the legal framework for protecting the rights of military personnel while on active duty. It resembles nonmilitary law as much as is possible. Military personnel have legal rights, especially when accused of offenses against military law. They are entitled to counsel (an officer designated to defend them); to a trial, called a court-martial, conducted according to established procedures; and to an appeal from adverse verdicts.

32. Other Suspensions of Your Rights • There are emergency situations in which a variety of rights may be temporarily suspended by local, state or even federal officials. During the Civil War, President Abraham Lincoln suspended the privilege of the writ of habeas corpus (see section 27) throughout the United States. He took this step against widespread and vociferous objection because judges were using the writ to release vast numbers of men drafted for service in the Union Army.

In the wake of natural disasters, such as hurricanes or earthquakes, special rules that suspend or abridge your personal rights may be put into effect. The public might be barred from a certain area during rescue operations, for example. Possibly, in the next decade, executive orders will be used to ban private cars in air pollution emergencies.

These suspensions of your rights raise legal questions. Practically speaking, they are usually of short duration and so are not subject to court tests. If they were tested, most courts would probably support them as necessary to the public safety. Only in the case of a flagrant and unreasonable suspension of your rights would the courts be likely to overrule the executive.

33. When You Must Help Police • If the local police call on you for help (see section 99), you have a legal duty to respond to such a call, and when you do you have the right of a police officer so long as you are acting at their direction and under their supervision. But you do not have the right to interfere with anyone else's rights unless you are recruited by the authorities. Your right to make a citizen's arrest is extremely limited and should never be exerted unless you are absolutely sure of what you are doing. You could be charged with false arrest (see section 39).

Your Obligations as a Citizen

34. Making the System Work · Certain basic obligations of citizenship are demanded of us all. Unless we meet these obligations we cannot live as we want to. As society gets more complex, as we expect more from the government by way of services—unemployment insurance, welfare payments, public health facilities, education at all levels, decent housing, old-age benefits, perhaps even a guaranteed minimum income—the government demands more from us.

The most obvious obligation or demand is that we pay taxes—local, state and federal. Next is the obligation each of us has to obey the laws adopted by the persons we have elected to our city councils, our state legislatures and the Congress. And in time of war persons who are physically capable must serve in the armed forces, unless their religion or deeply held conviction prevents them from doing so, in which case they must usually engage in some kind of work assigned for conscientious objectors.

Our legal system, with which this book is concerned, depends on public participation in many ways. Any kind of mass or widespread violation of laws will bring about the breakdown of public order. A breakdown of law and order ends in anarchy, a complete lack of order, which throughout history has been followed by enforced order and no law. A nation that wants a society built upon law must respect the laws it adopts or change them in an orderly way if they have lost their effectiveness.

Direct participation by the public in the operation of the legal system comes through service on juries. We Americans are curiously ambivalent in this respect. Our ancestors wrote into our Constitution what they regarded as a basic right or privilege: that every accused person shall be tried by a jury. Yet many of us will do almost anything to avoid serving on a jury when we are called upon by the clerk of the court. It is scarcely surprising that the caliber of our juries is not very high, or that signs point to a declining use of juries except where required in criminal trials.

The moral here is simply that as a people we are fortunate in having a legal system that allows us to enjoy many rights and privileges. The continued smooth operation of the system is essential to our continued enjoyment of them. And this requires that every citizen meet his obligation to understand and observe our laws and to fulfill the duties they place upon him.

—

CHAPTER THREE

Your Protection Against Wrongs

—

Ignorance of the law excuses no man;
not that all men know the law, but because 'tis
an excuse every man will plead.

—JOHN SELDEN

3

Your Protection Against Wrongs

Some Key Points in This Chapter—
Consult these sections for information on:

What a tort is and who can or cannot be liable for one, **35–38**
Intentional torts—false arrest, assault, battery, libel, **39–44**
Nuisances, trespass, misuse of your property, fraud, **45–49**
Defenses if you are sued for an intentional tort, **50–55**
Accidental wrongs—and how careful you must be, **56–62**
Assumption of risk, contributory negligence, other defenses
against negligence suits, **63–65**
If you are injured on the job or buy faulty merchandise, **66–70**
How to measure your money damages, **71**
Getting back your property or stopping wrongful acts, **72, 73**
What a lawsuit costs, **75**
What to do if you are the victim of a tort, **76–81**
How a civil suit is tried, **82–87**
How a civil judgment can be enforced, **88**

Charts in This Chapter
Statutes of Limitation for Starting a Civil Action, page 124
Garnishment of Wages, page 131

What a Tort Is and How
It Differs from a Crime

Most of us are generally aware of what crimes are (murder, arson, theft, bigamy, for example) but are vague about what lawyers call torts. There's a good reason: leading legal writers agree that no one has satisfactorily defined a tort. This is partly because torts are so common, so widespread and so varied. You are far more likely to be the victim of a tort than of a crime, and you are also far more likely to commit a tort than a crime. The purposes of this chapter are: (a) to explain torts; (b) to show how they differ from crimes; (c) to stress the importance, in the law of torts, of negligence, intent and liability; (d) to indicate what relief is available to you when a tort has been committed against you or your property; (e) to show you how to seek that relief by starting a lawsuit; (f) to explain how such a suit is tried; and (g) to show what defenses are available to you if you are sued.

35. Differences Between Torts and Crimes • A tort is a civil wrong against an individual. A crime, on the other hand, is an offense against the public at large, or the state. An automobile driver who carelessly bumps into your car in a parking lot and crumples the fender has committed a tort against your property. Because the law recognizes your legal right to freedom from injury to your property caused by other people's carelessness, you are entitled to sue the driver and be awarded damages for his breach of your right. But he has committed no crime.

Suppose, however, that after leaving the parking lot the same driver goes to a nearby bar, downs six whiskeys, then careens through a crowded city street at fifty miles an hour. Now he has committed at least these crimes: drunken driving, reckless driving and endangering the lives of others. But unless he actually damages another car or injures someone he has not violated the rights of any individual. His offenses are against the people as a whole. For these offenses he may be arrested and prosecuted by the state.

A crime, then, is a wrongful act against society. When a crime is committed, it is the state's responsibility to instigate, prosecute and bear the expense of legal action against the defendant, in the court handling criminal matters. The title to this kind of legal action, therefore, is usually *The People* v. *Smith* or *The State* v. *Jones*. For a serious crime, the penalty may be death, life imprisonment or imprisonment for a certain number of years, depending on the laws of the state in which it was committed. Other, less serious crimes—such as violation of the antitrust law or other laws in the commercial area—may be punishable by shorter terms of imprisonment or by a fine—and sometimes by both. Still other offenses, of course, are punishable only by fines. These fines are paid into the national, state or local treasury. Their purpose is to deter others from disobeying similar statutory requirements or restrictions. (For a complete discussion of crimes, see chapter 4, page 133.)

A tort, on the other hand, is an act that violates your private or personal rights. Unless the act that is a tort is also a crime, the state will do nothing about it. If you believe someone has violated your personal rights—but has not acted against the interests of the public as a whole— it is entirely up to you to seek relief by suing him in the civil courts. If the person who you believe has legally aggrieved you is found liable— that is, if the judge or jury finds that he did in fact injure you or your property—he may be required (a) to give you relief by paying you "damages" for the injury or property loss you suffered, (b) to discontinue his wrongful acts or (c) to restore to you what he took from you. In rare cases he may be imprisoned. All monetary damages awarded to you by the court in your suit are of course yours to keep. By the same token, the cost of hiring a lawyer to handle your case is your own personal expense whether you win or lose the case. Even a defendant who wins must bear his own legal costs.

If the tort is also a crime, two separate legal actions confront the wrongdoer: yours and the state's. We will discuss later the effect of these actions on each other. But they are independent of each other.

36. Elements of a Tort • A tort is usually committed when someone injures you physically, damages or misuses your property, attacks your reputation without justification or takes away your liberty and freedom of action without just cause. To recover damages for a tort you must prove either that the act was committed with *deliberate intent* (as when someone circulated a letter calling you a thief) or that it was the result of *negligence* (as in the case of the driver in the parking lot who carelessly hit your car when he had a duty to drive carefully).

In most cases you must prove that the act inflicted actual damage or injuries. A malicious act that does you no harm, such as a threat to punch you in the nose or a shove in a crowded subway, is not a sufficient cause for legal action.

84

Nor are you likely to recover damages from a neighbor when the healthy-looking elm tree in his yard crashes down on your roof in a windstorm. The crash was not something he intended, nor was it the result of his negligence.

A person who is proved to have committed a tort will be held responsible for all the damages proved to have resulted from his act. A motorist who sideswipes your car, causing you to swerve and hit a pedestrian, is responsible in damages both to you (for the injury to your car) and to the pedestrian (for his dental expenses in replacing the false teeth knocked out when your car hit him). A mugger who attacks you on the street, leading you, in defending yourself, to raise your umbrella so quickly that you hit a passerby, is responsible both to you (for the shock to your nervous system) and to the passerby (for the cost of stitching up his scalp). He is also guilty of a crime and can be arrested and prosecuted.

37. Who Can Be Held Responsible for Committing a Tort • Generally speaking, any person, young or old, mentally competent or not, is responsible for his torts: for the consequences of his actions to others injured by those actions. Here again is an interesting distinction between crimes and torts. As is explained in sections 137 and 338, children below a certain age are not usually liable for crimes they commit, on the ground that children of their age really don't understand the significance of their actions. For basically the same reason, persons who have been adjudged mentally incompetent are not liable for their crimes. But these same persons may be liable for their torts, whether they are deliberate or the result of carelessness.

Intent is an essential element in such torts as libel or trespass. Intent is an essential element in many crimes. But the same person who in the eyes of the law is not mentally competent to commit a crime, on the ground that an insane person lacks intent, may nonetheless be held liable for committing a tort. A lunatic who escapes from an insane asylum with a gun, breaks into a house, gets trigger-happy and shoots up the china and puts a bullet or two in the owner's thigh would be held liable for damages for trespass, battery and the value of the china he broke—if the homeowner chose to sue him. But he might well escape criminal prosecution either for breaking and entering the house or for assault and battery on the owner.

Almost all employers are liable for the torts of their employes if the employe committed the harmful act during the course of his employment. The law books are full of cases on both sides of this question of *course of employment.* The delivery truck driver who backs over a flower bed while delivering a package for his department store employer presents no problem: the department store is liable for the resulting damages. But suppose the driver notices that the package he is delivering has no string and is about to fall apart. He parks the truck, enters a stationery store, orders string and in an argument with the store owner over the price bangs his fist through a glass counter top. Is the department store liable to the stationery store owner for the cost of repairing the counter? Probably, on the ground that the driver was in the stationery store "in the course of his employment." But suppose that the driver, thirsty after the fight, stops again, this time at a bar, goes in for a beer and carelessly breaks the glass door down as he enters. Is the department store owner liable for the damages his truck driver caused the saloonkeeper? Probably not, on the ground that the visit to the bar is not in the regular course of the driver's employment.

The point to keep in mind is that the law usually holds an employer liable for what happens when his employe is carrying out his instructions and working on his behalf. But not all employers—especially not governmental ones. The doctrine of *sovereign immunity*—that the state cannot be sued except by its own consent—severely limits your right to sue governments and governmental bodies for the torts of their employes. The United States government and the governments of many states have in recent years passed laws that do permit such suits to be brought against them. In some instances separate courts, usually called courts of claims, have been established to handle these actions. But this ground has been given grudgingly, and you had better talk to a lawyer before you decide to press a claim against either the United States government or the government of your state. What may seem to you an open-and-shut case entitling you to substantial damages may prove to be much more difficult because of the legal complications created by sovereign immunity. Your ability to sue at all is an "act of grace" by the government concerned, and the courts are careful to ensure that the government's liability is kept within bounds.

38. Who May Not Be Held Liable in Tort Actions • Some people may not be held liable in tort actions. Among them are husbands and wives, who are not considered responsible for each other's torts, and parents, who are not usually liable for the torts of their children. Many people are not aware of this. But if your ten-year-old son carelessly knocks a baseball through a store window you are not legally responsible for the cost of replacing it—despite the owner's angry protests.

The situation changes, however, if a parent knows that his child has developed what lawyers call a vicious propensity to commit acts that injure other people or their property. If the neighborhood bully has a habit of going around hitting smaller children and stoning dogs and cats, and if his parents know about his habitual bad behavior, the court might find that it was their duty to restrain and control him. If they allow him to continue in his destructive ways, they might be found liable for damage he caused. In addition, some states have passed laws that do make the parents responsible for willful damage caused by their minor child (see section 330 and chart 23, page 375).

Of course, if it can be established that the husband or the parent actually thought up the tortious action, planned it and coerced or persuaded his wife or child into committing it, he will be held responsible for the act and liable for the damage it caused.

Police officers, sheriffs and other peace officers acting in the course of their official duties are not liable in tort unless they use excessive force or exceed their authority in discharging their duties. The police might be subject to disciplinary action by their superior officers, but generally they have no liability to you. The same general rule applies to many kinds of public officials working under actual or even implied orders from their superiors. You can't sue the overeager tax collector who charges you an excessive real estate levy. You may pay the money under protest and sue the senior official in charge, or the municipality, for a refund of your overpayment, but the collector is safe.

Intentional Interference with Your Personal Rights

Except for so-called acts of God (see section 244), any interference with your personal or property rights, whether intentional or through negligence, is a tort. Here we will discuss intentional interference, and we will take up the whole subject of negligence in sections 56–62.

39. Interference with Your Freedom of Movement · You have a right to unrestricted freedom of movement. This holds true unless you are under some legal restraint, such as confinement in a mental institution if you have been found incompetent or in a jail if you have been charged with or convicted of a crime. *False imprisonment* is the term the courts apply to any interference with your right of unrestricted freedom of movement. Another frequently used term is *false arrest*.

This tort, whatever it is called, means much more than interference with your right by police or other public officials, although it certainly does cover such interference. It means any detention that is not justified by law. It is this lack of right or justification that makes the arrest or imprisonment false. Let's say you are peacefully parading in a picket line that meets the requirements of peaceful picketing (see sections 386, 388), and a policeman orders you to go with him to the police station, saying, "You're under arrest." You do what he says because you think he has the authority to say so. Your freedom of movement has been interfered with, and it has been interfered with falsely because you have a right to picket. The arrest is false, and you may be entitled to sue the policeman or the city, as his employer, for interfering with that right.

You might be falsely imprisoned in many situations, such as being detained in a store by threats or by force because a shoplifter is known to be in the building and the management decides to examine all customers before they leave. False arrest suits based on this kind of detention have become so common that most stores now instruct their security guards not to approach a suspected shoplifter in the store but to wait until he has gone into the street.

Or you might not be allowed to leave a restaurant for an unreasonable amount of time because the waitress misplaced your money and you couldn't prove that you paid your bill. In both these cases your freedom of movement was restricted by the management without legal authority, that is, falsely. One court has gone a step further and said that if you restrict your own movements because you are afraid that someone who has threatened to damage your property can and will carry out his threat, you can sue him for false imprisonment.

Under all these situations you have an *action*—a right to sue—for damages. The amount of damages will depend on the actual injury you suffered. You are entitled to compensation for loss of time, any inconvenience or physical discomfort and any injuries to your health. If your false imprisonment was malicious—if your confinement was designed to harass you—your award could include *punitive* damages, that is, damages large enough to be a real deterrent to the defendant. But if you were falsely imprisoned along with many other persons because of stupidity or overeagerness (as in the shoplifting incident), and you were

88

merely inconvenienced, your damages would probably be *nominal,* that is, just enough to establish or protect your individual rights.

40. Misuse of the Legal Process • Similar to false imprisonment and false arrest, but quite different legally, are what are known as malicious prosecution and abuse of process. You have a right to freedom from the deliberate misuse of the law and the courts.

If you have been unjustly prosecuted for a crime because of someone's malicious accusations, you can sue. You have to prove that the case has been decided in your favor, that there was no real ground ("absence of probable cause") for the proceeding and that the person who started the proceeding was motivated by malice or that his primary motive was not simply to bring you to justice. In the case of false imprisonment or false arrest, you are improperly or falsely detained. In the case of *malicious prosecution,* which we have just described, you are properly detained but for improper reasons or motives.

An example of malicious prosecution is when your neighbor, out of sheer spite or dislike of you, goes down to the police station and accuses you of molesting his young daughter. He is believed; a warrant is issued for your arrest; you are arraigned, plead not guilty, are duly tried and are found innocent by the court. At the trial the testimony of your neighbor and his daughter reveals both his hostility to you and the fact that there was absolutely no basis for the action. You have an action for damages against your neighbor—but not against the police officer who arrested you or against the prosecuting attorney, because they were simply doing their duty.

Although suits for malicious prosecution were originally used only as protection against the improper bringing (and continuing) of criminal actions, they are now used increasingly when civil proceedings are brought for ulterior motives: as when someone starts a civil proceeding for some other reason than simply winning the suit he starts.

Your hostile neighbor may be afraid to accuse you falsely of committing a crime or may decide that he hasn't enough evidence against you to risk a countersuit for malicious prosecution. But he may decide that he can sue you for defamation of his character if he bribes several persons to testify that you have gone around the community spreading stories that he beats his children every night. If you win the action he brings against you and can establish that his real reason for suing you was to injure you financially—that is, that he had an ulterior motive—you may sue him in return for the tort of malicious prosecution, or the

89

wrongful bringing of civil proceedings. Your neighbor has interfered with your personal right of freedom from unjustified legal proceedings, and he is liable to you for damages you suffered in defending yourself in these proceedings.

Only slightly different is the tort known as *malicious abuse of process*. The principle is the same: misusing the legal process to harass someone. But abuse of process implies a valid legal proceeding brought for an invalid purpose, or for a purpose different from the one usually sought in the proceeding. If your neighbor sues you for trespass (see section 46) simply to force you to sell him a piece of your property that he's long desired, it is an abuse of process. You have a right to be free from such twistings of the law and may sue him for what it cost to defend yourself.

41. Interference with Your Person • You have a right to be free from bodily injury, however slight. You also have a right to freedom from threats of injury that you sensibly believe may be carried out. In recent times the courts have also devised ways to compensate you for suffering or distress that may be more mental than physical or that may be a combination of both.

Assault and battery are two of the oldest torts in legal history. The difference between them is simple. An *assault* is an open threat of bodily contact with someone, without his permission. The actual contact is a *battery*. If you get so mad at your neighbor that you go up to him with a baseball bat and say you'll knock out his brains, you have committed the tort of assault. If you lose control and actually hit him, you have committed the tort of battery. Actual contact is what distinguishes battery from assault, even though the contact may be only a touch or a stolen kiss, if made without permission. The contact may be with your body or anything attached to it, like your clothing or the chair you're sitting in.

The purpose of the courts is to keep the peace by providing a substitute for private fighting, to give you a legal alternative to retaliating physically if someone spits in your face or seizes your coat and shouts at you.

Just as you have a right to freedom from actual offensive contact with your person, so you have a right to freedom from fear of such contact. If someone brandishes a club in your face and starts to swing it as though he were going to hit you, you may sue him for damages for the tort of assault. The action is essentially for a mental, rather than a physical, interference with your rights: the "touching is of the mind, not of the body," as one court put it. Your damages are therefore for mental upset, fright, humiliation and for any physical illness that may result.

90

But your fear that you will be hurt must be reasonable. Even though you know your neighbor has been involved in several barroom brawls, you have no action against him if he walks menacingly up to your property line and shakes his fist at you but remains fifteen feet away. What is important is the immediacy of physical threat, not the way the threat is made.

42. Interference with Your Peace of Mind • The growth in the sciences of medicine and psychology has brought about an expansion of the idea of freedom from fear or apprehension. You may have an action against someone who intentionally inflicts mental suffering on you. For example, if someone falsely tells you that your wife has been struck by a car and rushed to the hospital, you may sue him for the emotional anguish you suffer as a result of his lies. Similarly, you may use this kind of suit to protect yourself against the high-pressure methods of collection agencies that harass you with abuse and accusations and threats of lawsuits.

If the woman who receives a series of lewd and obscene telephone calls could identify the caller, she would probably have an action against him for the mental distress she suffers. So would the person who receives telephone calls falsely reporting the death in wartime of a husband or son—and who suffers severe mental shock as a result. You have a right to freedom from the consequences of this kind of malicious act, and the courts protect that right by awarding damages—nominal, or small, if the harm is slight; punitive, or large, if the damage is great or the act particularly outrageous.

43. Interference with Your Privacy • Another right increasingly protected by the courts is the right to *privacy:* your right to be let alone. The right to privacy has been recognized in a large number of lawsuits and now exists in almost all states, either as a result of court decisions or by legislation. Interference with your right to privacy can take many forms. Perhaps the simplest examples of interference are the most obvious: searching your house without a warrant (such a search would also be a trespass, giving you additional grounds for suing the searcher; see sections 46, 303); eavesdropping on your telephone conversations by wiretapping your phone without the court's consent.

But there are less direct ways of interfering with your right to privacy that also give you the right to sue. One of these is giving objectionable publicity to private information about you. If the bank where you have your checking account published your name in your local newspaper in a list of persons who had overdrawn their accounts, you would have a right to sue the bank for invasion of your right to privacy—even though you really had overdrawn your account. Your relationship with your banker is contractual (see sections 166–185) and commercial, and he has no right to make public the private facts he knows about you.

44. Interference with Your Reputation · As important as any freedom to which you are entitled is freedom from unwarranted, untruthful attacks on your character. This kind of attack, if made in the presence of other people, constitutes *defamation,* for which you are entitled to nominal or punitive damages, as the case may be. If you are defamed orally, you have been *slandered*. If the defamation is in writing and shown to or seen by someone else, you have been *libeled*. Slander is the less serious of the two torts because it is fleeting. The spoken words of defamation exist only as they are uttered and then disappear forever. Libel is permanent as long as the letter, magazine article or book in which the words appear continues to exist, and the damages awarded are therefore usually larger. Generally speaking, defamatory statements made over radio and television are now considered libelous rather than slanderous.

You can recover damages for slander or libel without proving actual financial loss if you are accused of something as serious as having committed a crime or having a "loathsome" disease (such as syphilis) or if you're accused of being a butcher if you are a surgeon or a shyster if you are a lawyer. The reason is that, since the good reputation of a professional person is essential to his ability to make a living, the law assumes that such accusations will diminish that ability and will therefore damage him. Lawyers call this kind of attack slander or libel *per se*.

Remember that to entitle you to recover damages both libel and slander must be "published"—that is, communicated to others. If your neighbor calls you a thief over the backyard fence, with no one else present to hear him, he has not slandered you. Nor has he libeled you just by writing you a letter charging you with bigamy: he must show his letter to you to someone else.

Of course the attacks on you, written or oral, must be untrue to constitute libel or slander. Truth is almost always a perfect defense in an action for either tort. Freedom of speech is one of our most cherished rights. It wouldn't amount to much if we were not free to say things about others that we know to be true. The only exception to this—and it is a rare one—is when the statements were true but the sole motive in making them was to hurt you. The court might in this case hear a suit for the malicious use of true information. Spreading lies about others is different, however, especially when the lies may affect their ability to make a living or may hurt them in their family or public relationships.

You can go pretty far in expressing your opinion these days, but you risk a lawsuit if you go too far in commenting on your neighbor's personal traits. An amusing example was provided by the drama critic Heywood Broun, who wrote such a savagely critical attack on an actor's performance in a play that the actor sued Broun for libel. The lawsuit was still in the courts when the same actor appeared in another play. All concerned rushed to Broun's review to see what he had to say about the actor this time. The actor's performance, Broun wrote simply, "wasn't up to his usual standard."

Another defense, in actions for slander, is that the statement was *privileged;* that is, the person who made it had a special immunity from legal action. Legislators—such as United States congressmen and state senators and assemblymen—have absolute freedom of expression on the floor of the legislature. So if your congressman makes a speech in the House of Representatives accusing you of having supported the Nazis in World War II or of financing all Mafia activities in your state, all you can do is write him a letter or issue a statement to the press daring him to make the same charges off the floor of the House—when he won't have his defense of privilege and you may sue him for slander. But don't let your anger goad you into accusing him in public of being a liar and a cheat and a child beater, unless you can prove what you say, or you may find yourself being sued.

Similarly, judges while conducting their official duties are privileged to say whatever they want, whether in addressing witnesses, talking with counsel in court or charging the jury. Other public officials have more limited privilege.

In recent years another legal doctrine has grown up in connection with charges of slander and libel. This is the rule of *fair comment,* under which courts have held that public figures and elected and appointed officials must expect and accept a harsher degree of criticism about the conduct of their jobs than private persons. If a newspaper charged the state treasurer with incompetent handling of public funds, this criticism would probably fall under the fair comment rule, because the treasurer's competence is a legitimate subject of public interest. He could not recover damages in a libel suit against the paper. But if the same newspaper was to attack a privately owned firm of accountants as being slipshod in its work, the company could probably sue and recover successfully.

93

Intentional Interference with Your Property Rights

45. Nuisances and What to Do About Them • Just as you have a right to freedom from interference with your personal rights, so you have a right to freedom from interference with your property rights. You have a right to unrestricted enjoyment and use of your real and personal property. Your right to the "quiet enjoyment" of your property protects you not only from trespass on it by uninvited persons but from certain things that nearby landowners or tenants may do on their own property that cause you undue annoyance, inconvenience, discomfort or injury. These are called *nuisances*. A large number of nuisance cases fill the law books every year, and the number is likely to grow as the world becomes more populated and people live increasingly closer to one another.

There are two kinds of nuisances, public and private. The difference between them is the same one that is found throughout the law of torts: a public nuisance is one that interferes with the interest of your entire community, while a private nuisance is one affecting your interest only. Typical public nuisances are: someone in your neighborhood has a pond that he doesn't clean and from which bad smells often come; a tenant plays his stereo set or radio every night so loud that you and your neighbors in adjoining apartments can't sleep; someone shoots off fireworks in the streets. All these and similar uses of your neighbor's property cause distress to the whole community, not just to you.

A private nuisance, on the other hand, is conduct by your neighbor that interferes only with your freedom to enjoy the use of your property. The classic example is the "spite fence" erected by your neighbor, on his land, to keep out sunlight and air from your property and generally to make you feel confined and hemmed in when there is no reason for it. A neighbor who failed to maintain his septic tank, with the result that his sewage flowed onto your land, would be liable for a private nuisance against you. He would probably also be guilty of violating the local sanitation laws, but that violation would be an offense (see section 90). So by the same act he would be accountable for both a tort and an offense.

Your remedies are what you might expect. For both public and private nuisances you and your neighbors should yourselves seek an *injunction*— a court order to prevent someone from doing something (see section 73)—ordering the offensive conduct to be stopped. Or you may sue for

94

damages for the harm caused by the nuisance. Sometimes you may seek both. Frequently you will find that local ordinances prohibit the nuisance, so that it is worthwhile to consult the local public prosecutor and ask him to proceed in the name of the state against the property owner or tenant who is maintaining the nuisance.

You are hearing much more about public nuisances as the public is becoming more concerned about such problems as water and air pollution. The law frequently follows public sentiment, even though courts are often reluctant to put a stop to public nuisances that arise from commercial and industrial uses of property. Anyone who lives in the neighborhood of a chemical plant or a paper mill knows only too well the smells and the water pollution they can cause. The courts must balance the public's interest in industrial production against the public's interest in the enjoyment of clean air and water. Where courts lag, or tend to uphold industrial interests against those of the people as a whole, the legislature steps in and enacts statutes that force industry to devise and install antipollutants (see section 608). Much more such legislation is likely to be enacted in years to come. Meanwhile, you and your neighbors have a variety of weapons to use in really intolerable situations (see sections 610–615). Your lawyer should be consulted as to which of these weapons to use, when and how.

46. Keeping Others off Your Property · If someone comes onto your land or into your house or apartment without your permission, he has committed the tort of *trespass,* and you may sue him even though he does no damage whatever to your land, house or apartment. As the person legally in possession, you are entitled to the complete and unrestricted "quiet enjoyment" of your property, even though you may be only the tenant. Indeed, if you are the tenant you, not your landlord, are the only person who can bring the action for trespass. Again, the amount of the damages you will be awarded depends on the circumstances of the case. For trespass and nothing more your damages would be nominal, or very small, but enough to assert your rights and to warn others not to interfere with them.

In fact, you must assert your rights over your property or run the risk of losing some of those rights. For example, you own a field between a public road and a school, and children get into the habit of freely and openly crossing over your field in going to and from school. If they do so for a long period of time—usually from ten to twenty years—the public may be held to have won or gained the right to use your property. This is called a *prescriptive right*. You are said in effect to have surrendered your right to the exclusive use of your own property by failing ever to mention or complain about the trespassers (see section 302 and chart 19).

A famous example of this principle is Rockefeller Plaza, a short street that runs in front of the RCA Building in New York City. Although the street is privately owned it is generally open to traffic. But on one day a year it is closed to vehicles just to protect the owners' rights against any claim that the property has become a public way by default.

In some cases you may actually lose the ownership of property entirely if you allow others to occupy and use it as if it were their own over a long period of time (see section 302). For example, a mistake was made in a survey of your property years ago. A new survey shows that ever since you moved in, your neighbor has been using, as part of his croquet court, land that was actually yours. Ownership of that bit of land may therefore actually have passed to him.

Your right to the exclusive use of your property extends both upward and downward for a reasonable distance. Your neighbor may not legally build a house in a tree next to your property line if part of the tree house extends over your property. Nor may he legally tunnel under your property to reach a river on the other side in order to get water from it for his own use. An airline may fly high over your property without giving you an action for trespass—but the pilot of a small plane who regularly flies it barely over the treetops is trespassing. How high must the pilot fly to be free from damages for trespass? The question is one the courts have not settled.

The airplane problem more often arises where property owners next to an airport are harassed by the noise of aircraft taking off and landing. There is a technical tort of trespass, to be sure, but the property owners have usually sued for the tort of a public nuisance. The problem is like the one that confronts the family living near the chemical factory. And here, too, the courts are caught between the public's interest in encouraging the development of air travel and the property owners' right to enjoy their property free from excessive noise. Despite their very legitimate grievances, property owners usually come out on the losing side of these airport cases, providing an excellent demonstration of why you should check present and future development plans in an area before you buy a house (see section 277).

47. The Misuse of Your Personal Property • You also have a right to the unrestricted and uninterrupted enjoyment of your personal property,

96

just as you do the enjoyment of your real property. The law provides remedies for the intentional interruption of your right or interference with it. Interference with your personal property is known as the tort of *conversion*. It can be conduct intended to affect your personal property or conduct that, even though not intentionally wrong, is inconsistent with your right of ownership. Let's say that you sell your house, move out and leave some barrels in the cellar. If the buyer, believing you have abandoned them, sells them as junk, you may sue him for conversion. The purchaser of goods stolen from you or the auctioneer who innocently sells them is also a converter, because even though he did not know it he has interfered with your control of your property. You are entitled to recover the value of the goods from him. In effect, the defendant in these cases is required to buy the goods from you at a forced sale. This is the reason you yourself should avoid buying anything of questionable or suspicious origin.

But common sense should dictate your decision to sue for conversion. If someone removes your coat from your hanger at the office, but returns it half an hour later when he discovers it is not his, you would not win an action for conversion. But if he kept your coat a year, or intended to sell it to someone else when he took it, he would be liable.

Other common examples of conversion are: (a) Your property is borrowed and used without your permission: your neighbor, without your knowledge or permission, removes your lawnmower from your garage and uses it. (b) Someone intentionally alters the property you have loaned him: your wife lends her long evening dress to your neighbor's wife, who proceeds to convert it into a miniskirt. (c) Someone to whom you loaned your property uses it in a different way from that upon which you had agreed: you lend your car to someone to travel to the suburbs for the weekend, and he returns it a week later having traveled 500 miles. In all these cases, your control of your property has been interfered with, and you are entitled to sue for the tort of conversion.

48. Interference with Your Contractual and Business Relationships • You have a right to freedom from interference by others with the contractual relationships you have entered into. (For a full discussion of contracts see chapter 5, "Your Personal Property, Contracts and Purchases," page 185). This right extends to your family relationships too. If your mother-in-law persuades your wife to leave you, you may sue her for interfering with your marriage.

If you are a well-known artist, commissioned to paint a mural in a public building, and another artist induces the owner of the building to fire you and commission him instead, you may sue the other artist for interference with your contract rights—and sue the building owner for damages for breach of his contract with you. (You are unlikely, however, to recover your actual damages twice!) Malice or ill will need not be involved in this kind of interference, although a purely accidental interference might result in nominal, or very small, damages compared with the damages you might be awarded if you persuaded the court that the defendant set out to ruin your reputation as an artist and succeeded.

49. Fraud, Deceit and Misrepresentation • You have a right to freedom from being improperly induced or persuaded to do something, or not to do something, by someone's trickery. What is involved in this tort is: (a) a conscious or knowing false statement made to you, (b) by someone who knew the statement was false, (c) with the intention that you would rely on it, (d) followed by your actual reliance on it and (e) your suffering as a result. If you marry a girl because she says that she is worth a million dollars and she turns out to be penniless, your marriage contract can be set aside or annulled. If a policyholder obtained his life insurance policy by telling the salesman that he hadn't seen a doctor during the past five years, when in fact he had recently been treated for a bad heart, from which he died the week after taking out the policy, the company would be able to rescind the policy and avoid payment under it. The remedy will be different in each case. The main thing for the person suing to establish is that he was consciously tricked and that if he had been given the correct information he would not have acted as he did.

You should be wary when you are buying something, however, because courts recognize the right of a salesman to *puff,* or exaggerate, within reason, the merits of his product (see section 190). It might be difficult to prove that his exaggeration amounted to fraud or misrepresentation.

IF YOU ARE SUED: DEFENSES OF PRIVILEGE

50. When You Are the Defendant • Sections 39–49 have discussed your various rights to freedom of movement, to the peaceful enjoyment of your property, to freedom from invasion of your privacy and from unjustified attacks on your person and on your good name and reputation. For interference with any of these rights, the law provides you with a remedy, whether in the form of damages or in the form of an action to direct someone to stop his interference or to recover the property he improperly took from you.

Now let's assume you are the defendant in an action brought by someone charging you with having committed one or more of these torts. What defenses do you have? Much will depend on the specific tort with which you are charged and on the relationship between you and the person who is suing you (called the *plaintiff*). Under certain circumstances you may have acted in such a manner that the courts will protect you, even though you may have caused damage to the plaintiff: your action is said to be *privileged*. The term covers all the specific defenses that are taken up in sections 51–55.

51. If You Acted in Error • One defense, available to you in very limited circumstances, is mistake. Suppose you are a policeman carrying a warrant that seems valid but is technically faulty, and you make an arrest as authorized by the warrant. You may effectively plead that because of a mistake made in good faith you had the right to make the arrest and that therefore you are not liable in damages to the plaintiff whom you mistakenly arrested. Or suppose someone convinces you that the store across the street has been robbed and that the robber is still in the building. You rush in and arrest the person in the store, only to find at the police station that there was in fact no robbery and that you arrested the store owner. You are not liable to him, because you made an honest mistake while doing your duty.

But be careful, for the defense that you made a mistake will not protect you from liability for several torts. If you trespass on someone's land in the innocent and honest assumption that you own it or that you know the boundary when in fact you are mistaken, you have committed the tort of trespass and are liable to the true owner in damages despite your mistake. Also, if you buy a television set in the honest but mistaken belief that the seller owns it, you are liable for the tort of conversion if the real owner asks for it back and you refuse to give it to him.

52. If You Acted with Consent • *Consent* is a common defense against the charge that you have intentionally interfered with your neighbor's use of his property or his freedom of action. What the law says is that his consent means there was no tort at all. Your neighbor's consent may be *express,* as when the two of you regularly box together and one day you hit him so hard you knock him out; or *implied,* as when, after allowing you for months to enter his apartment to watch a television program, he suddenly sues you for trespass. In both these cases your defense would be effective.

In some circumstances, however, a defendant may not use the defense of consent. The best example is presented by the "statutory rape" situation. Statutes in most states provide that sexual intercourse with a girl below a certain age constitutes the crime of rape, and there are cases where the court has granted the girl an award of damages in a tort action for battery (see section 41), even though it was established that she gave her consent. In the same spirit—reasoning that they can't understand the nature of the act they consent to—the law considers infants and mental incompetents incapable of giving their consent.

As you might expect, consent brought about by mistake or fraud is no consent at all, and cannot be offered as a defense to a tort action. But the mistake must be about the essential nature of the act to be done, not merely about what inducement is being offered for permission to do it.

53. If You Acted to Defend Yourself or Others • Things you do in self-defense, the defense of others and the defense of your property may well be covered by privilege. For several hundred years it has been clear that you have a legal right to use reasonable force to defend yourself. This includes not only your right to protect yourself against someone who threatens to attack you but also your right to protect yourself against unwarranted imprisonment or confinement, whether intentional or not. But you must prove the facts that you claim created the privilege for you.

In defending yourself you should not use force greater than the force you fear or have suffered. If a child willfully kicks you, you may grab, shake or spank him to get him to stop. But you certainly cannot legally smash him in the face with your fist or a club. If someone fires at you or at a member of your family or threatens to do so with a gun you believe to be loaded, you have the right to shoot him, even to kill him. But if someone merely slaps you, you may strike him back but you have no right to shoot him, beat him senseless or to try to maim or kill him. In other words, take it easy. If you use more force than necessary defending yourself, you will lose the privilege of self-defense if charges of battery are brought against you.

Remember, too, that your right to defend yourself physically must be exercised at the time you are threatened, not later. If you are attacked by surprise and knocked senseless, the law gives you no right to revenge yourself later by beating up your assailant. All you can do is notify the police, charge him with one or more crimes and sue him for battery.

You have the legal right, but not the duty, to come to the aid of anyone you believe is in imminent danger of harm at the hands of another person—and to use all reasonably necessary force to protect him. Let's say you see a man cruelly and brutally beating up his child on the street. In coming to the help of the child you knock the father down and he suffers a concussion when his head hits a hydrant as he falls. Your actions would be regarded as privileged if he later sues you for the tort of battery. But you must be able to establish the facts: the "burden of proof," usually on the plaintiff (see section 84), would be on you.

54. If You Acted to Defend Your Property · In defending your property against trespassers and others who come onto your land not only to trespass but to steal or to damage your buildings, you are entitled to use as much force as seems necessary. You may attack the robber who refuses to leave, and you are certainly not liable if he falls and breaks his leg while running away. But if you shoot an unarmed burglar whom you have not even warned away, you would not have the privilege of defense of your property if he sued you for battery. You would probably be held to have used excessive force and he might be able to recover damages from you.

Think before you act. You are taking risks if, for example, as you come home from work you see your neighbor running off with your new skis and you then and there, on the spur of the moment, break open his front door, knock him down, grab the skis and take them back to your house. The wiser course would be to demand that he return them and then to call the police and your lawyer, who will put more effective and less dangerous machinery into operation. The risk of immediate action is that your neighbor may sue you and that you may have difficulty proving that he meant to steal the skis. You have a right to recover your own property, but you are not entitled to use excessive force in so doing.

This problem of recovering stolen goods particularly plagues store owners who are the victims of shoplifters. Nowadays stores frequently employ house detectives and other guards to stop suspected shoplifters. It is often difficult to prove that what looks like theft is not just carelessness. Moreover, if the suspect is detained in the store while the management calls in the local police, the suspect may have an action for false imprisonment. The increasing use of closed-circuit television enables the management more easily than before to identify shoplifters. But shoplifting remains a very considerable problem, precisely because of the accused's right of personal freedom. Management's detention of the suspect may not always be protected by the privileged right to recover its stolen goods.

55. If You Acted to Maintain Order • In certain circumstances the need to maintain discipline affords a defense to the person in charge. For example, the father is acknowledged as the person in charge of a family, and courts will not interfere with his rights to exercise reasonable and restrained force to maintain the order and discipline of the family. But the husband has long since lost his once near-absolute defense against a suit brought by his wife for unnecessary force. And it is doubtful today that a father's actions in punishing his children, even if well intentioned, enjoy the immunity from legal action that was once the case. A man may no longer physically mistreat his family and expect to avoid the law.

Children at school are under the supervision of school authorities acting in place of their parents. Rules governing school discipline are hard to establish and are just beginning to receive attention from the courts in the modern turbulence of academic life.

Similarly, ship captains are given wide latitude in using force to keep order while at sea—although they would certainly be liable for needlessly clapping in irons passengers whom they disliked but who had committed no offense. Soldiers, sailors and airmen are subject to the provisions of military law, which seeks to balance the necessities of military command and the requirements of elementary civil liberties.

ACCIDENTAL INTERFERENCE WITH YOUR PERSONAL
OR PROPERTY RIGHTS

56. Unintentional Interference with Your Rights • In the earlier sections of this chapter we were concerned with intentional interferences with your various rights as a member of society. In each of the torts discussed the harm was intended or the result of an intended act. But there is a large area of the law of torts that is basically different—the area of civil wrongs or torts that are the result of negligence, or mere carelessness. In our increasingly complex society, wrongs resulting from carelessness may become more numerous than intentional torts. In any case, you should remember one key difference between the two kinds of wrong:

to recover for someone's negligent conduct toward you, you must prove actual damages—you must establish that he really did injure your person or your property. By contrast, you will recall that in the cases of several intentional torts, such as trespass (see section 46), you are entitled to some damages just by proving that the tort was committed.

Here our concern is with unintentional interference with your personal and property rights. Unintentional interference can result either from negligence, which we will consider first, or from accident, which we will discuss later (see section 59).

57. What Negligence Is • Most lawyers agree that legal actionable *negligence* exists when: (a) you have a legal duty or obligation to conform to a certain standard of conduct to protect others against unreasonable risks; (b) you fail to conform to that standard; (c) your conduct is so closely related to the resulting injury that it can be said to have caused it—to have been its *proximate cause,* to use legal terminology; and (d) actual damage results from your conduct. If these four elements are all present in a situation in which you are involved, you may be sued and you will find it hard to defend yourself—although it is possible to win your case, as you will learn in sections 63–65.

These elements of negligence are reasonably clear. But you should recognize that the existence of "a legal duty or obligation" to others may depend on the circumstances of the case in which you are being sued. The first surgeon who sewed up a sponge in his patient's abdomen after removing his appendix must certainly have been surprised when the patient successfully sued him a year later for failing to conform to a "standard of conduct." On the other hand, would the courts find a parachutist negligent who failed properly to pull the cords on his parachute and crashed through your greenhouse, instead of landing harmlessly in your driveway? You have a legal duty to others only if the court or a statute says you do. You have no obligation if the court finds none.

Note that when a tort suit is tried, the standard of care expected of the defendant is defined by the judge; the jury, if there is one—otherwise the judge—determines the facts of the case and applies them in light of his definition (see section 85).

58. How Careful You Must Be • In groping around for guidelines as to whether you do or do not have a duty to act in a certain way, and in deciding whether your conduct meets the required standard, the courts compare your conduct with the presumed conduct of a reasonable or

103

prudent man. If this imaginary reasonable or prudent man would not have left the sponge in your stomach, the doctor who did so is liable. If he would have pulled the parachute cords so as to land in the driveway, the parachutist who damaged your greenhouse is liable. You are supposed to do what he would have done, and not to do what he would not have done. As A. P. Herbert, the English legal humorist, put it:

> He is an ideal, a standard, the embodiment of all those qualities which we demand of the good citizen. . . . He is one who invariably looks where he is going, and is careful to examine the immediate foreground before he executes a leap or a bound; who neither star-gazes nor is lost in meditation when approaching trapdoors or the margin of a dock; . . . who never mounts a moving omnibus and does not alight from any car while the train is in motion . . . and will inform himself of the history and habits of a dog before administering a caress; . . . who never drives his ball until those in front of him have definitely vacated the putting-green which is his own objective; who never from one year's end to another makes an excessive demand upon his wife, his neighbors, his servants, his ox, or his ass; . . . who never swears, gambles or loses his temper; who uses nothing except in moderation, and even while he flogs his child is meditating only on the golden mean. . . . In all that mass of authorities which bears upon this branch of the law there is no single mention of a reasonable woman.

A key element in a successful negligence suit is the connection between what you did and the injury that supposedly resulted from your act. The person suing you must prove that you caused injury to his person or property. He has what is called the burden of proof that your action (or failure to act) was responsible for the damage he suffered—that it was the *proximate cause* of the injury. Some courts in trying to decide whether an act was the proximate cause of subsequent damage have applied what is called the foreseeability test. They hold that your negligence is not the proximate cause unless the consequence was one that, in the light of all the circumstances, our reasonably prudent man could have foreseen as a probable result of his actions or his failure to act. If you park your unlocked car on the street with the key in the ignition switch (which is against the law) and the car is stolen by a person who then drives carelessly and injures someone, you may not be liable. The proximate, or intervening, cause of the injury was the act of the thief when he drove your car negligently, not your violation of the law when you left the keys in it.

59. Unavoidable Accidents · If you are involved in an unavoidable accident you are not subject to liability for negligence. As an example: You interfere in a dog fight, raise a stick and accidentally strike a man behind you. You didn't hit him intentionally, nor were you negligent, so you are not liable. Expressed differently, the man behind you has no right to freedom from being unintentionally struck by someone trying to stop a dog fight. Again, you would not be liable if while driving your car slowly and carefully down a residential street you struck a child who rushed in front of the car chasing a baseball. As you might guess, the great majority of accident cases involve automobiles; for an extended discussion of such accidents, see sections 242–260.

60. Standards of Care Required of Owners and Occupiers of Land •
Property owners must observe certain standards of conduct or care for the protection of others. Your neighbor is negligent if he uses his property in a way a reasonably prudent man would not use it and if as a result other people or their property are injured. If he burns brush on his property on a windy day without taking adequate precautions to keep the fire under control, and flames spread onto your land and destroy your outbuildings, you may bring an action against him for his negligence.

You also have the right to *lateral support,* which means that your neighbors may not dig along your boundaries in such a way as to deprive your land of its natural support so that it falls away onto theirs. Nor may the owner of land abutting or bordering on a public road build so close to the road as to endanger the safety of pedestrians or automobile drivers using the road. This kind of restriction is usually set forth specifically in local building codes and zoning regulations (see section 277).

61. Your Duty to Others Who Come onto Your Property • If you own or occupy property you have definite responsibilities to persons coming onto that property legally or otherwise. Even to a trespasser, someone entering your property illegally, you have an obligation to give warning of any genuinely dangerous condition known only to you. If your hobby is keeping live snakes, you'd be wise to post a warning sign so that casual trespassers realize there's danger in wandering around your property.

You owe a stricter responsibility to trespassing children because they are children and unlikely to realize or care about the fine points of the law of trespass. To protect young trespassers and to compensate them for injuries they may suffer in behaving like children, the courts have thrown over them a mantle called the *attractive nuisance* doctrine. The doctrine requires the property owner who maintains on his property anything attractive to young children, and dangerous to them because of

105

their immaturity and unawareness of possible risks, to exercise reasonable care in protecting them against the dangers of the attraction.

If you maintain a swimming pool in your backyard, you had better build a high fence around it or risk liability if one of your neighbor's children falls in and drowns. The point is that courts feel a trespasser should not be deprived of the protection of the law simply because he has come on your property without permission. When children are concerned, your duty is all the more stringent, because keeping on your property something that would tempt a child and yet is dangerous to him is almost, as one court put it, like baiting a trap that would draw him inevitably to his destruction.

There is a group of people called licensees who may come onto your property with your implied permission. They are different from trespassers who have no permission, and you have a somewhat stronger obligation to protect them. Persons taking shortcuts across your property; social guests; those who come into your store to get out of the rain; tourists visiting your factory at their own request; traveling salesmen calling at your home; solicitors for charities—all are licensees. You have a duty to warn them of dangerous conditions they would not anticipate or easily see. The law regarding your obligation to guests in your automobile is complicated and specialized; see section 255 for a discussion of its many byways.

Invitees are the people coming into your house, apartment, store or factory to whom you owe the maximum duty of protection, not only against risks you actually do know about, but also against dangers that you should know about if you exercised reasonable care. *Invitees* are persons who enter your property upon your business and upon your express or implied invitation. Store customers; patrons of restaurants, banks and places of amusement of all kinds; delivery men; plumbers; electricians and carpenters doing work at the owner's request—all are invitees. The list is of course much longer. But in most states it does not include policemen entering a property in search of a thief or firemen entering to put out a fire. They are regarded by most courts as licensees only (see section 303).

As in most tort cases, the court and the jury will carefully consider the facts in each situation before coming to a decision about whether or not the defendant was negligent. One rule commonly applied is that the standard of care required of the property owner is greater to the degree that the presence of people on his property is helpful or profitable to him. In other words, a store owner, who will make money as a result of

106

your visit to his store, has a greater duty to you than does a friend who invites you to his house as a social guest.

The store owner is not automatically held negligent, however. Let's say you fall and injure yourself in the supermarket because a jar of mayonnaise has been broken on the aisle floor. If you can prove that the mess had been lying there unattended for twenty minutes, you might recover. If the store manager can prove that he had sent a boy for sawdust and for a bucket and mop to clean up just before you entered the aisle, and that the jar had just fallen a moment or two before, you might not recover. The application of general rules is up to the court.

The liability to trespassers, invitees and licensees is the owner's or that of the person in legal possession. If someone is injured in your apartment the liability is yours, not that of the building's owner (see section 273).

62. When Negligence Is Obvious • Torts frequently occur under circumstances in which, although it is impossible to prove negligence on anyone's part, what happens is so extraordinary that negligence is presumed. As the courts say, the thing speaks for itself: *res ipsa loquitur.* Said one court, "We can imagine no reason why, with ordinary care, human toes could not be left out of chewing tobacco, and if toes are found in chewing tobacco, it seems to us that someone has been very careless." Accordingly, the tobacco company was held liable in damages to the plaintiff who was understandably unhappy with what he regarded as the undesirable condition of the company's chewing tobacco.

Of course, if the tobacco company could establish that the tobacco package contained no human toe when it left the factory and that it had been tampered with at the tobacco store where the plaintiff bought it, the presumption of res ipsa loquitur might be overcome. But such proof is hard. Where the entire manufacturing process is under defendant's exclusive control, the doctrine of res ipsa loquitur will more often than not be applied to permit recovery by a plaintiff suing to recover damages from a product that was presumably in an unfit condition when the manufacturer disposed of it (see sections 68, 192).

The doctrine of res ipsa loquitur may also be invoked where damage is caused by the breakdown of a mechanical device that is under the complete ownership and control of the defendant. For example, if an amusement park roller coaster collapses and injures passengers, there has been an obvious failure of maintenance and inspection even if no direct proof of negligence can be presented, and suits by the injured would be likely to succeed.

Defenses Against Negligence Suits

To almost all lawsuits involving negligence there are defenses that if established will either effectively negate the action or very substantially reduce the damages awarded. Most of these defenses are fairly simple.

63. Assumption of Risk · This defense exists when it is clear that the person complaining of the negligent conduct (or lack of care) was aware of it and ignored it at the time his injury occurred. When you buy a box seat at the ball park you obviously know that you are taking a risk; therefore, you have no action against the owner of the stadium for injury you suffer if you are hit on the head by a foul pop. If you go ice skating on your neighbor's pond and hurt your ankle when you hit rough ice, you have assumed the risk of such injury and cannot hold him liable.

64. Contributory Negligence and Comparative Negligence · The doctrine of contributory negligence applies in a situation in which both parties are negligent. The doctrine is that the plaintiff's own lack of care deprives him of his right to recover for the defendant's negligence toward him, even though it can be proved. An example of contributory negligence is a situation in which a construction worker who had failed to fasten his safety harness fell to his death from a faulty scaffold. Even if the construction company was negligent in not keeping the scaffold in good repair, if it can be proved that the safety harness would have saved the worker's life, his family might not recover damages because he "contributed" his own negligence by failing to fasten the harness.

This denial of recovery has been carried to extremes by some courts, which have ruled against the plaintiff even though his fault was clearly minor compared to that of the defendant.

Let's say that you lightly bump a truck in a parking lot. Unknown to you, the truck is loaded with nitroglycerin and explodes. The truck owner was certainly negligent in leaving his vehicle in such an exposed place with no warning of its dangerous cargo. But your own negligence in hitting his truck would under a strict application of the contributory negligence doctrine prevent your recovering damages for the injury to your car and yourself in the explosion.

The harshness of the contributory negligence doctrine has led to increasing use of the much fairer doctrine of *comparative negligence*.

Under this doctrine the court would certainly award you damages for the injury to you and your car in the situation just discussed. But the damages would be diminished or reduced somewhat by your own negligent striking of the truck. What the doctrine of comparative negligence does is to enable the court to apportion the damages according to the relative degree of negligence of the plaintiff and the defendant. (For further discussion of contributory and comparative negligence, see section 500; see chart 15, page 275, for states that have comparative negligence laws.)

65. Last Clear Chance · The defense of contributory negligence can sometimes be defeated by what is known as the *last clear chance* theory. It is as simple as it sounds. It permits you to recover damages, in spite of your own contributory negligence, if the defendant could still have avoided injuring you by exercising ordinary care. "Last clear chance" is really an application of the principles of proximate cause (see section 57). The theory is, that because the defendant had the last chance to avoid your injuries, it was negligent of him not to do so. It was his failure to act, not your own negligence, that was the proximate cause. His negligence in failing to avoid the accident becomes the direct and proximate cause of your injury. Accidents involving cars are those in which last clear chance and other defenses in negligence actions most often arise. For a fuller discussion, see chapter 6, "Your Automobile," page 237.

LIABILITY IMPOSED BY STATUTE

66. The Changing Law of Torts · Although the language of the courts may sometimes seem old-fashioned, and though the cases in the old law books seem astonishingly simple in this modern world, the law of torts affects you in your daily life more than you might think. Remember that a tort is an act or a failure to act, intentional or unintentional, that interferes with your freedom to enjoy your personal and property rights (see section 36).

In our complex, industrialized society, such interferences have become increasingly common in two areas with which the law was little concerned as recently as 100 years ago. One is the area of your employment and the injuries that are part of everyday life on your job, often through no one's fault. Another is the area of injuries you suffer when you buy a defective car, television set or pair of skates—injuries that may or may not be a result of negligence, but that you lack the time, money and ability to trace back to their original cause.

The courts have slowly moved into these new areas to give you remedies; and where they have moved too slowly or not at all, the legislatures have moved decisively to provide you with previously unknown opportunities to recover damages. We will deal with these two areas separately.

67. When You Are Injured on the Job • Time was, not so long ago, when it was very difficult for an employe to recover from his employer for injuries received on the job or on the business premises. The employe's rights were severely limited by old economic ideas and tight legal rules designed more to protect his employer from a flood of lawsuits than to protect him. In Germany in 1883, in England in 1897, in the United States in 1911 for federal government employes, statutes were passed which we know as workmen's compensation acts.

The principle behind these statutes and all the state statutes (which New York initiated in 1910) is that industrial accidents are an inevitable part of industrial society, that the individual employe cannot protect himself against them—much less against the economic loss he suffers as a result—whereas the employer has the resources to give this protection and to pass on to his customers the cost of the insurance.

Who is at fault for an accident is not an important issue. The state statutes impose a strict liability on the employer unless it can be proved that the employe is the direct cause of the accident. Even in those instances in which the employe's negligence may be the sole or the main cause the modern trend is to hold the employer liable, the more so because the money to compensate the injured employe is available in a fund to which the employer contributes and the cost of which he adds to the cost of his product and passes on to the consumer.

Workmen's compensation laws prescribe in detail the amount of money that can be recovered and the machinery for obtaining it. There are special workmen's compensation courts, or tribunals, that do nothing but hear and pass upon claims for compensation arising from all kinds of injuries suffered on the job. Bear in mind that the old common-law defenses of assumption of risk and contributory negligence are unavailable to your employer under these statutes, so long as your kind of employment is covered by them. It is also worth remembering that since the awards in these cases are limited by statute, an injured worker might not recover as much under workmen's compensation as he would if he ran

110

the risks inherent in a regular tort suit and took the case before a jury.

There are several federal liability and compensation laws. The most important of these, passed in 1906, is the Federal Employers' Liability Act covering all employes of common carriers by railroad whose employers are engaged in interstate commerce. The same kind of protection covers longshoremen and harbor workers, seamen and other maritime workers.

Some categories of employes are still not covered by one or another of these liability and compensation statutes, but the number who are not is steadily decreasing. Farm laborers and domestic servants, for example, must still rely on the traditional legal remedies to recover for injuries sustained "in the course of their employment," and their actions to recover for such injuries are at the mercy of the old-time defenses of assumption of risk and contributory negligence.

For more details on workmen's compensation laws, see sections 375, 430, 498.

68. When You Buy Faulty Merchandise · The other area where well-established rules of law are being expanded out of all recognition, if not actually abandoned, is that of the liability of manufacturers and sellers of all kinds of personal property, or merchandise. For literally hundreds of years, the Latin words *caveat emptor* were used by the courts to deny you legal satisfaction if you bought faulty or harmful merchandise. This was so even if you could easily prove that the watch you had bought couldn't be wound because it lacked a winder, or the horse was lame, or the toy might fire too quickly to be handled safely by your son. "Let the buyer beware," replied the courts, and for a long, long time you bought strictly at your peril.

Then the courts came to realize than even if you exercise ordinary care, you have no way of protecting yourself against some defective merchandise. Say you buy a car and test-drive it, and all seems to be well— but later the steering wheel falls off because of a misplaced or defective nut or bolt. You are innocent of any negligence or lack of care in buying the car that appeared to you to be in good condition. You could not have discovered the imperfect or defective part by exercising ordinary care. When you buy a new car you have no duty to hire a mechanic to go over it. By offering it for sale the manufacturer is saying, in effect, that it is a safe vehicle. Therefore, it is unreasonable to deny you recovery for the manufacturer's negligence—or for the negligence of one of his employes, which is in effect the same thing (see section 37). You now have an increasing ability to hold the manufacturer liable for damages you suffer because, as the courts say, he has released an inherently dangerous product into the channels of commerce.

The courts are more and more willing to say that you have the right to freedom from injury to your person or property because of the negligence of a company (meaning its employes) whose products you buy in reliance on its good reputation for skill and competence. And they will award you damages for unintentional interference with that freedom.

69. Who Is Responsible—Merchant or Manufacturer · In most cases, of course, you buy a product not from the manufacturer but from someone else. If the television set you buy from a store proves to emit dangerous radiations, your suit for damages (if you suffered any) should probably be against the manufacturer. The reason is that the dealer bought in good faith from the manufacturer. Under such circumstances the dealer may have a defense against your suit. He was not negligent toward you. But the manufacturer was. Still, you might be able to sue the dealer successfully for breach of warranty—in which case he in turn could probably recover from the manufacturer. You should consult a lawyer in deciding whom to sue. The manufacturer is required by the courts to assume a liability that the courts will not impose on the dealer. It may turn out that the dealer, too, will be able to sue the manufacturer for supplying him with TV sets that were returned in profusion or couldn't be sold in the first place because of health hazards.

In practice, merchants today will go much further than the law requires in such a situation. Many store owners, for the sake of keeping your goodwill, will permit you to return merchandise you find unsatisfactory, no matter how trivial your reason. But accepting the faulty merchandise back is one thing; accepting the liability for all the injuries it may inflict on you is something else again.

If the toy you buy for your child at Christmas explodes and seriously injures him, it is little help to be able to return it and demand another. If you want to collect damages to cover medical expenses and to compensate the child for his pain and suffering, you will almost surely have to sue the manufacturer—and perhaps the store owner as well. Let them fight it out as to who has to pay you. You have bought a toy in good faith. Someone is liable. You have the right to buy a toy in the expectation that if it is used carefully and in the way intended it will not injure your child. For the interference with that right, for the damages you suffer because of the interference, you have a legal action. The apportionment of the damages for such interference is the job of the courts—it is not yours to have to decide.

If the courts don't keep up with the times and continue to deny you and others like you relief when, even though you are innocent of any negligence, you suffer significant injury, the public authorities step in. They often do so by passing laws that make the manufacturer liable. A growing number of public officials are setting up agencies to protect consumers against the risks and the possible harm of buying faulty and dangerous merchandise. The targets of these agencies include merchandise that is fraudulently sold to you, such as medicines that are supposed to cure your ills but do no such thing (see section 196).

It is this increased interest in the consumer's rights that has led automobile manufacturers to recall defective cars. The companies hope to avoid the expense of lawsuits they fear will be brought by people injured while operating cars manufactured with these defects.

Of course the manufacturers could fight these suits in the courts. But several thousand defective automobiles could give rise to so many lawsuits in which the manufacturer would have to admit defective material or workmanship that it is simply too great an economic risk for him to run. It is fair to say that today the old warning of "let the buyer beware" (caveat emptor) has truly been replaced by a new warning, "Let the manufacturer beware."

70. The Importance of Liability · We have now discussed many but not all of the aspects of this strange and developing law of torts. We have described those that are intentional (sections 39–49) and those that are unintentional (sections 56–62). Underlying all is your right to recover for injuries you suffer from interference with your right to be free from a variety of wrongs, some well established and others just becoming established. If you feel that you have been wronged in any of these ways, you should carefully consider still another factor that will influence your decision whether or not to sue.

That is the question, which only your lawyer should decide, of whether there is any liability on the part of the person who has wronged you. He will be liable, and your legal action against him will succeed, only if he has actually violated a legal duty he has to you as an individual. (The only exception to this rule is in cases involving so-called "no fault" insurance statutes, under which it is not necessary to prove liability.) Forgetting momentarily the question of your responsibility for what happened, you can recover from him only where what he did or failed

113

to do violated the course of conduct that our old friend, the reasonably prudent man (section 58), would have followed.

If the conduct of the person you want to sue has not, judged by the presumed conduct of the reasonably prudent man, violated a duty to you, the chances are you have no action. Liability is essential: you can win your suit only if the person you are suing acted or failed to act in such a way as to make him liable. Liability results from conduct that violates or interferes with one of your rights that the law recognizes. If there is no such conduct there is no liability, no matter how aggrieved you may feel.

RIGHTING THE WRONG: VARIOUS REMEDIES AVAILABLE TO YOU

71. Measuring Your Money Damages • Let's say that your lawyer has decided that, on the basis of the facts you have given him, the person who has wronged you had a duty not to do so and that a court can therefore find him liable for violation of that duty. The question of which remedy you should seek becomes all-important. Underlying the answer to this question is the subject of damages.

Many intentional torts are crimes, and the typical criminal is not likely to be able to pay you damages. Take the case of the thief who breaks into your house or apartment (committing the crime of breaking and entering and the tort of trespass), threatens you with a gun (committing the crime of assault with a deadly weapon and the tort of assault) and steals $10 from your wallet (committing the crime of robbery). Police officers tell you he's a deadbeat with a long record and no funds.

You may of course sue him for one or more of the torts he committed against you. But your tort actions would have to be brought in a civil court (see section 35), entirely separate from the criminal action the prosecuting attorney will bring, and you would have to hire an attorney of your own. Although you are reasonably certain of winning your action, what good would it do you? What damages might you expect to be able to collect? The thief is *judgment-proof:* he has no funds you can collect. The cost of hiring a lawyer and going to court would be considerable, and you cannot realistically expect to recover even that cost, much less damages.

Another case involving ability to pay damages is the one in which

114

your local dry-cleaner, after negligently ruining the fur coat you stored with him for the summer, goes broke. You have an action against him in tort for negligently misusing his role as a bailee of your property (see section 201). But again, how are you going to collect the damages you are likely to be awarded by the court? The cleaner is also judgment-proof. You wouldn't even recover the expense of bringing your action. There would be no practical value in suing him.

Of course there may be other considerations. You have an action against the airline that negligently sends your suitcase on a plane going to Egypt instead of Chicago, and it is never seen again. Most airlines are financially solvent and have the funds to pay the award you win in court in your suit for negligence. But it's one thing if your suitcase was forty years old and about to fall apart and contained nothing of much value: your award in damages would scarcely compensate you for the expense of suing the airline. It's something entirely different if your suitcase contained a family jewel that was irreplaceable. Now, suing becomes worthwhile. Your award in damages might well be an amount at least equal to the value of the jewel unless the airline had specifically limited its liability for lost baggage. The airline is presumably not judgment-proof and can afford to pay you the established value of the jewel.

You must decide whether what you've lost is worth the expense of suing, and your lawyer will help you to make an intelligent decision.

72. Getting Back Your Property · But you're not limited to asking for money damages when you have been deprived of your property. You may try to get back the property itself. You may sue your dry-cleaner for the return of a watch he took when he had your coat for storing, or the airline for the return of the family heirloom that was inside the suitcase.

Whether the defendant is judgment-proof is not a factor here. You want a specific thing back, whatever the assets of the dry-cleaner or the airline, and whatever the cost of the legal proceeding. If what you want back can be found, your action is for restitution of your property. If you sue for the value of the watch, you may have trouble fighting off competing claims by other people who are suing the bankrupt dry-cleaner, people whose property he may have ruined or to whom he owes money. But you are likely to get your watch back—at a price, the price being the cost of the legal action.

73. Putting a Stop to Undesirable Acts · There are other torts for which money damages are not the relief you want. If you are bothered by the neighbor who persists in walking across your property despite all your requests that he stop, money damages don't help you much. What you want in such a case is a court order that he stop. Such an order is called an *injunction*. In a simple case like this you should have no trouble getting an injunction, but it will cost you the expense of hiring a lawyer and starting and carrying through with a court action. You'll probably be able to collect your actual court costs, but not your lawyer's fee.

Lawyers are in great demand these days, and their time is dear. Litigation, or going to court for a client, is expensive. So you should carefully consider and discuss with your lawyer which of the various legal remedies available will bring you the satisfaction you want at a cost you can afford. To enforce your rights in courts you need professional assistance, which costs money. The practical aspects of enforcing your rights are often more important to you than the principles involved.

74. The Importance of Insurance • One point to discuss with your lawyer in deciding whether to go to court and what sort of relief to seek when you go is whether the person who has wronged you is likely to be insured. In days gone by it might not have been worthwhile to sue the homeowner for injuries you suffered when you came onto his property at his invitation and broke your leg when you tripped on a loose stair carpet. If he didn't have the money to pay the cost of your medical expenses and the loss of your salary or wages while your leg was mending, the damages the court awarded you might be meaningless. But today many homeowners carry liability insurance, which covers or contributes to the payment of just such damage awards (see sections 493, 496).

We all know that an increasing number of automobile owners carry liability insurance—either voluntarily or because state laws require it— for their protection in lawsuits arising out of accidents involving their cars. (See chapter 6, "Your Automobile," page 237, for a more detailed treatment of the automobile cases). We have already mentioned workmen's compensation (section 67), which is a form of liability insurance required by statute, with the cost shared by industry generally. We have also seen that new areas and forms of liability are being imposed both by statute and by the courts on the manufacturers (who are also protected by insurance) of all kinds of products that contain defects the buyer or consumer cannot reasonably be expected to discover (see sections 68, 69). All these changes work to your benefit in recovering damages.

Don't confuse insurance coverage with liability, however. Though a defendant is insured for millions, you cannot recover a penny unless you

116

can persuade the jury that the defendant is liable for the damages you have suffered (see section 70).

What your lawyer can do to let the court know that the defendant has insurance is the subject of a very technical legal argument. Nevertheless, whether the person who has harmed you is insured is certainly a key element in deciding whether to sue. If the proposed defendant is on relief and probably has no insurance, one decision is clearly indicated. If your defendant is both apparently wealthy and (as in the case of a home-owner) is likely to be insured, the decision is clear too. But many of your problems will lie in between, making your decision more difficult.

75. The Cost of a Lawsuit • You should know something about the kind of arrangements you may want to make with your lawyer regarding his expenses if you decide to go to court. Keep in mind that litigation is an extremely wasteful use of a lawyer's time. Abraham Lincoln advised lawyers generally to avoid going to court if at all possible, by negotiating compromise solutions whenever possible.

Litigation is wasteful for several reasons. First, court calendars in almost all parts of the country are long and crowded: more legal actions are being brought than there are judges to handle them. Second, litigation involves many appearances in court by your lawyer that are purely routine, but that take him out of his office for at least an hour, depending on how near his office is to the courthouse. Third, no matter how skilled your lawyer is in the area of your lawsuit, he or someone he employs is going to have to do some research to make sure he knows the latest developments in the law on that subject. Fourth, your lawyer will probably have to spend some time checking on the facts you present to him and talking to other people who may be involved in the case.

So your lawyer spends a great deal of time in handling your litigation, and as Lincoln said, "Time is the indispensable thing the lawyer has to sell." You must therefore show that you can pay him before he can be expected to take your case, unless he is willing to do so voluntarily because of its special merits. And no lawyer can afford to take more than a few cases on a voluntary basis.

A great many of the tort actions that take place today involve relatively poor plaintiffs and defendants who, although not wealthy, are at least believed covered by enough insurance so that they can pay a damage award. A common basis for paying your lawyer in such actions is by an agreement to share your recovery with him, usually on the basis of his receiving a percentage of what you get.

117

If you sue for $15,000 for your expenses from hospitalization, medical care and loss of income resulting from an automobile accident, your lawyer would probably take the case if you agreed to pay him $5,000, or a third of the amount you hope to recover in the action. These agreements are entirely proper. But you should be on your guard against some few unscrupulous lawyers, popularly called ambulance chasers, whose entire practice consists of automobile cases and who supposedly follow ambulances around and enter into agreements with accident victims at the scenes of the accidents to act as their lawyers in suing the drivers or owners of the other cars.

In other kinds of tort actions, where you are seeking the return of a specific item (see section 72) or an injunction ordering your defendant to stop doing something (see section 73), you'll have to pay your lawyer a retainer to engage him to take your case. A *retainer* is simply a payment you make at the time your lawyer agrees to represent you that will partly or completely compensate him for his time and expenses. In most cases the retainer is only part payment; you agree to pay the lawyer the balance either in installments, at the end of the legal action or when the result you seek has been obtained. Incidentally, on this point American law is different from that in England. In civil actions in England, the successful party in a lawsuit will be awarded not only the expenses of the action but also his entire lawyer's fee. In most actions in this country, only the relatively small statutory expenses will be awarded to the successful party and he must still pay his own lawyer.

What to Do When a Tort Has Been Committed

76. Getting in Touch with Your Lawyer • When you are involved in a tort, committed by or against you, the first thing you should do in most cases is to consult a lawyer. If you are adequately insured, there are some situations, mostly involving accidents, in which it is safe just to report the accident to your insurance company and rely on it to assert or defend your rights. Once you have reported the facts to the company (and to the public authorities, as required by many states for automobile accidents), your responsibilities are pretty well taken care of. But you should keep in touch with the insurance company and make sure it is doing all it can to recover for you or to protect you if you are being sued.

But if you have any reason to believe that you are likely to be sued for a larger amount than your insurance provides for, you should retain a lawyer for your own protection. Or if, for example, your house burns down from a fire negligently set by your wealthy neighbor and your own fire insurance is inadequate to cover your loss, you'll have to get a lawyer if you want to sue the neighbor for the damages you have suffered.

In the type of tort not involving an accident, what is most important is giving your lawyer all the facts so that he can properly advise you. The facts are crucially important, and your ability to remember them accurately and report them fully to your lawyer will save you money and help him to advise and represent you more effectively.

He then has the responsibility of advising you as indicated in sections 70–75. First, he must consider how strong your legal case it—which really means deciding whether the person who has wronged you, intentionally or negligently, had a duty to conduct himself otherwise; that is, whether he has any legal liability toward you. Second comes the equally vital question of the seriousness of that liability: how much in damages is involved or whether you can obtain the injunction you seek. Third is the question of whether the legal relief your lawyer says he can obtain for you is worth what it will cost you to get it: the expenses of bringing the action plus the expense of appealing the case to a higher court if you should lose in the trial court.

You and your lawyer should have a full understanding of the legal steps ahead, how much they are going to cost and how you are going to pay for them.

77. The Advantages of Settlement · It goes without saying that you should always authorize your lawyer to settle your case out of court if possible. Often a disagreement with your neighbor that seems very serious to you, perhaps because you and he dislike each other, can easily be resolved by your lawyer and his talking together. Developing matrimonial crises can frequently be smoothed over or resolved in a satisfactory fashion by lawyers for the two parties (see section 359). Even once litigation has started, many opportunities will arise when settlement out of court can be arranged. Your lawyer should have your permission to settle your suit if he can.

Litigation is really civilized warfare, a substitute for violent conflict. But it is warfare nonetheless—to be avoided in the first place wherever possible, but once undertaken, to be waged determinedly and forcefully, yet always with an eye open to the possibility of gaining more by com-

119

promise than by pressing on to hoped-for complete victory with the risk of losing, despite all the signs in your favor.

78. Arbitrating Your Case • One question you and your lawyer should consider carefully before going to court is whether to resort to an arbitration of your claim for the damages you seek. In *arbitration* the parties to a dispute agree on an impartial arbitrator, who listens to all sides of the argument and makes an award that he considers fair.

Statutes of more than twenty states outline procedures for giving an arbitration award the full force of law. The recipient of the award simply goes to court for an order confirming the award—a simple matter unless it is contested. Once confirmed, it has the same legal force as a court judgment and can be enforced in the same ways (see section 88).

Arbitration has several advantages over litigation. First, it is less expensive. Second, it is quicker: there is no backlog of cases such as there is in all too many of the courts. Third, it is private, whereas all court proceedings are public. Fourth, when the quarrel is technical or of a sort that the average judge—let alone the average jury—would have trouble understanding, you may be better off selecting an arbitrator from the panel, or list, of thousands of experts maintained by the American Arbitration Association. A dispute about a highly complicated patent covering a recent scientific development, for example, would be better taken before an arbitrator than before most courts.

But like everything else, the case for arbitration is not so simple. In a variety of the more ordinary torts an arbitrator has no special competence. He will not necessarily do better for you than a jury or a judge and jury. If you have been crippled for life in an elevator that fell to the cellar from the twenty-fifth floor because the operator was flirting with a passenger and pulled the wrong switch, you're far better off taking your case to court than to an arbitrator. From your point of view juries are at their best in this kind of case because they are much more inclined to hold a sympathetic view of your plight and to be much harder on building owners—and on the insurance companies they are certain are behind the owners. So even though arbitration is cheap, quick and private, these advantages may be overcome by other factors.

Furthermore, arbitration has a disadvantage that legal action does not. Because the arbitrators and many of the witnesses are usually experts in their fields and rules of procedure are relaxed, the grounds for appeal are very narrow. You may appeal only if you can establish objections, such as: that the arbitrator exceeded his authority or failed to render

120

a final and definite award, disposing of all the issues before him; or that the award was procured through or as the result of corruption, fraud or actual misconduct by the arbitrator.

If a legal judgment goes against you, on the other hand, there are many grounds on which you may appeal. No decision to arbitrate should be made without considering all aspects of both arbitration and litigation.

79. Choosing the Right Court · If you and your lawyer have decided that your dispute cannot be settled amicably, compromised or arbitrated, he must choose the court in which to start your action. At least three factors will affect his choice: the nature of the wrong committed against you, the kind of relief you are seeking and where you can obtain jurisdiction over the defendant. The laws of all fifty states differ, and alongside of them is the United States, or federal, court system, which has its own rules and statutes (see sections 7, 8).

Simply stated, the federal courts are open to you in tort actions only if: (a) the wrong you are complaining of is a wrong under the United States Constitution or a federal statute; or (b) you are a resident of one state, the person who has injured you is a resident of another state and the amount you are suing for (if your hoped-for relief is damages) is over $10,000—the so-called jurisdictional amount.

For example, if you believe and your lawyer agrees that someone has violated your rights in an invention you have patented, you must sue in the federal courts because patents are issued only by the United States government. If you are a railroad trainman suing your employer for injuries you received in a train wreck you believe was caused by the railroad's negligence, you use the federal courts because the United States government and its courts have jurisdiction over railroads.

But if you want to sue the town you live in for injuries you suffered because the streets were badly maintained, you must use the state courts. As mentioned earlier (section 37), suits against a government itself, where permitted by statute, are most often brought in a special court created to handle such claims only, usually called the court of claims. Or if you are injured by a bus operated by a local bus company under a state license or franchise, you must sue in the state courts.

Suits you bring against your neighbor for almost all the torts discussed in this chapter are no concern of the federal government.

80. The Summons and Complaint · Your suit begins when your lawyer prepares and causes to be served upon the defendant a *summons and*

121

complaint. This is a written order that says the defendant must appear in the court designated in the summons to answer charges brought by you. The summons is not issued by the court itself. Your lawyer, as an officer of the court, is authorized to prepare it and to have it delivered to the defendant, usually by a process server. Under certain circumstances he may mail it to the defendant. In federal cases the summons must be served by a marshal. But the defendant must actually receive the summons if the court is to have jurisdiction over him.

Once he receives it he must answer the complaint, or at least respond to the summons by filing a notice of appearance or asking your lawyer for a delay in the date he is ordered to appear. If he does nothing at all he may find that a judgment in your favor has been entered against him because of his failure to appear.

The question of jurisdiction must be settled before you can get an enforceable judgment ordering the defendant to do something. If the court should decide it has no jurisdiction, you get no judgment.

If you are seeking an injunction against him, or a court order directing him to return your favorite watch, or a judgment that he should pay you damages, he must "appear" in court, either in person or represented by his lawyer. This is called a *general appearance.* If his only appearance is to challenge the jurisdiction of the court—to argue that the court chosen has no legal right to try the case—it is called a *special appearance.*

81. The Defendant's Answer—His Defenses • When the defendant in a tort action has received the summons, he should at once contact his own lawyer, who will draw up an "answer" to the complaint. The answer will probably set forth one or more of a wide variety of defenses available to him. The most basic would be a denial that the wrong you complained of ever occurred: this results in a simple "issue of fact." Another defense would be that the facts complained of do not constitute a tort. This defense is a simple "issue of law."

Another defense would be available to the defendant if he could establish that you had waited too long to bring the action against him. The mere passage of a certain period of time between the commission of the wrong against you and the service of a summons and complaint will constitute a defense to many tort actions (as well as to actions for breach of contract; see section 185) because of what is known as the *statute of limitations.* The statute prescribes different periods within which different actions may be brought (see chart 6, page 124; chart 10, page 217).

A broader doctrine may also be available as a defense—the doctrine of *laches*. The law does not favor plaintiffs who unreasonably delay asserting their rights. One reason is that the longer you delay, the stronger is the suspicion that you weren't as badly injured by the defendant's tort as you complain you were. Another reason is that the longer you delay, the harder it becomes for the defendant to establish his defense. With the passage of time memories become unreliable and facts become blurred, giving more force to charges that can't be proved. And finally, the defendant may show that he has done something—opened a new business, for example—that he would not have done if your suit had been brought expeditiously.

If the court believes that you have delayed unduly in starting your action and you offer no plausible reason for your delay, you may be "estopped" from pressing the action or obtaining a judgment in your favor. Your own conduct may bar you from the favorable judgment that you might have won if you had asserted your rights sooner and more vigorously. When you think you have been wronged, therefore—when you think you are the victim of a tort—consult your lawyer.

There are rare situations, however, in which you would be wise to postpone starting a lawsuit until close to the end of the period allowed by the statute of limitations. But under most circumstances the sooner you start your legal action, the better.

When You Go to Court

What follows is a simple explanation of what goes on in a typical tort action. Much of it will be familiar to detective story fans and to those who like television shows with courtroom scenes. It will help to give you a basic understanding of what will happen if you and your lawyer agree that your case should be litigated.

82. The Participants and Their Roles • Remember that each of the main actors in the courtroom drama has a distinct part to play. The *plaintiff* is the one who brings the action, the *defendant* the one against whom it is brought. In a criminal action, as mentioned in section 89, it is *The State* v. (for *versus,* meaning "against") *Sam Brown*. In a civil case, however, the plaintiff is named: *Joseph Smith* v. *Sam Brown*.

The role of each party's lawyer is to represent his client to the best of

123

STATUTES OF LIMITATION FOR STARTING A CIVIL ACTION

CHART 6

	Assault & Battery	Fraud & Deceit	Libel	Slander	Personal Injury	Wrongful Death	Trespass	Damage to Personal Property	Conversion	Medical Malpractice[1]	False Imprisonment	Malicious Prosecution	Breach of Sales Contract	Breach of Warranty
	IN YEARS													
ALABAMA	6	1	1	1	1	2	6	1	6	6 mo.	6	1	4	4
ALASKA	2	2	2	2	2	2	6	6	6	2	2	2	4	4
ARIZONA	2	3	1	1	2	2	2	2	2	3[2]	1	1	4	4
ARKANSAS	1	5	3	1	3[3]	3[3]	3	3[3]	3	2	1	5	4	4
CALIFORNIA	1	3	1	1	1	1	3	3	3	1	1	1	4	4
COLORADO	1	3	1	1	6	2[4]	6	6	6	2	1	6	4	4
CONNECTICUT	2	3	2	2	2-3	2-3	3	2	3	2	3	3	4	4
DELAWARE	2	3	2	2	2	2	3	2	3	2	2	2	4	4
D.C.	1	3	1	1	1	1	3	3	3	1-3	1	1	4	4
FLORIDA	4	4	4	4	4	2	4	4	4	4	4	4	4	4
GEORGIA	2	4	1	1	5	2	4	4	4	2	2	2	4	4
HAWAII	2	6	2	2	2	2	2	2	6	2	6	6	4	4
IDAHO	2	3	2	2	2	2	3	3	3	2	2	4	4	2
ILLINOIS	2	5	1	1	2	2	5	5	5	2	2	2	4	4
INDIANA	2	6	2	2	2	2	6	2	6	2	2	2	4	4
IOWA	2	5	2	2	2	2	5	5	5	2	2	2	5[6]	5[6]
KANSAS	2	2	1	1	2	2	2	2	2	2	2	2	4	4
KENTUCKY	1	5	1	1	1	1	5	5	5	1	1	1	4	4
LOUISIANA	1	1	1	1	1	1	1	1	1	1	1	1	1	1
MAINE	2	6	2	2	6	2	6	6	6	2	2	6	4	4
MARYLAND	1	3	1	1	3	3	3	3	3	3	3	3	4	4
MASSACHUSETTS	3	3	3	3	3	3	3	3	3	3	3	3	4	4
MICHIGAN	2	3	1	1	3	3	3	3	3	2	2	2	4	4
MINNESOTA	2	6	2	2	6	3[4]	6	6	6	2	2	2	4	4
MISSISSIPPI	1	6	1	1	6	6	6	6	6	6	1	1	4	4

(1) Many states require that action be brought within a specified number of years of the date of injury. This time limit varies from 2 to 8 years, according to the state.

(2) Limit runs from injury date with exceptions.

(3) Limit may be extended to 4 years in certain cases involving construction or improvement to real property.

(4) Limit runs from the time the act causing death occurred.

You may sue for redress of civil wrongs only during a period limited by law, as shown below (see section 81). Unless otherwise specified, the limit for fraud, personal injury and malpractice runs from time of discovery; for wrongful death, from time of death.

	Assault & Battery	Fraud & Deceit	Libel	Slander	Personal Injury	Wrongful Death	Trespass	Damage to Personal Property	Conversion	Medical Malpractice	False Imprisonment	Malicious Prosecution	Breach of Sales Contract	Breach of Warranty
	IN YEARS													
MISSOURI	2	5	2	2	5	2	5	5	5	2	2	2	4	4
MONTANA	2	2	2	2	2	3	2	2	2	3	2	2	4	4
NEBRASKA	1	4	1	1	4	2	4	4	4	2	1	1	4	4
NEVADA	2	3	2	2	2	2	3	3	3	2	2	2	4	4
NEW HAMPSHIRE	6	6	6	6	6[7]	2	6	6	6	6	6	6	4	4
NEW JERSEY	2	6	1	1	2	2	6	6	6	2	6	6	4	4
NEW MEXICO	3	4	3	3	3	3	4	4	4	3	3	3	4	4
NEW YORK	1	6	1	1	3	2	3	3	3	3	1	1	4	4
NORTH CAROLINA	1	3	1	1	3	2	3	3	3	3	1	3	4	4
NORTH DAKOTA	2	6	2	2	6	2	6	6	6	2	2	6	4	4
OHIO	1	4	1	1	2	2	4	2	4	1	1	1	4	4
OKLAHOMA	1	2	1	1	2	2	2	2	2	2	1	1	5	5
OREGON	2	2	1	1	2	3[4]	6	6	6	2	2	2	4	4
PENNSYLVANIA	2	1	1	1	2	1	6	6	6	[8]	2	1	4	4
RHODE ISLAND	6	6	6	1	3	2	6	6	6	6	6	6	4	4
SOUTH CAROLINA	2	6	2	2	6	6	6	6	6	6	2	6	6	6
SOUTH DAKOTA	2	6	2	2	3	3	6	6	6	2	2	6	4	4
TENNESSEE	1	3	1	6 mo.	1	1	3	3	3	1	1	1	4	4
TEXAS	2	2[6]	1	1	2	2	2	2	2	2	1	1	4	4
UTAH	1	3	1	1	4	2	3	3	3	4	1	1	4	4
VERMONT	3	6	3	3	3[7]	2	6	3	6	3	3	3	4	4
VIRGINIA	2	3[6]	2	2	2	2	5	5	5	2	2	2	4	4
WASHINGTON	2	3	2	2	3	3	3	3	3	1	2	3	4	4
WEST VIRGINIA	2	2	2	2	2	2	2	2	2	2	2	2	4	4
WISCONSIN	2	6	2	2	3	3	6	6	6	3	2	2	6	6
WYOMING	1	4	1	1	4	2	4	4	4	4	1	1	4	4

(5) Injuries to person, 2 years; injuries to reputation, 1 year.

(6) For breach of a written contract or contract under seal, see chart 10, page 217.

(7) For skiing injuries the limit is shorter.

(8) Any claim filed 4 years after the date of injury is to be paid out of a special catastrophe fund.

his ability. Litigation, as we said, is civilized or legalized warfare, and it's up to your lawyer to use every argument and every procedural device to win your case.

The jury, if there is one, has one basic job: to decide the facts and to apply the law to those facts as the judge instructs them.

The judge's responsibility is to maintain minimum order in the courtroom, to decide whether the evidence offered is relevant and, when both the plaintiff's and the defendant's lawyers have presented their clients' cases, to advise or instruct the jury regarding the law of the case.

Here is an example of how this interplay of law and fact, judge and jury, might work. In a libel action (see section 44) truth is an absolute defense. Let's suppose that you are suing a newspaper publisher for having printed an article saying that you are a bigamist and that the lawyer for the publisher has presented evidence about an unfortunate marriage that you entered into years ago and that you thought had long since been forgotten. When all the evidence has been heard, the judge will instruct the jury that the only question for it to decide is whether in fact that marriage did take place and was never legally ended; and that if the jury finds that these were the facts, it must render a decision in favor of the defendant publisher. If the jury concludes that the marriage never took place or was legally ended, it must find in your favor.

83. Preliminary Steps • Because so many cases are waiting to be tried these days, many lawyers and judges try to clarify the issues and thus shorten the trial itself through pretrial proceedings. The lawyers may offer evidence or the testimony of witnesses they have examined under oath in their own offices. Often pretrial proceedings show the lawyers that the case is not worth pressing, or that there is no defense, with the result that it may be settled then and there. Often, also, the judge at a pretrial hearing is able to persuade the parties to reach a compromise, saving the time and expense of an actual trial.

As the trial opens, if there is to be a jury it is selected by the opposing lawyers from a group (or panel) presented to them by the clerk of the court. Each lawyer wants jurors who have as little bias as possible or have a bias in his client's favor. Statutes in several states set forth the size of the jury, usually twelve members but now often reduced to six. Potential jurors from the panel are questioned by the lawyers. Each lawyer is entitled to reject a certain number of jurors, set by statute, without having to give any reason.

As soon as the trial begins, each lawyer makes a brief opening statement, outlining his client's version of the facts and explaining his theory of the case, so that the court will understand the significance of the evidence as it is presented during the trial.

84. The Plaintiff's Burden of Proof • Because it is always the plaintiff who brings the action, it is his job to persuade the court of the merits of his case: he bears what is called the *burden of proof.* In a criminal case the state must establish the guilt of the accused beyond a reasonable doubt. If the lawyer for the accused can raise such a doubt in the jury's mind that the accused was near the place where the crime was committed, at the time it is alleged to have been committed, the jury must return a verdict of not guilty. In a civil case, however, plaintiff need only establish the truth of his claim by "a fair preponderance of the evidence," that is, by presenting evidence that has a more convincing effect on the jury than the defendant's.

85. Presentation of Evidence • Each party's case is presented through documentary evidence, presented and identified by the attorneys as exhibits, and through the testimony of witnesses, if there were any, to the commission of the alleged tort. Witnesses are questioned in *direct examination* by the lawyer for the side calling them as witnesses and may be *cross-examined* by the opposing lawyer. The penalty for perjury, or not telling the truth on the witness stand, can be severe, because perjury is itself a crime, subject to punishment by fine or even by imprisonment.

Evidence is usually presented in this order: First, the plaintiff brings all his witnesses to the stand. They give testimony and are cross-examined. At this point the plaintiff rests his case, and the defendant may ask the judge to dismiss the case because the plaintiff has failed to prove that he has a "cause of action"—a reason to bring suit. If this motion is denied, as is most often the case, the defense then brings its witnesses to the stand to testify and be cross-examined. At the discretion of the judge, each side may put rebuttal witnesses on the stand to counteract or refute the testimony of the opponent's witnesses.

The lawyer who believes a witness is being asked a question that is improper for any one of several reasons is entitled to object to the judge. If the objection is granted, or *sustained,* the question must be withdrawn. If the objection is *denied,* the question stands, the witness must answer— and all the lawyer can do is to note an *exception* to the judge's ruling. The purpose of the exception is that if the verdict in the trial court is appealed, the judge's ruling can be called into question as an error that may persuade the appellate court to reverse the trial court's verdict.

It is customary but not essential for the lawyer for each side to summarize his client's case when all the evidence has been presented and all the witnesses have been examined and cross-examined. The judge then instructs the jury regarding the law, and the jury retires to come to a decision on the facts and to apply the law as the judge has explained it. While the jury's verdict in criminal cases must be unanimous, in civil cases (which include tort cases) it need not be. Statutes in various states set forth the size of the majority required in civil cases.

86. The Decision and Judgment • When the jury announces its verdict —or if there is no jury, when the judge has made known his decision— the lawyer for the successful party prepares for the judge's signature a document called the *judgment* or *decree* of the court. It may simply dismiss the action, if the defendant has won; or, if he has lost, order him to do something, stop doing something or pay money to the plaintiff. It will usually order the loser to pay the court costs—the fees and other expenses of the litigation—incurred by the winner, but not his legal fees.

87. Appealing the Court's Decision • Either party to the lawsuit may appeal a trial court's decision. But appeals are expensive. Unless the party appealing has no funds, his lawyer must file a printed record on appeal and a printed *appellate brief,* or argument as to his understanding of the law and where and how the trial court went wrong in applying the law. (An appeal *in forma pauperis,* in the form of a pauper, may be authorized upon petition to the appellate court. If granted, the appeal papers need not be printed; typewritten copies will be accepted.)

When an appeal is made, it asks the appellate court to reverse, or overrule, the verdict of the trial court on legal grounds, that is, on the grounds that the trial judge committed errors of law in allowing or disallowing evidence or in giving mistaken instructions to the jury. It is not the responsibility of an appellate court to look for errors of fact or to quarrel or disagree with the jury's findings of fact, unless the side appealing can show that, given the evidence, a reasonable person would not have come to the conclusion reached by the jury.

A notice of appeal must be filed within a period of time allowed by statute or by the rules of the court which have the force and effect of statute. The transcript of the full record of the original trial must be printed in a specified way and accompanied by a brief giving the reasons for seeking reversal of the trial court's verdict. An opposing brief is filed by a lawyer for the party that won the verdict in the trial court.

When the appeal is ready for consideration by the appellate court, lawyers for both sides are notified and given an opportunity to appear in person and present oral arguments. Oral arguments are not required, and in many cases the opportunity is not used. The decision for or against oral argument on appeal must be your lawyer's. His decision will depend on the nature of the case, its importance to you, the complexity of the legal issues, the prevailing custom among lawyers in your state and the rules of the court in which the argument is to be held.

In the case of an appeal of a "money judgment" (an order that the defendant pay a sum of money), the defendant may ask for a stay of judgment. The judge granting the stay usually will direct that the money be placed in escrow, or bonded, until the conclusion of the appeal.

88. Enforcing the Judgment • If no appeal is filed within the time allowed by the court rules or by statute, the judgment becomes final. All that remains is for the plaintiff to enforce the judgment, that is, to get what is coming to him. If you have won a money judgment and if the defendant doesn't pay, your lawyer must set machinery in motion to compel him to pay. Your lawyer will make out what is called a property execution form, take it with a copy of the judgment to a sheriff or a marshal and ask him to collect what is due you. It's up to the sheriff or marshal to make the defendant pay or to sell enough of his property to satisfy your judgment.

In some cases you may already have frozen some of the defendant's assets—even before the start of the lawsuit—by asking the court to issue a *writ of attachment* on all or part of his property. For example, if you were planning to sue for $10,000 in damages but feared the defendant might leave the state before you could obtain a judgment against him, the court might allow you to attach his bank account in that amount or some of his real estate of equivalent value. The attachment would make it impossible for him to spend the money or to dispose of the property until after the judgment in your favor had been executed. If the court should find in favor of the defendant, however, he might turn around and sue you for damages he had incurred as a result of the attachment.

Attachment can be a harsh remedy, and it does involve the possible risk of a countersuit by the defendant against the plaintiff. But it also makes it easier to reach the defendant's assets once you have obtained a judgment against him.

You may also have a statutory lien against some of the defendant's

129

property, in which case you will have less trouble in satisfying the judgment than you might otherwise (see section 459).

If the sheriff or marshal can't find the defendant, or if he can't find any of his property to sell, or if the property he finds and sells isn't enough to pay you the amount of your judgment, your lawyer institutes *supplementary proceedings*. He gets from the court an order commanding the *judgment debtor* to appear in court for an examination under oath of his assets. He then tells the sheriff to sell whatever assets are disclosed by the defendant.

If the defendant has no assets, your only remaining hope of collecting lies in obtaining a court order directing other people to pay you the money they may owe him. A common example is an order directed to the defendant's employer, garnisheeing his wages: ordering the employer to withhold and pay over to you part of the defendant's wages or salary for a period of time long enough to pay you your judgment in full.

Unlike attachment, garnishment can usually be invoked only after you have obtained a judgment in your favor. The percentage amount of a person's wages that can be garnisheed is strictly limited by statute in most states (see chart 7, page 131), and many states have also passed laws saying that an employe may not be discharged by his employer simply because his wages have been garnisheed.

Garnishment may well be called rough justice, and some states have outlawed it entirely. Nonetheless, there are still many places where it can be used as a most effective club over the heads of defaulting defendants (see also sections 379, 458).

Despite legal sanctions, the task of collecting the amount of a judgment is often difficult. One lawyer, whose client was awarded a $48,000 judgment against a railroad which neglected to pay, literally seized one of the railroad's locomotives. He got a court order authorizing him to seize the railroad's property and took it to a deputy constable. The two of them physically seized a switch engine and a caboose, and the deputy constable handcuffed himself to the caboose as a symbol of taking possession. Both the constable and the lawyer released themselves from the caboose when the lawyer was notified by the railroad that a $48,000 check was on its way in satisfaction of the judgment.

This question of how difficult it may be to obtain satisfaction of a judgment rendered by the court is one that any person considering a lawsuit should think over carefully and discuss with his lawyer. Some people find that because of the difficulty of reaching the defendant's assets, the investment in time and money required for litigation is not worthwhile.

GARNISHMENT OF WAGES

The amount of your salary that may be garnisheed by creditors is limited by law in most states. This chart shows the statutory limits. (See section 88.) "Disposable income" or "earnings" means that part of your pay remaining after the deductions required by law.

CHART 7	How Much of Your Wages Is Exempt from Garnishment?
ALABAMA	75%; but for consumer debts, 80% or 50 times the federal minimum hourly wage, whichever is greater
ALASKA	75% of disposable income or $114 per week, whichever is greater[1]
ARIZONA	50% of money earned within 30 days preceding writ; 75% of disposable income or 30% of federal minimum hourly wage, whichever is greater
ARKANSAS	(1) $500 ($200 if unmarried) of money earned within 60 days preceding writ; or (2) 60 days' wages if less than above; $25 per week absolute exemption
CALIFORNIA	50% of the money earned within 30 days preceding writ of garnishment
COLORADO	70% (35% if unmarried)
CONNECTICUT	75% of disposable income or 40 times federal minimum hourly wage, whichever is greater
DELAWARE	85% of wages (except when process is for debts to state)[1]
D.C.	75% of disposable wages or 30 times federal minimum hourly wage, whichever is greater[1]
FLORIDA	75% of disposable income or 30 times federal minimum hourly wage, whichever is greater
GEORGIA	75% or 30 times federal minimum hourly wage, whichever is greater
HAWAII	95% of the first $100 of monthly wages; 90% of the next $100; 80% of monthly wages over $200 (50% in some cases)[1]
IDAHO	75% or 30 times federal minimum hourly wage, whichever is greater
ILLINOIS	(1) $65 a week ($50 if unmarried); or (2) 85% of gross wages; or (3) 75% of disposable earnings or 30 times federal minimum hourly wage, whichever is greater
INDIANA	75% or 30 times federal minimum hourly wage, whichever is greater (resident householders may qualify for higher exemptions)
IOWA	75% or 30 times federal minimum hourly wage, whichever is greater (no one garnishment may exceed $250 a year)
KANSAS	75% or 30 times federal minimum hourly wage, whichever is greater
KENTUCKY	75% or 30 times federal minimum hourly wage, whichever is greater (50% if judgment is for food, medicine or certain other essentials)
LOUISIANA	75% (minimum exemption is $70 per week)
MAINE	Earnings may not be garnisheed
MARYLAND	$120 or 75% of wages, whichever is greater[2]
MASSACHUSETTS	$125 of weekly earnings
MICHIGAN	60% (40% if not a head of household), subject to certain limitations[1]
MINNESOTA	75% or 40 times federal minimum hourly wage, whichever is greater (plus earnings within 30 days preceding writ if necessary for family support)[1]
MISSISSIPPI	75%
MISSOURI	75% or 30 times the federal minimum hourly wage, whichever is greater; 90% for resident head of household
MONTANA	All wages earned by head of household, or a person over 60, within the 45 days preceding writ of garnishment (with limitations)[1]

CHART 7 (cont.)	**How Much of Your Wages Is Exempt from Garnishment?**
NEBRASKA	75% of disposable earnings or 30 times federal minimum hourly wage, whichever is greater; 85% for head of household
NEVADA	75% of disposable weekly wages or all disposable weekly earnings in excess of 30 times the federal minimum hourly wage, whichever is greater[3]
NEW HAMPSHIRE	$40 of weekly wages owing for services rendered before issuance of writ of garnishment; all of wages earned after issuance of writ
NEW JERSEY	$48 a week plus 90% of excess[4]
NEW MEXICO	75% of disposable weekly wages or 40 times minimum hourly wage rate, whichever is greater
NEW YORK	90%; but if earnings are less than $85 per week, garnishment is not permitted
NORTH CAROLINA	No specific provision
NORTH DAKOTA	75% of weekly wages or 40 times federal minimum hourly wage rate, whichever is greater
OHIO	75% of disposable earnings or 30 times federal minimum hourly wage, whichever is greater, within 30 days preceding writ[1]
OKLAHOMA	75%, but all earnings for 90 days following judgment may be exempt if necessary for family support
OREGON	75% of disposable weekly wages or 40 times federal minimum hourly wage, whichever is greater
PENNSYLVANIA	None, but garnishment is only allowed in execution of an order against a husband for support of his wife & family
RHODE ISLAND	$50 a week
SOUTH CAROLINA	All wages for 60 days after issuance of writ of garnishment if necessary for family support. Judge has discretion to exempt earnings
SOUTH DAKOTA	No specific provision
TENNESSEE	(1) Head of family: 50% of weekly earnings or $20 a week, whichever is greater, but no more than $50 a week; (2) others: 40% of weekly earnings or $17.50 a week, whichever is greater, but no more than $40 a week
TEXAS	Wages may not be garnisheed
UTAH	75% of weekly wages or 40 times the federal minimum hourly wage, whichever is greater
VERMONT	No specific provision
VIRGINIA	75% of weekly wages or 30 times minimum hourly wage, whichever is greater
WASHINGTON	75% of weekly wages or 40 times Washington State minimum hourly wage, whichever is greater
WEST VIRGINIA	80% of disposable earnings or 30 times federal minimum hourly wage, whichever is greater
WISCONSIN	75% of weekly wages or 30 times the federal minimum hourly wage, whichever is greater
WYOMING	75% of disposable earnings or 30 times the federal minimum hourly wage, whichever is greater[1]

(1) An employe may not be fired or suspended solely on the ground that his wages have been garnisheed.

(2) In Caroline, Kent, Queen Anne's & Worcester counties, 75% or 30 times federal minimum hourly wage, whichever is greater.

(3) All wages are subject to garnishment under court orders for support, bankruptcy or payment of state or federal taxes.

(4) The court may fix a larger percentage if annual income exceeds $7,500.

CHAPTER FOUR

Your Protection Against Crime and Criminal Charges

It is better, so the Fourth Amendment teaches,
that the guilty sometimes go free than that
citizens be subject to easy arrest.

—WILLIAM O. DOUGLAS

4

Your Protection Against Crime and Criminal Charges

Some Key Points in This Chapter—
Consult these sections for information on:

Chart in This Chapter

Basic Things You Should Know About Criminal Law

Criminal law and procedure are a distinct and highly specialized field. Even if, as a law-abiding person, you have little direct contact with criminal law, it nonetheless affects your everyday life, because the high crime rate in all communities means that much of your tax dollar is spent fighting crime. Because the field is so specialized, many lawyers have little experience with criminal law. It will help you to know enough about the basic principles of criminal law to understand how it works and how best to protect yourself, your family and your friends against crime or the accusation of crime.

So varied are the crimes that men and women—and children—commit that no one book can cover them all. Those discussed in this chapter are the ones you hear most about. Crimes and offenses are presented in four broad groups, starting with the most serious and ending with the least serious. Crimes against the public generally, the country, the state and the different branches of government are considered first, in sections 93–119. Then, in sections 120–128, we take up offenses against your person. Sections 129–131 involve crimes against real property. Sections 132–136 discuss offenses against personal property. Sections 137–149 set out various defenses to criminal charges. Sections 150–157 concern criminal procedure.

89. What a Crime Is • A *crime* or *offense* (the two terms are used interchangeably in this book) is an act or omission defined and made punishable by law. To this very simple definition two points should be added: A crime is not a crime if committed by someone who is legally incompetent. And a crime is not a crime unless, at the time it was committed, a law was in effect saying the offense was a crime. If the speed limit in your state has been seventy miles an hour but by statute is lowered to sixty, effective at some future date, you may until that date legally travel at seventy. No criminal law is constitutional which is *ex post facto*—that is, which says something is illegal that was legal when it was done.

The distinction between a crime and a tort (see chapter 3, section 35) is that a crime is regarded as an injury to society whereas a tort is regarded as an injury to individuals only. The state brings the alleged criminal into court; the state protects the public by setting criminal procedures in motion. The criminal action in court is designated *The State* (or *The People*) v. *John Doe*. But if you as an individual have been wronged, in a way that may or may not involve a violation of a criminal law or statute, you must bring the legal action yourself, in a civil court. The action is designated *Jane Smith* v. *John Doe*.

Of course, an act may be both a crime and a tort. A motorist who drives so fast down a street that he loses control of his car, which runs up on the sidewalk and smashes into your store, would doubtless be prosecuted for one or more criminal offenses. But you would have your own right of action against him for the damages to your property. If he's insured you may or may not need to sue him to redress the wrong he did to your property. In theory, however, the public prosecutor has no choice but to have the driver arrested and charged with the commission of a crime, if only that of reckless driving.

90. Classification of Crimes or Offenses • Offenses with which criminal law is concerned fall into several different classifications, of which the following seem to be the most descriptive in terms of substance and procedure: *felonies* and *misdemeanors,* both of which are crimes and leave a person convicted of them with a criminal record; and *violations,* which are not crimes although they are punishable offenses.

Felonies are generally described as offenses that are punishable by more than one year's imprisonment. You will sometimes see these felonies referred to as capital crimes or infamous crimes. These terms have little or no legal significance today. All other crimes, which carry less severe penalties, are misdemeanors. Violations are punished less severely than crimes. The distinction between felonies and misdemeanors, on the one hand, and violations, on the other, is really the difference in the severity of punishment which is provided for the crime or offense in the law defining the crime. Typical felonies are ones we often read about: murder, rape, larceny, arson, burglary and treason.

Another important difference between felonies and misdemeanors and all other lower offenses lies in your right to trial by jury: if you are suspected of having committed a felony or a more serious misdemeanor, you are brought before a grand jury, indicted (if the grand jury believes you may be guilty), arraigned (see section 153), given a chance to plead in any one of several ways ("guilty" and "not guilty" are the most common pleas) and offered a jury trial. But if your offense is relatively minor —a less serious misdemeanor or a violation—you are arraigned or brought into court at the motion of the local prosecuting attorney and given a chance to plead; you may or may not have the opportunity to be tried by a jury.

Misdemeanors are offenses which, because they are regarded as less dangerous to society, less evil in themselves, carry a lighter penalty than felonies. Society, therefore, throws fewer protections around those accused of misdemeanors and violations. You are guilty of committing a *battery* if, unprovoked, you start a fistfight with your neighbor and punch him in the nose. If he calls the police and you are summoned to appear before the local magistrate the next morning, you will not be offered a jury trial, unless battery is punishable in your state by imprisonment for more than six months.

When you leave your car an hour too long in a restricted parking area, you have violated a local parking ordinance—but the worst that can happen is that the policeman or meter maid will issue you a *summons* directing you to pay the appropriate fine by mail or in person by a stated date. In the case of your fistfight with your neighbor, your summons orders you to appear in court on a certain date at a certain time, "to answer the charges against you." You ignore such a summons at your peril: the judge may issue a *bench warrant* for your arrest.

91. Parties to Crimes: Principals, Accessories and Accomplices • Those who actually commit or perpetrate the crime, whether a felony or a misdemeanor, are called *principals*. *Accessories before the fact* are those who, although absent when the act was committed, nevertheless participated in it by procuring, counseling or ordering the principal to commit the act. Accessories before the fact are now commonly regarded as principals. Because the law doesn't try to distinguish among those involved in the relatively minor offenses called misdemeanors, perpetrators, abettors and inciters are all considered as principals. *Accessories after the fact* are those who, knowing a crime has been committed, assist the principal to avoid capture or arrest or to escape. But if the crime is treason, all involved are treated as principals, because the offense is so serious.

An *accomplice* is a person who knowingly and willingly participates in the commission of a crime, whether a felony or a misdemeanor. If a person can be charged and convicted of the same offense as that charged against the principal offender, he is an accomplice. For example, suppose two people rob a bank, one of them standing outside the bank to warn the other of passersby, then driving the getaway car. The driver is an accomplice and can be charged and convicted of the crime of robbery just as readily as the one who actually took the money.

If the one who took the money shoots and kills the bank's armed guard, the driver would also be charged with felony in some states. In others he would be an accomplice only to the crime in which he participated.

92. Crime and Responsibility · Crimes remain crimes even if they are not punished. The fact that many offenses and infractions go unnoticed or unpunished neither justifies them nor constitutes a legal defense for those who commit them. Many parents serve beer to their minor children, knowing it is against the law to do so. Many people knowingly exceed the speed limit when driving. In some of the New England states old blue laws remain on the statute books, laws passed in early colonial days, when customs were much stricter than today. These and other laws are violated every day, but society is rarely concerned, and the police and the prosecutors are often too busy with serious offenses to proceed under these old and generally ignored laws. Nonetheless, the crime remains a crime, and anyone who violates the law may be called to account for it.

Moreover, an unsuccessful attempt to commit a crime is in itself a crime. It involves an intent to commit a crime and the performance of some act preliminary to its commission, and it is punishable despite the failure to consummate the intended crime.

OFFENSES AGAINST JUDICIAL AUTHORITY, PUBLIC JUSTICE AND THE GENERAL WELFARE

93. Treason · "No crime is greater than treason," the United States Supreme Court has said, because it threatens the very existence of the nation. It is the one offense defined in the Constitution (Article III, Section 3): "Treason against the United States, shall consist only in levying war against them, or in adhering to their enemies, giving them aid and comfort."

But the framers of the Constitution—recognizing that charges of treason were often made with little supporting evidence—immediately added: "No person shall be convicted of treason unless on the testimony of two witnesses to the same overt act, or on confession in open court." This requirement of the testimony of two witnesses results in very few prosecutions for treason.

94. Conspiracy • In the so-called draft-card cases of the 1960s the government prosecuted for the crime of conspiracy. A *conspiracy* is an agreement between two or more persons to bring about an illegal result or a legal result by illegal means. In the draft-card cases the government charged that the several defendants conspired with each other to counsel and persuade young men to violate the selective service or draft laws, an illegal result.

In the case of the so-called Chicago Seven the charges were conspiracy and crossing state lines to incite riots, at the convention of the Democratic Party in 1968. Here both an illegal result and an agreement to achieve it by illegal means were charged.

Keep in mind that the conspiracy is a separate and distinct offense from the act that is the purpose of the conspiracy. A person may be convicted both of the crime of conspiracy and of the crime actually committed by the conspirators. A man may be convicted both of conspiring with others to violate the antitrust laws and of violating them.

95. Sedition • The crime of *sedition* has the same purpose as treason but lacks the element of an overt act. Sedition involves actively urging the overthrow of the state, not simply discussing revolution as a philosophical matter. Clearly it comes close to the borders of freedom of speech, and as a result there have been few prosecutions for the crime of sedition in modern times.

Generally speaking, you may safely write an article or make a speech saying that monarchy is the best kind of government and that you wish the United States were a monarchy—but you may not add that you are starting a political movement to bring about a monarchy by force and violence and that you urge everybody to join you in bringing about the downfall of the constitutional form of government in order to establish a monarchy.

96. Contempt • The crime of *criminal contempt* has been charged in many recent cases. Very simply, it is a challenge to the dignity and authority of a court or of a legislative body. If it takes place in court itself, in the courtroom and before the judge, there is no question that the judge has the right to order the immediate punishment of the offender. What has not been established, and will not be known until appeals from the contempt orders in several cases have been decided by higher courts, is how severe a sentence the trial judge may impose and whether the provocation or degree of contempt shown justifies the length of the

139

sentence imposed. What must be balanced off are the beliefs on the part of some defendants and their lawyers that they have a right to impress the jury by any method, including disruption, against society's need that court proceedings be conducted according to at least minimal standards of order and decorum.

Contempt of a legislative body is also a crime. Such a body must have the means of getting information about the subjects with which it is authorized to deal. As part of its legislative function it has the power to summon witnesses and to compel them to attend hearings and produce and disclose facts and documents. A witness who refuses to respond to such a summons may be punished for contempt.

The legislature may delegate to any committee properly established the power to issue summonses and to punish for contempt. But the person summoned may not be forced to answer questions or to produce documents he thinks may tend to make him subject to criminal prosecution. This is the reason for the many citations of the Fifth Amendment to the U.S. Constitution by witnesses called before congressional committees (see section 25).

The legislative committee's questions must also be limited to areas within the scope of the purpose for which the committee was established. It is unlikely that a committee set up to look into new leglislation for wildlife refuges could legally demand answers from officials of the dock workers' union about corrupt labor practices. Contempt of Congress is a misdemeanor by law.

The examples of contempt we have been discussing, in court and before a legislative committee, are *direct contempt*. *Indirect contempt* is contempt outside the courtroom: a violation of a court order or improperly talking with a juror. It is the ignoring or demeaning of a valid court order. It is a misdemeanor.

Civil contempt is contempt that affects an individual rather than the dignity of the court. In a case where a divorced man fails to make support payments that are owed to his former wife for the care of their children, he may be liable for civil contempt. He can escape punishment by making the payments. Criminal contempt, on the other hand, because it is an offense against the judicial system itself, cannot be so lightly excused.

97. Perjury · The judicial process would not work very well if people felt free to give false testimony in court. Accordingly, there are penalties to discourage such conduct. If in a judicial proceeding someone willfully gives false testimony or information under oath, in matters material to the issue involved, he has committed the offense of perjury. It is a felony in many instances, and the perjurer, if convicted, may be sent to jail. No prosecution for perjury follows if mistaken testimony is given in good faith or if the false statement has nothing to do with the case. You may, for example, tell a white lie about your age—unless, of course, your age as given makes you a minor when in fact you're an adult, and this information is material to the case.

Although perjury is most often associated with judicial proceedings, you should take care not to perjure yourself—knowingly make material false statements—on important affidavits and documents such as tax returns, customs statements and so forth. This is called *false swearing,* which is perjury outside of or apart from a judicial proceeding.

If A intentionally persuades B to commit perjury and B does so, A may be prosecuted for the offense of *subornation of perjury.* It is also a felony. Note that two things are necessary to constitute this crime: the inducement by one person and the act of perjury by the other.

98. Escape and Associated Crimes • *Escape* is the crime of getting away from lawful custody without the use of force. *Breach of prison* is the crime of getting away from legal custody by the use of force. If you get into a street fight with several demonstrators and are taken to the police station for booking but manage to skip out the back door in the general confusion, you have committed the crime of escape. If you make your escape by breaking open the door of the paddy wagon, you are guilty of breach of prison.

The theory underlying these offenses is that if you have been deprived of your liberty by authority of law, you have a duty to submit to confinement until freed by due course of law, no matter whether you are committed to await a trial, are being punished after conviction or are confined for any other purpose authorized by law.

If the policeman who arrests you carelessly leaves the door of the paddy wagon unlocked so that it swings open and you jump out and get away, he is guilty of the offense of *permitting escape* from legal custody. The offense is a misdemeanor in some states, a felony in others. It is a felony if the policeman acted as he did in order to let you make your getaway. If you believe a friend has been improperly seized by the police and you stage a fight and spring your friend from the patrol car, you have committed the crime of *rescue.* It is classified either as a felony or as a misdemeanor, depending on the nature of the crime with which your friend was charged.

141

99. Your Duty to Help Police • You have a duty to help law officers make arrests or prevent crimes if they ask you to, and your failure or refusal to do so is a misdemeanor. This obligation was well known throughout the West in frontier days, when the sheriff often collected several citizens into what was called a posse to accompany him as he apprehended an outlaw. The posse had roots far back in England and was a recognized and quite legitimate method of enlarging the number of law enforcers in emergencies.

The same considerations exist today. A policeman may jump into your car and order you to "follow that cab." Even if you are on your way to a big date, you had better do as he asks. Modern statutes recognize that administration of the law is handicapped or frustrated by refusal to give an officer the assistance he is authorized to demand.

100. Probation, Parole and Bail • Probation and parole are both conditional release. If someone who has been released from jail on probation or parole violates the terms of his release, the penalty is revocation of the release, and the violator is again taken into custody.

A prisoner who is released on bail must obey the terms of his release. *Bail* (see section 152) is money that is put up as security for the prisoner's being on hand when his case is brought to trial. The crime of *jumping bail* is failure to appear. The bail money is forfeited, and the person who forfeits is again subject to arrest. In some states jumping bail is a separate offense from the original charge, a felony or a misdemeanor depending on the seriousness of the offense for which the defendant was originally charged and awaiting trial.

101. Compounding a Crime • Because a crime is an offense against society as a whole, the individual victim has no right to enter into an agreement with a criminal that would prevent or avoid or delay his prosecution by public authority. The burglar who breaks into your house at night and steals your silverware may decide the next day he's made a big mistake and offer to return all he stole if you'll agree not to tell the police about his crime. You may accept the return of the silverware, but if you agree not to tell the police you are *compounding* a crime and may yourself be prosecuted for a felony.

If you know that a crime is about to be committed and you don't try to stop it, or if you know that a crime has been committed and you don't report it to the proper authorities, you may be charged with *misprision of felony*. This offense is seldom prosecuted today, but you should at

142

least understand that you run a risk when you fail to prevent the commission of a crime if you can or fail to report its commission as soon as possible after you know of it.

102. Extortion and Blackmail • Originally, *extortion* was an offense, usually only a misdemeanor, that could be committed only by a holder of public office. It is the corrupt collection of an unlawful fee by an officer using the power of his office as pressure. The unlawfulness may consist in the fact that the fee extorted was not due at all or was not yet due or was more than was due. Laws in many states broaden out extortion to include what is commonly called *blackmail,* which is really extorting money by threats of criminal prosecution or by the destruction of a person's social standing or reputation.

The building inspector who demands $100 or even $10 for certifying your building as safe and sound is guilty of the offense of extortion. The man who says that unless you pay him $1,000 he'll publicize an event in your past you'd rather keep forgotten is blackmailing you—it's extortion by a private individual.

103. Criminal Libel • The great majority of cases involving libel are civil wrongs or torts; they are actions for damages caused by the publication of untrue defamatory statements or actions for injunctions to stop the publication of such statements (see section 44). But there remains the misdemeanor of *criminal libel.* Although it closely resembles civil libel, there are significant differences. For instance, if a man maliciously makes insulting statements about a dead person, he may be prosecuted for criminal libel, but he could not be sued for damages. The purpose of the law in a case like this is to keep the peace, to avoid stirring up anger—and perhaps violence—on the part of the surviving relatives of the deceased. Also, the tort of libel is committed only when the libelous statement is made to a third person. Criminal libel, however, is committed even if the only person reading the statement is the person who is insulted. Depending on the law in your state, if you write a paper saying a man is a traitor and a thief, and you show it only to him, you may be prosecuted for criminal libel: you have endangered the public peace. If you show that same paper to someone else, you have published it and subjected yourself to the possibility of a civil suit for damages.

Truth remains the perfect defense to an action for libel, whether criminal or civil—except in the case where the defamatory statement was made out of a desire to harm. And in an action for criminal libel you have the same defenses of privilege as you have in the tort action for civil libel (see section 44).

104. Forgery · Forgery is the act of fraudulently making a false document, which has apparent legal significance, with the intent to defraud. Be careful not to confuse forgery with other offenses, such as getting money under false pretenses by pretending that a document is what it is not. If a man obtains a life insurance policy by presenting the valid birth certificate of his deceased brother, in order to establish a younger age than his own and receive a lower premium rate, he has defrauded the company. He has obtained a policy under false pretenses, but he has committed no forgery. If he writes a check on a bank where he has no funds, or insufficient funds, the check is written with intent to defraud, but it is no forgery. If, on the other hand, he steals someone's checkbook and so cleverly signs the owner's name that the bank makes payment on it, he has committed (in addition to the offense of theft) a forgery. Moreover, once the forger passes the check, he has committed another offense: *uttering a forged document.* The writing of the check is a forgery; uttering it is a separate offense. In some states these two offenses have been merged into one statutory offense of forgery.

105. Counterfeiting · Although very similar to the offense of forgery, *counterfeiting* is a distinct crime. It consists of the making of any kind of false money which appears to be genuine or of any paper or document that is a false obligation or other security of the United States or of any foreign government. It is a felony. Paragraph 5 of Article I, Section 8, of the United States Constitution expressly reserves to the Congress the right to coin money, and Paragraph 1 of Article I, Section 10, specifically denies the states this right. But Congress has never denied the states the right to punish for the crime of counterfeiting. As a result, counterfeiting is an offense both under federal laws and under the laws of many states.

Federal law makes it a crime not only to make false money but also to pass false money off as genuine and even to make or possess machinery that can be used to produce counterfeit money, whether paper or coin. Here, then, is another area in which society seeks to protect itself by spelling out specific offenses against itself and by providing stiff penalties—fine and imprisonment—for their commission.

106. Bribery · *Bribery* is the offering, giving, soliciting or receiving of money, or some other valuable thing, to influence a person to act in a

HOW TO SPOT A COUNTERFEIT BILL

The best way to detect a counterfeit bill is to compare it with a real one of the same denomination. The paper on which real bills are printed contains small red and blue fibers. The portrait on a genuine bill is sharp and distinct with regular, unbroken background lines. The Treasury seal is printed in the correct color (*see below*) and its sawtooth points are sharp and even. The serial numbers are evenly spaced and aligned and printed in the appropriate color (the same color in which the Treasury seal is printed). The appearance of counterfeit bills is generally poor.

FEDERAL RESERVE
SEAL AND LETTER

TREASURY
SEAL

TYPE OF NOTE
SHOWN HERE

SERIAL
NUMBER

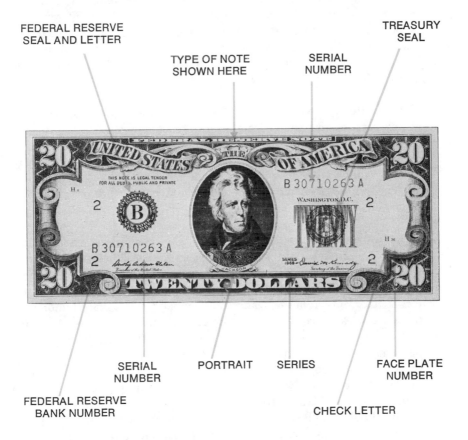

SERIAL
NUMBER

PORTRAIT

SERIES

FACE PLATE
NUMBER

FEDERAL RESERVE
BANK NUMBER

CHECK LETTER

Three types of U.S. paper currency are in circulation:

Type	Color of Treasury Seal and Serial Number	Denominations
Federal Reserve Note	Green	$1, $2, $5, $10, $20, $50, $100[1]
United States Note	Red	$2[2], $5[2], $100
Silver Certificate[2]	Blue	$1, $5, $10

1. Larger bills not issued after 1946.
2. No longer issued.

manner contrary to his duty, or to reward him for so acting. Originally the offense applied only to corrupt giving to judges. Then it was broadened to cover bribes to all public officials. And in recent years it has been extended to include giving to and receiving from people generally for illicit purposes, such as paying money to voters to vote a certain way or to an athlete to throw a game. By law, bribery has become a felony.

107. Misconduct in Office · The necessity that the public's business, in governmental offices of all kinds, be conducted with minimum standards of honesty has led to the recognition by the courts of three different kinds of offenses: (a) doing an act which is wrongful in itself, called *malfeasance,* (b) doing an otherwise lawful act in an unlawful manner, called *misfeasance,* or (c) omitting to do an act required by the duties of the office, called *nonfeasance.*

108. Interference with a Jury · *Embracery* is an attempt by wrongful and corrupt means to influence a juror in reaching a verdict. We speak of this old but relatively rare offense these days as tampering with the jury or a juror. It is a misdemeanor, as is the somewhat more common offense of *tampering with a witness,* or doing anything with the intent of influencing his testimony or of inducing him not to appear as a witness when he is legally bound to do so.

109. Obstruction of Justice · *Obstruction of justice* is a general phrase used to cover offenses in which a conscious effort is made to interfere with the proper functioning of the courts and of police officers. A common offense is interfering with a policeman who is making an arrest. *Resisting arrest* is a misdemeanor that probably takes place hundreds of times a day as policemen around the country arrest vagrants, drunkards who get disorderly, suspected dope pushers and others. If you think a policeman is in the wrong when he starts to arrest you, "tell it to the judge" in night court or the next morning. You'll only create further trouble for yourself if you get into a fight with the policeman, who can have you charged with disorderly conduct and obstructing justice.

You should also be aware of the risk of trying to destroy or suppress evidence. Let's say you know that the police are about to search your neighbor's house for a quantity of illegal or unlicensed alcohol. If, in the hope of sparing your neighbor embarrassment, you enter the house while he is away and remove the alcohol and hide it, you are suppressing evidence and may be charged with that misdemeanor.

146

110. Disturbing the Peace • Society has an obvious interest in preserving the peace and tranquility of the community. Any willful act committed without lawful justification which unreasonably disturbs the public peace or tends strongly to create or encourage disturbance is a *breach of the peace*. In some states the offense is called *disorderly conduct*. Just as disorderly conduct is hard to define, so it is hard to defend. Police can and often do use the charge of disturbing the peace as a very flexible weapon in their arsenal of ways to keep the peace, and judges are not likely to show sympathy for those who have allowed themselves to get into a situation where they are brought into court on this charge.

111. Unlawful Assembly • Unlawful assembly is an offense only in some states. It is an assembly or gathering of three or more persons (a) with the intent of committing a crime by force or (b) with the intent of carrying out a common purpose in such a manner that reasonable persons in the neighborhood would fear a breach of the peace. All involved may be guilty of misdemeanors.

112. Riot • A *riot,* on the other hand, is strictly defined as the actual execution, by three or more unlawfully assembled persons, of their common purpose in such a way as to create public alarm. Note that a riot can follow from a peaceful meeting which mushrooms into an unlawful assembly. Rioters are guilty of misdemeanors.

Inciting to riot, itself a misdemeanor, is using words or signs or any other means to provoke a riot. The legal definition of riot clearly does not apply to many of the disturbances that have taken place in cities and on campuses recently, since it requires some common purpose. Participants in such spontaneous civil disorders are more likely candidates for arrest for breach of the peace, theft, battery or arson, among other offenses.

113. Forcible Entry and Detainer • Forcible entry and detainer is sometimes called *criminal trespass*. A civil trespass (see section 46) is the deliberate walking on another person's property without his permission. If you cross your neighbor's field you have committed the tort of trespass, but you have not committed a crime. But if you break down his fence to get on his land and refuse to leave when he orders you off, you may be held guilty of the misdemeanor of criminal trespass.

114. Weapons Laws • Carrying weapons is something you can do in some states with no worry whatsoever. But in other states, and in many

147

cities, you are clearly violating the law (see chart 5, page 66). Most states do make it a felony to carry a concealed weapon. The statutory differences concern the carrying of unconcealed weapons.

Be careful not to take the apparent permissiveness of the Second Amendment to the United States Constitution too seriously (see section 21). It says that "A well-regulated militia, being necessary to the security of a free State, the right of the people to keep and bear arms shall not be infringed." The United States Supreme Court has said that this amendment means only that the right to "keep and bear arms" shall not be regulated by the Congress; it does not prevent regulation by the states.

The assassination of prominent leaders of the United States during the 1960s, and the large number of incidents of rifle and pistol shooting that we hear and read about so often, indicate that the offense of carrying weapons is being committed daily all over the United States. In self-protection, the people (through laws passed by the legislatures) are likely to punish this offense more and more severely. The police could hardly search every person they suspect, even if the law gave them the right to do so. Punishment may therefore be the most effective instrument of control. You should check the statutes in your state and the ordinances passed by your city and town before you decide to carry a gun or pistol with you at any time.

Here, as in other cases, the criminal law makes no exceptions for the "good guys" as opposed to the "bad guys." A small store owner who keeps an unlicensed or illegal pistol on his premises may well be prosecuted when he uses it to shoot a holdup man in the leg just as surely as if he had used it for some nefarious purpose. Again it is wise to protect yourself by obeying the law.

115. Vagrancy • The soaring welfare costs of the second half of this century should not blind us to the existence in many states of what are known as vagrancy laws. These laws make it an offense for one who is capable of self-support not to support himself. The intent of the legislation in New York State, for example, was said by a court to be "to compel individuals to engage in some legitimate and gainful occupation from which they might maintain themselves, and thus remove the temptations to lead a life of crime or to become public charges."

A *vagrant* by this definition is a man or woman "without visible means of support," who, although capable of earning a legitimate living, does not do so or makes no effort to do so. It is not unlikely that this basic concept, of a man's duty to keep himself from being a public burden, will attract revived interest in the courts, especially as the welfare laws are rewritten to ensure that everyone has an absolute minimum of financial support.

116. Bigamy • Society's interest in protecting and preserving the integrity of its strongest unit, the family, has led in almost every nation outside the Muslim world to strong legislation against *bigamy* (or polygamy): the state of having more than one spouse at the same time. In the United States the offense is a felony. It is also a felony knowingly to marry a married person.

For the purpose of defining bigamy, a previous marriage is valid unless it has been pronounced void or annulled or dissolved by judgment of a court. The only exception is the case in which one spouse has deserted the other and has disappeared for a period of time defined in state statutes. The period varies from five to thirty years; seven is the most common (see chart 39, page 677). But before you undertake a second marriage under such circumstances, you should consult a lawyer and obtain a court order permitting you to do so.

117. Adultery • An almost universal ground for divorce is *adultery,* sexual intercourse between a married person and someone other than his or her spouse. *Fornication,* or illicit cohabitation, is sexual intercourse between two persons not married to each other. The penalties laid down for these offenses vary widely from state to state, but they are almost never prosecuted by the state as crimes.

118. Incest • Incest is sexual intercourse between persons who are closely related to each other, generally persons "of the same blood"— parent and child, brother and sister, in some states uncle and niece or aunt and nephew. It is a felony, regardless of whether both parties have undertaken the sexual relationship willingly. The offense of incest, of course, is only a reflection of society's conviction that such relationships are to be punished for society's sake. Marriage between persons of such close relationship is not permitted, and there is medical and legal logic in also punishing sexual acts between them.

119. Other Sex Offenses • Several offenses against public morals and public decency should be mentioned, even though they are seldom the subject of modern prosecution. Society has increasingly come to believe that these offenses are essentially private, not public, and that adult indi-

149

viduals should be free from interference with their sexual activities as long as no obvious public harm results. Sodomy in any form, such as homosexuality, pederasty or lesbianism, is an offense which not very long ago was a felony and severely punished. Acts of sodomy include sexual activities between individuals of the same sex or different sexes, activities that have historically been regarded as "unnatural" and, therefore, to be penalized.

Not to be overlooked are the better-known sexual offenses of *prostitution,* the performance of sexual acts for hire; *indecent exposure,* or exposure of the private parts in a public place; and *indecent assault,* or the act of taking sexual liberties against the will of another, though short of actual intercourse. The offense of *abduction,* which is the act of taking away a child or woman by fraud or violence either for immoral purposes or to force the victim into marriage, is seldom prosecuted in the United States today.

It has become increasingly difficult to draw a line between what is and is not permissible in literature and in public performance on the stage and screen. Public standards change from age to age, and what was prohibited in one era is permitted in another. The courts are most reluctant to engage in what might even remotely be regarded as censorship, because of the privileges of freedom of speech guaranteed by the First Amendment to the United States Constitution. But the courts have indicated no intention of carrying that guarantee beyond a reasonable point. It is reasonable to expect that the courts will recognize and protect the right of persons to be free from the receipt of admittedly pornographic material in the mail.

These matters are in the shadowy zone where individual freedoms and public concerns clash, and society's many interests conflict. Not even your lawyer will be able to guide you in all cases, but if you seek protection for yourself or your family, you certainly should consult him.

CRIMES AGAINST YOUR PERSON

120. Homicide · Our society regards the killing of one human being by another as the most serious of all crimes. In the great majority of states, however, the killing of an unborn child is not a criminal offense. (Abortion is discussed in section 125.) Nor are actions which result in death long after the event. An old rule, that death a year and a day beyond the act said to have caused it was not homicide, has been questioned. But a man who dies of a cerebral hemorrhage five years after he was hit on the head would almost surely not be regarded as a homicide victim, even if the autopsy showed that the blow may well have been the remote cause of his death.

The major categories of homicide are (1) *criminal homicide,* which is either murder or manslaughter, (2) *negligent homicide* and (3) *innocent homicide,* which is either justifiable homicide or excusable homicide (see section 122).

121. Murder · The hallmark of murder is malice: without malice there is no murder. But some murders seem more heinous than others. *Murder in the first degree* is either an intended killing that was premeditated and deliberate—a murder planned for its own sake—or a so-called felony-murder. A *felony-murder* is one committed during the perpetration of a felony or serious offense, such as arson, rape, robbery or burglary, or as the consequence of a "depraved act," such as detonating a bomb in a public place.

Murder in the second degree is a killing also motivated by malice but in which the intent to kill did not exist until just before the killing itself and for which there was no real justification. Suppose a married man falls in love with a blonde beauty and asks his wife for a divorce; she refuses, and he kills her in a rage. He is guilty of murder in the second degree.

122. Manslaughter and Lesser Killings · Just as there are two categories of murder, so there are two categories of manslaughter. *Voluntary manslaughter* is a killing in which there was no intent until just before the act, which was not motivated by malice and for which there was some provocation—as when, having been violently assaulted, you respond violently and kill your attacker. Killing a person while resisting his attempt to arrest you unlawfully would be voluntary manslaughter, as would the killing of a wife in the classic situation of a man unexpectedly returning home from a trip and catching her in the act of adultery.

Involuntary manslaughter is a killing in which there is no malice but which might have been avoided. The offense is committed most often during the perpetration of a misdemeanor. It is a lesser offense because the original offense was lesser. Felony-murder, you'll recall, is a killing that takes place during the commission of an offense that is a felony. The rapist whose victim dies as a result of the rape or because of his violence

151

in raping her is guilty of a felony-murder. But suppose a man picks a fight with someone he suspects of trying to seduce his wife and during the fight knocks his opponent down so hard that he hits his head on the pavement and dies. In picking the fight in the first place the man committed an offense that is only a misdemeanor. Chances are he would be charged only with involuntary manslaughter because of the resulting unplanned but clearly avoidable death.

Negligent homicide, or automobile homicide, as it is increasingly called, is a killing resulting from the negligent operation of a passenger vehicle, especially an automobile. If in careless or negligent driving a man kills a pedestrian, the driver of another car or a passenger in his own car, the offense is negligent homicide. In most states it is only a misdemeanor. The driver may, however, be vulnerable to a civil suit for wrongful death brought by the widow or the family of the man he has killed (see section 328). Gross and wanton negligence that results in death is a more serious matter and is usually considered a crime.

Justifiable homicide is not a crime either. It is a killing that takes place under lawful orders, so to speak: killing of an enemy in wartime, killing of a condemned criminal by a hangman or an executioner. A police officer, or a citizen ordered by him to help catch a suspected criminal, commits no crime if he kills the criminal to prevent escape. Nor do you commit a crime if you shoot and kill the robber who breaks into your home and refuses to leave on your command (see sections 147–149). But often the circumstances surrounding this kind of killing are not clear-cut, and reasonable restraint in the use of force is essential in all situations. A homeowner who shoots and kills a suspected prowler outside his house at night may find himself open to criminal charges if the victim turns out to be a delivery boy or a neighboring youngster taking a shortcut home. The courts do not encourage the use of deadly force.

123. Suicide · About all that can be said about suicide is that it has been historically regarded as a crime, for which, clearly, the law can impose no punishment. An attempted suicide is in many states a misdemeanor, one which courts are increasingly reluctant to penalize because of the almost general acceptance today that such an attempt is the result or manifestation of extreme mental illness, demanding psychiatric care.

124. Rape · An almost universally recognized felony, *rape* is forcible sexual possession by a man of a woman, other than his wife, without her consent and against her will. The woman who consents to the act through fear, or because she is mentally deficient, or whose consent is meaningless because she is unconscious from sleep, alcohol or narcotics, is the victim of the offense of rape, even if the rape was merely attempted and not consummated.

Statutory rape is sexual intercourse between a man of any age and a girl below the age of consent. The age of consent is usually eighteen (see chart 28, page 428). If the girl is below that age, it makes no difference even if she was more than "the willing victim"; sexual intercourse with her subjects the man to the charge of rape and, if he is found guilty, to imprisonment. The offense is a felony.

125. Abortion · Abortion is the intentional destruction or deliberate premature bringing forth of a human fetus in such a way that it is bound to die. Until recently, abortion was permitted by the state laws only in very limited circumstances, as, for example, to protect the life of a pregnant woman. Historically, an abortion performed without such legal justification was a criminal act and a felony.

In recent years the idea that a woman has the right to choose whether or not to bear a child and that, if she unintentionally becomes pregnant, she has the right to a safe legal abortion has gained widespread acceptance. In 1973 the U.S. Supreme Court—in a case that held the Texas abortion law to be unconstitutional—set down the guidelines for state abortion laws that would not infringe upon the right of a woman and her physician to decide whether or not she should have an abortion.

The Court divided the human gestation period into three parts or trimesters, each encompassing approximately three months of the nine-month total. The right to privacy governing the doctor-patient relationship was found to be of paramount importance in the stage of pregnancy prior to the end of approximately the first trimester. In this stage the decision as to whether to abort and the implementation of the decision must be left to the judgment of the pregnant woman's attending physician, free from interference by the state. In the stage of pregnancy subsequent to approximately the end of the first trimester, the state may, if it chooses, impose regulations that are aimed at protecting the health of the woman. For the stage subsequent to the time when the fetus is capable of surviving outside the woman's body—even though artificial aid may be necessary—the state in promoting its interest in potential human life may regulate or even prohibit an abortion unless it is necessary for the preservation of the life or health of the woman.

Since 1973 most states have enacted new abortion laws that attempt

153

RESTRICTIONS ON THE RIGHT TO ABORTION

The laws in many states still do not conform to the requirements of the Supreme Court ruling, and many of these laws have been declared unconstitutional or are being challenged in court. You should consult a lawyer or public official to determine the law in your state. In this chart, it is assumed that the abortion decision must be made by the woman and her physician. Such a requirement is not considered to be a restriction.

CHART 8	First Tri-mester[1]	Second Tri-mester	Third Tri-mester		First Tri-mester[1]	Second Tri-mester	Third Tri-mester
				MISSOURI	Yes	Yes	Yes
ALABAMA	Yes	Yes	Yes	MONTANA	No	Yes	Yes
ALASKA	Yes	Yes	Yes	NEBRASKA	No	No	Yes
ARIZONA	Yes	Yes	Yes	NEVADA	No	No	Yes
ARKANSAS	Yes	Yes	Yes	NEW HAMPSHIRE	Yes	Yes	Yes
CALIFORNIA	Yes	Yes	Yes	NEW JERSEY	Yes	Yes	Yes
COLORADO	Yes	Yes	Yes	NEW MEXICO	Yes	Yes	Yes
CONNECTICUT	Yes	Yes	Yes	NEW YORK	No	No	Yes
DELAWARE	Yes	Yes	Yes	NORTH CAROLINA	No	Yes	Yes
D.C.	Yes	Yes	Yes	NORTH DAKOTA	No	Yes	Yes
FLORIDA	Yes	Yes	Yes	OHIO	Yes	Yes	Yes
GEORGIA	No	Yes	Yes	OKLAHOMA	Yes	Yes	Yes
HAWAII	No	No	No	OREGON	Yes	Yes	Yes
IDAHO	No	Yes	Yes	PENNSYLVANIA	No	No	Yes
ILLINOIS	Yes	Yes	Yes	RHODE ISLAND	No	No	Yes
INDIANA	Yes	Yes	Yes	SOUTH CAROLINA	No	Yes	Yes
IOWA	No	Yes	Yes	SOUTH DAKOTA	No	Yes	Yes
KANSAS	Yes	Yes	Yes	TENNESSEE	No	Yes	Yes
KENTUCKY	No	Yes	Yes	TEXAS	No new statute has been enacted[2]		
LOUISIANA	Yes	Yes	Yes	UTAH	No	Yes	Yes
MAINE	Yes	Yes	Yes	VERMONT	Yes	Yes	Yes
MARYLAND	Yes	Yes	Yes	VIRGINIA	No	Yes	Yes
MASSACHUSETTS	No	Yes	Yes	WASHINGTON	Yes	Yes	Yes
MICHIGAN	Yes	Yes	Yes	WEST VIRGINIA	Yes	Yes	Yes
MINNESOTA	No	Yes	Yes	WISCONSIN	Yes	Yes	Yes
MISSISSIPPI	Yes	Yes	Yes	WYOMING	Yes	Yes	Yes

(1) The states define the time periods for each trimester differently; for example, the first trimester may be defined as 10, 12 or 13 weeks depending on the state.

(2) The old law permitted abortion only to save the mother's life.

to conform to the standards set by the Supreme Court, but many of the restrictions on the right to an abortion contained in these laws have been found to be invalid. Other states have refused to enact new laws.

Statutes prohibiting all abortions not necessary to save the woman's life, prohibiting all advertising of legal abortions or prohibiting the use of an abortion procedure known as saline amniocentesis have been found to be invalid. Also found to be invalid are statutes that require that an abortion in the first trimester be performed in a hospital, that a hospital committee approve the abortion where such approval is not necessary for other surgical procedures, that two consulting physicians approve the abortion, that the husband of a married woman or the parents of a minor give their consent to the abortion, that there be efforts made to preserve the fetus after it has been aborted and that to be eligible for an abortion the woman be a state resident for a certain period of time.

Publicly funded hospitals and health care facilities may not refuse to perform abortions, although an individual may refuse to participate in an abortion if it would be against his or her moral or religious beliefs to do so. One issue that is quite troubling in this area is whether private or religiously affiliated hospitals and facilities that receive some federal funds may refuse to perform an abortion if it is against the moral or religious policy of the facility. Many states have statutes that permit a hospital or other facility to refuse to provide abortion services for these reasons. In some geographic areas this effectively cuts off the opportunity for a pregnant woman to have a safe, convenient legal abortion, since the hospital or facility that refuses to perform the abortion is the only health care facility in the area.

Congress recently enacted a provision of the Medicaid program that prohibits the use of Medicaid funds to pay for abortions not necessary to save the life of the pregnant woman. A federal district court in New York has found this provision to be unconstitutional because it unfairly discriminates against women who choose to have abortions, since funds are provided for the care of women who choose to bear a child.

The laws in many states still do not conform to the requirements of the Supreme Court ruling, and many of these laws have been declared unconstitutional or are being challenged in court. You should consult a lawyer or public official to determine the law in your state.

126. Assault and Battery • As we said earlier (section 41), an *assault* is an open threat of bodily contact with someone; the actual contact is a *battery*. Assault and battery are both torts and crimes, which means that the victim has a right to sue his assailant and that the state may also bring an action for the offenses, which are felonies or misdemeanors depending on the laws of individual states. A battery necessarily includes an assault.

Aggravated assault is assault with intent to murder, rob, rape or do serious bodily harm. For example, the man who knocks you down in a fight over who was the greatest baseball player of all time has committed a simple assault and battery. But the man who knocks you down in a fight while trying to snatch your watch is guilty of assault with intent to steal or rob—an aggravated assault, which is generally a felony.

127. Mayhem • *Mayhem* is the malicious maiming or disfiguring of a person. In some states it is an offense only when the disfigurement was intended. In these states the man who breaks your nose in a spontaneous street fight is guilty merely of assault and battery; if he breaks your nose because he wants revenge for a real or imagined insult, he is guilty of mayhem, which is really a form of aggravated assault and is a felony.

128. Kidnapping • *Kidnapping* is the act of abducting or stealing away a man, woman or child through force or fraud and detaining him against his will. It is one of the gravest of offenses and in several states is a capital crime—that is, one punishable by death.

After the famous kidnapping and murder of the Lindbergh baby in the 1930s, kidnapping was made a federal crime. Federal agents may now enter a kidnapping case after seven days even if it cannot be proved that a state line has been crossed. Any abduction of a person may be regarded as kidnapping, even though no ransom is demanded for his return.

CRIMES AGAINST REAL PROPERTY

129. Arson • *Arson* is the malicious burning of another person's property. Originally the only "property" involved in arson was a dwelling or a building connected with or in an enclosure with a dwelling. But statutes in many states have broadened the crime so that arson includes the burning of buildings other than dwellings. It is not arson to burn your own building—but don't burn your house down to collect insurance on it; to do so is a separate statutory offense.

Arson is widely recognized as a felony. It is the malicious setting fire that counts, whether the building is partially or entirely destroyed.

130. Vandalism · Willful damage to another person's property is also an offense. It's called by several names. Malicious mischief covers a wide variety of these offenses, which are only misdemeanors.

Vandalism is the one we read about most often, especially in connection with public buildings such as schools. *Vandalism* in this sense is the willful or malicious causing of damage, by throwing rocks through windows, ripping off doors, flooding basements or whatever.

The willful destruction of any property, real or personal, is unlawful and punishable by fine and perhaps imprisonment, depending on the extent of the damage done.

131. Burglary · In earlier times the offense of *burglary* was one committed only against another person's house or an adjacent building and at night. It was defined as the breaking and entering of the dwelling of another in the nighttime with intent to commit a felony. Modern statutes have greatly changed this rather strict definition.

You should check the criminal statute in your state to find out whether someone who breaks into your store at midday on Sunday and robs your safe has committed burglary. He will doubtless be charged with the offense of larceny (see section 132), but the fact that he broke in during the daytime, and that he broke into your store rather than into your home, may mean that he cannot be charged with burglary.

Whatever the statutory provisions, there must be what the law quaintly calls a burglarious intent. Someone breaking into your house at night just to admire your new oil paintings, and without doing anything harmful while there, would not be committing burglary. The offense would be trespass—a tort for which you might sue the offender (see section 46)— but it would not be criminal trespass since there was no intent to commit a crime.

So while burglary used to be an offense against the sanctity of the home, and a very serious one, it is now more of an offense against your property generally—really against the full enjoyment of your property. But the old ideas prevail in many localities, and you should carefully check your state statutes and consult a lawyer if you want to learn precisely what the offense consists of where you live. Burglary is a felony in all states, though in some there are varying degrees of burglary and the lesser ones are only misdemeanors.

132. Larceny • *Larceny* is the felonious taking and carrying away of someone else's personal property, without his consent, with the intention of permanently depriving him of its use or possession. There are several necessary parts to this offense, which is either a felony or a misdemeanor depending on the value of the property stolen.

In defining larceny, the word *felonious* means fraudulent; felonious larceny is a taking with intent to steal. If you remove your neighbor's lawn mower from his garage to trim your lawn, intending to return it when you've finished, you have not committed the offense of larceny.

Both a taking and a carrying away are essential. By going into your neighbor's garage without his knowledge or consent and laying your hands on the lawn mower, you have taken it—that is, you have established your (unlawful) possession of it. But there's no larceny until you remove the mower to your property intending never to return it.

The property taken need only have been in the possession of someone else. If you and your neighbor are having a genuine dispute over who owns the lawn mower, and in entering his garage at night and removing the mower to your property you think you are merely getting back what is yours, you are nevertheless guilty of the offense of larceny. The crime is directed against possession, not legal title or technical ownership.

Larceny is directed only against personal property. If you chop down a tree on someone else's property you have not committed larceny. But if you're walking along the road and see a pile of logs in a field and you take a few home for your fireplace, you would be guilty of larceny. Because domestic animals are now regarded as personal property, it is larceny to take home a dog, cat or heifer that you find on a stroll. But wild animals are not regarded as being in the possession of anyone.

Larceny can be the result of a trick or a fraud. A friend who has long admired your portable color television set, and who asks to borrow it—when in reality his intention is to get it from you and keep it—is as guilty of larceny, if he succeeds, as though he had actually stolen the set.

Abandoned property is not the subject of larceny, but lost property is. Making the distinction between something that has been abandoned and something that has been lost is not always easy. A 25-cent piece you find on the street is legally regarded as abandoned, and there is no way you can be expected to find the owner. But it would be different if you found a $1,000 bill. In that case it's likely that the person who dropped it would report its loss to the police, so that before treating the bill as your own you should try to find the owner.

The distinction between lost and abandoned property can be described in another way. The law in this area starts from the assumption that a person who abandons something does not really intend to recover it, whereas the person who loses or misplaces something does hope to recover it. The owner of abandoned property has discarded his ownership; the owner of lost property has not.

The same thing is true of a package that is left on the overhead rack in a train. You may not legally take the package as yours. It is regarded not as abandoned but only as lost or mislaid. Railroad companies operate lost-and-found departments to which their employes refer such packages so that careless passengers know where to go when they realize they have mislaid them. Lost-and-found items are usually held by the railroad for a certain period of time, then sold at auction. The title or ownership you would get by buying items at such an auction would be "good against the world," because what was once merely mislaid has now, by passage of time, been deemed abandoned.

Larceny may also result from a mistake, depending on the facts. Intent is the controlling factor. Let's say you order a raincoat from a store and pay cash for it but ask to have it sent to you. When the package arrives, you find that what has been delivered is a much more expensive coat. You have an obligation to return what was obviously sent you by mistake. Failure to return it would be larceny, because when you discovered the mistake you intended to take and to keep something that was not yours.

The difference between *grand larceny* and *petit,* or *petty, larceny* depends only on the value of what has been stolen. Check the statutes of your own state for the dividing line. The practical significance is that grand larceny is a felony and petty larceny is only a misdemeanor.

133. Robbery · *Robbery* is taking something from a person by violence or intimidation. The element of force is the difference between robbery and simple larceny. The pickpocket who adroitly lifts your wallet while you are standing in a crowd is guilty of larceny, not robbery. The mugger who stops you on the street, knocks you down in a scuffle and snatches your wallet has committed the offense of robbery. It would be armed robbery if the mugger threatened you with a gun; that would be intimidation. Robbery is widely regarded as a felony.

159

134. Receiving Stolen Property • Accepting property acquired by larceny or robbery is now a distinct statutory offense, generally a felony, depending in some states on the value of the property that was stolen. Most of the statutes require that the offense have several elements: (a) the accused must actually have received the property; (b) it must have been stolen and remain stolen at the time of its receipt; (c) the receiver must have known that the property was stolen; and (d) he must have received it with criminal intent—that is, intent to prevent the owner from getting it back.

The typical receiver today is what newspapers and books refer to as a fence. He is the one who encourages the criminal to steal or commit larceny in the first place because of his assurance to the thief that he can sell or dispose of the stolen property.

Knowledge by the receiver that the property is stolen may be implied by the courts from the circumstances of the case. If property is in fact stolen, the receiver accepts it "with knowledge" if (a) he knows it was stolen, (b) he believes it was stolen or (c) his suspicions are aroused and he does not check further for fear that he will discover it was stolen. Suppose a used-car dealer is offered a car exactly like one described in a recent newspaper story about the theft of a car from a nearby parking lot. He either knows or believes that the car offered to him was stolen. His acceptance of that car would in all likelihood subject him to the charge of receiving stolen property. The situation would be different if the theft of the car from the parking lot happened some time earlier and the dealer only vaguely remembered the details in the newspaper account.

Even if the car now offered him for sale in his used-car lot seems in fine condition and he believes he can sell it quickly at a good profit, he'd be wise to check carefully to make sure the person offering him the car has legal title to or ownership of it. Statutes in many, if not all, states require the registration with the state of documents of title to automobiles, and the dealer should have little difficulty learning whether the car is actually owned by the person who wants to sell it. But all documents can be forged, and to protect himself from the possible charge of receiving stolen property a dealer should report to the proper authorities any case that seems suspicious.

135. Embezzlement • Embezzlement is a relatively modern offense. It is the illegal use or taking of personal property by someone to whom it was entrusted or who acquired it legally. The bank teller who uses your deposit to bet on the races or to pay his personal expenses, the securities dealer who mingles with his own money the funds you gave him to invest in the stock market, the building manager who takes your cash rental payments and uses them for himself, the state treasurer who puts public funds in his own bank account—all these persons may be found guilty of embezzlement. In each case the money came into the hands of the embezzler legally; there was no larceny.

The tendency today is to tighten these laws, particularly as regards public officials and professional men, such as lawyers who receive their clients' funds in the course of their professional duties. Some courts will go so far as to infer embezzlement where a lawyer mingles his client's funds with his own or a public official fails to deposit public funds in a distinct bank account.

136. Obtaining Property by False Pretenses · This is an offense which means pretty much what it says. It is a statutory offense which may be either a felony or a misdemeanor, depending on the value of the property falsely obtained. The property these statutes refer to is what one court has described as "personal, movable things," not real estate. The "false pretense" may range from clear misrepresentation or fraud (see section 49) to simply writing a bad check.

The person making the false statement must do so intending to defraud, and the false statement must be one of fact, not of opinion. The grocer who sells you a sack of what he calls and labels Idaho potatoes, when in fact the potatoes were grown in his own field in New Hampshire, is guilty of the offense of taking your money under false pretenses. But if he says he believes a sack of potatoes is from Idaho without being certain, the statement is merely one of opinion, and he has committed no offense against you. No offense is committed if you buy a horse on the assurance that he runs fast when in fact he's awfully slow. Such a statement is mere "puffing," which all salesmen are expected to indulge in and which you should learn to guard against (see section 190).

It is an offense to obtain property by writing a check when you know you have no funds in your bank account or when you know you have insufficient funds to cover the check. Banks expect occasional overdrafts and seldom do more than charge a penalty, but intentional persistent overdrawals may expose the drawer to criminal charges (see section 440).

Some states in recent years have combined the offenses of larceny, embezzlement and false pretenses under the heading of theft. Your lawyer will advise you of your state's statutes.

Defenses to Criminal Charges

Conviction for the commission of a crime is not only a matter of establishing that the crime was committed as charged. If that were the only proof necessary, criminal law would be simpler, and harsher, than it is. But there is a wide assortment of defenses available to persons charged with crimes under certain circumstances. If one or more of these defenses can be established, the defendant may not be formally charged at all or his defense, if established, may result in a dismissal of the charge by the court or at least in a much lighter penalty after conviction than if there were no defense at all. These defenses are described below.

137. Infancy or Immaturity · Even the severe doctrines of the old common law recognized not only that some persons are physically incapable of committing a crime but also that even though physically capable, some may lack the criminal capacity which is an essential ingredient of any crime. Common law, and the statutes of most states, say that an infant under the age of seven has no criminal capacity. These statutes also provide that there is a presumption against criminal capacity on the part of the infant between the ages of seven and fourteen, though the presumption may be proved wrong or rebutted. The age of "no criminal capacity" has been raised to nine in Texas, ten in Georgia and twelve in Arkansas.

For example, in many states a six-year-old child who steals candy from the local drugstore may not be charged with the crime of robbery or theft. He is conclusively presumed not to have criminal capacity, even if he is uncommonly bright for his years and knows very well that he is doing something wrong. If the police should charge him with the crime of theft, all his lawyer needs to do is establish that at the time the child stole the candy he was under the age of seven. By establishing that one fact, the child's lawyer has raised a perfect defense.

However, if the child at the age of seven continues on his path of stealing from stores, or from anyone else (apart from his parents), the charge of theft cannot so easily be dismissed. The presumption that he has no criminal capacity, which his lawyer would raise, can be overcome by the prosecutor's establishing the facts of a series of carefully planned robberies, all tending to prove that the child knew he was doing wrong.

What becomes of the juvenile offender, what treatment he receives, varies tremendously with his age and with the nature of the offense he is

162

charged with committing. The United States Congress and the legislatures of all states have established procedures, although very different ones, for the special treatment of such offenders as juvenile delinquents.

The philosophy behind all these statutes is the same: the young offender should not be regarded as a criminal and put behind bars either as a penalty or as a means of protecting society. He should, instead, be regarded as needing protection (from himself) and rehabilitation. Also, in order to help him get back on his feet and live a normal life, the legal proceedings that follow his arrest for having committed an offense should not be made public, and his name should not be revealed.

At whatever age the state law distinguishes between the treatment of an accused person as an adult criminal or as a juvenile delinquent (see chart 29, page 432), the effect of the juvenile delinquency statute is that the child is in the hands of a court that is different from others, or at least in the hands of a judge who treats the charge and the offender differently.

In some states juvenile courts have exclusive jurisdiction over all offenses committed by juveniles. In others they have jurisdiction over all offenses except those which, if committed by an adult, would be punishable by death or by life imprisonment. In the first group of states, any offense committed by any person of the age making him a juvenile offender can be tried only in a juvenile court; in the second group, even if the offender is a juvenile he must be tried in a regular criminal court if the penalty would be death or life imprisonment.

What all these provisions mean, as a practical matter, is that the juvenile delinquency statutes have raised the age at which a person is considered to lack criminal capacity from fourteen to sixteen, seventeen or even twenty.

The blessings of being treated as a juvenile delinquent are mixed. Too often young people are thrown into the embrace of the juvenile system whether they want it or not, whether or not it's best for them, without the benefit of a lawyer and even without notification of their constitutional rights. And the control that system has over the delinquent may stretch far beyond the time he has to spend in prison if he has been found guilty of a relatively minor felony or misdemeanor. A young person may have to remain in the custody of the juvenile court for several years. But if the offense was minor he might not be imprisoned for more than a few months. Consequently the United States Supreme Court, in 1967, insisted that a person charged as a juvenile delinquent must be advised of his Constitutional rights, of his right to a lawyer if he

163

wants one and of his right to cross-examine the witnesses who testify to the offense he is supposed to have committed.

Nonetheless, infancy is in fact a most effective defense, especially in all crimes less serious than those punishable by death or life imprisonment. A lawyer's advice is essential to anyone who might consider using infancy as a defense.

For a more detailed discussion of the treatment of juvenile offenders, see sections 338–342.

138. Coercion • Coercion of a wife by her husband is a gradually disappearing defense. There was a time when a wife who committed a crime in the presence of her husband was presumed to have done so because he directed or forced her to. This defense was the result of an age-old doctrine that, human nature being what it is, wives do what their husbands compel them to do. The presumption still hangs on in some states, but the ever increasing realization that a modern wife is in control of her own actions means that she has lost her "presumption of innocence," innocence that the law inferred just because she was a married woman.

139. Mistake of Law • Almost everyone has heard that "ignorance is no defense in the eyes of the law" or "ignorance of the law is no excuse." In great part this is true. If you are caught exceeding the speed limit by ten miles an hour, you will not get very far with either the arresting officer or the judge before whom you appear if you complain that you didn't realize how fast you were going or that you thought the state speed limit had been raised.

But as with so many legal generalities, there are exceptions to the rule that ignorance is no defense. The exceptions arise in what may be called the nonpenal area. You buy a house in a new community and, unaware that the law requires you to go to the town clerk's office and fill out a description of your personal property for tax purposes, you fail to do so. No criminal penalty will attach to your failure if you can establish that your ignorance or mistake of law was genuine. You committed no crime.

Some states will excuse you if you rely on the advice of a lawyer which turns out to be wrong. But for the most part you are responsible for finding out what the law is. Consult a lawyer, or a real estate agent or town official, to learn your obligations as a property owner and a taxpayer. Be careful about carrying firearms; in states and cities requiring a license, ignorance or mistaken knowledge of the licensing law will not constitute a defense to the charge of violating it.

164

140. Mistake of Fact · An honest mistake of fact will often serve as a defense against a criminal charge. When you cross over into your neighbor's yard to take back the lawn mower you loaned him and accidentally take someone else's, your mistake would excuse you from being convicted of larceny. If you pick up someone else's overcoat at a restaurant, you have made a mistake of fact. In both these cases you intended no crime: you did not mean to take what was not yours.

Curiously, many of the mistake-of-fact cases come up in connection with the charge of bigamy. Be careful about remarrying unless you are certain that your first marriage was effectively annulled or that your divorce is absolutely final. It is risky for a man or woman whose spouse has simply disappeared to marry again without consulting a lawyer and obtaining a judicial determination that the necessary period of time has passed for the former spouse to be presumed dead. (See sections 362–365 and charts 26, page 415, and 39, page 677.)

141. Duress · At the opposite end of the scale from offenses committed under a mistake of law or fact are offenses committed under *duress* or *threat*. Because criminal intent is such an important element of a crime, courts will excuse certain offenses where intent is lacking. If a bank robber leaps into your car as you are waiting for a traffic light to change, points a gun at you and orders you to drive him to the airport at seventy miles an hour, you will not be held responsible for the offenses you commit in carrying out his orders: violating the speed laws and serving as accessory after the fact in helping him to escape. The fact that you acted under compulsion or duress will excuse you for almost any offense except taking someone else's life. If the gunman orders you to run over a policeman who tries to stop your car, you are expected to disobey the order even at the risk of your own life.

142. Necessity · Force of circumstance may result in a forgivable crime. In a famous English case, two seamen were cast away in a storm in a small boat with a seventeen-year-old boy. All their food was eaten in a few days. Eight days later, having had nothing to eat or drink for some time, they deliberately killed the boy, whose condition was very bad, and fed on him for four days, until they were picked up by a passing ship. They were charged with and found guilty of willful murder, but in consideration of all the circumstances the court commuted their sentence from death to six months' imprisonment.

The principle to keep in mind, again, is that whatever the circum-

165

stances, the courts are most reluctant to find in them an excuse for taking another's life.

143. Consent · If the victim of a crime consents to its commission, is the perpetrator guilty of a crime? As you might imagine, it all depends on the circumstances. In the easy case, submission under fear or compelled consent is no consent at all. The man who sticks a gun in your back as he robs you on the street and orders you to keep quiet as a policeman passes by cannot set up the defense that your silence meant that you consented to being robbed. The blackmailer who gets money from you by threatening to expose something of which you are ashamed has no defense that you consented to his unlawful action. And there are cases in which even clearly established consent will not excuse commission of a crime. The best example is statutory rape (see sections 124, 307): sexual intercourse with a girl below the statutory age is rape, even though she may actually have solicited the intercourse.

Where consent is procured by trickery, it is no defense. Your neighbor across the hall has long wanted your rare violin, which he knows you wouldn't give or sell to him. So he asks you to loan it to him for an evening. You do so, and he refuses to return it. When you sue him to recover possession, he cannot claim as a defense that you voluntarily turned it over to him. He has committed the offense of larceny by trickery. Fraudulently induced consent is no defense.

144. Insanity · Mental disease or defect is a defense to the charge of commission of a crime. That much is easy to say. But enormous problems arise in the use of this defense, because there is no neat or generally accepted definition of insanity. There can be no crime without an intention to commit one, and most of us understand that an insane person is incapable of forming any intention that would make him responsible for his actions. So if the defense of insanity is raised by a defendant and the jury finds that in fact he was insane, no conviction will result.

But the great strides in recent years in the field of psychiatry have vastly complicated this defense of insanity. It is now believed that, as is the case with other diseases, there are degrees of mental illness. A simple neurosis, if there is such a thing, would scarcely support a defense of insanity. For example, the otherwise normal person whose history of several convictions for theft might lead him to be termed a kleptomaniac could not successfully plead insanity if charged with murder. By contrast,

166

the individual whose conduct would lead a psychiatrist to say he suffered from a persecution complex—exaggerated or acute schizophrenia—might well be able to plead insanity.

In other words, the degree of the defendant's mental illness must be considered in relation to the gravity of the crime with which he has been charged. The law's presumption is that a really "depraved mind," a mind suffering from the most serious sort of mental disease, simply cannot have the necessary intent to commit a crime. In such cases the tendency across the country is not to sentence such a person to prison but to commit him to a mental institution where he will receive treatment until the authorities running the institution believe he has been sufficiently cured to be allowed to return to society.

There is an important distinction between insanity at the time of the crime and mental incompetence to stand trial. A defendant who pleads insanity at the time of the crime and is deemed competent to stand trial may not be prosecuted again if he is acquitted by reason of insanity—even if he recovers his sanity. A person cannot be charged twice for the same offense (see section 28). An acquittal, however, might result in an automatic commitment to a civil mental hospital. On the other hand, if the defendant is deemed mentally incompetent to stand trial (which is not a plea at all to the charge), he can be prosecuted if and when he becomes mentally competent.

145. Drunkenness · As a defense to a criminal charge, the fact that the accused was intoxicated is effective only to the extent that it determines the existence of criminal intent. What we loosely call the habitual drunkard, the person who has succumbed to or been overwhelmed by the narcotic alcohol, is regarded in modern medical thought as being mentally ill, and he may by that fact have an effective defense. A mind that is drugged lacks criminal intent, and most courts would so hold today. Such persons present few extreme problems in criminal law, because real drunkards are unlikely to commit a serious crime. They are usually arrested on vagrancy charges and sentenced to prison or a treatment center.

Consequently, the element of drunkenness most often arises in criminal law as a collateral or side issue in the commission of another offense. In the case of drunken driving, clearly the fact of being drunk not only is no defense but is the essence of the offense. But take the man with no prior criminal record who gets drunk with friends at an anniversary party. Unaware of what he's doing, he joins his friends on a spree and ends up smashing a neighbor's windows. He awakens the next morning in jail with no recollection of what he did. This man is unlikely to get more than a fine for breach of the peace. Drunkenness in this case will perhaps reduce the possible severity of the sentence; it certainly will not increase it.

146. Narcotics Use • To plead the influence of drugs as a defense is questionable. Drug addiction—the uncontrollable physical need for such drugs as heroin and morphine—is widely regarded as a mental disease, and victims are committed to public institutions for treatment rather than to prisons as a penalty. It is the use of drugs themselves and their sale to others that is a crime in all states. What happens to the drug addict, what he does under their influence, is not what is criminal. In the extreme case of addiction, the necessary intent to commit a crime is lacking, as is probably the ability.

147. Defenses to Homicide • In some circumstances it is not illegal to kill or wound. If those circumstances can be established, they constitute a defense to any charge that a crime was committed.

Certain acts of killing are justified because they are not only permitted but directed by the public as a whole, for its protection. An example is the soldier who kills one of the enemy in time of war and within the rules of war. The soldier has a duty to kill the enemy if he is attacking or if he refuses to surrender on warning. This duty has been recognized as long as there have been armies. But slowly and painfully rules of war have been established, and these rules the soldier also has a duty to observe. Under no circumstances is the killing of unarmed civilians justifiable, and the Department of the Army is wholly within its rights in bringing charges against men who violate this rule.

Such a defense also applies to the public executioner who carries out a sentence of death in a capital case. Although the Supreme Court has struck down the death penalty as a form of cruel and unusual punishment except in certain circumstances, more carefully drawn state or Federal laws may reintroduce capital punishment for certain serious crimes. In any case, the public hangman is regarded as doing his duty and may not be charged with the crime of murder, even if later developments establish that the executed man or woman was innocent.

But this defense, of public duty, is very strictly construed or interpreted. It is the duty of a prison guard to keep order in prison, but he may not legally use excessive force in so doing. Excessive flogging of a disobedient convict by a guard has been held to constitute criminal assault and battery, and a guard who kills a prisoner may be charged with murder.

Perhaps the most common situation involving the defense of public duty arises where a police officer or a citizen acting on a policeman's direction kills someone who he believes has committed a serious crime and is resisting arrest. The private citizen who acts on his own in trying to arrest someone he thinks is guilty of a crime is running a great risk. If he has to use deadly force in making the arrest, he is almost sure to be charged with the crime of murder himself, and the courts have been very reluctant to accept the defense that he was doing his public duty. The citizen should call on the police and give them help if they ask for it, rather than act by himself (see sections 33, 39, 99).

In general, the police officer who has good reason to believe one of the more serious felonies has been committed—murder, manslaughter, arson, rape, robbery, burglary, mayhem, kidnapping, felonious assault—may use whatever force is necessary to arrest the offender. But he will be held strictly accountable if he uses more force than is necessary: if the person he believes guilty of one of these offenses puts up no real resistance but shouts a series of obscenities at the police officer, the officer is not justified in killing him or even in beating him up, and he may not use the defense of public duty if he is charged with a crime for using excessive force.

148. If You Acted to Prevent a Crime • Your freedom of action as a private individual in preventing the commission of a crime is similar to your freedom of action in bringing about the arrest of someone you believe or know has actually committed a criminal offense. A lot depends on the circumstances. Let's say that you are out in the country hunting deer, and you come around a bend in the road and see a man lying on the ground and another man standing over him with a raised hatchet. You shout a warning, but it is not heeded, and you shoot the man with the hatchet before he swings it, and kill him. Then you would probably have an effective defense of crime prevention.

The force you may legally use to prevent a crime must be in some degree proportionate to the severity of the crime itself. If, on returning from your hunting trip, you see someone about to rob your neighbor's mailbox, you had best content yourself with shouting a warning or firing your gun over his head to scare him off.

Remember that it is risky business at best for a private citizen to assume the job of a peace officer. In times of increasing defiance of the law there may well be occasions when you not only can but should take the responsibility of preventing crimes you believe are about to be committed. But in the vast majority of cases your action should consist of alerting or calling in the police. You should act on your own only when the police are not available or when the crime seems likely to occur so quickly that you have no time or means of calling the police. And even then you should do everything possible to avoid the use of deadly force, force intended or likely to cause death or great bodily harm.

149. If You Acted in Self-Defense · In defending yourself, other people and your own property, you are entitled to use nondeadly force to whatever extent the circumstances warrant. You may, if you can, beat up the mugger who attacks you on the street or the thief you see stealing your companion's wallet or the burglar who enters your house to steal your jewelry. In all these cases the amount of force you may legally use depends on what a reasonable man would think necessary. You may not, when held up for your money, draw a gun and shoot the holdup man— but you may hit him over the head with the butt of the pistol. As a thief puts his foot across your doorstep you may not legally fire at him with a shotgun. But you may shoot a burglar in your house who refuses to leave or threatens to attack you (see section 53).

It is when you believe your life is in danger that the law becomes less clear. Much depends on the reasonableness of your belief. Suppose you are known to be nervous and high-strung. You excitedly confuse being jostled in a crowd with someone's sticking a gun in your back and you turn around savagely and kill your supposed attacker with a knife. Then you have abused the privilege of self-defense and are subject to prosecution for manslaughter. A similar situation might arise if you shot and killed a supposed trespasser or intruder without trying to determine his identity or purpose.

The other side of the coin is, of course, that you cannot be expected to remain calm and detached when someone is clearly trying to kill you. As a wise judge put it, "Detached reflection cannot be demanded in the presence of an uplifted knife." You have both a right of self-defense and an obligation to preserve the life of others. The law does not expect you to surrender meekly to someone who is about to shoot you; but the law does expect you to avoid deadly confrontations wherever possible and, when you are threatened, to use only as much force as will enable you to save your own life. If someone else is killed as a result, you have acted in self-defense and cannot be successfully prosecuted for taking his life.

Basic Things You Should Know About Criminal Procedure

Perhaps no other field of law has seen so many changes in recent years as that of criminal procedure. Perhaps no other field is so highly specialized. In no other field are the services of a lawyer more necessary, and in none other are there so few lawyers with experience and firsthand knowledge of the specialty. Here are some of the features that set criminal procedure apart from so many other areas of the law.

150. The Court System · We mentioned before (see section 3) that the federal system on which the government of the United States is based produces two parallel court systems. One is the court system of the United States government itself. Its courts, called federal courts, exist in three levels, or tiers: the district, or trial, courts, of which there is at least one in each state; eleven circuit courts of appeal; and the United States Supreme Court. The federal district courts try criminal offenses against federal laws only: the United States Constitution and statutes enacted by the United States Congress.

The state courts exist side by side with the federal courts but are concerned largely with offenses against the state constitutions and statutes enacted by the state legislatures. In many of our large cities there are municipal courts for trying offenses against state laws and municipal laws or ordinances, just as in hundreds of our smaller rural areas there are police courts and courts presided over by justices of the peace, who try minor offenses such as traffic violations. The responsibility or jurisdiction of these lower municipal and other courts is set forth in state statutes.

It is important to keep in mind that in addition to the two parallel court systems, there are two parallel sets of laws. An act that is an offense under a federal law may or may not be an offense under a state law. If you are thought to have violated a federal law you will be arrested and brought into court by a United States marshal and charged by a United States attorney for the district in which you live. This action will be brought in the U.S. district court and will be conducted under the federal rules of criminal procedure.

If, on the other hand, you have done something that appears to violate a state law—such as using excessive force in a fight with your neighbor, which may be regarded as criminal assault and battery—you

171

will be arrested by a police officer and, depending on the seriousness of the offense, charged by him or by the local prosecutor in one of several state courts. The trial will be conducted by a magistrate or criminal court judge under the state rules of criminal procedure. The state and federal rules are similar, but there are many important differences.

151. Rights of the Accused · What makes criminal procedure so different today from what it was even a few decades ago is a series of decisions by the United States Supreme Court regarding the rights, under the United States Constitution, of persons accused of crimes of any kind. As a result of these decisions, both federal and state courts must allow every accused person to consult an attorney, even if he can't afford one, and every person taken into custody must be notified of his right to remain silent and of his right to have an attorney present throughout the process of his arraignment (see section 152) or preliminary hearing and throughout the trial.

It is worthwhile repeating the rights of every citizen charged with a crime, as described earlier in section 26.

If you are arrested, the police must inform you of your rights and give you an opportunity to phone a relative, friend or lawyer.

You have the right to a lawyer's services from the moment of your arrest and need not say anything until after you have consulted him.

You have a right to know the charges against you.

You have a right to a reasonably prompt hearing before a magistrate.

If you are held for trial, you have a right to have reasonable bail set as security for your release—except for certain crimes or at the discretion of the court.

You have a right to a reasonably prompt jury trial.

You have a right to confront and cross-examine your accusers and to call witnesses on your own behalf.

You cannot be tried twice for the same offense.

If you are convicted, you cannot be subjected to cruel or unusual punishment.

These rights may be waived, but it is foolish to waive them. When one's liberty is at stake, the only sensible thing to do is to make use of every available means of defense. In criminal law and procedure, it is impossible fully to defend oneself without having one's own lawyer.

To illustrate the steps that are followed in a criminal prosecution and the rights available to a person accused of committing a crime, let us trace a hypothetical case that might happen to anyone.

152. Arrest and Arraignment • Let's suppose you leave the car you borrowed from a friend in a parking lot, and as you start home you notice, but pay no real attention to the fact, that the trunk space in the rear looks as though someone had tried to open it. You slam down the trunk lid to make sure it's closed. On your drive home you absentmindedly go through a red traffic light and are immediately stopped by a policeman. You can't find the car's registration. He takes a dislike to you and is aggressive and unpleasant. You and he get into an argument and he decides your behavior is suspicious. He orders you to open the trunk of the car. You obey, and he finds in the trunk a large paper bag whose contents seem to be drugs. He ignores your statement that you have no idea how the bag got there. He places you under arrest and takes you to the police station.

Right at this point is where the recent Supreme Court decisions apply to you. You should make no statement of any kind before talking to a lawyer. The police and the prosecutor must warn you that you have a right to remain silent, and that anything you say may be used against you at your trial, if there is one.

At the police station you are booked on charges of illegal possession of narcotics, of driving without a registration and of endangering the lives of others by failing to obey traffic regulations. You are fingerprinted and put in a cell, and later an assistant prosecutor comes to interrogate you.

You should demand the opportunity to telephone your lawyer. If you don't have a lawyer, telephone a member of your family or a friend and ask that one be sent to see you. The offense with which you are charged, illegal possession of narcotics, is a crime and may be a felony, punishable by both fine and imprisonment. Even so you are probably entitled to be released on bail, although your release must be ordered by a magistrate or criminal court judge. By this time it's fairly late in the evening, and you may not be brought before a magistrate until the next day.

However, the attorney who gets to see you that night can arrange bail (see sections 26, 27). The most common form of bail is a *bail bond,* a promise by a bonding company to pay a certain amount of money to the court if you do not appear when you are supposed to. The cost of such a bond is something like 10 percent, depending on the size of the bail. To purchase a bail bond, you have to pay the premium, 10 percent or less, and put up or pledge securities or other property of value as collateral. All of this must be arranged by your lawyer working with your family or friends. You must remain in jail until you've appeared before the magistrate, bail has been posted and you have been released by him.

If you can't afford a lawyer, you probably can't afford bail either. In some states bail may not be required where an investigation by probation officers indicates that you have no prior criminal record, that your character and reputation are good and that you will be unable to support your wife and children or other dependents if you have to remain in jail because you can't afford bail. If you are in a small, local court in your hometown or village, you may be well known to the presiding judge, and he may release you without bail, on "your own recognizance."

When your lawyer gets in touch with you, you should answer all his questions as fully and frankly as possible. You should agree to pay him something if you can, because he is going to have to put in a lot of time on your case, and he has his own bills to pay. Once you and he agree that he is to represent you, anything you tell him is confidential. He cannot be made to tell anyone else what you tell him; your communications with him are said to be privileged.

Under the circumstances of your case as we have outlined it, your lawyer certainly will advise you to plead not guilty to the charge of illegal possession of narcotics when you appear in a day or so before a magistrate for a preliminary hearing, called the *arraignment*. The other charges against you are minor and could be disposed of quickly. But you have no easy way of proving that you didn't put the bag in the trunk.

The magistrate's job is simple. Because the charge against you is a major one, he lacks authority to try the case himself. What he must decide is, first, whether a crime has been committed and, second, whether there is *probable cause* to believe that you, the defendant, committed it. If he decides that neither is the case, he has authority to release you and order the charge dropped. The police officer who arrested you will doubtless state in his complaint or information at the arraignment, that he found the narcotics in your car and that you had no explanation for their being there. The crime you are charged with is illegal possession. On the facts before the magistrate he has little choice but to order your case to go to higher authorities for submission to the grand jury.

He will first, however, advise you that you have a right to a hearing in his court. This is a procedure under which the police or the prosecuting attorney or a representative of the district attorney's office produces witnesses, under oath, to support the charges in the information that has been filed against you. At this time you and your lawyer are entitled to cross-examine. In our hypothetical case, your lawyer might take this opportunity to move that the charges be dropped because the evidence against you was obtained illegally (see section 154).

174

The magistrate may or may not grant you the right to post bail. Much will depend on the amount or value of the narcotics in your borrowed car and what the district attorney or prosecutor may tell the magistrate regarding narcotics activity in your community at the time of your arrest. For the purposes of this discussion, let's assume the police and the prosecutor say the value of the narcotics is $250,000.

153. The Grand Jury and Indictment · In this situation, then, the magistrate sends your case up to the grand jury. A grand jury is a body of as many as twenty-three persons, often chosen by lot from the citizens of the county or other district where the court is located. Unless extended by court order, the life of a grand jury is limited to the term of the court, usually one year. The grand jury's duty is to inquire into crimes committed in that county and to make accusations, called *indictments,* in accordance with the law. Its legal adviser is the prosecuting attorney, whose advice the jury is free to accept or ignore. The proceedings are usually recorded by a stenographer—a fact of immense importance later on in your trial if the grand jury should indict you.

The grand jury has the authority to conduct investigations on its own, in addition to its better-known task of considering matters submitted to it by a magistrate or criminal court judge after a preliminary hearing. Except in federal cases, a grand jury can receive only legal evidence (excluding hearsay), and every element of an alleged crime must be proved so that all the evidence before it would, if not contradicted and not explained, result in a lawful conviction of the defendant at a trial.

As you can imagine, your lawyer must really pitch in once your case goes to the grand jury. He may not have had sufficient time to establish all the facts, particularly if he has been retained or appointed at the last minute. He must now, with whatever help you can give, do his best to find out how that paper bag got into the trunk of the car you had borrowed. He will need to talk at length to the friend from whom you borrowed it; he must find out when the trunk was last open. He should try to learn whether there are any fingerprints on the car or on the paper bag and whose they are—a difficult task, because the prosecutor may refuse your lawyer's request to examine the car and the paper bag.

Your lawyer is going to have to find out a lot about the friend who loaned you the car, more than you may know. He will try to learn whether there has been any narcotics activity in the neighborhood, a job that will prove hard unless he has some knowledge of the underworld. He'll have to question the parking lot attendants to learn whether there's

175

anything suspicious in their background and whether on the day you left the car there they noticed anyone suspicious in the area. To uncover all possible information that will help establish your innocence, your lawyer may have to hire private investigators, which will be expensive.

If we assume that by the time you are called before the grand jury your lawyer has been unable to produce any hard evidence that will refute the charges against you, and he therefore believes the chances are that you will be indicted, he may well advise you not to appear before the grand jury at all. Such appearances can be risky, particularly when all the evidence seems to point toward your guilt. You have an absolute right not to appear, and your failure to appear is not supposed to put you in any unfavorable light. Moreover, if you appear before the grand jury, your own lawyer is not allowed to be present.

However, the prosecuting attorney will be there, and he will have the opportunity to question you extensively. You must testify under oath, and your testimony will be recorded stenographically. All this gives the prosecuting attorney an opportunity to prepare his case against you for trial. You will have to go over the same ground again at the trial itself, and the danger that there will be minor inconsistencies in the two versions of your story is very great.

Also, in appearing before the grand jury you must sign what is called a *waiver of immunity,* which means that if during your appearance something should come up regarding any other offense you may have committed, you may also be subject to prosecution for that offense. The United States Constitution provides that no person may be compelled to incriminate himself; this is the immunity you waive by appearing before a grand jury.

Let us now assume that the grand jury finds that if your possession of narcotics cannot be explained, you may be guilty of the crime of illegal possession. It will prepare an indictment: a legal document charging you with that crime. This indictment will be formally presented to a magistrate or criminal court judge at another arraignment.

If your lawyer has learned little more than he knew when he was first brought into the case, he will not be able to do more than appear with you and represent you at the hearing. You must be present yourself, because you are charged with the commission of a crime. He will almost surely urge you to plead not guilty, and the magistrate will set the case down for trial at a specific date. There are situations in which your lawyer may advise you to plead guilty to a lesser offense than the one you were originally charged with, in hopes of your receiving a lesser penalty.

176

This entire matter of so-called plea bargaining is crucial today because of the enormous and increasing number of crimes to come before the courts and the inability of the judicial system to cope with the case load that confronts it. Prosecutors are harassed; they lack the time and the personnel to investigate all crimes and to assemble enough evidence for a conviction. Accordingly, prosecutors often permit the accused person to plead guilty to a lesser crime than the one with which he was first charged—and consequently to receive a lesser penalty—just in order to expedite the proceedings and dispose of the case quickly. But in our hypothetical case, the prosecutor is unlikely to accept a plea of guilty to a lesser crime. Besides, you have committed no felony and certainly don't want a felony conviction on your record because of the very serious potential consequences of having a "criminal record."

If the bail set seems too high, your lawyer will ask the judge to reduce it. If you can find the money for the bail bond—reduced or not— you may return to your home and your job. If you should be unable to raise bail, you would have to remain in jail until the date scheduled for your trial on the court calendar.

In the case of the most serious felonies, for which the penalty is death or life imprisonment, the law does not specifically prohibit bail, but some judges set bail so high that it cannot be obtained, thereby keeping the alleged criminal in jail to prevent him from committing another crime while out on bail. "Excessive" bail is forbidden by the Eighth Amendment to the U.S. Constitution, but who is to say what is excessive? An appeals court has the authority to declare bail excessive but it is unlikely to substitute its judgment for that of the trial judge unless he is clearly abusing the whole purpose of bail.

154. The Trial and Presentation of Evidence • A criminal trial is not significantly different from a civil trial (the various steps of which were discussed in chapter 3, sections 82–88). Your case generally will be tried before a jury, and the first problem for your attorney will be to see to it that the jurors are not prejudiced or biased. He can challenge *for cause* (because they indicate bias) and *peremptorily* (because he thinks, for any of various reasons, that they should not be on the jury). Your state statute will say how many peremptory challenges he may have. Challenges for cause are unlimited in number. In our hypothetical case your attorney may question the jurors as to their attitude toward narcotics, or especially the mere possession of narcotics, since this is the substance of the charge against you.

177

After the jury has been selected, the prosecutor will make an opening statement, describing the case, what he intends to prove and, perhaps, how he will go about proving it. Your lawyer may follow with a statement of your defense, stressing that there is no evidence whatever directly linking you with the narcotics traffic and that you have never used narcotics or even handled them in any way.

Your lawyer owes you the duty of doing everything possible to help you. He must try at the very least to discredit the prosecutor's only evidence. The key to the prosecution's charge against you is the paper bag found in the back of your borrowed car. But there is grave legal doubt whether the policeman who arrested you had the right to search the car at all. The Constitution protects you against unreasonable search and seizure. The question is, was the policeman's search lawful? Courts generally recognize that policemen may "stop and frisk" someone they have reason to believe may have committed a felony or even a misdemeanor; also, the policeman who sees someone whose conduct suggests he's about to rob a passerby may stop and "frisk" him to see whether he is carrying a gun.

In your case, however, the policeman had no basis for searching your car just because you went through a traffic light and couldn't find the automobile's certificate of registration. He had no right to search your car himself—and indeed he didn't actually do so. But by forcing you on his orders to open the trunk of the car, he compelled you to put yourself in a legally incriminating position.

Generally, prior to the trial, your lawyer will make a motion to suppress the evidence of the paper bag containing narcotics on the ground that it was illegally obtained and its admission deprives you of your constitutional rights. The judge may then hold a hearing and ask your lawyer and the prosecutor to submit legal arguments on the point. (If by any chance your lawyer does not make this pre-trial motion, he will most likely object to the introduction of the paper bag as evidence when the prosecutor offers it in the course of the trial.)

If the judge denies your lawyer's objection and directs the trial to proceed, your lawyer will "take an exception" to the judge's ruling, which makes that ruling reviewable later by an appellate or higher court. Appellate courts are sometimes more sensitive than trial courts to the importance of protecting constitutional rights during the criminal process.

If your lawyer's motion is denied, the prosecutor will put the policeman who arrested you on the witness stand and examine him directly. The policeman will go over the circumstances under which he arrested

ELECTRONIC SNOOPING—
FOR AND AGAINST THE LAW

Wiretapping and electronic surveillance by law enforcement agencies under a court order is one of modern society's most powerful weapons against crime. But illegal and illegitimate electronic snooping by private individuals is on the increase. Some sophisticated devices are shown below.

The most commonly used listening device is the telephone bug, shown in the diagram at the left located approximately under the number four on the dial. This tiny piece of electronic wizardry automatically records anything you say or anything said to you over the phone. It may also be used as an open mike to listen in on conversations in the room where the phone is located. The unauthorized use of a telephone bug or tap is against the law.

Commonly seen today in banks and large office buildings is the closed-circuit TV camera. But it can also be used for secret electronic surveillance. Only a foot long, the camera can easily be hidden behind a curtain or a one-way mirror in a public restaurant, a hotel lobby or the like.

Perhaps the most famous of the bugs is the exotic olive-in-the martini microphone with transmitter. The mike is at the left end of the olive, where the hole should be, and the antenna is concealed inside the toothpick. The sending range of the olive is a mere fifty feet, however.

The proliferation of illegal bugging devices in recent years poses a problem for law enforcement officials and has given rise to a whole new breed of electronics professionals who help businessmen to spy on their competitors and private individuals on one another.

you and tell the whole story in a manner most harmful or prejudicial to you. Your lawyer then has the opportunity to cross-examine the policeman and will try to make him appear foolish or unnecessarily harsh in getting so upset over a minor traffic violation. Your lawyer will also do everything he can to discredit the reasons the policeman had for ordering you to open the trunk of the car and to establish for the jurors that there was simply no reason to link you to the paper bag.

Let us assume now that your lawyer gets word that a witness, learning of your arrest, later went to the police and stated that he saw someone place a paper bag in the trunk of your borrowed car. Your lawyer asks the prosecutor to disclose the identity of the witness, but the prosecutor denies that there was one, and the judge does not order a hearing—after excluding the jury—to establish the truth of your lawyer's allegation.

The prosecution finishes presenting its case and when your lawyer has completed his cross-examination of prosecution witnesses, he will normally move that the case against you be dismissed. If the judge denies the motion, as is usually the case if the prosecutor has done his homework, your lawyer will proceed to present the case for the defense.

The question whether you should testify on your own behalf depends on several things. If your lawyer, and any investigator engaged by him, has been unable to find any clue as to how, or why, that paper bag was put in the trunk of the car, if the friend from whom you borrowed the car seems innocent of any connection with your plight, it becomes increasingly vital that your honesty and credibility be established. If your lawyer believes that you will make a good impression and that under aggressive cross-examination by the prosecuting attorney you can stick to a consistent and believable story, he will urge you to take the witness stand. But you are not required to, and courts keep repeating that the jury is to draw no conclusions from a defendant's failure to testify.

Character witnesses will be important in your case, which resolves itself into a conflict between your statement that you have no idea how the paper bag got into the car and the fact that it was there. Your own character witnesses may, of course, be cross-examined by the prosecutor.

At the end of the trial—after the cross-examination of rebuttal witnesses if there are any (see section 85)—it is customary for your lawyer to make a closing statement on your behalf and for the prosecutor to sum up his case to the jury. Your lawyer may want to point out to the jury that nothing the prosecution has said or charged directly connects you with the bag of narcotics. There is almost certainly a missing link in the case, which would explain where the narcotics came from.

180

155. The Charge, Verdict and Sentence • At the end of the trial your lawyer will also probably want to ask the judge to make certain statements to the jurors when the judge *charges* them as to the law they must apply. The judge tells the jury what the law is and how it relates to the facts that the jury is asked to determine; the jury decides what the facts were. Your lawyer wants to be sure the judge includes in his charge that the jury must find that the prosecution has established your guilt beyond any reasonable doubt.

In order to convict, the jury must conclude beyond a reasonable doubt that you were the knowing possessor of narcotics. Without criminal intent, there is no crime. If someone slips a stolen diamond into your pocket, unknown to you, you are not guilty of illegal possession of stolen property. If the jury has any reasonable doubt that you knew the paper bag containing the narcotics was in the car, it must find you not guilty. In some states a jury's verdict of guilty need not be unanimous to convict, and the Supreme Court has upheld the constitutionality of that procedure.

If the jury should find you not guilty, or acquit you, you are free once again. Your lawyer will, if the laws of your state permit it, demand that fingerprints and other police records be returned to you or destroyed.

If the jury finds you guilty, there are several things your lawyer can still do for you, even before you have been sentenced, depending on the laws in your state. He can get in touch with the court's probation officer, on whose recommendation the judge will rely heavily in deciding on the severity of your sentence. The fact that this has been your first offense will certainly be helpful to you. The court will not want to give you more than the minimum sentence the statute requires, so as to enable you as soon as possible to return to society as a useful employed person.

156. Motions After Trial and Appeal • Your lawyer again has the opportunity to try to have you released on bail, or to have your bail lowered, while he takes certain legal steps in your behalf. He may file in the trial court a motion for a new trial. His ground, or reason, would be that the verdict was against the law or against the weight of the credible evidence.

If the motion for a new trial is not granted, your lawyer has one remaining move to make, an appeal. He files a notice of appeal to the appellate court, arguing that the trial court erred, especially in failing to grant your motion to suppress the evidence against you on the ground that you were the victim of unlawful search and seizure and in not holding a hearing on the question of whether the prosecutor suppressed the identity of a witness who could clear you. His appeal does not challenge the verdict of the jury; it reached a reasonable conclusion on the basis of the evidence.

Appeals take time to complete. If you have been sentenced to prison or fined by the trial court, your lawyer may be able to have you freed on bail or have payment of the fine postponed until the result of the appeal is known. He applies to the trial court for what is known as a certificate of reasonable doubt, doubt whether your conviction will stand up on appeal. If the probation officer advises the trial court that your record shows you to be a responsible person, that you will not run away if freed on bail, you will in all likelihood be set free. An important consideration, if there is a good chance that your conviction will be reversed, is that by the time the appeal is determined you might have already finished the prison term to which the trial court sentenced you. A reversal of your conviction by the appellate court would therefore be of no practical value, and an obvious injustice would have been done to you.

If your appeal to the state appellate court should fail, your only recourse is to seek the help of the United States Supreme Court or the lower federal courts. You were originally charged with violation of a state statute against the illegal possession of narcotics. But you and your lawyer believe that the evidence against you was improperly seized in a manner that violated your constitutional rights against unreasonable search and seizure and also that the prosecution willfully suppressed the name of a witness who could have exonerated you of the crime—a violation of your constitutional right to due process of law, guaranteed by the Fourteenth Amendment.

There are two ways of proceeding. Your lawyer can file a petition for a *writ of certiorari* in the U.S. Supreme Court within ninety days of your conviction being affirmed. But the Supreme Court's jurisdiction is purely discretionary and will be exercised only if it believes that a case presents a substantial constitutional question.

If this route to the Supreme Court is unsuccessful, your lawyer can file an application for a writ of *habeas corpus*. This is a method of testing the legality of your imprisonment under the federal statutes and under the United States Constitution (see section 27). The procedure is technical, and it is by no means always effective, but in the circumstances of your case it is well worth trying. The grounds for your writ of habeas corpus would be only the charge of the failure of the prosecution to disclose the name of a witness; federal courts no longer review claims of unconstitutional search and seizure presented by state defendants in federal habeas corpus petitions. Your lawyer can, it should be noted, file a habeas corpus petition in the federal district court without first proceeding to the Supreme Court.

The federal court, if it finds any substance in the charge that you are being unlawfully detained, may review your entire case, freed from the pressures under which the state trial court operated and from the state appellate court's understandable reluctance to reverse a state court's considered finding. If the federal court finds any real flaw in the way your case was handled—such as the crucial and, to you, damaging failure of the prosecutor to disclose the name of a witness—it will grant the writ and release you, which means setting aside the order of the state court. It may direct the state court to retry you, keeping in mind that the heart of the case against you was unconstitutionally presented.

Needless to say, if at any time during any of the procedural steps outlined above as typical in a criminal trial, your lawyer should come upon evidence establishing that someone put the paper bag in the borrowed car that day, whether to "frame" you or simply to get rid of it for fear of his own prosecution (for example, the unknown witness, who had been unaware of the trial, learns about your situation and comes forward), he would present that evidence to the proper authority.

If the evidence turned up before your arraignment or preliminary hearing, your lawyer would discuss it with the prosecuting attorney, in hopes of persuading him to drop the charges against you entirely. If the evidence turned up during the course of the trial itself, your lawyer would doubtless alert the prosecuting attorney, then request a conference with the trial judge in his chambers and seek to have the charges withdrawn. If the evidence turned up after the jury had reached its verdict and the judge had sentenced you, your lawyer would file a motion for a new trial on the ground of newly discovered evidence.

There are ample procedural devices for upsetting the results of a trial if it can be established that new evidence has been discovered that casts questions on the whole proceeding to which you have been subjected. One of these remedies which is often available—but which would not be in your hypothetical situation—is a *writ of error coram nobis,* an attack on the judgment of conviction based on the claim that it was obtained through fraud, force or pressure. The trial court would hear or review the application for the writ, and if the charges were found to be truthful, you would be immediately released and your conviction set aside.

157. Essentials of Criminal Procedure • We have now taken you through the barest outline of an imaginary criminal proceeding. Not every legal procedure has been discussed, but enough steps have been mentioned to indicate some of the complications and risks in this field of criminal law and procedure. Let's touch on a few, by way of review, so that you have a realistic sense of what is involved:

a. No one simple law or simple legal system is in issue: there are federal constitutional provisions and state constitutional provisions, federal statutes and state statutes, and parallel federal and state court systems, codes and procedures.

b. If you are arrested you have a number of specific rights based on Supreme Court interpretations of the Fifth and Fourteenth Amendments. Among the most important of these are your right to legal advice from the moment of your arrest and your right to remain silent until you have talked to a lawyer. It is the duty of police to inform you of these rights.

c. Your financial ability to hire a lawyer is less important than it was ten years ago. The United States Supreme Court has said that you are entitled to one, and one way or another you should be able to get one. Perhaps the discussion of criminal procedure in this chapter will persuade you that you are foolish if you fail to get one at the first whiff of trouble with the criminal law. All sorts of different organizations are springing up around the country to make lawyers available to persons charged with criminal offenses and unable to pay legal fees (see section 622).

d. Your right to bail—to be free on bail, pending a final decision or verdict on the charges brought against you—is subject to the courts' increasing unwillingness to grant bail as a matter of course, except where the court is able to utilize the services of social workers and others who can advise it regarding the need of bail in different circumstances.

e. As we said in the chapter on torts (section 75), litigation is expensive. From reading about the many things your lawyer must do for you in the course of representing you in any criminal proceeding, you will appreciate how many hours he must spend talking with you as his client, investigating the facts, talking with witnesses, appearing in court, making various motions and actually conducting your defense. If you are or expect to be under criminal prosecution, don't talk to anyone until you've first seen a lawyer. And don't be surprised if he asks for fees in advance; this is fairly standard procedure for criminal lawyers today, partly because if a client is found guilty, he may not have the ability or the desire to pay his lawyer.

CHAPTER FIVE

Your Personal Property, Contracts and Purchases

Any legal liability for breach of a contract is a disagreeable consequence which tends to make the contractor do as he said he would.

—OLIVER WENDELL HOLMES, JR.

5

Your Personal Property, Contracts and Purchases

Some Key Points in This Chapter—
Consult these sections for information on:

Charts in This Chapter

Your Right to Own, Enjoy and Dispose of Personal Property

158. What Property Is • Property is anything that you can own exclusively with the protection of the law. Ownership need not of course be by an individual; it can be by any of several kinds of groups whose right to own property the law recognizes: partnerships, corporations, the state and agencies created by the state.

To become property, the object must be something that can be controlled. Water flowing in a river is not property: ownership is in the bank of the river and in many cases in half the riverbed. The bank and the bed of the river can be controlled and rights in them will be protected by the courts; hence they are property. Oxygen in the atmosphere cannot be exclusively controlled and is not property. But it can become your property if you extract the oxygen from the air and confine it under pressure in a metal cylinder or container. You have then reduced it to controllable form and you may sell it to a hospital, laboratory, factory or to anyone.

Practically anything else you can think of is property of one kind or another—real or personal. *Real property* is land and things under the land (minerals) or growing on it (trees) or permanently attached to it (buildings). *Personal property* is every other kind of property: minerals after they have been taken out of the ground, trees after they have been felled and bricks from a chimney of a house that has been torn down.

You will often see other adjectives used to describe personal property. *Corporeal,* or *tangible,* property means physical things, movable things such as animals, furniture or automobiles. *Incorporeal,* or *intangible,* property commonly includes rights to tangible things. Bonds, mortgages, leases—all are legal documents that, although they themselves are movable and tangible, nevertheless have value only for what they represent or for the rights that they describe.

A bond represents the obligation of the issuer to repay you the principal amount you have loaned him, plus the interest, at the times and in the amounts set forth in the bond. A mortgage represents the obligation of the owner of the property, the mortgagor, to repay you, as mortgagee, the principal amount of the loan and the interest, at the times and in the amounts set forth in the mortgage. The mortgage also contains provisions covering the rights in the property, that is, security for them in the event that the borrower (or mortgagor) defaults (see sections 292, 298).

187

A lease represents your right to occupy the landlord's premises or property and your obligation to pay him rent for that right, as set forth in the lease. In these two cases of borrowers and one of lessee or tenant, one individual or a corporation owns the real property. The personal property, the lease that is the evidence of your interest in the real property, is owned by you and has value to you, but quite a different value and interest from the real property itself.

159. Acquisition and Legal Protection of Personal Property • You may acquire personal property in several ways: by inheritance, by purchase, as a gift, by finding it or by making it. But you do not legally own anything you acquire by theft or fraud. Stolen or misappropriated property that comes into your possession may be returned to its rightful owner with no payment to you, even though you were ignorant of the fact that it was wrongfully acquired and paid for it in good faith (see section 189).

You may own personal property individually or together with other persons. A joint bank account that you have with your wife gives each of you an equal share in the account and may give the entire account to the survivor. If a partnership of which you are a member owns property in the name of the partnership, your share of that property will be spelled out in the partnership agreement (see section 404). And of course by investing in a corporation, you and the other stockholders all own a part, however small, of its assets (see sections 406, 475).

Property that has been in your possession for any length of time usually requires no proof of ownership. You can sell your sofa without having to produce a document showing you own it. But it's wise to hold on to such documents for a while after you make major purchases. A bill of sale will serve for most purposes. In the case of certain kinds of property that are dangerous if misused, such as guns and automobiles, state laws require that they be registered or licensed, and in most cases you should have the registration certificate with you at all times (see section 21 and chart 5, page 66).

The Constitution of the United States prohibits any state from depriving you of your property "without due process of law." You may use your property as you see fit, sell it, give it away or discard it, and you may dispose of it to your relatives or friends upon your death. You have an action for damages against anyone who harms or ruins your property or uses it without your permission. If it is stolen or wrongfully taken from you, you may sue the thief or wrongdoer in a civil action seeking restitution or damages for conversion (see section 47) or for fraud and deceit (see section 49). In addition, the public authorities have the responsibility of prosecuting the thief in a criminal action.

160. Lost, Abandoned, Misplaced and Found Property • You have lost property when you have involuntarily parted with it and hope or expect to get it back. A person who knowingly takes over lost property deprives the owner and may be guilty of larceny. Abandoned property, which the loser does not expect to recover, is another matter (see section 132). A finder is not obliged to return abandoned property. Often property is found under circumstances that give the owner some chance of recovering it. If a wallet or an umbrella you carelessly leave on the train is found by the trainman or stationmaster, it will be placed in a lost-and-found department and held there for a while. But this is done as a convenience to customers, not because the law requires it.

In a world increasingly cluttered up with machinery, people have got into the habit of abandoning machines they don't want in order to avoid the expense of having them hauled away. In cities abandoned cars have become such a nuisance because they are unsightly and a traffic hazard that municipal ordinances and some state laws impose a fine on the owner of this kind of abandoned property. In the country the sight of abandoned cars is increasingly becoming an eyesore. As we grow more sensitive to these conditions around us, we must expect more laws to be passed requiring us as citizens to share some of the responsibility of improving our environment: of selling our old cars to junk dealers who will take them off the streets. Your freedom to dispose of your personal property just as you wish (by throwing your trash out your apartment window onto the street below) may have to yield to the public's need of safe, sanitary and reasonably attractive surroundings.

PATENTS, TRADE SECRETS, COPYRIGHTS AND TRADEMARKS

161. Patents and "Design Patents" • A personal property right that is protected largely by statutes rather than by case law or constitutional provisions is the property you have in the product of your own mind or brain: a thing you invent, design, write for publication or manufacture for sale. The importance of this little-understood and highly specialized field of law is indicated by the fact that it is specifically mentioned in the United States Constitution. Article I, section 8, reads: "The Congress shall have power: . . . To promote the progress of science and useful arts, by securing for limited times to authors and inventors the exclusive right to their respective writings and discoveries." The significance of this constitutional provision is that the federal government has sole jurisdiction and responsibility over patents and copyrights.

A patent is your exclusive right as an inventor to make, use and sell your invention for a certain period of time. The word *exclusive* is all-important. It means that during the prescribed "term of years" no one else may legally make, use or sell your invention and that the courts will protect your sole rights in your invention. The term of years is seventeen for most patents and fourteen for so-called design patents. To be patentable, your invention must consist of a new and useful process, a machine, a manufacture (usually referred to as an article of manufacture) or a composition of matter. Design patents are awarded for original and ornamental designs for articles of manufacture and include a wide variety of designs for such things as furniture, fabrics, jewelry, vehicles and industrial equipment.

Patent law is a specialty within the entire legal field, and if you are seeking a patent on something you have invented or want to get some notion of the patentability of an idea for an invention, you should consult a patent lawyer. Don't delay. If a description of your proposed invention has been published in the United States or elsewhere it is not patentable by you, even though you may not know of that publication.

What your patent lawyer does first, if he believes your invention or idea for one can be patented, is to conduct a *patent search* in the search room and scientific library of the U.S. Patent Office in Washington, D.C., where the more than four million patents issued in the United States are on file, as well as almost complete sets from major foreign countries.

If the search turns up no previously issued patent similar to the one you are seeking, your lawyer will prepare for your signature and then file a patent application. The application fee is now $65. The law provides for appeal procedures if your application is denied. If it is granted, you must pay a final fee of $100 for the patent itself, which is good for seventeen years from the date of issuance, which often comes long after the date of filing the application. The words "patent pending" that appear on many articles mean that a patent has been applied for but not yet granted. A device for which a patent has been granted usually carries one or more patent numbers. The United States district courts are the

190

ones where patent suits are brought, that is, suits charging that one's patent rights are being violated, or *infringed*.

Upon payment of a filing fee of $20 design patents may be obtained for three and a half years at a final fee of $10, for seven years at a final fee of $20 or for fourteen years at a final cost of $30. Design patent applications are handled differently by the Patent Office from applications for mechanical, or utility, patents and provide protection that is limited to the form or design of the device as disclosed in the design patent. On the other hand, a mechanical patent extends to all devices that embody the principles of the invention and is not confined to the particular design that the inventor happens to have disclosed.

A patent, like any other item of personal property, may be assigned to or shared with others. This fact is of great importance to the solitary inventor operating on his own, who so often lacks the funds to exploit or take full advantage of his invention. If you invent a complicated piece of machinery that costs hundreds of thousands of dollars to build and even more to market effectively, your patent may seem to be of little value to you. Time and again, inventors find themselves in this situation and too quickly sell or assign their patent rights to others well able to make the investment in anticipation of reaping millions a few years later. It often happens that an inventor without business experience who needs funds sells and assigns his entire right, title and interest in his patent, in which case the assignee, or buyer, becomes the sole owner and can do anything with it that he wants.

You should be aware, however, that you have the alternative of continuing as the legal owner of the patent and, for a fee, licensing someone to use part of the patent or to use the patented object in a certain way or in a certain part of the country. The license must be in writing. The term for which you license the use of part or all of your patent rights cannot effectively last longer than the life of the patent itself.

If you are the pleased possessor of a patent that appears valid and someone or some corporation violates your rights, you have several legal remedies, depending on the nature of your patent and on the nature of the infringement. The choice of which remedy to use will be decided by you and your lawyer. As we say in section 75, all litigation is expensive. Patent litigation is particularly so because it involves complex technical questions and may require not only general counsel (who functions like a medical general practitioner) but a patent trial counsel as well (who functions like a medical specialist). So you should assist your lawyer to the best of your ability in his efforts to reach a compromise.

191

If you do decide to go to court, it may be best for you to seek only an *injunction,* or court order commanding the person infringing your patent rights to stop what he is doing; for example, to stop producing and marketing a silent lawn mower that is a clear-cut copy of one you patented. You may also seek to recover damages for infringement of the patent. In many cases, damages are measured by what would have been a reasonable royalty in all of the circumstances if you had granted a license under the patent when the infringement began.

These are questions to discuss with your lawyer, in addition to the other usual questions involved in any litigation (see sections 76–81): which court to sue in, whether to ask for a jury, whether there is any effective defense against your action, such as *laches* (unnecessary delay on your part in asserting your rights as a patent holder). The patent laws bar any recovery for an infringement committed six years or more before you start your suit (see section 81).

162. The Law of Trade Secrets • Innovations in business and trade, including inventions that could be patented, may in appropriate circumstances be protected as trade secrets. The law of trade secrets goes far back in the common law and reflects the basic principle that the courts will protect a person against wrongful appropriation of his private and secret knowledge. Such wrongful appropriation may arise by breach of a confidential relationship with the owner of the trade secret, by breach of an agreement not to use the trade secret without the consent of its owner, by theft of documents or by espionage. The owner of the trade secret has no rights against the use of his trade secret by another who has independently discovered it or who has secured knowledge of the trade secret in a proper manner and without any commitment to the owner of the trade secret. At such time as a trade secret is disclosed to the public or becomes generally known to others in the trade, all rights in it are lost.

In some situations, protection of an invention as a trade secret may be the basis for a successful business. For example, the formulas for Coca-Cola syrup have been maintained as a trade secret for generations, far longer than the 17 years afforded by a patent. In many other situations, however, the only effective protection may be via the patent law.

The law of trade secrets is not confined to inventions that can be patented. For example, you cannot patent a way of doing business: it's neither mechanical nor a design. But if you develop a method of marketing and selling ice cream that puts you far ahead of all your competition, the courts will protect you against an official of your company who accepts employment with one of your competitors in order to teach him how to use your methods in his business. You would have an action against the official for breach of a confidential relationship in passing on, and benefiting from, your trade secret. And you would have an action against your competitor who knowingly profited by it.

163. Trademarks and Trade Names • A *trademark* is a visible symbol that serves to identify and distinguish your particular brand of goods from similar goods made by others. It may be a name, phrase, sign or a combination of these elements, and it has distinct value as personal property. Federal law enables you to register trademarks used on goods you sell in interstate commerce. Most states also have laws providing for the registration of trademarks, usually on goods sold only within their boundaries.

Your federal trademark application must be made to the Commissioner of Patents in Washington, D.C. It should include your name, home address, citizenship and the location of your company (or those of a corporation if you have formed one to sell your product). It should state the type of merchandise or service for which the trademark is requested and should contain a description and a drawing of the trademark signed by you. The fee for filing the initial application is $35 and for filing a renewal application $25. Your application will not be granted or may be challenged by competitors if the trademark you submit too closely resembles others already in existence for which it could be mistaken or if it uses words that are in common or general use in describing the particular class of product.

Once it has been approved and registered, a trademark becomes your exclusive property for twenty years, with the right of renewal for additional twenty-year periods. It may be transferred, licensed, bought and sold, and you may bring suit for infringement in a U.S. district court against others who use the trademark without your permission or who employ symbols that too closely resemble it.

Trade names, under which persons, partners and corporations conduct their business over a long period of time, acquire an identity or public image that can be protected by the laws of unfair competition. An example of a trade name is the Sun Oil Company, while its name for the gasoline it sells, Sunoco, is a trademark. Trade names cannot be registered under our patent laws, but the courts will protect them if they have acquired well established meaning.

164. Literary Property and Copyright • The law of copyright is in a state of flux. In October 1976, the President of the United States signed a new law that becomes effective January 1, 1978. The new law changes the old law, enacted in 1909, in a number of significant ways.

Let's say you have written a biography of a man who died only recently. You send it to a publisher and are told that the time is not right for publishing it. The subject of your biography is identified with a currently unpopular cause. You're convinced, however, that, in time, your book would sell many copies. What should you do?

Until January 1, 1978, the main thing is not to let your book get into the hands of anyone who is likely to print it. So long as you keep your manuscript to yourself, showing it only to a few people and making it clear to them that it remains your property, the law will protect that property against anyone who tries to take advantage of it or use it without your permission. You have what is called a common-law right of property in the product of your brain and pen, and you can use the traditional legal remedies if that right is violated. You can go to court for an injunction to stop an unauthorized publication, either before or after it is printed. If a "pirated" edition has been printed, you should be able to obtain a judgment awarding you the pirate's profits.

One change that will occur on January 1, 1978, is that this common-law right disappears, to be replaced by a statutory right that comes into existence as soon as you have written down your story. You will be able to register, in the Copyright Office, your copyright in your manuscript. Unpublished books cannot be registered under the 1909 law.

The law of copyright protects you against the unauthorized printing, reprinting, publishing, copying, selling, translating, conversion, arrangement, adaptation, delivery or performance of any work you have copyrighted. What you may copyright as set forth in the 1909 act are:

a. Books, including composite and cyclopedic works, directories, gazetteers and other compilations.

b. Periodicals, including newspapers.

c. Lectures, sermons, addresses (prepared for oral delivery).

d. Dramatic or dramatico-musical compositions.

e. Musical compositions.

f. Maps.

g. Works of art; models or designs for works of art.

h. Reproductions of a work of art.

i. Drawings or plastic works of a scientific or technical character.

j. Photographs.

k. Prints and pictorial illustrations, including prints or labels used for articles of merchandise.

l. Motion-picture photoplays.

m. Motion pictures other than photoplays.

Under the 1909 law, the total term of copyright is fifty-six years, an initial and a renewal term of twenty-eight years each. Starting January 1, 1978, unexpired existing copyrights will have a total term of seventy-five years, twenty-eight years and a renewal term of forty-seven years. The renewal term is lost upon failure to renew. Copyrights obtained after January 1, 1978, will be for the life of the author plus fifty years, and there is no need to renew.

To obtain a copyright, all you need do is to affix a copyright notice on your work and have it publicly exhibited or distributed. After you have obtained your copyright, you should register it in the Copyright Office, Washington, D.C. 20559. Application forms may be obtained free from the Copyright Office. Each form contains detailed instructions for filling out and filing the application and the appropriate fee, which, for a book, is now $6. After January 1, 1978, the filing fee for all registration applications will be $10.

The copyright notice, essential for obtaining copyright, consists of either a three-part or a two-part notice. The three-part notice, which must be used on works in copyright Classes, listed above, *a* to *e*, *l* and *m*, consists of: (1) the word "Copyright," the abbreviation "Copr." or the symbol ©; (2) the name of the copyright owner; and (3) the year date of the work's publication. The two-part notice, which may be used with works in Classes *f* to *k*, consists of the symbol © and the name of the copyright owner. The symbol © is important because it gives protection for your work in more than 50 countries under the Universal Copyright Convention. On printed material the notice should appear on the title page or the page following.

Under the new law there is a strict time limit within which a copyright must be registered after publication with notice. If not so registered, attorneys fees—recoverable under copyright law—and certain damages cannot be obtained from infringers.

If your copyright is violated, the U.S. copyright law gives you the following remedies to select:

a. An injunction restraining the infringement.

b. Damages *and* profits. The criteria for their determination are explicitly stated in the statute, with a statutory penalty yardstick set forth as an alternative to actual damages and profits.

c. Impounding of the infringing articles during the action.

d. Destruction of the infringing copies and plates. Moreover, a U.S. district court can invoke criminal penalties for willful infringement or fraudulent notice of copyright, but these drastic penalties are seldom used.

Be careful not to "sleep on your rights." A three-year statute of limitations (see section 81) applies to copyright actions: you must start your action within three years of the alleged infringement.

165. International Copyright • A word should be said about international copyright conventions or treaties. The following are the treaties that concern you as an author:

a. The Universal Copyright Convention, which was signed in 1952 and became effective in the United States in 1955, provides that each signatory country shall give to works of citizens of other signatories, and to works first published there, the same copyright protection it gives to works of its own citizens. More than 50 countries have signed.

b. Very similar are the provisions of the Convention on Literary and Artistic Copyright, or the Buenos Aires Convention, signed at the Fourth International Conference of American States at Buenos Aires in 1910. The difference is that this convention is open only to republics of the Western Hemisphere (thus excluding Canada, which is a dominion of the United Kingdom). Most Western Hemisphere republics have signed.

c. Last, there is the Bern Convention, signed in Bern, Switzerland, in 1886 and amended several times since. Almost sixty countries have signed. The United States has not. The Bern Convention now provides that authors of any signatory country enjoy in other signatory countries the rights granted by such other countries to their own citizens. Authors of a country that has not signed the convention may obtain rights under it if they publish their works first or simultaneously in any country that has signed. For this reason many U.S. publishing firms bring out their authors' books simultaneously in Canada, which is a member.

CONTRACTS

166. The Promises Men Live By • Harry Scherman once wrote a readable and instructive book about economics with this phrase as its title. What interested him was the extraordinary number of times that we do things or fail to do things simply because we count on someone else to do something or not to do something. Many of these undertakings and expectations of ours are never put in writing.

You enter a restaurant and order an expensive steak to be cooked "rare." The management serves you one that is well done, and you send it back to the kitchen because it's not what you asked for. You get another, which you accept. At the end of the meal you pay your bill and give the waitress a tip. For another example, without even requesting it, you receive in the mail a credit card from a large oil company that entitles you to buy its gasoline on credit and to use the facilities of a chain of motels. You fill up your tank with the company's gas and take a weekend trip, stopping for two nights at one of the chain's motels, where you eat all your meals. When you leave you sign a slip of paper charging all the expenses to the oil company. Or again, a friend gives you a hot tip about the stock market; you call your broker and place an order for 100 shares at $50 a share.

In each of these situations a whole series of actions having substantial economic consequences was set in motion with no formal agreement on either side, without even a spoken promise by either side to do anything. But both sides confidently expect that what should happen will happen: The restaurant management undertakes to serve you a steak cooked the way you order it and relies on you to pay the price shown on the menu. The oil company relies on you to pay for the expenses of your trip when you get its bill in the mail. Your broker relies on you to send him a check for $5,000 (plus his commission) when you receive a notice that he has bought in your name the 100 shares you ordered. In each case you have made an oral undertaking; you have given an implied promise to pay: for the meal, for the gas and motel expenses, for the stock. These cases, and hundreds like them, are covered by the law of contracts, the area of the law that most closely touches our everyday lives and that we largely take for granted.

167. What a Contract Is • A *contract* is a legally enforceable agreement between two or more persons involving mutual promises to do or not to do something. The law of contracts is the area where law and business most often meet and where the courts try to protect you in your business dealings by giving you legal weapons against those who fail to honor their agreements with you. Because we do business in so many ways, there are many kinds of contracts. Some of them are discussed below, not to give you answers to all the questions you may run into in

197

your various business affairs, but to give you some idea of the principles involved as you handle such affairs.

168. Oral and Written Contracts • Obviously, there are both *oral* and *written* contracts. As the examples suggest, a tremendous amount of business is conducted by means of oral contracts, which though never reduced to writing, create legally binding obligations the courts will enforce. But some contracts must be in writing if they are to be enforceable (see section 180). And not all written contracts are enforceable, either because they are illegal or against public policy or because the parties are not legally competent to make them (see section 176).

169. Express and Implied Contracts • In *express contracts* the terms have been agreed upon between the parties, whether orally or in writing makes no difference. Your verbal agreement to hire a plumber to install new faucets in your bathroom at a stated price that includes materials and labor is a binding express contract. Once the plumber installs the faucets you have a legal obligation to pay him the amount you and he agreed upon. The courts will enforce that obligation. You might have several defenses (see section 185) if he were to sue you for failure to pay him—that is, for breach of your contractual undertaking to pay—but the fact that the contract between you was not a written one would not be one of them.

Implied contracts, on the other hand, are the contractual obligations you undertake without ever mentioning the word *contract* or *agreement*. When you entered the restaurant and ordered the steak, you became just as legally obligated to pay the management as though you had signed a two-page contract to do so. The law distinguishes between two kinds of implied contracts: those *implied in fact,* as in the restaurant situation, and those *implied in law*.

Contracts *implied in law* are not really contracts at all: there was no agreement. But in order to do justice the law imposes an agreement on the parties. For example, you lend your neighbor your car for a week while you are on vacation so that he can enjoy the convenience of driving to and from work instead of riding on the train. But your neighbor gets other ideas and drives 2,000 miles to visit an old girl friend in a distant city. If he doesn't pay you for adding on all that extra mileage, you may well have an action against him for breach of an implied contract to pay you for the use of your car farther than you had expected him to. You also may be able to sue him for violating the terms of your bailment agreement (see section 197) and perhaps a tort action for conversion, or the wrongful use of your property (see section 47).

170. Why Written Contracts Are Better • You will realize by now that written contracts are in many cases preferable to oral ones, whether express or implied. The reason is the difficulty of establishing the terms of an oral contract; the problem of persuading a court when you sue on the oral contract that your version of the facts is the right one. It is this very difficulty that resulted hundreds of years ago in what is called, both in England and in the United States, the statute of frauds. This statute requires certain contracts to be in writing if they are to be enforced by the courts (see section 180). But whether the contract you are about to enter into is or is not covered by the statute of frauds, you should as a matter of course put it in writing if at all possible.

171. Unilateral and Bilateral Contracts • Contracts may be unilateral or bilateral. Under our definition of a contract, "a legally enforceable agreement between two or more persons involving mutual promises to do or not to do something," a unilateral, or one-sided, contract may seem contradictory, and in a way it is. Nevertheless there are many such contractual situations; a typical one is in the area of rewards. Let us say that your dog is lost and you put an advertisement in your local newspaper saying that you will pay $50 for its return. If someone reads your ad, finds the dog and returns it, you must pay him the $50. The courts reason that his action in returning the dog constitutes an agreement to the terms of the contract you proposed. A *unilateral contract*, therefore, is one that consists of a promise by one person and an act by the other carrying out the terms of that promise.

A *bilateral contract*, on the other hand, consists of the exchange of mutual promises. Let's say, in the lost dog situation, that you tell your neighbor you will pay him $50 if he will agree to look for your dog, and he so agrees: you and he have entered into a bilateral contract. If he then goes home and does not search for the animal at all, you may sue him for breach of contract.

172. Voidable and Unenforceable Contracts • A contract may be as formal as possible, in writing, signed by legally competent parties, with a host of witnesses—and yet be void. A common ground for declaring a contract void is that it is against public policy.

A *voidable contract* is one that can, but will not necessarily, be set

199

aside by a court. If one party to a contract is senile or otherwise incompetent, it will not be enforced against him if he raises the defense of incompetency when he is sued or if he simply refuses to perform under the contract. But if no such defense is raised or if he performs his obligation, the contract will stand. Similarly, a contract induced by fraud or mistake can be avoided if the person who contracted because of the other party's fraud wishes to get out of it. But he is free to live up to the contract if he wants.

An *unenforceable contract* is one for which there is no remedy if it is breached. Because the statute of frauds requires written contracts for the sale of land, your oral contract to buy land is unenforceable. If your written contract is broken by the other party but you wait ten years before you sue, you will find your suit barred by the statute of limitations (see section 185 and chart 10). Your contract was formal, in writing, valid and binding when you made it, but it is now unenforceable.

173. Essentials of an Enforceable Contract • The word *enforceable* means that your contract will be enforced by the courts: that you have legal remedies to protect you if the other party should fail to live up to its terms. Some contracts that appear to be enforceable may be only moral obligations, however. You and your wife may enter into an agreement with another couple to play bridge next Wednesday evening. You might go so far as to put the agreement in writing, with all kinds of "whereas" clauses and statements about the time of the bridge game, the number of rubbers you intended to play and so forth. It might even state that you were giving up an opportunity to go to the movies with your children and that the other couple was missing their favorite television show.

But these conditions alone would not involve the courts if the agreement was broken. You would have to establish some actual harm done to you if the other couple failed to show up or left your home at the end of only one rubber. All the right might be on your side, all the wrong on the other side. Even so, the courts would give you short shrift if you sought either to compel the other side to play bridge or to pay damages for their failure to abide by the terms of the contract.

These are the essentials of an enforceable contract: (a) There must be mutual assent by the parties. (b) There must be consideration. (c) The parties must be legally competent to contract. (d) The object to be achieved by the contract must be lawful. (e) The contract must require performance within an agreed period of time. (f) The contract must be in the form required by law. These requirements are discussed below.

174. The Importance of Assent • Mutual assent is perhaps the most basic requirement of all. You and the person with whom you are contracting must agree on what the contract is all about. Suppose the fellow in the apartment across the hall offers to sell you his television set but says nothing about the expensive and essential antenna that is installed outside his window. If you assume his offer includes the antenna but nothing is mentioned about it, either in your oral agreement or in the brief paper you both sign to formalize your contract, there really is no contract. Your minds have not met. Should you sue him for breach of contract for failure to hand over the antenna when he delivers the television set to you, chances are he would be able to defend himself successfully on the grounds that there was a mistake as to the terms of the contract, and hence no meeting of the minds.

When you enter into a contract, therefore, make sure that every item is included. A binding enforceable contract is one that covers all the terms you agreed upon and only those terms; it is a contract that reflects the mutual assent of both parties.

Mutuality of assent is often expressed differently. There must be a firm offer and an equally firm acceptance of that offer. Offer and acceptance are what make up assent. The difficulty mentioned in the example just given might have been avoided if your neighbor across the hall had said to you: "I'll sell you my television set, without the antenna, for $350," and you had replied, "I'll pay you $350 for the television set *and* antenna." Here there would clearly be no contract, because you and your neighbor had not agreed on anything. Actually, he made you one offer and you countered with another offer.

But a contract might well have resulted if your reply to his offer was, "I'd sure like to have the antenna too, but $350 is such a good price for your marvelous television set that I accept," or if he had answered you by saying, "I'm going away for five years and need the money, so you can have everything for $350." Under neither of these last two instances is the situation as clear as it might be, but mutuality of assent is reasonably close and the court is likely to find there is a binding contract. The important thing is, what did the parties actually mean—to be bound or not to be bound, at the time they exchanged their promises?

175. Consideration for the Promise • Next and crucially important to an enforceable contract is what is known as *consideration:* whatever it is that underlies and induces the promise. A promise by itself does not constitute a contract and cannot be enforced against the person making the promise, called the *promisor*. To make the promise enforceable, something must be given up by the person to whom the promise is made, called the *promisee*. Something already given up by the promisee before the promise was made will not support the promise.

The written promise by an elderly invalid to reward his faithful nurse for all she has done by making her a bequest in his will cannot be enforced against the invalid's estate when he dies. Either the services were rendered voluntarily or she had already been paid for them, and no promise to pay more for them is enforceable.

Suppose, on the other hand, that an invalid asks his widowed daughter to give up her home and live with him and take care of him in his declining years. In return he promises her a bequest of $10,000. Here we have a unilateral contract (see section 171) that is enforceable against the invalid's estate if the daughter accepts it by doing what he asks. No matter that the daughter may be thought to have a moral obligation or duty to take care of her elderly father. She has no legal obligation (welfare laws aside—see section 355), and she is giving up not only her home but her own freedom of action in coming to live with and take care of her father *in reliance on his promise* to make her a bequest in his will. Her act gives consideration to his promise and results in an enforceable contract.

You probably remember seeing, in contracts you have read, a phrase like "for $10 and other valuable consideration, receipt of which is hereby acknowledged." This kind of phrase is very common in leases and contracts of sale. It is included in these and other contracts—even though, as often happens, no money actually changes hands—just to make the contract enforceable. It is an assertion of consideration that, although it can be challenged and perhaps even disproved, goes far to support a contract that has no other apparent consideration. One might truthfully say that "a little consideration goes a long way." The reason is that courts are reluctant to "go behind" the terms of a contract, to question the parties' statement that they have given and received consideration.

The assertion that there is consideration, small though it may be in relation to the size of the subject matter of the contract, is further protected against attack by what is known as the parol evidence rule. This is a rule of evidence that makes it extremely difficult to challenge the language of a written contract by "parol," or oral, testimony. Let's say that your contract for the sale of your house states that "in consideration of the payment (to you) of $10 and other good and valuable consideration, receipt of which is hereby acknowledged," you agree to sell your house for $10,000—even though the house is actually worth at least $25,000. If you change your mind, you are going to have a hard time avoiding the contract unless you can establish some defense, such as fraud, mistake or duress (see section 185). The court will not accept your oral statement that you were not paid $10 when you signed the contract. (For more about the parol evidence rule, see section 180.)

Nor will it, in the absence of one of the possible defenses just mentioned, accept or listen to the testimony of experts that $10,000 is a ridiculous price for your $25,000 house. You made your contract voluntarily; you acknowledged receipt of some consideration; you must honor your freely incurred contractual obligation.

It is possible to imagine cases in which a court will regard the consideration as so inadequate as to make the contract unconscionable. But be careful. Read what you sign and make sure it reflects the facts.

Many of us these days are solicited by our schools, colleges, churches and other charities for pledges to their money-raising campaigns. Occasionally you will be asked to sign a statement that you are making your pledge "in consideration of" the pledges of other contributors. The reason for this language is to make you believe that your pledge is legally enforceable against you during your life and against your estate if you die before you have made all the payments you agreed to. There may be consideration, legally speaking, behind your pledge. Your pledge is a unilateral promise made voluntarily. Your obligation may be a legal one as well as a moral one, and many courts would enforce it, maintaining that each of the other pledges serves as a consideration for yours. If your pledge were a large one and the school or charity to which you made it had acted in reliance on it—perhaps by contracting for a new building or hiring staff for a new program—the courts would be all the more likely to view your obligation to pay as a binding one.

176. Legal Capacity of Parties to a Contract: Minors and Other Incompetents • For a contract to be enforceable, the parties must be legally competent to contract at the time they contract. Certain groups of people do not have legal capacity (see sections 336, 356), and contracts they entered into while under such legal disability may be disavowed by them or on their behalf—and affirmed by them if and when the disability is removed. These contracts are voidable at the option of the legally incompetent person or party.

Check the laws of your state in chart 28, page 428, to determine when a minor ceases to be a minor for contract purposes. In a few states it is twenty-one; most have reduced it to eighteen. A minor or infant is not legally competent to enter into a contract. What this means is that the minor, if sued for breach of his contract, may successfully plead the defense of infancy, or legal incapacity. In most cases the court will accept the defense and refuse to enforce the contract.

Minors who leave home or whose parents refuse to support them are called *emancipated*. Their contracts are equally voidable, unless the contracts are for the *necessities* of life: food, clothing, shelter, medicine and education. Also, emancipated minors are entitled to keep their wages, whereas the wages of minors living at home are the legal property of their parents.

In brief, you make a contract with a minor for nonnecessaries at your own risk. The courts have always assumed the duty of protecting minors against their presumed inability to do what is best for them and their proved tendency to commit themselves to unwise contracts. If you are an automobile salesman and are about to make a sale to a buyer who seems very young, you should obtain proof that he is of age. If you don't, his contract with you is worth little if he wants to violate it. Even if he offers you cash on the barrelhead you have no protection: should he decide a month later that he doesn't like the car, he is legally able to return it and demand his money back. A court might permit you to keep part of what he paid you as compensation for the use of your property, but that's all you could expect. If the terms of the sale provide for installment payments, and he fails to make more than a few and you sue for the balance, his defense of legal incapacity will be upheld. (You can, however, get a court order instructing him to return the car to you.)

When the minor who bought the car from you reaches his majority, he may either ratify or get out of the contract. If he continues to make the payments required by the contract and to use the car, a court will hold that he has ratified it: he does not have the right to return the car six months after he has reached his majority and then demand his money back. But if within a short time after the date of the crucial birthday he decides to get out of the contract, he may be able to do so.

This legal right of a minor to plead lack of legal capacity while a minor and either to ratify or to avoid the contract on becoming of age is personal to him. If he dies his contracts may be avoided by his heirs and personal representatives; if he becomes insane, by his guardian. But you, the other party to the contract, are regarded as able to protect yourself, which includes having the sense not to enter into contracts with minors. You are under no legal disability and are bound by the contract if the minor chooses to hold you to it. The minor gets the best of both worlds. That is what the law intends and that is what the courts enforce.

Much the same protection is provided by the courts for two other categories of persons presumed incapable of entering into contracts: insane persons and persons obviously under the influence of alcohol or narcotics. Their contracts, except those for necessities, are voidable. You may sell half a dozen shirts to someone you think is acting peculiarly, and you'll probably be able to collect the purchase price if you go to court. But if the person has legally been declared insane and has had a guardian appointed for him, his contracts thereafter are absolutely void and you will not be able to collect.

What is involved in all these cases is simple enough: the protection by the courts of persons who may be unable to protect themselves. Of course not all underage people are wasteful and improvident. Of course not all very elderly persons are senile and incompetent. And some town drunks have moments of lucidity, even sobriety. But you should be aware of the laws protecting minors, mental incompetents and addicts. Although it is possible to have business dealings with them, you should realize the chance you are taking. You cannot enforce their promises in court; if they won't honor their contracts there's nothing you can do about it. The risk is all yours.

177. Legal Capacity of Corporations · Another category of "persons" you should be wary of with regard to contracts is corporations (see section 405). A corporation is a creature of the state, authorized by statute. Its actual powers are only those specifically set forth in its charter or articles of incorporation and the implied powers necessary to carry them out. A corporation has no other powers, and a contract it enters into to do something not authorized in its charter is beyond its powers, or *ultra vires,* as lawyers say. You most likely cannot enforce such a contract against the corporation: if you sue to enforce it the corporation has the defense of legal incapacity. The contract is regarded as void by some courts. Much depends on the circumstances. If the contract has been in existence for some time and the terms have been fully carried out by both parties, it cannot be revoked or disaffirmed. But if all that has happened is that both parties have signed, and little if anything has been done to carry out the provisions of the contract, the corporation may effectively plead ultra vires, or lack of capacity, in a suit by either party.

In dealing with corporations let common sense be your guide. Look suspiciously at an offer by a book publisher to sell you a mink coat. You can assume, however, that an automobile manufacturer has the authority to buy your property for a new factory.

Be especially careful about contracts with municipal corporations, because their powers are very strictly interpreted by the courts. For example, the laws of many states limit the rate of interest a municipality in the state may pay on its bonds. Chances are that limit does not exceed 7 percent. A proposed bond issue with an interest of 7½ percent would be illegal because it would be beyond the powers of the municipal corporation. If you bought such a bond and the city defaulted, you could not collect the 7½ percent interest it had agreed to pay. The city lacked legal capacity to enter into such a contract.

Questions as to corporate powers can be extremely complicated as can be many other issues related solely to corporate law, which accounts for the fact that so many lawyers spend so much time interpreting them. Where there is any doubt in your mind regarding the legal capacity of the corporation, public or private, to contract as it proposes to do, you should consult a lawyer before you sign the contract.

178. Lawful Object of a Contract • The requirement that what your contract commits you or the other party to do must be lawful scarcely needs discussion. Gambling contracts and contracts that tend to create a monopoly are unlawful and will not be enforced. If you have any doubts as to the legality of your proposed contract, ask your lawyer.

179. Performing the Contract on Time • If a contract is to be enforced by the courts it must contain a statement of the time within which it is to be performed. In the case of most common oral contracts, however, the courts are willing to infer an agreement between the parties that the contract will be performed within a reasonable time, depending on the nature of the acts to be performed and the customs of the community in which the contract is relevant.

180. When Contracts Must Be in Writing • The requirement that certain contracts must be in writing was first adopted by the British Parliament in 1677, in an act known as the statute of frauds (a more accurate title would have been the "statute to prevent frauds"). Practically every state in the Union has adopted most of its provisions. The language of the statute is confusing. In effect, it says that no legal action may be taken to enforce the following contracts unless they are in writing: (a) a contract by an executor or administrator of an estate to pay the debts or liabilities of the deceased out of the executor's or administrator's own property; (b) a contract to pay someone else's debt; (c) a contract made in consideration of marriage, that is, a contract that promises something upon someone's marriage; (d) a contract for the sale of land or any interest in land; (e) a contract that by its terms cannot be performed within one year of the date of its signature by both parties.

In addition, all the states except Louisiana have adopted a further provision of the old statute of frauds; it is part of the Uniform Commercial Code. Although the amount may vary in different states, an oral contract for the sale of goods worth $500 or more shall not be enforceable unless: (a) the buyer accepts part of the goods and actually receives them or (b) the buyer gives something in part payment. Otherwise, some written memorandum of the contract or sale must be signed by the party to be charged or by his agent.

These modern descendants of the statute of frauds are important in your everyday life. Your promise to pay your daughter $100 a month for life if she marries your partner's son must be in writing. Your contract to sell your house and grounds or part of your property must be in writing. Your contract to pay for your grandchild's college education when he enters as a freshman two years from now must be in writing.

In a way the parol evidence rule (see section 175) backs up and gives strength to the statute of frauds. It makes no sense to require you to put certain contracts in writing if you or the other party may go into court and complain you didn't intend to enter into the contract or that it doesn't mean what it says. A written contract, in brief, may not be altered by oral testimony or evidence.

One exception is oral evidence offered to prove that no contract was actually entered into or that the contract admittedly entered into resulted from fraud, mistake, duress, undue influence, legal incapacity of one or both parties or illegality of the object of the contract. Parol, or oral, evidence is also occasionally heard by a court to help interpret the terms of a contract that may be misleading or confusing.

But these two exceptions only prove the rule. The courts adopted the parol evidence rule to give permanence to written contracts and to protect your rights under them from idle or fraudulent attempts to upset those rights. Read carefully the terms of the written contract you are asked to sign: the chances are you will not be able to change them later if you don't like them.

181. When You May Assign Your Contract • Generally speaking, you

AGREEMENTS THAT MUST BE IN WRITING

This chart shows what agreements must be in the form of a written contract if they are to be enforced by the courts in the various states, according to the so-called statute of frauds (see section 180). All agreements to convey real estate must be in writing.

CHART 9	Contracts Not to Be Performed Within:	Leases for a Period of More Than:	Sales of Goods Worth More Than:		Contracts Not to Be Performed Within:	Leases for a Period of More Than:	Sales of Goods Worth More Than:
				MISSOURI	1 year	1 year	$500
ALABAMA	1 year	1 year	$500	MONTANA	1 year	1 year	$500
ALASKA	1 year	1 year	$500	NEBRASKA	1 year	1 year	$500
ARIZONA	1 year	1 year	$500	NEVADA	1 year	1 year	$500
ARKANSAS	1 year	1 year	$500	NEW HAMPSHIRE	1 year	1 year	$500
CALIFORNIA	1 year	1 year	$500	NEW JERSEY	1 year	3 years	$500
COLORADO	1 year	1 year	$500	NEW MEXICO	___³	3 years	$500
CONNECTICUT	1 year	1 year	$500	NEW YORK	1 year	1 year	$500
DELAWARE	1 year	1 year	$500	NORTH CAROLINA	___¹	3 years	$500
D.C.	1 year	1 year	$500	NORTH DAKOTA	1 year	1 year	$500
FLORIDA	1 year	1 year	$500	OHIO	1 year	___⁴	$500
GEORGIA	1 year	1 year	$500	OKLAHOMA	1 year	1 year	$500
HAWAII	1 year	1 year	$500	OREGON	1 year	1 year	$500
IDAHO	1 year	1 year	$500	PENNSYLVANIA	___¹	3 years	$500
ILLINOIS	1 year	1 year	$500	RHODE ISLAND	1 year	1 year	$500
INDIANA	1 year	3 years	$500	SOUTH CAROLINA	1 year	1 year	$500
IOWA	1 year	1 year	$500	SOUTH DAKOTA	1 year	1 year	$500
KANSAS	1 year	1 year	$500	TENNESSEE	1 year	1 year	$500
KENTUCKY	1 year	1 year	$500	TEXAS	1 year	1 year	$500
LOUISIANA	___¹	___¹	$500²	UTAH	1 year	1 year	$500
MAINE	1 year	1 year	$500	VERMONT	1 year	1 year	$500
MARYLAND	1 year	1 year	$500	VIRGINIA	1 year	1 year	$500
MASSACHUSETTS	1 year	1 year	$500	WASHINGTON	1 year	1 year	$500
MICHIGAN	1 year	1 year	$500	WEST VIRGINIA	1 year	1 year	$500
MINNESOTA	1 year	1 year	$500	WISCONSIN	1 year	1 year	$500
MISSISSIPPI	15 months	1 year	$500	WYOMING	1 year	1 year	$500

(1) No requirement.
(2) Unless proved by two witnesses.
(3) Common law.
(4) All leases must be in writing.

may assign your rights under any contract you enter into, except one for personal services. If you are the world's greatest operatic tenor and enter into a contract to sing for the season at the Metropolitan Opera, you may not assign your contract: it is personal to you. What the Metropolitan wants is your unique ability to sing and your worldwide reputation. In the same sense, your doctor or lawyer may not turn you over to someone else without your permission. Nor can you legally assign your contract to teach at a designated school. The test is whether the services to be rendered under a contract are personal. If so, the contract may be assigned only with the approval of both original parties. You also cannot assign your contract to marry.

Other contracts are freely and orally assignable unless the law specifically requires that the assignment be in writing. A railroad ticket, which is the symbol of the railroad's contract to carry you as a passenger, is easily assignable by you or by the railroad. You may sell or give away your ticket. Simple delivery of your ticket completes the assignment. If the railroad is merged into another company, the successor company assumes the obligation to carry you or the person you gave your ticket to.

You may, however, include in a contract a clause stating specifically that the contract may not be assigned or setting forth special conditions under which it may be assigned. If the contract is valid, such a clause will be upheld by the courts.

182. How Contracts Are Discharged • Performance of the terms of a contract by both parties to it *discharges* the contract. What was anticipated has been done, and no further obligations remain. But because contracts are entered into in such a variety of ways, to achieve such a variety of results, and because conditions so often change and relationships between the parties alter, the legislatures and the courts have recognized various methods of discharging a contract short of full performance. Some of these ways will be mentioned, just to give you an idea of what might be done under your contract if you want to do something different from what it actually provides. Most of these methods of discharge will be obvious.

a. *Failure of consideration.* You remember how important consideration—the giving up of something to support a promise—is to a contract (see section 175). Suppose the widowed daughter who was promised a bequest of $10,000 in her father's will if she would live with and take care of him unexpectedly falls in love again, marries for a second time and moves in with her new husband, who refuses to live with his father-in-law. The contract her father made is discharged for failure of consideration, and his promise is no longer enforceable (see section 185).

b. *Inability to perform.* Some contracts are discharged because performance has become impossible. Your contract to sell your television set to your neighbor is discharged if a fire in your apartment destroys it. You cannot perform, and the law, sensibly, does not require you to do what you cannot (see section 185).

c. *Rescinding of the contract.* A contract may be rescinded: you engage the services of an engineer to survey your property to find out exactly how much you've got, but before he does anything you decide you don't need the survey. You and he can simply agree orally that the "deal is off," and there is no longer a contract between you. But if he has done any work, if he has started on the survey, rescinding the contract will require some payment by you for work done and as consideration for his giving up his rights under the contract.

d. *Cancellation and surrender of the contract.* The situation is very similar in a cancellation of the contract and a surrender of the contract itself. Your writing "canceled" on the check you accepted when you sold your lawn mower and your delivery of the uncashed check to the buyer discharges the contract and his obligation. If you got a simple IOU from the buyer, surrender of the note must be accompanied by a new agreement between you to release his obligation on the contract.

e. *Substitution of a new contract.* Substituting a new contract will discharge an old one. You contract with a builder that he shall build a house for you according to a set of specifications set forth in the contract, the price to be paid partly in cash and partly by his accepting a mortgage from you. But later on, you and he agree on different specifications and on payment in cash only. Here there is a new contract, consisting of those terms of the original that remained unchanged and of the new terms. The second contract is substituted for the old, which is thus discharged. Neither you nor the builder can then enforce the old contract in its original form.

f. *Novation.* Substitution of new parties, which lawyers call *novation,* also discharges a contract. By mutual agreement, supported by adequate consideration, a new contract comes into being. If you owe your brother $100 and he owes your sister $100, the three of you may agree that you will pay your sister $100, thus ending your brother's obligation to her. Your contract with your brother is discharged, as is his contract with her.

g. *Accord and satisfaction.* When one of the parties is not satisfied with the performance of the other, accord and satisfaction is a way of discharging the contract. Suppose a patient and his doctor agree that the doctor will remove the patient's appendix for $500. He does so, but the patient is unhappy with the way he did it and refuses to pay him more than $350. The doctor threatens to sue the patient for $500, and the patient indicates he's prepared to make nasty charges about the doctor in court. After a while the doctor realizes the expense of suing will more than eat up the $150 difference. He says he'll accept $350 in full satisfaction of his claim. The patient agrees and sends him a check for $350, which the doctor cashes.

Here we have what is called an *accord and satisfaction*. An agreement by a creditor (the doctor) for the discharge of an obligation by a performance different from what the creditor is owed under the contract is an *accord*. The completion of that accord—in this case by the patient's paying the doctor the $350 and the doctor's accepting it—is the *satisfaction*. Consult your lawyer, however, if you're ever in such a situation; not all courts will agree to such a discharge of the original obligation.

h. *Account stated.* Despite its formal sound, an account stated is familiar to most of us. Your monthly bank statement is one. It reflects what you have put in as deposits and what the bank has paid out at your direction in the checks you wrote. If you raise no question about the monthly statement when you receive it, or within a reasonable period of time thereafter, any legal action you bring against the bank a year later for what you think is a mistake will not be enforced unless the bank has defrauded you or acted in bad faith.

Another example of an account stated is the bill you get from your local grocer at the end of the month, to which he has attached a list of all the items you bought that month and charged. Your payment of the bill, or your failure within a short while to question items you think are improperly charged to you, strips you of the right to challenge the accuracy of the bill.

i. *Release from the contract.* Occasionally a creditor may be willing to release the debtor from his contractual obligation. If you are owed $1,000 from a contract debt of $5,000 and your debtor suffers an accident, making it difficult or impossible for him to pay you the remaining $1,000, you may be willing to forgive such repayment. In such a situation, you should sign a paper saying that you are releasing him from completing his contract and agree not to sue him for the balance due. To make sure that the paper will have the effect you want it to, it would be well to state some consideration as your inducement to surrender what is legally yours.

183. When a Contract Is Broken • *Breach of contract* is any unjustified failure to perform the terms of a contract when performance is due. If you fail to make only the last monthly payment on a contract that calls for forty-eight payments, you are guilty of just a partial breach. Similarly, the contractor you hired to build a swimming pool who walks off the job without caulking the cracks in the cement has only slightly breached his contract. You would still have to pay him, perhaps deducting from the contract price an amount representing the modest cost of labor and materials necessary to caulk the cement. But if your swimming pool contractor quit after merely digging a hole in the ground, most courts would hold that he had breached the contract totally and that you had no duty to pay him.

A total or material breach of contract may be treated as a partial breach only. In these times, when it is so hard to get plumbers and contractors and electricians who will perform a job when they say they will, many of us are driven to accept the breach. If the plumber doesn't come when he says he will, his breach of contract is material. But you don't know of a better plumber so you overlook his breach and wait until he arrives. If the leak you engaged him to repair gets worse and starts to flood your bathroom, you'd better do what you can to get another plumber, good or bad, and fight with the first one later. You have an obligation not to increase your damages (see section 195). Of course, if after having agreed to do work for you, the contractor repudiates his agreement for no reason, he is guilty of total breach of contract.

184. Remedies for Breach of Contract • If your contract has been breached, the law allows you damages in order to award you a sum of money that will put you in the same position as if the contract had been performed. Your damages will be slight, or *nominal,* if you have suffered no real financial loss or if your loss is so speculative it cannot be proved. *Punitive* or *exemplary* damages—to punish the defaulting party or to make an example of him so that others will be warned—are seldom awarded in contract actions.

But circumstances may be such that damages are not the remedy you want. Specific performance is sometimes better. Suppose you are rummaging through an antique dealer's store and find one old chair that closely matches a set of yours. The design is rare; you want *that* chair. You make the dealer an offer, which he accepts, and he agrees to deliver the chair in three weeks after reconditioning it. Three weeks pass, but you don't receive the chair. You go to the store and ask why he did not deliver it. He indicates he's had a higher offer than the one you made and says he's not going to honor his contract with you.

You could sue him for damages, but damages won't get you the chair. Your more effective remedy is an action for *specific performance:* an action asking the court to order the dealer to live up to his contract by delivering to you that one chair. The remedy of specific performance is one that you and your lawyer will want to consider when the subject of the contract has unique qualities that cannot be measured in money alone.

Contracts for personal services, however, cannot be enforced by the remedy of specific performance. The remedy is available only in areas where the court can supervise and ensure performance. If you operate a restaurant and hire a world-famous chef who breaks his contract with you, your only remedy is an action for damages. Courts know better than to try to ride herd on such notoriously temperamental characters as chefs, portrait painters or professional football players.

But you may have another weapon against the chef, an *injunction.* If he leaves your restaurant in a huff, in violation of your contract with him, and goes to work for the restaurant across the street, you may bring an action asking the court for an order forbidding him to cook for your competitor during the term of his original contract with you. The courts won't order him to cook for you, but they may order him not to cook for anyone else in the area.

185. Defenses to Actions for Breach of Contract • There is a whole battery of defenses to actions for breach of contract. Many are obvious. Others are more technical, but you should know about and keep them in mind whether you are the one who is trying to enforce the contract (the plaintiff) or the one who is trying to avoid its enforcement (the defendant).

a. *Statutes of limitation.* In all states statutes of limitation specify the maximum time within which you may start a legal action for breach of contract. The usual period is six years, but you should check chart 10, page 217, and consult your lawyer if you believe the period has elapsed. In other words, even though your contract with the man who was to build your house was valid and signed and witnessed, and even though the builder never even broke ground on your property and thus was guilty of total breach of your contract—if you have waited more than six years to bring your lawsuit against him, he has an effective defense against you. This same sort of defense may take other forms, but the principle remains: you may not "sleep on your rights," or you will lose them.

b. *Misleading conduct.* Your own conduct may contribute to depriving you of your right to sue for breach of contract. For example, if the same builder knew that your wife had died after the contract was entered into and that you had moved to Florida where you had bought a house and settled down to live, you might well be regarded as *estopped,* or prevented, by your own actions from enforcing the original building contract. You should have told him that you were just going away for a time and fully intended to return and live in the house when he finished building it, as you expected him to do under the contract.

c. *Misunderstanding and mistake.* A misunderstanding or mistake by both parties will also serve as an effective defense in an action for breach of contract, because it means there was no real meeting of the minds in the first place, and without a meeting of the minds, there is no contract (see section 174). Say that you own two cars—a four-year-old station wagon and a late-model compact. You tell a friend that you will sell him your "second car" for $1,000 and he accepts the offer and pays you $100 down on the transaction. But he thought you were offering to sell the compact, whereas you meant to sell the station wagon. A suit to enforce the agreement by either one of you against the other would be subject to the defense of mutual mistake. Assuming the facts are this simple, the contract will not be enforced.

You cannot expect to take advantage of a mistake made by someone else in order to get the better of him. If you are an automobile salesman and receive a telegram from an old customer offering to buy for his teen-age son a ten-year-old used Cadillac for $10,000, you would not be able to enforce the "contract" against him by sending him a telegram saying, "Your offer accepted." No ten-year-old Cadillac is worth $10,000; $1,000 might be a fair, reasonable price. You may not hold him to the price that is clearly the mistake of the telegraph company.

Usually the mistake that enables you or the other party to avoid the contract must concern the subject matter of the contract itself (the two different cars) or the nature of the agreement (you think you are contracting to buy a house, but the other party thinks the agreement is only to rent it) or the identity of the parties (you and your son have identical names, and the seller of a piece of real estate thinks you are the buyer, whereas in reality it is your son). Where the mistake is real, and not an excuse for nonperformance or the result of carelessness, the court will usually permit the contract to be canceled.

214

d. *Fraud.* If your contract is the result of fraud, it is unenforceable. An antique dealer persuades you to buy a chest of drawers by telling you that it is Early American in manufacture, when in fact it was produced last month in the factory of a clever furniture producer well known for his copies; the dealer will not be able to enforce the contract against you. But be careful that he is not simply *puffing* (see sections 136, 190). If he says that the chest of drawers is one of the finest examples of Early American manufacture, although it is actually an early copy by a manufacturer who died in 1810, the dealer's statement might not be regarded as a real misrepresentation or fraud. A certain amount of "sales talk" is legally permissible in describing an object for sale.

e. *Duress.* The use of force or threats to make either party sign is always a defense to an action for breach of contract. The real estate dealer who forces a homeowner to enter into a contract for the sale of his house for less than its value by threatening to go to the local prosecutor and establish that forty years ago the homeowner was convicted of arson, cannot enforce the contract against him. The homeowner entered into the contract under duress; there was no true meeting of the minds. His assent was forced; his contract will not be.

f. *Inability to perform.* Some contracts may become impossible to perform, and the courts don't try to hold you to the impossible. Let's say you have always wanted to spend the summer on a part of the coast you have known since childhood. You contract to rent a particular cottage overlooking the spot where you learned to swim. Two weeks before the time arrives for you to move in, a tidal wave sweeps ashore and wipes out the cottage. Your contract is unenforceable. It's not the cottage owner's fault that he can't produce the cottage for you. Under such circumstances, there is no remedy for breach of contract: the cottage owner's defense of impossibility of performance will be upheld by the courts. He must, however, return any rent you have paid.

g. *Failure of consideration.* As we have already suggested (see section 182), failure of consideration is a valid defense to an action for breach of contract. Remember that there is no contract without consideration: an undertaking by one person to support another's promise. If the consideration fails, the contract "fails," that is, it cannot be enforced.

Suppose you and your neighbor agree that in consideration of his putting up a fence between your property and his, you will mow his lawn with your new and highly efficient power mower. If by July 1 he has done nothing to show he means to build the fence, you are entitled to hold off when he asks you to start to work on his lawn. If he continues to delay doing anything, you had better delay also. If by August 1 he has still done nothing, you are probably correct to mow your lawn only and forget his. Your promise to mow his lawn was clearly contingent upon his commitment to put up the fence. His failure to carry out his part of the bargain is a *failure of consideration,* excusing you from carrying out your obligation under the contract.

But you would be wise to say or do something that indicated your willingness to carry out your part of the contract: to tell him that you're just waiting for him to start building the fence before you start cutting his lawn. Don't put yourself in the position of not being willing, able and ready to perform your part of the bargain; otherwise he may accuse you of failure of consideration. Remember that his and your undertakings are mutual and support each other: the failure of one, without an adequate explanation, excuses the failure of the other.

h. *Illegality of the contract.* The last and in a way the most obvious defense to an action for breach of contract is illegality of the subject matter or the thing to be performed. If the contract is illegal, it cannot be enforced. That statement is simple, and most cases of illegality are simple. A contract to operate a gambling syndicate is illegal. A contract to sell narcotics to schoolchildren (or to adults, for that matter) is illegal. A contract to pay someone to testify falsely in court (with the fancy name, *subornation of perjury*) is illegal. A contract to lend money at an interest rate higher than the laws of your state allow (see section 454) is usurious, hence illegal.

Not all cases are so simple. What about a contract that was legal when you entered into it, but has since become illegal? For example, you inherit twelve acres of land and you can't afford the taxes. So you enter into a contract with a builder under which you agree to sell him half the property, six acres, so that he can put up three houses, the final price to be paid after the sale of the houses. The buyer understands that the zoning regulations as then in effect require that only one house can be built on any two-acre lot. In other words, he is assured that the community will continue to have "two-acre zoning." He starts to build three houses. But as construction is well under way, the local office of a national civil rights group wins a case in the highest court of your state establishing that such zoning is discriminatory. Now you have a very different situation. Your contract with the builder becomes unenforceable, despite good faith on both sides. You had better consult a lawyer, in this and any similar case in which the "ground rules" change between the time you enter into the contract and the time of its performance.

LIMITATIONS OF SUITS FOR BREACH OF CONTRACT

You may sue for breach of contract only during a limited period of years after the contract has been breached (see section 185). These legal limitations are shown below. They do not apply to contracts for the sale of goods (for these see chart 6, page 124).

CHART 10	Limitations in Years				Limitations in Years		
	Oral	Written	Sealed[1]		Oral	Written	Sealed[1]
				MISSOURI	5	10	10
ALABAMA	6	6	10	MONTANA	5	8	8
ALASKA	6	6	10	NEBRASKA	4	5	5
ARIZONA	3	6[2]	6[2]	NEVADA	4	6	6
ARKANSAS	3	5	5	NEW HAMPSHIRE	6	6	20
CALIFORNIA	2	4	4	NEW JERSEY	6	6	16
COLORADO	3 or 6[3]	3 or 6[3]	3 or 6[3]	NEW MEXICO	4	6	6
CONNECTICUT	3	6	6	NEW YORK	6	6	6
DELAWARE	3	3	3	NORTH CAROLINA	3	3	10
D.C.	3	3	12	NORTH DAKOTA	6	6	6
FLORIDA	4	5	5	OHIO	6	15	15
GEORGIA	4	6	20	OKLAHOMA	3	5	5
HAWAII	6	6	6	OREGON	6	6	6[4]
IDAHO	4	5	5	PENNSYLVANIA	6	6	20
ILLINOIS	5	10	10	RHODE ISLAND	6	6	20
INDIANA	6	10	10	SOUTH CAROLINA	6	6	20
IOWA	5	10	10	SOUTH DAKOTA	6	6	20
KANSAS	3	5	5	TENNESSEE	6	6	6
KENTUCKY	5	15	15	TEXAS	2	4	4
LOUISIANA	10	10	10	UTAH	4	6	6
MAINE	6	6	20	VERMONT	6	6	8
MARYLAND	3	3	12	VIRGINIA	3	5	10
MASSACHUSETTS	6	6	20	WASHINGTON	3	6	6
MICHIGAN	6	6	6	WEST VIRGINIA	5	10	10
MINNESOTA	6	6	6	WISCONSIN	6	6	20
MISSISSIPPI	3	6	6	WYOMING	8	10	10

(1) A sealed contract, considered more formal than an ordinary written contract, is impressed with a seal at the time it is executed.

(2) The limit is 4 years on written contracts executed outside the state.

(3) Depending on the terms of the contract.

(4) The limit is 10 years for sealed instruments entered before August 13, 1965.

217

SALE AND PURCHASE OF GOODS

186. When You Buy or Sell • A sale or a purchase is a contract. The law of sales, therefore, is governed by many of the principles of the law of contracts, as modified by two statutes. The first was the Uniform Sales Act. The second, under which we operate today, is the Uniform Commercial Code, which has been adopted in all states—although not uniformly, despite its name. You should check the statute in your state whenever you have a question regarding a transaction under the code.

Just as with any other contract, the following characteristics are essential for a purchase or sale to be legal: (a) there must be mutual assent, resulting from an offer and an acceptance of that offer (see section 174) communicated to the person who made the offer; (b) the parties to the contract must be legally competent (see section 176); (c) there must be consideration (see section 175); and (d) the subject matter of the contract must be legal (see section 178). If any of these aspects of the contract is lacking, the purchase or sale is unenforceable in court.

When you go into a store and ask the clerk for a book you want to buy, when you order the book by phone or when you place a written order and the order is accepted, a *contract of sale* comes into being. But when you go to an automobile showroom and place an order for a particular model, of a particular color, that the dealer doesn't have on hand but agrees to get for you, you must sign a contract to buy.

Check the statute in your state to learn whether the contract you plan to enter into must be in writing: the answer depends on the value of what you are buying. If the value exceeds $500 (see chart 9), the contract must be in writing to be enforced in court. A sales slip or a receipt will serve for many purposes, but if you are buying something of considerable value you would be wise to insist upon a more formal contract that spells out exactly what you're buying, the price, when the price is to be paid and when delivery is to be made.

187. Who Has Title or Ownership • What is important to you in the typical sale or purchase situation is the moment when the merchandise becomes yours—"when title passes," as the courts say. The reason is that until the merchandise is yours the seller normally bears the loss if anything happens to it. The intent of the buyer and seller is not always easy to discover, and the following seven rules under the old Uniform

Sales Act are mentioned only as a guide. If a serious question of owner-ship arises, consult a lawyer to find out which of these rules are retained in the Uniform Commercial Code adopted in your state. The Code is generally less concerned than the Uniform Sales Act with technicalities of title.

a. You agree to buy a specific item, such as a lawn mower, from your local dealer, who has it in stock. But you have no place to keep it for a month and leave it in his store. Title passes to you at the time of your agreement, and if the store is destroyed by fire the loss is yours.

b. However, if the lawn mower you are buying is secondhand and repairs are required to put it into working condition, the dealer retains title and he suffers the loss if his store is destroyed before he has finished making the repairs.

c. If the dealer gives you the option of returning the lawn mower after a week's trial instead of paying for it, you get title to the lawn mower when it's delivered to you. While you have the mower on trial the loss is yours if it is stolen. But if you decide you don't like the machine and return it within the week (or, if no time was specified as the trial period, within a reasonable time), title passes back to the dealer and loss there-after is borne by him.

d. If your agreement with the dealer is for him to deliver to you the lawn mower on approval, title passes to you only when you indicate your approval or when you retain the mower beyond a reasonable time with-out giving notice of your rejection.

e. If you go to a lumberyard and place an order for a definite number of square feet of lumber of a specified kind, which you are to pick up at the yard yourself and take home in your station wagon, the lumber thus described is said to be unconditionally appropriated to the contract and title then and there passes to you. If the yard burns up that night, the loss of the value of your lumber is yours.

f. If the lumberyard is on the other side of town from your home and the owner agrees to deliver the lumber to your house or pay the cost of transportation to your house, title does not pass to you until the lumber has actually been delivered to you.

g. If you are a dealer in flowers and garden products and you place a firm offer for 1,000 tulip bulbs to be shipped to you by an airline you specify, title passes to you as soon as the bulbs are delivered to that airline.

188. Methods of Shipment and Liability for Loss • In dealing with shipments of goods before and after purchase, you will want to understand some of the language used to identify different kinds of shipping arrangements between the parties. These arrangements are often expressed by initials.

Most familiar to us is a c.o.d. shipment. You go to a department store and order a new sofa for your living room. You don't have a charge account at the store, so you arrange for a "collect on delivery" shipment. You pay no money at the store, but the department store's delivery man is instructed not to deliver the sofa into your house unless you pay him when he arrives, usually in cash, although these days he might be authorized to accept your check. But if the delivery truck has an accident on the way to your home and the sofa is smashed, the loss is yours (see rule (a) in section 187).

If you order an automobile from a distant factory, in this country or overseas, two methods of payment are used, each with a different legal significance as far as risk of loss is concerned. The document generally used in connection with the shipment is called a *bill of lading,* which simply embodies the instructions given by the shipper to the shipping company or the railroad—the common carrier. The bill of lading is a receipt given by the carrier to the shipper. It is also a contract between the shipper and the carrier covering the terms of the transportation. A copy is sent to the buyer, and it is hence an indication of ownership: the person who presents it at the place of delivery is entitled to receive the shipment.

Your contract with the manufacturer or seller may be f.o.b. (free on board) or f.a.s. (free alongside ship). Under such a contract you, as the buyer, obtain title when the seller delivers your automobile to the railroad or ship. If the Modern Motor Company, which has its factory in Detroit, contracts to sell you one of its cars f.o.b. Detroit, title to the car passes to you when the car is delivered to the railroad freight yard at Detroit. Any damage to the car while it is being shipped to you is your problem, not the Modern Motor Company's.

But if you live in Lincoln, Nebraska, and order an automobile from a European manufacturer and the contract reads "c.i.f. Lincoln" (*c.i.f.* means cost, insurance and freight), the manufacturer must deliver the car to the carrier and pay the freight to the point of destination, in this case Lincoln. He must send you the invoice or contract, an insurance policy covering the entire shipment, the bill of lading and a receipt showing that the freight was paid. Title passes to you only when the manufacturer has done all these things.

189. What Happens If the Seller Doesn't Own the Goods He Sells You • Generally speaking, a seller cannot pass on better title than he has. A thief cannot pass on good legal title to the watch he stole from you. If you find the watch in someone else's possession, you have the right to demand its return. The courts will order its return to you, even if the person who bought from the thief acted in complete good faith. Such a buyer is called an *innocent purchaser for value*. His only remedy would be to sue the thief for the price of the watch—if he could find him.

But suppose you are in the business of selling cosmetics through salesmen around the country, keeping your company's name a secret because you went through bankruptcy some time ago and the fact, if known, might lead potential buyers to avoid your line. You have "clothed" your salesmen with apparent authority to sell the cosmetics in their possession, and if they make contracts that you don't like or that violate their agreements with you, you cannot assert your right to reclaim the cosmetics from a purchaser who bought from them in good faith. (You'll read more about such a situation in sections 393, 394.)

190. What Happens If the Goods You Buy Are of Poor Quality • A question that is being discussed more and more these days is that of your rights and remedies as a buyer of goods that turn out to be sleazy, dangerous or, at the very least, not what you thought they were when you bought them. When you enter into any contract you and the other party have a duty to perform according to the understanding, express or implied, between you. These undertakings regarding quality of the merchandise being bought or sold are called *warranties*. The air-conditioner you buy carries a warranty to cool the air in your room, and if it doesn't you have an action against the seller for breach of warranty.

But be careful. Every salesman is entitled to and should be expected to build up his product, to exaggerate its qualities. Such overemphasis of the good points is called *puffing,* and mere puffing does not constitute a warranty. If the shoes you buy are advertised as comfortable and long-lasting, you have no action for breach of warranty if you don't like the way they feel and they give signs of wearing out after a year's time. Nor would you have an action against the real estate agent who, when he sells you a house, says it has a clear, fine view of the ocean, though the stretch of land where the house is located is misty and foggy a great many days of the year. Such statements by sellers are merely exaggerations, which you should learn to take with a grain of salt and to protect yourself against by making reasonable inquiries (see sections 49, 136, 277).

Also remember that to succeed in a suit for breach of warranty you must do more than prove that you personally were not satisfied with the performance of the product you bought. You must prove that the product did not do what it was supposed to do to the satisfaction of an average, reasonable person. You might have had special needs in mind that the warranty was never supposed to cover.

Warranties are either express or implied. The seller of a sweater labeled "pure cashmere" has made an *express warranty* that in fact the sweater is cashmere. You have the following choices if you buy it and later find it is not cashmere at all: you may (a) return the sweater and sue the seller for the purchase price, (b) keep the sweater and sue for breach of warranty for the difference between what you paid for the sweater and what it is actually worth or (c) refuse to accept the sweater on delivery to you and sue for breach of warranty.

Other express warranties are equally simple: you buy an electric can opener that the seller says will operate on either direct current or alternating current, but when you plug it into the old-fashioned direct current electrical system in your apartment it burns out. This is a clear breach of an express warranty. An express warranty can be either written or oral.

Implied warranties, on the other hand, are ones the law implies for the sake of society. Although the courts were groping toward the imposition of implied warranties in the process of modernizing old legal doctrines like caveat emptor, or "Let the buyer beware" (see sections 68, 69), they did not move fast enough to protect masses of consumers in our increasingly intricate economy. The old legal theory that there had to be some kind of a contractual relationship to permit recovery for breach of an implied warranty of quality has largely been replaced by legislation that gives more protection to the consumer. Today if you buy a can of spoiled vegetables that make you ill, you have a legal action against the manufacturer. The law implies a warranty of quality: that what you buy is reasonably fit for the purpose for which it was sold (that the vegetables are fit to eat) and that what you buy is of salable quality.

These implied warranties and others we'll mention later were set forth in the Uniform Sales Act and, generally speaking, are carried over into the Uniform Commercial Code (see section 186). Every sale, the code says, implies the following kinds of warranties: (a) that the seller has the legal right to sell the goods to you and that you will have the exclusive possession of what you buy—that no one else has any lien or charge against the goods, (b) that the goods are fit for the purpose you and he had in mind in making the sale and (c) that if you ordered from a sample or a description, what you will receive is like the sample or is as it was described to you.

191. Mail Order and Door-to-Door Sales • When you order merchandise by mail, it is important that what you receive is what you ordered from the description in the catalog or, if you placed your order on the basis of a sample of a material sent with the mailed advertisement, that what you receive is actually made from the same material. If the merchandise you are sent does not conform to what you ordered by description or by sample, there has been a breach of an implied warranty.

These same considerations apply to sales made by door-to-door salesmen. These men represent the manufacturer directly, whether they are his employes or individuals acting as his agents. Statements they make about their products—statements that aren't just puffing—are made with the manufacturer's apparent authority, and you may sue the manufacturer for breach of warranty in sales by door-to-door salesmen just as readily as for breach of warranty in sales by salesmen in a store.

192. Injury from Defective Products • When the product you receive turns out to be not only of a different quality from what you ordered but actually harmful, you may have an additional action in tort (see sections 68, 69). There are many court decisions awarding money damages to buyers who, for example, found thumbtacks in their piece of pie or were injured by exploding soft drink bottles. The courts today are determined to protect the consumer by one method or another: they will entertain lawsuits against a person or corporation that they assume has some responsibility for injuries caused by defective merchandise, whether it's the storekeeper seller, the restaurant owner or the manufacturer who produced whatever caused the injury.

The principle that someone is responsible has won wide acceptance, first in torts and now increasingly in sales. You have a right, assuming you exercise reasonable sense and care, to be free from loss or harm suffered from the purchase of defective merchandise; and the courts will protect that right, awarding you damages from the seller or the manufacturer, whichever seems most equitable.

193. Installment or Time or Credit Sales • Recent years have seen an extraordinary growth in the use of means other than cash for paying for purchases of all kinds. Some economists even believe that cash will gradually disappear. So it is useful to know some of the legal considerations involved in the use of credit. Different legal instruments have been designed for credit sales.

Perhaps the earliest was the *chattel loan,* formerly called a chattel mortgage. When you buy a new car with money borrowed from a bank or the dealer's credit organization, you receive a bill of sale and a certificate of title for the car, but you sign a chattel loan (sometimes called a "leasing security agreement" or a "conditional sales agreement"), which designates the car as security for the debt. You take the vehicle home and use it just as though you had paid for it in full; it is as much your property as your mortgaged house.

If he wishes, the dealer may take the chattel loan down to the county clerk's office and record it for his own protection. In fact, this is seldom done today. But if the dealer did record the loan and you subsequently sold the automobile to a neighbor before paying off your debt to the dealer, the new buyer would not have any better title to it than you had. If the dealer then repossessed the vehicle from him the buyer might sue you for damages for what he had paid you for it. For more information on chattel loans, see section 452.

More frequently used today is the *conditional,* or *installment,* sale. Many of us are familiar with it because we use it when buying appliances. You buy an electric dishwasher for $400, paying $100 in cash and signing an installment, or conditional, sales agreement in which you promise to pay the dealer the $300 balance in twelve equal monthly installments. The agreement says that the dealer legally owns the dishwasher until you have paid the full $400, even though you have full use and possession of it. To protect himself the dealer will have the conditional sales agreement recorded by the appropriate public official —then his ownership also is "good against the world." Furthermore, and most important, the installment, or conditional, sales agreement usually provides that the dealer may repossess the dishwasher from you if you fail to keep up your agreed monthly payments.

Legal rights in credit sales is a complicated subject that you should discuss with your lawyer if you are about to enter into any important sales transaction involving the use of credit. One important aspect of this whole matter of installment or time or conditional sales, the interest you pay on what you borrow, is separately considered in section 454.

194. Legal Remedies of the Buyer • Because a contract of sale and a contract to sell resemble other contracts, the remedies available to both sides for nonperformance are similar to the usual remedies for breach of contract (section 184). If the seller fails or refuses to deliver the merchandise you have contracted to buy, you have an action against him for nondelivery—for damages for breach of contract.

Ordinarily your damages will be the amount of the loss you suffered because of the seller's breach of contract. Let's say you have a contract with the Fit-Tight Necktie Company to buy 1,000 neckties at $1 each, which you then plan to stamp with your novel design and sell to the Fascinating Neck Decoration Company for $5 a tie. But Fit-Tight doesn't perform and you have to pay the Men's Beautifying Company $2 a tie in order to comply with your contract with Fascinating Neck Decoration Company. You have suffered a loss of $1,000, and that $1,000 could be the amount of your damages.

Under some circumstances you as a buyer may be entitled to *specific performance*—that is, delivery to you by the seller of the exact thing you had contracted to buy. For example, you collect rare stones and enter into a contract with a dealer to buy a particular stone at a particular price. He refuses to perform his part of the contract because someone offers him a higher price than you did. You may then have an action for the specific performance of his contract with you. If you are successful, the court will issue an order directing him to sell that particular stone to you for the price you and he agreed upon.

But in some situations an action to *rescind* the contract may be better for you. If the seller of the rare stone doesn't perform, and you find you can buy a similar stone for a lesser price than you had thought possible, it might be well to treat the contract with him as rescinded. A rescission would also be available if you found that the original seller had lied to you about the kind of stone you thought you were buying. When you sue to rescind the contract, your aim is to have the contract set aside and any money you have paid returned to you, so that you are in the same position as you would have been if the contract never existed. You may also try to collect damages for any wrong done to you by the seller in improperly inducing you to enter into the contract in the first place.

Another remedy you may have, when title to the goods has already passed to you but the seller refuses to deliver, is a suit for *conversion,* the wrongful withholding or use of your property. You may even use a very old legal remedy called *replevin,* an action to recover possession.

For a breach of warranty by the seller you have a choice of remedies: (a) You may keep the goods and sue the seller for damages for breach of warranty, or return them and decline to pay the price if you have not already paid it. (b) If title to the goods hasn't already passed, you may refuse to accept them and sue for breach of warranty. (c) You may rescind the contract and decline to accept the goods, or if they've been accepted, you may return them or offer to return them and recover the price or any part of it that you've paid.

195. Legal Remedies of the Seller • If the buyer refuses to pay the agreed purchase price, the seller has several courses of action available. The choice of one or another remedy depends on the circumstances in each case, especially on such questions as who has possession of the merchandise and who has title to it.

If a customer whom you know comes into your store, buys $50 worth of merchandise and takes it with him, asking you to send him a bill, you have made a very common kind of credit sale. Title or ownership of the merchandise passed to the customer: you surrendered title in consideration of his implied promise to pay you the $50 purchase price within a reasonable time. Should the buyer fail to pay after you have sent him a bill, you have an action against him for damages for breach of contract, in this case $50. The law tries only to put you in the same position you would have been in if the buyer had fulfilled his contract.

As another example, suppose your business is raising beef cattle, and your buyer agrees to buy ten steers at a price of $1,000 each, but for some reason he refuses to accept the steers when you're ready to deliver them to him. You then have to sell the steers at $500 each because that's the best price you can get. Your damage award in a successful action for breach of contract would be $5,000. Keep in mind that even though a buyer defaults on a contract and becomes liable for damages, the seller has a legal obligation to keep the damages down—to *mitigate* them, as lawyers say. Merely because the buyer who contracted to buy your steers for $1,000 each defaults, you do not have the right to neglect them until they die and then to sue him for the full contract price of $10,000.

Of course the seller has the same right as the buyer to rescind the contract (see section 194). If you have a contract to sell the vegetables you grow in your garden to a canning company in another state, and you ship $1,000 worth to the company by rail only to learn that the company has gone broke and is both unable and unwilling to pay you, you may stop the goods in transit. You notify the railroad company that you are rescinding the contract with the buyer and order the vegetables returned to your possession. Again, you must resell them at the best price you can get and try to recover the difference in a legal action against your original buyer. If the vegetables have become unsalable because of the shipping back and forth, you might be able to recover the full contract price.

196. Government Protection of Consumers • Today unscrupulous manufacturers, dealers and salesmen are being held responsible by statute for a wide variety of conduct for which there previously were few legal remedies, and those remedies that did exist were too expensive to aid the consumer. As we have stressed elsewhere (see section 75), going to court is a very expensive way of asserting your rights. The ghetto resident whose meat store sells him "hamburger" meat that is one quarter bread or stuffing can't afford to sue the store owner. Nor can he afford to sue the department store that sells him a "genuine horsehair" sofa cushion that in reality is stuffed with excelsior.

In recent years, therefore, the government has stepped in to help the consumer. Statutes have been adopted that impose penalties and fines for false and misleading advertising and for falsely labeling merchandise. Federal, state and local agencies have been established to enforce these laws and, from a number of individual citizen complaints, to detect new patterns of consumer-damaging practices by manufacturers and merchants, and to take action to stop these practices. In some areas officials have been appointed, at senior levels of government, to serve as *ombudsmen,* who receive complaints from the public and investigate them.

Both the United States government and the governments of several states have consumer protection bureaus for just such purposes. They work with older, established offices and agencies such as the Federal Trade Commission, which is concerned with business practices of all kinds; the Food and Drug Administration, which is responsible for licensing the sale of certain new drugs and making sure that harmful foods are not sold and that the advertising of food and drugs is reasonably honest and true; the Post Office Department, which tries to prevent the use of the mails to defraud innocent people by schemes to get their money in illegal promotions; and, of course, the Department of Justice in Washington and the attorneys general of the various states, which work to step up and intensify enforcement of all kinds of laws. Ask your congressman what consumer protection offices are available in your state. Remember that these new offices exist to control and stop undesirable and unfair actions by manufacturers and sellers.

But these offices are no substitute for traditional legal weapons available to you if you believe a serious wrong has been done that has caused

227

you substantial damage. By all means register your complaint with a consumer protection bureau to put an end to a false advertising campaign, but be aware that the bureau is concerned only with the present and the future—not with the damages you have suffered as a result of something that has already taken place. For financial relief you will have to sue. Consult your lawyer to determine whether you have a basis for legal action.

Use and Protection of Property You Entrust to Others

197. What a Bailment Is · A *bailment* is a delivery of personal property to another person for a specific purpose, under an express or implied contract (see section 169) that when that purpose has been achieved the property will be restored to the person who delivered it. The *bailor* is the one who delivers the property; the *bailee* is the one to whom it is delivered.

The number and variety of bailments in our everyday lives are enormous. When you lend your lawn mower to your neighbor to cut his lawn, leave your watch to be repaired, send your shirts to the laundry to be washed, check your hat and coat in a restaurant, place your furniture in storage, board your dog or turn over your securities as collateral for a loan, you have in each case created a bailment.

There are certain general rules that cover your rights in almost every conceivable bailment situation. They are:

a. The bailee does not own the property entrusted to him. Only possession of the property is transferred, and possession reverts to the owner when the purpose of the transfer is fulfilled.

b. The bailee may not use the goods without permission or in a manner of which the owner would not approve.

c. The bailee may not dispose of the goods without the owner's permission, unless the owner fails to fulfill the terms of the contract despite having received a warning notice.

d. The bailee must be warned of hidden defects in or dangerous characteristics of the property, known to the bailor, that might cause personal injury or property damage.

e. The bailee must take reasonable care of the property in order to keep it in good condition, such as oiling machinery, keeping boats watertight while afloat and feeding animals entrusted to his care.

f. The bailee may be liable for loss of or damage to property caused by his own negligence, depending on the circumstances under which it came into his keeping, as explained below.

g. However, the bailee is generally not liable for loss of or damage to property due to forces beyond his control, including the negligence of others; "acts of God," such as floods or tornadoes; acts of public enemies, such as strikes and riots; or seizure of the property by the government.

h. But the bailee is nearly always liable for loss of or damage to the bailed property, whatever the cause, if the mishap occurs while he is using the property without the owner's authorization.

i. The bailee must return the exact article he received, unless the agreement calls for him to change the form of the property (as when a garment is left with the tailor to be altered) or unless the goods are *fungible,* that is, of a nature that makes it impossible to distinguish them from other similar goods (as when a neighbor returns a pound of sugar which is not the identical sugar she borrowed).

198. Conversion · *Conversion* is the wrongful use or the wrongful taking of personal property that has been entrusted to you. A bailee may be charged with the civil wrong of conversion if he violates the rules governing entrusted personal property, described in the sections above and below. An analysis of conversion and the property owner's legal recourse against the convertor are presented in sections 47, 71.

199. Responsibility for Loaned or Borrowed Personal Property · Where no payment or other consideration is offered or expected, a promise to lend personal property is not enforceable (section 175). Once the property is in the possession of the borrower, however, a contractual relationship is established in which the rights and obligations of the parties are as follows:

a. If you lend personal property for your benefit, as when you turn your lawn mower over to a neighbor who offers to repair it for you free, he is legally bound to fulfill his promise and you may sue him if he fails to do so. He is not allowed to use the property without your permission. He is not responsible for damage or loss if he guards it with reasonable care. However, if he is guilty of gross negligence (see sections 57, 58), such as leaving the lawn mower on the curb overnight, he may be liable for any damage or loss that results.

229

b. If you borrow personal property for your own benefit, you may use it only for the purpose for which it was loaned. Thus, if a neighbor lends you his car for an hour to drive your children to school, he can charge you with conversion (see section 47) if you drive it elsewhere or lend it to a third party without his permission.

You must also exercise scrupulous care, not just reasonable care, in using and guarding the borrowed property. If you fail to do so, you are fully liable for any damage or loss attributable to your negligence (see section 71).

You are also liable for loss or damage, whatever the cause, if it occurs while you are using the borrowed property in a manner not authorized by the owner. Thus, if you drive the borrowed car to the beach without the owner's permission and it is struck by a runaway truck or overturned by rioters, you must pay for the damage even though you were powerless to avoid the disaster.

200. Responsibility for Rented or Leased Personal Property • (Liability for accidents in rented automobiles is discussed in section 252.) As in the case of goods offered for sale, goods offered for rent carry with them express or implied warranties (see section 190) that they are fit for the use for which they were intended. If the goods are defective, the owner is responsible for all personal injury or property damage they may cause, unless he can prove that the defect was created by the user's negligence.

Unless there is some other agreement the bailor (owner) is also responsible for major repairs that become necessary during the rental, or bailment, period, such as repair of defective brakes, fuel pumps and engines, but the bailee (renter) may be responsible for minor repairs, such as fixing a flat tire.

Again, unless the rental contract specifies otherwise, the bailee is liable for any damage or loss to the rented property caused by his negligence, as well as for any personal injuries or property damage he may inflict on others through his negligent use of the rented property. Because of this it is wise to discuss liability insurance coverage with a car rental firm or similar company before you rent.

201. Responsibility for Property Left for Cleaning, Alteration or Repair • A bailee who accepts personal property for servicing in return for a charge has entered into a contract that may be enforced against him if he fails to perform the cleaning, alterations, repairs or whatever

230

else he promised to do to the goods (see sections 390, 391). The bailee must use reasonable care in handling the goods.

However, the bailee's acceptance of the goods is no guarantee as to the quality of the work he performs. If the job has been so ineptly done as to constitute an obvious breach of contract—for example, your shirts are returned from the laundry with the grime still in the collars or your watch still doesn't run after the watchmaker repairs it—you have a right to demand that the work be redone properly, to refuse to pay for it or to demand the return of your money if you have already paid. But if the work has simply been done badly—the ironed shirts have wrinkles in them or the repaired watch doesn't keep perfect time—you have very little claim against the bailee.

Under the principle of caveat emptor ("Let the buyer beware"; see sections 68, 190) the burden of selecting a competent workman falls on the customer, and if he turns out to be a bungler there is little you can do about it legally. Your best protection, then, is the bailee's hoped-for desire to do a good job in order to keep your business.

If a bailee fails to complete the work on your property by the time promised—as when a cleaner fails to return in time a dress promised for a special occasion or the mechanic has not repaired your crippled car by the day you have to start your trip—all you can do is to sue for breach of the bailment contract. Unless you can show that his breach has seriously injured you or that it was clearly understood between you that timely performance was an essential part of the contract, your damages are likely to be nominal.

If you fail to pay for work done to your personal property when the job is completed, the bailee may refuse to surrender it, holding it under a workmen's or artisan's lien until payment is made (see section 392). If you still do not pay for the work, the bailee may sell the property to recover the money owed him, returning the surplus to you, minus storage charges, interest on the debt and the costs of the sale.

The bailee must exercise ordinary care to safeguard the entrusted property, and is liable for theft, fire or other damage due to his negligence, even if the contract specifically states that he will not be responsible for such mishaps. However, he may limit his liability to a specific sum for each article by posting a notice to that effect on the wall of his shop or by printing it on the receipt or claim check he gives you. If the article is destroyed because of the bailee's negligence, he is not obliged to pay you more than its fair value, as of the time and in the condition received, or more than the maximum price established in your contract.

202. Responsibility for Property Left in Checkrooms and Public Places • A *public place* is a store, theater, restaurant, meeting hall, sports arena, school or any other place to which the public is admitted. The owners or operators of a public place will be held liable for the loss or damage to property entrusted, or *bailed,* to them if they fail to take reasonable precautions, many of which are prescribed by law, to protect the property of their patrons from physical harm caused by fires, moving objects and structural defects that might cause the collapse of floors, staircases and the like, and to safeguard the property from the depredations of thieves, pickpockets, drunkards and unruly persons.

But if reasonable precautions are taken and the statutory requirements met, the management is not responsible for loss of personal property, whether or not attributable to the negligence of the owner or his employes. Thus, if you leave your handbag on a theater seat during intermission, or hang your coat on a hook in a restaurant, you have no claim against the management if it is stolen, even if a theater usher had promised to keep an eye on the handbag or a waiter helped you off with your coat and hung it up for you.

If you leave your personal property in a checkroom in a public place and receive a claim check for it, the management or the checkroom operators are liable for loss or damage to it.

203. Responsibility for Property Left in Storage or Safekeeping • The rules are much the same whether or not the bailee is paid for his services in the storing or safekeeping of goods. Unless the storage or safeguarding agreement specifies otherwise, the bailee may not use the goods without the bailor's permission, except where such use is necessary under the circumstances of the bailment: as when an attendant at a commercial parking lot drives your car from one space to another in order to let another car out.

The bailee must exercise reasonable care in protecting your property, which allows the parking lot attendant to douse your engine if it starts smoking, or a boarding kennel to call a veterinarian if your dog suddenly becomes ill.

The bailee is responsible for any damage or loss to stored property caused by his negligence, even when the storage receipt or contract states (usually in very small print) that he is relieved of such liability. But the bailee is not responsible for damage arising from such causes as floods, arson and riots that occurred despite the reasonable care he exercised.

The bailor has an obligation to inform the bailee of any danger inherent in the property left in storage or safekeeping, and if he neglects to do so he may be liable for any personal injury or property damage that results. Thus, if you forget to tell the kennel keeper that your dog is vicious or the furniture warehouse that there is a loaded revolver in your desk drawer, you may be liable if the dog bites or the gun goes off.

If personal property is being stored or taken care of without cost, the bailee need keep it only a reasonable time when no time limit has been agreed upon. If a time limit has been agreed upon and the bailor fails to show up by the termination date, the bailee's only obligation is to keep the property for a reasonable time thereafter. After giving notice to the bailor, he may then sell it and send the bailor the fair value of the property, or hold it for him if he has lost the bailor's address.

204. Responsibility for Property in Transit · If personal property is transported as a favor, without cost, as when a friend agrees to transport your dog or desk in his station wagon, the rules of performance and liability are practically identical with those that apply to personal property loaned for the benefit of the lender (see section 199). The transporter must carry out his agreement once he accepts the property, but he is not responsible for any damage that befalls it, unless he handles it with gross negligence. If the property presents a hazard unknown to the transporter —if the dog has a tendency to bite or the desk has a loose leg—the shipper, if he failed to give prior warning to the transporter, is responsible for any personal injury or property damage that may result.

If personal property is carried for a fee by a *private carrier*—that is, an individual or company who is not in the transportation business but who contracts to carry the goods in this particular instance—the carrier's liabilities are much the same as those of a bailee who stores goods (see section 203). He is liable only for damage or loss that results from his negligence or from his failure to use reasonable care in the performance of his task.

If personal property is carried for a fee by a *common carrier*—a railroad, airline, trucking company or shipping line, whose business it is to transport goods for anyone who hires it—the carrier is responsible under all circumstances for loss or damage to the property, as well as for unreasonable delay in delivering it, with two exceptions: (a) The carrier is not liable if the loss, damage or delay was caused by events beyond his control, such as floods, tornadoes, fire caused by lightning, snowstorms that block roads and airports, riots, strikes or seizure by the government. (b) Nor is the carrier responsible if the damage or loss is caused by the

BAILMENTS—WHEN YOU
ENTRUST YOUR PROPERTY TO OTHERS

When you lend your property to a friend or neighbor or leave it with someone to be repaired, cleaned or stored, you create a situation known legally as a bailment. More specifically, a bailment arises any time you deliver your personal property to someone for a particular purpose with the express or implied understanding that once that purpose has been achieved the property will be returned to you. The four examples below illustrate how bailments work in different situations.

If your next door neighbor borrows your lawn mower, he must take reasonable care of it. He must return it to you in the same condition as when you lent it — or reimburse you for any damage. Should he lose it, he must buy you a new one. If, however, you failed to warn him about a loose cutting bar or other dangerous defect, you are liable for any injury he may have sustained as a result.

If you leave your clothes with a dry-cleaner, you expect them to be cleaned and returned to you for a specific price. The cleaner must reimburse you if he damages or loses your clothes. But if you fail to pick up your clothes within a reasonable amount of time—despite several notices from the cleaner—he may have the right to sell or otherwise dispose of them.

If you leave your pet poodle at a kennel for a few days, the owner of the kennel is under an obligation to provide proper care for your dog. You will pay him in return. If he beats or abuses your dog, you may recover damages. If he sells your dog, you may sue for its return. On the other hand, if your dog has a vicious temper—and you forget to warn the kennel owner—you may be liable for any injuries your dog may inflict.

If you place your furniture in storage, the storage company agrees to keep it for a given length of time for a certain price. The company may not use the furniture for its own benefit while it is being stored. When the time expires, the company must return the same items to you in their original condition. If any of the furniture is missing or damaged, you may demand compensation.

shipper's negligence or fraudulent concealment, as when shipped china breaks because it was not packed in proper cushioning material or because it was falsely labeled as unbreakable to obtain a cheaper rate.

A common carrier has a right to know the nature of the goods presented for transportation. It may restrict itself to transporting goods of a certain type, size or weight and may refuse to accept merchandise that is improperly packed or that it considers dangerous or perishable. But within these limitations the carrier may not discriminate. It must accept all goods presented for transportation by anyone, and may be sued for damages for refusal to do so.

A common carrier that transports passengers is obligated to carry a reasonable and specified amount of baggage for each passenger free of charge. However, the carrier is responsible only for the baggage the passenger checks with it and not for the hand luggage carried by the passenger while in transit.

A carrier has a right to set a reasonable limit to the amount of money it will pay for lost or damaged goods under the terms of its contract. It is therefore wise to read the bill of lading (see section 188) or baggage stub you receive when you ship goods or deliver your bags to an airline. If the value of the property exceeds the stated liability limit, it is usually possible to insure the goods for their full value by paying an additional fee. However, the carrier is obligated to pay only the reasonable value of the lost or damaged property and not a higher value that the owner or shipper may have set on it, even if he has paid transportation charges based on a higher declared value. If the shipper suffers a loss because of the carrier's unreasonable delay in delivering goods, the carrier is liable for damages—but the carrier would not be responsible for delays over which he had no control.

If shipped goods are not called for by the shipper or the person to whom they are being sent within a reasonable or specified time after the carrier has notified him of their arrival, the carrier may impose storage charges and ultimately may sell the goods at auction in order to recover expenses incurred.

205. Responsibility for Property of Guests in Hotels • In a few states a hotelkeeper's liability for a guest's luggage and personal property is limited by law. But in most states the hotelkeeper is responsible for all damages, loss or theft of a guest's personal property or money, and must compensate him for its full value, unless the loss was due to an act not caused by the negligence of the hotel.

235

Even in these states, however, the hotel's liability may be limited by contract, if the limitations are brought to the guest's attention by posting them in the hotel register or the hotel rooms and a safe is provided in the hotel office in which the guest may store money, jewelry and other valuables when not in use. Liability for valuables kept in the hotel safe may also be limited to an announced sum, usually $500, unless a higher value is declared by the guest and the hotel agrees to accept the risk before the deposit is made, or unless the hotel has been grossly negligent in guarding the safe and its contents.

If a hotel guest is unable or fails to pay the bill for the room, meals and services rendered to him, the hotel may retain his baggage and other personal property as security for payment of the claim. This *hotelkeeper's lien* covers not only the property fully owned by the delinquent guest but any of his property found in the hotel room, even if not fully paid for.

206. Responsibility for Personal Property Left in Pledge or Pawn • A *pledge* or *pawn* is personal property put in the keeping of a lender as security for a loan of money. The owner may redeem, and the lender is obligated to return, the pledged article at any time during the specified period of the contract, upon payment of the principal and interest. The bailee may not use the property held under lien unless the agreement specifies otherwise; he must take reasonable care of it and is liable for any loss or damage it suffers due to his own negligence.

If the owner of the property fails to redeem the pledge and pay the interest charges when due, the lender may foreclose on his lien and offer the property for sale to satisfy the loan. But unless the agreement provides otherwise, the lender must notify the owner of the time and place of the sale in order to give him an opportunity to buy the property back. If he fails to give such notice the owner may hold him liable for conversion (see section 47) in selling his property without authority.

Laws governing licensed pawnbrokers are generally stricter than those governing others who lend on security. Depending on the statutes of the state in which they operate, they may charge loan interest ranging from 2 percent to 10 percent per month. They are generally required to hold unclaimed property for at least a year. Some states allow the pawnbroker to sell unredeemed property privately, while others require him to offer it at public auction after due notice in the newspapers. In some states surplus proceeds of the sale may be kept by the pawnbroker; in others he must turn the surplus back to the owner after first deducting the unpaid balance of the loan, interest and the costs of sale.

236

CHAPTER SIX

Your Automobile

"The law is a ass, a idiot . . ."

—CHARLES DICKENS

6

Your Automobile

Some Key Points in This Chapter—
Consult these sections for information on:

Charts in This Chapter

Owning an Automobile

An automobile is a very special type of personal property. For most people it is the second largest single investment made in a lifetime, the largest being a home. Automobiles are vital to many people's livelihood and well-being yet at the same time are the greatest single cause of property damage, personal injury and death. Hence their use and misuse bring more people into contact with the law than any other activity.

207. Buying and Selling Automobiles • The laws that govern purchase and sale of automobiles are generally the same as those that apply to the buying and selling of any other type of personal property; these are discussed in sections 186–196. Listed below are the areas in which problems most frequently arise and the sections in which the answers may be found:

a. Purchase of cars by or for minors, sections 176, 336.
b. Installment purchase of cars, section 193.
c. Chattel mortgages on cars, section 208.
d. Getting title to the car you bought or ordered, section 212.
e. Seller's misrepresentation of the condition of the car, section 49.
f. Warranties on new and used cars, sections 215, 216.
g. Sale of mortgaged cars, section 210.
h. Dangers of buying a mortgaged car, section 210.
i. Purchase of stolen cars, section 189.

208. Financing Your Automobile • No matter where you borrow money, you want to pay the lowest possible total interest. The cheapest source is your own savings account, which will cost you substantially less than money borrowed elsewhere—just the interest your money earns at the savings bank.

The next cheapest way is to borrow against your life insurance policies, since you pay a flat rate of interest, usually 5 to 6 percent, which is fixed as of the date of the policy and is payable only on the amount of the loan outstanding. The total interest payment is reduced each time you repay a part of the principal. Such borrowing requires self-discipline, however, since you yourself decide how fast you want to repay the loan. The insurance company imposes no penalty for failure to meet the installments, and you must resist the temptation to skip payments.

239

The most common source of funds for buying an automobile is a commercial bank. The bank gives you a chattel loan on the car—sometimes called a leasing security agreement or a conditional sales agreement (see sections 193, 452)—and usually makes no charges other than interest. The interest is deducted from the face amount of the loan on the entire principal borrowed, with no reduction in the total amount of interest as the money is repaid. Thus, the interest you actually pay is more than it appears to be (see explanation in chapter 10, "Your Money, Credit and Investments," section 454).

In borrowing from an automobile finance company or loan company the procedure is much the same as in dealing with a bank, except that the interest rate is apt to be higher and additional charges may be tacked on. Although such carrying charges are regulated by statute in most states, it is unwise to sign the loan agreement unless you know exactly what the charges represent and how they compare with similar charges by other automobile-financing organizations in your locality.

If you fail to pay the installments to the bank or the finance or loan company on the date due, an additional late charge is exacted. If no payments are made for the period of time specified in the contract, the automobile may be repossessed (see section 193).

209. Keeping Up Payments If Your Car Is Destroyed or Stolen • As explained in section 193, the buyer of goods purchased on installments or under a chattel loan is fully responsible for them, even though he may not yet own them. So you are obliged to continue payments even if your car is destroyed or stolen. You should, therefore, have adequate collision, fire and theft insurance on a car bought on time payments or under a chattel loan, even where state laws do not require it.

210. Selling or Buying a Car on Which Payments Are Still Owed • If you wish to sell a car with a chattel loan on it or on which installment payments have not been completed (see sections 193, 452), you should pay off the loan or remaining installments and obtain a release of lien, because until you do so you do not hold a clear, unencumbered title to the car (see section 187). Or you may get the consent to sell from the bank, company or individual to whom the money is owed. Such consent must be set out in writing, signed by the creditor and made a part of the bill of sale to the buyer, who assumes the unpaid debt.

If you buy a car on which money is owed without getting the consent of the creditor, he may repossess it, paying you the fair value of the car but minus the amount he is owed and the cost of repossession. Your only recourse, in such an event, is to sue the seller for fraud (see section 49) and try to recover the money you paid him. You can sometimes find out whether money is owed on a car from the clerk of the city, town or county in which the seller resides, because chattel loans are often recorded with the clerk's office (see section 452).

211. Required Automobile Insurance • Every state (see chart 16, page 288) has laws that make liability insurance either compulsory or highly advisable (see section 263). Where it is compulsory, failure to carry coverage will result in revocation of your automobile registration. (The insurance company is required to notify the motor vehicle bureau if your policy has lapsed.) In states where insurance is not compulsory, it is still advisable to carry insurance. In those states, if you have an accident and are not insured, you will be required to post a cash bond in court to cover your possible liability.

It should also be noted that insurance companies are often late in notifying the motor vehicle bureau when a policy has lapsed, so you may be exposed to the hazards of uninsured drivers during the interim.

The amount of insurance a car owner may want to have, beyond the minimum amount specified by law, is discussed in section 264. The courses open to an automobile owner who is unable to obtain insurance coverage through normal channels are discussed in section 266.

212. Registration of Automobiles • Forty-nine states (see chart 11, page 242) require you to have a certificate of title as proof of ownership, in order to prevent the sale, purchase, use or operation of stolen vehicles. The certificate usually has on it a description of the vehicle, the name and address of the mortgagee and the date and amount of the mortgage.

When you buy a new automobile, the dealer supplies a manufacturer's certificate of origin, which is the equivalent of a certificate of title. When you buy a used automobile, the certificate of title is assigned to you by the seller and turned over to the state motor vehicle bureau, which issues a new certificate in your name.

Most states require that if you install a new motor in your car, you notify the motor vehicle bureau of the number of the new block, attaching a bill of sale to the notification.

In addition, all states require annual registration of motor vehicles and payment of license fees. In some states the registration certificate must be

OWNERSHIP AND REGISTRATION OF YOUR CAR

CHART 11	Proof of Ownership		Registration	Who Gets License Plates When Car Is Sold?
	Is a Certificate of Title Required?	If So, Who Issues It?	How Long Is Out-of-State Registration Valid?[1]	
ALABAMA	No		30 days	Buyer
ALASKA	Yes	Department of Public Safety, Box 960, Anchorage 99501	90 days or until employment	Buyer
ARIZONA	Yes	Motor Vehicle Division, Department of Transportation, Phoenix 85007	6 months or until employment or school enrollment	Buyer
ARKANSAS	Yes	Motor Vehicle Division, P.O. Box 1272, Little Rock 72203	10 days after employment[2]	Seller
CALIFORNIA	Yes	Department of Motor Vehicles, Sacramento 95806	Until expiration but no more than 1 year	Buyer
COLORADO	Yes	County clerk (in Denver, Motor Vehicle Department)	30 days after employment or establishing residence	Seller
CONNECTICUT	Yes	Commissioner of Motor Vehicles, Wethersfield 06109	60 days after establishing residence	[3]
DELAWARE	Yes	Motor Vehicle Division, Dover 19901	90 days after establishing residence or until employment or school enrollment	Buyer
D.C.	Yes	Bureau of Motor Vehicle Services, Washington, D.C. 20001	Until expiration of reciprocity	Seller
FLORIDA	Yes	Division of Motor Vehicles, Tallahassee 32304	Until 10 days after establishing residence or school enrollment	Seller
GEORGIA	Yes[4]	Motor Vehicle Division, State Department of Revenue, Atlanta 30334	7 days after establishing residence	Buyer
HAWAII	Yes	County treasurer or director of finance	10 days[5]	Buyer
IDAHO	Yes	Motor Vehicle Division, Dept. of Law Enforcement, Boise 83703; county assessor	Until establishing residence	Seller
ILLINOIS	Yes	Secretary of State, Vehicle Services Department, Springfield 62756	Until expiration of reciprocity agreement or establishing residence	Seller
INDIANA	Yes	Bureau of Motor Vehicles, 401 State Office Bldg., Indianapolis 46204	60 days	Seller
IOWA	Yes	County treasurer	90 days or until employment or establishing residence	Buyer
KANSAS	Yes	County treasurer	Staggered system for autos	Seller
KENTUCKY	Yes	County clerk	Until expiration of reciprocity or establishing residence	Buyer
LOUISIANA	Yes	Department of Public Safety, Motor Vehicle Division, Baton Rouge 70896	Until expiration of reciprocity agreement or employment	Buyer
MAINE	Yes[6]	Motor Vehicle Division, Capitol Street, Augusta 04333	Until expiration of reciprocity	Seller
MARYLAND	Yes	Motor Vehicle Administration, Glen Burnie 21061	30 days after employment or establishing residence	Seller
MASSACHUSETTS	Yes[7]	Registry of Motor Vehicles, Boston 02114	Until expiration of reciprocity agreement	Seller
MICHIGAN	Yes	Secretary of State, Lansing 48918	Until establishing residence	Seller
MINNESOTA	Yes[8] [9]	Commissioner of Public Safety, Motor Vehicle Division, St. Paul 55155	Until expiration of reciprocity agreement or 60 days after establishing residence	Buyer
MISSISSIPPI	Yes	Car dealer or designated financial institution	30 days	Buyer[10]
MISSOURI	Yes	Motor Vehicle Registration Unit, Jefferson City 65101	Until establishing residence	Seller

(1) If 2 conditions are stated, the first to occur governs.

(2) Tourists are allowed 90 days if they obtain a visitor's permit after 30 days.

(3) Plates go to Department of Motor Vehicles.

(4) For 1963 and later model vehicles.

(5) A nonresident may obtain a permit to operate his vehicle with his out-of-state reg-

The chart below shows the laws on automobile ownership and registration in the various states. For more detail, contact your state department of motor vehicles.

	Proof of Ownership		Registration	Who Gets License Plates When Car Is Sold?
	Is a Certificate of Title Required?	If So, Who Issues It?	How Long Is Out-of-State Registration Valid?[1]	
MONTANA	Yes	Registrar of Motor Vehicles, Deer Lodge 59722	Until employment, establishing residence or school enrollment	Seller
NEBRASKA	Yes	County clerk	Until expiration of reciprocity or establishing residence	Seller
NEVADA	Yes	Department of Motor Vehicles, Registration Division, Carson City 89711	45 days after establishing residence	Seller
NEW HAMPSHIRE	Yes[4]	Director of Motor Vehicles, Concord 03301	Until expiration of reciprocity agreement	Seller
NEW JERSEY	Yes	Motor Vehicles Director, Trenton 08625	60 days after establishing residence	Seller
NEW MEXICO	Yes	Department of Motor Vehicles, Santa Fe 87503	90 days, or 30 days after establishing residence	Buyer
NEW YORK	Yes[9]	Department of Motor Vehicles, South Mall, Albany 12228	30 days after establishing residence	Seller
NORTH CAROLINA	Yes	Commissioner of Motor Vehicles, Raleigh 27602	Until expiration of reciprocity agreement or employment	Seller
NORTH DAKOTA	Yes	Registrar of Motor Vehicles, Bismarck 58501	Until employment or establishing residence	Buyer
OHIO	Yes	Clerk of county court	Until expiration of reciprocity	Seller
OKLAHOMA	Yes	Oklahoma Tax Commission, Oklahoma City 73194	60 days until establishing residence or employment	Buyer
OREGON	Yes	Motor Vehicles Division, Department of Transportation, Salem 97310	Until expiration	Buyer
PENNSYLVANIA	Yes	Bureau of Motor Vehicles, Harrisburg 17122	Until expiration of reciprocity agreement or 30 days after establishing residence	Seller
RHODE ISLAND	Yes[9]	Registry of Motor Vehicles, Providence 02903	Until expiration of reciprocity[11]	Seller
SOUTH CAROLINA	Yes	Motor Vehicle Division, State Highway Department, Columbia 29216	10 days after establishing residence	Buyer
SOUTH DAKOTA	Yes	Department of Public Safety, Public Safety Building, Pierre 57501	60 days or until employment or school enrollment	Buyer
TENNESSEE	Yes	County court clerk	Until expiration of reciprocity, establishing residence or 30 days after employment	Seller
TEXAS	Yes	Dept. of Highways and Public Transportation, Motor Vehicle Division, Austin 78779	Until expiration of reciprocity agreement or establishing residence or employment	Buyer
UTAH	Yes	Motor Vehicle Division, Salt Lake City 84116	Until establishing residence or employment	Seller
VERMONT	Yes[12]	Department of Motor Vehicles, Montpelier 05602	Until expiration of reciprocity agreement or 6 months after employment	Seller
VIRGINIA	Yes	Division of Motor Vehicles, Richmond 23261	30 days	Seller
WASHINGTON	Yes	Department of Motor Vehicles, Olympia 98504; county auditor	60 days	Buyer
WEST VIRGINIA	Yes	Department of Motor Vehicles, Charleston 25305	30 days	Seller
WISCONSIN	Yes	Vehicle Registration, Department of Transportation, P.O. Box 7909, Madison 53707	Until expiration of reciprocity agreement or establishing residence	Seller
WYOMING	Yes	County clerk	30 days	Seller

istration until that registration expires.
(6) For 1975 and later model vehicles.
(7) For vehicles less than 10 years old.
(8) For initial registration of out-of-state vehicle.
(9) For 1973 and later model vehicles.
(10) But if the car is sold to a licensed dealer, the plates must be surrendered.
(11) If the owner has an established place of business in the state and uses his vehicle in that connection he must register it.
(12) For 1972 and later model vehicles.

attached to the steering column or dashboard where it can be plainly seen. In other states it may be kept in the glove compartment or on the driver's person. Failure to produce the certificate upon the request of a police officer is an offense that may lead to the driver's arrest or to difficulties in respect to other offenses.

The automobile license plate or plates given to the owner must be securely fastened to the vehicle, kept clean, unobstructed and easily readable and illuminated at night. If your registration certificate or license plates are lost or stolen, you should immediately notify the state bureau that issued them (see chart 11, page 242) and obtain duplicates or make application for new ones.

In some states the license plate remains with the car when ownership is transferred, but many states require that the purchaser apply for a new plate (see chart 11).

213. Out-of-State Registration Certificates and License Plates • If you visit another state, you are not required to register your car there so long as the vehicle is registered in your home state. In some localities, however, you may be required to obtain a visitor's permit or sticker.

The length of time you may continue to use your car in another state without obtaining local license plates varies widely, frequently depending on reciprocity agreements among the states (see chart 11).

If you move to a new state, you must obtain a local registration certificate and license plates within a specified period of time (see chart 11).

214. Your Obligation to Maintain a Mechanically Safe Automobile • State laws and U.S. Department of Transportation regulations require that your car be properly equipped and in good working condition. Equipment required on new cars in all states includes: headlights strong enough to illuminate objects at 500 feet; tail lights visible at 500 feet; side marker lights; license plate illumination; a hydraulic braking system with residual braking capacity in case of failure; a brake failure warning light and other hazard warning lights; an effective parking brake; a horn audible at 200 feet; two-speed windshield wipers plus a defroster and defogger; a mirror giving a clear, unobstructed view to the rear; an energy-absorbing steering column; a padded dashboard with recessed knobs; safety glass throughout; headrests to prevent whiplash injury; lap and chest safety belts in front and lap belts in back, with a warning buzzer that sounds if front belts are not fastened; an exhaust and muffler system in good repair that meets pollution control standards;

energy-absorbing front and rear bumpers designed to withstand collision at speeds of five m.p.h. and two and one-half m.p.h. respectively.

Equipment that is forbidden by law in most states includes muffler cutouts; sirens, bells, whistles or gongs; a red light showing from the front of the car; a television set whose screen is visible to the driver; and signs, posters or stickers on the windshield, except those specifically authorized by law.

Periodic inspection of vehicles is mandatory in most states and is required at periods of one or two times yearly (see chart 12, page 246). Such inspections usually include checks of brakes, lights, muffler, windshield wipers, tires, horn and most of the other items enumerated above. You must repair or replace anything found defective. The authority to make inspections is conferred by the various states on cities, towns, counties or licensed private garages and service stations.

215. Warranties on New Cars and Replacement of Parts • Every automobile manufacturer issues a warranty (more fully explained in section 190), which guarantees that defective parts will be replaced or repaired at no cost to the buyer within a specified period of months after the purchase or within a specified number of miles driven, whichever occurs first.

Registered dealers in all states are required to honor the warranty, if it so specifies. However, it need be honored only if the defect was not caused by any action of the driver. Thus, your muffler will be replaced if it fails to function properly through no fault of yours, but not if it was punctured by a stone while you were driving. Furthermore, the warranty does not compensate you for your loss of the use of the vehicle while it is being repaired or for the cost of substitute transportation.

If you are unlucky enough to buy a "lemon" that is almost continuously in the garage for one mechanical failing or another after the expiration of the warranty, neither the manufacturer nor the dealer has any obligation to replace the vehicle, if it can be proved—as it nearly always can—that due care was exercised in its manufacture and that the large majority of similar models suffered few of the defects afflicting your particular car.

If, however, it becomes apparent that a particular part or assemblage in the entire line is defective, rendering the cars unsafe to drive, the manufacturer is obligated by federal law to recall all vehicles of that model and to replace the defective equipment at no cost to the owners. Failure to do so might subject the manufacturer to payment of damages to victims of accidents caused by the defective part (see sections 68, 192).

AUTOMOBILE INSPECTION LAWS

CHART 12	Does State Require Inspection?	If So, How Frequently?
ALABAMA	No, but cities have the authority to maintain inspection stations & enact local inspection laws.	
ALASKA	No, but state police may inspect any vehicle at the roadside if there is a reasonable cause to believe vehicle is unsafe.	
ARIZONA	No, but an annual inspection of engine exhaust emissions is required in Maricopa and Pima counties.	
ARKANSAS	Yes	Annually
CALIFORNIA	No, but a peace officer may inspect any vehicle at the roadside if there is reasonable cause to believe vehicle is unsafe.	
COLORADO	Yes	Every 12 months
CONNECTICUT	Only for used out-of-state vehicles being registered in Connecticut & Connecticut cars more than 10 years old before resale or transfer. There are also provisions for voluntary annual inspection & spot highway inspection.	
DELAWARE	Yes	Annually during month on license plate sticker
D. C.	Yes	Annually
FLORIDA	Yes	Annually
GEORGIA	Yes	Annually. Newly registered vehicles must be inspected within 5 days unless displaying valid out-of-state sticker.
HAWAII	Yes	Vehicles 10 years or older, every 6 months; others, annually
IDAHO	No	
ILLINOIS	Trucks only	Every 6 months
INDIANA	Yes	Annually. Vehicles must be reinspected if sold or transferred or if state police consider an inspection warranted following an accident.
IOWA	Yes, required prior to first registration in Iowa & on all transfers.	
KANSAS	Yes, required prior to resale. Any police officer may stop a vehicle for inspection if there is reasonable cause to believe vehicle is unsafe.	
KENTUCKY	Yes	Annually. Vehicles not previously registered in state (except new vehicles from licensed Kentucky dealers) must be inspected before registration.
LOUISIANA	Yes	Annually
MAINE	Yes	Every 6 months
MARYLAND	Only for used passenger cars upon resale or transfer, or when moving to Maryland from another state.	
MASSACHUSETTS	Yes	Twice a year, Apr. 1–May 15 & Sept. 1–Oct. 15. A vehicle registered between inspection periods must be inspected within 7 days of registration.
MICHIGAN	No, but there are provisions for random inspection by state police & for individual inspection by local police if there is reasonable cause to believe vehicle is unsafe.	
MINNESOTA	No, but municipalities may provide for inspection & the state highway patrol may conduct a spot inspection.	
MISSISSIPPI	Yes	Annually

Well over half the states require automobile inspections on a regular basis, as shown in the chart below (see also section 214).

	Does State Require Inspection?	If So, How Frequently?
MISSOURI	Yes	Annually, no more than 60 days prior to renewal of registration
MONTANA	No	
NEBRASKA	Yes	Annually
NEVADA	Only for select vehicles in pilot program, Washoe County	
NEW HAMPSHIRE	Yes	Twice a year: 1st inspection during month of birthdate of owner & then every 6 months. Newly registered vehicles must be inspected within 10 days of registration.
NEW JERSEY	Yes	Annually during the month of renewal of registration
NEW MEXICO	Yes	Twice a year
NEW YORK	Yes	Annually
NORTH CAROLINA	Yes	Annually. All vehicles purchased outside state or brought into state for registration must be inspected & display certificate within 10 days.
NORTH DAKOTA	Random inspection by state highway patrol	
OHIO	Random inspection by state highway patrol	
OKLAHOMA	Yes	Annually
OREGON	No, but state police may conduct roadside inspections.	
PENNSYLVANIA	Yes	Twice a year
RHODE ISLAND	Yes, for all vehicles over 1 year old; may be required for any vehicle found defective in a police road check.	At least once a year, but no more than twice a year
SOUTH CAROLINA	Yes	Annually
SOUTH DAKOTA	Yes	Annually
TENNESSEE	No, but state law permits inspection by cities.	
TEXAS	Yes	Once a year & after an accident
UTAH	Yes	Once or twice a year
VERMONT	Yes	Twice a year
VIRGINIA	Yes	Immediately after 1st registration & every 6 months thereafter
WASHINGTON	No, except as result of citation for defective equipment or spot check by state patrol.	
WEST VIRGINIA	Yes	Annually. New vehicles purchased in state must be inspected within 3 days; vehicles purchased out of state, within 10 days after entry into state.
WISCONSIN	No, but compulsory spot checks are conducted by state & local officers for defective or missing equipment.	
WYOMING	Yes	Annually

216. Warranties on Used Cars • If the manufacturer's warranty on a new car has not yet expired before the car is resold, its privileges usually pass on to the new owner. However, some warranties specify that to render the warranty effective the second owner must pay a service charge or share the cost of repair or replacement of defective parts.

Where the manufacturer's warranty has expired, most dealers will issue their own warranty on used cars, good for a period of days or for a number of miles driven after the purchase date. In such a case it would be wise to have the seller's guarantees set down in writing and signed by. him. If he refuses to give you a written guarantee, you may not be able to recover if he defaults.

The terms of used-car warranties vary widely, from free replacement or repair of parts to fifty-fifty sharing of the cost between owner and seller to arrangements whereby the owner gets a 10 to 15 percent discount on the cost. These figures may be deceptive, however, since unscrupulous dealers have been known to jack up the prices of repairs to the point where the owner actually pays the whole cost. Before enforcing your warranty on a used car, it would be wise to get an independent estimate of the cost of repairs or replacement at another garage.

The used-car business is so notoriously unregulated that about the only assurance you have of the mechanical quality of the vehicle you buy is the reputation of the dealer. Usually it is safest to deal with a registered dealer, a new-car distributor who operates his used-car lot in connection with his showroom. Since he has too much to lose by selling poor merchandise, he usually wholesales his defective trade-ins to non-registered dealers.

217. Warranties on Parts and Tires • Most new or reconditioned automobile parts are sold with printed warranties, offering replacement at no cost if they prove defective within a specified time period or number of miles driven. The defect must be inherent in the construction of the equipment, however, and not caused by any action of the driver.

Although tires carry similar guarantees, covering several thousand miles of use, the guarantees are difficult to enforce against manufacturers because it is almost impossible to prove that a blowout was not caused by striking a stone, curb or other obstruction, or that the undue wear on the tread was not the result of wheel misalignment or some other malfunction of the vehicle. About the best you can expect from your tire warranty is a prorated discount on the cost of replacement, representing the difference between the cost of the new tire and the value

REQUIRED AUTOMOBILE SAFETY FEATURES

State and federal laws place an increasing responsibility both on automobile manufacturers and on automobile owners to produce and maintain mechanically safe cars. The diagram below shows safety features required by federal statute and often checked during periodic state inspections. Details of inspection requirements vary from state to state.

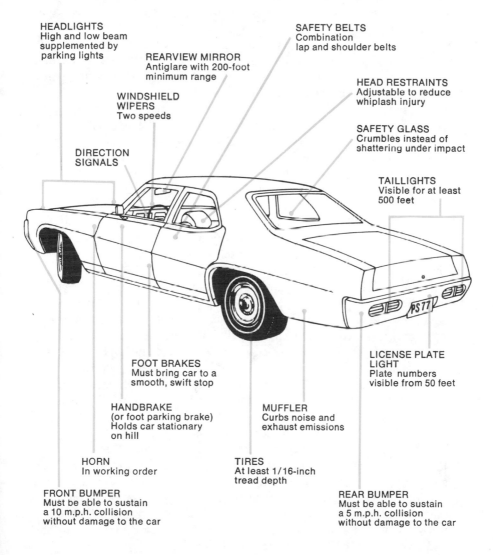

HEADLIGHTS
High and low beam supplemented by parking lights

REARVIEW MIRROR
Antiglare with 200-foot minimum range

WINDSHIELD WIPERS
Two speeds

DIRECTION SIGNALS

SAFETY BELTS
Combination lap and shoulder belts

HEAD RESTRAINTS
Adjustable to reduce whiplash injury

SAFETY GLASS
Crumbles instead of shattering under impact

TAILLIGHTS
Visible for at least 500 feet

LICENSE PLATE LIGHT
Plate numbers visible from 50 feet

FOOT BRAKES
Must bring car to a smooth, swift stop

HANDBRAKE
(or foot parking brake) Holds car stationary on hill

MUFFLER
Curbs noise and exhaust emissions

HORN
In working order

TIRES
At least 1/16-inch tread depth

FRONT BUMPER
Must be able to sustain a 10 m.p.h. collision without damage to the car

REAR BUMPER
Must be able to sustain a 5 m.p.h. collision without damage to the car

Generally inspections are held once or twice annually to see that legally required safety equipment has been installed and is operating properly. For details see chart 12, page 246.

of the used tire, which depends on the number of miles it has been driven and the amount of tread it has left.

218. Dealing with the Automobile Mechanic • Although talk about licensing automobile mechanics has been rife for years, no state has yet enacted a law requiring such licensing. You must therefore rely on your own judgment, or the reports of neighbors or friends, as to the competence of a mechanic to whom you entrust your car.

The mechanic who accepts your car for servicing or repair has only two legal obligations. The first is to exercise reasonable care to see that no harm comes to your car. This means that if it is stolen, destroyed by fire or otherwise damaged while in the mechanic's possession, he is obligated to pay you for what the car was worth in view of its age and condition. He is also required to pay for or repair other damage he may cause while doing his work, such as denting a fender or scratching the paint. However, the mechanic may escape liability if the damage was caused by forces over which he had no control, such as floods, hurricanes or riots and similar disturbances. (For more details on the obligations of bailees, see sections 197–206.)

The mechanic's second obligation is to perform the work he has agreed to do. This is no guarantee of the quality of the work performed. If the job is so improperly done as to be useless, as when parts of the wrong size or specifications are installed, or the starter still fails to set the engine running after he has repaired it, you have a right to refuse payment until the work is redone properly or to demand the return of your money if you have already paid. But if the work is simply bungled, as when your brakes squeal or the engine still knocks after the mechanic has endeavored to correct the defects, you have little claim against him. Although there is an implied contract to do repairs in a "good and workmanlike manner," proof is the problem—not to mention legal expenses involved in suing, even if your claim is good (see section 75). It is the kind of situation where legal remedies are not entirely satisfactory, and your best recourse is not to use that mechanic again.

After repairs are completed to the mechanic's satisfaction, if you fail to pay for work done he may claim a workman's or mechanic's lien and refuse to surrender your car until payment is made. You then have two alternatives if you are dissatisfied with his work: you may either pay the bill and then sue the mechanic for breach of contract or breach of warranty or performance (sections 183, 184) or you may refuse to pay and seek a court order for the return of the car.

219. Licenses to Drive • No one may legally drive a motor vehicle anywhere in the United States without carrying in his possession a driver's or operator's license issued to him by his state of residence or, if he is a foreigner, by the proper authority in his own country. Failure to produce the license when requested by proper authority may subject the driver to arrest and fine. Your driver's license is recognized as valid in all other states you visit, and in some foreign countries, although in the latter you may also have to produce proof of your financial responsibility.

The same is not necessarily true of learner's and junior driver's permits or of chauffeur's licenses and other professional permits. You should be extremely cautious about letting your son or daughter drive with a junior driver's permit outside your home state or perhaps county, even if you are in the car. If the permit is not valid and you are in an accident, you may find that your insurance company will not honor the policy, with disastrous financial consequences for you (see section 260).

Learner's permits are usually issued for a limited time and often require that a licensed driver sit beside the learner and that no other passenger be in the vehicle. In states that issue junior driver's permits, the young driver must pass the driving examination and also obtain the permission of his parent or guardian. The junior driver is usually permitted to operate the vehicle only during daylight hours, driving to and from school, or with an adult in the car.

Driving examinations required to obtain a license vary from one state to another (chart 13, page 252). They usually include vision tests, tests on traffic rules (section 220) and tests of recognition of colors, road signs and traffic signals, and require a demonstration of driving ability.

Restrictions on driver's licenses that may be imposed for various physical disabilities include "with glasses," when the driver cannot meet the vision standards without their aid; "outside mirror," when the driver is blind in one eye or has impaired hearing that might prevent him from hearing an automobile horn; "daytime only," when the driver has difficulty seeing at night; "steering wheel knob," when the driver does not have full use of both hands; and various "special mechanical devices," when the driver has physical defects that prevent him from driving ordinary vehicles.

For more detail on requirements for a driver's license, see chart 13.

REQUIREMENTS FOR A DRIVER'S LICENSE

CHART 13	What Is Minimum Age for Unrestricted License?	Does State Issue Junior License? If So, At What Age?	Is a Learner's Permit Required? At What Age Can One Be Obtained?	What Tests Are Required for Original License?
ALABAMA	16	14[1]	Yes: 15	Written, driving, eye
ALASKA	18; 16[3]	No	No	Written, driving, eye
ARIZONA	18; 16[4]	No	In some cases: 16 & 7 months with parental consent	Written, oral, driving, eye
ARKANSAS	18; 16 if parent signs application	14[5]	Yes: 14	Written, oral, driving, eye
CALIFORNIA	18; 16[7]	14, restricted license	In some cases: 15[7]	Written, road sign, driving, eye
COLORADO	21	16, minor's license[8]; 18, provisional license	Yes: 15¾; 15½ if taking driver education	Written, driving, eye
CONNECTICUT	18; 16[7]	No	For motorcycles only	Written, oral, driving, eye
DELAWARE	18; 16[7]	No	Yes: 16	Written, driving, eye
D.C.	18; 16[3]	No	Yes: 16	Written, oral, driving, eye
FLORIDA	18; 16[10]	15, restricted license	Yes	Written, driving, eye, hearing, road sign
GEORGIA	16	No	Yes: 15	Written, driving, eye
HAWAII	18; 15 with parental consent	No	Yes: 15	Written, driving, eye
IDAHO	16 with parental consent	14[7]	In some cases: 16	Written, road sign, driving, eye
ILLINOIS	18; 16[10]	No	Yes	Written, driving, eye
INDIANA	18; 16½ with parental consent; 16 & 1 month[7]	No	Yes: 16 if taking driver education	Written, driving, eye
IOWA	18; 16[7]	14[11]	No	Written, driving, eye
KANSAS	16	14	Yes	Written, driving, eye
KENTUCKY	18; 16[3]	No	Yes: 16	Written, driving, eye, hearing, physical disability
LOUISIANA	17	15[12]	No	Written, driving, eye
MAINE	18; 17 with parental consent	15 with driver education[11]	Yes: 15[7]	Written, oral, driving, eye
MARYLAND	18; 16[10]	No	Yes	Written, driving, eye
MASSACHUSETTS	18	17; 16½ with driver education[13]	Yes: 16	Written, driving, eye
MICHIGAN	18; 16[10]	14 with parental consent[8]	Yes: 14	Written, oral, driving, eye
MINNESOTA	18	16, provisional license	Yes	Written, driving, eye

(1) For lightweight motorcycles only.
(2) License expires on driver's birthday.
(3) With written parental consent.
(4) With notarized parental consent.
(5) Driver under 16 must be accompanied by licensed adult.

252

Every state requires that you carry a driver's license if you are to operate a motor vehicle on the public highways (see section 219). Details of the licensing laws of the states as to age and other qualifications are outlined below.

Is Licensee's Photograph Required?	How Many Years Is License Valid?	Are Any Tests Required for Renewal?	How Long Is a Non-resident License Valid?
No	4[2]	No	30 days
Yes, on license	3[2]	No	90 days
Yes, on license	3[2]	Yes: written, eye	Until employment; visitors need permit after 10 days
No	2[6]	No	Until application for Arkansas license plates; visitors need permit after 30 days
Yes (color), on license	4[2]	Yes: written, eye	10 days after establishing residence
Yes (color), on license	3[2]	Yes: eye (written in some cases)	30 days after establishing residence or employment
Yes, on licenses issued after July 1, 1977	2[6]	No	60 days after establishing residence
Yes (color, every 4 years)	4[2]	Yes: reexamination	90 days after establishing residence
Yes (color)	4[9]	Yes: eye (special tests persons 70 and over)	Reciprocal basis; visitors need permit after 14 days
Yes (color)	4[6]	Yes: eye, hearing, road signs	Until establishing residence or employment
Yes (color), on license	4[2]	Yes: eye	30 days or immediately if employed
No	2 (ages 15–24 & over 65); 4 (ages 25–64)[2]	Yes: eye, written	Until expiration
Yes (taken at sheriff's office, no charge)	3[2]	Yes: written, eye	90 days, or until establishing residence or employment
No	3[9]	Yes: written, driving, eye (every 9 years; every 3 years after age 69)	90 days after establishing residence
Yes	4[6] (under age 75); 2[6] (over age 75)	Yes: written, driving, eye (persons over 75)	60 days or until establishing residence
No	2 (16–20 & over 65); 4 (21–64)[2]	Yes: eye	Until establishing residence
Optional	4[2]	Yes: written, eye	Reciprocal basis
No	2[6]	No	Reciprocal basis
Yes (color), on license	2[2]	Yes: eye	90 days
No	2[2]	No	Reciprocal basis
No	4[2]	No	120 days, or 30 days after establishing residence
Yes (color)	4[2]	Yes: eye	Reciprocal basis
No	2, 3 or 4[2]	Yes: eye, written	Until establishing residence
Yes (color)	4[2]	Yes: eye	60 days after establishing residence

(6) License expires on last day of driver's month of birth.
(7) With driver education course completed.
(8) Must be renewed annually.
(9) License expires on anniversary of date of issuance.

253

CHART 13 (cont.)

	What Is Minimum Age for Unrestricted License?	Does State Issue Junior License? If So, At What Age?	Is a Learner's Permit Required? At What Age Can One Be Obtained?	What Tests Are Required for Original License?
MISSISSIPPI	15	No	Yes: 15	Written, road sign, driving, eye
MISSOURI	16	15½ if taking driver education	No	Written, road sign, driving, eye
MONTANA	18	15[7], 16–18, provisional license with parental consent	Yes	Written, driving, eye
NEBRASKA	16	No	Yes: 15; 14 for school permit	Written, driving, eye
NEVADA	18; 16 with parental consent	No	Yes: 15½	Written, driving, eye
NEW HAMPSHIRE	18; 16[7]	No	No	Written, oral, driving, eye
NEW JERSEY	17	16 for agricultural work	Yes: 16[7]	Written, driving, eye
NEW MEXICO	16; 15[7]	No	Yes: 15	Written, driving, eye
NEW YORK	18; 17[7]	16 (not valid in New York City)[13]	Yes	Written, driving, road sign, eye, driver training
NORTH CAROLINA	18; 16[10]	No	In some cases: 15	Written, road sign, driving, eye
NORTH DAKOTA	16	14	Yes: 14	Written, driving
OHIO	18; 16[7]	14 in hardship cases	Yes	Written, driving, eye
OKLAHOMA	16; 15½[7]	No	Yes: 15½	Written, driving, eye
OREGON	16	14[11]	Yes: 15	Written, driving, eye
PENNSYLVANIA	18; 17[7]	16[13] with parental consent	Yes	Oral, driving, eye, physical
RHODE ISLAND	18; 16[10]	No	Yes	Written, driving, eye
SOUTH CAROLINA	16	15	No	Written, oral, driving
SOUTH DAKOTA	16	14[12]	In some cases: 14	Written, driving, eye
TENNESSEE	16	14[16]	Yes	Written, driving, eye
TEXAS	18; 16[7]	15 if taking driver education	No	Written, driving, eye
UTAH	16[7]	No	Yes	Written, driving, eye
VERMONT	18	16	Yes: 15	Written, driving, eye
VIRGINIA	18; 16[10]	No	Yes: 15⅔ with parental consent	Written, oral, driving, eye
WASHINGTON	18; 16[7]	No	In some cases: 15½	Written, driving, eye
WEST VIRGINIA	18	16[3]	Yes	Written, driving, eye
WISCONSIN	18; 16[7]	No	Yes: 15½	Written, driving, eye
WYOMING	18; 16 with parental consent	No	In some cases: 15	Written, driving, eye

(10) If parent signs application and driver education course has been completed.
(11) Valid only for driving to and from school.
(12) Valid only certain hours.
(13) Valid only certain hours unless accompanied by parent.

Is Licensee's Photograph Required?	How Many Years Is License Valid?	Are Any Tests Required for Renewal?	How Long Is a Non-resident License Valid?
No	2[6]	No	60 days, unless a tourist, student or serviceman
Yes (color), on license	3[9]	Yes: eye	Reciprocal basis
Yes	4[2]	No	90 days
No	4[2]	Yes: written, eye	30 days of continuous residence
No	4[2]; 2 if over 70	Yes: eye, driving (persons over 70)	45 days after establishing residence
No	4[2]	Yes: eye	Reciprocal basis
No	2	Yes: eye (every 10 years)	Reciprocal basis
No	2[6]	Yes: written, eye	30 days after establishing residence
No	3, staggered expiration dates	Yes: eye	60 days after establishing residence
No	4[2]	Yes: written, driving, road sign, eye[14]	30 days after establishing residence
Yes (color), on license	4 or 2, staggered expiration dates	Yes: eye (persons under 21 or over 70)	60 days after establishing residence
Yes (color), on license	4[2]	No	Reciprocal basis
Yes (color), on license, as of 1977	2[6]	No	Until establishing residence
Yes (color), on license	2[2]; 4 with photo license	No	Until establishing residence
No	4[6]	No	30 days after establishing residence
No	2[9]	Yes: eye (every 4 years)	30 days after establishing residence
Yes (color), on license	4[2]	Yes: eye	Until establishing residence
Yes, on license	4[2]	Yes: eye[15]	90 days after establishing residence
No	2[2]	No	90 days after establishing residence
Yes, for renewal	4[2]	Yes: eye	30 days after establishing residence
Yes (color), on license	4[2]	Yes: written, eye	60 days after establishing residence
Optional	2[2]	No	6 months on reciprocal basis
Yes (color)	4[9]	Yes: eye	30 days
Yes	2[2]	Yes: eye (statement of physical condition)	1 year or until establishing residence
No	4[9]	No	30 days on reciprocal basis
No	2[2]	Yes: eye (every 4 years)	Reciprocal basis until establishing residence
Yes	3[2]	Yes: eye	30 days after employment or establishing residence

(14) Written and driving tests waived if no traffic offense in previous 4 years.
(15) All tests required if traffic offense in previous 4 years.
(16) Valid only for daylight driving to school, grocery store and church.

220. Traffic Rules and Regulations • While traffic regulations are not identical in all states, they generally adhere to the following basic patterns:

a. *Traffic signs and signals.* Keep within the statutory speed limits or the speed limits posted along the road. Observe the Yield, No Passing, One Way and other posted instructions. Do not cross a yellow line when it is on your side of the center line.

At traffic lights come to a stop when the yellow signal appears, unless you are going too fast to stop with safety, and do not proceed until the green light comes on and cross traffic has cleared the intersection. Do not make a left turn unless the left-turn signal appears. Where there is no left-turn signal, do not make a left turn on a green light if oncoming vehicles are too close to the intersection for you to make the turn safely.

At stop signs come to a full stop (except in states which permit rolling stops), and do not proceed until it is safe to do so.

Come to a complete stop at a flashing red light and slow down at a flashing yellow light, then proceed when it is safe. Come to a complete stop at a railroad crossing when the warning lights are lit or the crossbar is down, and do not proceed until the lights are off or the bar is lifted, even if you can see no train coming.

Obey the instructions of police even if they are contrary to traffic lights, signs or traffic regulations.

b. *Straight driving.* Drive on the right-hand side of the road or in the extreme right lane of a multilane highway, except when passing another vehicle or preparing to make a left turn. In a few states you need not keep to the right on highways that have three or more lanes going in the same direction.

Following too close to a vehicle ahead of you can result in a crash if it stops suddenly. Allow a distance equal to the length of your car (about sixteen feet for standard sizes) multiplied by every ten miles of speed, and even more space if weather or road conditions are unfavorable.

c. *Passing.* If another driver wants to pass you, move to the right to let him by and do not increase speed until he has passed you completely and returned to the right-hand lane.

Signal your intention to pass another car, either by signal lights or hand signals, well before you overtake it.

Always pass other vehicles on the left. Passing on the right is permissible only when the vehicle overtaken is about to make a left turn or on a very wide highway in a state where it is not compulsory to keep in the right-hand lane. Passing on the shoulder of the road is prohibited.

Passing is prohibited on two-lane highways within 100 feet of an intersection, railroad crossing, bridge or tunnel; on a hill or curve when the view ahead is unclear or obstructed; when an oncoming car is too close or traveling too fast to allow you to get by the car ahead of you safely; and when prohibited by highway signs or a yellow stripe on your side of the center line. In all cases you must have from 500 to 600 feet of visibility, depending on the state.

d. *Turning.* Signal your intention to turn at least 100 feet before reaching the intersection. When turning, move over into the appropriate lane in plenty of time to make the turn. Right turns must be made from the extreme right-hand lane or side of the road, left turns from the lane or portion of the road closest to the center line on two-way roads, or from the extreme left lane on one-way roads.

Do not make U-turns on curves or hills, or anywhere else that does not allow clear visibility for 500 feet in each direction or where prohibited by city ordinance.

e. *The right of way.* Cars proceeding on more important streets and highways have the right of way over cars entering from side streets, less important thoroughfares or access roads leading from other main highways.

At intersections the car entering the intersection first has the right of way. If two cars enter at the same time, the car to the right has the right of way. Cars turning left must yield the right of way to oncoming vehicles proceeding straight ahead.

Emergency vehicles, such as police cars, fire trucks and ambulances, have the right of way over all other traffic when they sound their sirens or bells. Other vehicles must pull over to the right-hand side of the road and stop to let them through.

When a school bus has stopped to let children off, all other vehicles, from any direction, must come to a stop until the children have crossed the road; the bus should not be passed until its doors are closed and its warning lights are turned off.

Cars in funeral processions have the right of way at intersections when their headlights are lighted. The driver of the leading vehicle must obey Stop signs and traffic control lights. But once he has proceeded across the intersection all other vehicles in the procession may follow without stopping.

Pedestrians have the right of way over motor vehicles if they are lawfully crossing the roadway within any crosswalk, marked or unmarked, or if they have started across while the traffic light was in their favor.

Pedestrians must yield the right of way to motor vehicles when crossing a street or highway at any place but a designated crosswalk, when entering a crosswalk before the traffic light is in their favor or when crossing a road where a pedestrian overpass or tunnel has been provided.

Blind pedestrians carrying white canes or led by dogs have the right of way under any circumstances, and motorists must stop to let them pass.

Motorists and pedestrians must yield the right of way if another person makes it unsafe to proceed, despite the fact that the other person may be driving or walking in violation of the law.

f. *Stopping.* Never stop abruptly, if you can avoid it. To do so is to invite a rear-end collision with the car behind you.

Signal your intention to stop, either with the hand signal or with your emergency flashing lights.

Do not stop on a highway or in a traffic lane if there is a shoulder or other place off the road to which your vehicle can be driven. If it is impossible to pull off the road, turn on your emergency flashing lights as a warning to other cars or, if possible, have a passenger walk 100 feet back on the highway to wave off oncoming vehicles, and raise the hood of your car as a distress signal.

g. *Parking.* Parking is prohibited on sidewalks, in front of driveways, on crosswalks, in safety zones, at bus stops, on the street side of parked vehicles (double parking) or other obstructions jutting out into the street, in tunnels, on bridges and overpasses, within fifteen feet of a fire hydrant, within twenty feet of a fire station, within thirty feet of an intersection, Stop sign or traffic signal, within fifty feet of a railroad crossing and wherever a No Parking sign is posted.

For parallel parking your wheel should be within twelve inches of the curb. For parking uphill the front wheels should be toed out if there is a curb but toed in if there is none. For parking downhill the front wheels should always be toed in.

If you park at night on unlit country or suburban roads, you must usually display dim lights, front and rear.

h. *Miscellaneous rules.* Headlights must be dimmed at night within 500 feet of an approaching vehicle, and the bright beam may not be turned back on until the vehicle has passed.

Backing up is prohibited on limited access highways, at intersections and wherever else it cannot be done safely without interfering with another vehicle.

Opening doors of a vehicle on the side on which traffic is moving is prohibited unless it is safe to do so.

Overcrowding in the front seat, usually interpreted as occupancy by more than three adults, is prohibited as an interference with the driver. It is illegal for the driver's view to be obstructed by people, by goods or by objects set or hung before the front or rear window. Overloading a vehicle to the point of imperiling mechanical safety is also illegal.

Riding in a house trailer while it is being moved is prohibited.

221. Local Traffic Ordinances and Driving Regulations • Driving laws and regulations may be enacted by states, counties, townships and municipalities. While they are generally based on the commonly recognized regulations outlined in section 220, they vary not only from one jurisdiction to another but also within a jurisdiction, depending on the nature of the area you are passing through (residential or business district, school zone or open road), the time of day or week (daylight or dark, quiet period or rush hour, weekday or Sunday), weather and road conditions (fair, raining, icy) and temporary conditions (construction on the highway, accidents on the road and other unusual obstructions).

Signs indicating the maximum permissible speed need not be posted along a road if they are identical to those specified by state or municipal law, but the motorist must be warned if the speed limit is lower than that established by law, as in the vicinity of a school while classes are in session, or if there are any unusual traffic rules that must be followed (such as keeping to the left when a major access road enters the highway from the right).

As with all other types of misdemeanors and infractions, ignorance of the law does not excuse you if you violate a driving or traffic regulation, even in a strange state or locality. You can usually obtain copies or digests of the ordinances and regulations in any area from the local police or sheriff's office or from the state motor vehicle authority

222. Driving with Due Care • In addition to setting forth traffic rules and regulations (see section 220), the driving statutes of all states require that you exercise due care behind the wheel. This is your most important legal obligation in operating an automobile.

The warnings are not simply paternal admonitions; they have serious legal significance, for the "due care" requirement takes precedence over all other driving regulations. If you fail to heed it and an accident ensues, you may be found negligent and required to pay damages for personal injuries or property destruction (sections 57, 71), even though you have broken no published traffic law. Moreover, your negligence may substantially reduce your ability to collect damages in a lawsuit arising from the accident.

The due care cannot be spelled out in detail in the statute books, because it deals with the standard of care required of the driver in particular circumstances, few of which are ever identical (see sections 57, 58). It has been interpreted by the courts as meaning that the driver must operate his vehicle as a prudent person would in a given situation, seeking to avoid unreasonable risk of harm to himself and others.

For examples, if the speed limit on a street is thirty miles per hour, you may not drive that fast if the road is crowded with pedestrians. Again, although the law says that you have the right of way if you reach an intersection first, you may not make a turn if another car is coming toward you at high speed. A green light gives you permission to go, but you must try to stop if a car crosses in front of you against the red light.

Not all examples of "due care" infractions are so clear-cut. For example, you may sound your horn to warn animals off the edge of the road, but not if they are skittish horses and reason tells you that they may bolt across the highway. You must look behind you and sound your horn before backing out of a driveway, but these precautions are not sufficient if you know there are children playing in the vicinity, since you cannot see below the level of your back window.

In many instances, questions as to whether or not a driver exercised due care can be settled by the courts only after all the circumstances of the case have been aired. (For more details on due care, see sections 56–59).

223. Reckless Driving · If you are guilty of violating a traffic ordinance, you are generally charged with an infraction. If you fail to meet a standard of care that is imposed on you by statute, you will be charged with *reckless driving,* a violation which is usually defined as "willful and wanton disregard for the safety of persons and property." In some circumstances you may be charged with both a lesser violation and reckless driving.

Reckless driving charges are usually arguable, and if the penalty is severe, it may be to your advantage to retain a lawyer and defend yourself against the accusation.

224. Traffic Laws for Pedestrians · The traffic ordinances and rules governing pedestrians are not as carefully spelled out as those governing motor vehicles, and they tend to vary widely among jurisdictions.

In some states and cities it is illegal for pedestrians to jaywalk through vehicular traffic, to cross the street anywhere but at intersections or designated crosswalks, to cross against red lights or unless Walk signs are lit. When walking on a highway, pedestrians are generally required to keep close to the left-hand shoulder of the road, where they can see and be seen by oncoming vehicles. Many states forbid hitchhiking, making it illegal for pedestrians to solicit rides or for motorists to pick them up.

The obligation to exercise due care is as legally binding on pedestrians as on motorists (see section 222). A person on foot may not step off the curb until he has made sure that there are no nearby vehicles coming at him from either direction. He may not cross at an intersection until traffic has come to a stop, even if the lights are in his favor. He may not walk with an umbrella or any other object obscuring his vision, nor take any other kind of risk in traffic that a prudent person would avoid.

Failure to observe these precautions or the traffic ordinances can lead to tickets and fines. If an accident results, the careless pedestrian may be unable to recover damages because of his contributory negligence and in some instances may himself be sued for damages for whatever personal injuries or property destruction results (see section 64).

225. Your Legal Defense Against Traffic Violation Charges • Charges of traffic violations are difficult to combat, for unless you have witnesses to testify to the contrary, the court will probably accept the statement of the arresting officer as the truth. Nor have you any discretionary authority to break the law. If you are ticketed for illegal parking while you are getting change to put in the meter, or for speeding while rushing someone to the hospital, the court may recognize these as mitigating circumstances and dismiss the charge. But it is not required to do so.

In most states and municipalities it is not necessary to appear in court to answer for minor traffic offenses. The fine can simply be mailed to the court. But this is an automatic admission of guilt, which appears as such on your driving record, and in view of the growing tendency of automobile insurance companies to raise rates or cancel policies for even minor convictions (see section 266), you should think twice before accepting this easy way out, particularly if you have a bad record of violations.

If you plead not guilty but are convicted, you have a right to appeal the sentence to a higher court, although the cost and time involved rarely make such action worthwhile unless your driver's license has been suspended or revoked as a result of your conviction.

226. What Not to Do When Charged with a Traffic Violation • Unless you want a bigger fine or even a jail sentence, don't try to bribe a police officer, refuse to give him your driver's license and auto registration, tear up the ticket or drive away before the ticket has been made out and given to you. These are all crimes (see section 90).

You have every right to protest your innocence, but if you do so in abusive language you run the risk of an additional, heavy fine if you are found guilty. However, except for giving the officer your name and address and those of the passengers in the car, you are not required to answer any questions he may ask you or to explain your actions, and you should not do so if you believe your statements may incriminate you. In fact, if the violation is a serious one, the officer must warn you that anything you say may be used as evidence against you, and his failure to do so may result in dismissal of the case (see section 151).

For situations involving driving and the use of alcohol, see section 231.

227. Suspension or Revocation of Your Driver's License • Permission to drive is legally considered a privilege, not a right, even in the case of people whose livelihood depends on it. The state may suspend or revoke the driver's privilege when the court finds it is abused, creates a danger to others or is used in connection with, or results in, a felony (see section 90).

Common causes of suspension or revocation are: (a) manslaughter while driving (see sections 122, 229); (b) driving while drunk or drugged (see section 231); (c) hit-and-run driving; (d) serious violation of the motor vehicle laws; (e) habitual negligence in driving, including repeated violations of the speed laws; (f) incompetence or physical inability to drive safely; (g) causing a serious accident while driving recklessly or unlawfully; (h) failure to carry accident and liability insurance as required by law (chart 16, page 288).

Your driver's license may be suspended for a stated period, during which it is unlawful for you to operate a motor vehicle, or it may be suspended indefinitely or revoked entirely. If temporarily suspended, the license automatically becomes valid again when the suspension period has lapsed. If indefinitely suspended or revoked, you must appeal to the licensing authority to have the license reinstated or a new one issued.

Owing to the reciprocity agreements signed between various states and the notices they send each other, a motorist committing a serious driving violation outside his home state may not be able to escape the consequences of his act. Thus, a New York motorist convicted of drunken driving in California may well have his New York license suspended.

In addition, many states now file notices of driving convictions with the National Driver Register maintained by the United States Department of Transportation in Washington, D.C. Before a court passes sentence for a driving violation or a state motor vehicle bureau issues a driver's license, a query may be sent to the Register, whereupon a complete record is returned listing all of the individual's driving infractions throughout the United States. If his previous record is bad enough, a motorist may lose his driving privileges for even a minor violation or be denied a driver's license in one state if his license has been revoked or suspended in another.

228. Speed Traps • Some areas maintain traffic regulations—such as fifteen-mile-per-hour speed limits where such low speeds are patently ridiculous—that are antiquated or were deliberately established by local authorities to trap unwary drivers and mulct them of fines. Although state authorities and automobile clubs campaign against such abuses, there is little you can do if caught in such a situation but pay the fine, since you have no right to violate the law no matter how unreasonable it may seem.

229. Vehicular Homicide • The charge of vehicular homicide may arise in any case in which a human being is killed by a motor vehicle. The term itself does not imply guilt or criminal offense. The homicide may be deemed accidental, as when the victim unexpectedly dashes into the path of an oncoming vehicle; it may be held manslaughter (see section 122), if the driver causes the death while violating a traffic law; or it may be held murder, if the driver deliberately plows his car into someone on the highway.

230. Driving When You Know You Are Ill • While there are no laws forbidding driving when you are ill, it may be taken as evidence of negligence on your part if you do so and then become involved in an accident.

231. Driving While Intoxicated • In all states drunken driving is one of the most serious crimes a motorist can commit, since more than half of all traffic fatalities and injuries are caused by motorists who have been drinking. Even if you have caused no accident, when caught behind the wheel in a tipsy condition you may be arrested, fined and jailed, and your license may be suspended or revoked.

Police use various methods to determine whether a driver is inebriated. They may observe his attitude, his appearance, the condition of his clothing and the state of his breath, noting also whether his eyes are bloodshot or his face flushed. They may test his ability to enunciate clearly, to read, to walk, to turn and to pick up coins. These tests may in some states be recorded on television tapes for later showing to a judge or jury.

There are also chemical tests of breath, blood and urine. In some states a person is presumed to be intoxicated if chemical tests reveal that his blood contains as little as $\frac{1}{10}$ of 1 percent of alcohol, a level that may be reached by a man of average height and weight after drinking two stiff martinis, five ounces of liquor or five bottles of beer in an hour.

There is no question of the right of police to record their visual observations of a suspected driver's condition. But the right to force him to undergo physical or chemical tests involves a thorny legal problem, since it can be construed as forcing a person to testify against himself, which is prohibited by the Constitution of the United States (see section 25). But all fifty states have now enacted "implied consent" laws, which entitle the police to make the tests without the driver's permission, provided no brutality is used, on the theory that the driver automatically consented to such tests in advance when he was awarded a driver's license or took his car onto a public thoroughfare. A driver does not have to allow the tests, however, but if he refuses them his license may be suspended or revoked even if the court should later find him innocent of the charge of driving while intoxicated.

232. Ownership and Operation of Motorcycles • Since the passage of the U.S. Highway Safety Act of 1966, more than two thirds of the states have adopted regulatory codes governing motorcycles, and eventually all states are expected to comply with the act's provisions. The laws governing ownership, operation and licensing of motorcycles are generally modeled after those pertaining to automobiles.

Your automobile driver's license does not entitle you to operate a motorcycle; you must pass special tests to do so. Motorcyclists are required to obey the same traffic laws and regulations as automobile drivers, and they are entitled to exactly the same consideration as an automobile in traffic, despite their smaller size.

It is illegal in most states for motorcyclists to drive between lanes of slow-moving or stopped cars or to weave in and out of traffic. As an aid to visibility at night, some states require that reflective material be used on the motorcycles or attached to the driver's clothing. In addition, motorcyclists are generally required to wear protective safety helmets and to protect their eyes either by means of a windshield on the motorcycle, spectacles with lenses of safety glass or plastic, goggles or a face shield attached to the helmet.

Specific information about ownership and operation of motorcycles may be obtained from the state authorities.

233. Ownership and Operation of Automobile Trailers • The laws governing passenger car trailers vary in detail from state to state, and you should check with local authorities to see what rules apply where you live. In general, all trailers must be registered and must carry license plates. In many states the fee depends on the weight of the trailer.

Lights, and in some cases directional signals, are required. If your trailer weighs more than a certain amount, an independent braking system is required by law in many states. Hitches and safety chains are frequently required to meet certain legal specifications. In some states a passenger car pulling a trailer must observe lower speed limits than would otherwise be the case, and riding in a moving trailer is forbidden.

AUTOMOBILE ACCIDENTS

Even if you suffer no personal injury or property damage, an automobile accident can be one of the most serious misfortunes that ever befalls you. In addition to the shock of the experience itself, it can result in civil and criminal action, jail sentences and serious financial loss.

The cost and the things that can happen to you as the person who caused an accident, or the amount you can recover as the victim of an accident, depend to a large extent on what you do and say after the mishap. You owe it to yourself to take careful note of the postaccident procedures recommended in the following paragraphs.

234. Hit-and-Run Accidents • Hit-and-run driving is a serious crime for which you may be fined or jailed, or both, even if you were totally innocent of causing the accident. If you panic and drive away, get back to the scene as soon as you have recovered your wits, or report to the nearest police station. Such action may substantially mitigate the penalty for the crime you committed in leaving.

265

If you witness a hit-and-run accident, it is your duty to notify the police and to give them whatever information you have of the event and a description of the fugitive driver and car.

235. If You Are Involved in an Accident • There are several things you should do immediately or as soon as possible after an accident:

a. Stop at once and give all the help you can to anyone who is hurt, but avoid moving injured people. If possible, have someone call an ambulance or doctor.

b. Notify the local police authorities immediately if someone is injured or killed.

c. Obtain the names and addresses of all witnesses or as many as possible, as well as the badge numbers of police officers and the names and addresses of doctors or ambulance services, if any are present.

d. Exchange driver's licenses, registration certificates and insurance-company information with the other driver, in the case of a collision, as well as the names of other occupants of the cars. If any of them have been injured, make a note of the type and extent of their injuries. If a pedestrian is involved, exchange names and addresses with him and make note of his injuries.

e. If at all possible, arrange to have photographs taken of the damaged car or cars, as well as of skid marks and other physical evidence.

f. If you are injured, try to be examined by your regular physician as soon as possible.

g. If you collide with an unattended vehicle or other object, try to locate the owner and report the accident. When this is not possible, leave a note on the car or object with your name and address. If you have injured a farm animal or pet, try to locate the owner.

h. Report the accident within twenty-four hours to your automobile insurance company or broker.

i. Report the accident to the local police or proper authorities within forty-eight hours of the mishap, and fill out an accident report, if required (see chart 14, page 269 and section 238).

236. Don'ts After a Major Accident • Since these are circumstances in which the services of a lawyer are crucial, it's recommended that you don't do any of the following things:

a. If the accident is a serious one and you believe you may have to bear some share of responsibility for causing it, don't make any statement whatever to the police, other motorists, bystanders or anyone else, until you have consulted a lawyer. The emotional upset resulting from the mishap may induce you to say things that are self-incriminating, distorted or actually not in accord with the facts, and whatever you may say may be taken down and used in evidence against you. Under the constitutional provision against self-incrimination you are not required to say anything (see section 25), and, in a criminal proceeding, no inference may be drawn from your silence.

b. If you are the victim of an accident, don't accept any money from the person causing it in payment for injury or property damage, until you get legal and medical advice. The extent of the injury or damage may be greater than you first believe, or you may be entitled to recover more money than you realize, and the acceptance of cash may be regarded by the law as full settlement of your claim.

c. Don't talk to insurance adjusters, or accept an immediate cash settlement from them, or sign a release or any other papers they may present, without an attorney's advice. Adjusters must try to settle your claim at the lowest possible cost to their companies, and they may go to considerable lengths in their efforts to do so. Even if the settlement the adjuster offers is a reasonable one, it will probably be available at a later date. Be careful of the statements you make even to your own insurance company adjuster, since the company may also represent the other party to the accident. It is possible in such circumstances that your statement may end up being used against you.

237. The Possibility of Hidden Injuries • Even if you suffer no apparent injuries, it is a wise precaution to consult a doctor. A severe jolt may have caused whiplash injury to the neck and spinal cord, which can ultimately cripple you, although it may not become apparent for days or weeks after the accident. Or a bump on the head may have created a hairline fracture of the skull or brain damage not immediately evident.

If you are the victim of an accident in which you have been shaken up, it is unwise to accept settlement or sign a release until your doctor is sure that no complications will result and that no permanent injury has been caused. Don't act prematurely, even if the insurance adjuster pleads that "you are holding things up," accuses you of malingering or threatens that "if you don't accept settlement now, you may end up with nothing." Such statements are without legal foundation, and once you accept settlement and sign a release it may be difficult, or even impossible, to reopen the case if your injuries prove to be more serious than they originally appeared.

267

238. Filling Out the Accident Report • All states require that accident reports be filled out in case of injury or death to anyone involved. If there is no injury or death, accident reports are required only if the property damage exceeds a fixed figure (see chart 14, page 269).

The report must be as accurate as you can make it, since it may be used later when negligence, liability and damage claims are being determined. If you have any difficulty in preparing the report accurately, get assistance from your automobile insurance agent or your lawyer.

The items in the report that should be most carefully filled out are:

a. Location and time of the accident, conditions of the road and traffic and a diagram of the surroundings, locating the cars and pedestrians and their movements.

b. Directions from which the vehicles and pedestrians were approaching prior to the accident.

c. The point of collision and the spots where the vehicles came to rest after collision, including measurements of distances in feet or inches.

d. Name and address of the other driver or the pedestrian; license and registration numbers; names and addresses of witnesses, including occupants of the cars, and any statements they may have made; badge numbers of the police officers present.

e. Nature and extent of injuries to passengers and pedestrians.

f. Nature and extent of the damage to the vehicles.

239. Accidents Involving Out-of-State Cars or Drivers • A driver who is involved in an accident outside his own state cannot escape a lawsuit for any damages which may have resulted. Under the Non-Resident Service of Process Law, which is in effect throughout the United States, if you own or drive a car you automatically appoint the secretary of state of your home state to be served with process on your behalf. This means that you agree to recognize the service of legal papers on him as being the same as service on you in respect to any accident you may have been involved in outside the state.

If an out-of-stater wants to sue you, his lawyer will send one copy of the summons to your state secretary and one by registered mail to you. Under the law the summons is enforceable, and you must either appear (or have a lawyer appear) in your defense in the courts of the state in which the accident occurred or run the risk of having a judgment entered against you by default. If such a judgment does result, it will almost certainly be enforced against you by the courts of your own state, and you will have to pay (see section 88).

HOW TO REPORT AN AUTOMOBILE ACCIDENT

Laws in all states require that automobile accidents involving more than a specified amount of property damage be reported. Some states also require preliminary reports. (See also section 238.)

CHART 14	Preliminary Reports			Written Reports		
	Must You Make Preliminary Report?	If So, When?	To Whom Must Report Be Made?	Time Limit for Filing	Where to File	Amount of Property Damage Requiring Report
ALABAMA	Yes	Immediately	Local police	10 days	Safety Responsibility Unit, P.O. Box 1471, Montgomery 36102	$50
ALASKA	Yes	Immediately	Local police, state trooper	48 hours	Division of State Troopers	$100
ARIZONA	Yes	Immediately	Local police, sheriff	5 days	Motor Vehicle Division, Department of Transportation, 1801 W. Jefferson St., Phoenix 85007	$300
ARKANSAS	Yes	48 hours	State police, municipal police in cities	5 days	Department of Revenue, Little Rock 72203	$50, preliminary; $100, written
CALIFORNIA	Yes	24 hours if injury; immediately if death	Highway patrol	15 days	Department of Motor Vehicles, Financial Responsibility Office, P.O. Box 2431, Sacramento 95811	$250
COLORADO	Yes	Immediately	Local or state police	10 days	State Motor Vehicle Division of Department of Revenue, 140 West Sixth Ave., Denver 80204	$100
CONNECTICUT	No			5 days	Department of Motor Vehicles, Wethersfield 06109	$400
DELAWARE	Yes	Immediately	State or local police	Not required		$250
D.C.	Yes	Immediately	Police	5 days	Bureau of Motor Vehicles, Washington, D.C.	Material damages, preliminary; $100, written
FLORIDA	Yes	Immediately	Police, sheriff, highway patrol	5 days	Department of Highway Safety & Motor Vehicles, Kirkman Building, Tallahassee 32304	$100
GEORGIA	Yes	Immediately	Local police	10 days	Bureau of Safety Responsibility, Department of Public Safety, P.O. Box 1456, Atlanta 30301	$25, preliminary; $100, written
HAWAII	Yes	Immediately	Police	Not required		$300
IDAHO	Yes	Immediately	State or local police, sheriff	Not required		$250
ILLINOIS	Yes	Immediately	Police	10 days	Department of Transportation, Springfield 62766	$100
INDIANA	Yes	Immediately	Police	5 days	State Police	$200
IOWA	Yes	Immediately	Sheriff, police, highway patrol	3 days	Department of Transportation, Lucas State Office Building, Des Moines 50319; chief of police in cities over 15,000	$250

CHART
14
(cont.)

	Preliminary Reports			Written Reports		
	Must You Make Preliminary Report?	If So, When?	To Whom Must Report Be Made?	Time Limit for Filing	Where to File	Amount of Property Damage Requiring Report
KANSAS	Yes	Immediately	Police, sheriff, highway patrol	15 days	Motor Vehicle Department, State Highway Commission, State Office Building, Topeka 66612	$200
KENTUCKY	No			10 days	Department of Justice, Frankfort 40601	$200
LOUISIANA	Yes	Immediately	State police	10 days	Financial Responsibility Division	$200
MAINE	Yes	Immediately	Sheriff, police	2 days	Secretary of State, Augusta 04333	$200
MARYLAND	No			15 days	Motor Vehicles Administration, 6601 Ritchie Highway N.E., Glen Burnie 21061	$100
MASSACHUSETTS	No			5 days	Registrar of Motor Vehicles, 100 Nashua St., Boston 02114; local police department	$200
MICHIGAN	Yes	Immediately	Sheriff, state or local police			$200
MINNESOTA	Yes	Immediately	Police, sheriff, highway patrol	Promptly	Commissioner of Public Safety, Transportation Building, St. Paul 55155	$100
MISSISSIPPI	No			5 days	Commissioner of Public Safety, Jackson 39205	$100
MISSOURI	Yes	Immediately	Police, sheriff, damaged party	10 days	Director of Revenue, Jefferson City 65101	$100
MONTANA	Yes	Immediately	Police, highway patrol	Not required		$100
NEBRASKA	No			10 days	Department of Motor Vehicles, Lincoln 68509	$250
NEVADA	Yes	Immediately	Sheriff, highway patrol, chief of police	10 days	Department of Motor Vehicles, Driver's License Division, Safety Responsibility Section, Carson City 89711	Any damage, preliminary; $250, written
NEW HAMPSHIRE	No			5 days	Director, Division of Motor Vehicles, Concord 03301	$100 ($50 if uninsured)
NEW JERSEY	Yes	Immediately	Police	5 days	Director, Motor Vehicle Division, 25 South Montgomery St., Trenton 08625	$200
NEW MEXICO	Yes	Within 5 days	State or local police and Dept. of Motor Vehicles	5 days	Department of Motor Vehicles, Santa Fe 87501	$100
NEW YORK	Yes (for death or injury)	Immediately	Local police	10 days	Commissioner of Motor Vehicles, Department of Motor Vehicles, South Mall, Albany 12228	$200
NORTH CAROLINA	No			5 days	Division of Motor Vehicles, Motor Vehicles Building, Raleigh 27602	$200

	Preliminary Reports			Written Reports		Amount of Property Damage Requiring Report
	Must You Make Preliminary Report?	If So, When?	To Whom Must Report Be Made?	Time Limit for Filing	Where to File	
NORTH DAKOTA	Yes	No specific limit	Local police, sheriff, highway patrol	10 days	Highway Commissioner, Bismarck 58505	$300
OHIO	Yes	Immediately	Sheriff, police, highway patrol	5 days	Ohio Department of Highway Safety, Columbus 43215	$150
OKLAHOMA	No			10 days	Department of Public Safety, P.O. Box 11415, Oklahoma City 73111	$100
OREGON	Yes	72 hours	Sheriff, police	Not required		$200
PENNSYLVANIA	Yes, if death, injury, road hazard	Immediately	Police	5 days	Bureau of Accident Analysis, Harrisburg 17123	$200
RHODE ISLAND	Yes	Immediately	State or local police	10 days	Registry of Motor Vehicles, Providence 02903	$200
SOUTH CAROLINA	Yes	Immediately	Police, highway patrol	5 days	Motor Vehicles Division of State Highway Department, Drawer 1498, Columbia 29216	$100
SOUTH DAKOTA	Yes	Immediately	Sheriff, highway patrol, peace officer, city police	10 days	Department of Motor Vehicles, Old Post Office Building, Pierre 57501	$250
TENNESSEE	Yes	Immediately	Sheriff, local police, highway patrol	10 days	Department of Safety, P.O. Box 945, Nashville 37202	$200
TEXAS	Yes	Immediately	Sheriff, police, highway patrol	10 days	Statistical Services, Texas Department of Public Safety, P.O. Box 4087, Austin 78773	$25
UTAH	Yes	Immediately	Local peace officer	5 days	Financial Responsibility Division, Department of Public Safety, Salt Lake City 84114	$200
VERMONT	No			3 days	Motor Vehicle Commissioner, Montpelier 05602	$100
VIRGINIA	Yes	Immediately	State or local police	5 days	Division of Motor Vehicles, Box 27412, Richmond 23269	$250
WASHINGTON	Yes	24 hours	Police, sheriff, highway patrol	Not required		$100
WEST VIRGINIA	Yes	Immediately	Police	5 days	Department of Motor Vehicles, Charleston 25305	$100
WISCONSIN	Yes	Immediately	State patrol, traffic authorities	10 days	Department of Motor Vehicles, 4802 Sheboygan Avenue, Madison 53702	$200
WYOMING	Yes	Immediately	Police, highway patrol	5 days	Accident Records Division, Highway Department, Cheyenne 82002	$250

240. Legal Action That Can Be Taken Against the Driver After an Accident • As a motorist you may be involved in a civil action (see sections 76–88) or a criminal action (see sections 150–157) or both.

A *civil action* is one brought by an injured plaintiff demanding damages from the defendant driver or defendant owner or both, for personal injury or damage to his automobile or property. If the plaintiff is killed in the accident, the action may be brought by his family or next of kin.

A *criminal action* is one brought by the government demanding punishment for violation of the laws. It need not involve an accident at all.

If you are involved in a traffic accident while violating the traffic laws, as you would be if you hit someone while speeding, you may be involved in both a civil action by the victim and a criminal action by the government, thereby risking both damages and a fine or imprisonment for the same mistake.

241. When to Consult a Lawyer After an Accident • Under the terms of your contract with the automobile insurance company, provided you comply with all the conditions stated in your policy, it must represent or defend you in all matters concerning personal injury or property destruction arising from an accident in which you are involved and for which you are covered in the policy (see section 262). But there are practical limits to the extent of the insurance company's real interest in your case. Thus, whether you need a lawyer depends on the situation.

a. If a criminal action (sections 89, 90) is brought against you (reckless driving or manslaughter, for example) that may lead to a jail sentence or suspension or revocation of your license, you need a lawyer. The insurance company must defend you only in civil actions.

b. If the accident produced no apparent injury to anyone and the property destruction you caused or suffered is fully covered by property liability insurance, you should receive full protection from your insurance company.

c. If the property destruction is greater than the insurance coverage— as when $20,000 worth of property is destroyed but your property liability insurance limit is only $5,000—you should seek legal advice, since the insurance company is primarily interested in what it has to pay and only to a lesser degree in amounts exceeding your coverage. Since it's not always possible to judge the extent of damages from the outset, use your common sense. If you think you have done a lot of damage or that your exposure is great, talk to your lawyer.

d. If the accident results in injury to yourself or anyone else, you

272

certainly should let your lawyer know the details immediately. If you have injured someone, your lawyer will advise you as to what action the insurance company should take to defend you against charges of negligence and claims for damages that may be brought against you. If you have been injured, he will advise you of the extent of your rights and the ways to enforce them and to claim appropriate damages. The question as to whether you need a lawyer, in addition to your own insurance company, to prosecute or defend any lawsuits in which you may become involved is discussed in section 259.

LIABILITY AND DAMAGE CLAIMS ARISING FROM AUTOMOBILE ACCIDENTS

242. Negligence and Liability • It has long been the rule that the negligent party is liable for damages that occur in an accident. Except for mishaps that are ruled unavoidable or perhaps acts of God (see sections 59, 244), the law's view has been that every accident is the result of someone's negligence—that is, the performance of an illegal or reckless act that a reasonably prudent person would not have committed, or the failure to perform, in the face of danger, a legally required or precautionary act that a reasonably prudent person would have performed.

In this traditional view, the person whose negligence causes an accident is held responsible to make payment for resulting property damage and personal injury and, in some cases, even for resulting death. If the accident is caused by the negligence of more than one of the parties involved, either or both may be held liable.

In an increasing number of states, however, the introduction of new no-fault insurance laws (see section 261) means that you will no longer have to prove that the other driver was negligent in order to recover damages for injuries you suffer in an automobile accident.

The major types of negligence contributing to automobile accidents, with a statement as to who is liable in each case, are described in sections 245–257, which follow. However, these do not begin to exhaust all of the possibilities, or the many exceptions to the rules. In fact, from 65 to 80 percent of all civil court cases tried in the United States revolve around the question of negligence in automobile accidents. (For more details on negligence, see sections 56–65, 70.)

243. Measuring Damages • How much can an automobile accident cost in damage claims? If it is serious enough and the state in which it occurred has no limitation on the amount of damages that may be awarded (chart 15, page 275), an automobile accident can result in a devastating financial setback, perhaps the worst you will ever experience. Briefly stated, the possibilities are as follows:

a. If you cause damage to property or another automobile, you are required to replace or repair it, and you may also have to compensate the owner for the loss of its use, or the cost of substitute transportation, until it has been repaired.

b. If you injure someone, you may be required to pay his medical and hospital bills, compensate him for the pain and suffering he endured and pay the value of his future loss if he is disabled temporarily or even incapacitated for life.

c. If you kill someone, you may be sued for compensation to the limit of liability allowed by the state under its "wrongful death" statutes. Should the victim be the breadwinner for his wife and children, you may have to pay the equivalent of the support he would have provided.

How much you will actually have to pay is determined either by the laws of the state (chart 15, page 275), by private negotiation and settlement or by a court and jury. If the amount exceeds your liability insurance, your bank account, house and other assets may be seized, and if these proceeds are still insufficient, a portion of your earnings may be garnisheed for as many years as necessary to make full compensation.

In one case a driver was sued and the verdict was for $23,500 more than his insurance. His house was sold and, after payment of the mortgage, yielded $10,500. He paid off the balance in weekly payments of $50 for five years. So the importance of having adequate insurance protection in advance (see section 264) and of consulting a lawyer immediately after a serious accident (see section 259) cannot be overemphasized.

244. Unavoidable Accidents • If an accident was unavoidable, no one is held liable. However, there are fewer truly unavoidable accidents than you might think, since more often than not a mishap can be traced to some person's negligence, error or wrongdoing. Clear-cut examples of unavoidable accidents include those caused: (a) by natural phenomena, as when a car is wrecked in a flash flood or when a rock on a hillside weakened by erosion falls and crashes into a vehicle, and (b) by unforeseeable events, as when a child at play dashes into the path of an

STATE LAWS AFFECTING LIABILITY AND DAMAGE CLAIMS

Most liability and damage claims arise from automobile accidents. State laws affecting such claims are summarized below. For detail on the headings, see sections 243, 249, 254, 255.

CHART 15	Does Guest Suit Statute Apply?	Does Family Car Doctrine Apply?	Does Principle of Contributory or Comparative Negligence Apply?	Within How Many Years Must You Sue for Property Damage?	Within How Many Years Must You Sue for Personal Injury?	Within How Many Years of Death Must You Sue for Wrongful Death?	Maximum Recoverable in Suit for Wrongful Death
ALABAMA	Yes	No	Contributory	1	1	2	No limit
ALASKA	No	No	Contributory	6	2	2	No limit
ARIZONA	No	Yes	Contributory	2	2	2	No limit
ARKANSAS	Yes	No	Comparative	3	3	3	No limit[1]
CALIFORNIA	No	No	Comparative	3	1	1	No limit
COLORADO	No	Yes	Comparative	6	6	2[2]	No limit[3]
CONNECTICUT	No	Yes	Comparative[4]	2	2	2[2]	No limit
DELAWARE	Yes	No	Contributory[4]	2	2	2	No limit
D.C.	No	Yes	Contributory	3	1	1	No limit
FLORIDA	Yes	No[5]	Contributory[4]	3	4	2	No limit
GEORGIA	Yes	Yes	Comparative	4	2	2	No limit
HAWAII	No	No	Comparative	2	2	2	No limit
IDAHO	Yes	Yes	Contributory	3	2	2	No limit[6]
ILLINOIS	Yes	No	Contributory	5	2	2	No limit
INDIANA	Yes	No	Contributory	2	2	2	No limit
IOWA	Yes	Yes	Contributory	5	2	2	No limit
KANSAS	No	No	Contributory	2	2	2	$50,000 & costs
KENTUCKY	No	Yes	Contributory	5	1	1	No limit
LOUISIANA	No	No[7]	Contributory	1	1	1	No limit
MAINE	No	No	Comparative	6	6	2	No limit[8]
MARYLAND	No	No	Contributory[4]	3	3	3	No limit
MASSACHUSETTS	No[9]	No[5]	Comparative[4]	2	3	3	No limit
MICHIGAN	Yes	Yes	Contributory[4]	3	3	3	No limit[8]
MINNESOTA	No	Yes	Comparative[4]	6	6	3[2]	No limit[8]
MISSISSIPPI	No	No	Contributory	6	6	6	No limit

(1) Only pecuniary damages may be recovered.

(2) From date of accident that led to death.

(3) If the decedent left no spouse, minor child or dependent parent, limit is $45,000.

(4) State has a "no fault" automobile law.

(5) There is a presumption that owner is liable for negligence of anyone driving his car.

(6) Liability of vehicle owner for death caused by another driver is limited to $10,000 for   275

CHART 15 (cont.)

	Does Guest Suit Statute Apply?	Does Family Car Doctrine Apply?	Does Principle of Contributory or Comparative Negligence Apply?	Within How Many Years Must You Sue for Property Damage?	Within How Many Years Must You Sue for Personal Injury?	Within How Many Years of Death Must You Sue for Wrongful Death?	Maximum Recoverable in Suit for Wrongful Death
MISSOURI	No	No	Contributory	5	5	1	$50,000
MONTANA	No	Yes	Contributory	2	2	3	No limit
NEBRASKA	Yes	Yes	Comparative	4	4	2	No limit
NEVADA	Yes	Yes	Contributory	3	2	2	No limit
NEW HAMPSHIRE	No	No	Contributory	6	2	2	$120,000[10]
NEW JERSEY	No	Yes	Comparative	6	2	2	No limit[1]
NEW MEXICO	Yes	No	Contributory	4	3	3	No limit
NEW YORK	No	Yes	Comparative	3	3	2	No limit[1]
NORTH CAROLINA	No	Yes	Contributory	3	3	2	No limit
NORTH DAKOTA	Yes	Yes	Contributory	6	6	2	No limit
OHIO	No	No	Contributory	2	2	2	No limit[1]
OKLAHOMA	No	No	Comparative	2	2	2	No limit
OREGON	Yes	Yes	Contributory[4]	6	2	3[2]	$25,000
PENNSYLVANIA	No	No	Contributory[4]	6	2	1	No limit
RHODE ISLAND	No	No	Comparative	6	3	2	No limit[1]
SOUTH CAROLINA	Yes	Yes	Contributory	6	6	6	No limit
SOUTH DAKOTA	Yes	No	Comparative	6	3	3	No limit[1]
TENNESSEE	No	Yes	Contributory	3	1	1	No limit
TEXAS	Yes	No	Contributory	2	2	2	No limit
UTAH	Yes	No	Contributory	3	4	2	No limit
VERMONT	No	No	Comparative	3	3	2	No limit
VIRGINIA	Yes	No	Contributory	5	2	2	No limit
WASHINGTON	Yes	Yes	Contributory	3	3	3	No limit[1]
WEST VIRGINIA	No	Yes	Contributory	2	2	2	$10,000[11]
WISCONSIN	No	No	Comparative	6	3	3	No limit
WYOMING	Yes	No	Contributory	4	4	2	No limit

death of one person, $20,000 for death of more than one person.

(7) But father is liable for negligence of unemancipated minor child living at home.

(8) But damages may include only pecuniary loss, plus pain and suffering prior to death.

(9) While owner's liability for guest is not restricted by statute, the courts have ruled that a nonpaying guest can recover damages only if he can prove gross negligence.

(10) If the decedent left no spouse, minor child or dependent parent, the limit is $30,000.

(11) Without evidence of pecuniary loss; with evidence, an additional $100,000.

oncoming vehicle at the last second or when a spike lying on the road pierces a tire, causing the vehicle to turn over. Accidents of this kind are often called acts of God.

However, if the flood was caused by the collapse of a faultily constructed dam, or the rock was pushed by someone whose indentity is known, or the driver who struck the child was going too fast and therefore was unable to stop, or the spike was left on the road by a repair crew, the person who caused the accident, in each instance, may be at least partially liable and may be sued for damages.

Other types of accidents that the courts have ruled unavoidable include: (c) accidents caused by a driver's instinctive, uncontrollable reaction to unexpected happenings, as when a gust of wind flattens a sheet of newspaper across his windshield, causing him to stop suddenly without signaling or to jerk the wheel and veer off the road, striking someone; (d) accidents that are caused by sudden, unexpected illness of the driver; and sometimes (e) accidents caused by other accidents, as when a car in a collision is thrown into another lane, causing it to be struck by an oncoming vehicle. Chain collisions, involving several vehicles, fall into the last category. The driver of the first or second vehicle may be liable for causing the accident but probably not for damage to the other cars in the pileup.

245. Accidents Caused by Conditions of the Road • State and municipal statutes require that signs or lights be placed along the road or signalmen be stationed to warn motorists of any obstructions due to work on the road or to natural causes, such as landslides and floods. Thus, if you plow into an unmarked, unlit excavation in the road at night, the government agency that ordered the excavation or the contractor may be liable for any damages you suffer.

This does not exempt you from your responsibility to drive prudently. If you are driving in daylight and see the excavation some distance ahead, but then cannot avoid it because you fail to slow down, you are negligent, and the rule of comparative negligence (see sections 64 and 500) applies, even though you were not warned initially. Nor is the state responsible for accidents caused by wet and icy surfaces. Under the "due care" statutes (see section 222), you must adapt your driving to weather conditions and the presence of blind corners and narrow bridges.

246. Accidents Caused by Pedestrians • Legally the pedestrian is as fully liable as a motorist for accidents caused by his own negligence or his failure to obey the traffic ordinances and rules of the road that apply to him (section 224), and he may be required to pay for resulting personal injury or property damage suffered by the motorist.

In actuality, however, the courts, holding that a comparatively frail human body is no match for the steel body of a car, tend to give the person on foot the benefit of the doubt. As one judge put it, a pedestrian in the road may stop traffic "even as Moses held back the Red Sea." He is entitled to as much space as will afford him free passage, and "his heart, as well as his body, should be free from attack." This means that even if a pedestrian should cross the road illegally and fail to respond to your horn, or panic and run back in front of your car, the burden of proving that you were not responsible for causing the accident might still be on you. The fact that the pedestrian was negligent might not free you from liability, especially if it was found that you had been driving carelessly.

247. Accidents Caused by the Condition of the Car • Because you have a duty to maintain a safe automobile (see section 214), you are usually responsible for accidents caused by mechanical failures. If you know that your car has a defect that would make it dangerous to drive, you have no right to take it on the road. Thus, if you apply the brakes to avoid a pedestrian and your car swerves into him, you are liable for damages if you knew your brakes were faulty, and you may be held liable even if you did not know.

The defect does not have to be a major one. Verdicts for damages have been rendered in cases of accidents resulting from worn tires, missing lights, broken rearview mirrors and cracked windshields.

Your negligence may not hurt you if it can be proved that the mechanical defect did not cause the accident. In one case a motorist who injured a child darting out from behind a parked car was held not liable, although he admitted that his brakes were worn. The court ruled that the motorist could not have avoided hitting the child even if the brakes had been in perfect working order.

248. Accidents Caused by the Condition of the Driver • According to the laws of most states, motorists who are under the influence of liquor or drugs automatically risk full or partial liability for accidents in which they are involved. You may also be held liable for an accident if you drive while drowsy, fall asleep, engage in lovemaking while at the wheel or fail to keep your eyes on the road for any other reason.

Drivers with weak eyes, bad hearing, arthritic hands or one arm or leg who have passed the driving tests and employ the corrective mechanical devices specified on their driver's licenses (see section 219) bear no greater liability than other motorists for accidents in which they are involved. But the law does demand that they take extra precautions to counteract the effects of their particular disabilities. Thus, a speed deemed reasonable for a normal driver in a given situation might be considered excessive for a physically handicapped motorist.

If a driver dies or suffers a sudden, unexpected attack of illness while at the wheel—such as a dizzy spell, blackout, spasm of pain or heart attack—which causes him to lose control and strike someone or something, the accident is usually held unavoidable, provided he has no previous and continuing history of such ailments. He is not liable for the damage caused, since he had no warning or reason to expect the attack. If, however, the ailment is chronic and the driver knew that it might recur at any time, he or his estate may be held liable.

249. Accidents in Which More Than One Person Is at Fault • The states follow two different rules in awarding damages when more than one party is at fault, as detailed in chart 15, page 275. Most states accept the theory of *contributory negligence*. Under this theory the plaintiff who sues for damages arising from an automobile accident must prove that the accident happened through no fault of his own and entirely through the fault of the defendant. If the defendant proves that the plaintiff was also negligent, even in the slightest degree, the plaintiff can recover nothing for the damage he suffered.

Each person's negligence cancels out the other's, even though one driver may have been 99 percent in the wrong and the other only 1 percent. In one case a drunken truck driver who, without signaling, cut recklessly across traffic to make a left turn, was held not liable for colliding with a driver who sought to pass him, because the latter had failed to slow down at the intersection.

To avoid such seeming inequities, a few states have adopted the rule of *comparative negligence*. By this rule if the plaintiff is found 25 percent to blame and the defendant 75 percent to blame, the defendant must pay 75 percent of the plaintiff's damages but could escape payment of the other 25 percent. (For more details see section 64.)

250. Liability When Driving Your Own Car • In seeking to collect damages for personal injury or death (see section 122) caused by an automobile, the burden of proof is always on the plaintiff. In order for the plaintiff to win his case against you, if you were at the wheel of the car that inflicted the damage, he must prove by "the fair preponderance of credible evidence" that the accident was caused by your negligence and that he contributed little or nothing to it. If you can prove that the accident was caused by factors beyond your control (sections 59, 244) or that the plaintiff was partly responsible (section 249), you may escape liability for damages, either wholly or partially. But if the plaintiff was on foot at the time of the mishap, he is likely to receive more consideration than if he were the driver of the other car (see section 246).

251. Liability When Driving a Borrowed Car • The driver's potential liability in this case is exactly the same as when he is driving his own car (see section 250). In addition, most states have enacted consent statutes, which stipulate that in accidents caused by the driver's negligence the owner is also liable for resulting damage and injury if his car was borrowed with his consent. In these states the owner is generally exempt from liability only if the borrower lends the car to a third person after he has been expressly forbidden to do so or if he uses the car for a purpose to which the owner has not agreed—for example, if he has borrowed a neighbor's car to run a local errand but drives it to another city instead.

Even in states that have no consent statutes the owner may be liable if he knowingly lends his car to an unfit driver, such as a child or a chronic alcoholic, or if he lends a car which he knows to be defective without warning the borrower. In the latter instance, the owner may be liable also for injuries suffered by the borrower, on the grounds that "when a person lends he ought to confer a benefit, not do a mischief."

You run considerable risk when you lend your car, but if you must do so, be certain your automobile insurance policy covers its use by others.

252. Liability When Driving a Rented Car • Here, too, the driver's potential liability is the same as if he were driving his own car. The rental company might also be found liable, as owner of the car, and for this reason drivers of rented cars are covered by insurance policies taken out by the companies, the costs of which are included in the rental rates.

One thing to bear in mind, however, is that there is a difference between a rented car and a leased car. If you lease a car (for May through October, let us say, or for every weekend), the company providing the car may insist that you take out your own policy.

280

253. Liability When Driving an Employer's Vehicle • When accidents are caused by the negligence of employes driving their employer's cars, buses or trucks on the latter's business, liability falls on the employer as well as on the employe. Legally, the employer is absolved from liability if the employe was using the vehicle for purposes not related to his job or had no permission, either expressed or implied, to drive it. In practice, however, it is frequently difficult for the employer to establish such a defense or to make it stick, particularly in the common situation where the employe retains the car during nonworking hours. When he is allowed to take the car home, it is a reasonable assumption that he may use it for his own convenience, which, in effect, puts him in the status of a borrower of the vehicle (see section 251).

254. Liability of Members of Your Family Driving Your Car • Most states either have "family car" statutes or recognize the family doctrine (chart 15, page 275), whereby the owner of a car is liable for any accidents caused by members of his family if he has given consent for them to drive it. Express permission is not required in every instance. Implied consent may be assumed if it is usual for a wife, son or daughter to drive the family car. The courts tend to regard use of the car—and the liabilities it may incur—as an aspect of the comfort and convenience a parent commonly provides his family. So if Junior causes an accident while drag-racing in your car, more than likely you will be required to pay the bill.

In states where parents are not held liable (chart 23, page 375), their children whose negligent driving caused an accident are. No matter how young they are, they may be successfully sued for whatever money, property, gifts or inheritances they possess or later acquire and may be required to satisfy judgments for up to twenty years after the accident.

A vital precaution every parent should take is to enlarge his automobile insurance coverage to include his children as they become old enough to drive, as well as other members of his household who are permitted to use his car, such as servants.

255. Liability to Guests in Your Car • Most states (chart 15, page 275) have enacted "automobile guest" laws whereby drivers of private automobiles are ordinarily absolved of all liability to nonpaying guests who ride with them. To recover damages for personal injury in these states the guest must prove that the car had been driven not just carelessly but with wanton recklessness or that the driver knew his car was dangerously unsafe but had not informed the guest of its condition.

In states that do not recognize the "automobile guest" doctrine the negligent driver is liable for injury to his guests, except, in some instances, where the driver is the guest's husband or wife. However, a guest may be unable to recover damages if he is guilty of contributory negligence (see section 64) in an accident—for example, if he fails to warn of an avoidable danger of which the driver is unaware or if he does not demand to be let out of a car that is being recklessly driven. The law, as you can see, approves of backseat driving.

If an accident is caused by a guest's reckless act, such as grabbing the steering wheel or distracting the driver's attention from the road, the guest is solely liable for the consequences, including injury sustained by the driver.

The term *guest* can be a tricky one. If you drive a party of friends on a trip or in a car pool with the understanding that they will share the cost of gasoline, highway tolls and similar expenses, they are not guests but business visitors, and you are liable for their safety. Your automobile liability insurance may not apply to injuries they suffer due to your negligence, and the few dollars they contribute to your expenses may later cost you thousands in a courtroom.

256. Liability to Paying Passengers • A paying passenger in a car or taxi will always recover for any personal injuries or damage to his property suffered when the vehicle in which he is riding is involved in a collision—unless he somehow deliberately caused the accident or unless it was caused by an act of God. The liability for payment falls on the person or persons adjudged responsible for having caused the accident: the driver of the passenger's car, the other motorist or both.

257. Special Rules of Liability Involving Children • The courts of most states have set various ages below which a child is held not capable of a proper understanding of danger. Thus, the sounding of horns, reduction of speed and other precautions that a driver normally uses to avoid adult pedestrians may not be sufficient to absolve him of liability in the case of children. Although some courts hold that children who are old enough to be allowed to cross the road by themselves or play in the street are old enough to understand and obey the traffic rules, the wisest precaution a motorist can take, as one judge has put it, "is to assume that playing children will do the most reckless thing imaginable, and proceed accordingly."

In recent years the "attractive nuisance" description (section 61) has been applied to cars. One driver who left his car with the key in the ignition while he ran into a store was held liable when some children started the car and it hit a pedestrian.

258. Out-of-Court Settlement • In recent years—even with no-fault insurance—a high percentage of people who suffered injuries in automobile accidents retained lawyers. This is because no-fault insurance applies only to injuries for which damages do not exceed $500. Most of the cases were settled out of court, however.

The reasons for this are obvious. First, the backlog of cases is so great that many of them take five or six years to reach trial, and few claimants have either the financial resources or the patience to wait that long. In addition, important witnesses may have died or moved away in the interim. Second, the costs of litigation are high, for both parties (see section 75). Third, it is rare that a settlement fair to both parties cannot be reached out of court (see section 77).

259. When You Need a Lawyer • If you are the injured party in an automobile accident in which the other driver admits his fault, and your claims for personal injury or property damage are small, chances are that you can reach a fair settlement with the driver's insurance company, or the driver himself if he carries no liability insurance, without the aid of a lawyer. If you do not know how much you may reasonably claim in damages and other compensation, you should seek the information from a lawyer, although you need not necessarily retain him to represent you. If the other driver refuses to admit that he was responsible for the accident, or if he or his insurance company refuses to pay your full claims, you can have a lawyer take the matter to court or you can, if your claims are not substantial, take your case to small-claims court yourself.

Your own insurance company has no obligation to represent you as a plaintiff seeking damages, although it may take legal action against the other driver on its own behalf to recover any monies it pays you in compensation for damage to your car or personal injuries if you carry collision, family liability or similar coverage (see section 262). If your own insurance company refuses to pay you what you consider fair compensation for your property damage and personal injuries under your policy, you will need a lawyer to take legal action against the company.

If you have no liability insurance and are involved in an auto accident, you should consult a lawyer whether or not you believe the accident was solely your fault. If you are sued and the damages asked for are larger than you think justified or than you can afford to pay, you should certainly retain a lawyer to defend you.

If you carry liability insurance and are the defendant in an auto accident, your insurance company is obligated to represent and defend you, and you do not ordinarily need a lawyer of your own, although there is no harm, and possible advantage, in consulting your own lawyer to explore the ramifications of the case. However, you should retain your own lawyer to work with the insurance company attorneys in the following situations:

a. If the plaintiff's claims exceed the amount of your liability coverage, so that if a judgment were entered against you for the plaintiff's full claims the balance of the compensation would have to be paid out of your own pocket. If you carry only $20,000 in liability insurance and the plaintiff demands $150,000, your insurance company must still defend you against the claim, but it may not do so with as much zeal as your own lawyer, since it has no financial obligation for any amount above the $20,000 for which you are insured, and it may feel that the $20,000 is as good as lost against such a large claim if the plaintiff has a good case against you. However, if the insurance company is plainly careless or negligent in defending you, and you lose the suit or are forced to settle too quickly, you may have a legal claim against your company. You need an attorney to pursue such a claim.

b. If you decide it is to your advantage to sue the other driver before he sues you, or if you want to enter a countersuit against the plaintiff. Your insurance company is not obliged to follow your wishes in these respects.

c. If your insurance company's willingness to settle with the plaintiff implies liability on your part, which may also expose you to charges of criminal liability. The insurance company's obligation to defend you extends only to civil actions, not to criminal prosecution.

260. When the Insurance Company Has a Right Not to Defend You • There are some situations in which your company is not required to act in your defense: (a) if you attempt to settle the case without your insurer's approval; (b) if the company finds that you misrepresented yourself when you applied for your policy; (c) if you make a false statement in reporting the accident to the insurance company; (d) if you fail to send to the insurance company promptly any legal notices served on you with regard to the accident; or (e) if you fail to report an accident promptly.

A case in New York involved a small boy who darted out into the street and was clipped by the fender of a passing car. Some weeks later the driver of the car was sued. His company refused to accept liability, claiming that, not having been notified, it could not investigate the case properly. This position was upheld by the highest court in the state.

AUTOMOBILE INSURANCE

261. Proof of Negligence vs. No-Fault Auto Insurance • Until several years ago no victim of an automobile accident, in any state, could collect compensation from automobile liability insurance for death, bodily injury or property damage unless he could prove that the accident was caused by an insured driver's negligence (see sections 70, 242)—and the same situation continues to prevail in many states today.

This necessity of proving that a driver was at fault creates an avalanche of litigation, which swamps the nation's courts, costs billions of dollars in legal fees and helps to raise the cost of auto insurance to new heights every year. It also frequently causes injustice to victims of accidents in which it is difficult to prove negligence, in which both drivers were partly negligent or in which it is impossible to determine who was at fault, as in chain collisions that may involve dozens of cars. In addition, the system tends to delay compensation, causing hardship to victims, because insurance companies have the right, as well as the obligation to their stockholders, to resist payment or defer it in the hope of making a cheaper settlement.

To alleviate these problems and injustices, almost half the states have adopted the so-called no-fault automobile insurance laws (see chart 16, page 288). While the exact provisions of these laws differ from state to state, their key elements are similar: (1) If you have no-fault insurance, you need not prove that the other driver was negligent to recover. (2) Your own insurance company will promptly pay you, within certain statutory limits, for direct economic loss you have suffered—medical expenses, loss of wages, substitute household services, and, in case of death, a variety of survivor's benefits. (3) In most no-fault states property damage is not covered. (4) You still have a right to sue other parties in the accident. If you can prove their negligence you can recover for losses that were not covered or not sufficiently compensated for by no-fault insurance (property damage or suffering, for example). However,

YOU AND THE LAW

this right to recover is usually limited to certain maximum amounts. (5) Coverage generally extends to members of your household, drivers who are using the car with your permission, passengers, and pedestrians struck by your car. In some states it may extend to occupants of other vehicles.

262. Types of Automobile Insurance • The major categories of automobile insurance are (a) *bodily or personal injury liability* insurance, which covers the insured for any damages he may have to pay, up to the amount specified in the policy, for injury or death to others resulting from negligent operation of his vehicle; (b) *property damage liability,* which covers the insured up to a specified amount for any damage to the property of others caused by his car; (c) *collision* insurance, which compensates the owner for repair of his own car that was damaged in an accident, whether he is at fault or not; (d) *comprehensive coverage,* which pays for damage to the car from any accidental cause, such as flood, fire, theft, vandalism, windstorm or freezing, but not normal wear and tear on it or, frequently, mechanical breakdown; and (e) reimbursement for towing costs.

The most common type of policy is for liability insurance, usually covering both bodily injury and property damage up to certain stated amounts. Other risks that can be selected for coverage include medical payments to the owner for injuries suffered in a car accident; disability income, should he be permanently disabled; a death indemnity payable to his family should he be killed; family liability, to compensate for death or injury to members of the owner's family; guest medical payments, to cover doctor and hospital bills of others injured in the owner's car; uninsured motorists coverage, whereby the insurance company makes good any damages, up to the amount provided by law, awarded to the policyholder by the court if the motorist who caused the accident is uninsured and without sufficient resources to make full payment; and hit-and-run coverage, similar to uninsured motorists coverage, which applies when neither the owner nor the operator of the vehicle that caused the damage can be identified.

The various coverages mentioned above are usually available in two types of insurance packages, referred to as special automotive and family automotive policies. The special policy, which also may be written to include members of your family who drive your car, costs about 10 percent less than the family policy but offers less protection.

Among the types of coverage offered by the family policy that the

286

special policy does not, or may not, include are the following: coverage of you and members of your household when driving borrowed, rented or leased cars; coverage when other persons use your car with your permission; compensation to members of the family whom you (or other members of the family) accidentally injure while driving; and automatic coverage when you attach a trailer to your car.

When you buy a car on credit or through a bank loan (see sections 208, 452), the only insurance the creditor is likely to require is collision and comprehensive coverage, which protects his security interest in the automobile, and sometimes credit life insurance or disability insurance, to ensure that he will receive the balance of the payments if you should become disabled or die before the debt is discharged. This insurance does not protect you or your family in case you are injured in an auto accident and does not safeguard you from damage claims of other people you may injure, nor does it satisfy your state's financial responsibility laws (see section 211). Only liability insurance will provide you with the latter types of coverage.

263. Financial Responsibility Laws • Only a few states have compulsory insurance laws, which require you to obtain minimum liability insurance for bodily injury and property damage before you can register your car. The other states have so-called financial responsibility laws (see chart 16, page 288), under which you can legally drive your car without automobile liability insurance. But if you are unfortunate enough to be involved in an automobile accident that results in injury or property loss (beyond a specified amount) and don't have liability insurance, the financial responsibility statute requires you to post a cash bond, which may range from $5,000 to $35,000. In the great majority of states you must post the bond immediately, regardless of whether you are later found liable for damages.

In any state failure to possess adequate liability insurance or to post the bond after an accident will result in the suspension of your driver's license for as long as three years. In many states you must obtain liability insurance to the amount specified by statute before your license will be reinstated. The practical effect of these laws is to make automobile liability insurance highly advisable, even though it may not be technically required in all states.

264. How Much Insurance You Need • Your insurance company need not pay more in damages to the victim of an accident for which you are

AUTOMOBILE INSURANCE AND PROOF OF FINANCIAL RESPONSIBILITY REQUIRED BY LAW

CHART 16	Type of Law[1]	What Results of Accidents Are Covered?	Minimum Property Damage Liability	Liability for Injury or Death[2]
ALABAMA	Security	Injury, death, over $50 damage	$5,000	$10,000/$20,000
ALASKA	Security	Injury, death, over $200 damage	$10,000	$25,000/$50,000
ARIZONA	Security	Injury, death, over $300 damage	$5,000	$10,000/$20,000
ARKANSAS	Security (voluntary no-fault insurance)[3]	Injury, death, over $250 damage	$5,000	$10,000/$20,000
CALIFORNIA	Financial responsibility	Injury, death, over $250 damage	$5,000	$15,000/$30,000
COLORADO	No-fault insurance (compulsory)[3]			
CONNECTICUT	No-fault insurance (compulsory)[3]			
DELAWARE	No-fault insurance (compulsory)[3]			
D.C.	Security	Injury, death, over $100 damage	$5,000	$10,000/$20,000
FLORIDA	No-fault insurance (compulsory)[3]			
GEORGIA	No-fault insurance (compulsory)[3]			
HAWAII	No-fault insurance (compulsory)[3]			
IDAHO	Security	Injury, death, over $100 damage	$5,000	$10,000/$20,000
ILLINOIS	Security	Injury, death, over $250 damage	$5,000	$10,000/$20,000
INDIANA	Security	Injury, death, over $200 damage	$10,000	$15,000/$30,000
IOWA	Security	Injury, death, over $250 damage	$5,000	$10,000/$20,000
KANSAS	No-fault insurance (compulsory)[3]			
KENTUCKY	No-fault insurance (compulsory)[3]	Injury, death, over $200 damage	$5,000	$10,000/$20,000
LOUISIANA	Security	Injury, death, over $200 damage	$1,000	$5,000/$10,000
MAINE	Security	Injury, death, over $200 damage	$10,000	$20,000/$40,000
MARYLAND	No-fault insurance (compulsory)[3]			
MASSACHUSETTS	No-fault insurance (compulsory)[3]			
MICHIGAN	No-fault insurance (compulsory)[3]			
MINNESOTA	No-fault insurance (compulsory)[3]	Injury, death, over $100 damage	$10,000	$25,000/$50,000
MISSISSIPPI	Security & future proof	Injury, death, over $100 damage	$5,000	$10,000/$20,000
MISSOURI	Security	Injury, death, over $100 damage	$2,000	$10,000/$20,000

(1) "Security" means that each driver involved in an accident must prove his ability to pay for any damages that may be charged to him as a result. "Future proof" requires a similar showing of financial responsibility by persons who have been convicted of serious traffic offenses or have failed to pay judgments against them.

288

This chart summarizes state laws requiring that automobile owners offer proof of financial responsibility within specific limits of liability (see section 263).

	Type of Law[1]	What Results of Accidents Are Covered?	Minimum Property Damage Liability	Liability for Injury or Death[2]
MONTANA	Security & future proof	Injury, death, over $250 damage	$5,000	$25,000/$50,000
NEBRASKA	Security	Injury, death, over $100 damage	$5,000	$10,000/$20,000
NEVADA	No-fault insurance (compulsory)[3]			
NEW HAMPSHIRE	Security	Injury, death, over $300 damage	$5,000	$20,000/$40,000
NEW JERSEY	No-fault insurance (compulsory)[3]			
NEW MEXICO	Financial responsibility	Injury, death, over $100 damage	$5,000	$15,000/$30,000
NEW YORK	No-fault insurance (compulsory)[3]			
NORTH CAROLINA	Security & compulsory	Injury, death, over $200 damage	$5,000	$15,000/$30,000
NORTH DAKOTA	Security	Injury, death, over $200 damage	$5,000	$10,000/$20,000
OHIO	Security	Injury, death, over $100 damage	$7,500	$12,500/$25,000
OKLAHOMA	Security	Injury, death, over $100 damage	$5,000	$5,000/$10,000
OREGON	No-fault insurance (voluntary)[3]			
PENNSYLVANIA	No-fault insurance (compulsory)[3]		$5,000	$15,000/$30,000
RHODE ISLAND	Security	Injury, death, over $200 damage	$10,000	$25,000/$50,000
SOUTH CAROLINA	No-fault insurance (compulsory)[3]	Injury, death, over $100 damage	$5,000	$15,000/$30,000
SOUTH DAKOTA	Future proof (vol. no-fault insurance)[3]	Injury, death, over $250 damage	$10,000	$15,000/$30,000
TENNESSEE	Security & future proof	Injury, death, over $200 damage, or conviction of moving traffic violation	$5,000	$10,000/$20,000
TEXAS	Security (voluntary no-fault insurance)[3]	Injury, death, over $250 damage	$5,000	$10,000/$20,000
UTAH	No-fault insurance (compulsory)[3]			
VERMONT	Security	Injury, death, over $100 damage	$5,000	$10,000/$20,000
VIRGINIA	Security & future proof (vol. no-fault)[3]	Injury, death, over $250 damage	$5,000	$25,000/$50,000
WASHINGTON	Security & future proof	Injury, death, over $200 damage	$5,000	$15,000/$30,000
WEST VIRGINIA	Security	Injury, death, over $100 damage	$5,000	$10,000/$20,000
WISCONSIN	Security	Injury, death, over $200 damage	$5,000	$15,000/$30,000
WYOMING	Security	Injury, death, over $250 damage	$5,000	$10,000/$20,000

[2] The first figure is the minimum showing of financial responsibility required by law for death or injury of one person in an accident; the second is the minimum for all persons injured or killed in one accident.

[3] No-fault automobile insurance provides for payment of an injured party without proof of liability (see section 261).

held liable than the dollar amount of the liability coverage provided for in your insurance policy. If you have $10,000 in auto liability insurance and the court awards $50,000 in medical expenses and other compensation to the person injured by your car, you must pay him the additional $40,000 out of your own pocket—which could ruin you financially. Therefore, even if your insurance policy is large enough to satisfy your state's statutory requirements, it may not be sufficient to cover the risk.

There is no hard-and-fast rule for determining the amount of auto liability insurance you should actually have. Some experts say that you should carry as much as you can afford. Others say that it should be roughly equal to your net worth, so that if, for example, your assets total $100,000, you should have at least that much in auto liability coverage. But the authorities agree that most drivers are dangerously underinsured and that the minimum auto insurance and financial responsibility requirements that prevail in most states are too low in view of the increasing size of the awards made to accident victims by courts and juries. The cost of the additional insurance is surprisingly small.

265. Factors That Affect Your Insurance Costs • In a few states automobile insurance companies may charge whatever premiums they like without regulation by any government authority. In the majority of states, however, changes in rates must be approved by the state insurance commissioner after a waiting period, and sometimes public hearings. In other states new rates may be filed and put in effect immediately, pending subsequent review by the commissioner.

Where you live is a determining factor in the size of the premium you pay on your automobile insurance. States that have enacted no-fault auto insurance laws generally have lower rates than states that are otherwise similar. Each state is divided into rating territories based on population density, traffic congestion and other factors that influence the accident rate. The premium paid by an individual car owner reflects the number and cost of accidents caused by all drivers in his rating territory. Cities and their suburbs are usually placed in separate rating areas.

The cost of each accident claim in your territory also contributes to the cost of your insurance. Car repair charges, hospital and medical bills and jury awards vary widely from area to area, and you will pay more for your insurance in a community where the average accident bill is high.

Once a community's overall insurance bill as been determined, based on the number of accidents and the size of the claims, the cost is shared by all the insured car owners in the community. But it is not shared equally. Your own particular insurance premium within your territory is influenced by how likely you and other drivers in your family are to have an accident. Thus, individual or family premiums may be affected by the following factors:

a. *How your car is used.* Cars that are driven to and from work, or that are used for business purposes throughout the day, are usually more exposed to accidents than cars used only for family convenience and pleasure, and usually require higher insurance rates. There are farmer discounts for cars used primarily in farming and ranching, since their accident rates tend to be relatively low.

b. *The kind of car you drive.* Sports cars, extrahigh-horsepower vehicles and souped-up automobiles of normally lower horsepower are involved in proportionately more accidents than standard models, and many insurance companies impose higher premiums on them.

c. *Your driving safety record.* Statistics show that drivers who have had accidents or been convicted of traffic violations in the past are more likely than those with clear safety records to have accidents in the future. Thus, under the "safe driver" plans in effect in most states you may save up to 20 percent on your auto insurance if you and others in your family have not been responsible for any traffic accidents or been convicted of any serious traffic violations for three years.

d. *Your sex.* Men have more accidents than women. In most states a woman between thirty and sixty-four years of age may be eligible for a 10 percent saving on the premium if she is the only person in the household who drives the car.

e. *Your age.* Accident rates are highest among young drivers. Thus a male driver under twenty-five or a female under twenty-one may be charged considerably more than drivers above those ages, and a male driver under twenty-one more than a female driver of the same age.

f. *Your marital status.* Among young drivers, those who are married have fewer accidents than those who are not. Thus young married men are likely to enjoy lower premium rates than single men of the same age.

g. *Driver education discount.* Because they learn good driving habits, young drivers below the age of twenty-five or twenty-one (depending on the state) who have completed recognized courses in driver education may be entitled to special discounts on their auto insurance premiums. To be recognized the driver education course must meet the standards set by the National Conference on Driver Education of the National Education Association.

h. *Good-student discount.* Premium credits ranging up to 25 percent

291

are available in many states to youthful drivers who maintain good grades in schoolwork. To qualify for the discount, a youth must be at least sixteen years old and be a full-time student in a high school or college.

i. *Two or more cars discount.* If you own two or more private passenger cars, you may qualify for a discount on your insurance premiums, provided the cars are all insured with the same company.

266. Cancellation of Your Insurance • An insurance company is not legally obligated to sell you insurance and has a right to cancel your policy for any reason within sixty days after it goes into effect. After that the company generally may not cancel the policy unless you fail to pay the premiums or your auto registration or driver's license (or the license of another member of your family who drives the car) has been suspended. The company may also cancel your policy if it discovers that you obtained the policy fraudulently—by not disclosing prior accidents, for example. In any event it must give you notice of cancellation and, in most states, tell you the reason.

In most states the insurance company is not required to renew your coverage after the original policy expires. It might refuse if you have a bad record of accidents or traffic violations or are considered a poor risk. Many people don't report minor accidents for fear of losing coverage, but evidence of this dangerous practice can be used by the company to bar your recovery after a more serious accident, which is the time when you need it most.

Even if you have had no accidents or traffic tickets during the preceding year, the insurance company may refuse to renew your coverage if you belong to a group that tends to produce above-average accident claims, such as new or young drivers, or if you live in an area where the company finds insurance premium rates inadequate (see section 265).

Recently a few states have enacted laws that provide that an insurance company may not refuse to renew an automobile policy unless it has substantial reasons, such as your failure to pay premiums. In those states the company must tell you its reason, just as it would have to when cancelling your policy. If you are rejected or not renewed by one insurance company, it may be difficult to persuade another standard company to insure you.

If you are unable to obtain auto insurance through the usual channels, you may still get it through your state's assigned risk program or by dealing with insurance companies that specialize in covering poorer risks at higher premiums.

The *assigned risk plan* authorizes the state to order an insurance company, not of your choosing, to provide you with at least liability insurance under a quota system. Assigned risk plans vary from state to state, but generally the insurance company is not obligated to sell you liability insurance over a certain statutory amount. In most states the company is also not obligated to sell you coverage for collision, fire, theft and other types of losses, and its duty to defend you in court may be limited to accidents in which you cause bodily injury or property damage to other people; and you will pay a higher than average premium rate, depending on your driving record during the preceding thirty-six months.

If your record remains clean for that length of time, you may request that the insurance company change your status from an assigned risk to a standard risk basis. In order to encourage insurance companies to restore good risks to regular status, most states give them a credit toward their assigned risk quotas for each new driver they provide with insurance on a regular basis.

If you want more insurance coverage than is available under the assigned risk program but can't obtain it on a regular basis, your alternative is to buy it from a so-called substandard or nonstandard company that specializes in covering poor risks. Such companies may charge from 35 to 75 percent more in premiums than standard companies and may require far more liability coverage than you feel you need.

267. Selecting Your Automobile Insurance Company • Your safest course in choosing an insurance company is to deal with a reputable broker. If you buy insurance directly from the company or want to check on the company your broker recommends, ask your state insurance department about it or consult *Best's Guide,* which describes and rates every insurance company in the nation.

One factor to consider is the promptness with which the insurance company settles legitimate claims, since even some reputable companies may be very dilatory. There is no unimpeachable source for such information, so your best course is to rely on the word of a broker whom you trust or on friends who have had experience with various companies.

268. Dealing with Your Insurance Company and Claims Adjuster • After an automobile accident (see section 235) one of your primary duties is to notify your insurance agent as soon as possible. You should also inform him immediately if your car is stolen or damaged in any way, such as by fire, flood or other natural causes, by vandalism or by un-

293

known causes while it is parked. Give the agent as many details as possible, preferably in writing. Date your report and keep a copy, so that the company cannot later deny that you gave it prompt notice.

If your car is damaged through the fault of another driver, his insurance company must pay for the repairs in full, under his property damage liability coverage. If your car is damaged through your own negligence or by persons unknown or through an act of God, such as flood, lightning or other natural phenomena, your insurance company must pay for the repairs (minus the $50 or $100 deductible amount that your policy specifies), provided you have the proper collision or comprehensive coverage. If your car is damaged by an uninsured driver, your company will pay for your repairs only if your policy specifically provides for such coverage. (Types of coverage are discussed in section 262.)

Do not make repairs until the insurance company authorizes them. Otherwise you run the risk of having the bill challenged. When it receives your notification, the insurance company—either your own or the other driver's, depending on the circumstances—will ask you to bring your car to its inspection center, if it can be driven, or will send an inspector or claims adjuster to examine the car where it is or will ask you to submit to it two or more signed estimates from mechanics, garages or body shops, indicating what the repairs will cost. Even if you are not asked to do so, you should obtain such estimates in case the company challenges the cost of the repairs later on.

The question of whether the company is obliged to pay for the damage under the terms of the policy is a separate one. But if the company does acknowledge liability, and if it accepts one of the estimates, as is usually the case, it will send you a check for the amount. But if it refuses to pay the full amount, you may retain a lawyer and sue, which is expensive, or take the case to a small claims court (see section 8) yourself.

If your car is stolen, or totally destroyed by fire or other cause, the insurance company must pay you its fair value, as described in section 492. If the amount offered is less than you think the car is worth, you may sue the company for a larger amount. If your stolen car is recovered in damaged condition, the procedure for recovering from the insurance company is the same as for any damaged car.

If you injure someone else in an automobile accident or cause damage to his car or other property, your insurance company will ordinarily handle the matter entirely (see section 241), although you are required to furnish all available information and possibly appear in court to testify if a suit for damages comes to trial. If you are found liable, the company

294

will pay the judgment up to the amount of your liability coverage. If the victim's claims for injury or property damage exceed the amount of your coverage, however, you should consider getting a lawyer to represent you even though your insurance company has a duty to defend you (see section 259).

If you, your passenger or a member of your family is injured in an automobile accident as the result of another driver's negligence, his liability insurance will compensate you for your injury (pain, loss of limb, etc.), your medical bills and your loss of income while you are laid up. Sometimes the other driver's insurance company will deny his liability, in which case you may have to sue him and prove that he was negligent. You may also have to sue him if your claims for compensation exceed the amount of his insurance coverage. If your collision damage and medical bills are paid by your own insurance company in such an accident, your company may then sue the other driver's insurance company to collect what it has paid out. Your policy probably requires you to cooperate with your company in this suit. If you are injured by your own negligence, your insurance company must still make the payments if you carry the appropriate coverage.

Do not sign a release, accept a settlement or even talk to the claims adjuster until you know the full extent and cost of your injuries and property losses. The settlement will be paid in one lump sum, fully discharging the company. Any statement you make about injuries to anyone but your doctor, lawyer or members of your family may later be used as evidence against you.

Most reputable insurance companies will pay legitimate and provable medical and loss-of-income claims promptly. But some companies go to great lengths to reduce compensation. Do not be beguiled into accepting quick and unfair settlements by the insurance adjuster's claim that it is the only way to get your money quickly or that he is not authorized to settle for more, or be browbeaten by his accusations that you are unreasonable or are malingering and may be subject to prosecution for fraud. If you don't accept the offered settlement, some companies may not communicate with you or answer your letters or telephone calls, other than to acknowledge them, for months at a time.

If you run into this kind of treatment and the insurance company refuses to pay for future medical treatments that your doctor considers necessary or for compensation that you believe legitimate, you should consult a lawyer about your claims. Unfortunately, the courts are so clogged with such litigation that it may take as long as four years in some states for your case to come to trial. But if your claim is fairly substantial and you have the patience and resources to wait, your chances of obtaining a fair settlement are excellent; it will probably be made by the insurance company out of court just before the case is scheduled for trial.

For a more general discussion of considerations in dealing with insurance companies, see chapter 11, "Your Insurance," sections 481–485.

269. What to Do If Your Car Is Stolen • If your car is stolen from your own property or garage or from a public street or a municipal parking lot, you should immediately notify the police and your insurance company. If it is not recovered within a reasonable time and you are covered for theft, the insurance company must pay you the car's *fair value,* the price it is worth in view of its age and condition.

If the car is recovered in damaged condition, the insurance company must reimburse you for the cost of the repairs if you have such coverage. But if the car is recovered in another city, the insurance company need not pay you for your expenses in going there to pick it up or in having the automobile driven back, or for the cost of the substitute car you may have been forced to rent while your own vehicle was missing.

Nor will the insurance company be required to pay more toward the cost of repairs than the fair value of the car. If you have a battered old sedan worth only $250, and the garage to which you take it charges $700 to repair the damage from an accident, your insurance company need not pay you more than the $250 the car is worth. In any situation, be careful to ascertain just how much you may be likely to recover and whether the sum will cover your costs.

If the automobile is stolen while parked in a commercial garage or parking lot where you have turned your keys over to an attendant, the operator of the facility is responsible for the car and for reporting the theft to the police. If the vehicle is recovered, he must reimburse you for any damage it may have suffered and for the cost of substitute transportation if you need your car for your livelihood.

If it is not recovered after a reasonable time, he must pay you its fair value, unless the theft occurred during riots or under certain other conditions that he was powerless to prevent (section 203). However, you should immediately notify your insurance company, since if you are covered for theft, the company is responsible for making good the damage or loss if the garage or parking lot operator fails to do so. Your insurance company may then sue the parking lot's insurance company, and you must cooperate in the suit.

296

CHAPTER SEVEN

Your Home, Apartment and Real Estate

A boundary line is none the worse for being narrow.

—FELIX FRANKFURTER

7

Your Home, Apartment and Real Estate

Some Key Points in This Chapter—
Consult these sections for information on:

Charts in This Chapter

Renting Your Home or Apartment; Relations Between Landlord and Tenant

270. What It Means to Rent · If you live in a large city, or if your job requires you to move from place to place frequently, you may spend years of your life as a tenant in apartments or houses that you rent from the landlord. When you rent you are simply paying the owner of the property a fee for using it in somewhat the same way as if it were yours. But your rights are much more limited than they would be if you owned the property (see sections 46, 273, 303).

Your legal status as a tenant depends on what sort of agreement you reach with your landlord. The agreement is usually set down in writing and is called a *lease*.

The most common kind of tenancy is *tenancy for a fixed period*. This simply means that you can occupy the house or apartment for an agreed period of time—a certain number of weeks, months or years—according to the terms of the lease. Unless you or the landlord violate part or all of the lease agreement, you must continue to pay rent and the landlord must allow you to occupy the property for the agreed period of time.

Another kind of rental agreement you may make with your landlord is called a *tenancy at will*. In this situation either the landlord or the tenant may end the agreement when he wishes, though most states have laws requiring that the one must give written notice to the other a certain number of days before the projected termination date. If you are a tenant at will, you should consult a real estate agent or lawyer to find out what notice is required in your state.

If you stay on in your rented house or apartment after the period specified in your lease has expired, the landlord may have the right to evict you. While he may permit you to remain for another full term, he may also have the right to compel you to remain for a new full term. In any case you have become what is known as a *holdover tenant* (see section 276). The laws governing the rights and obligations of holdover tenants differ from state to state, and you should check them if you don't intend to renew your lease when it expires. It is also important that you make plans to leave the rented premises on or before the last day of the lease. If your departure is delayed by illness or for some other reason, you should try to make an agreement with your landlord that would permit you to stay on for a short period without obligating yourself to the whole term of the original occupancy. The court probably will not protect you if you are late in moving out simply because of inconvenience.

Local rent control laws may give you the right to stay on the premises indefinitely after your lease has expired at the same rent you paid before, in which case you become what is known as a *statutory tenant*. Or the same laws may set up special legal procedures which the landlord must take to compel you to move out. Once again, it's wise to find out what the law is in your state or locality.

271. Dealing with the Rental Agent • Once you have decided to rent, your next job is to find a suitable house or apartment. Sometimes the landlord will advertise premises for rent directly, but in most cases you will find yourself dealing with him through a real estate agent or broker (see section 278). He is paid a commission by the landlord for the service he provides in finding a tenant.

When you are looking at a house or apartment for rent, remember that the agent's first duty is to his client: the landlord. Don't take as gospel everything he tells you about the property, because the owner cannot be bound by the agent's misstatements—unless you can prove that he knew about them—but only by the printed words of the lease you sign. What's more, the courts recognize that anyone engaged in selling is entitled to a certain amount of sales talk, or "puffing." If the agent taking you through a house on a cold winter day points out the charming fireplace in the living room and the fine view and tells you the site is cool and breeezy in the summer, you won't be able to get out of your lease if the fireplace smokes, the view is blocked when trees are in leaf or the house and yard are muggy and stifling during July and August (see section 190).

Although brokers are regulated by the state and may have their licenses suspended or revoked as a result of misconduct or fraud, your best protection is to get references beforehand. There are several ways you can check on the reliability of a broker. You may ask friends or neighbors who have recently rented, you may talk to a local banker or lawyer or you may check with the local Better Business Bureau or local real estate board. But remember that your only binding agreement with the landlord is the lease itself. In fact, most leases state that any oral agreements not specifically included in writing are not binding.

272. What's in Your Lease • When you arrive at the real estate agent's office to sign the lease, he is likely to hand you a printed form that he will describe as "standard." The particular terms of your rental, such as

300

the description of the house or apartment, the term of the lease and the amount of rent will have been typed in. Although an oral lease is binding if you are renting for less than a year, it's still desirable to have your agreement with the landlord in writing. Leases for more than a year must be in writing under the statute of frauds (see section 180); otherwise they may not be enforceable.

The important thing to remember about a standard lease form is that it has been written for landlords and obviously contains clauses that are more favorable to them than to tenants. It may contain some terms that a court would not enforce against you and may not contain others that could be enforced against the landlord if they had been included. So even though you have a printed "standard" form in front of you, there may still be some room for bargaining. To make sure you are protected, you should read it carefully before signing.

You'll be better prepared to do this if you know beforehand what the lease is likely to contain and what the provisions mean. If you have any doubts about the lease, you should ask your lawyer to look it over.

Like any contract, the lease should be dated and should include the full names and addresses of the parties—you and the landlord.

The lease should also state the amount of the rent and how and when it is to be paid. Most leases give the total amount of the rent and divide it into installments, payable in advance on the first of each month or other stated period. If the lease doesn't call for advance payment, the rent will be due on the last day of the period for which it is paid. The lease will probably provide that if rent is not paid on time the landlord may start eviction proceedings against you or sue you for damages or both (see section 275). In localities that have rent control laws there may be a ceiling on the rent that may legally be charged for your apartment; be sure that this ceiling has not been exceeded in your lease.

The term of your lease should be set forth—whether it is for a year, two years or a longer period. In some states long-term leases must be recorded just as deeds are (see section 283). Be sure that the lease contains precise beginning and ending dates for your tenancy and tells when you can take possession of the unoccupied premises. This precaution will help you to avoid the possibility that an earlier tenant may still be occupying the place you have rented after the expiration of his lease. You may want to insist on a provision that postpones the beginning of your term until you can occupy the property.

The lease should describe the premises being rented in enough detail so that there can't be any mistake about what you are entitled to. If

301

you're renting an apartment, a statement of the street address and apartment number should be enough, but you may want the lease to pinpoint what public or semipublic areas of the building you may also use. For example, if the apartment building has a laundry room, garage, storage cubicles in the basement or swimming pool, you should have your right to use these facilities spelled out, as well as the total amount of any extra charges that may be involved. The lease should also describe any personal property, furnishings, household or garden equipment that are included in the rental. Sometimes an inventory of the landlord's property is attached to the lease and made a part of it. You may be responsible for any items that are missing or damaged when you move out.

Most leases call for an *advance deposit*—usually a month's rent—that you must pay the landlord as security to ensure that you will live up to the terms of the lease and return the premises to him in good condition. The landlord is usually required to put this deposit in a special bank account or trust fund and to pay interest on it. If the lease provides that the deposit is considered security against damages, the landlord may hold onto it after you have left until his claims, if any, are satisfied. If either you or the landlord breaks the lease before it has expired, you are still entitled to the return of your security deposit subject to his claims for actual damages (see section 276).

A particularly important part of your lease is the clause that tells who will be responsible for *repairs and upkeep*. Your obligation may vary widely depending on the kind of property you are renting and what the lease says, so be sure that your duties and the landlord's are clearly described. The landlord is generally responsible for major structural repairs, such as putting on a new roof, rebuilding a cracked foundation or replacing plumbing or drainage tiles.

If you are renting a house, you will be held responsible for ordinary small repairs to keep the property in the same condition in which you found it and for keeping the grounds in good condition. If the place you are renting or any of the equipment that goes with it is in disrepair when you are ready to sign the lease, you should ask for a provision stating that the landlord will correct these conditions before you take occupancy—or that you can return the premises in the same state of disrepair in which you found them. Any improvements that the landlord has promised to make before you move in should also be described in detail in the lease.

If you are renting an apartment, the landlord's duties will probably be greater. He is responsible for the repair and maintenance of common

HOW TO PROTECT YOUR HOME
FROM BURGLARS

From 1960 to 1975 burglaries increased by more than 250 percent. Observing the basic precautions outlined below can help make your home a less inviting target.

Key Points in Protecting Your Home

The keys to protecting your house or apartment from burglars are prevention—the installation of locks, grilles and the like—and awareness of the need for security. Locks are no good if you and all members of your family don't use them habitually.

Like anyone else, the burglar prefers to enter your home through the doors, so make these your first line of defense. They should be sturdy and equipped with dead-bolt locks *(see below)*. Don't neglect doors to an attached garage or sun porch; once inside them, a burglar can work unobserved on the connecting door to the house. Replace regular glass with safety glass for greater protection.

In a house, ground floor and basement windows should be fitted with locks or grilles; a burglar can open an ordinary window latch in a matter of seconds with a table knife. It is vital, however, that all members of your family be able to open the grilles easily from the inside in case of fire. In an apartment, be sure your window grilles don't block access to the fire escape.

Outside floodlights will help discourage nocturnal burglars. An electric eye or timing attachment will turn on the lights automatically at sundown.

When you go away on vacation, arrange to have mail, newspaper and milk deliveries stopped. Set up several inside lights with timing devices so that they turn on and off at different times during the evening, to simulate normal activities. A radio playing in the daytime will also discourage many burglars.

Don't carry identification on your key ring. If the wrong person should find the keys, he could walk right in. Keep your car and house keys separate; if you put your car in a lot be sure to leave only the ignition key. If you lose your keys, change your lock or the tumblers in your lock. Never give keys to strangers, such as workmen, tradesmen or domestic help; it's too easy to make copies. Arrange to be home when repairs are necessary or deliveries are made, or have a friend substitute for you. Never leave keys in such obvious hiding places as under the mat or in the mailbox.

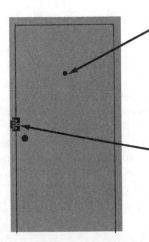

1. Don't open your door automatically when the bell rings. Look through the window or the peephole in the door. Even better than a peephole is a 180-degree viewer, which allows you to see down the hall, down to the floor, and about 12 feet on each side. Be sure you know your caller. Ask for identification if you have any doubts.

2. Use a double lock or a dead bolt at all times. Lock it even when you are at home or going out for only a few minutes.

3. Windows that are accessible from outside should be fitted with keyed window locks.

areas in and outside the building, like halls, stairways and courtyards, and—depending on the laws and customs of the state or area—he may also be responsible for regular maintenance work inside your apartment. In localities where the landlord's responsibilities are defined by statute he may be required to paint the inside of your apartment periodically and to make repairs to leaky plumbing, faulty wiring, flaking plaster and so forth. He is responsible for any damage or injury that results from his failure to keep the public parts of the building in good repair.

The important thing to remember here is that the landlord can't be held responsible for any damages arising out of his failure to do repair work inside your apartment unless you have told him the work is needed. To protect yourself, let him know by letter and keep a copy. If you notify the landlord that repairs for which he is responsible are needed and he still does not make them, you may be able to sue him for breach of contract. It's also possible that if the landlord refuses, you may legally have the work done yourself and then charge him for it—but whichever of the courses you plan to take, you should definitely consult a lawyer first. Only if the premises become really unlivable can you pack up, move out and cancel your lease (see section 274). But you can avoid almost all these problems if you take the trouble to find out the responsibilities imposed on each of you by state and local laws and to be sure that any other duties are carefully explained in the lease.

The *sublet clause* in most leases today requires you to have the landlord's written permission to sublet the house or apartment or sign over the entire lease to another person. If the clause simply calls for written permission, the landlord can say no without any explanation at all. You're better off, therefore, if the lease reads that the landlord's consent "shall not be unreasonably withheld." In this case you should be able to sublet unless the landlord can show a good reason for his objection. If you go ahead and sublet the premises anyway to a reliable substitute tenant, the landlord can only accept the new tenant or terminate the lease—he can't insist on continuing the lease and at the same time unreasonably refuse you permission to sublet the property. But be careful in any situation like this. You should consult a lawyer and know the local law before you intentionally do anything that's contrary to the terms of the lease, even if you're sure you are in the right.

There are other reasons for being cautious when you sublet, even with permission. If the new tenant doesn't live up to the obligations of the lease, you will still be liable to the landlord unless he's given you a release—even if he has accepted rent money from the subtenant. And when you arrange to sublet, don't forget your security deposit. Depending on the circumstances, you should arrange with the landlord to have the money repaid to you at the expiration of the lease, or you should have an equal amount paid to you by the subtenant and arrange with the landlord to return the security to him. Whatever the situation, try to release yourself as much as possible from any obligation under the original lease. Renting rooms in your house or part of your apartment is not considered subletting, but the landlord may forbid it by another clause in the lease.

Many leases contain a *renewal clause* of one sort or another. One kind of renewal clause gives the tenant the option of renewing the lease when it expires, either at the same rent or at a higher rent to be negotiated with the landlord. Another kind, less common today, binds the tenant to a second lease on the same terms unless he gives the landlord adequate notice that he is leaving. The important thing to remember is that these provisions of the lease are binding. Read the renewal clause carefully so that you won't be trapped into a new lease you don't want or be deprived of the opportunity to renew a lease you'd like to continue.

If you're renting an apartment, the printed lease will probably contain a section called *landlord's rules and regulations*. These usually deal with such matters as keeping baby carriages and bicycles in the public halls, making excessive noise late at night and so forth. If the rules are reasonable a court will uphold them, and if you violate them the landlord may be allowed to end the lease. On the other hand, even if the landlord does not enforce the rules against other tenants, you may not be able to get out of the lease, since courts have often said that these rules are made for the landlord's convenience and not as a protection for you.

Your lease may contain a clause saying what the rented premises are to be used for, and the landlord can usually hold you to this. If you are thinking of setting up a home business of some kind in your rented house or apartment, make sure it's not forbidden by the lease. Any illegal use of the premises, whether mentioned in the lease or not, will allow the landlord to terminate the lease and evict you.

If you are renting a house, the lease may call for you to carry insurance or even to pay some or all of the taxes on the property. If there is no such clause, the law assumes that the landlord is responsible.

Once the terms of the lease have been agreed on, all that remains is for you and the landlord to sign it. If the landlord does not sign himself, be sure his representative has the authority to do so on his behalf.

273. Once You're In—Your Rights and Obligations as a Tenant • Your most important right as a tenant is to what the law calls *quiet enjoyment* of the property you have leased from the landlord. This means that, with some exceptions, a tenant has the same rights to the house or apartment he is renting as if he owned it. Within the four walls of your house or apartment—or on the surrounding grounds if they are part of the rented property—you may invite anyone you wish or carry on any activities that are legal and not expressly forbidden by law or by the lease you have signed with the landlord. If you live in an apartment building, it is understood that you have the right to use the public areas of the building, such as the halls, vestibules, elevator and basement laundry rooms.

Of course you do not have the right to destroy or radically alter rented property, as you would if you owned it. If you were to cut down the landlord's shade trees to make room for a croquet court or knock out the front wall of his colonial house to install a picture window, any court would view favorably his suit to dispossess you and to recover damages.

Generally speaking, the landlord does not have the right to enter the property whenever he pleases without your permission. But he does have the basic right to collect his rents and to enforce any other terms of the lease, and he does have the right to come onto the premises to demand payment of the rent or to make repairs in an emergency. And he may, with your permission, visit the premises to make sure they are being kept in good condition.

If the landlord should force his way onto the rented premises or harass you unreasonably with constant demands and complaints, a court would undoubtedly find this a breach of your right to quiet enjoyment of the property. In this situation you might bring an action for trespass against the landlord, sue him for damages or cancel your lease and move elsewhere. A landlord never has the right, without your permission, to enter your rented house or apartment simply to check on your housekeeping and to snoop. If your life style is so extreme as to represent a health hazard or to constitute a continuing nuisance to nearby tenants, however, he may take legal steps to have you evicted (see section 275).

Under the terms of your lease or the laws in your locality the landlord is required to provide you with services and may be responsible for certain kinds of repairs. If you live in an apartment building, the landlord is required to supply water and heat and to keep the public areas of the building safe and in good repair. If you live in a rented house, however, more of the responsibility falls on you. For example, if a visitor to your apartment slipped and fell on the icy sidewalk in front of the apartment building and injured himself, a court would probably find that because the landlord was responsible for maintaining the public areas in and around the building, he would also be responsible for any damages your friend might have incurred in the fall. If, on the other hand, the same friend were to slip and injure himself on the icy pathway in front of your rented house, the responsibility would probably be yours.

The landlord's failure to provide the services for which he is responsible can be dealt with in much the same way as his violation of your right to quiet enjoyment of the premises. If he should fail to provide you with adequate heat, for instance, you might sue him for damages, heat the premises at your own expense and deduct the cost from the rent, or you might terminate the lease and leave the premises. In an area where rent control laws apply, you might also seek a reduction in your legal rent because of the landlord's failure to provide services. Before taking any of these steps, however, you would be wise to consult a lawyer, particularly if you are being asked by other tenants to take part in a *rent strike,* which involves deliberately not paying your rent as a means of forcing the landlord to live up to his obligations.

The landlord's obligation to make repairs inside your rented house or apartment varies from place to place and from lease to lease (see section 272). Even if he is required to make repairs, you have a duty to notify him when they are needed. If you neglect to tell the landlord that the porch of your house has a rotten board, and a visitor subsequently puts his foot through the porch floor and injures himself, the landlord will probably not be liable to the visitor, unless it can be shown that the landlord received from some other source a warning of the defective condition of the board.

If you suffer damages as the result of an inherent defect in the property that the landlord knows about at the time you take possession but does not tell you about, he is liable. He may even be liable if the court finds that he should have known about the defect because it was his duty to be aware of the condition of the premises. So if the corroded pipes in your apartment that he knew about burst and ruin your carpeting and upholstery, you have a good chance of recovery.

Responsibility for carrying insurance on the premises also varies from one case to another. Unless in the lease the tenant explicitly assumes responsibility for carrying insurance, courts will usually hold that the landlord is responsible for insuring the rented premises against damage or destruction by fire. Of course it is your obligation as tenant to insure your personal belongings against fire and theft and to carry liability insurance if you wish to protect yourself against suits for damages by any guests or employes of yours.

Obviously the landlord is not responsible for damages suffered by friends or employes of yours in accidents that occur on the rented premises as a result of your negligence (see sections 61, 304).

You have no right to make major or substantial changes in the apartment or house that you are renting unless the lease specifically allows you to or unless you obtain the landlord's permission in writing. If you knock out an interior wall or have a fishpond built in the garden, the landlord may go to court to force you to restore the premises to their original condition when your lease comes to an end. If he is pleased with the changes you have made, however, he may keep them without reimbursing you for any of the expense involved. If you install minor fixtures such as shelves, curtain rods or a simple room divider, however, these remain your property and you may usually take them with you at the termination of the lease (see section 276).

274. Breaking Your Lease · As long as the landlord allows you to possess and quietly enjoy the rented property and fulfills the obligations he has undertaken in the lease, it is difficult for you to break a written lease for a fixed period of time. If your arrangement with the landlord is a tenancy at will (see section 270), you can of course bring the lease to an end simply by giving the landlord notice at the prescribed interval before you want to vacate the premises. A landlord and tenant can always end a lease by mutual agreement—whether the lease is written or not.

While a legal document is not necessary to terminate a lease, it would be wise to obtain a written statement from the landlord so that he could not later claim that you broke the lease without his agreement and that you owe him rent for months or years after your departure. Technically, however, your surrender of the property and the landlord's acceptance of it—often symbolized by your returning of the key to the premises to him—is sufficient to show that the lease has come to an end.

A tenant may terminate the lease without the landlord's agreement if the landlord has either interfered with the tenant's quiet enjoyment of the property or failed to meet his obligations in such a way that the property has become unlivable or so changed in nature from its condition when the tenant rented it that it is no longer usable. Lawyers call this *constructive eviction,* and most courts consider it a basis for breaking a lease. If your apartment was without heat or water for a day or two because of a boiler breakdown, there would probably not be an eviction, and you would not be able to break your lease. But if there was a consistent lack of heat and hot water over a period of months, you would probably be able to terminate your lease and perhaps to recover damages from the landlord as well. Courts have also allowed tenants to break their leases when the landlord has let the property deteriorate or become filthy or infested with rats or vermin. A violation of fire department regulations may also constitute a basis for breaking the lease.

The continued intrusion of an overcurious lady landlord into an apartment rented by a group of working girls might well constitute constructive eviction and justify their breaking their lease. If you rented a country house with a broad lawn, the landlord's subsequent return without your permission to deposit piles of lumber and farm equipment on it might also constitute such an eviction and entitle you to break your lease. In a case of this sort the courts would probably rule that even though he did not interfere with your use of the house, by depriving you of the use of a large part of the property he had effectively *evicted* you from all of it.

A tenant may also terminate his lease if the rented property is destroyed or so severely damaged by fire or storm that he can no longer occupy it—provided that the damage was no fault of his. When the rented premises are condemned for public use by a city, state or other governmental agency, the lease may usually be canceled without liability to either party (see section 299).

If you do leave the apartment or house that you have rented before the expiration of your lease, the landlord may decide to sue you for damages equal to the rent from the time of your departure until the end of your lease. He is not normally required to search for a new tenant; that burden falls upon you.

Whatever the supposed basis for breaking your lease, you should consult a lawyer before you act. Legal decisions in your state may favor the landlord despite the interference with your rights which you think he has caused.

275. When the Landlord Can Evict You • In popular parlance—despite the legal meaning of the word described in the previous section—a landlord *evicts* a tenant when he takes legal steps to throw him out of the property he has been occupying. The landlord has the right to evict any tenant who is violating a substantial provision of his lease. The most common reason for eviction is the tenant's failure to pay rent, but a landlord may also go to court and ask that the tenant be dispossessed if he stays on the property without permission after the termination of his lease, if he is using the rented property for any illegal purpose or if the landlord can prove to the court that the tenant is objectionable or is violating the building regulations.

The question of whether you may always be evicted for a violation of the landlord's rules and regulations as set forth in the lease (see section 272) is a difficult one that has been decided differently by different courts. In one case a court ruled that a landlord could evict a lady tenant who kept a dog in violation of the "no pets" rule in her lease. But in a similar case in another state the tenant was allowed to keep her dog and her apartment, despite an almost identical clause in her lease. If you value your apartment and the landlord complains of a violation, your best course is to do as he asks and obey the regulation. If you want to make a fight of it—at considerable expense—you should first discuss the matter with an experienced real estate lawyer in your area.

The details of the eviction proceedings are governed by state and local laws and vary from one area to another. Generally speaking, however, the tenant must be given notice that the landlord is starting legal action against him—as in any other civil case—and an opportunity to correct whatever situation is the basis of the suit. If your landlord is seeking a dispossess order because you have not paid the rent, for example, you may end the proceeding at any time before the court issues a final eviction order by paying the amount you owe plus some possible court costs. But if you continually fail to pay your rent, so that the landlord is forced to start proceedings against you again and again in order to get his money, some state laws give him the right to evict you even if you offer to pay.

You do have the duty to pay your rent promptly, and that duty does not cease to exist even if the landlord has willingly accepted payment later in the month than is specified in the lease. If at any time he requests you to pay on the date specified and you fail to do so, he may start eviction proceedings against you, although a court might well regard his acceptance of many late payments from you as estopping, or barring, him from the right to evict you for one late payment.

If you should be evicted in the middle of the month for some reason other than nonpayment of rent, you would be entitled to a partial refund of any rent you may have paid in advance.

If you should fail to answer your landlord's complaint or to convince the court that you are observing the terms of your lease, the court will render a decision in favor of the landlord. At this point the court will issue a warrant to the local sheriff, marshal or other law enforcement officer ordering him to remove you and your property from the apartment. Unless you make prompt arrangements for the removal of your furniture and personal property, you run the risk of considerable loss or damage to your possessions.

If you feel that you have been unjustly evicted, without a lawsuit, you can bring a civil suit against your former landlord to recover damages. Again, however, because of the time and expense that may be involved, you should discuss the matter thoroughly with a lawyer.

276. When Your Lease Runs Out • Unless your lease has an automatic renewal clause (see section 272) or unless you have negotiated a new lease with the landlord, you have a duty to move out of the house or apartment you have been renting on the day the lease expires and to return possession of the premises to the landlord. This is usually symbolized by handing him or mailing in the key. In some states the law allows a tenant whose lease expires on Sunday all of Monday to move out.

When you leave the premises at the end of your lease you usually have the right to take all your personal property with you, even if you still owe the landlord back rent. In most states, unlike a hotelkeeper, he does not have a lien on your belongings to satisfy your debt to him.

If you do not move out at the expiration of your lease, the landlord may do one of two things. If he wants the premises back for his own use or to rent them to somebody else, he may take you to court and have you evicted in much the same manner as he would for violation of the lease. If he wishes to keep you on as a tenant, however, he may regard you as a holdover tenant (see section 270) and hold you to a new lease equal in length to the one that has just expired. In other words, if you stay on after the expiration of a two-year lease, the state or local law may allow the landlord to bind you as a tenant for the term of the lease or one year at the same rent. For this reason you should be extremely careful to arrange to vacate the premises by the end of the lease period, unless you want to stay on for the prescribed time.

The laws of some states make you a tenant at will (see section 270) instead of a holdover tenant if you stay on after the end of the lease. Under this arrangement, either you or your landlord may terminate your tenancy by giving whatever notice the law requires—usually at least thirty days.

The laws governing holdover tenancies may also work in favor of the tenant. If you stay on and pay rent after the expiration of your lease, and the landlord accepts the payment, a court will probably hold that you have established your rights as a holdover tenant and may stay on for a term equal to that of the original lease. During this period of time the landlord is powerless to remove you unless you fail to pay rent or violate some other obligation of your tenancy.

In certain localities where rent control laws prevail, a tenant who stays on after the expiration of his lease becomes what is known as a *statutory tenant*. A statutory tenant may keep possession of the premises indefinitely as long as he continues to pay whatever maximum rent is stipulated by the law and does not give the landlord any other legal cause to evict him (see section 275).

Let's say, however, that your lease has come to an end in the normal course of events and you are preparing to move out. Aside from having some place to go and from having the moving men lined up, your primary consideration should be the condition in which you leave the rented premises. Most leases call for the premises to be left *broom clean,* and this means pretty much what it says. While you would not be expected to leave walls, woodwork and floors sparkling and spotless, the landlord might well deduct from your security deposit the cost of removing large quantities of trash and debris. The law also recognizes that the house or apartment will have suffered a certain amount of reasonable wear and tear during the period you occupied it, whether the lease specifically takes note of this or not. Interpretations of what "reasonable wear and tear" means vary, but they generally adhere to the principles of common sense. If you practiced knife throwing in the den and splintered a section of wood paneling, or if you used the basement room as a workshop and bolted down power equipment through the linoleum, you would almost certainly be responsible for restoring the damaged areas to their original condition. If the amount of your security deposit was not sufficient to cover the cost of repairs, the landlord could proceed against you in court for the amount of the difference.

You do have the right to take with you fixtures that you have installed, provided that their removal does not do serious damage to the house itself. In disputes over fixtures, the court will often have to judge whether your additions have become such an integral part of the structure that to remove them would damage the premises. For example, there would be no objection to your removing curtain rods, venetian blinds and even shelves where such removal would leave relatively small holes in the walls. But if you had installed a carved mantelpiece in the living room whose removal would leave a gaping hole above the fireplace, you might be required to leave it in the house. At the very least, you would be held responsible for the landlord's costs in restoring the room to its original condition.

And as you leave, don't forget to collect your security deposit—or what's left of it!

Buying Your Home

277. When You Look for a House · There are many more nonlegal considerations in looking for a new home than there are legal ones. A wealth of material is available to instruct the prospective buyer on such questions as whether it is wiser to buy an old house or a new one, how to check the structural qualities and design features of a house, whether you should prefer a new development or an established neighborhood. There are certain practical questions that should be mentioned here, however, because failure to answer them may lead to expensive and troublesome legal complications later on. For your own protection, look into these points:

a. *Tax rates.* What are the current tax rates, how much have they gone up in recent years, how are they figured, what are the prospects for the future? If large-scale building and civic improvement programs are planned, how will these affect taxes?

b. *Zoning ordinances.* What kinds of uses are permitted in the neighborhood where you plan to buy? What is the minimum acreage allowed per house? Are there laws that will prevent you from expanding or remodeling the house you plan to buy? If you are buying a plot of land only, are there any restrictions that will make it difficult or expensive to build on or to use it for the purpose you intend? How easily can zoning laws be changed, and what is the likelihood that they might be: for example, might a quiet old residential community be rezoned for commercial purposes?

c. *Public services.* What kind of police and fire protection, utilities, sewage, sanitation and other services of this kind can you expect? Again, what is the outlook for the future? Will you be required to convert from a septic tank to a new local sewage system within the next few years— probably at considerable expense? How is the water supply? What are the chances of a hike in utility rates?

d. *Transport and highways.* Are any new state or federal highway

313

PRACTICAL POINTS IN BUYING A HOUSE

In addition to the legal considerations described in this chapter, there are a number of practical points you should carefully consider when you buy a house. Your evaluation of the property should take into account the quality of the neighborhood, the appearance of the house and yard and the quality of the exterior construction, the quality of the interior construction including plumbing and wiring and the arrangement of interior living space in terms of your family's particular needs.

TREES
Trees are desirable for shade and privacy.

GUTTERS
Gutters and downspouts should be adequate and connected with a drain that directs water away from the house.

FOUNDATION
Foundation should extend six inches above ground level.

ROOFING
Roofing material should be of good quality.

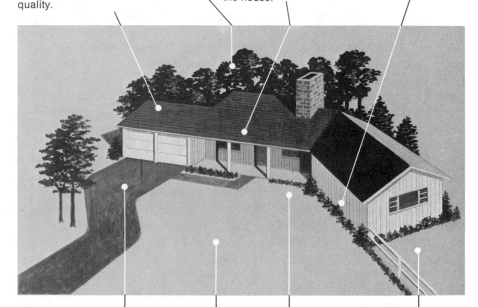

DRIVEWAY
Should be large enough for guest parking.

LARGE YARD
Size affords privacy and space for play.

LANDSCAPING
Flowers or shrubs may screen house.

DRAINAGE
Drainage should not allow surface water to stand.

Some basic considerations in judging the quality of a house from its exterior appearance are shown in the drawing above. Equally important is a thorough examination of interior construction for possible flaws.

projects planned that might result in the condemnation of the property you plan to buy or in lowering its value by making the neighborhood less desirable? Is the city likely to route a new bus line past your house or a subway under your street? What about plans for new airports in your vicinity, with the unavoidable concomitant of jet noise and fumes? Is there any chance that commuter service may be discontinued or radically cut back?

It is difficult if not impossible to get firm, reliable answers to all these questions. But by consulting with real estate agents, local officials, community planners and lawyers in the area who specialize in the real estate field, you should be able to get a pretty good idea of what lies ahead—or may lie ahead—for the area where you plan to buy. You can then plan for the future or turn your attention elsewhere before you make any binding commitment.

278. The Role of the Real Estate Broker • Once you are ready to look for a house in earnest, you will probably find it easiest to work through a real estate agent or broker. He knows the market in the area where you want to live and will be able to advise you about property values, the local tax base and other matters of concern to you (see section 277). If you describe your wants and needs to him realistically, he can save you time and frustration by guiding you to those properties for sale that are most likely to meet your qualifications.

In almost all states the real estate broker is a licensed professional who has received special training and passed a qualifying examination in order to practice. These examinations usually require a comprehensive knowledge of state statutes concerning the transfer of property. The salesmen in his office may also have passed qualifying examinations at a less demanding level, allowing them to work for a broker but not to run their own businesses (see chart 34, page 492).

As in any profession, there are some bad eggs in the brokerage business. But if you choose carefully, selecting a firm that has been in business for some years and perhaps checking with a local bank or real estate lawyer, you should have no problems with the broker.

Bear in mind, however, that the broker is not a neutral party. He has been retained by the owner of real property to sell that property, and he is acting as the owner's agent (see section 393). He is paid by the owner when he makes a sale—and only then. Although he may be extremely helpful to you, his primary responsibility is to the man who hired him and his primary aim is to sell. He will naturally stress the

315

desirable aspects of a house he is showing you, and courts will not hold him responsible in tort for normally enthusiastic claims he may have made. The law accepts a certain degree of overstatement, or puffing, as natural in a salesman (see section 190).

It is another matter, of course, if he makes an intentional misrepresentation of fact to induce you to buy the place. This is fraud (see section 49), and you might be entitled to sue him for damages or for rescission of the contract of sale (see section 184). This is a situation that is not likely to arise, however, if you make a careful check of the property—perhaps with the assistance of a professional house inspector—before you make a commitment. Buying a house is a big step, and you should not be hurried into it.

Sometimes the buyer will hire the broker, in which case the broker is responsible primarily to him and the buyer pays the commission on the sale if the broker finds a house for him. But the more normal arrangement is for the seller to retain and pay the broker. In no circumstances should the broker represent both parties to a sale unless he does so with their full knowledge and agreement. If two brokers are involved—one for the buyer and one for the seller—they usually split the commission.

The broker and the seller can make any agreement they choose as to what his fee or commission is to be. Generally it is from 1 to 7 percent of the total selling price of the house.

279. When and Why You Need a Lawyer • There is no clear answer to the question, "Do I need a lawyer to buy a house?" The fact is that you can select a house, bargain for it, sign the contract for sale (see section 281), attend the closing and complete the purchase (see section 288), take possession and live there happily ever after without the help of a lawyer. Many of the people who buy houses every year do it just that way. Against this preponderance of practice, however, you should weigh the considerations that the purchase of real estate may be the largest investment you will ever make, that there are legal problems that may arise (see sections 280–289) and that you should have a lawyer's advice on any important legal document you sign. So if you value peace of mind and future security, get a lawyer to help you in your purchase of a home.

If you do decide to seek a lawyer's help, be sure to get a man with experience in the real estate field so that he will know the fine points of the law in connection with deeds, contracts for the sale of real property, mortgages, encumbrances on title (see section 284) and the like. The bar association in the locality where you plan to buy will recommend experienced real estate lawyers to you. If you are getting a lawyer, get him early. He can assist you from the moment you start negotiating for a house, not just at the closing.

To make sure that you will not be unpleasantly surprised, discuss the lawyer's fee before you engage him. The usual minimum is not more than 1 percent of the total purchase price of the property. If you are buying a $25,000 home, you may spend $250 on the lawyer's fee. If the negotiations are particularly complicated the amount will of course be higher, but the lawyer will give you fair warning.

280. The Real Estate Binder • Your negotiation with the real estate broker, with or without the help of a lawyer, presents few legal problems and is largely a matter of horse trading. When you have agreed on a price, however, it is more than likely that the broker will ask you to make a deposit and sign a preliminary agreement. This paper is commonly called a *binder,* an *offer to buy* or simply a *deposit receipt.* To be prudent, you should not sign it without consulting a lawyer first.

The effect of the binder is supposed to be temporary; it acknowledges your intention to buy and the seller's intention to sell while a contract for sale is being drawn up. Some real estate lawyers object to the use of binders, saying that either the agreement is not in fact legally binding, in which case you gain no protection by signing it or, if a binder is so drawn up that it is legally binding, it may be so inflexibly worded that it will handicap your negotiations at the contract stage and may prevent you or your lawyer from securing more advantageous terms.

Despite these drawbacks, binders are widely used. Perhaps your best course is to follow the customs of the community but to be sure, if a binder is required, that you have it carefully examined by an experienced real estate lawyer before you sign it.

281. The Contract • The law requires that contracts for the sale of real estate, to be enforceable, be in writing (see section 180). Even if this were not so, however, in any transaction as important as the purchase of a house it is to the advantage of both parties to have their rights and duties spelled out as fully as possible. The contract binds both buyer and seller to go through with the deal on mutually agreed terms, but it also gives the buyer time to arrange for a mortgage loan (see section 290), to make sure that there are no defects in the seller's title to the property and to arrange for title insurance (see section 285); and it gives the seller time to arrange for moving out of his former home before the actual transfer of ownership—called the *closing*—takes place.

The contract for sale is customarily drawn up by the seller's lawyer or by the real estate broker who represents the seller. For this reason it is a normal precaution for the buyer to have it checked by his own lawyer to make sure that it adequately protects his interests.

A typical contract might contain the following provisions:

a. Names and addresses of the buyer and seller (see section 306).

b. A description of the property to be sold, including its address, dimensions, block, lot number, survey sheet number (if any) and any other details that will help to identify it clearly. Many buyers have discovered too late that because of inaccurate descriptions they have not purchased the property they thought they had.

c. The total sales price, the amount of the deposit (see section 282), the method of payment and the amount and the kind of mortgage, if any (see section 291).

d. A statement that the sale is conditional on the buyer's being able to obtain the kind of mortgage specified. The contract should clearly state that if the buyer cannot get the kind of mortgage he needs within a specified period of time, the contract may be canceled and the buyer will be entitled to the return of his deposit. If the buyer lets this deadline pass without notifying the seller of his failure to obtain a mortgage loan, however, he will be bound by the contract.

e. A description of the kind of deed the seller will give the buyer (see section 283).

f. A statement of any known encumbrances or defects in the seller's title (see section 284), with the buyer's agreement to take title subject to them.

g. A list of the personal property and fixtures that are part of the sale, including furniture, appliances, tools and garden equipment and the like. If this is overlooked, the new homeowner may arrive to find himself without a stove or refrigerator or minus the handsome bookcases he had admired in the den.

h. A note of the financial adjustments to be made between the parties —usually at the closing—for such things as fuel oil left in the tank or insurance premiums prepaid as of a certain date.

i. Any guarantees the seller is willing to make about the condition of the house. In the case of an old house, the buyer usually accepts the property "as is." But for a new house, the contract frequently contains guarantees of material and workmanship for at least a year after purchase.

318

j. The time and place of the *closing*—or actual transfer of title—which may take place weeks or even months after the contract is signed (see section 288). In the case of a new house still under construction, the contract should also give a date on which the buyer may actually take possession of the premises and provide either for a penalty payment or for the return of the buyer's deposit and cancellation of the contract if the house is not ready for occupancy on the date specified.

282. The Deposit and Escrow • A normal deposit, or down payment, on a house is 10 percent of the total purchase price, depending somewhat on the needs of the parties and the condition of the real estate market. The amount of the deposit is set forth in the contract, and the buyer should be sure that any previous payments he has made under a so-called binder (see section 280) are also listed in the contract.

Where particularly complicated financing is involved, the buyer or his attorney may request that the seller or his attorney set aside the deposit money in a special account, called an *escrow fund,* where it cannot be touched until the other provisions of the contract have been carried out. This is a matter of negotiation in most cases. The seller may be glad to comply or he may have an urgent need to use the deposit money at once, perhaps as a deposit on a new house he hopes to buy. Your lawyer can advise you on the possibility and the importance of having the deposit held in escrow in your particular case, and if so for how long.

283. The Importance of Your Deed • A *deed* is the legal document that transfers the ownership of property from one person to another. The deed is drawn up by the seller's attorney and is signed by the seller. After the closing (see section 288) the deed should be recorded with the county register of deeds. The purpose of this recording is to put the world on notice that you are now the owner of the property and to provide a public history of ownership—called a *chain of title* by lawyers—of any specific piece of real estate. In giving you a deed the seller cannot give you better title to the property than he himself had. If there is any defect in his title (see section 284); you assume ownership subject to the same limitation of your property rights.

There are three common categories of deeds. The contract for sale of the property will reflect the agreement between buyer and seller as to what kind will pass between them.

A *full covenant and warranty deed* is the most desirable from the buyer's point of view. It means that the seller guarantees there are no

319

defects in his title to the property. If it later turns out that there are, the buyer may be able to sue him for damages, which the seller's title company usually must pay unless the defects were caused by the seller. There are many kinds of defect in title that will not interfere with a buyer's quiet enjoyment of the property, however, and you should not necessarily be apprehensive if the seller will not or cannot give you a full covenant and warranty deed.

A *bargain and sale deed with covenant against grantor's acts* simply means that the seller guarantees that he has done nothing to cause a defect in the title, but that he cannot be responsible for any defect caused by a former owner which he knows nothing about. In most cases this kind of deed is perfectly satisfactory.

A *quitclaim deed* gives the buyer the least protection. In it the seller simply says that he is selling whatever title he has in the property. While this sounds risky, quitclaim deeds are commonly used to transfer the ownership of property in some parts of the country. The best advice on whether it is safe to accept a quitclaim deed will come from your lawyer.

You should also discuss with your lawyer the question of how your deed should read, that is, whose names should be listed as the new owners of the property. If you and your wife are buying a house together and the deed contains both your names, you will own the property as *tenants by the entirety*. This means that neither of you can sell the house without the other's agreement, and that when one of you dies the other becomes full owner. If there are specific reasons that this isn't desirable—if, for example, you want to be able to leave the house to your son when you die— then you should be sure that you are named as sole owner in the deed. But here legal help is essential, since community property laws in some states may defeat your intention anyway. The names of the buyers should be agreed on and set forth in the contract, since it may be difficult to change the type of ownership after you have received and recorded the deed. (For more details on joint ownership, see section 306.)

Remember that a deed will not protect you unless it has been recorded. If you receive a deed from a swindler and fail to record it, and he then sells the property again and gives another deed to John Smith, who does record it, Smith, not you, is the legal owner of the property. Even evidence of the fact that you received your deed first will not help you; it is placing the deed on the public record that counts.

284. Possible Defects in Your Title • There are several ways in which your rights of ownership in property, your *title,* can be limited or restricted. Many of these, however, do not prevent you from occupying your property and peacefully enjoying it, nor do they prevent you from reselling it, as long as the new purchaser agrees to accept the defects, or *encumbrances,* just as you have. Common defects in title include easements and covenants and restrictions. Zoning laws and encroachments may also limit the uses you can make of your property.

An *easement* simply means that someone else has the right to use part of your property for a special purpose. A previous owner may have granted an easement to the electric company, allowing it to run power lines over a corner of the property. Or a neighboring landowner may have the right to pass over your property to reach the main highway. This kind of easement is commonly referred to as a *right of way.*

There may be certain *covenants and restrictions* on the use of the property that were written into an earlier deed and that affect all future owners. A typical restriction might state that the land could only be used for residential purposes, for example. As long as the restriction is not illegal, the courts will enforce it. Restrictions on the sale of property on racial or religious grounds have recently been struck down by the U.S. Supreme Court as being unconstitutional, however.

Zoning laws impose statutory restrictions on the use of land. They may be changed or repealed in the future, however, so it is wise to discuss with your lawyer the effect they may have on your property rights.

In crowded neighborhoods where houses are closely jammed together, *encroachment* may exist. This might mean, for instance, that the eaves of a neighbor's garage extend over your property line, or that your porch actually sticks out into the public right of way. In a contract for sale of the property the buyer will normally agree to accept existing encroachments unless they make the property unfit for its intended use.

There may also be other *hidden defects* in title that would come to light only after extensive searches through the register of deeds, sometimes going back many generations. It might be that the property you plan to buy was transferred many years ago by a forged deed, or that a deed was signed by a minor who was not legally competent to sign it (see section 176), or that the deed was delivered after the signer had died and the property should have passed to his heirs. If a distant relative of that former owner were now to turn up and challenge your title to the property, you might find yourself in very serious trouble. It is because of this danger that the institution of title insurance has grown up.

285. Insuring Your Title • Title insurance companies now exist in most parts of the country. Your lawyer or the real estate broker can recommend one that serves the area in which you plan to buy property. The purpose of title insurance is to protect the buyer—and the person or institution who has lent the buyer money—against losses that may result from legal suits based on defects in his title, hidden or otherwise.

There are two basic kinds of title insurance coverage; the buyer pays the premiums on both. The difference between them is an important one.

The *mortgage policy* protects the lender of mortgage money, usually a bank, life insurance company or mortgage company (see section 290). The lender usually requires that the borrower take out this coverage as a condition of the loan. It does not protect the buyer against losses he may suffer as the result of a title defect, and it lasts only until the mortgage is paid off. It covers only the amount of the mortgage.

The *owner's policy,* or *fee-title policy,* protects the buyer-owner. This kind of coverage is not required by the lender, but it may be well worth the extra premium payment to a buyer whose ownership is challenged or impaired because of some defect in the chain of title. The owner's policy continues in force indefinitely after payment of the single premium.

The cost of title insurance averages about 1 percent of the purchase price for each kind of coverage, but this varies with the area and the complexity of the title search the company finds it must make. The premium on the mortgage policy is one of the expenses the buyer will be expected to pay at the closing (see section 288).

286. Rights and Duties of the Buyer and Seller • Once a contract for the sale of real property has been signed, the buyer and seller have the same obligation to perform as do the parties to any contract—and the remedies available to them if the contract is breached are also the same (see sections 183–185).

If the seller reneges and refuses to transfer title, and the buyer is forced as a result to buy a more expensive house or suffers other financial losses, he may sue for damages for breach of contract. If the buyer wants that particular house, he may apply to the court for specific performance of the contract (see section 184). If the court finds in his favor, it will order the seller to deliver a deed according to the terms of the contract. If the seller still refuses, the court itself may issue a deed naming the buyer as the new owner of the property.

When the seller is willing to sell, but the buyer and his attorney or the title insurance company find that the title to the property is so defective as to make it "unmarketable," and consequently refuse to accept it, the buyer is entitled to the return of his deposit plus the expenses of his title search and anything else the seller may have agreed to in the contract. The question of what makes a title unmarketable is a complex one that the courts must decide on the basis of the facts in each case. Generally speaking, however, if someone other than the seller has an enforceable legal claim to the property which would prevent the buyer from using it as he had intended, the title is not marketable.

If the buyer finds a less expensive or more attractive house after he has signed the contract, he too is required to stick to his bargain. If he defaults, the seller can sue him for the purchase price or for damages he has suffered as a result of the loss of the sale.

287. Other Considerations Between Contract and Closing • During the period between the time you sign the contract and the date when the title actually passes, you should attend to some other details in addition to your mortgage (see sections 290–293) and your title search or title insurance arrangements. You may want to have the property surveyed if there is any doubt about the boundaries as described in the contract. Your lawyer should check to make sure there are no lawsuits pending against the seller that might result in the seizure or attachment of the property (see section 301). The county clerk's records should be checked to be sure there are no mechanic's or artisan's liens outstanding against it that might take priority in case of the seller's default or bankruptcy (see section 296). If these items are not included in the search made by the title company—in some states they are—they are additional reasons for you to engage a lawyer, since he will know where to go for this important information.

288. The Closing: When Ownership Changes • The closing is the climactic moment in your purchase of a house, for it is here that you actually assume legal ownership of the property. The closing is a meeting between the parties to the contract for the sale of the property, their lawyers and others who have an interest in the sale—such as a representative of the bank that is putting up the mortgage money, the real estate agent and a man from the company that is issuing title insurance (see section 285). They gather to make sure that all the necessary documents have been prepared in accordance with the contract, to affix signatures and to agree on the apportionment of various expenses that the buyer and seller have agreed to share under the terms of the contract.

When all the details have been settled and the terms of the contract complied with, the seller signs the deed and delivers it and the previous mortgage to the buyer. At the closing the buyer also pays the other costs, often quite substantial, that are involved in the purchase of real estate. These are commonly referred to as *closing costs* (see section 289). The closing usually takes place in the office of the bank that is making the loan or that of the title company or that of the seller's attorney. (For a detailed discussion of mortgages, see sections 290–293).

Here are some of the things you may expect to happen at a typical closing:

The bank representative will produce the bond and the mortgage (see section 290). These papers will be examined by the buyer's attorney, and if they are in order, the buyer and his wife (whether or not she is a party to the purchase) will sign them. The representative of the bank will then hand over to the buyer the check for the amount of the loan. If the mortgage loan is guaranteed either by the Federal Housing Administration or the Veterans Administration (see section 291), the bank or mortgage company representative will also present the buyer with FHA or VA forms for his signature.

The representative of the title insurance company will produce policies insuring the lender (and the buyer as well, if he has requested coverage) against defects in title (see sections 284–285). These will be examined and checked against the description of the property in the deed and against the survey, if one was made.

If the house being bought is a new one, the seller—who is probably also the builder—will deliver a *certificate of occupancy* to the purchaser. This is a document issued by the local building department which states that the house has been constructed in accordance with local regulations and with the plans submitted by the builder for approval before construction was begun. The builder will also deliver whatever written guarantees of his materials and workmanship may have been called for in the contract. These papers, too, will be examined by the buyer's lawyer.

The attorneys for the two parties will figure out how much each owes toward such apportioned expenses as real estate taxes, fire insurance, fuel already in the tank and so forth (see section 289).

The seller's lawyer will produce the deed (see section 283) for examination by the buyer and his attorney, by the bank's representative and by the representative of the title company. The written description of the property in the deed should be carefully compared with that in the contract, with any survey that may have been made by the buyer or by the title company and with the descriptions in ear-

324

lier deeds to the same property examined by the title company in its search. This is the last chance the buyer will have to make sure he is getting exactly the piece of property he wants and expects to own. Errors creep in between the best intentioned of parties, and once a deed has been accepted and registered by the buyer it is expensive and difficult to change at best—and sometimes impossible. If the seller should die before the unintentional mistake could be corrected, for example, his executor (see section 588) might not be authorized to correct it, and his heirs might not want to, and the buyer would have no legal recourse.

When the buyer and his attorney have satisfied themselves that the deed is properly drawn up, the seller and his wife, if she is a joint owner or co-owner or has dower rights in the property (see section 306), sign the deed and hand it over to the buyer. Either he or his lawyer or the representative of the title company should see to it that the deed (and the mortgage, if state law requires it) is recorded with the proper authority as soon as possible after the closing. An unrecorded deed may not give the buyer legally enforceable title to his new property (see section 283).

The buyer endorses the bank's or other mortgagee's check over to the seller and gives him his own check for any balance still due on the purchase price.

This describes the course of a traditional closing. With the boom in housing sales in the last few decades, however, the procedures have become less personal in many parts of the country. Often the buyer and seller never meet face to face, and the new owner may receive his signed deed and a statement of closing costs by mail from a representative of the bank or title company. But the legal considerations and the significance of the documents remain the same.

After a traditional closing has taken place, the buyer's attorney will draw up and send to him a summary of the transaction, called a *closing statement*. This simply states when and where the closing took place and records all the sums paid out by the buyer including payments on the purchase price and closing costs, and the purpose of each expenditure.

289. The Closing Costs • It has become a truism that the average buyer is surprised and frequently embarrassed by the amount of money he is expected to pay out of pocket when he takes title to his new house. Since many of these closing costs are incidental to the buyer's obtaining a mortgage loan, he is clearly responsible for them. Other closing costs may be a matter for negotiation between the buyer and the seller or their attorneys. The costs a buyer may reasonably be expected to pay fall into three categories.

a. *Costs of financing* include all payments made to the lender in connection with the mortgage loan, including payments to the seller or his attorney in case a purchase money mortgage is involved (see section 291). They may include:

1. *Mortgage service charge.* This is the fee charged by the lender for the preparation of the mortgage bond. The amount of this charge varies in different parts of the country.

2. *Title insurance premium.* This may cover only the title insurance required by the lender for his protection (see section 285). A wise buyer will obtain title insurance for his own protection as well, since the lender's policy expires with the mortgage.

3. *Appraisal fee.* The lender will normally have the property appraised at the buyer's expense before granting the mortgage loan.

4. *Survey cost.* Whether the bank requires a survey or the buyer's attorney feels one is necessary, the expense usually falls on the buyer.

5. *Cost of credit report.* Most lending organizations require a credit check of the buyer, at his expense, before granting a loan.

6. *Recording fee.* In most localities the lender will record the mortgage with the appropriate public official for a nominal fee, which is charged to the buyer.

7. *Tax.* Some states subject mortgages to a tax based on the principal amount lent.

8. *Escrow account.* Some lenders require the buyer to deposit money regularly in an escrow account from which the lender will pay property taxes, insurance premiums and the like as they fall due. If a loan is insured by the Federal Housing Administration (FHA) this is mandatory (see section 291). The initial payment into such an account will be due at the closing and may be substantial.

b. *Payments to the seller* include the balance of the purchase price due at the closing if the down payment and mortgage loan don't cover the whole cost of the property, plus the buyer's share of the apportioned expenses listed below. These apportionments are usually spelled out in principle in the contract (see section 281) and computed exactly by the attorneys for the buyer and seller at the closing. They include:

1. *Real estate taxes.* If the seller has paid taxes for the whole year and title passes on June 30, for example, the buyer must repay him half the annual amount. If the closing were to take place on December 1, the seller would recover only one twelfth of the amount he had paid.

2. *Insurance premiums.* Most property owners have prepaid fire, casualty and comprehensive insurance policies in force when they sell. These are often transferred to the buyer, who pays back to the seller a share of the premium proportionate to the unexpired term of the policy.

3. *Fuel.* The buyer reimburses the seller for any unused oil remaining in the tank.

4. *Escrow account.* If the buyer is taking over the property subject to an existing mortgage that involves an agreement between the prior owner and the mortgagee for an escrow account, he must reimburse the seller for his contribution toward future payments. For example, if the seller has put $300 more into the account than has been paid out on the closing date, he is entitled to be reimbursed to this extent by the buyer.

c. *Other costs* that may fall due at closing include the premium on title insurance taken out for the buyer's own protection, legal fees for the buyer's lawyer, cash payment to the seller for any personal property that may come with the house (as when you buy some of the previous owner's furniture or garden equipment) and the nominal fee for the very important recording of the deed (section 283).

If you are buying a house it would be wise to discuss these costs with your lawyer or with the lender and real estate broker before the closing, so that you will have some idea of what to expect before the big day arrives. If you are represented by a lawyer, he will supply you with the detailed breakdown of your actual costs—the closing statement—a few days after the actual closing takes place.

YOUR HOME MORTGAGE

290. What a Mortgage Is • Few people today can afford the full purchase price of a house, and consequently most real estate is bought with the aid of mortgage loans. Savings banks, savings and loan associations, life insurance companies and mortgage companies all specialize in lending money for the purchase of real estate. The amount such organizations are willing to lend will depend on their appraisal of your financial stability, the locality, the current interest rate on mortgage loans and the appraised value of the property you want to buy. You, as the buyer, agree to repay the principal amount of the loan plus interest at a fixed rate on a monthly basis for as long as thirty years. The key provision of a mortgage loan is that the property which is the *subject of the mortgage*—that is, the property you are borrowing money to buy—becomes the security for the loan.

A mortgage loan ordinarily involves two parts. The *bond* is simply the written agreement between the lender (the *mortgagee*) and the borrower (the *mortgagor*) stating the amount of money involved and the terms under which it is to be repaid. Specifically it should spell out the principal amount of the loan, the interest rate, the duration of the loan and the periods at which payments are due (see section 292). The bond is signed by the mortgagor and has the same legal effect as an ordinary contract or note (see sections 167, 451). The *mortgage* itself is a separate document in which the borrower gives the lender an interest in the property as security for his loan. If the borrower fails to repay the loan as agreed in the bond, the lender can take legal steps to assert his right in the property in order to recover his money (see section 298). To protect the lender's interest in the property, the mortgage is recorded with the appropriate local official.

The laws of the states differ on just what rights the lender, or mortgagee, gets when the mortgage is signed. In the great majority of states today, the lender simply gets a lien on the property as security for his loan. The differences that do exist have little pratical consequence unless the borrower defaults, in which case both parties must seek legal advice about their rights (see section 298).

Since most contracts for the sale of real estate contain a clause that makes the actual transfer of ownership conditional on the buyer's getting the kind of mortgage loan he requires (see section 281), the lender will customarily send the borrower a *letter of commitment* outlining the terms of the loan which he has agreed to make. Once he has this letter in his possession, the buyer can proceed to the closing. If he cannot obtain a loan that he is able to bear, the buyer is released from his obligation to purchase the house under the terms of the contract for sale—but only if the contract contained this kind of conditional clause.

A person who has purchased property through a mortgage loan may obtain another mortgage on it if he can find a lender who is willing to assume the risk. This is called a *second mortgage*. The rights of the lender under the second mortgage are subject to the rights of the holder of the first mortgage. Let's say you borrow $20,000 from the Able Mortgage Company to buy your house and you give the company a first mortgage. Two years later you want to make substantial improvements in the property and you borrow $8,000 from the Baker Building and Loan Association, giving them a second mortgage. If you later fall on hard times and can't meet the payments to Able so that they foreclose the first mortgage, Baker's rights under the second mortgage are good only if Able sells the house for more than you owed, in which case Baker may recover what he can from the surplus. Second mortgages are not popular with many lenders and are usually issued only at higher interest rates and for shorter periods of time (see section 291).

291. Kinds of Home Mortgages • Existing mortgages and first mortgages fall into three general categories: conventional mortgage loans, mortgage loans guaranteed by the Federal Housing Administration (FHA) and mortgage loans guaranteed by the Veterans Administration (VA). Purchase money mortgages and second mortgages, which often represent secondary sources for financing the purchase of a house, are also discussed at the end of this section. For our purposes, the terms "mortgage" and "mortgage loan" mean the same thing.

Conventional mortgages account for more than 70 percent of the mortgage loans granted by lending institutions for the purchase of houses or other real estate. In a conventional mortgage loan the lender takes the full risk that accompanies any kind of loan transaction and charges the highest legal interest that the market will support. Most banks will lend up to 80 percent of the appraised value of the property to be bought, but the percentage is controlled by state law and by the age, condition and value of the house. Because the lender bears all the risk, his credit examination of the borrower is likely to be stricter than in the case of FHA and VA loans. Because he has more flexibility in raising his interest rates to meet the current market level, the lender is more likely to accept a conventional mortgage in times of high interest rates than he is to accept an FHA or VA mortgage, on which the interest is limited. While lenders may agree to a term of thirty years on a conventional mortgage, terms of twenty to twenty-five years are more common. Prepayment provisions and other terms of the mortgage are at the lender's discretion (see section 292).

FHA mortgages differ from conventional mortgages in two very important ways. First, the lender (still a private bank or mortgage company) is insured by the FHA, under the Department of Housing and Urban Development, against losing money on the mortgage loan. Second, interest rates, the percentage of the appraised value that can be lent and other terms of the mortgage loan, including prepayment provisions (see section 292), are much more closely regulated by federal law.

Under an FHA loan, premiums on the mortgage insurance amounting to one half of 1 percent a year on the outstanding principal amount of the loan (no interest is figured in for the purposes of the premium) are paid by the borrower. But the insurance protects the lender (mortgagee). Since the bank or loan company is thus protected, in theory it should be willing to grant loans more readily for longer terms or at a lower rate of interest—or both. In fact, however, when interest rates for conventional mortgages go up, lending institutions are unwilling to lend money at lower interest even when they are receiving this additional protection.

Many lenders overcome this disadvantage by charging a discount, popularly called *points,* on mortgage loans made at an unfavorable interest rate. *But FHA regulations prohibit the home buyer from paying a discount.* If, as a prospective home buyer, you are ever asked to pay points—refuse. On the other hand, it is perfectly legal for a seller or builder who seeks FHA and VA loans for his prospective customers to pay the required points to the lending institution. As a wise purchaser, you should simply be aware that in this sort of situation the money is coming from someone's pocket. If the seller is compensating the lender for low interest rates, the price he is charging you for the house will reflect the cost of the points (to the lender) above and beyond the normal purchase price.

VA mortgages involve many of the same advantages and disadvantages as FHA-insured mortgages. Guaranteed by the Veterans Administration, VA mortgages are available only to eligible veterans of the United States armed forces. (The rules regarding eligibility should be checked with your local VA office.) VA mortgages frequently require no down payment whatsoever, and interest rates are low. Because of this, lenders often want to charge a discount, or points, as in the case of FHA loans, and this charge must be assumed by the seller of the property. For a comparison of FHA and VA loans, see chart 17, page 331.

Another kind of mortgage frequently mentioned is a *purchase money mortgage.* What this means is that the seller of the house has accepted a mortgage from the buyer as security for the buyer's future payment of the difference between the total price of the property and the amount of cash he advances. Although no money changes hands, the seller has in effect "lent" the difference to the buyer in return for the mortgage.

Frequently a purchase money mortgage may also be a second mortgage (see section 290), offered by the seller in order to complete the sale of his property. White has agreed to buy Green's house for $25,000. He makes a down payment of $2,500, and the bank agrees to lend him

FHA AND VA MORTGAGES

The Federal Housing Administration and the Veterans Administration guarantee mortgage loans for the purchase of single-family homes under the terms shown below (see section 291). Eligibility does not expire.

CHART 17	FHA Mortgages	VA Mortgages for World War II Veterans	VA Mortgages for Korean War Veterans	VA Mortgages for Other Veterans
Who is eligible?	1. Persons who have satisfactory credit records, the cash needed at closing of the mortgage and enough steady income to make monthly mortgage payments without difficulty 2. Servicemen who have been on active duty for at least 2 years 3. Veterans who were on active duty for at least 90 days and who received honorable discharges	1. Veterans who served between September 16, 1940, and July 25, 1947, and were honorably discharged after at least 90 days' active service[1] 2. Surviving spouses of persons who served during the above period and who died as the result of service 3. Members of the Women's Army Auxiliary Corps who served for at least 90 days and who were honorably discharged for disability incurred in the line of duty[2] 4. Certain U.S. citizens who served in the armed forces of a U.S. ally	1. Veterans who served between June 27, 1950, and January 31, 1955, inclusive and were honorably discharged after at least 90 days' active service[1] 2. Surviving spouses of persons who served during the above period and who died as the result of service	1. Veterans who served between July 25, 1947, and June 27, 1950, and veterans who served after January 31, 1955, for a period of 181 days or more and were honorably discharged[1] 2. Surviving spouses of persons who served during the above periods and who died as the result of service 3. The spouse of any member of the armed forces serving on active duty who is listed as missing in action, or is a prisoner of war, and has been so listed for more than 90 days 4. Service personnel who have served at least 181 days in active duty status, even though not discharged
What is the maximum loan?	97% of first $25,000 of appraised value and closing costs (100% for servicemen and veterans); 90% of next $10,000; 80% of balance over $35,000; maximum loan is $45,000[3]	No maximum loan, but the loan may not exceed the reasonable value of the property as determined by the VA. Closing costs may not be included in the loan		
What is the down payment?	Difference between sale price and insured mortgage as described above	There is no VA requirement for a down payment if the purchase price does not exceed the reasonable value of the property, but the lender may require one		
What is the allowable interest rate?	8% (rate changes in accordance with market conditions)	8% (rate changes in accordance with market conditions and VA regulations)		
What is the maximum term?	30 years	30 years, 32 days		
What is the maximum service charge for loan?	1% of the amount of loan	There is no VA charge for securing a loan, but the lender may charge reasonable closing costs, which are usually paid by a borrower,[4] and also a flat charge of up to 1% of the mortgage loan amount for other origination costs		
Is there a prepayment penalty?	No	No	No	No

(1) Or who served a lesser period and were discharged for a service-connected disability.

(2) This applies only to persons so discharged from the Women's Army Auxiliary Corps prior to its integration with the Women's Army Corps.

(3) If mortgage covers a home approved for FHA mortgage after building begins and before the home is a year old, mortgage limit is 90% of first $35,000 and closing costs and 80% of remainder; maximum loan is $45,000.

(4) Closing costs generally include VA appraisal, credit report, survey, title evidence and recording fees.

331

$17,500 (70 percent of the purchase price) in return for a first mortgage on the property. But White does not have the $5,000 balance of the purchase price. Because he is anxious to dispose of the house and move on to a new job in another town, Green may accept a second mortgage as security for the $5,000 White still owes him. White signs a note agreeing to repay the principal and interest at a prescribed rate. Because the holder of a second mortgage places himself in a relatively risky position, a seller should consult his attorney before accepting one.

The acceptance of a purchase money mortgage can mean considerable inconvenience for the seller, who may then be saddled with the chore of checking up on the buyer's insurance and tax payments as well as keeping after him for the monthly payments on principal and interest. A seller who does accept a purchase money mortgage may want to put it in the hands of a mortgage company, for management on a fee basis, to relieve himself of these cares.

292. The Provisions of Your Mortgage • Every mortgage has certain standard provisions which protect the interests of the lender (the mortgagee), whose lawyer draws up the documents involved.

The borrower promises to pay off the loan and interest in the amounts and on the dates set forth in the bond; he agrees to carry fire insurance on the house as required by the lender (see section 487); he agrees that the entire amount of the loan will fall due if he defaults on his payments or otherwise violates the terms of the bond—except in situations covered by the loan modification clause mentioned below; he agrees not to make any major changes that might affect the value of the property, such as tearing down any of the buildings on it, without first getting the consent of the lender.

The mortgage agreement will normally spell out what *grace period* is allowed—that is, how much time the borrower has to make up a delinquent payment—and what legal notice the mortgagee must give him before starting foreclosure proceedings (see section 298). It is particularly important that the borrower clearly understands his rights in this area. If you have any questions, discuss the terms of the mortgage agreement with your lawyer.

The three central provisions of the mortgage agreement, and those which are the subject of most of the negotiation between the lender and the borrower, are the *principal amount* (how much is to be lent), the *rate of interest* (the cost of the loan to the borrower) and the *term* of the loan (how long the borrower has to repay.)

The question of how much to borrow and how long you should take to repay the loan is a financial rather than a legal one and depends greatly on your own circumstances, the state of the economy and other variable factors. The old theory that it is best to make as large a down payment as possible and to keep the term of the loan as short as possible —thus saving on interest charges—has given way to more flexible thinking in recent years. You should discuss the ins and outs of this decision with your lawyer, accountant or other financial adviser.

The repayment provisions of most mortgages today call for equal monthly payments for the duration of the loan. These monthly installments include payments both on the principal amount of the loan and on the interest. A certain amount to be set aside against taxes and insurance charges is often added to the payment. Under this system of regular payments, known as *amortization*, the proportion of each installment that goes toward payment of the interest is very high at the beginning of the loan period and becomes increasingly smaller as time passes. Most lending organizations publish detailed tables setting forth the exact amount of each payment to be allocated for interest and principal payments. During the early years of the mortgage loan the borrower may find it advantageous (if the agreement permits) to prepay a certain number of installments, either to shorten the term of the loan or to reduce interest charges. This, too, is a question for discussion with financial advisers. Interest paid on a mortgage loan is a deductible item on federal income tax returns.

Many mortgages todays contain provisions helpful to the borrower:

The *open-end* provision allows the mortgagor to borrow more money in the future under the same mortgage agreement without going to the trouble and expense of refinancing or taking out a second mortgage. This is particularly advantageous if interest rates have gone up since the orignal mortgage was drawn up.

The *prepayment provision* allows the borrower to pay off part or all of the outstanding amount of the mortgage before the due date. This can be an advantage to the borrower during a time of falling interest rates, or when he wants to resell his house without a mortgage on it. Conventional loans will frequently include a prepayment clause that provides for a penalty charge to the borrower if he exercises his right to prepay. FHA and VA loans all have clauses allowing prepayment.

Some mortgage loan agreements contain *modification provisions* that permit the borrower to miss a certain number of payments without risking foreclosure. The mortgagee in this case simply extends the period of

333

the mortgage to compensate for them. This can be particularly helpful in cases of illness or short-term financial setbacks.

Package provisions allow the borrower to include in the mortgage the cost of large appliances that will be permanently installed in the house he is buying.

293. Buying Property That Already Carries a Mortgage • If you decide to buy a house on which the owner has an existing mortgage, it may be either necessary or desirable for that mortgage to continue in effect. Perhaps the mortgagee will not allow the original owner to prepay the balance of the mortgage loan without a penalty, in which case the property will still remain subject to the terms of the original mortgage. Or perhaps you want to assume the balance of an original mortgage loan issued at interest rates more favorable than the current ones. If interest rates are falling, lenders are less likely to allow prepayment; if rates are rising, they may insist on it.

Whatever the reason, you may decide to buy the property *subject to the mortgage,* or you may agree to *assume the mortgage.* In either event, your liability to the existing mortgagee bank will be no different from what your liability would have been had you executed a new mortgage in the first instance. The mortgagee could foreclose against your property if you defaulted and could sell it to recover the full balance due on the debt. But where you take title to an existing mortgage, the bank has double security because, if you default, it can also look for payment to the prior owner (who originally executed the mortgage), since the bank would not have released him from his obligation under the mortgage agreement when you bought, *unless* the bank had then agreed in writing to accept you in his place.

BUILDING YOUR OWN HOME OR BUYING A NEWLY BUILT HOME

294. Before You Build • Many families today buy new houses that are part of a development or subdivision. The contract to buy the house may be signed months before the house is completed, and the financing may be handled by the representatives of the builder or developer. Other families may be able to afford the expense of a custom-built house designed by an architect engaged specially for the purpose. If you are contemplating either course, there are key legal points to keep in mind.

The special considerations involved in buying a development house are discussed in section 297. For the moment let's assume that you are planning to build your own, custom-designed house on your own land.

Because of the comparatively greater expense of custom-building your own house, it's more important that you have a lawyer's advice than in the case of a routine purchase.

Before you get far involved in planning, you must know what legal restrictions there are on the use of the property where you want to build and the manner in which your house may be constructed. This requires that you find out the details of the local zoning laws and building code.

Zoning laws are enacted by local legislatures with the aim of protecting and enhancing the interests of all property owners. They usually restrict the purposes for which a piece of property may be used or the number or kind of structures that can be built on it. Frequently they limit the height of buildings or require that they be built a certain distance from the property line. You—and your architect—must obviously be aware of any such restrictions before you start to draw up plans for a mansion with towers, turrets, ponds, stables and a racetrack, all of which are contrary to local zoning laws.

How the house may be built will be regulated by the local building code. This sets standards for materials and workmanship and is designed to protect the health and safety of people who buy or build in the neighborhood. If you employ a local architect he will be familiar with the building code and will not be likely to specify iron pipe where copper is required or fifteen amp wiring where twenty is required. If you employ an out-of-town architect, be sure that he has checked the local zoning laws and building code.

In most communities, plans for a new house must be approved by the local building department. If the plans comply with the requirements of the zoning laws and the building code, you will be issued a building permit. If the plans are not approved, then it's back to the drawing board —at a considerable expense to you in time and money. But whatever happens, don't proceed without a permit. Not only can the work be stopped indefinitely, but you may be fined and in extreme cases even imprisoned for violating the local ordinance.

295. What the Architect Does for You • An architect is a specially trained professional who is licensed to practice by the state (see section

335

398). His primary task, of course, is to design a house that pleases you, that meets your needs and that complies with the local zoning regulations and building code.

But the architect can and will do more than this. Once plans have been drawn up to your mutual satisfaction, he will submit the blueprints and specifications to various builders for bids; he will advise you on your final choice of a builder and perhaps on the terms of your contract with the builder (although you should also review the contract with your lawyer); he will supervise the contractor's work and check the bills he submits; and when the house is completed he will examine it in detail to be sure that the work has been done properly. If everything is in order he will issue an *architect's certificate,* stating that the builder has fulfilled the terms of the contract.

Once you've reached an agreement with an architect, most courts would take the view that he is acting as your agent (see section 393). This means that you may be bound by his actions or agreements in dealing with the builder, provided they aren't so unreasonable or incompetent as to represent a kind of architectural "malpractice" on his part. So be sure that you have a clear understanding with your architect about what you want done, what materials you are willing to accept, what changes in the original specifications he has the authority to make and what you are willing or able to spend.

Another question you should settle at the beginning—just as you would with a doctor or lawyer—is that of the architect's fee. It may run as high as 15 percent of what the house costs—and since custom-built houses are expensive, this can easily be a substantial amount. Remember, too, in your dealings with the architect that he cannot guarantee his estimate of the cost of building the house. If you ask him to design a $60,000 home he will try to come close; but the contractor's bid will be the first firm indication about price that you'll receive—and it can grow disastrously before the job is completed unless you are careful (see section 296).

What can you do if the architect you have engaged doesn't perform to your satisfaction? You may sue him for breach of contract (see section 183) and try to recover in damages the amount of money it will cost you to have new plans drawn or the amount of other losses you may have suffered as a result of his actions. This is a costly procedure, however, and you may find it difficult to prove that he did not exercise the standard of care required (see section 58). As in all such situations, your best bet is to make sure that you hire a reliable and experienced architect and that you and he have a clear understanding of what you want and how much you can afford to spend.

296. Dealing with the Builder • The specifications you or your architect send to the builder and his firm bid—which states that he will undertake to build the house as described for a specific amount—are the basis for your contract with him. But there are many other factors in a building contract which you should discuss carefully with the architect and your lawyer before signing. Here are the most important:

a. *Method of payment.* Because they are expending large amounts for supplies and labor costs, most contractors prefer to be paid at specified intervals as construction proceeds. This common kind of arrangement is called a *step contract.* A typical agreement might call for one payment when the foundation is complete, another when the roof is on and a final payment when the local building inspector issues a *certificate of occupancy,* which states that the house meets the requirements of the building code. There are many acceptable variations of such a payment scale.

b. *Completion date.* Builders are notoriously lax about completing work on the date agreed upon, and courts generally are lenient about enforcing strict completion dates because they know that unforeseen circumstances, ranging from labor difficulties to bad weather, can slow down a construction job. If you really want to be sure that you will get your house by a given date, you must insist that the contract specify in writing that "time is of the essence of the contract." This phrase will show the builder (and a court, if he defaults) that you mean business about having the job finished on time. This provision will have even more force if you can persuade the builder to agree to a clause stating that he will pay a certain amount in damages for each day work continues beyond the scheduled completion date.

c. *Completion bond.* It is wise to request that the builder post a bond guaranteeing that he will complete the job according to the terms of the contract. You will have to pay the premium, which should run about 1 percent of the cost of building the house, but it is well worth it in terms of the protection you receive. Many is the builder who has gone out of business leaving the unhappy landowner with nothing more for his money than a hole in the ground and a pile of lumber.

d. *Changes in specifications.* Perhaps the greatest cause of disputes and disappointments arising between the owner and the builder is cost increases that result from changes in plans or specifications, or the builder's charges for "extras" that were not covered by the original bid.

337

Charges of this kind can easily double the cost of building your own house. For this reason your contract with the builder should state clearly that all the work to be performed is included in the contract price and that you are only to be charged for changes approved by you, in writing, at an agreed cost. Remember that your architect's agreement to such changes can also make you legally responsible for their cost.

e. *Satisfactory performance.* Any standard contract you sign with a builder should routinely include a clause in which he guarantees to do the job described in a satisfactory manner. Remember, however, that your idea of a satisfactory job may be quite different from the contractor's—and if your disagreement should reach a court of law, the question of whether his performance was satisfactory will be decided *not* on the basis of your opinion but on the basis of whether the average reasonable man would be satisfied in the same circumstances. Obviously, if your contract called for a three-bedroom house with a fireplace, a court will not force you to accept a two-bedroom house with a Franklin stove. But if the question has to do with the color of tile used in the bathroom, or whether your kitchen counter tops are Formica or wood, you may have to accept a ruling in favor of the builder. This is an important reason for checking the progress of the job at regular intervals.

One other important point should concern you if you are hiring a contractor. Under the laws of every state, anyone who supplies materials or labor for building, altering or repairing your house has a claim against the property as security for your debt. This is called a *mechanic's lien* (see section 392). It can actually lead to the sale of your house by court order to satisfy the debt (see section 301).

A problem frequently arises when your builder *subcontracts* parts of the job to smaller outfits. Let's say that you contract with the Stix Construction Company to build your house. In turn, and quite legally, Stix subcontracts the electrical work to the Watts Electric Company. The house is completed on time and to your satisfaction. You pay Stix and happily move in. But Stix doesn't pay Watts for his part of the job. Even though you have acted in complete good faith, Watts has a mechanic's lien against your new house! If Watts can't get his money from Stix, he may be able to force the sale of your house to recover. If Stix has not furnished you with a security bond at the time you made the contract, your right to recover against him may be a Pyrrhic victory.

Most lawyers agree that the best way to cope with this situation is to avoid it. Before you pay the contractor, therefore, you should ask him for a list of all his suppliers and subcontractors and obtain releases from them waiving their rights to the mechanic's lien or affidavits stating that they have been paid. If the general contractor is reputable, they should have no objection to this procedure. Your architect and lawyer can help you with the details.

297. Buying a Development House · The answer for most families who want a newly built house without the expense and headaches of building their own is to buy a house that is under construction or about to be constructed in a housing development.

The legal steps involved in buying such a house are generally the same ones covered in sections 277–289. The primary difference is that the details of the financing are usually arranged by the builder or developer, and the contract you sign and the deed you receive are virtually identical with those of the other buyers in the development. It is still wise to have the contract, deed, bond, mortgage and other papers reviewed by a lawyer, although it is a fact that most people who buy development houses do not hire one.

An essential step before buying a development house is to check the reputation and past performance of the builder. Many people have been swindled by builders who move into an area, throw up a development of substandard houses, collect their money and then simply disappear. When the houses begin to deteriorate—or if the local building inspector won't even issue a certificate of occupancy—the disappointed owners have no legal remedy because they can't find anyone to sue. So ask the builder for references and check his standing with local banks, credit bureaus, the Better Business Bureau or other consumer service organizations. Here are some other points you should consider when you buy a development house:

a. Be sure the contract describes a house that is the same as the model house you were shown by the salesman. A copy of the plans and specifications should be made a part of the contract if possible.

b. You may want to have the plans and specifications checked by an architect before you sign the contract, to be sure that his trained eye doesn't uncover hidden defects in the design of the house that you have overlooked.

c. Although the mortgagee conducts inspections, get the builder's agreement to let you (or an architect you hire) make periodic inspections of the premises while construction is under way, just as you would if you were building your own home. In this way you can detect early signs that things are not on schedule or according to specifications.

339

d. Have your contract notarized and recorded at the county clerk's office. This gives you a lien on the property and puts you ahead of other, unsecured creditors if the builder should default.

Ways You May Lose Your Home

298. If Your Mortgage Is Foreclosed · Almost all mortgage loan agreements (see section 292) provide that the total amount of the loan will fall due if the homeowner fails to meet his regular monthly payments or defaults on his real estate taxes or his insurance payments. In such a situation the mortgagee, or lender, may foreclose the mortgage and sell the mortgaged property to satisfy the debt.

There are three possible procedures by which a mortgage can be foreclosed. The most common requires that the lender go to court, prove that there has been a default under the mortgage agreement and obtain a court order to sell the property. In the second situation the bank or lender has a *power of sale* under the terms of the mortgage agreement, and can proceed to auction off the property without a court order simply by following the procedures outlined by the law of the state where the foreclosure is taking place. A third situation arises in the few states where a mortgage agreement gives actual ownership—legal title to the property—to a trustee who holds in trust for the lender and can sell the property to satisfy the loan.

In all cases the result is the same: the property is sold to the highest bidder and the proceeds are applied against the homeowner's debt to the mortgagee. If the property sells for less than the debt, the mortgagee can go to court and obtain a *deficiency judgment* against the homeowner for the difference. This may have to be satisfied by garnishing his wages or attaching his personal property (see section 88 and chart 7, page 129). All in all, foreclosure can mean disaster for the borrower-homeowner.

Today, however, there is little reason why the careful borrower should suffer from a mortgage foreclosure. If you ever find yourself in a situation where you doubt your ability to continue your mortgage payments at the present rate, you should at once consult your lawyer or a financial adviser and then talk over your problem frankly with the bank or other lender who holds your mortgage. Here are some of the factors you will want to discuss:

REDEEMING PROPERTY AFTER FORECLOSURE

Many states allow you to redeem mortgaged real estate even after the foreclosure sale by paying the purchase price plus costs and interest. Others allow you to redeem it up to the date of the sale. The chart below shows the time allowed in your state.[1] (See section 298.)

CHART 18	Time Allowed for Redemption		Time Allowed for Redemption
		MISSOURI	Until date of sale
ALABAMA	1 year	MONTANA	1 year
ALASKA	1 year	NEBRASKA	Until confirmation of sale
ARIZONA	6 months	NEVADA	1 year
ARKANSAS	1 year	NEW HAMPSHIRE	1 year
CALIFORNIA	1 year	NEW JERSEY	Until date of sale
COLORADO	6 months	NEW MEXICO	9 months
CONNECTICUT	Until date of sale	NEW YORK	Until date of sale
DELAWARE	Until date of sale	NORTH CAROLINA	Until date of sale
D.C.	Until date of sale	NORTH DAKOTA	1 year
FLORIDA	Until date of sale	OHIO	Until confirmation of sale
GEORGIA	Until date of sale	OKLAHOMA	Until date of sale
HAWAII	1 year	OREGON	1 year
IDAHO	1 year	PENNSYLVANIA	Until date of sale
ILLINOIS	6 months	RHODE ISLAND	Until date of sale
INDIANA	1 year	SOUTH CAROLINA	Until date of sale
IOWA	1 year	SOUTH DAKOTA	1 year
KANSAS	Until date of sale	TENNESSEE	2 years
KENTUCKY	1 year[2]	TEXAS	Until date of sale
LOUISIANA	Until date of sale	UTAH	6 months
MAINE	1 year	VERMONT	6 months
MARYLAND	Until date of sale	VIRGINIA	Until date of sale[3]
MASSACHUSETTS	Until date of sale	WASHINGTON	1 year
MICHIGAN	6 months	WEST VIRGINIA	Until date of sale
MINNESOTA	6 months	WISCONSIN	1 year
MISSISSIPPI	No right of redemption	WYOMING	3 months

[1] These figures apply when property is sold to satisfy the debt. If the property remains in the possession of the mortgagee, rights of redemption vary and may continue longer.

[2] Applies only if property is sold for less than two thirds of its appraised value.

[3] Unless set at 6 months by the court when foreclosure decree is issued.

341

Most mortgage agreements allow for an automatic grace period during which overdue payments may be made. If your problem is short term, this provision should take care of it.

Banks are increasingly willing to help borrowers who have defaulted on their payments. If your credit rating is good and the circumstances justify it, the bank or other lender may agree to one of several proposals. In some cases the mortgagee will accept payment of the interest only, until the borrower's financial situation improves. In other cases the payments you have missed may be rescheduled so that they can be made up in the future. And possibly the mortgagee might agree to refinance the entire loan over a longer period to allow for smaller monthly payments.

If no such arrangement can be made, and things do come to the point of foreclosure, one further possibility exists. Many states have passed laws allowing the homeowner to redeem his property if he pays the balance due—usually with penalties and costs added—within a given period after the default. If the necessity should arise, you can check the applicable law with your lawyer to find out how much time is allowed. For details on the time allowed for foreclosure proceedings in your state, see chart 18, page 341.

299. If Your Property Is Condemned · All governments—federal, state and local—have the power to take your private property for a public use. This can include your house, your farm, your summer place or undeveloped acreage you own. This power of condemnation, or *eminent domain,* is a harsh one and often seems unfair, but courts and legislatures recognize it on the basis that the welfare of society as a whole must come before the welfare of any individual.

There are, however, limitations on this power. The government may take your property *only* for a use that benefits the public as a whole; it may not take more of your property than is necessary for the use intended; and it must compensate you for the fair market value of the property taken. The courts have extended the public use doctrine to mean that the government itself may take property or give the right to private persons or corporations for such purposes as building railroads or power plants—again on the theory that such enterprises work for the benefit of all the people.

If you receive a notice that condemnation proceedings are being started against your property and you want to contest them, you should immediately consult a lawyer. He will appear with you at a court hearing and may dispute the authority of the governmental agency that has started the proceedings, or try to persuade the court that your property is not being taken for a valid public use or isn't needed for the project planned.

If your arguments are not accepted and the court issues a condemnation order, you will be required either to negotiate privately with the governmental agency about the compensation you will receive or to appear at a hearing before a commission, jury or court to determine your just compensation. These procedures differ according to the laws of the various states, but the end result will be court confirmation of a compensation award. If you and your lawyer feel that there are valid legal grounds for further resistance, you may appeal the condemnation order, the award or both to a higher court.

300. If Your Taxes Are Delinquent · In general, any property owner who is buying his home under the terms of a mortgage loan is not likely to become the victim of a tax sale. This is because the mortgagee (the bank or mortgage company that has lent money for the purchase of the property) will see to it that real estate taxes are paid on time in order to protect its own interest in the property.

But if you alone are responsible for knowing when your real estate taxes are due, you must be extremely careful to keep them paid up to date. Delinquency can lead to a tax sale even if you have not received a bill for the amount due. The laws of many states require neither personal notice nor a legal proceeding against the property owner before the taxing authority can authorize a sale. You are really on your own in knowing about and meeting this obligation.

The law does offer the delinquent taxpayer some protection. In most states you can prevent a tax sale by paying the overdue amount at any time until the sale actually takes place. In addition, state tax statutes sometimes allow the original owner to redeem his property even after such a sale has taken place by paying the back taxes plus a penalty and the various costs and expenses of conducting the sale. The amount of time allowed for an owner to redeem his property in this way differs from state to state, and if you are threatened with a tax sale or find that some of your property has already been subjected to a tax sale, consult a lawyer at once.

301. If You Fall into Debt · There are several ways in which your ownership of a house or other real estate can be threatened by your creditors. Most of them involve the imposition of a lien on your property according to state or federal laws or as the result of a judgment against you.

343

A *lien* gives your creditor a legal interest in your property as security for the money you owe him. If you do not pay, it can be foreclosed like a mortgage and your house and land can be sold to satisfy the debt.

Most of the people to whom you owe money—called *general creditors* —can obtain an interest in your property only by suing you and obtaining a judgment in their favor in court after a trial. Once a judgment has been rendered against you, your general creditor becomes a *judgment creditor.* That judgment becomes a lien on all the property you own in the county where the case was tried. If you fail to pay your creditor the amount of the judgment he has obtained against you, he can obtain another order directing the sale of your house at public auction to satisfy the judgment. Once this sale has taken place, the law of your state may allow you a certain period of time in which you can still redeem your property by paying the full amount of the debt, plus other costs.

Many people in financial difficulties have tried to preserve their houses or other real estate from the clutches of creditors who have obtained judgments against them by transferring the ownership of the property to relatives or friends for an amount that does not reflect its fair value. The law calls this a *fraudulent conveyance* and will not respect it. If a court finds that you have disposed of the property for no, or insufficient, consideration in an effort to keep it from your creditors, it will declare the transfer invalid and will still order the house sold to satisfy the debt.

A court judgment is the only way a general creditor can get at your house *unless* you have signed a document, a first or second mortgage (see section 291), which specifically gives him an interest in it as security for a debt. This is why it is essential that you consult your lawyer before signing any papers a creditor may put before you.

Some states protect the house and property that are actually used as the family's dwelling place from creditors under what are referred to as *homestead laws.* These laws vary greatly in the amount or value of the property they protect, and in some cases their provisions are so antiquated that they provide the homeowner with little real security. If you are afraid that your property may be threatened, however, you should ask your lawyer about the homestead laws in your state.

There is another class of creditor, known as *lien creditors,* that can legally move against your property without obtaining a court judgment. Their interest in your property is created by state or federal statutes. The federal government has a statutory lien on your property for unpaid taxes, and a local taxing authority has an enforceable lien on your house and land for unpaid real estate taxes (see section 300). Workmen or suppliers are entitled by law to a mechanic's lien on any property you own on which they have worked or for which they have supplied materials (see sections 296, 392).

Another threat to your property arises if you find it necessary to go into personal bankruptcy (see section 463). In states where your home is protected against judgment creditors by homestead laws it may also be safe from your creditors in bankruptcy. Otherwise it must be sold and the proceeds distributed to them as directed by the court.

302. If Your Property Is Used or Occupied by Others • The popular expression "squatter's rights" still has a legal significance that all homeowners and property owners should be aware of. If someone else regularly uses or occupies your land without your permission—and if you don't order him to stop using it—you may find that after a certain amount of time has passed, the laws of your state will grant him the right to continue using or occupying it whether you like it or not.

The amount of time that must pass before you lose all or part of your interest in the land ranges in most states from ten to twenty years. All such laws require that the land be used or occupied continuously during this period and that the use or occupancy be completely open and hostile to the owner. If you give permission for the use or occupancy, the doctrine does not come into play (see chart 19, page 346).

The results of this *adverse possession,* as lawyers call it, can vary considerably. If you own a large tract of rural land and one spring the neighboring farmer moves his fences over a few yards and uses part of your back lot for pasturage without your noticing or objecting, he may become the legal owner of the acreage involved after the time has elapsed. On smaller lots, a misunderstanding between neighbors about the property line may lead to eventual conflicts over ownership. You may build a shed which you believe is on your property, but which your neighbor says encroaches on his. He demands that you remove it, but you refuse. Not wanting the expense of a lawsuit, he takes no further action, and twenty years pass. Neither he nor a new owner of his lot could now sue you; you have gained title to the land on which the shed stands through adverse possession. (For further information, see section 46.)

Knowing what can happen is the best protection against losing any of your property or your property rights in this way. If you have surveyed your land and know its boundaries, and if you are vigilant about its unauthorized use, you should be safe from subsequent claims arising from adverse possession.

345

WHEN OTHERS OCCUPY YOUR LAND

Under the laws of adverse possession, others who use or occupy your land openly and unchallenged may claim ownership of it after a certain period of time has passed (see section 302). This chart shows the statutory period by states.

CHART 19

Number of Years of Possession After Which Original Owner Can No Longer Claim the Property as His

State	Years	State	Years	State	Years
ALABAMA	20	KENTUCKY	15	NORTH DAKOTA	20[11]
ALASKA	7[1]	LOUISIANA	30[5]	OHIO	21
ARIZONA	10[2]	MAINE	20	OKLAHOMA	15
ARKANSAS	7	MARYLAND	20	OREGON	10
CALIFORNIA	5	MASSACHUSETTS	20	PENNSYLVANIA	21
COLORADO	18[3]	MICHIGAN	15	RHODE ISLAND	10
CONNECTICUT	15	MINNESOTA	15	SOUTH CAROLINA	10
DELAWARE	20	MISSISSIPPI	10[6]	SOUTH DAKOTA	20
D.C.	15	MISSOURI	10	TENNESSEE	20[12]
FLORIDA	7[4]	MONTANA	5	TEXAS	25
GEORGIA	20	NEBRASKA	10[7]	UTAH	7
HAWAII	20	NEVADA	5[8]	VERMONT	15
IDAHO	5	NEW HAMPSHIRE	20	VIRGINIA	15
ILLINOIS	20	NEW JERSEY	20[9]	WASHINGTON	10
INDIANA	10	NEW MEXICO	10	WEST VIRGINIA	10
IOWA	10	NEW YORK	10	WISCONSIN	20[13]
KANSAS	15	NORTH CAROLINA	20[10]	WYOMING	10

(1) In an action against the United States or the state of Alaska, 10 years are required.

(2) Statute applies to not more than 160 acres or acres actually enclosed.

(3) Without color of title. With color of title, statutory period is 7 years if occupancy can be established and assessed taxes were paid during this period.*

(4) Adverse possession for 30 years confers the title even against persons with disabilities.

(5) Under just title acquired "in good faith," 10 years of possession are required.

(6) Occupancy is not necessary to establish adverse possession; possession, cultivating or pasturing is sufficient.

(7) A municipal corporation may begin action at any time to regain grounds or city or town lots.

(8) The statutory period is 2 years for mining property.

(9) There can be no adverse possession of land owned by the state or its subdivisions.

(10) Under known and visible boundaries. With color of title, the statutory period is 7 years.*

(11) If taxes and assessments are paid, title may pass in 10 years.

(12) With color of title, the statutory period is only 7 years.*

(13) When occupancy is based on a written decree, the statutory period is 10 years. Against the state it is 40 years.

---

*"With color of title" means that the person occupying the land is the apparent owner, even though his title is in fact defective.

303. Your Rights as a Homeowner • Everyone who owns a home has a time-honored right to the undisturbed possession and *quiet enjoyment* of his property. This means that—with the exceptions described below and in the next section—you may invite onto your property anyone you want and keep off it anyone you don't want, and that you may use your property for any legal and reasonable purpose that doesn't interfere with your neighbor's or the public's rights.

As far as private persons are concerned, you have an almost absolute right to keep them off your property if you don't want them there. Anyone who comes onto your land against your will is committing the tort of trespass (see section 46). You may order him off, and if he refuses to leave you may use reasonable force to remove him. Your right against trespass includes things as well as people. If your neighbor dumps heaps of old leaves and branches over the fence into your yard, he has committed a trespass against you. You may sue a trespasser for damages or report him to authorities if his trespass is also a crime. There are times, of course, when people may legally come on your property without permission. If your neighbor enters your land to beat off a brush fire that is threatening his own property, for example, the courts would not be likely to find in your favor if you sued him for trespass. (For a more detailed discussion of trespass, see sections 46, 54, 61.)

Your right to bar public officials from your property is more limited. The Constitution protects you against unreasonable searches and seizures (see section 22), but police officers with a search warrant properly issued by a judge or magistrate have the right to search your house without your permission. In fact, if you don't let them in they can break down the door if necessary to complete the search. If the police search your house without a proper warrant, or if their search goes further than the warrant allows, you may sue them in a civil court for damages (see section 38). You are also entitled to recover any property seized during an illegal search. Evidence obtained in the course of an illegal search is not admissible in court (see section 154).

Police may also come onto your property to make a legal arrest— either with or without a warrant for the arrest. If he has no warrant, however, the policeman must reasonably believe that the person he is pursuing has committed a crime in his presence. He can't simply batter down your door and arrest you on the say-so of a malicious neighbor. If you are the victim of an illegal arrest, your remedy is to seek a writ of habeas corpus for your release, if necessary (see section 27), or perhaps a civil suit for damages for false arrest (see section 39).

State and local laws also grant to some other public officials, such as fire inspectors, health inspectors and the like, the right to enter and inspect your house. Laws of this kind usually require that inspections be made at a reasonable time and that the inspectors show proper identification and authority if they are requested to do so. If you refuse admittance to legally constituted inspectors they may not force their way in, but must get a court order commanding you to admit them. Such an order can be enforced against you by the sheriff or other law officers.

Your right to the quiet enjoyment of your property can also be violated by all kinds of activities that do not involve actual trespass. Your neighbor may habitually burn rubber tires in his backyard or play his radio at top volume late into the night. He may accumulate old refrigerators and bedsprings on his front porch or plant a tree that blocks the sunlight from your patio. All these things are nuisances—at least from your point of view. They may also constitute the civil wrong of nuisance (see section 45). You may go to court and ask for an order that your neighbor stop his objectionable activities, or you may ask for damages or both. Because the facts are different in almost every case, it is impossible to give a general prediction about a court's decision in a nuisance suit. If you feel that some outside activity is reducing the value of your property or interfering with your quiet enjoyment of it, your best move is to discuss the specific situation with your lawyer. (For more on the law of nuisances, see section 45.)

304. Your Duties as a Homeowner · Your duties as a homeowner are relatively simple. You have a duty to pay your taxes (see sections 300, 305). You have a duty not to act in ways that will damage your neighbor's property or interfere unreasonably with his quiet enjoyment of it (see sections 45, 46). You have a duty to exercise reasonable care toward people who come on your property, either at your invitation as your social guests or simply with your permission.

Your duty toward people who enter your home is deeply involved with the law of torts (see sections 60, 61). Courts have argued for years about what standard of care you owe to various persons who come onto your property—and the result has often been to confuse the situation as much as to clarify it. Generally speaking, you should use and main-

348

tain your property with the same amount of care expected of the average prudent person, and you should warn visitors of any dangerous conditions you know of. If you do this, a guest or tradesman injured on your property would have a hard time proving negligence in a lawsuit against you for damages (see section 70).

You have a higher duty toward two classes of people, however—those invitees the law calls business visitors and children.

A *business visitor* is anyone who comes onto your property at your invitation and for your financial profit. Customers in a store or patrons at an amusement park are business visitors. If you invite a customer to your home for dinner in hopes of winding up a profitable deal with him, he is a business visitor. If your wife gives piano lessons, the pupils who come to your house are business visitors. Because they are there for your benefit, the courts give these people greater protection against possible injury from your carelessness.

Let's say that you have invited an important client to your home for dinner. You have also invited a neighboring couple to round out the group. In the course of a pleasant evening you expect to do some profitable business with your client. While your client and the neighbors are sitting on your porch swing before dinner, the swing unexpectedly collapses and all three suffer injuries. Your neighbors probably could not collect damages, since unless you knew the swing was untrustworthy you were not negligent. But the client might recover. Because he was a business guest, you had a duty to him to *make sure* that the swing was in good condition before he sat in it.

The courts also require you to exercise more care toward children than you would toward ordinary visitors on your property, because children are assumed to have less understanding of possible dangers and, in fact, to be attracted to potentially dangerous objects or places. Many municipalities require fences around swimming pools for this reason. Under the legal doctrine called *attractive nuisance*, some courts have found property owners liable for injuries to children on their property even when the children were trespassers. This doctrine has resulted in some decisions that seem extremely unfair, and it is applied differently by the courts of different states. To be safe, if you know of a dangerous object or a condition on your property—an uncovered well, an abandoned outbuilding or mine site, a piece of rusty farm equipment—where children do come to play without your permission, or if this object might attract children to your property, you had better fence it off, cover it up or remove it, for your own protection as well as that of the children.

349

With the exception of this attractive nuisance doctrine involving children, you have no duty to exercise reasonable care toward trespassers. Your only duty toward a trespasser is not to injure him intentionally if you know he is on your land and not to use unreasonable force in throwing him off. Of course, the law will not allow you to act with such extreme carelessness that you injure even a trespasser if you are aware of his presence. If you and a friend are target shooting in your back pasture and a vagrant staggers across your line of fire, you have a duty to stop shooting until he is out of the way.

305. Your Real Estate Taxes • As a homeowner, your most basic and certainly most unpleasant obligation is to pay real estate taxes on your property. These taxes are imposed by the county or by the town or municipality in which your property is located. You may also be subject to special assessments—charges for specific local improvements like new sewer pipes or improved street lighting. To add inconvenience to your expenses, taxes owed to these various taxing authorities are in many localities due on a number of different dates throughout the year. You should keep a list of these due dates handy, because the consequences of missing them may be severe (see section 300). If you have any question about due dates you should discuss it with your lawyer or your local taxing authority.

The amount of tax you must pay depends directly on two factors. The first of these is the *tax rate,* which is set by your local government and in many states cannot exceed a certain statutory amount. The tax rate is a percentage of the assessed value of your property. If your house and lot are assessed at $16,000, a tax rate of 10 percent would require you to pay $1,600 a year in taxes.

The second—and to you the more important—factor affecting your taxes is the *assessment.* This is the value of your property for tax purposes, as estimated by assessors who work for the local taxing authority. The assessment of your property's value may change from time to time. For example, if the local tax rate is 6 percent, an increase in the assessed value of your property from $16,000 to $21,000 will increase your taxes for that year from $960 to $1,260—a jump of $300. But there are legal means described below by which you can challenge your tax assessment if you think it is too high.

The laws governing assessment procedures differ from one state to another, but the general outline is the same in most places. If you want to challenge the assessment on your property, it is important for you to know the laws of your community. In general, this is what happens:

Every year the board of assessors in your community draws up a preliminary list of assessments. It should include every piece of real estate in the tax district, together with the name of the owner and the assessed value of the property.

On a date specified by law and usually announced in the local newspapers, this list of assessments is posted for examination by the public. The board of assessors may also be required to notify you by mail if there is an increase in your assessment.

If there has been an increase, you will have until a certain date to file a written and sworn protest. On a day previously announced, you may have to appear before a board of review to explain why you think your new assessment is unfair or illegal. If you plan to protest your assessment, it is wise to have the assistance of a lawyer from the beginning, because the statements you make in your written presentation to the review board will serve as the basis of any future court action.

The most common legal grounds for objecting to an assessment are that it is *unequal*—your house is assessed for more than the other, similar houses in your neighborhood—or that the property is assessed at more than its actual value.

Once all the protests have been heard and considered by the board of review, a final list of assessments is made public. If the board has not responded to your plea for a reduction, your only recourse is to go to court—presenting the same reasons and evidence as in your initial protest—to seek a reversal or modification of the board's decision. This must be done within a limited time after publication of the final list.

Once your taxes have been finally established, it is your obligation to pay them as they fall due or within a limited grace period if the law provides it. The consequences of failure to pay can be extremely serious—ranging from penalty and interest payments to the loss of your home (see section 300). So as a homeowner you should be sure that you clearly understand the extent and due dates of your real estate tax obligations. and be prepared to meet them promptly.

306. Your Wife's Ownership Rights • Depending on the laws of your state and the specific circumstances of your marriage, your wife may be the joint owner of your house or she may have legal rights which don't amount to ownership but which do give her the use of the property after your death. These are matters to be discussed in detail with your lawyer when you and your wife plan your estates (see sections 527–554).

If your name and your wife's both appear on the deed, then you both own the house as *tenants by the entirety*. Neither of you can sell the house without the other's consent, nor can either of you leave it to anyone else by will. If you die, your wife automatically becomes the sole owner of the house—and vice versa.

If you live in a community property state (see section 317), matters become more complicated. Here it doesn't matter whose name appears on the deed; the law considers that you own the house jointly—it is part of your community property. This means that neither of you can sell the house without the other's consent. Differences arise about its disposition on your death, however. In some states, *all* the community property goes to the surviving spouse—which means that your wife would become the sole owner. In others, the community property would be divided fifty-fifty between your wife and your estate, so that you might be able to leave half ownership of the house to someone else in your will. Your wife might be able to defeat your intention, however, by exercising her *right of election*—her legal right to take that part of your property which would have gone to her if you had died without a will (see section 542 and chart 38, page 650).

Even if your wife is not a part owner of your house, she may have an interest in it after your death. State laws of descent and distribution entitle her to a certain share of your property (see sections 555–559 and chart 42, page 696). In addition, over a third of the states recognize what is called the wife's *right of dower*. This means that she is legally entitled to the use of one third of her husband's real estate as long as she lives. Oddly, this right applies even to property which her husband had sold unless she also signed the deed. This is why it is so important when you are *buying* property to see that both the seller and his wife sign the deed.

Some states give the husband a similar right in the property of his dead wife. This is called the right of curtesy. For details of the dower and curtesy laws of the various states, see chart 20, page 353.

Still another right recognized in some states is called the widow's *right of homestead*. This right entitles the widow and her minor children to occupy the husband's house or other property as long as she lives, even if he has left it to someone else in his will or his creditors have claims against it. She does not own the property, but simply has the use of it during her lifetime. This is called a "life tenancy" or a "life estate."

If you and your wife are divorced, your jointly owned property is divided as ordered by the court or according to the terms of a prior separation agreement (see section 361). Whatever interest in your property the law granted her because she was your wife—such as dower or homestead—ceases to exist with the dissolution of the marriage.

EXTENT OF YOUR DOWER, CURTESY AND HOMESTEAD RIGHTS

The laws of dower and curtesy define the rights of a husband or wife to part of the deceased spouse's property. Homestead laws define the property set aside for the use of a surviving spouse and minor children, free from the claims of creditors. (See section 306.)

CHART 20	Does Husband Have Right of Curtesy or Dower?	Does Wife Have Right of Dower?	Does State Have Widow's Homestead Law?	Homestead Rights	
				Limit of Value	Limit of Area
ALABAMA	No	Yes: if children survive, life estate in ⅓ of husband's real property; if no children, life estate in ½ *	Yes	$2,000	160 acres
ALASKA	No	No	Yes	$12,000; house trailer $8,000	¼ acre in city or town; 160 acres elsewhere
ARIZONA	No	No	Yes	$15,000; house trailers $8,000	None
ARKANSAS	Yes: same as dower[1]	Yes: ⅓ of husband's personal property & life estate in ⅓ of husband's real property[2]	Yes	$2,500	1 acre in city, town or village; 160 acres elsewhere
CALIFORNIA	No	No	Yes[3]	$20,000, head of family; $10,000	None
COLORADO	No	No	Yes[3]	$7,500	None
CONNECTICUT	No	No	No		
DELAWARE	No[4]	No[5]	No		
DISTRICT OF COLUMBIA	Yes: life estate in ⅓ of wife's real property*	Yes: life estate in ⅓ of husband's real property*	No		
FLORIDA	Yes: 30%	Yes: 30%	Yes	None	½ acre in city or town; 160 acres elsewhere
GEORGIA	No	No	Yes	$500 (in city or town); $200 elsewhere	50 acres in country[6]
HAWAII	Yes: ⅓ of wife's personal property & life estate in ⅓ of her real property**	Yes: ⅓ of husband's personal property & life estate in ⅓ of his real property*	Yes	$20,000, head of family; $10,000	1 acre
IDAHO	No	No	Yes	$10,000, head of family; $4,000	None
ILLINOIS	No	No	Yes	$5,000 ($10,000 in some statutes)	None

353

CHART
20
(cont.)

	Does Husband Have Right of Curtesy or Dower?	Does Wife Have Right of Dower?	Does State Have Widow's Homestead Law?	Homestead Rights	
				Limit of Value	Limit of Area
INDIANA	No	No	No		
IOWA	No	No	Yes[3]	$500	½ acre in city or town; 40 acres elsewhere
KANSAS	No	No	Yes	None	1 acre in city or town; 160 acres of farmland
KENTUCKY	Yes: ½ of wife's property[7]	Yes: ½ of husband's property[7]	Yes	$1,000	None
LOUISIANA	No	No	Yes	$15,000	160 acres
MAINE	No	No	Yes	$3,000	None
MARYLAND	No	No	No		
MASSACHUSETTS	Yes: life estate in ⅓ of wife's real property**	Yes: life estate in ⅓ of husband's real property**	Yes	$30,000	None
MICHIGAN	No	Yes: life estate in ⅓ of husband's real property*	Yes	$3,500	1 lot in city, town or village; 40 acres elsewhere
MINNESOTA	No	No	Yes[3]	None	½ acre in city, village or borough; 80 acres elsewhere
MISSISSIPPI	No	No	Yes	$15,000	160 acres
MISSOURI	No	No	Yes	$5,000	None
MONTANA	No	No	Yes	$20,000	¼ acre in city or town; 320 acres of farmland
NEBRASKA	No	No	Yes	$4,000	2 lots in city or village; 160 acres in country
NEVADA	No	No	Yes	$25,000	None

| | Does Husband Have Right of Curtesy or Dower? | Does Wife Have Right of Dower? | Does State Have Widow's Homestead Law? | Homestead Rights | |
				Limit of Value	Limit of Area
NEW HAMPSHIRE	No	No	Yes	$2,500	None
NEW JERSEY	Yes: life estate in ½ of wife's real property*	Yes: life estate in ½ of husband's real property*	No		
NEW MEXICO	No	No	Yes[3]	$10,000	None
NEW YORK	No	No[8]	Yes	$2,000	None
NORTH CAROLINA	No	No	Yes	$1,000	None
NORTH DAKOTA	No	No	Yes[3]	$40,000 in town; no limit in country	2 acres in town; 160 acres in country
OHIO	Yes: life estate in ⅓ of real estate held by wife during her lifetime but not at death	Yes: life estate in ⅓ of real estate held by husband during his lifetime but not at death	Yes	$1,000	None
OKLAHOMA	No	No	Yes[3]	$5,000 in city; no limit elsewhere	1 acre in city; 160 acres in country
OREGON	No	No	Yes	$12,000; house trailer $10,000	1 block in city; 160 acres elsewhere
PENNSYLVANIA	No	No	No		
RHODE ISLAND	Yes: if children survive, life estate in wife's real property*	Yes: life estate in ⅓ of husband's real property*	No		
SOUTH CAROLINA	No	Yes: life estate in ⅓ of husband's real property[9],*	Yes	$1,000	None
SOUTH DAKOTA	No	No	Yes: right belongs to family	$15,000	1 acre in town; 160 acres in country
TENNESSEE	Yes: if issue survive, life estate in all wife's real property**	Yes: life estate in ⅓ of husband's real property*	Yes	$1,000	None
TEXAS	No	No	Yes	$10,000	200 acres in country; one or more lots elsewhere

CHART 20 (cont.)	Does Husband Have Right of Curtesy or Dower?	Does Wife Have Right of Dower?	Does State Have Widow's Homestead Law?	Homestead Rights	
				Limit of Value	Limit of Area
UTAH	No	No	Yes	$4,000 plus $1,500 for wife plus $600 for each child	None
VERMONT	Yes: if only 1 child, ½ of wife's real estate; otherwise, ⅓**	Yes: if only 1 child, ½ of husband's real estate; otherwise, ⅓**	Yes	$5,000	None
VIRGINIA	Yes: ⅓ of wife's real property*	Yes: ⅓ of husband's real property*	Yes	$3,500	None
WASHINGTON	No	No	Yes[3]	$10,000	None
WEST VIRGINIA	Yes: life estate in ⅓ of wife's real property*	Yes: life estate in ⅓ of husband's real property*	Yes	$1,000	None
WISCONSIN	Yes: ⅓ of wife's real property**	Yes: ⅓ of husband's real property*	Yes	$25,000	Not more than 40 acres nor less than ¼ acre
WYOMING	No	No	Yes	$4,000	None

* Right of dower or curtesy applies to real property owned by the deceased spouse at any time during the marriage.

** Right of dower or curtesy applies to real property owned by the deceased spouse at the time of his/her death.

---

(1) If estate is ancestral and there are no descendants, the husband is entitled to only ⅓ of property for life as against collateral heirs.

(2) If the husband leaves no descendants, the wife is entitled to absolute possession of ½ real and personal property as against collateral heirs and ⅓ as against creditors. But if the real estate is ancestral, the dower right is only for life.

(3) Statute gives both widows and widowers homestead rights.

(4) If the wife left no will, the husband is entitled to life estate in ½ of the wife's lands if children survive and to life estate in all if no children survive.

(5) If the husband left no will, the wife is entitled to life estate in ½ of real estate owned by her husband at time of his death if children survive, or life estate in all if no children survive.

(6) Plus 5 acres for each child under 16.

(7) Plus life estate in ⅓ of all real property held during the marriage but not at death.

(8) Except for wives married prior to September 1930: ⅓ husband's real estate.*

(9) Or absolute possession of ⅙ of husband's lands.

———

CHAPTER EIGHT

Your Family

———

We must think things not words, or at least we must
constantly translate our words into facts for which
they stand, if we are to keep to the real and the true.

—OLIVER WENDELL HOLMES, JR.

8

Your Family

Some Key Points in This Chapter—

Consult these sections for information on:

Charts in This Chapter

COURTSHIP, ENGAGEMENT AND MARRIAGE

American society is undergoing so many changes that to give you an understanding of family law presents many problems. Most of us believe that the family is our basic social unit, and existing laws reflect that belief. Yet the fact that one out of every three first marriages ends in divorce seems to indicate that our attachment to marriage as our basic social institution is weakening. Many states are broadening the grounds for divorce and even adopting statutes that make it possible to get a divorce by mutual agreement between husband and wife. The law, as so often happens, is being molded to keep up with changing social customs. In recent years the distinction between the rights of adopted and natural children has practically disappeared—another reflection of changing customs. A further remarkable change is taking place right now in woman's position in society—one that is reflected in many legal areas. One of the impulses behind the liberalization of abortion laws is many women's conviction that they have a right not to bear children: a conviction completely contrary to age-old beliefs concerning the purposes of marriage and the rights of unborn children.

But as the French say, the more things change, the more they remain the same. We will, therefore, lay before you the laws regarding you and your family, pointing to the many that have not changed, stressing those that are either really new or very different. All this book can give you is a general overview. Your lawyer is the one to consult when you have personal problems in any one of the several areas covered by this chapter.

307. Legal Aspects of Adolescent Dating • There are no laws specifying the minimum age at which a girl or boy can begin going out with members of the opposite sex. Parents have a right to forbid their teen-age daughter (or son, for that matter) from dating if they consider her too young, and the child has a duty to obey. If the child disobeys the order, parents have a right to discipline her to the same degree that they might punish her for disobeying other reasonable commands (see section 323). Parents may ban visits to their homes by unwelcome suitors. But if a minor child persists in defying the parents' commands, there is no legal way they can stop her short of charging her with juvenile delinquency (see section 338), if she is below a specified age (see chart 28, page 428), or seeking to have her declared a wayward minor (see section

359

342), if she is above the age at which delinquency laws can be applied.

Most states have laws barring sexual intercourse between persons not married to each other. But boys and girls who willingly engage in the act are unlikely to be punished by the court if they are above the age of consent, which ranges from fourteen to eighteen, depending upon the state and sex of the participants (see chart 28, page 428). But a girl above the age of consent who is paid for her sexual services may be charged as a prostitute, or she may be charged as a public nuisance if she lavishes her favors too promiscuously without payment.

However, if a girl is below the age of consent, her male partner is automatically guilty of statutory rape, even though she may have entered the sexual act willingly or actually have solicited it. If the sexual act results in pregnancy, and the male admits his responsibility or it can be proved against him, he is responsible for the girl's medical and hospital bills prior to the child's birth and for the support of the child until it reaches eighteen or twenty-one, depending on the state, even if the father himself is a minor or below the age of consent. There is, however, no law in any state that requires him to marry the girl.

308. Engagement to Marry and Breach-of-Promise Suits • A proposal to marry and its acceptance are recognized by law as a binding contract, generally subject to the same rules that apply to other contracts (see section 173). If the man and woman mutually agree to end their engagement, the contract is automatically annulled. In the past, if one fiancé sought to break the engagement and the other refused, the latter could sue the former for breach of promise in an effort to compel the unwilling partner, usually the man, either to go through with the marriage or to pay compensatory damages. The damages asked for included reimbursement not only for the jilted woman's actual monetary losses but for her humiliation and injury to her feelings, as well as for the loss of financial benefits she would have derived from the marriage. This right led to many abuses. Sympathetic juries tended to award damages far in excess of any conceivable injuries suffered, and unscrupulous women tried to inveigle men into rash promises of marriage for the purpose of blackmailing them by threatening to sue for breach of promise. The great majority of these so-called heart balm cases were settled out of court in order to avoid damaging publicity.

But these suits became so notorious that some states now allow them only when the woman is pregnant by her fiancé, while other states have banned them altogether. Even in states that still permit breach-of-promise suits the amount of damages awarded may be limited by statute. Furthermore, in many of these states a man or woman may break off an engagement for a variety of reasons without being subject to suit.

In a few states, damage suits for interference or alienation of affection may still be launched by a jilted fiancé against third parties who have been instrumental in breaking up an engagement. Thus, a man may demand damages from another man who won his fiancé from him by offering her greater luxuries than he could provide, and a woman can sue a rival who lured her betrothed away through sexual seduction. However, such suits may not be entered against parents who advise a son or daughter not to go through with a marriage, since they have a right to counsel their children. Nor are the suits likely to be successful against friends or relatives of the betrothed who counsel against a marriage, if they offer the advice sincerely and are not motivated by malice against the jilted partner.

309. What Happens to the Gifts When an Engagement Is Broken • The gifts that might have been exchanged by the man and woman even if they had not become engaged may be kept by the recipients. But gifts, including the engagement ring, that were given solely in the expectation that the couple would be married, properly should be returned to the donors, since the basis for the gift is gone.

The question of whether a person has a legal right to recover wedding gifts that are not voluntarily returned has been decided differently by different courts, however. In most instances engagement rings are ordered returned to the donor, but some courts have allowed the woman to keep the ring if it was the man who repudiated the marriage agreement. In one notable instance a man who tried to recover the ring, gifts and money for household furniture from his fiancée, who had broken their engagement, found his case thrown out of court on the ground that it was a breach-of-promise suit, which was banned in that particular state. But courts in other states with similar laws have ruled exactly the reverse.

310. Common-Law Marriage • As the state has gradually taken over the authority once exercised by the church in the private lives of all citizens, many rules have been adopted regarding the marital status: who may marry, at what age, the property rights of husband and wife and how a marriage may be ended. For a long time men and women have lived together for a period of time without taking the trouble to "get married." These arrangements are called common-law marriages because English courts recognized that by living together the couples voluntarily assumed rights and obligations to each other that society should protect and enforce. Several states still recognize common-law marriages (see chart 27, page 420).

311. Who May Marry • Certain persons who are closely related to each other may not legally marry (see chart 27). The reason is the conviction that children of a marriage between such close relatives may not be healthy. Moreover, some states (see chart 27) prohibit marriage between persons of different races. Although many of these laws are still on the books, the Supreme Court has declared them unconstitutional.

312. At What Age You May Marry • The age at which persons may marry is set forth in state statutes. As you will see from chart 27, the ages vary from state to state; nevertheless persons below this age may in most cases get married with their parents' approval.

313. How to Get Married • To get married you must first appear before the clerk of the city or town in which you live and apply for a license to marry. Many states (see chart 27) require that the marriage license not be issued for several days after you apply, whereas in others you can be married the same day. A number of states further require that each person seeking a marriage license submit a physician's statement that he or she has been examined and is free from certain communicable diseases, particularly venereal disease. In some cases a blood test will be performed by the state or county medical officer.

After the marriage license has been issued, the marriage ceremony may be performed by a priest, rabbi or minister; by a clerk or a justice of certain courts; or, in some states, by elected public officials (chart 21, page 363). Valid marriages may be performed at sea by a ship's captain, but a couple so married would be wise to go through another ceremony, civil or religious, after obtaining a license when the ship docks.

314. The Domicile • The domicile, or home, of the married couple is the place where the husband resides, and it is his right and responsibility to choose it. If on occasion the wife lives apart from her husband but does not intend a separation from him (see section 361) her domicile is still her husband's, although the courts are increasingly acknowledging the concept that a career woman may establish her own domicile.

WHO MAY PERFORM A MARRIAGE CEREMONY

After a license has been obtained from the proper authority, a marriage ceremony may be conducted by the persons listed below, depending on the law of the state in which the wedding takes place (see section 313).

CHART 21	Clergyman	Public Official	Judicial Official
ALABAMA	Licensed minister of the gospel, pastor of any Christian society. Marriages may be solemnized by religious sect according to its rules.	No	Judge of supreme, appellate or circuit court within the state; probate judge
ALASKA	Minister or priest of any church in state; officer of the Salvation Army. Marriages may be solemnized by any religious society according to its rules.	No	Marriage officer appointed by presiding judge of superior court or any judicial official within his jurisdiction
ARIZONA	All licensed or ordained clergymen	No	Judge of court of record, justice of the peace
ARKANSAS	Any regularly ordained & registered minister or priest	Governor or mayor of city of first or second class	Judge of court of record, justice of the peace of county
CALIFORNIA	Any priest, minister or rabbi, age 18 or older	No	Judge, including retirees or resignees, or commissioner of court of record or justice court
COLORADO	Marriages may be solemnized by any religious denomination according to its rules.	Yes, if powers include solemnizing marriage	Any judge of court of record
CONNECTICUT	Ordained or licensed minister	No	Any judge or justice of the peace
DELAWARE	Any minister of the gospel or minister in charge of a recognized church. Marriages may be solemnized by any religious society according to its rules.	Mayor of Wilmington, if one party is a resident of Delaware	Clerk of peace
DISTRICT OF COLUMBIA	Any appointed or ordained minister of the gospel. Marriages may be solemnized by any religious society according to its rules.	No	Any judge of court of general sessions or any court of record, clerk of court of general sessions
FLORIDA	Ordained minister of the gospel or elder in communion with some church. Quaker marriages are valid.	No	Any judicial officer, clerk of circuit court, or notary public
GEORGIA	Any minister of the gospel	City recorder	Any judge or justice of the peace
HAWAII	Any minister, priest or officer of any religious denomination in accord with rules of that society.	No	Any justice, judge or magistrate of state or federal court within state

CHART 21 (cont.)	Clergyman	Public Official	Judicial Official
IDAHO	No particular form of ceremony is necessary.		
ILLINOIS	Minister of the gospel in regular standing. Marriages may be solemnized by any Quaker or any other religious society according to its rules.	No (except supt. of public instruction for deaf & dumb)	Judge of court of record
INDIANA	Minister of the gospel or priest. Quakers & German Baptists may solemnize according to rules of their societies.	Mayor of city	Judge of court of record, justice of peace
IOWA	Ordained or licensed minister of the gospel	Mayor of city or town in which marriage is performed	Judge of supreme, district, superior or municipal court; justice of the peace
KANSAS	Licensed preacher, age 21 or older	No	Any judge or justice of the peace
KENTUCKY	Any minister or priest. Marriages may be solemnized by any religious society according to its rules.	No	Judge of circuit, county, city or police court; justice of the peace
LOUISIANA	Any minister of the gospel or priest of any religious sect	No	Judge of supreme court anywhere in state; district court judge, parish judge, justice of the peace, city court judge within own parish
MAINE	Any ordained or licensed clergyman. Quaker marriages are valid.	No	Notary public, justice of the peace
MARYLAND	Minister except for Quakers, who must sign a special form of certificate	No	Clerks, deputy clerks of circuit court
MASSACHUSETTS	Qualified resident clergyman or rabbi. Marriages may be solemnized by any religious society according to its rules.	No	Magistrate, authorized justice of the peace
MICHIGAN	Minister of the gospel who is pastor of a church or who continues to preach	Mayor of city in which marriage is performed	Judge of probate or municipal court, justice of peace
MINNESOTA	Ordained minister of the gospel in regular communion with any religious society	No (except in state school for deaf & blind, supt. of dept. for deaf & dumb)	Judge of court of record, justice of the peace
MISSISSIPPI	Any minister of the gospel in good standing	No (except for member of the board of supervisors within respective counties)	Judge of supreme, circuit or county court; justice of the peace

364

	Clergyman	Public Official	Judicial Official
MISSOURI	Licensed or ordained clergyman of the gospel who is a U.S. citizen. Religious society according to its own customs	No	Any judge of a court of record
MONTANA	Priest or minister of the gospel. Marriages may be solemnized by any religious society according to its uses.	Mayor of city	Judge of supreme or district court, justice of the peace
NEBRASKA	Minister of the gospel. Marriages may be solemnized by any religious society to which parties belong, according to its rules.	No	Any judge, justice of the peace
NEVADA	Licensed minister of the gospel. Marriages may be solemnized by any religious society according to its rules.	No	Judge of the supreme or district court, justice of the peace
NEW HAMPSHIRE	Ordained minister of the gospel or rabbi. Quakers are allowed to solemnize marriages according to their usual practices.	No	Justice of the peace
NEW JERSEY	Minister of any religious society, institution or organization	Mayor, Chairman of Township Committee, village president	Judge of the U.S. District, county, county district, criminal, juvenile, domestic relations or municipal court
NEW MEXICO	Ordained clergyman of any sect. Marriages may be solemnized by any religious society according to its rules.	No	Civil magistrate
NEW YORK*	Clergyman, minister or leader of certain ethical culture societies	Mayor, recorder	City magistrate, police justice, judge of court of record or municipal court, town justice
NORTH CAROLINA	Ordained minster of any religion or denomination	No	Magistrate
NORTH DAKOTA	Ordained & licensed minister of the gospel, priest, pastor of church. Marriages may be solemnized by any religious society according to its rules.	No	Justice of county, judge of court of record, within respective jurisdiction
OHIO	Ordained & licensed minister of any religious society or congregation. Marriages may be solemnized by any religious society according to its rules.	Mayor	Judge of county court
OKLAHOMA	Ordained minister, priest or other ecclesiastical dignitary	No	Judge or justice of court of record
OREGON	Minister or priest	No	Any judicial official within his jurisdiction

*When either of the parties is under 21, the marriage must be performed by a clergyman, a mayor, judge of a court of record or municipal court or district court.

CHART 21 (cont.)	Clergyman	Public Official	Judicial Official
PENNSYLVANIA	No statute makes a ceremonial marriage necessary.		
RHODE ISLAND	Licensed minister or licensed elder. Quaker & Jewish marriages are valid.	No	Justice or associate justice of supreme, superior or family court; supreme, superior or district court clerk; police court justice in Providence; warden in New Shoreham
SOUTH CAROLINA	Minister of the gospel or rabbi	No	Any officer authorized to administer oaths
SOUTH DAKOTA	Minister of the gospel or priest of any denomination	Mayor	Judge of supreme, circuit, municipal or district county court, justice of the peace
TENNESSEE	Minister	Governor, chancellor or speaker of state senate or house	Judge, including resident federal judge; justice of the peace; retired chancellors or judges of courts of record
TEXAS	Licensed or ordained minister, rabbi, officer of religious organization authorized to perform marriage ceremony	No	Judge of court of record, justice of the peace
UTAH	Minister or priest in regular communion with religious society	Mayor of city, county clerk	Justice of supreme, district, city or juvenile court, justice of the peace
VERMONT	Minister of the gospel residing in Vermont	No	Justice in county of his jurisdiction
VIRGINIA	Minister authorized by circuit or corporation court. Marriages may be solemnized by any religious society according to its rules.	No	Any person authorized by circuit or corporation court
WASHINGTON	Licensed & ordained minister or priest of any chuch or religious denomination	No	Judge of supreme court of appeals or superior court, justice of the peace (between certain hours only)
WEST VIRGINIA	Authorized & licensed minister	No	Judge of court of record
WISCONSIN	Ordained or licensed clergyman of any religious denomination or society	No	Judge of court of record
WYOMING	Ordained or licensed minister of the gospel. Marriages may be solemnized by any religious society according to its rules.	No	Any judge, court commissioner, justice of the peace

366

Relations Between Husbands and Wives

315. The Marriage Contract · In the eyes of the law marriage is a contract whereby a man and a woman agree to enter into a union for life for their mutual benefit, to provide each other with companionship, sexual gratification and economic help and to procreate and raise children. The fact that none of these considerations may be mentioned at the time of marriage doesn't make them any the less binding. They are inherent in the marital contract. Many of them result from customs and religious doctrines that are almost 2,000 years old and have been incorporated into present-day laws by both our legislatures and our courts.

316. The Rights and Duties of Husbands and Wives · The obligations of husband and wife to each other are a matter more of custom and tradition than of law. But the husband has one clear and unavoidable obligation: to support his wife and children in accordance with his financial ability. This is a legal obligation, affirmed both by the courts and by statutes. All fifty states have adopted the Uniform Reciprocal Enforcement of Support Act, which enables a wife to get a court order in the state where she lives directing her husband who has left the state to pay her money to support her and the children. That court order is enforceable in the courts of any other state. If he violates such an order, the husband may be fined or imprisoned in the state where he has settled, but many men, by keeping on the move, manage to elude the law.

The wife's obligations are to maintain a home for her husband, to care for him, to provide companionship and to gratify his basic needs. These mutual obligations of husband and wife to each other are historically known as the marital *consortium*. The consortium is protected by the law: an injury to the husband or wife which incapacitates him or her for any period of time gives the other spouse the right to include "loss of consortium," or loss of the services of the injured spouse, as another element in a suit for damages.

317. Property Rights of Husbands and Wives · The rights of the husband and wife to each other's property depend on many things. Occasionally a marriage is preceded by an *antenuptial agreement* regarding the property of the couple. Such an agreement is more likely to be made when the woman has considerable property of her own that she wants to remain in her own name or that she wants to tie up in such a manner that her future husband can have no control over it. Although it is much less common today than it was when a married woman's property was regarded as belonging to her husband, the antenuptial agreement is still used, particularly in the eight so-called community property states: Arizona, California, Idaho, Louisiana, Nevada, New Mexico, Texas and Washington. In these states the husband's and wife's earnings are legally considered to be merged; that is, they become their common property.

Antenuptial agreements are also frequently used in second marriages where both parties have children by their first husband or wife and want to ensure that neither partner will expect to inherit the other's estate.

In general, however, marriage no longer affects the separate property of husband and wife. With rare exceptions married women today may buy, hold and sell both personal and real property in their own names as freely as men. They may enter into contracts, obtain credit and carry on their own businesses. They have the sole use of their earnings. They have really become economically emancipated, just as they became politically emancipated when they received the right to vote.

The rights of husbands and wives to each other's property in the event of the death of one of them are discussed at length in sections 533, 542, 558. Each is entitled to share in the other's estate, as prescribed by statute (see chart 20, page 353). Unmarried couples, even those who have lived in longlasting partnerships, are not covered, however. The survivor must make his claim—usually unsuccessfully—in court.

318. The Husband's Responsibility for His Wife's Debts • The husband is obligated to pay debts his wife incurs in running the household: bills for food, clothing, furnishings and so on. His only protection, if he's married to a spendthrift wife, may be to advertise in local newspapers that he will no longer honor her bills and to write to the stores she frequents not to give her any more credit. A wife normally has no legal obligation to pay her husband's bills. Both husbands and wives are responsible for jointly signed notes, tax returns and the like.

319. Lawsuits • Husbands and wives may sue each other to establish property rights or to press claims arising from business transactions between them. But only a few states (see chart 22, page 369) permit tort suits (see section 38) of one against the other, both as to personal injury and property damage. Neither a husband nor a wife is responsible for the other's torts or civil wrongs.

368

LAWSUITS BETWEEN SPOUSES

The laws of many states do not allow husbands and wives to sue each other for torts (for an explanation of torts see sections 35-38). The chart below indicates the law in your state. (See also section 319.)

CHART 22	Can You Sue Your Husband or Wife for a Tort?		
ALABAMA	Yes	MISSOURI	No
ALASKA	No	MONTANA	No
ARIZONA	No	NEBRASKA	No
ARKANSAS	Yes	NEVADA	No
CALIFORNIA	Yes	NEW HAMPSHIRE	Yes
COLORADO	—[1]	NEW JERSEY	No[3]
CONNECTICUT	Yes	NEW MEXICO	Yes
DELAWARE	No	NEW YORK	Yes
D.C.	No	NORTH CAROLINA	Yes
FLORIDA	No	NORTH DAKOTA	Yes
GEORGIA	No	OHIO	Yes
HAWAII	Yes	OKLAHOMA	Yes
IDAHO	Yes	OREGON	—[4]
ILLINOIS	No	PENNSYLVANIA	No
INDIANA	No[2]	RHODE ISLAND	No
IOWA	No	SOUTH CAROLINA	Yes
KANSAS	Yes	SOUTH DAKOTA	Yes
KENTUCKY	Yes	TENNESSEE	No
LOUISIANA	No	TEXAS	No
MAINE	No	UTAH	No
MARYLAND	No	VERMONT	No[3]
MASSACHUSETTS	No	VIRGINIA	No[3]
MICHIGAN	No	WASHINGTON	No
MINNESOTA	Yes	WEST VIRGINIA	No
MISSISSIPPI	No	WISCONSIN	Yes
		WYOMING	No

(1) Wife may sue husband for torts.
(2) Wife can sue husband for damage to separate property.
(3) Spouse may sue other spouse when action is for injuries from automobile accident.
(4) For willful torts but not for torts caused by negligence.

369

Husbands and wives may not testify or give evidence against each other in any criminal proceeding. This rule is very old and probably based on the theory that such testimony would be unreliable. But civil actions are a different matter. In lawsuits involving divorce or in suits concerning third parties spouses' testimony against each other is allowed.

RELATIONS BETWEEN PARENTS AND CHILDREN AND SCHOOLS

320. Rights of Unborn Children · Children conceived but still unborn have the same rights of inheritance (see section 560) as children who have been born: when a parent dies leaving no will, all the children share equally in his estate, even the unborn, or posthumous, child born after his death. But this statutory right of the unborn child to inherit may be cut off by the terms of the parent's will (see section 533). In other words, a parent may legally direct that his estate be distributed only to those children actually born prior to his death.

An unborn child has other legal rights, depending on the laws of individual states and court interpretations of those laws. Particularly important is the right of a child to sue for damages resulting from injuries inflicted before birth on his mother—whether maliciously or negligently. The modern trend is to support such a right of the child.

321. Rights of Minors · A minor is a person who has not yet reached the age of majority, that is, the age at which he is entitled to the management of his own affairs and enjoyment of civic rights. This age varies from state to state (see chart 28, page 428). But merely to say that a person is a minor is not very helpful. Minors have a variety of rights, and there are many things they may not legally do. Chart 28 indicates these rights and prohibitions and the ages at which minors may and may not do these things: marry, vote, go to work, be sentenced for a crime or misdemeanor, drive a car, buy alcoholic beverages. Minors may enter into contracts, but usually the contracts cannot be enforced against them until they reach the age of majority. Even then, the contract must be ratified to make it enforceable (see section 176).

322. When a Child Is Legitimate · A child born to parents who are married at the time of his birth is presumed to be legitimate. A child

370

born to an unmarried woman may become legitimate, when state statute allows, if the mother marries the natural father and he acknowledges that he is the father.

Parents who are unable to have children for one or another medical reason occasionally resort to artificial insemination: the mechanical insertion of male sperm into the womb. No questions arise as to the legitimacy of a child where the sperm is from the mother's husband. But if the sperm is from another man, doubts often arise as to the child's legitimacy. To ensure that child's full legal rights the husband should formally acknowledge the child as his own. Complicated legal questions are involved, and women considering artificial insemination should first obtain legal advice.

323. Parents' Right to Discipline Children • Parents have the right and the duty to discipline their children and may use reasonable force to do so, but they may be prosecuted for the use of excessive force. Under the statutes of many states, a child who is being abused or mistreated by his parents may be taken under the protection of the courts and placed in the care of another family or institution that will bring him up properly. The parents will be compelled to bear the expense of such care.

324. Parents' Obligation to Support Legitimate Children • The parents of a legitimate child, especially the father, have a centuries-old obligation to support the child according to their financial ability. This duty usually continues until the child reaches his or her majority. Where the marriage falls apart, for whatever reason, the father's legal obligation of support continues. If he should desert his family and flee to another state, his wife should consult a lawyer for help in taking advantage of the Uniform Reciprocal Enforcement of Support Act (see section 316).

The primary duty of support is the father's. But if he is dead or physically or mentally incapable of providing support, the duty falls on the mother. If both parents are dead or incapacitated, and no grandparent or other relative or individual comes forward to volunteer to care for the child, the court will place the child in an institution and require regular reports regarding the child's progress and welfare.

325. Support of an Adopted Child • Adoption is a legal proceeding in which a court declares someone a child's legal parent who is not his natural parent. If the child's natural parents are alive, they must consent to the adoption order. The court order of adoption, which is necessary even if both natural parents are dead, has the effect of giving the adopted child all the rights of a natural child. The adopting parents owe the adopted child the same duty of support and care as they owe a natural child. Most states give an adopted child full rights of inheritance from his adopting parents, but in a few states these rights are not entirely clear (see chart 24, page 394). Wills drawn by adopting parents in those states should contain a clause stating the parents' wish that adopted and natural children receive equal treatment in the distribution of their estate. Statutes differ regarding the rights of adopted children to inherit from their natural parents (see chart 24).

326. Support of an Illegitimate Child · An unmarried mother is legally responsible for the support of her illegitimate child. The only way she can compel assistance from the child's father is to bring a *paternity suit* against him—a legal proceeding to have a court declare the man the child's father. By the use of blood tests, if the man can be found, and of other evidence paternity can sometimes be established. Once it is, the court will order the man to contribute to the child's support. The amount of his contribution varies from state to state and depends on what other persons he is supporting and other circumstances.

327. Care of Neglected or Deserted Children · Parents whose income is so meager that they cannot provide their children with adequate food and clothing can get help from public welfare agencies.

Parents who mistreat or abandon their children will find similar public agencies stepping in, taking over responsibility for the children and seeing to it that a minimum of support and care is provided. Welfare officials and probation officers have wide authority to investigate conditions at the homes of neglected or deserted children and to recommend to the court that the children be sent to an institution, usually operated by a charitable or religious agency, for decent care. The agency will either care for the child on its own premises or place him in a foster home supervised by the agency.

Of course parents may on their own initiative place their children in care of these agencies. In either case, the parents are required to pay as much as they can for the expenses of the agency in providing food, clothing, room and medical care for the children.

328. Suits by Children for Injury or Death of a Parent · The family of a breadwinning husband or wife who is killed or totally disabled as the result of a crime, accident or civil wrong has a right to recover damages from the person or agency responsible for his death or disablement. Usually the surviving spouse brings the suit. But if both parents are dead, the minor children may start a legal action through a guardian ad litem (see section 336), a guardian appointed to defend or prosecute for a child in a suit to which he is a party. The damages sought may include reimbursement not only for the victim's medical and funeral bills, the pain and suffering he endured before death and the spiritual value of the lost parent to the children (see section 71), but also—and most important—for his prospective lost earnings.

Each child's share of the compensation awarded for the deceased parent's lost earnings is usually based on the duration of his right to support during his minority. For example, if the age of majority is twenty-one in the state in which the family lives and there are two surviving children, eighteen and fourteen years old, the older child would be entitled to three years' support, or 30 percent of the amount allocated to the children, while the younger would be entitled to seven years' support, or 70 percent of the amount.

329. Recourse for Injuries Inflicted on Your Children • A parent has a right to defend his child from physical attack to the same degree that he has a right to defend himself. This right includes the same restriction that he not use more force than is necessary to stop the attack. Thus, if you see your son being beaten by an older boy, you may pull the assailant off, but you may not strike him unless that's the only way you can get him to stop. Or if your child is jostled by an adult, you may shove the man away—even knock him down, if necessary—but you may not beat him senseless.

Nor may a parent assault another adult in revenge for injury done to his child. If your son reports that a neighbor struck him, you may not proceed to the neighbor's house and beat him. Your proper recourse is to report the assault on your child to the police, who will investigate it as a criminal matter. You may also want to consider bringing a tort suit for battery against the neighbor, but this is a matter for you to discuss in detail with a lawyer. The cost of litigation is high, and the rewards may not amount to much (see section 75).

Suits for injury to children resulting from accidents, assaults or other civil wrongs must be brought by their parents or by a guardian ad litem. In addition to other damage claims that may be made (see section 71), the parent may also sue for the loss of his child's services, affection and company while the child is incapacitated. If the evidence shows that the injury was the result of the child's own negligence, however, such claims may well not be honored, unless the court recognizes that the source of the injury constitutes an "attractive nuisance" (see sections 61, 304).

330. Parents' Responsibility for Damage and Injuries by Children • Unless there are specific statutes to the contrary in your state (discussed later in this section), a parent is generally not liable for most damages and injuries caused by his minor child. However, the parent may be liable for his child's acts: (a) if he fails to restrain the child reasonably from continuing wrongful conduct of which the parent is aware; (b) if the parent directs, participates in, consents to or ratifies the act; (c) if the child is acting as the parent's agent in committing the act; or (d) if the parent negligently entrusts a dangerous instrument to a child.

To illustrate: If your son engages in a fight with another boy and knocks out his teeth, you are not responsible for the dental bills, unless your child has a record of beating up other children and you have done nothing to stop him, or you have encouraged him to fight, or you have watched the fight and done nothing to stop it, thereby giving tacit consent. You might also be liable if your son injures someone with his bicycle while on an errand for you (thereby acting as your agent); if he shoots someone with an air rifle you gave him or with a real gun that you left within reach; or if he hits someone with a hammer, if he is too young to understand that the instrument could be dangerous.

The same rules apply to property damage. You would not be liable if your child, playing with a pack of matches he had found in the street, set fire to a neighbor's garage. But you might well be responsible if you knew he had set fires before and you had done nothing to cure him of the habit or if you saw him playing with the matches and did nothing to stop him.

Suppose your child, who ordinarily is well behaved and disciplined, engages in vandalism or malicious acts of destruction. In most states you would not be required to pay for the damage since a parent is not responsible for the acts of his children, except under the circumstances described above. However, an increasing number of states (listed in chart 23, page 375) have enacted parent liability laws that require a parent to pay for all or part of any property damage done by their children, regardless of the circumstances. The details of these laws vary from state to state, but the parents' liability is usually limited.

By far the most common instruments of personal injury and property

PARENTAL LIABILITY LAWS

Under common law, parents are not liable for the torts of their children. But many states have enacted laws imposing such liability in certain circumstances and within certain limits. These laws are summarized below. (See also sections 38, 330.)

CHART 23	Are Parents Liable for Torts of Children	If So, Until Child Reaches What Age?	What Is Limit of Parental Liability for Each Tort?	To What Kinds of Torts Does Liability Extend?
ALABAMA	Yes	18	$500[1]	Intentional, malicious or willful destruction of property; injury to person
ALASKA	Yes	18	$2,000[1]	Malicious or willful destruction of property
ARIZONA	Yes	18	$500	Malicious or willful destruction of property
ARKANSAS	Yes	18	$1,000	Malicious or willful destruction of property
CALIFORNIA	Yes	18	$2,000	Willful misconduct
COLORADO	Yes	18	$1,000[1]	Malicious or willful destruction of property
CONNECTICUT	Yes	18	$1,500	Malicious or willful destruction of property
DELAWARE	Yes	18	$300	Malicious property damage
D.C.	No			
FLORIDA	Yes	18	$1,000	Malicious or willful destruction of property
GEORGIA	Yes	18	No stated limit	Willful or wanton torts resulting in property damage
HAWAII	Yes	18	No stated limit	All torts
IDAHO	Yes	18	$300	Malicious or willful destruction of property
ILLINOIS	Yes	19	$500[1]	Malicious or willful injury to property or persons (no liability for child under 12)
INDIANA	Yes	18	$750[1]	Intentional, willful or malicious acts
IOWA	Yes	18	$1,000	Unlawful acts
KANSAS	Yes	18	$1,000[1,a]	Willful or malicious destruction of property
KENTUCKY	Yes	18	$2,500	Willful defacement or damage of property
LOUISIANA	Yes	18	No stated limit	All torts
MAINE	No			
MARYLAND	Yes	18	$1,500	Willful or malicious destruction or theft of property; injury to person
MASSACHUSETTS	Yes	17	$500	Damage caused by child's willful acts (no liability for child under 8)
MICHIGAN	Yes	18	$500	Willful or malicious destruction of property; injury to person
MINNESOTA	No			
MISSISSIPPI	No			

CHART 23 (Cont.)	Are Parents Liable for Torts of Children	If So, Until Child Reaches What Age?	What is Limit of Parental Liability for Each Tort?	To What Kinds of Torts Does Liability Extend?
MISSOURI	Yes	21	$300	Willful damage
MONTANA	Yes	18	$300[1]	Willful or malicious damage
NEBRASKA	Yes	19	No stated limit	Willful or intentional infliction of personal injury or destruction of property
NEVADA	Yes	18	$3,000	Willful misconduct resulting in property damage or personal injury
NEW HAMPSHIRE	No			
NEW JERSEY	Yes	16	$250[3]	Willful, malicious or unlawful destruction of property; injury to person
NEW MEXICO	Yes	18	$1,000[1]	Malicious or willful destruction of property
NEW YORK	Yes	18	$500	Willful, malicious or unlawful destruction of property (no liability for child under 11)
NORTH CAROLINA	Yes	18	$500	Willful or malicious destruction of property
NORTH DAKOTA	Yes	18	$1,000[1]	Willful or malicious destruction of property
OHIO	Yes	18	$2,000[1]	Willful destruction of property or malicious assault of person
OKLAHOMA	Yes	18	$1,500	Willful or malicious destruction of property
OREGON	Yes	18	$1,500	Intentional torts
PENNSYLVANIA	Yes	18	—[4]	Willful, tortious act resulting in injury to person; theft, destruction or loss of property
RHODE ISLAND	Yes	18	$500	Willful or malicious destruction of property; injury to person
SOUTH CAROLINA	Yes	17	$1,000	Malicious destruction, damage or theft of property
SOUTH DAKOTA	Yes	18	$300[1]	Willful or malicious acts
TENNESSEE	Yes	18	$500[1]	Willful or malicious destruction of property
TEXAS	Yes	18	$5,000[1]	Willful or malicious destruction of property resulting from parental neglect (no liability for child under 12)
UTAH	No			
VERMONT	Yes	17	$250	Willful or malicious destruction of property; injury to person
VIRGINIA	Yes	18	$200	Willful or malicious destruction of property
WASHINGTON	Yes	18	$1,000	Willful or malicious destruction of property
WEST VIRGINIA	Yes	18	$300	Willful or malicious destruction of property
WISCONSIN	Yes	18	$1,000	Willful, malicious or wanton property damage; injury to person
WYOMING	Yes	17	$300	Willful or malicious destruction of property (no liability for child under 11)

(1) Plus attorney's fees and court costs.
(2) No limit if act is result of parental neglect.
(3) $1,000 for damage to railroad or public utility property.

(4) $300 for one person damaged; $1,000 maximum for all persons damaged as a result of one act.

damage among older children, as among adults, are automobiles. The rules governing the driver's liability in case of accidents are fully reviewed in sections 242–257. But their application to minors may be briefly summarized as follows: If your child is licensed to drive and solely through his own negligence causes an accident while at the wheel of his own car, he and his insurance company are liable; you and your insurance company have no liability. If your child causes an accident while at the wheel of your car, you are not liable if you have expressly forbidden him to drive the car. In all other instances, you are usually liable under the family car doctrine (see section 254).

331. The Obligation to Educate Children • Every state in the nation requires a child between certain ages either to attend school or to receive a proper education outside of school. State statutes differ (see chart 28, page 428), but generally the child must attend school from the ages of six or seven to sixteen or seventeen or until he has finished the work of a specified grade, whichever comes first.

All states provide elementary and high schools for children, which they may generally attend at no cost until they graduate or reach the age of majority. If there is no public elementary or high school in the district in which the child lives, the state or local government must usually pay for the child's transportation to a school in a nearby district. The situation has been complicated in many areas by court-ordered busing of children to achieve racial balance in formerly all-black or all-white schools. The U.S. Supreme Court has reversed lower court decisions mandating busing, but it has also upheld busing in some instances.

It is the duty of parents or guardians to see that a child attends school during the ages specified by law or to provide an equivalent education outside of school, as explained below. If a child is absent from school unreasonably, truant officers may summon his parents to court to explain the absence or place them under bond, to assure his regular attendance. If a child refuses to attend school and becomes an habitual truant, his parents or school authorities may bring him before a juvenile court and have him sent to a state reform school or similar institution (see section 341) until he reaches the statutory age limit.

Despite the compulsory attendance laws, a public school is not obligated to accept a child who does not meet the local and federal standards of age, health, residence, intelligence, vaccination and cleanliness, and may expel or suspend a child who does not abide by the rules or code of decorum established by the local school board. If the refusal of admission or expulsion seems capricious or unreasonable, the parents may sue the school board to compel it to accept or reinstate the child. It is a federal offense for public school authorities to refuse to enroll a child in a school because of his race or religion.

A parent may of course send his child to a state-approved private or parochial school, instead of public school, or to a special school for the handicapped if the child is blind, deaf, crippled, slow to learn or if he suffers from other physical or mental deficiencies. The state or municipality that does not provide special schools for handicapped children will often contribute toward the expense of educating such children in specially equipped private institutions.

However, the state is not obligated—indeed, it is forbidden—to pay the tuition of normal children in private or parochial schools. Under the constitutional doctrine of the separation of church and state, public monies may not be used to support parochial schools. The economic plight of these schools is forcing a reconsideration of this doctrine as applied to education. Various devices are being used to avoid its limitations, such as providing public funds for transporting all children to schools (including parochial ones) and using public funds for scholarships at colleges of all denominations and to help students buy schoolbooks.

The question of educating children at home instead of at school is the subject of much legal controversy. The child whose residence is so remote and isolated that school attendance is impossible, or who is physically or mentally handicapped and has no special school available to serve him, may usually be educated at home. The state may even pay a parent or other qualified person to teach him. Otherwise, however, the state and courts regard home education of children as culturally inadequate, no matter how well qualified the parents or private tutors may be, on the ground that home education deprives the child of the social setting and the training and adjustment to group life and group activity that only a school can provide. The parents generally may not refuse to send a child to school on religious grounds (except for absence during religious holidays) or because they disapprove of subject matter schools teach, such as evolution and sex education.

No state requires a child to go to college or to continue his schooling beyond high school, nor are parents legally required to provide their children with advanced schooling, no matter how well they can afford it or how important the family's station in life. Curiously, however, if the parents are separated or divorced, the father who can afford to pay for his child's higher education may be required to do so.

332. Rights of Schools and Teachers to Discipline Children • Local boards of education, school superintendents and principals have a right to establish rules and regulations governing the conduct of students under their jurisdiction as long as they are "reasonable," designed to achieve proper ends and in line with state educational policies. The courts are increasingly limiting such rules to those that deal with the behavior and decorum of students and are more and more reluctant to uphold rules about clothing, the length of boys' hair and girls' skirts and the like.

The school may, to some extent, regulate the conduct of students away from school in certain circumstances. It may forbid students to leave the school grounds or to eat at nearby restaurants during school hours, deny them the right to belong to certain types of social organizations and punish them for fighting with or molesting other children on their way to and from school.

Punishments imposed by schools for violations of the rules may range from detention after school or withdrawal of privileges, such as membership in school-sponsored clubs and athletic teams, for minor infractions; to temporary suspension or permanent expulsion, for major violations. Expulsion, however, may require a formal hearing and action by the school board.

The right of a school or teacher to administer corporal punishment to a student or to lay hands on him in any way varies from one state and one school district to another. Some states and districts forbid any form of corporal punishment. Others give teachers the same authority to discipline children as parents have (see section 323), which means that corporal punishment is permitted if it is reasonable, administered for a good cause and in the interests of correcting the child's behavior and is proportionate in its severity to the child's age, size, sex and physical condition.

For example, a teacher might be entitled to slap the hands of a student throwing spitballs at another, but would not be justified in doing so for the pupil's failure to pronounce French verbs correctly. A teacher may use whatever force is necessary to break up a fight between sixteen-year-old boys, but may not use the same force to end a scrap among six-year-old girls.

There is some legal question about the right of schools and teachers to punish students who misbehave by lowering their grades or denying them academic credit. Few court decisions on the subject exist.

Parents have a right to bring suit against school authorities for disciplinary action taken against their children, and they may institute both criminal charges of assault and battery (see section 126) and a civil suit for damages (see section 41) against teachers who administer corporal punishment. The law presumes, however, that educational authorities have acted correctly in administering punishment, and the burden of proving the contrary lies on the complaining parents. Unless the administrators or teachers have flagrantly abused their authority, such actions are unlikely to succeed. Moreover, a teacher has the same right to defend himself against an assault by a student as he has against anyone else who attacks him (see sections 53, 149), and he may prefer criminal charges against the student and, under some circumstances, sue the parents for damages (see section 330).

If you feel that your child has been mistreated by a teacher at his school, by far the wisest course is to ask for an interview with the principal and discuss the matter with him. Only if you can't get results this way should you consider legal action, in which case, as always, you should get the advice of a lawyer.

333. The School's Financial Liability for Injuries to Students •

As government agencies (see section 38), school districts are not legally responsible for damages caused by their negligence or the negligence of their employes, *unless* the state has enacted legislation making local school districts liable for injuries to children entrusted to their care. Some states have given local school boards the option of assuming such responsibility and taking out liability insurance (see chart 31, page 448). Where no such liability is recognized, parents cannot recover damages from school districts for accidental injury to their children while under the school's jurisdiction.

Even in states where the school may not be sued, however, school administrators and employes may be held individually responsible for accidents that result from their negligence. Members of a school board have been ordered to pay damages for death or injury to students in a school bus accident because the driver had a record of drunkenness and reckless driving. A teacher was held liable for an explosion that resulted when he allowed students to mix chemicals in a laboratory without supervision. A custodian was required to pay the medical bills of a child who was injured on a swing that the custodian knew had a broken link.

But in no school district, whether it accepts liability or not, is the board or its personnel responsible for injuries resulting from a student's own negligence or disobedience. Thus, a child could not recover damages if he was injured jumping from a moving school bus on a dare, breaking into a laboratory against orders to mix explosives or playing on a faulty swing despite warnings not to. Nor is the school or its personnel responsible for injuries a child suffers as part of the normal risks of an activity he takes part in voluntarily. Parents who have given their son permission to join the school's football squad, for example, have no grounds for legal action if he accidentally breaks his leg in a scrimmage.

334. If Your Child Wants to Get a Job • For most of recorded history there were no laws about a child's right to work. But cruel conditions of child labor that attended the development of industry in the 1700s made it necessary to pass laws protecting minors from employment in mines and factories. Such laws first simply limited the number of hours children under a certain age could work. Only much later were laws passed absolutely prohibiting employment of children below a certain age. Then came laws permitting children of designated ages to be employed in limited kinds of work considered not dangerous. For the laws in your state covering employment of children, see chart 33, page 466. (See also section 371.)

335. Parents' Rights to Their Children's Earnings • Parents are entitled to all of a minor child's earnings. In fact, if the parents insist, the employer may be required to pay the child's wages directly to them. In years gone by courts even allowed a child's earnings to be seized by creditors to satisfy the parent's debts. When a minor is injured in an accident, a parent may sue to recover damages for loss of the child's services—in addition to any other damages demanded (see section 71). The father has first priority on the child's earnings and on money recovered for loss of his services. If the father is dead or deserts his family, the mother is entitled to the earnings. In these days of relative prosperity and growing independence among young people, working minors normally keep most or all of their earnings for their own use—possibly with the understanding that they will contribute toward their school, transportation or recreational costs. But the parents' legal right to these earnings still remains.

336. Debts, Contracts, Lawsuits of Minors • Parents are not responsible for debts incurred by minor children, unless the parents have guaranteed payment or the debts involve the purchase of necessaries that the parent has failed to provide. However, the term *necessary* is a flexible one. One court required a father to repay money his son borrowed for university tuition, on the ground that higher education was necessary to the boy's station in life, even though the father disapproved of it.

Minors may also be held responsible for the debts they incur for necessaries, but they are not obligated to repay debts incurred for other things. An automobile dealer who sells a car on the installment plan to an underage student, who uses it for pleasure, takes a ridiculous risk unless payment is guaranteed by the parents. Contracts entered into by minors cannot be enforced against them because they may be disavowed by the minor until he attains majority. For a more extended discussion of minors' contracts, see section 176. Many insurance companies will issue policies to minors, however, and many banks will allow minors to open accounts in their own names.

A minor child may not institute lawsuits or be sued in his own name except for debts he has incurred for necessaries. All civil actions taken either for or against him, whether involving property, debts, contracts, accidents, negligence or other civil wrongs, must be prosecuted or defended by his parent, guardian or a special *guardian ad litem* (a guardian for purposes of the litigation appointed by the court), depending on the laws of the particular state.

337. Property Rights of Minor Children · Parents have no right to any property that comes to their child in the form of a legacy or bequest or by right of inheritance. Such property, including the income from it, belongs entirely to the child. But property inherited by minors must be managed by a guardian or trustee named in the will or appointed by the probate court, who administers it in accordance with instructions given in the will or by the court. The property is not turned over to the child until he reaches the age of majority (twenty-one, in most states; see chart 28, page 428) or the age specified in the will for termination of the trust (see sections 545, 594.)

More often than not in these situations, the child's parent is appointed trustee for his inherited property, but he may not use the child's principal or income to defray the cost of supporting him, unless he is specifically permitted to do so by the terms of the will or by court order. He is merely a custodian of the property, and, except for a trustee's fee to which he may be entitled for managing the property (see section 548), he is expected to turn the property over to the child intact at the proper time. If the parent is financially unable to support the child or faces an unusual expense on his behalf which he cannot afford, such as straightening the child's teeth or sending him to college, he should seek a court order permitting him to use the child's money. If he spends the money without court permission, when the child comes of age he may sue the parent to recover the amount spent, requiring him to prove that he had no alternative to using the child's funds.

The statutes of all states include "descent and distribution" laws (see chart 42, page 696), which set forth the portion of a deceased parent's estate to which the children are entitled. These statutes are discussed in sections 555–570. The most important point to remember here is that all states permit children to share in their parents' estates and set forth the exact percentage they receive if their parents die without a will. Except in Louisiana, however, a parent may disinherit a child by a carefully (or carelessly) drawn will.

When Children Get in Trouble with the Law

338. Legal Status of Minors Who Do Wrong • Below a specified age—which is usually eighteen, but may range from sixteen to twenty-one, depending on state laws—a child may not be convicted of any crime except murder (sections 92, 137), no matter how serious it may be. This is not to say that he goes uncorrected or unpunished, but that he is treated as a juvenile delinquent, whose case must be handled under special laws —in many states by special juvenile courts—and that if he is convicted for the first time he may not be regarded as a criminal or acquire a criminal record. A child may be charged with juvenile delinquency not only for commission of misdemeanors and felonies, as explained in sections 90, 137, but also for truancy from school; for sexual license, which might be condoned in an adult; for incorrigibility, if his parents find him difficult or impossible to control; and for a wide variety of other misbehavior. In fact, in some states a child may be adjudged delinquent for using obscene language, smoking cigarettes, patronizing a public poolroom or attempting to marry without his parents' consent (see chart 28, page 428).

A young offender who has passed the age at which he is treated as a juvenile delinquent may be tried and convicted as an adult in most states and situations. However, the consequences of acquiring a criminal record can be so serious and have so disastrous an effect on his future that courts and legislatures lean over backward to prevent him from becoming, or being branded, a criminal. If he is a first offender who has not yet reached a proscribed age (eighteen to twenty-one, depending on state laws) and has no prior record of juvenile delinquency, he may be treated as a "youthful offender" (see section 342).

For a survey of state juvenile court systems and laws dealing with juvenile offenders, see chart 29, page 432.

339. Preliminary Investigation of Juvenile Offenders • Fully half the cases involving juvenile offenders never reach a judge. The proceedings start with the filing in the juvenile court of a *petition* instead of the complaint, information or indictment that commence adult criminal proceedings (see sections 150–153). The petition, which may be filed by law officers, the district attorney, school officials, parents or anyone having knowledge of the circumstances, sets forth the alleged facts of the child's wrongdoing, his name, age and residence, and the names and residence of his parents or guardian. The petition is then turned over to the court's probation department or to a child welfare agent appointed for the purpose, which conducts a full investigation into the facts and circumstances of the case, as well as into the child's environment, character and family history. In many states this investigation may include physical and mental examinations of the child. If the probation staff decides that the child was wrongly accused or that his delinquency was not serious, it may dismiss the charge, in the former instance, or, in the latter, put the child on informal probation in charge of his parents or guardian or refer him to a private agency for treatment. Only if the investigation shows that the delinquency is serious is the case passed on to the juvenile court for formal hearing before a judge.

During the period of investigation or while he is awaiting formal hearing, the child is usually released into the custody of his parents or guardian. In some cases bail (see sections 26, 100, 152) may be required, but usually he is released free of bail. However, if the child's home conditions make his release inadvisable, or if bail is unavailable and his offense is too serious to allow his release, he may be detained. Most states (see chart 29, page 432) require that children below a specified age who are detained be placed in special children's homes or shelters or be given special accommodations. But in a few states they may still be detained in jails or police stations, together with adults.

340. Juvenile Court Procedure • A *juvenile court* or *family court* (it goes by different names in different localities) is one that hears only cases involving children young enough to be classed as juvenile delinquents and, in some instances, older youths below the age of majority (as explained in section 342). In most jurisdictions the juvenile court is a separately constituted tribunal, with its own judges and officers. In a few jurisdictions, however, cases involving children may be heard by judges of criminal and other courts, who sit as juvenile courts for the purpose of the hearing. But whether heard by full-time or part-time juvenile court judges, court proceedings involving children are usually quite different from those involving adults. One major exception to this rule is the area of traffic violations, where in many states a minor with a driver's license may be tried in traffic court or before a magistrate, and be fined or have his license suspended or revoked exactly like an adult.

Juvenile hearings are informal. They are usually held in the privacy of the judge's chambers, in an office specially set up for the purpose or in a "closed" courtroom, to which newsmen and the public are not admitted. There is very rarely a jury. Usually the only people present or admitted to the court are the judge, probation officers, the child and his parents or guardian and witnesses who may be called. The child's case may be represented by a lawyer, if the parents and guardians desire. The judge may question the child about his part in the delinquent act, take the testimony of witnesses and listen to the recommendations and objections of the defense attorney, if there is one. He may also question the parents about their relations with the child and the extent of the discipline they exert. But the judge is apt to rely most heavily on the probation officer's analysis of the case and his recommendations. The entire hearing rarely takes more than half an hour. The proceedings may or may not be officially recorded. But the identity of the child may not be published in the newspapers in most states, and the court records are kept confidential, unavailable to anyone but the probation staff, the child's parents and lawyer and the court itself.

Informality is all very well, but it can be carried so far that it results in the denial of basic constitutional rights. The U.S. Supreme Court has ruled that the constitution requires, in cases involving juveniles as well as in cases involving adults: (a) that the offender must have written notice of the charges against him; (b) that he must be advised of his right to have his own lawyer; (c) that he has a right to meet his accuser and to cross-examine him; (d) that he must be accorded the privilege against self-incrimination, that is, he cannot be made to give evidence against himself. This Supreme Court decision will go a long way toward protecting the rights of juvenile offenders.

341. Punishment of Juvenile Offenders • Most juvenile courts are authorized to dispose of juvenile offenders in one of four ways: (a) The court may dismiss or discharge the child. (b) It may place the offender on probation or under the supervision of a probation officer and return him to his family. (c) It may place him in an agency or foster home. (d) It may commit the child to a reformatory or training school. In addition, the court may order restitution of property or reparation for damage done, such as requiring the child to replant the garden he has torn up or to work for a storekeeper free for a specified number of days in compensation for the goods he has stolen. But rarely, if ever, may a child be fined, except for traffic violations.

An order of the juvenile court concerning the treatment of a delinquent child may subsequently be vacated or modified by the judge in the interests of the child's welfare. Even if the charge against a delinquent is dismissed, he may be ordered back to court and placed on probation if he continues his offensive behavior. A juvenile on probation must report to his probation officer at regular intervals. Also, the judge may order him to attend school regularly, perform certain household chores or work details, stay away from disreputable persons or places, remain within a specified geographic area, keep regular hours and be home or in bed by a certain time each night. Failure to observe these orders may result in more severe punishment.

If a delinquent child is placed in a foster home, the court will require his natural parents to pay what they can toward his expenses and toward the medical or psychological treatment the court orders (see section 324). The parents' failure to pay may be punishable as contempt of court (see section 96). Committing a juvenile to a training school or some other corrective institution is usually ordered as a last resort, when probation or foster home treatment seems likely to be ineffective or has been tried before without success.

342. Special Treatment of Wayward Minors and Youthful Offenders • Some people believe that wrongdoers who, though they are not yet twenty-one, are too old to be treated as juvenile delinquents should not be regarded as criminals and should not have a criminal conviction on their record. Statutes in New York State, for example, provide special treatment for such persons. A *wayward minor* is defined as any person between the ages of sixteen and twenty-one who either: (a) is habitually addicted to the use of drugs or the intemperate use of intoxicating liquors; (b) habitually associates with dissolute persons; (c) is found

386

of his (or her) own free will and knowledge in a house of prostitution, assignation or ill fame; (d) habitually associates with thieves, prostitutes, procurers or disorderly persons; (e) is willfully disobedient to the reasonable and lawful commands of parents, guardian or other custodian and is morally depraved or is in danger of becoming morally depraved; (f) deserts his home or place of abode without just cause and without the consent of parents, guardian or other custodian; or (g) so conducts himself as to willfully injure or endanger the morals or health of himself or of others.

Such a person may be declared a wayward minor after a hearing and either placed on probation for two years or, if not considered fit for probation, committed to a religious or charitable institution for a period of up to three years. The fact that a person has been declared a wayward minor will not disqualify him from holding public office, and such declaration is not to be regarded as being the same as a conviction for a crime.

Whereas a wayward minor has not actually committed a crime but seems likely to if he does not change his course, a *youthful offender* is a person under a specific age set by law (see chart 29, page 432) who has committed a crime not punishable by death or life imprisonment and who has not previously been convicted of a felony. In states where these laws exist, a special procedure is established to prevent the case from getting the usual criminal procedure treatment.

For example, the boy in his late teens who is accused of arson may request the court's permission to be treated as a youthful offender, or the judge or district attorney may suggest such a request. The case cannot be publicized in any way while the request is being considered. If the request is granted, the original charge or accusation is changed from "arson" to "youthful offense." The trial of the offense is not public. Because a youthful offense is not a crime, even if the offender is found guilty he has not legally committed a crime and so has no criminal record. His file is not available to the public, but it is to other judges. Finally, the punishment for youthful offenders is limited to confinement for not more than three years in a religious, charitable or reformative institution of the offender's own religious faith, to probation under court supervision or to some other appropriate action.

As is the case with wayward minors, youthful offenders are not disqualified from holding public office, and a determination of a youthful offense is not a conviction of a crime. The whole purpose of such special treatment is to prevent persons under a certain statutory age from starting out adulthood as criminals.

387

343. When Children Need Legal Guardians • In the eyes of the law, minors are incapable either of taking care of themselves and their property or of asserting their rights. Of course this is not true in many cases, but the time-honored legal fiction is designed to protect people under the age of majority from their own errors in judgment and from exploitation by older and more experienced persons.

Because minors lack this legal capacity (see section 336), every child has a natural or a legally appointed guardian. The father is the child's natural guardian. The mother is the natural guardian if the father is dead or has abandoned the child, if the child is illegitimate or if the parents are divorced. The parents may in their wills name a relative or friend to serve as a guardian in the event of their death. If they fail to do so, the probate court will appoint one, usually the adult who is nearest of kin.

In most states, if the child is over fourteen, he may nominate his own guardian. Any guardian, even a parent or a guardian named in a will, may be removed and replaced by the court if circumstances and the child's welfare make a change advisable. Actually, two guardians may be named in a will or appointed by the court, although this is not a common occurrence: a *guardian of the person,* to take care of the child himself, and a *guardian of the property,* to take charge of his assets. In addition, if the child should be involved in a lawsuit, as either plaintiff or defendant, a special *guardian ad litem* must be appointed by the court.

Guardianship of the person ends when the child, or *ward,* to use the legal term, reaches his or her majority or gets married. Guardianship of property also ends in most states when a female ward is married, but usually continues until a male ward reaches his majority, even if he marries. Other legal functions of guardians and their accountability to the court are discussed in section 549.

344. Relations Between Legal Guardians and Wards • The rights and responsibilities of guardians and wards with respect to each other are the same as those of parents and children—with several significant exceptions. The guardian is not entitled to his ward's earnings, nor is he liable for the ward's support. The cost of maintaining the ward, either independently or in the guardian's home, is paid from the child's own property, as authorized by the court. The extent and place of the child's general education may be determined by the guardian, but not his religious education; the court usually requires the child to be brought up in the faith of his parents. The guardian is entitled both to repayment of the expenses he incurs for his ward and to compensation for his services, either in the form of a commission on the amount of receipts and disbursements of the ward's property or in the form of a fixed allowance, as determined by state statutes and the courts.

345. Trustees of Children's Property • Because a minor may not legally manage his own property, anyone who makes a will leaving money or property to a minor should name a trustee to administer the property until the child reaches his majority or a designated age beyond that time. The trustee appointed may be the child's parents or parent, a friend, lawyer, bank or trust company. (The functions, rights and duties of trustees are discussed in sections 545–548.) If no trustee is named in the will or if the child receives property by inheritance without a will, the property is administered by a guardian appointed by the probate court, as described in section 557.

346. The Meaning of Adoption • Adoption is the process that creates the legal relationship of parent and child between persons who are not so related by birth. When any adoption is finally legalized, the adopting parents and children bear the same relationship and have exactly the same rights and obligations to each other as do natural parents and children (except for certain inheritance rights, as described in section 562). Moreover, adoption is permanent. Once formalized, it can be undone only in exceptional circumstances (see section 353).

347. The Importance of Retaining a Lawyer in Adoption Proceedings • Adoption proceedings are so complicated (see section 350) that it is both impractical and unwise to attempt an adoption without the aid of an attorney. He is needed to prepare the necessary documents, to give advice about the legal status of the adopted child and to follow the matter through from the adoption petition to the final adoption decree from the court. Equally important is the lawyer's role in investigating the circumstances and supervising the papers and conditions of the adoption, so as to safeguard the interest of the adopting parents and the adopted child. Most recognized adoption agencies have their own lawyers, but their primary responsibility is to protect the agency and to a lesser extent the adopted child. Frequently adoptions are arranged without the help of

389

adoption agencies. Persons adopting children under these circumstances are especially advised to consult a lawyer to make sure that all legal requirements have been met (see chart 24, page 394).

348. Where Adopted Children Come From • The great majority of children put up for adoption are of illegitimate birth. The mother may voluntarily surrender the child for a variety of reasons: because she did not want it in the first place; because it might interfere with her future prospects for marriage; because she is too young or too poor to take care of it; or because she wants to give it a better chance in life with both a mother and father to rear it. The courts favor the adoption of illegitimate children, whatever the reason, on the grounds that a married couple is better able than an unwed mother to raise a child properly and that the stigma of illegitimacy is an unfair handicap for any child. But an illegitimate child may never be adopted without its mother's consent unless she neglects or abandons it or is too unsound of mind to care for it properly.

Adoption of stepchildren is also common. A husband or wife may adopt the child or children born to the other spouse in a prior marriage. Such adoptions usually present few legal difficulties and are encouraged by the courts. They have the important advantage of giving the stepchild the same last name as the other children in the family and putting him on a legal par with them.

If the child was born out of wedlock or if one of his natural parents is dead, only the consent of the mother or of the surviving natural parent is required. If the adopted child's natural parents have been divorced, the consent of both is needed, even though only one was awarded custody of the child. If the divorced father has been paying the mother for support of the child, the court may require him to continue full or partial support payments even after the child is adopted by the wife's new husband. In a case where the child's natural father is reluctant to consent to his adoption by the stepfather, one could probably negotiate his consent by agreeing that support payments by him may be stopped. When there is any conflict, a complete discussion with your lawyer is essential. If the child is more than ten to sixteen years of age, depending on state laws, his own consent to the adoption may also be required.

Legitimate children are sometimes put up for adoption by physically incapacitated parents or by parents without the means to take care of them, who seek to give the child advantages they cannot provide. But the courts are unlikely to approve such adoptions unless the reasons are valid and compelling and the child, if he is old enough, consents.

349. Who May Adopt a Child • Although the laws of the fifty states vary, all states now recognize that the welfare of the adopted child gets first consideration. Many of the regulations and practices governing adoptions may be modified or set aside by courts when they believe it is in the child's best interest to do so. With this reservation in mind, the rules governing the qualifications required of people who want to adopt a child may be summarized as follows:

a. The foster parents must be married and living together, and both must consent to the adoption, although both need not actually adopt the child. Some states allow adoption only by married couples who physicians certify are unable to bear children of their own. Other states bar adoption by parents with natural or adopted children living with them. Unmarried, separated or widowed persons are permitted to adopt children in most states, but such adoptions are rare because most agencies consider two parents necessary for the child's welfare.

b. The foster parents must be adults, usually ten to fifteen years older than the child, but not too old to care for him properly. Some states forbid adoptions when the wife is over thirty-five or the husband over forty. In other states the maximum allowable age of the foster parents depends on the age of the child. Thus, a thirty-six-year-old woman might be allowed to adopt a fourteen-year-old child, but not a younger one.

c. Close relatives of the foster child are given preference over strangers. In fact, parents with children of their own may adopt their minor nieces, nephews, cousins, in some states which would ordinarily bar their adoption of children not related to them.

d. The character, temperament, physical and mental health and social standards of the adopting parents must in the opinion of the court be adequate to give the child a secure and decent home and a proper upbringing.

e. The adopting parents must also have the financial means to support and rear the child. Once adopted, however, the foster child shares the family's fortunes, and the adoption is not affected if the parents subsequently become impoverished.

f. Some states require that foster parents and children be of the same race. Others require that the foster parents be of the same religion as the child's natural parents. Requirements of this kind have recently been challenged on constitutional grounds, and their validity is not clear.

350. Legal Steps in Adopting a Child • The procedure is much the same in all states. The prospective adopting parents file a *petition* in the appropriate court, identifying the child to be adopted and supplying all other information required by law. The petition must be accompanied by the written consent of the welfare agency, if one is involved, and of the child's natural parents, if they are alive. Parental consent is not needed, however, if the parents are mentally incompetent or have abandoned the child or if a court has removed the child from their custody because of cruelty or neglect. Only the natural mother's consent is required for adoption of an illegitimate child. In most states the consent of the child who has reached the age of fourteen is also needed.

A *judicial hearing* is then held, in which the court examines the qualifications of the adoptive parents and either grants or denies the petition.

Either before or after the hearing, a *probationary period,* or trial period, is required in all but one state. During this waiting time—which lasts from six to twelve months, depending on the state—the child lives with the foster parents, and the state welfare agency keeps an eye on them to see how the relationship develops and whether the foster parents are willing and able to care for the child as they should. If the welfare authorities, the foster parents or the child is unhappy with the arrangement, the agency may remove the child from the foster parents' custody or request the court to do so.

If all parties concerned are satisfied with the relationship, the welfare agency asks the court to issue a permanent adoption decree.

Adoption proceedings are strictly confidential. The hearing takes place in a closed courtroom, without spectators, and the records of the hearing may be examined only by court order. A new birth certificate called a certificate by adoption is issued for the child under his new family name, recording the date and place he was born (not the date or place of his adoption) and the ages of his foster parents at the time of his birth, with no mention of his natural parents. The old birth certificate is sealed and filed and may be opened only by order of the court or at the request of the adopted child himself, when he is of legal age. Thus, if the adoption takes place when the child is too young to remember his previous life, he may never know that he is adopted, or the names of his real parents, unless his foster parents choose to divulge the information if, in fact, they know it. The purpose is to give the child a maximum sense of security and identity with his new family.

State laws regulating adoptions are shown in chart 24, page 394.

351. Private Adoption Versus Agency Adoption of Children • Private adoption is an arrangement by which a natural parent or parents give up a child and consent to its adoption by specific individuals. Such adoptions sometimes involve legitimate children (whose parents surrender them for the reasons described in section 348), but the majority of cases involve illegitimate children.

The adoption of the illegitimate child may be arranged by the unwed mother, by a friend or relative or, frequently, by the doctor who delivers the child. Often the adoption is agreed upon during the mother's pregnancy and the identity of the adopting parents is withheld from the mother by the doctor, so as to avoid complications later on. The parents who propose to adopt the baby may provide the mother with support during her pregnancy and pay for her medical and hospital bills during delivery, as well as for her postnatal care. But it is illegal for them to "buy" the baby or to give money to the mother, the doctor or the intermediary, for any purpose other than those pertaining to the expenses of pregnancy and birth.

Private adoptions may sometimes be justified on the ground that the unwed mother might seek an illegal and perhaps dangerous abortion if this alternative were not available to her. The mother-to-be may be comforted by the assurance in advance that the child will be taken off her hands at birth and put in the care of responsible people who want it and will raise it as their own. Adopting parents usually have the benefit of obtaining a baby more quickly and at a younger age through private adoption than through a welfare agency. They may also be able to check the backgrounds of the child's natural parents.

But the dangers frequently outweigh the advantages. The adopting parents have no recourse should the mother change her mind and decide to keep the baby after they have paid for her care and medical bills, and they may have less protection should the mother seek to recover her child after adoption. Nor is there anyone to whom they can "return" the baby if it turns out to be physically or mentally defective. Once privately adopted, the child is theirs forever, as if it were their own flesh and blood.

Agency adoption occurs when one or both natural parents give their child to a state welfare or licensed adoption agency for placement or when the court orders a child put up for adoption because of cruelty or neglect. From the adopting parents' viewpoint there are several disadvantages of adoption from an agency: they may have to wait a long time to receive a child; the child may not be as young as they might have wished; the child the agency selects for them may not be the one they would have chosen, if given a choice; they may not obtain as much

ADOPTION LAWS

CHART 24	Above What Age Is Child's Consent to Adoption Needed?	How Long Is the Probationary Period Before Adoption Order Becomes Final?	Which Court Has Jurisdiction?	May the Child Inherit from Its Adoptive Parents If They Die Without a Will?	Does the Adopted Child Retain the Right to Inherit from Its Natural Parents If They Die Without a Will?
ALABAMA	14	6 months	Probate court	Yes	Yes
ALASKA	10	6 months	Superior court	Yes	No
ARIZONA	12	1 year	Superior court	Yes	No
ARKANSAS	14	6 months	Probate court	Yes	Yes
CALIFORNIA	12	6 months	Superior court	Yes	No
COLORADO	12	6 months	Juvenile division of district court; in Denver, juvenile court	Yes	No
CONNECTICUT	14	12-13 months	District probate court	Yes	No
DELAWARE	14	1 year	Superior court	Yes	No
D.C.	14	6 months	Superior court	Yes	No
FLORIDA	12	90 days	Circuit court of county	Yes	No
GEORGIA	14	3 months	Superior court	Yes	No
HAWAII	10	1 year	Circuit court	Yes	No
IDAHO	12	No probationary period	District court	Yes	No
ILLINOIS	14	6 months	Circuit court	Yes	Yes
INDIANA	14	Discretionary	County court with probate jurisdiction	Yes	No
IOWA	14	1 year	District court	Yes	NSP*
KANSAS	14	No probationary period	District court	Yes	No
KENTUCKY	12	90 days	Circuit court	Yes	No
LOUISIANA	16	1 year	Juvenile court	Yes	Yes
MAINE	14	1 year	Probate court	Yes	Yes
MARYLAND	10	Not more than 1 year	Circuit court of county; in Baltimore, equity court	Yes	No
MASSACHUSETTS	12	6 months if under 14	Probate court	Yes	No
MICHIGAN	10	1 year	Probate court	Yes	No
MINNESOTA	14	6 months	Juvenile court	Yes	No
MISSISSIPPI	14	6 months	Chancery court	Yes	No
MISSOURI	14	9 months	Circuit court, juvenile division	Yes	No

*No statutory provision.

In this chart, the adopted child's inheritance rights refer only to the situation in which neither of the adopting parents is related to the child by blood. If a child is adopted by a stepparent who is married to his natural parent, the child may inherit from both.

	Above What Age Is Child's Consent to Adoption Needed?	How Long Is the Probationary Period Before Adoption Order Becomes Final?	Which Court Has Jurisdiction?	May the Child Inherit from Its Adoptive Parents If They Die Without a Will?	Does the Adopted Child Retain the Right to Inherit from Its Natural Parents If They Die Without a Will?
MONTANA	12	6 months	District court	Yes	Yes
NEBRASKA	14	6 months	County court	Yes	No
NEVADA	14	6 months	District court of county	Yes	No
NEW HAMPSHIRE	11	6 months	Probate court	Yes	No
NEW JERSEY	10	1 year	Superior court or juvenile & domestic relations court	Yes	No
NEW MEXICO	10	6 months	District court	Yes	Yes
NEW YORK	14	6 months	Family court	Yes	No
NORTH CAROLINA	11	1 year	Superior court	Yes	No
NORTH DAKOTA	10	6 months	District court	Yes	No
OHIO	12	6 months	Probate court	Yes	No
OKLAHOMA	12	6 months	District court	Yes	NSP*
OREGON	14	6 months	Court with probate jurisdiction	Yes	No
PENNSYLVANIA	12	6 months	Orphans' court; in Philadelphia, family division	Yes	No
RHODE ISLAND	13	6 months	Under 18, family court; over 18, probate court	Yes	Yes
SOUTH CAROLINA	NSP*	6 months	Court of common pleas	Yes	No
SOUTH DAKOTA	12	6 months	Circuit court	Yes	Yes
TENNESSEE	14	1 year	Chancery & circuit courts	Yes	No
TEXAS	11	6 months	District court	Yes	Yes
UTAH	12	1 year	District court	Yes	No
VERMONT	13	6 months	Probate court	Yes	Yes
VIRGINIA	13	6 months	Chancery court	Yes	No
WASHINGTON	13	6 months	Superior court	Yes	No
WEST VIRGINA	11	6 months	Juvenile or circuit court	Yes	Yes
WISCONSIN	14	No probationary period	County court	Yes	No
WYOMING	13	6 months	District court	Yes	NSP*

information about the child's parentage and background as they want.

But the advantages of the agency adoption usually outweigh the disadvantages. The agency makes certain the child is legally available for adoption and that the irrevocable consent of the natural parents is obtained, which decreases the possibility that they may try to reclaim him later. The child's background and physical condition have been examined by the agency, lessening the chances that he will turn out to be physically or mentally defective. The agency also makes an effort to match characteristics to ensure that the newly adopted child will fit harmoniously into his foster parents' home. During the probation period, agency workers visit the child and foster parents periodically to make sure they are adapting to each other satisfactorily. If the arrangement is working out unsatisfactorily, for any basic reason, the agency will relocate the child. The agency's files are strictly confidential. It is forbidden by law to divulge the identity or place of residence of the adopting parents to the natural parents, which greatly lessens the chances of the latter's interfering at some future date.

352. The Danger of Adopting a "Black Market" Baby • The practice of buying and selling illegitimate or unwanted children is less common than it once was, but the "black market" in babies still exists. Among the most frequent victims of the racket are young unwed mothers who go to other cities or states to bear their children, in order to avoid embarrassment at home, and who are frightened into surrendering their babies through threat of exposure or legal punishment.

Buying or selling children is a crime in all states. Not only may the seller (or buyer) be fined or imprisoned, but there is also a strong probability that the child will be removed from the custody of the parents who have adopted it. As explained in the previous section, the only payments adopting parents may make in a private adoption are the legitimate medical and hospital expenses of the mother and reasonable lawyer's fees. Even after the adoption has been fully legitimized by the courts, the natural mother may sometimes recover the child if she can prove that she gave it up because of duress, threats or misrepresentation.

353. When Adoption May Be Revoked • An adoption decree may be set aside at the court's discretion, even years after it was issued, if there is evidence of fraud or misrepresentation by the adopting parents, as might happen if a man lied about his age or religion in order to obtain a child or hid the fact that he had a criminal record.

Occasionally adoptions may also be abrogated by mutual consent of all parties, if the court deems it to be in the best interests of the child. But if mutual consent is lacking and there is no evidence of fraud or misrepresentation, the child cannot be taken away from the adopting parents, nor can they get rid of it, except in the following circumstances:

Adoption may be revoked against the will of the adopting parents, in some circumstances and in some states, if they become habitual criminals or are imprisoned for crimes; if they abandon or neglect the child; if they become too physically or mentally incapacitated to care for the child; if they become so impoverished that they can no longer provide it with the necessities of life; or if the child is so desperately unhappy with his new parents that the court might find the situation dangerous to his physical or emotional health.

By far the most common cause of adoption annulment actions is the natural mother's change of mind. If her consent to adoption was given before the birth of the child, in some states she may still be allowed a change of heart when the child is born, and even in states where the consent is technically binding the courts are unlikely to force her to give up the baby. But what happens if she wants to get her child back later on because her economic situation has improved, or because she has married and is able to provide a home for it or simply because she longs for it? When the child is still in custody of the welfare agency or its adoption is in the probationary state (see section 350), the court may return it to her if it decides such action is in the child's best interest. She may get the child back even after the adoption has been fully legalized if the adopting parents consent and the court approves the action as being in the best interests of the child.

However, if the adopting parents are not willing to give up the child, the natural mother may not recover it unless she can prove that her consent to the adoption was wrung from her by duress, fraud or misrepresentation or that the foster parents had illegally paid for the baby or had otherwise violated the adoption statutes. Even then, the court may choose not to return the child if it is happy in its foster home and is getting proper care and love.

Nevertheless, tragedy may arise if the natural mother learns the whereabouts of her child. There are many cases in which natural mothers have invaded the homes where their children were living, harassed the adopting parents and even resorted to kidnapping. This is why the laws, adoption agencies and courts are so intent on keeping the identity of the adopting parents secret from the natural parents and why it is so important for adopting parents to obey the adoption laws scrupulously. If they neglect to follow the adoption procedures to the letter, they may be inviting heartbreak in later years.

354. Adoption of Adults • The laws of many states make it entirely legal for adults to adopt other adults as their children, providing the adopting parent is at least ten to fifteen years older than the adopted child. Adult adoptions are usually performed for the purpose of continuing a family name, of making the adopted person eligible for inheritances or for sentimental reasons. The legal procedure is similar to, but considerably simpler than, that involved in child adoption, described in section 350. The consent of the parties to the adoption is needed, but no investigation is required by welfare agencies.

YOUR OBLIGATIONS TO RELATIVES OTHER THAN YOUR CHILDREN

355. Support of Your Impoverished Relatives • Whether or not you have a legal duty to support your poor relations depends on what state you live in and on the degree of your relationship to the person in question. All states require you to support your wife (or husband) and minor children (see sections 316, 324). One third of them don't require you to contribute to the support of any other relatives, even if they are so poor that they must otherwise be supported at public expense. In the majority of states, however, you are responsible for the support of certain relatives besides your spouse and minor children. In some of these states you are required to support only your impoverished adult child. In others you may also be liable for the support of your grandchild, mother, father, brother, sister, grandfather and grandmother, if there are no closer relatives to take up the burden, or you may be required to share the responsibility with other relatives. If you do not provide support, and the relative becomes a public charge, the state or county may sue you for the expense of his or her maintenance. If you want to know the laws of your own state, you should consult a lawyer.

356. Legal Protection of Incompetent Relatives • Legally, *incompetency* means the inability of a person to manage his own affairs. It may be brought about by accidents or by physical illness. More often it is the result of a mental debility, such as subnormal intelligence, insanity, senility or addiction to alcohol or drugs. The state seeks to protect incompetents and their property from the consequences of their own lack of judgment, and from the greed of other persons, by providing guardians (sometimes called committees) to manage their affairs.

A person may be declared incompetent and a guardian appointed only upon application to the proper court and submission of evidence that he is indeed unable to manage his affairs rationally. The proof must be convincing, because the law is extremely reluctant to deprive a man of his liberty or the control of his property.

The fact that your aged grandfather is forgetful, wants to marry a teen-ager, is overly generous in giving away his money or makes unwise investments may not be acceptable proofs of incompetency, since many rational people act the same way. But if he is unable to remember where he lives or what property he owns; if he wanders into the snow in a bathing suit, throws his money into sewers or invests in property on Saturn—he doubtless would be declared incompetent. Most cases fall somewhere between these two extremes, making a decision a knotty problem for the court. For once a person is declared incompetent he reverts to the legal status of a minor (see section 321). He cannot be charged with crime, marry, enter into contracts, dispose of his property or income (although he still owns it) or make or alter his will. His personal freedom may be restricted and he may be institutionalized.

Guardians for incompetents are appointed by the court, with the preference going to the next of kin. If the court deems it in the incompetent's best interests, however, it may appoint a more distant relative, a lawyer or other stranger or an institution or a bank to serve as guardian. If the guardian proves to be dishonest or inept or otherwise becomes disqualified to serve, the court may revoke a guardianship appointment and make a new one.

There are two types of guardians, in most states, who may or may not be the same individual. The *guardian of the person* is responsible for the physical care and welfare of the incompetent. The *guardian of the property* manages his money and property, pays his bills out of his funds, signs his checks, and deposits or invests his income. The guardian of the property is required to put up a bond, operate under court supervision and present periodic accountings to the court. He may be charged with malfeasance for failure to abide by the rules or be ordered to make restitution if his unauthorized actions result in a loss.

399

In practice, the distinctions described above are not always clear-cut. In the common situation where an older parent is in the care of a nursing home, the staff of the home fills the role of guardian of the person and the children act—with or without formal court approval—as guardians of the elderly parent's property.

357. Commitment of the Insane and Mental Incompetents • The laws of the states differ so widely with respect to commitment of mental incompetents that some of the procedures mentioned below may not apply to all states and situations.

A person may apply to a hospital or mental institution for *voluntary commitment* if he thinks he is mentally ill. If he is a minor, his parents or legal guardian may do so on his behalf. The voluntary patient may request discharge at any time. But the hospital has a right to keep him for further observation for a period of days specified by state law, and to recommend the continuation of treatment or prolonged commitment to another institution if it thinks his condition warrants it.

Involuntary commitment, without the patient's consent, may be either judicial or nonjudicial. *Nonjudicial commitment,* which is only a preliminary procedure, occurs when a close relative or person with whom the patient lives obtains certification from one or more doctors that the patient needs professional attention and applies for his admission to the hospital. In case of emergency—if a man suddenly goes berserk and begins assaulting people on the street, for example—the application can be made by a policeman or other peace officer, without medical certification. The hospital may release the patient shortly after his admission if its examination shows that he does not need help. If the hospital decides the patient does need treatment, he may not be released without a court hearing, which must be held within a specified period of time after admission, usually thirty days. If the hospital decides the patient needs prolonged psychiatric care, it must within a reasonable time apply to the court for an order authorizing his retention. The patient or his relatives may appeal the order.

Judicial commitment procedures begin when relatives, friends, a mental hospital or health officials—or even the patient, himself, in rare instances—file a commitment petition with the court. The court orders the patient examined by one or more qualified doctors or psychiatrists or by a special committee of experts, sometimes referred to as a "commission in lunacy." If the experts recommend commitment, a hearing is usually held at which the experts testify, as well as laymen who know the patient and his behavior. The patient may be represented by counsel and has a right to a jury trial in many states, if he requests one. In some, a jury trial is mandatory. If the court or the commission in lunacy finds the patient to be mentally ill, he is committed to a mental hospital either for temporary observation or for an indefinte period, and his property is put in the hands of a guardian, committee or conservator.

358. Discharge from Mental Hospitals • When the superintendent or administrative head of the institution finds that a patient is cured or no longer dangerous, he may be discharged from the hospital to which he is committed, or he may be put on parole, or "convalescent status," or granted a "trial visit" with his family, for six or twelve months, to determine whether he is ready for full discharge. In many states no prior notice of discharge or parole need be given to the court unless the patient is also under indictment for a crime. If the patient violates the terms of his parole or convalescent status or has a mental relapse during the period, he may be returned to the hospital. A patient who is being held against his will, or his relatives, may also apply for a writ of habeas corpus (see section 27), challenging the legality of his detention. If the court finds any injustice or legal flaw in the commitment procedure or hearing, it may order his release.

If Your Marriage Is in Trouble

359. When Things Go Wrong • Not all marriages are made in heaven. With the best will on both sides, some married couples find themselves so incompatible that continuing to live together is harming them both and creating unhealthy strains on their children. It is at this point in a marriage that outside advice should be sought. Marriage counselors, clergymen, doctors—all are willing to help you when marital troubles assume unbearable proportions. Lawyers are available also.

But though many lawyers who practice in the matrimonial field spend much of their time counseling, their proper function is both different and narrower. The lawyer's job is to advise you of your rights and obligations as a husband or wife, to explain the many laws that are involved in continuing or dissolving the marital relationship, to point out to you the legal consequences of ending your marriage. The lawyer will want to leave the decision to you, not advise you what decision to make. That decision you should reach yourself, perhaps in consultation with your clergyman or doctor. You should have in mind the legal consequences of the various choices your lawyer will point out to you. All we shall try to do here is to set forth some of these choices in a general way so that you will be able to discuss them more intelligently if you should need to consult your lawyer.

360. Some Basic Definitions • A *separation,* which can be of several kinds, does not end a marriage. If you and your spouse simply part company and maintain separate living quarters, your marital rights and obligations are in no way changed. If you both voluntarily enter into a legal agreement to keep separate quarters, divide your property and make provisions for bringing up your children, the separation agreement controls your actions. But you remain married. If either party violates the separation agreement, the other may sue for breach of contract (see section 183). If the separation is not by mutual agreement, but is the result of a suit by one spouse against the other, the terms of the separation agreement are decreed by the court. If either spouse violates this judicial separation, the other can enforce it by a court order. Certain marital rights, but not all, are ended.

Annulment (sometimes called the poor man's divorce) is a court order that says that your marriage is a nullity: that you were never legally married. It restores both parties to the single status they originally enjoyed. The annulment decree reaches back to the time of the marriage and says it never occurred. The rights of all concerned are settled as of the time of the marriage that never took place.

A *divorce decree,* on the other hand, says that your marriage is ended from the time the decree becomes final. It does not look back; it does not say there was no valid marriage. It says there is no marriage from a stated time on. The rights of the parties are settled as of the time of the final decree.

A *void marriage* is one that was illegal from the beginning, usually because it violated well-known laws. The man who, while still married to one woman, knowingly marries another, is guilty of bigamy and the second marriage is void. Even if the second "wife" remains with him for years, she cannot legally become his wife unless he divorces his first wife and remarries. The marriage is a nullity; it is void and creates no rights or obligations in either party.

A *voidable marriage* is different. It may be terminated or ended at any time by proper legal procedure, but will remain valid unless proceedings are brought to end it. You marry a man who says he's twenty-one years old and has just inherited a fortune. Actually he is only eighteen and will not inherit anything until he reaches the age of fifty. He has deceived you. You have been defrauded into entering into a marriage because of a misrepresentation of a major fact. You may go to court and ask to have your marriage contract set aside on the ground that it was fraudulently brought about. Unless you can prove fraud, however, your marriage will remain valid.

From these brief definitions, you will see that three broad courses are available where a marriage appears to be failing. Separation, formal or informal, is a step, but only a step on the way to ending the marital relationship. Annulment is a judicial declaration that there never was a marriage in the first place. Divorce means the marriage is ended when the decree becomes final.

361. Separation • The simplest separation is where a husband and wife agree informally to keep separate houses. The husband remains duty-bound to support his wife and children, and neither can remarry without obtaining an annulment or a divorce. Indeed, the husband is entitled to return home at any time to be with his wife. A form of separation that has different legal consequences is desertion, where the husband or wife leaves home without the other's consent. It is surprisingly common, because a great many states (see chart 25, page 408) make it possible to obtain a divorce when either spouse has deserted the other for a number of years.

The husband who deserts his wife, or his wife and children, can be compelled to support them, even if he has moved to another state. She may sue him for separate maintenance and obtain a court order that gives her custody of the children and control of the home and furnishings, and requires him to pay her alimony and money to support the children. Also, the wife who is successful in a separation action is generally entitled both to alimony during the legal proceedings and to payment of her attorney's fees by the husband. A separation action may be brought against a wife or a husband for several reasons other than desertion—the same sort of reasons that are the basis for divorce in states that have liberalized their divorce laws.

Many couples who have agreed to separate have their lawyers prepare a formal separation agreement, which sets forth in writing their understanding as to division of property, alimony and child support payments, custody of the children and the couple's continuing rights and duties toward each other. This is a private contract between them which would continue in effect even if they were subsequently divorced, unless they mutually agreed to change it or unless it were merged into the divorce decree. If either one breaks the agreement, the other may sue for breach of contract, asking the courts to enforce the terms of the agreement.

If a couple cannot agree on the terms of a separation agreement, one spouse may go to court and sue the other for separation, citing grounds that are valid in the state where the suit is being heard (see chart 25, page 408). If the court finds that grounds for a separation exist, the parties then introduce evidence of their needs and resources on which the court can base the terms of a separation decree. A judicial separation will cover such matters as alimony and child support, but until recently it would probably not concern itself with a property settlement between the husband and wife. The terms of the decree are dictated by the court and can be changed by a subsequent order of the court. They may become the basis for the terms of an eventual divorce decree.

You should keep in mind that separations often settle little. If a married couple has come to a parting of the ways, even a legal separation leaves both parties in an unsatisfactory status as far as their future actions are concerned. The separation agreement does not cut the legal marriage tie. That tie is likely to become thinner and thinner and finally to snap when one party or the other decides to remarry, in which case, of course, a divorce is necessary.

362. Annulment · Annulment has a long and respectable history. It was and still is the only method recognized by the Roman Catholic church for ending a marriage. Canon law, as the laws of the church are called, permits a church-sanctified marriage to be annulled but does not permit a divorce. Many of the states (see chart 30, page 440) have adopted the philosophy of the Roman Catholic church and permit marriages to be annulled where they do not permit the marriage to be ended by divorce.

The philosophy or thinking behind annulment is that the marriage contract that results from fraud is no contract and may be set aside if the fraud is established. Among the principal frauds that may lead to annulment are: concealment of previous marriage or divorce (particularly when the religion of one spouse forbids marriage to a divorced man or woman); refusal to have children (the expectation of a family is implicit in the marriage relationship); refusal to go through with a religious ceremony after a civil wedding; financial misrepresentation; concealment of pregnancy (when the child is not the husband's); misrepresentations as to chastity; concealment of disease; misrepresentation of character (for the purpose of obtaining consent to marriage); marriage for ulterior motives (for the purpose of obtaining the property of another, for example; or in order to gain admission to the United States or to become an American citizen; or to legitimize an unborn bastard child).

Many states, however, have extended the grounds for annulment to include such postmarital developments as insanity of either spouse subsequent to the marriage; inability of either spouse to engage in normal sexual intercourse; sterility of either spouse discovered after the marriage, unless it was caused by a postmarital accident or disease; discovery of unsavory facts about a spouse's past life that would have prevented the marriage if they had been known; failure to make good on financial promises made before marriage; refusal of a spouse to abide by a premarital agreement to change his or her religion or to raise the children in a certain religion. Generally speaking, in states with strict divorce laws the grounds for annulment are broad, whereas states with liberal divorce laws have strict annulment rules.

Annulment proceedings may be barred if they are not instituted within a reasonable time after the marriage, depending on the nature of the fraud or complaint. If a woman continues to live with her husband for several months after discovering he is diseased or had lied to her about not being previously married, or a man waits for five years after finding out his wife refuses to have children, the right to annulment on those grounds has probably been waived. Nor is the court required to grant an annulment even when the application is timely and the grounds are legitimate, if it is not in the public interest. Thus, an annulment may be refused to an underage couple who married in defiance of the law, if the wife is pregnant or their parents refuse to take them back. The courts have considerable discretion in annulment cases to determine what is in the best interests of society and those involved.

Annulment resembles divorce in many respects: the former spouses are free to remarry; custody of the children is decided by the court, although the husband is usually obligated to support them; each spouse regains his or her property; and joint property is divided between them. But annulment has several disadvantages as compared with divorce. In a few states (see chart 30, page 440) and situations the children of annulled marriages are legally considered illegitimate and lose their right to inheritance. The woman whose marriage is annulled is usually not granted alimony, nor does she have any rights to her former husband's estate or to any share of his property.

363. Divorce · Dissolution of marriage by divorce is the method most widely used. Divorce is more common than annulment for a simple reason: the longer the marriage lasts, the more difficult it is to establish that it resulted from fraud, which is the most common ground for obtaining an annulment. By far the greatest cause of divorce is simple incompatibility—the inability of the husband and wife to get along. By its nature, incompatibility is a condition that doesn't develop or become recognized and accepted until after the husband and wife have tried to live together for some time.

Conditions of life in the twentieth century, with the dramatic shift from a rural to an urban society, have done much to undermine the idea that a marriage is an institution that, once entered into voluntarily, should not be broken. Divorce laws in our fifty states vary widely, as you will see from chart 25, page 408. No matter how "liberal" your state's divorce laws may be (*liberal* here means how easy the state makes it to obtain a divorce), you must be sure to follow these statutory provisions carefully.

Various forms of "do-it-yourself divorces" have recently appeared on the market. They range from storefront counseling operations to books on how to cut legal costs to the bone, to kits that include the necessary forms with instructions on how to fill them out and get a divorce without a lawyer. The pitfalls of do-it-yourself divorces are serious. No matter how simple the issues may seem, one party tends to dominate, and the other comes out the loser. Many rights—health insurance, pension rights, social security benefits—may be forfeited. An agreement regarding visitation rights may become unworkable if one parent moves out of state. Lawyers cannot anticipate every future event, but they are better equipped to protect the rights of parties in a divorce action than the parties themselves. Too much is at stake to take any chances.

364. Getting a Divorce · To obtain a divorce under the laws of any state you must be a resident of that state. What complicates things is the different lengths of time the various states require for you to establish residence: you may become a resident in Nevada by living there for only six weeks, whereas you must live for five years in Massachusetts to become a legal resident of the Bay State.

No divorce decree is binding on both parties unless both appear before the court which issues the decree. *Appear* is a word we all use regularly, but to a lawyer it has a special meaning. It means putting yourself under the jurisdiction of the court, either by your personal appearance in the court itself or by having a lawyer appear for you, authorized to represent you. In cases in which both husband and wife are known to be alive, a court cannot permanently dissolve their marriage unless both the husband and wife, or lawyers representing them, appear before it. If only one party appears, a divorce decree does not bind the other, and a remarriage by either would be bigamous.

In the great majority of cases the divorce proceeding is started by the wife, who establishes residence in the state whose divorce laws seem most favorable to her by actually going there. The husband has his lawyer file a "notice of appearance" and the divorce proceeding goes on with both parties technically "before the court." Such a procedure will usually be respected by any court throughout the United States.

At one time Mexican divorces were popular with U.S. citizens because Mexican divorce laws contained no minimum residence requirements. Now, however, a three-month period of residence has made these divorces less attractive.

A divorce action or proceeding is similar to any other civil action (see sections 79–88). It starts with the filing of a summons and complaint. The summons is a paper directed to the defendant, usually the husband, advising him that an action has been brought against him and ordering him to appear in court to answer the charges in the complaint. The complaint contains a statement of the wife's grievance, or her reason for requesting the divorce: adultery, desertion, conviction of a felony, cruelty or any other grounds that are legally valid in the state where the action is being tried.

More and more states, however, are doing away with the principle of "guilt" in divorce cases by passing *no-fault divorce laws* which do not rely on traditional grounds such as adultery. These statutes vary in their details, but all of them make it unnecessary for one spouse to prove the other was at fault in order to get a divorce. They recognize the right of the parties to terminate a dead marriage by mutual agreement, and they reduce opportunities for revenge and recrimination in the proceedings, as well as cutting costs and tempering bitterness.

Frequently the wife will ask the court for an order instructing her husband to pay alimony *pendente lite,* for support during the time it takes to litigate her divorce action. Such requests are often granted. If the husband wants to contest the divorce action he files an answer. There may be a pretrial hearing or a conference in which the judge tries to narrow the issues. There may even be a jury in some cases, but most divorce proceedings are tried, if at all, with as little publicity as possible. At the end of the jury trial, if there is one, or after reviewing the evidence

RESIDENCE REQUIREMENT AND GROUNDS FOR DIVORCE OR SEPARATION

CHART 25

	Residence Requirement Before Commencing Action	No fault*	Adultery	Desertion (Length of Absence)	Mental or Extreme Cruelty	Physical Cruelty	Impotence	Physical Defect	Nonsupport (Willful Neglect)	Insanity (Length of Commitment)
ALABAMA	State resident, none; nonresident, 6 months	D/S	D/S	D/S (1 year)	S	D/S	D/S	D/S	D/S (2 years)	D/S (5 years)
ALASKA	1 year[2]	D	D	D (1 year)	D	D	D	No	No	D (18 months)
ARIZONA	90 days	D/S	No-fault doctrine applies							
ARKANSAS	60 days	No	D/S	D/S (1 year)	D/S	D/S	D/S	No	D	D (3 years)
CALIFORNIA	6 months in state, 3 in county	D/S	There are 2 grounds for divorce or legal separation: (1) irremediable breakdown of the marriage; & (2) incurable insanity							
COLORADO	90 days	D/S	No-fault doctrine applies							
CONNECTICUT	1 year[3]	D/S	D/S	D/S	D/S	D/S	No	No	D/S (1 year)	D/S (5 years)
DELAWARE	6 months	D	D	D	D	D	No	No	D	D (5 years)
DISTRICT OF COLUMBIA	1 year	No	D/S	D/S (1 year)	S	S	No	No	No	No
FLORIDA	6 months	D	There are 2 grounds for divorce: (1) irremediable breakdown of the marriage; & (2) mental incompetence							
GEORGIA	6 months	D	D	D (1 year)	D	D	D	No	No	D
HAWAII	1 year in state, 3 in circuit	D/S	No-fault doctrine applies							
IDAHO	6 weeks	D	D	D	D	D	No	No	D	D (3 years)
ILLINOIS	1 year[4]	No	D	D (1 year)	D	D	D	No	No	No
INDIANA	6 months in state, 3 in county	D	No	No	No	No	D	No	No	D (2 years)
IOWA	1 year	D/S	An irremediable breakdown in the marriage is the single cause for dissolution of marriage or legal separation							
KANSAS	60 days	No	D/S	D/S (1 year)	D/S	D/S	No	No	D/S	D/S (3 years)[5]
KENTUCKY	180 days	D/S	No-fault doctrine applies							

In the chart below, D indicates a ground for divorce, S a ground for legal separation. Where a number of months or years is given, it indicates the length of time the condition must last before it becomes a ground for divorce or separation.

Alcoholism	Drug Addiction	Pregnancy at Marriage (by Other Man, Unknown to Husband)	Bigamy¹	Conviction of a Felony or an Infamous Crime (Length of Sentence)	Separation (Length of Time)	Other Grounds
D/S	D/S	D/S	No	D/S (7 years)	No	Crime against nature (D/S); living under final separation decree for 2 years (D)
D (1 year)	D	No	No	D	No	
						Separation decree is convertible into divorce decree
D/S (1 year)	No	No	D/S	D/S	D (3 years)	
D/S	No	No	No	D/S (Life)	D/S (18 months)	Fraudulent contract (D/S)
D (2 years)	D	No	D	D (1 year)	D (6 months)	Homosexuality; lesbianism; willful refusal to perform marriage obligations (D)
No	No	No	No	D/S (2 years)	D (1 year)	
D	D	D	No	D (2 years)	No	Consanguinity; force, fraud or duress in obtaining marriage; mental incapacity at time of marriage (D)
D	No	No	No	No	D (5 years)	
D (2 years)	D (2 years)	No	D	D	No	Attempt on the life of the spouse by poisoning or other means showing malice; communication of venereal disease (D)
No	No	No	No	D	No	
D/S	No	No	No	D/S	No	Incompatibility (D/S); gross neglect of duty (D/S); any cause the court deems sufficient (S)

CHART 25 (cont.)

	Residence Requirement Before Commencing Action	No fault*	Adultery	Desertion (Length of Absence)	Mental or Extreme Cruelty	Physical Cruelty	Impotence	Physical Defect	Nonsupport (Willful Neglect)	Insanity (Length of Commitment)
LOUISIANA[6]	1 year	No	D/S	D/S	D/S	D/S	No	No	D/S	No
MAINE	6 months	D[7]	D	D (3 years) /S (1 year)	D	D	D	No	D	No
MARYLAND	1 year (but if ground is insanity, 2 years)	No	D	D/S (1 year)	S	S	D	No	No	D (3 years)
MASSACHUSETTS	1 year[8]	D	D	D (1 year) /S	D	D	D	No	D/S	No
MICHIGAN	6 months in state, 10 days in county	D/S	No-fault doctrine applies							
MINNESOTA	1 year[9]	D	A course of conduct detrimental to the marriage is cause for dissolution (1 year)							D (not specified)
MISSISSIPPI	1 year	D[10]	D	D (1 year)	D	D	D	No	No	D (3 years)
MISSOURI	90 days	D/S[11]	D/S	D/S (6 months)	D/S	D/S	No	No	No	No
MONTANA	90 days	D/S	No-fault doctrine applies							
NEBRASKA	1 year	D/S	No-fault doctrine applies							
NEVADA	6 weeks	D/S	No	S (90 days)	No	No	No	No	No	D (2 years)
NEW HAMPSHIRE	1 year[12]	D/S	D/S	D/S (2 years)	D/S	D/S	D/S	No	D/S (2 years)	No
NEW JERSEY	1 year	No	D/S	D/S (1 year)	D/S	D/S	No	No	No	D/S (2 years)
NEW MEXICO	6 months	D	D	D	D	D	No	No	No	No
NEW YORK	1 year	No	D/S	D (1 year) /S	D/S	D/S	No	No	S	No
NORTH CAROLINA	6 months	No	D	S	S	S	D	No	No	D (3 years)
NORTH DAKOTA	1 year[13]	D/S	D/S	D/S (1 year)	D/S	D/S	No	No	D/S (1 year)	D/S (5 years)
OHIO	1 year in state, 90 days in county	No	D	D (1 year)	D	D	D	No	D	No
OKLAHOMA	6 months in state, 30 days in county	D/S	D/S	D/S (1 year)	D/S	D/S	D/S	No	D/S	D/S (5 years)

Alcoholism	Drug Addiction	Pregnancy at Marriage (by Other Man, Unknown to Husband)	Bigamy¹	Conviction of a Felony or an Infamous Crime (Length of Sentence)	Separation (Length of Time)	Other Grounds
D/S	No	No	No	D/S	D/S (1 year)	Public defamation; attempt on spouse's life; spouse charged with a felony but has fled from justice (D/S)
D	D	No	No	No	S (1 year)	
No	No	No	D	D (1 year)	D/S (3 years)	Any cause rendering marriage void at outset (D); excessively vicious conduct (S); separation for 12 months with no prospect of reconciliation (D/S)
D	D	No	No	D (5 years)	No	Living apart for justifiable cause (S)
D (1 year)	D (1 year)	No	No	D	No	Continuous separation for 1 year under a decree of separate maintenance (D)
D	D	D	D	D	No	Insanity or idiocy at time of marriage unknown to plaintiff; parties related within prohibited degree (D)
No	No	No	No	No	D/S (2 years)	Separation by mutual consent for 1 year (D/S)
						Any cause the court deems sufficient (S)
No	No	No	No	No	D/S (1 year)	Incompatibility (D)
D/S (2 years)	No	No	No	D/S (1 year)	D/S (2 years)	Membership in religious sect that professes the conjugal relation is unlawful; refusal to cohabit for 6 months (D/S)
D/S (1 year)	D/S (1 year)	No	No	D/S (18 months)	D/S (18 months)	Deviant sexual conduct without consent of complainant
No	No	No	No	No	No	
No	No	No	No	D/S (3 years)	No	Living part for 1 year under decree of separate maintenance or written separation agreement (D)
S	S	D	No	D (1 year)	D (1 year)	Crime against nature & bestiality (D); maliciously turning the other out-of-doors (S)
D/S (1 year)	No	No	No	D/S	No	
D	No	No	D	D	No	Fraudulent contract; spouse obtained a divorce in another state; any gross neglect of duty (D)
D/S	No	D/S	No	D/S	No	Fraudulent contract; gross neglect of duty; spouse obtained divorce in another state not releasing plaintiff from marital obligations (D/S)

CHART 25 (cont.)

	Residence Requirement Before Commencing Action	No fault*	Adultery	Desertion (Length of Absence)	Mental or Extreme Cruelty	Physical Cruelty	Impotence	Physical Defect	Nonsupport (Willful Neglect)	Insanity (Length of Commitment)
OREGON	6 months	D/S	No-fault doctrine applies							
PENNSYLVANIA	1 year	No	D/S	D (2 years)	D/S	D/S	D	D	No	D (3 years)
RHODE ISLAND	1 year	D/S	D/S	D/S (5 years)[14]	D/S	D/S	D/S	No	D/S (1 year)	No
SOUTH CAROLINA	1 year	No	D	D (1 year)	No	D	No	No	No	No
SOUTH DAKOTA	None[16]	No	D/S	D/S (1 year)	D/S	D/S	No	No	D/S (1 year)	D/S (5 years)
TENNESSEE	6 months; 1 year for armed services	No	D	D/S (1 year)	S	S	D	D	S	No
TEXAS	State, 6 months; county, 90 days	D	D	D (1 year)	D	D	No	No	No	D (3 years)
UTAH	3 months	No	D	D/S (1 year)	D	D	D	No	D/S	D
VERMONT	6 months[17]	No	D/S	D/S (7 years)	D/S	No	No	No	D/S	D/S (5 years)
VIRGINIA	6 months	No	D	D/S (1 year)	D/S	D/S	No	No	No	No
WASHINGTON	None[16]	D/S	No-fault doctrine applies							
WEST VIRGINIA	1 year	No	D	D (1 year)	D	D	No	No	No	D (3 years)
WISCONSIN	State, 6 months; county, 30 days	No	D/S	D/S (1 year)	D/S	D/S	No	No	D/S[18]	D/S (1 year)
WYOMING	60 days[9]	No	D/S	D/S (1 year)	D/S	D/S	D/S	D/S	D/S (1 year)	D/S (2 years)

(*) No-fault divorce laws generally cite incompatibility, irreconcilable difference or an irretrievable breakdown of the marriage relationship as legitimate grounds for divorce. As indicated on the chart, in some states the no-fault doctrine also applies in suits for legal separation.

(1) In most states where bigamy is not a ground for divorce, the bigamous marriage is void or subject to annulment (see chart 30).

(2) But there is no requirement if the plaintiff is a resident of the state and the marriage was solemnized in the state.

(3) Does not apply if cause of divorce occurred after taking up residence in the state or if the plaintiff was married in the state.

(4) But if the cause of action arose within the state, the required residence is only 6 months.

(5) Confinement need not be continuous.

(6) Immediate divorce may be granted only for adultery or conviction of a felony and sentence to death or imprisonment at hard labor. Divorce may not be granted on any other grounds unless separation from bed and board has been decreed and one year has elapsed after the separation without reconciliation.

412

Alcoholism	Drug Addiction	Pregnancy at Marriage (by Other Man, Unknown to Husband)	Bigamy[1]	Conviction of a Felony or an Infamous Crime (Length of Sentence)	Separation (Length of Time)	Other Grounds
No	No	No	D	D (2 years)	No	Uncondoned fraud, force or coercion; related within a degree prohibited by law (D); husband turned wife out of home (S)
D/S	D/S	No	No	D/S[15]	D/S (5 years)	Marriage originally void or voidable by law; any gross misbehavior & wickedness repugnant to & in violation of the marriage contract (D/S)
D	D	No	No	No	D (3 years)	
D/S (1 year)	No	No	No	D/S	No	Persistent refusal to cohabit
D	D	D	D	D	No	Conviction of infamous crime (D); attempt on life of spouse by means showing malice (D); refusal by wife without reasonable cause to move to state with husband & willfully absenting herself for 2 years (D); 2-year separation under decree of separate mainte-nance (D); wife thrown out of home by husband (S)
No	No	No	No	D (1 year)	D (3 years)	
D	No	No	No	D	S	Separation for 3 years under decree of separate maintenance (D)
No	No	No	No	D/S (3 years)	D/S (6 months)	Intolerable severity (D/S)
No	No	No	No	No	D (2 years)	Sodomy or buggery (D)
D	D	No	No	D	D (2 years)	
D/S (1 year)	No	No	No	D/S (3 years)	D/S (1 year)	
D/S	No	D/S	No	D/S	D/S (2 years)	Vagrancy of husband; conviction of a felony or infamous crime prior to the marriage unknown to other party (D/S)

(7) No-fault divorce may not be granted un-less the parties have received counseling.

(8) Unless a waiver is granted by the court, a divorce suit may not be filed unless the par-ties have been living apart for 30 days.

(9) Unless the marriage took place in the state and the plaintiff has resided in the state since then.

(10) Petition must be on file 60 days before divorce is granted.

(11) Fault grounds come into effect only if one party denies irretrievable breakdown of marriage.

(12) If both parties were residents of the state when the cause of action arose, there is no time requirement.

(13) Five years' residence is required for di-vorce on the ground of insanity if the insane party is confined outside the state.

(14) A shorter period may be granted by the court.

(15) If party is deemed to be civilly dead.

(16) Plaintiff must be a resident of the state or stationed there in the armed forces.

(17) Two years' residence is required if ground is insanity.

(18) Ground for wife only.

and the papers submitted by the lawyers for both parties, the judge will, if the evidence so indicates, issue a decree of divorce.

365. Kinds of Divorce Decrees • The divorce decree may be interlocutory or final, depending primarily on the law of the state where it is obtained. An *interlocutory decree* is one that does not become final for a period of time specified in the decree: thirty, sixty or ninety days. During that period the parties are not divorced and may not legally remarry. If they do, they may be held in contempt of court for having violated the terms of the court order. But when the period has expired, the divorce decree becomes final (see chart 26, page 415).

The divorce decree not only frees both parties to the marriage. It settles such major questions as who has custody of the children (usually custody is granted to the wife, with the right given the husband to visit the children regularly and to have them live with him for part of the year) and how much money the husband is to pay to support the wife and children. More and more, however, the courts are considering the concept of the two parents having joint custody.

Many husbands and wives who are getting divorced consult lawyers well ahead of the divorce proceeding and enter into a separation agreement that sets forth all the provisions regarding custody and support of children and alimony and division of their property (see section 361). This agreement—which should say nothing about a divorce because in most states an agreement to obtain a divorce is against public policy—may be *merged*, or joined with, the actual divorce decree, or court order. It must then be followed unless altered or amended by the court on the basis of information supplied by one of the parties. For example, divorce decrees frequently contain rather generous property settlements by a husband who is so anxious to marry someone else that he goes overboard in arranging support for his wife and children. Later he becomes ill or his business suffers, and he can't afford to make such large payments. He can go back to the court and move that the decree be altered to reduce the amounts he is required to pay for support. The wife is entitled to argue that he should be forced to keep up the payments they had originally agreed upon. The court must decide where the equities lie and modify the original decree as it thinks best.

But the separation agreement need not be merged with the decree of divorce. It may survive the divorce as a private contract between the parties regardless of their marital status—and if this is the case its terms can only be changed by their mutual agreement.

DIVORCE AND REMARRIAGE:
TIME LIMITATIONS IMPOSED BY LAW

The laws of many states provide for a waiting period before issuance of the final decree, either from the filing of the divorce action or from the issuance of an interlocutory decree (see section 365). These periods are shown below.

CHART 26	Time Required Between Filing of Suit & Final Decree	Time Required Between Interlocutory & Final Decree	Time That Must Elapse After Final Decree Before Parties May Remarry	
			Plaintiff	Defendant
ALABAMA	None	None	60 days	60 days
ALASKA	30 days[1]	——	None	None
ARIZONA	20 days	——	None	None
ARKANSAS	30 days	——	None	None
CALIFORNIA	6 months	——	None	None
COLORADO	90 days	——	None	None
CONNECTICUT	90 days	None	None	None
DELAWARE	——	None	None	None
D.C.	Final decree entered after expiration of time for noting appeal		None	None
FLORIDA	20 days	——	None	None
GEORGIA	None	None	At the discretion of the court	
HAWAII	——	None	None	None
IDAHO	None	None	None	None
ILLINOIS	None	None	None	None
INDIANA	None	None	None[2]	None
IOWA	None	None	1 year unless shorter time is granted by court	
KANSAS	60 days	——	30 days	30 days
KENTUCKY	None	None	None	None
LOUISIANA	None	None	None	None
MAINE	60 days	None	None	None
MARYLAND	None	None	None	None
MASSACHUSETTS	——	6 months	None	None
MICHIGAN	None	None	None unless provided for in decree	
MINNESOTA	30 days for defendant answer	None	None	None
MISSISSIPPI	None	None	None	None[3]
MISSOURI	30 days	None	None	None
MONTANA	20 days	None[4]	None	None
NEBRASKA	60 days	6 months	None	None

415

CHART 26 (cont.)	Time Required Between Filing of Suit & Final Decree	Time Required Between Interlocutory & Final Decree	Time That Must Elapse After Final Decree Before Parties May Remarry	
			Plaintiff	Defendant
NEVADA	None	None	None	None
NEW HAMPSHIRE	None	None	None	None
NEW JERSEY	None	None	None	None
NEW MEXICO	None	None	None	None
NEW YORK	None	None	None	None
NORTH CAROLINA	None	None	None	None
NORTH DAKOTA	None	None	At the discretion of the court	
OHIO	None[4]	None	None	None
OKLAHOMA	10 days[9]	None	6 months	6 months
OREGON	90 days[5]	60 days or until appeal has been settled		
PENNSYLVANIA	None	None	None	None[6]
RHODE ISLAND	60 days	6–7 months	None	None
SOUTH CAROLINA	3 months	——	None	None
SOUTH DAKOTA	60 days	None	None	None[7]
TENNESSEE	None	None	None	None[6]
TEXAS	60 days	None	30 days	30 days
UTAH	3 months	3 months	No remarriage pending appeal, otherwise 3 months	
VERMONT	——	None	None	None
VIRGINIA	None	None	No remarriage pending appeal[8]	
WASHINGTON	90 days	——	None	None
WEST VIRGINIA	None	None	None	None
WISCONSIN	60 days[5]	6 months	6 months after final decree	
WYOMING	None	None	None	None

(1) Court can order mediation.

(2) But if the divorce was obtained by default on notice by publication only, the plaintiff may not remarry for 2 years.

(3) But if the ground is adultery, court may prohibit remarriage.

(4) But the proceedings may be held up by the court for 90 days after the grounds have been established if there are minor children involved or if the court feels the parties should attempt a reconciliation.

(5) Unless court decides otherwise or divorce is uncontested and there are no children.

(6) But if the ground is adultery, defendant may not marry corespondent during lifetime of plaintiff.

(7) If the ground is adultery, defendant may not remarry during lifetime of plaintiff.

(8) If the ground is adultery, final decrees may forbid remarriage, but the court may revoke this ban for good cause after 3 months.

(9) 30 days with children.

366. The Defense of Condonation • There are relatively few cases in which only one spouse seeks a divorce and the other resists the action. But these cases do occur and you should be aware of possible defenses in order to take whatever action you and your lawyer think best.

Condonation is probably the most common and effective defense. To condone something is to forgive it or to act as though it never happened. The wife who knows very well that her husband is having an affair with his secretary but for the sake of the family or from deep affection for her husband, irrespective of his behavior, ignores it and continues to treat him as her husband is said to condone his action. By doing so, she deprives herself of the right to bring against him an action for divorce based on adultery. The husband is carrying on an adulterous relationship. But the mere fact of that relationship will not be ground for a divorce by the wife if she condones or ignores it.

Condonation of a single act or set of acts may not necessarily be claimed as a defense by the erring husband or wife, however, if the condonation was accompanied by the understanding that he would, for example, mend his ways and instead he goes out and repeats the act. A new offense would revive the old one. A woman may forgive her husband for an act of adultery and welcome him back to her bed, but if he subsequently steps out of line again he has renewed her grounds for divorce. The point is simply that neither husband nor wife may in one breath ignore the spouse's behavior and in the next go to court complaining of the behavior and asking for a divorce.

367. Collusion • In states with strictly limited grounds for divorce (as opposed to no-fault states), a couple may not legally get a divorce by following a scheme to "put one over on the court." If both husband and wife agree they'll cooperate in getting a divorce soon, they had better be careful. They should remember that society—and the courts—are on the side of marriage as an institution; the courts will not tolerate a clever (or stupid) scheme to end a marriage. In a state where the only ground for divorce is adultery, a husband and wife may agree to stage a scene in which a private investigator bursts into a motel bedroom and finds one of them in bed with a prearranged lover. This is collusion. It is a scheme to bring about the end of a marriage, and such a scheme is against public policy. The court that finds evidence that a divorce proceeding is the result of an agreement between husband and wife may not grant the divorce. If the defendant in a divorce suit should have a sudden change of heart, evidence of collusion would be an effective defense.

368. Alimony and Other Kinds of Property Settlement • Remember society's or the state's concern: the financial well-being of husband and wife and of the children, if there are any. Historically, the husband has been the sole or principal source of support for the family entity, large or small. While the marriage lasts he has an absolute obligation to support his wife and children to the best of his ability. The courts have little difficulty enforcing that obligation.

But once the marriage heads toward the rocks and dissolution appears likely, the courts are confronted by a very different situation. Apart from any question of moral responsibility for the dissolution of the marriage, which is only in part the court's business, is the question of who is to be financially responsible for all the persons involved after the marriage has been dissolved. It is interesting that the emancipation of women and their increasing recognition as legally responsible individuals have not yet diminished society's conviction that the husband (or the former husband) is primarily responsible for his wife (or former wife) and the issue of their marriage.

Alimony is nothing more than a requirement that the presumed money-maker—the husband—should continue to be responsible for supporting his wife even after she has filed suit for divorce. The wife who is independently wealthy or who has a job that pays her enough to live on may not be awarded alimony today. (Indeed, there are an increasing number of cases in which wealthy wives are required to support impoverished husbands if the wife is the guilty party in a divorce proceeding.) But in those cases that are still in the majority today the judge in a divorce proceeding has a clear responsibility: to hold the husband to his financial responsibilities; and to see to it that, whoever may have been at fault in the failure of the marriage, the persons are adequately provided for whose livelihood depended on the marriage.

Alimony is for the wife's support, both during and after the divorce proceedings. The amount of alimony awarded and the terms of the award will differ in every case according to the facts. Often alimony will stop if the wife remarries. In some cases awards are variable, providing for adjustment according to the incomes of the parties or other changes in their circumstances.

The husband's obligations to support the children of the (dissolving) marriage are separate and are limited to the period of the minority of the children. The child support agreement may also contain provisions for the payment of school and college expenses or medical bills by the father or for other special payments. Often a generous child support arrangement can be balanced off against a relatively low alimony settlement, with the wife gambling that she will remarry soon in any case. When the husband has substantial wealth, he cannot be forced to settle any of it on his children as part of a divorce proceeding, but the chances are the wife's lawyer will negotiate with his lawyer for him to turn over part of his estate to the children as part of the overall property settlement that will be incorporated into the final divorce decree issued by the court (see section 365).

369. Children of Divorce • A final word as to what happens to the minor children of a dissolving marriage. Their fate depends on what the parents decide, subject to approval by the judge before whom the divorce proceeding is brought. Circumstances vary so much that any generality is likely to be misleading. But one thing should be said clearly. Judges with any considerable experience in matrimonial cases, in family courts and elsewhere, still usually share a conviction that women should be given legal custody of children, especially of young children. Judges will therefore insist that the mother be given custody unless the father comes up with strong and convincing evidence that she is not a fit person or not competent to care for the children. The judge may often require a report from a probation officer on the relative merits of the parents when they are unable to agree between themselves.

Whenever a divorce occurs, it can be either a new start for all involved or just another sad experience. As society has gradually tolerated divorce for a growing number of reasons, husbands and wives have found increasing opportunities to obtain advice and assistance in deciding on the best arrangements for themselves and their children after the divorce has been granted. In the final analysis their determination to consider the interests of their children, at a time of intense emotional strain, is what will hold the best hope for their children's future. In determining what courses are open to them and what arrangements can be made in the best interests of the children they may seek the counsel of a trusted family lawyer who can anticipate difficulties before they arise. The courts stand ready to approve sound arrangements, even to help toward bringing about sound arrangements. But courts are impersonal and harassed. The husband and wife who have found the going too rough to continue on together owe it to their children to work out a plan that gives the children the best of both of them and to obtain the court's approval of what they themselves have decided upon, thinking not of the past nor the present but of the future.

MARRIAGE LAWS

| | At What Age May You Legally Be Married? | | | | What Relatives Are You Prohibited from Marrying?[2] |
| CHART 27 | With Parental Consent[1] | | Without Parental Consent | | |
	Male	Female	Male	Female	
ALABAMA	17	14	19	18	Stepparent, stepchild, stepgrandchild, half niece, half nephew, son-in-law, daughter-in-law
ALASKA	16	16	18	18	
ARIZONA	16	16	18	18	First cousin
ARKANSAS	17	16	18	18	First cousin
CALIFORNIA	—[6]	—[6]	18	18	
COLORADO	16	16	18	18	
CONNECTICUT	16	16	18	18	Stepparent, stepchild
DELAWARE	18[1]	16	18	18	First cousin
DISTRICT OF COLUMBIA	16	16	18	18	Stepparent, stepchild, stepgrandparent, grandchild's spouse, father-in-law, mother-in-law, son-in-law, daughter-in-law, spouse's grandparent or grandchild
FLORIDA	18[1]	16	18	18	
GEORGIA	18[1]	16	18	18	Stepparent, stepchild, father-in-law, mother-in-law, daughter-in-law, son-in-law
HAWAII	16	16	18	18	
IDAHO	16	16	18	18	First cousin
ILLINOIS	16	16	18	18	First cousin

All states require that persons must be a certain age to obtain a marriage license, and many prohibit marriages between close relatives (see sections 311–313). The marriage laws of the various states are summarized below.

Are Interracial Marriages Prohibited?[3]	Is a Blood Test Required to Obtain a License?	Is There a Waiting Period Between Application & Issue of License?	How Soon After Issue of License May You Marry?	How Long Is License Valid After Issuance?	Are Common-Law Marriages Recognized?
Yes	Yes	No	Immediately	30 days	Yes
No	Yes[4]	Yes: 3 days	Immediately	75 days	No
No	Yes	No	Immediately	NSP*	No[5]
No	Yes	Yes: 3 days	Immediately	NSP*	No[5]
No	Yes	No	Immediately	90 days	No
No	Yes	No	Immediately	NSP*	Yes[7]
No	Yes	Yes: 4 days	Immediately	65 days	No
Yes	Yes	No	24 hours[8]	30 days	No[5]
No	Yes	Yes: 3 days	Immediately	NSP*	Yes
No	Yes	Yes: 3 days	Immediately	30 days	No, unless effected before 1968
Yes	Yes	Yes: 3 days[9]	Immediately	NSP*	Yes
No	Yes	No	Immediately	30 days	No
No	Yes	Yes if both parties under 18: 3 days; otherwise no	Immediately	NSP*	Yes
No	Yes	No	Immediately	30 days	No

	At What Age May You Legally Be Married?				What Relatives Are You Prohibited from Marrying?[2]
CHART 27 (cont.)	With Parental Consent[1]		Without Parental Consent		
	Male	Female	Male	Female	
INDIANA	17	17	18	18	First cousin, first cousin once removed, great-uncle, great-aunt, grandnephew, grandniece
IOWA	16	16	18	18	First cousin, stepparent, stepchild, grandchild's spouse, father-in-law, mother-in-law, son-in-law, daughter-in-law
KANSAS	18[1]	18[1]	18	18	First cousin
KENTUCKY	18[1]	18[1]	18	18	First cousin, first cousin once removed, great-uncle, great-aunt, grandnephew, grandniece
LOUISIANA	18[1]	16	18	18	First cousin
MAINE	16	16	18	18	Stepparent, stepchild, spouse of grandparent or grandchild, father-in-law, mother-in-law, son-in-law, daughter-in-law, spouse's grandparent or grandchild
MARYLAND	16	16	18	18	Stepparent, stepchild, spouse of grandparent or grandchild, father-in-law, mother-in-law, son-in-law, daughter-in-law, spouse's grandparent or grandchild
MASSACHUSETTS	18[1]	16	18	18	Stepparent, stepchild, spouse of grandparent or grandchild, father-in-law, mother-in-law, son-in-law, daughter-in-law, spouse's grandparent or grandchild
MICHIGAN	18[1]	16	18	18	First cousin
MINNESOTA	18[1]	16	18	18	First cousin, first cousin once removed, great-uncle, great-aunt, grandnephew, grandniece
MISSISSIPPI	—[6]	—[6]	17	15	First cousin, stepparent, stepchild
MISSOURI	15	15	18	18	First cousin
MONTANA	16	16	18	18	First cousin
NEBRASKA	18	16	19	19	First cousin
NEVADA	16	16	18	18	First cousin, first cousin once removed, great-uncle, great-aunt, grandnephew, grandniece

Are Interracial Marriages Prohibited?[3]	Is a Blood Test Required to Obtain a License?	Is There a Waiting Period Between Application & Issue of License?	How Soon After Issue of License May You Marry?	How Long Is License Valid After Issuance?	Are Common-Law Marriages Recognized?
No	Yes	Yes: 3 days	Immediately	60 days	No, unless effected before 1958
No	Yes	Yes: 3 days (may be waived in some cases)	Immediately	20 days	Yes
No	Yes	Yes: 3 days	Immediately	NSP*	Yes
No	Yes	Yes: 3 days	Immediately	30 days	No
No	Yes	No	72 hours	NSP*	No
No	Yes	Yes: 5 days	Immediately	60 days	No
No	No	Yes: 2 days	Immediately	6 months	No
No	Yes	Yes: 3 days	Immediately	60 days	No
No	Yes	Yes: 3 days	Immediately	30 days	No, unless effected before 1957
No	No	Yes: 5 days	Immediately	6 months	No, unless effected before April 27, 1941
No	Yes	Yes: 3 days	Immediately	NSP*	No, unless effected before April 5, 1956
No	Yes	Yes: 3 days, except with court order	Immediately	10 days	No, unless effected before March 31, 1921
No	Yes	Yes: 5 days	3 days	180 days	Yes
No	Yes	No	Immediately	NSP*	No, unless effected before 1923
No	No	No	Immediately	NSP*	No

CHART 27 (cont.)	At What Age May You Legally Be Married?				What Relatives Are You Prohibited from Marrying?[2]
	With Parental Consent[1]		Without Parental Consent		
	Male	Female	Male	Female	
NEW HAMPSHIRE	14	13	18	18	First cousin, stepparent, stepchild, spouse of grandchild, father-in-law, mother-in-law, son-in-law, daughter-in-law
NEW JERSEY	18[1]	16	18	18	
NEW MEXICO	16	16	18	18	
NEW YORK	16	16	18	18	
NORTH CAROLINA	16	16	18	18	Double first cousin
NORTH DAKOTA	16	16	18	18	First cousin
OHIO	18[1]	16	18	18	First cousin, first cousin once removed, great-uncle, great-aunt, grandnephew, grandniece
OKLAHOMA	16	16	18	18	First cousin, stepparent, stepchild
OREGON	17	17	18	18	First cousin
PENNSYLVANIA	16	16	18	18	First cousin, stepparent, stepchild, spouse's grandchild, son-in-law, daughter-in-law
RHODE ISLAND	18[1]	16	18	18	Stepparent, stepchild, father-in-law, mother-in-law, son-in-law, daughter-in-law, spouse's grandparent or grandchild, stepgrandparent, stepgrandchild[1][3]
SOUTH CAROLINA	16	14	18	18	Stepparent, stepchild, father-in-law, mother-in-law, son-in-law, daughter-in-law, spouse's grandparent or grandchild, stepgrandparent, stepgrandchild
SOUTH DAKOTA	16	16	18	18	First cousin, first cousin once removed, stepparent, stepchild
TENNESSEE	16	16	18	18	Stepparent, spouse of grandparent or grandchild, spouse's grandparent or grandchild, son-in-law, daughter-in-law, grandnephew, grandniece

Are Interracial Marriages Prohibited?[3]	Is a Blood Test Required to Obtain a License?	Is There a Waiting Period Between Application & Issue of License?	How Soon After Issue of License May You Marry?	How Long Is License Valid After Issuance?	Are Common-Law Marriages Recognized?
No	Yes	Yes: 5 days	Immediately	90 days	No, unless effected before Dec. 1, 1939
No	Yes	Yes: 3 days	Immediately	30 days	No, unless effected before Dec. 1, 1939
No	Yes	No	Immediately	NSP*	No
No	Yes	No	24 hours[10]	60 days	No
Yes	Yes[11]	No[12]	Immediately	NSP*	No
No	Yes	No	Immediately	60 days	No
No	Yes	Yes: 5 days	Immediately	60 days	Yes
No	Yes	Yes: 3 days if either below age of consent	Immediately	30 days	Yes
No	Yes	Yes: 7 days	Immediately	30 days after medical exam	No[5]
No	Yes	Yes: 3 days	Immediately	60 days	Yes
No	Yes[14]	No	Immediately [15]	NSP*	Yes
No	No	Yes: 24 hours	Immediately	NSP*	Yes
No	Yes	No	Immediately	20 days	No, unless effected before July 1, 1959
Yes	Yes	Yes: 3 days if either under 18; otherwise none	Immediately	30 days	No[5]

425

CHART 27 (cont.)	At What Age May You Legally Be Married?				What Relatives Are You Prohibited from Marrying?[2]
	With Parental Consent[1]		Without Parental Consent		
	Male	Female	Female	Female	
TEXAS	14	14	18	18	Stepparent, stepchild, any relative by adoption
UTAH	16	14	21[16]	18	First cousin, first cousin once removed, great-uncle, great-aunt, grandnephew, grandniece
VERMONT	16	16	18	18	Stepparent, stepchild, father-in-law, mother-in-law, son-in-law, daughter-in-law, spouse's grandparent or grandchild, stepgrandparent, stepgrandchild
VIRGINIA	16	16	18	18	Stepparent, stepchild, son-in-law, daughter-in-law, spouse's niece or grandchild, brother or sister by adoption
WASHINGTON	17	17	18	18	First cousin, first cousin once removed, great-uncle, great-aunt, grandnephew, grandniece
WEST VIRGINIA	18[1]	16	18	18	First cousin, double first cousin
WISCONSIN	16	16	18	18	First cousin[17], first cousin once removed, great-uncle, great-aunt, grandnephew, grandniece
WYOMING	18[1]	16	18	18	First cousin

*No statutory provision.

(1) A number of states have established 18 as the lawful minimum age for marriage. In those states marriage below that age usually must have court approval, and parents may be required to give their consent under oath before a judge or witnesses.

(2) In every state it is illegal for a man to marry his sister, half sister, mother, daughter, granddaughter, grandmother, great-grandmother, aunt or niece. A woman may not marry her brother, half brother, father, son, grandson, grandfather, great-grandfather, uncle or nephew. Many states also prohibit marriages between more distant relatives. These are listed in the chart.

(3) Although the Supreme Court ruled on June 12, 1967, that laws prohibiting interracial marriages are unconstitutional, 5 states still retain such statutes. Whether these have any final legal effect is open to question.

(4) A physical examination is also required.

(5) The state, however, recognizes common-law marriage contracted in another state and recognized valid in that state.

(6) There is no statutory minimum age limit; both parental consent and court order are required.

(7) Colorado recognizes pre-1963 common-law marriages but status of post-1963 common-law marriages is unclear.

Are Interracial Marriages Prohibited?[3]	Is a Blood Test Required to Obtain a License?	Is There a Waiting Period Between Application & Issue of License?	How Soon After Issue of License May You Marry?	How Long Is License Valid After Issuance?	Are Common-Law Marriages Recognized?
No	Yes[4]	No	Immediately	21 days after medical exam	Yes
No	Yes	No	Immediately	30 days	No
No	Yes	No	5 days	60 days	No
No	Yes	No	Immediately	60 days	No[5]
No	Yes	Yes: 3 days	Immediately	30 days	No[5]
No	Yes	Yes: 3 days	Immediately	NSP*	No
No	Yes	Yes: 5 days	Immediately	30 days	No
No	Yes	No	Immediately	NSP*	No

(8) But there is a 96-hour waiting period if both parties are nonresidents.

(9) There is no waiting period if both parties are over 18 or if the female, regardless of age, signs an affidavit of pregnancy.

(10) Provided that at least 10 days have passed since the blood test. If court order waives the blood test requirement, 10 days must pass from issuance of license.

(11) A physical examination showing freedom from uncontrolled epilepsy, tuberculosis, idiocy and insanity is also required.

(12) But in some counties if both parties are non-residents there is a 48-hour waiting period.

(13) But marriages between Jews permitted by their religion are recognized regardless of their family relationship.

(14) A physical examination showing freedom from infectious tuberculosis is also required.

(15) But there is a 5-day waiting period for female nonresidents.

(16) Since the age of majority in Utah is now 18, it is possible males may be permitted to marry at 18 without parental consent.

(17) Marriage to a first cousin is permitted if the female is 55 or over.

AGE AT WHICH A CHILD ATTAINS ADULT STATUS

M = male; F = female; NSP = no statutory provision;
JL = junior license; PL = provisional license

CHART 28	Age of Majority	Age at Which You May Legally:				
		Marry (without Parental Consent)	Marry (with Parental Consent)	Vote	Buy Liquor	Drive
ALABAMA	19	19M, 18F	17M, 14F	18	21	16
ALASKA	19[3]	18	16	18	19	18, 16[4]
ARIZONA	18	18	16	18	19	18, 16[4]
ARKANSAS	18	18	17M, 16F	18	21	18, 16[4], 14 JL
CALIFORNIA	18	18	—[5]	18	21	18, 16[6], 14 JL
COLORADO	21	18	16	18	21 (18 for 3.2% beer)	21, 18 PL, 16 JL
CONNECTICUT	18	18	16	18	18	18, 16[6]
DELAWARE	18	18	18M, 16F	18	20	18, 16[6]
DISTRICT OF COLUMBIA	21	18	16	18	21 (18 for wine under 14% content & beer)	18, 16[4]
FLORIDA	18	18	18M, 16F	18	18	18, 16[7]
GEORGIA	18	18	18M, 16F	18	18	16
HAWAII	18	18	16	18	18	18, 15[4]
IDAHO	18	18	16	18	19	16[4], 14 JL[6]
ILLINOIS	18	18	16	18	21 (19 for wine & beer)	18, 16[7]
INDIANA	18	18	17	18	21	18, 16½[4], 16 & 1 month[7]
IOWA	18	18	16	18	18	18, 16[6], 14 JL
KANSAS	18	18	18	18	21 (18 for 3.2% beer)	16, 14 JL
KENTUCKY	18	18	18	18	21	18, 16[4]
LOUISIANA	18	18	18M, 16F	18	18	17, 15 JL
MAINE	18	18	16	18	18	18, 17[4], 15 JL[6]
MARYLAND	18	18	16	18	18	18, 16[7]
MASSACHUSETTS	18	18	18M, 16F	18	18	18, 17 JL, 16½ JL[6]
MICHIGAN	18	18	18M, 16F	18	18	18, 16[7], 14 JL
MINNESOTA	18	18	18M, 16F	18	21	18, 16 PL
MISSISSIPPI	21	17M, 15F	—[5]	18	21 (18 for wine & beer)	15
MISSOURI	NSP	18	15	18	21	16, 15½ JL[6]

428

There are many acts that a person under a specified age may not legally perform or that are not legally binding on him. This chart summarizes the age laws of the states in respect to these common acivities.

Execute a Deed to Real Property	Enter into Contract	Write a Will	Work	Work with a Work Permit	Ages of Compulsory Education	Age at Which Juvenile Delinquency Codes No Longer Applicable	Age of Consent (Statutory Rape)
19[1]	19[1]	—[2]	17, 19 in mines	16	7–16	18	16
19	19	19	16	NSP	7–16	18	16
18	18	18	16	14	8–16	18	18
18	18	18	16	14	7–15	18	16
18	18	18	16	15	6–16	18	18
21	21	18	16	14	7–16	17	16
18	18	18	18	16	7–16	16	16
18	18	18	16	14	6–16	18	12
21	21	21M, 18F	18	14	7–16	18	16
18	18	18	18	16	7–16	18	18
18	18	14	18	14	7–16	17	14
18	18	18	18	16	6–18	18	16
18	18	18	14	NSP	7–18	18	18
18	18	18	16	14	7–16	17M, 18F	16
18	18	18	18	14	7–16	18	16
18	18	18	16	14	7–16	18	16[8]
18	18	18	16	14	7–16	18	16
18	18	18	18	14	7–16	18	14[9]
18	18	16	18	16	7–15	17	17
18	18	18	16	NSP	7–17	18	14
18	18	18	18	16	6–16	18	16
18	18	18	18	16	7–16	17	18
18	18	18	18	14	6–16	17[10]	16
18	18	18	16	14	7–16	18	16
21	21	18	14	NSP	NSP	18	18[11]
18	18	18	16	14	7–16	17[10]	16

		Age at Which You May Legally:				
CHART 28 (cont.)	Age of Majority	Marry (without Parental Consent)	Marry (with Parental Consent)	Vote	Buy Liquor	Drive
MONTANA	18	18	16	18	18	18, 16 PL[4], 15 JL[6]
NEBRASKA	19[12]	19	18M, 16F	18	19	16
NEVADA	18	18	16	18	21	18, 16[4]
NEW HAMPSHIRE	18	18	14M, 13F	18	18	18, 16[6]
NEW JERSEY	18	18	18M, 16F	18	18	17, 16 agricultural license
NEW MEXICO	18	18	16	18	21	16, 15[6]
NEW YORK	18	18	16	18	18	18, 17[6], 16 JL[14]
NORTH CAROLINA	18	18	16	18	21	18, 16[7]
NORTH DAKOTA	18	18	16	18	21	16, 14 JL
OHIO	18	18	18M, 16F	18	21 (18 for 3.2% beer)	18, 16[6], 14 JL for hardship cases
OKLAHOMA	18	18	16	18	21	16, 15½[6]
OREGON	18[12]	18	17	18	21	16, 14 JL
PENNSYLVANIA	21	18	16	18	21	18, 17[7], 16 JL[4]
RHODE ISLAND	18	18	18M, 16F	18	18	18, 16[7]
SOUTH CAROLINA	18	18	16M, 14F	18	21 (18 for wine & beer)	16, 15 JL
SOUTH DAKOTA	18[12]	18	16	18	21 (18 for 3.2% beer & nonintoxicating wine)	16, 14 JL
TENNESSEE	18	18	16	18	18	16, 14 JL
TEXAS	18	18	14	18	18	18, 16[6], 15 JL[6]
UTAH	18[12]	21M[15], 18F	16M, 14F	18	21	16[6]
VERMONT	18	18	16	18	18	18, 16 JL
VIRGINIA	18	18	16	18	21 (18 for 3.2% beer)	18, 16[7]
WASHINGTON	18	18	17	18	21	18, 16[6]
WEST VIRGINIA	18	18	18M, 16F	18	18	18, 16 JL[4]
WISCONSIN	18	18	16	18	18	18, 16[6]
WYOMING	19	18	18M, 16F	18	19	18, 16[4]

(1) Anyone 18 years old and married is considered an adult.
(2) At 18 a person may bequeath personal property; at 21, real property.
(3) A married woman is considered an adult.
(4) With parental consent (state may require written consent).
(5) There is no statutory minimum age limit; both parental consent and court order are required.
(6) With driver education.
(7) With parental consent and driver education.
(8) Age 14 as of January 1, 1978.
(9) Age 16 if the man is 21 or over.

Execute a Deed to Real Property	Enter into Contract	Write a Will	Work	Work with a Work Permit	Ages of Compulsory Education	Age at Which Juvenile Delinquency Codes No Longer Applicable	Age of Consent (Statutory Rape)
18	18	18	18	16	7–15	18	16
19[13]	19[13]	19	16	14	7–16	18	16
18	18	18	17	14	7–17	18	16
18	18	18	16	14	6–16	18	16
18	18	18	18	16	6–16	18	16
18	18	18	16	14	6–17	18	13
18	18	18	18	16	6–16	16	17
18	18	18	18	16	7–16	16	16
18	18	18	16	14	7–16	18	18
18	18	18	18	16	6–18	18[10]	16
18	18	18	16	14	7–18	16M, 18F	18
18[13]	18[13]	18	18	14	7–18	18	18
10	18	18	18	16	8–17	18[10]	14
18	18	21	10	14	7–16	18	16
18	18	18	16	NSP	7–16	17	16
18	18	18	16	14	7–16	18	16
18	18	18	18	14	7–17	18	18
18	18	18[13]	15, 17 in mines	NSP	7–17	17	17
18	18	18	18	14	6–18	18	14
18	18	18	16	14	7–16	16	15
18	18	18	16	14	6–17	18	16
18	18	18	18	under 18	8–18	18	18
18	18	18	16	under 16	7–16	18	16
18	18	18	18	12	7–18[16]	18	18
19	19	19	16	under 16	7–17	19	18

(10) With respect to acts allegedly committed prior to the given age, state may continue jurisdiction.

(11) If the female is over 12, the statute applies only to virgins.

(12) A married person of any age is considered an adult.

(13) Earlier if married.

(14) Not valid in New York City.

(15) Since the age of majority is now 18, it is possible males may be permitted to marry at 18 without parental consent.

(16) Or until graduation from high school if this occurs before the age of 18.

CHART 29	What Court Has Jurisdiction?	Where May Appeals Be Heard?	Until What Age Does Juvenile Court Have Jurisdiction?[1]
ALABAMA	Juvenile court, circuit court and district court	Circuit court	19 for act committed prior to 17, continued to 21
ALASKA	Juvenile court	Superior court	18; 21 at discretion of court
ARIZONA	Juvenile court (division of county superior court)	Court of appeals	18, continued to 21
ARKANSAS	Statutory court under supervision of county judge	Circuit court, then supreme court	18
CALIFORNIA	Juvenile court (division of superior court)	District court of appeals, then state supreme court	18, continued to 21
COLORADO	Juvenile division of district court (in Denver, juvenile court)	Court of appeals, then state supreme court	18 (except jurisdiction is withdrawn in specified felony actions below that age)
CONNECTICUT	Juvenile court	Superior court	16
DELAWARE	Family court	Superior court, then state supreme court	18, continued to 21
DISTRICT OF COLUMBIA	Juvenile court	Court of appeals, then U.S. Court of Appeals for the District of Columbia	18, continued to 21
FLORIDA	Juvenile court or county judge serving as juvenile court judge, depending on county	District court of appeals	17, continued to 21
GEORGIA	Juvenile court or superior court, depending on county	Superior court, court of appeals, state supreme court	17, continued to 21 for educational & correctional purposes
HAWAII	Family court (division of circuit court)	State supreme court	Delinquency, 18; dependency or neglect, 20 (child under 21 cannot be judged delinquent except on written recommendation of psychiatrist)
IDAHO	District court (magistrate division)	District court, then state supreme court	18, continued to 21

In most states juvenile courts have jurisdiction over offenders below a certain age (see sections 338-342). These court systems and their powers are outlined below.

What Provisions Are There for Placing Child in a Foster Home or Institution?	Are Fines or Restitution Imposed?
Foster care is handled by welfare departments & social agencies. There are state training schools.	Fines up to $250 & restitution as deemed appropriate may be imposed.
Welfare agency may place juveniles in homes or correctional school. All homes are private; there is 1 state correctional school.	Fines are used infrequently. Restitution is often ordered under the supervision of the probation agency.
There is 1 state institution for boys; institutional care for girls is contracted. There are 2 institutions for mentally retarded.	Only if child is remanded to adult court are there fines, usually for traffic citations. Restitution is standard procedure.
State institutions for delinquent children. Court may commit child to public or private institution or call on welfare department to support custody.	Fines are not imposed on children. Restitution is used as condition of probation where appropriate. Damages are recoverable by civil action in court of appropriate jurisdiction.
Public & private institutions & foster homes. Public institutions include probation camps & California Youth Authority.	No fines, but county counsel of Los Angeles has ruled that payment to general fund of county is authorized in juvenile court as condition of probation. Traffic violation may result in fine of not more than $25.
Private & public institutions, under supervision of State Parole Board. Welfare Department handles placement of dependent & neglected children & pays costs if necessary.	Fines up to $300 are authorized by statute. Restitution is ordered where appropriate as a condition of probation.
Public & private institutions for delinquents. Welfare Department places neglected children in public & private foster homes.	Fines are not imposed on children. Restitution is used as a condition of probation where appropriate.
Courts have authority to commit to private & public institutions. Dependent & neglected children are committed to Department of Public Welfare.	Fine or restitution may be imposed as a condition of probation.
Children's Center; National Training School for Boys. Dependent & neglected children are committed to Department of Public Welfare.	The court is authorized to impose fines & penalties. Restitution is occasionally ordered as an adjunct to probation.
Children may be placed in foster homes or in public & private institutions. Courts have no jurisdiction over mental incompetents.	No fines, except in 1 court. Restitution may be ordered.
Delinquent children are placed in state training schools or in foster homes under court supervision. Private institutions for neglected & dependent children, who are committed to Department of Public Welfare if necessary.	Most courts do not assess fines but almost all require restitution by either child or parent. Parents are civilly liable for vandalism or damage done by their child.
Training school for delinquent children. Private foster homes for dependent children are arranged by State Department of Social Services.	Neither fines nor restitution are authorized.
1 public institution & several private ones. A summer camp & private home commitment are available. Foster homes are provided through Department of Public Assistance.	Neither fines nor restitution are authorized.

CHART
29
(cont.)

	What Court Has Jurisdiction?	Where May Appeals Be Heard?	Until What Age Does Juvenile Court Have Jurisdiction?[1]
ILLINOIS	Circuit & county courts have concurrent jurisdiction.	Appellate court	Delinquency, 17; neglect, 18
INDIANA	Juvenile court (under jurisdiction of circuit court)	Appellate court	18, continued to 21
IOWA	Juvenile court with concurrent jurisdiction in criminal court for children less than 18 accused of crime	State supreme court	18
KANSAS	Juvenile court	Court of appeals, then state supreme court	18, continued to 21
KENTUCKY	Juvenile court (division of county court)	Circuit court	18 (except moving motor vehicle violation involving a child 16 or older)
LOUISIANA	Juvenile court	Court of appeals (but adult criminal convictions go to state supreme court)	16 (except those 15 or older who are charged with capital offense), continued to 21
MAINE	District courts (designated juvenile courts when so acting)	Superior court, then state supreme court	17
MARYLAND	Circuit court sitting as juvenile court (in Montgomery County, district court sitting as juvenile court)	Court of appeals (in Montgomery & Allegany counties, appeals heard in circuit court)	18 (in Baltimore City, 16), continued to 21
MASSACHUSETTS	District court in separate juvenile session (in Boston, full-time juvenile court)	Superior court	7–17, continued to 18
MICHIGAN	Juvenile court (division of probate court)	Circuit court, then state supreme court	17, continued to 19
MINNESOTA	Juvenile court (in counties of over 200,000, division of district court except St. Louis County; elsewhere, division of probate court)	From juvenile district court, state supreme court; from probate courts, district court	18
MISSISSIPPI	Youth division of county court or chancery court, depending on county	From county court to chancery court, then state supreme court	Delinquency, 10–17, continued to 20; neglect, birth–17, continued to 20
MISSOURI	Juvenile court (division of circuit court)	Court of appeals; in some cases, state supreme court	16, continued to 21

What Provisions Are There for Placing Child in a Foster Home or Institution?	Are Fines or Restitution Imposed?
Court probation department establishes foster care & shelter. Illinois Youth Commission maintains diagnostic center, maximum security institution, cottage-type school & forestry camps.	NSP[2]
Private & public institutions; foster homes under court supervision or under guardianship of Welfare Department	Fines are not authorized. Restitution may be ordered as a condition of probation where appropriate.
Public & private institutions; foster homes recommended by Board of Social Welfare or obtained by private investigation	NSP[2]
3 state institutions. Counties have access to various private institutions for special problems.	Fines may be imposed on traffic offenders, not to exceed $150 per offense.
Children may be committed to Department of Child Welfare, to foster homes or to other available homes or institutions.	Fine or restitution may be ordered paid by child but not by parents. Court costs are not allowable.
3 correctional schools; foster homes provided by Department of Public Welfare; limited psychiatric facilities available under Department of Hospitals	Fines may be imposed only on traffic offenders.
Children may be committed to training center, to custody of welfare department or to family.	Court has power to impose fines but may not commit to jail or prison for failure to pay.
State training schools, forestry camps & diagnostic center. Foster care is provided by State Department of Public Welfare.	Fines are not authorized. Restitution by child may be required as a condition of probation. In Montgomery County, court may require parents to pay restitution if it is not feasible to require child to make restitution himself.
Youth Service Board youth centers, county training schools for truants & school offenders; 14 court clinics under Department of Mental Health; out-patient & in-patient centers; family service agencies. Citizenship Training Groups, Inc., is for rehabilitation of boys 12–17 in Boston. Neglected children are committed to State Welfare Department.	Court may impose restitution or fine. Fines may be imposed only for motor violations, however.
Public & private institutions. Private boarding homes are used to a considerable extent.	Fines are considered unconstitutional. Restitution may be ordered as a condition of probation where appropriate.
State institutions for delinquents; other public & private institutions; home training schools in 2 largest counties; private boarding homes under Welfare Department supervision	Fines are not imposed on children. Restitution may be ordered as a condition of probation where appropriate.
State training schools, private institutions & foster homes	No fines except in contempt cases. Costs cannot be assessed against minor or parents in youth court proceedings. Under separate statute parents are liable for $300 in damage done by their children.
Commitment to private or public institutions; foster homes through court services or Division of Welfare	No fines in juvenile court. Restitution may be ordered as a condition of probation.

CHART
29
(cont.)

	What Court Has Jurisdiction?	Where May Appeals Be Heard?	Until What Age Does Juvenile Court Have Jurisdiction?[1]
MONTANA	Juvenile court (division of district court)	State supreme court	18, continued to 21
NEBRASKA	County court unless separate juvenile court established by referendum in counties over 39,000	From separate juvenile courts to supreme court; from county courts to district courts	18
NEVADA	District courts (designated juvenile courts when so acting)	District court, then state supreme court	18, continued to 21
NEW HAMPSHIRE	District court or municipal court	Superior court	18, continued to 21 for neglected children
NEW JERSEY	Juvenile & domestic relations court	Appellate division of superior court	18
NEW MEXICO	Children's court or family court division of district court	Court of appeals	18, continued to 21, unless terminated earlier on court order. Court has jurisdiction over offenses committed before 18th birthday.
NEW YORK	Juvenile court (division of family court)	Appellate division of supreme court in family court's jurisdiction	Male, 16; female, 18. Court may assume jurisdiction over those on probation up to 21.
NORTH CAROLINA	District court	Court of appeals	18
NORTH DAKOTA	Juvenile court (division of district court)	State supreme court	18
OHIO	Juvenile division of court of common pleas or separate juvenile court	Court of appeals, then state supreme court	18 (21 if offense was committed before age 18 or child was ward of court)
OKLAHOMA	District court	Delinquency cases, court of criminal appeal; other cases, state supreme court	18, continued to 21
OREGON	Juvenile court (as division of circuit court, district court or department of domestic relations of circuit court, depending on county)	County court to circuit court; circuit court to court of appeals	18, continued to 21
PENNSYLVANIA	Court of common pleas	Superior court	18, continued to 21

What Provisions Are There for Placing Child in a Foster Home or Institution?	Are Fines or Restitution Imposed?
4 public & 4 private institutions, including detention center, youth forest camp & foster homes	No fines in juvenile court. Restitution for damage done may be ordered at judge's discretion.
Private & public institutions, including state training schools. Foster care is through county welfare departments & private agencies.	No fines in juvenile court proceedings. Restitution of property stolen or damaged may be ordered when it is in interest of child's reformation or rehabilitation.
Nevada Youth Training Center; Nevada Girls' Training Center; additional county facilities	NSP[2]
State youth development center. After 18, court may commit to youth development center, houses of correction, jail, for remainder of minority. Private homes & institutions are also available.	NSP[2]
Court controls 1 state home for boys, 1 for girls, several diagnostic & treatment centers.	Fine & restitution may be imposed on children where appropriate.
Court authority to transfer legal custody to child care agency	No fines. Restitution may be required of juveniles & costs levied against parents.
Public & private institutions; private boarding homes for neglected & abandoned children	Courts generally require restitution in delinquency cases as part of probation therapy. In support cases court may require such payments on account of support arrearage.
Department of Public Welfare commits children to juvenile detention homes & community-based residential care.	No provision for fining juveniles. Restitution may be required if judge feels it is appropriate in rehabilitation process. Parents are liable for damages, but suit for recovery must go through adult court.
1 state institution for delinquent & neglected children. Court & Welfare Department place children in foster homes.	No fines. Restitution is usually required as a condition of probation.
4 state institutions. Counties have child welfare boards, most of which operate children's homes; some use foster homes, some use both, or private care agencies.	Fines up to $50 may be levied on children. Restitution may be used as corrective.
Foster & institutional care for neglected, dependent & delinquent children provided by Department of Public Welfare; limited private facilities in Tulsa & Oklahoma counties	Fines are imposed on children only for violation of court order. Restitution is used in some cases as a condition of probation.
Private & public institutions, foster homes for delinquents used at county expense; neglected & dependent children accepted by county welfare commission for foster care	No fines. Restitution may be ordered as a condition of probation where appropriate.
State owned & operated institutions; privately owned & operated institutions; private, mostly sectarian, institutions	Fines & costs are generally not imposed on children. Restitution is sometimes a condition of probation.

CHART 29 (cont.)	What Court Has Jurisdiction?	Where May Appeals Be Heard?	Until What Age Does Juvenile Court Have Jurisdiction?[1]
RHODE ISLAND	State family court	State supreme court	18, continued to 21
SOUTH CAROLINA	No overall structure for juvenile court	Circuit court or state supreme court, depending on county where case originated	The age limit varies among the courts, but generally it is 17, continued to 21.
SOUTH DAKOTA	Circuit court	State supreme court	18
TENNESSEE	County court sitting as juvenile court & separate juvenile courts established by statute	Circuit court, then district court of appeals, then state supreme court	18, continued to 21
TEXAS	Juvenile court	Court of civil appeals, then state supreme court	Delinquency, 10–17, continued to 21; dependency, 10–16
UTAH	Juvenile court or district juvenile court	State supreme court	Dependency & neglect, 18; delinquency, 18, continued to 21
VERMONT	Municipal courts (designated juvenile courts when so acting)	State supreme court	Delinquency, 12–16, continued to 18; neglect, 18
VIRGINIA	Juvenile & domestic relations court under jurisdiction of county or municipal judge	Court of record (only final order is appealable)	18, continued to 21
WASHINGTON	Juvenile court (division of superior court)	State supreme court	18, continued to 21
WEST VIRGINA	Circuit court of county (unless additional court of record is created)	State supreme court of appeals (but from courts of limited jurisdiction first to circuit court)	18, continued to 21
WISCONSIN	A county judge has jurisdiction in each county.	Circuit court, then state supreme court	18
WYOMING	Juvenile court (under jurisdiction of district court judge); concurrent jurisdiction in municipal court	State supreme court	18

(1) These age limits are not inflexible, since for certain serious felonies or at the discretion of the juvenile court, children who fall within them may nonetheless be transferred to the regular criminal court for trial under regular criminal statutes and procedures.

What Provisions Are There for Placing Child in a Foster Home or Institution?	Are Fines or Restitution Imposed?
Neglect & dependency cases committed to Child Welfare Services; Boys' & Girls' Training School for delinquent & wayward children	No fines in juvenile cases. Restitution is worked out by court wherever possible.
NSP[2]	Fines & restitution are at the discretion of the court.
State training schools & youth forestry camps for delinquents; private institutions or homes for foster care of delinquent, dependent or neglected children	Court may impose fine up to $50. Restitution may be required as a condition of probation where appropriate.
State Preparatory School maintained by Department of Education for older dependent children; 4 state correctional schools; mental health facilities in various parts of state	Fines may be assessed up to $50 for delinquency.
Public & private institutions. 1 school for delinquent boys, 2 for girls. 2 homes for dependent & neglected children. Several counties have county institutions; some private foster homes.	Fines are not imposed on children. Restitution may be used only as a condition of probation where appropriate.
State Industrial School for delinquent children; private group boarding homes for girls, ranch types for boys, under Welfare Department supervision; private child care agencies; child welfare divisions of county welfare departments	Fines may be imposed in "limited amounts." Restitution may be ordered in appropriate cases, either independently or as a condition of probation. Work assignments may be used to fulfill restitution obligations.
1 state institution for juveniles. Private institution or foster home placement made through commitment to Department of Social Welfare.	No statutory provision for fines in Juvenile courts. Court costs may be assessed againt parents. Restitution may be ordered as a condition of probation.
4 state training schools. Foster homes used for dependent & neglected children.	Court may impose fines up to $100 & require restitution when deemed appropriate.
State diagnostic center; 2 state correctional institutions for girls & 2 for boys; 5 forest camps. Public Assistance Department provides suitable foster homes.	No fines. Restitution may be ordered as a condition of probation when appropriate.
Industrial School or Forestry Camp for boys, Industrial Home for girls; private boarding homes or West Virginia Children's Home for neglected children	Children are not fined in juvenile court. Restitution is extensively used in proper cases.
State boys' school & girls' school; commitment made by State Department of Public Welfare; private & sectarian institutions used extensively	No fines or costs in juvenile cases
Boys' & girls' reform school; children's mental hospital; state children's home; state hospital for the insane; foster care by Welfare Department; some use of private & church institutions	Court may impose fines when authorized by specific statute. Court may require restitution.

In some instances children who are already under the jurisdiction of a juvenile court at the statutory cutoff age may continue under its jurisdiction until they are older than the initial limit.

(2) No statutory provision.

439

WHEN A MARRIAGE MAY BE DECLARED VOID OR ANNULLED

CHART 30	Nonage (Underage at Time of Marriage)	Prior Existing Marriage	Prohibited Degree of Relationship	Violation of Miscegenation Statute[1]	Consent Obtained Under Fraud	Consent Obtained by Force or Duress
ALABAMA	Annulment is not provided for by state statute, but courts can annul marriages. Grounds include: insanity at time of marriage, fraudulent intent not to perform marriage vows, bigamy, incest and interracial marriage. Interracial and bigamous marriages are void without a decree or any legal proceedings. Where male is under 17 years or female under 14, the marriage is voidable while either is underage.					
ALASKA	Yes	Yes	Yes	No	Yes	Yes
ARIZONA	Yes	Yes	Yes	No	Yes	Yes
ARKANSAS	Yes	Yes	Yes	Yes	Yes	Yes
CALIFORNIA	Yes	Yes	Yes	No	Yes	Yes
COLORADO	Yes	Yes	Yes	No	Yes	Yes
CONNECTICUT	An incestuous marriage is void. A marriage in which either party is an imbecile and the woman is under 45 years of age violates the criminal law but is voidable only for fraud. In other cases the common law determines whether or not a marriage is voidable.					
DELAWARE	Yes	Yes	Yes	No	Yes	Yes
DISTRICT OF COLUMBIA	Yes	Yes	Yes	No	Yes	Yes
FLORIDA	No statutory grounds; courts can annul on common-law grounds.					
GEORGIA[4]	Yes	Yes	Yes	Yes	Yes	Yes
HAWAII	Yes	Yes	Yes	No	Yes	Yes
IDAHO	Yes	Yes	Yes	No	Yes	Yes
ILLINOIS	Incestuous marriages are void. There are no statutory grounds for annulment, but the courts may grant relief on grounds of fraud, duress, mental incapacity or because the marriage is prohibited by statute.					

The chart below sets forth the grounds for which a marriage may be declared void or annulled in the various states (see section 362) and shows the effect of annulment on children born of the marriage.

Lack of Under-standing	Inability to Consummate Marriage	Other Grounds	Status of Children Born Before Annulment	Time Limit for Bringing Suit to Annul
Yes	Yes		NSP*	NSP*
Yes	No	Any ground that would render the marriage contract null and void.	NSP*	NSP*
Yes	Yes		NSP*	A suit to annul on ground of nonage must be brought before party bringing suit reaches legal age. Otherwise, NSP.*
Yes	Yes		Legitimate	Limit varies depending on ground.[2]
Yes	Yes	Marriage entered into as jest or dare or while intoxicated.	Legitimate	6 months to 2 years, depending on ground.
Yes	Yes	Marriage entered into as jest or dare or while intoxicated.	Legitimate	90 days to 1 year, depending on ground.
Yes	Yes		Legitimate[3]	NSP*
No	No	Drunkenness brought about to induce consent.	Legitimate[7]	NSP*
Yes	Yes	Concealment of a loathsome disease.	Legitimate	2 years for inability to consummate; otherwise, NSP.*
Yes	Yes		Legitimate[5]	Limit varies depending on ground.[2]

441

CHART **30** (cont.)	Nonage (Underage at Time of Marriage)	Prior Existing Marriage	Prohibited Degree of Relation- ship	Violation of Mis- cegenation Statute[1]	Consent Obtained Under Fraud	Consent Obtained by Force or Duress
INDIANA	Yes	Yes	Yes	No	Yes	No
IOWA	No[6]	Yes	Yes	No	No	No
KANSAS	NSP*	Yes	Yes	No	Yes	No
KENTUCKY	Yes	Yes	No	Yes	Yes	Yes
LOUISIANA	No	Yes	No	Yes	Yes	Yes
MAINE	Yes	Yes	Yes	No	No	No
MARYLAND	No	Yes	Yes	No	No	No
MASSACHUSETTS	[11]	Yes	Yes	No	No[20]	No[20]
MICHIGAN	Yes	Yes	Yes	No	Yes	Yes
MINNESOTA	Yes	Yes	Yes	No	Yes	Yes
MISSISSIPPI	Yes	Yes	Yes	No	Yes	Yes
MISSOURI	There are no statutory grounds for annulment, but a marriage may be annulled by the courts for causes existing at the time of marriage, including fraud, duress and incapacity of either party to consummate marriage. Incestuous and bigamous marriages and marriages in which either party is insane are void from the outset.					
MONTANA	Yes	Yes	Yes	No	Yes	Yes
NEBRASKA	Yes	Yes	Yes	No	Yes	Yes
NEVADA	Yes	Yes[13]	Yes[13]	No	Yes	No[14]

Lack of Under-standing	Inability to Consummate Marriage	Other Grounds	Status of Children Born Before Annulment	Time Limit for Bringing Suit to Annul
Yes	No		Legitimate	NSP*
Yes	Yes		Legitimate[8]	NSP*
No	Yes	Wife, at time of marriage, conceals pregnancy by man other than her husband.	Legitimate[5]	NSP*
Yes	Yes		Legitimate[8]	Limit varies depending on ground.[9]
Yes	No	Mistake as to other person.	[10]	NSP*
Yes	No		Legitimate[8]	NSP*
No	No		Legitimate	NSP*
Yes	No		Legitimate[3]	NSP*
Yes	No[20]		Legitimate[12]	For nonage, up to age of consent; otherwise, NSP.*
Yes	No		NSP*	NSP*
Yes	Yes	Failure to procure license unless followed by cohabitation; pregnancy of wife by another at time of marriage, if husband did not know.	Legitimate[8]	NSP*
Yes	Yes	Marriage entered into under influence of alcohol or drugs.	Legitimate	1 year to lifetime of spouse, depending on ground.
Yes	Yes		Legitimate[21]	If ground is physical incapacity, 2 years from marriage; otherwise, NSP.*
Yes	Yes	Any ground that would render marriage contract null or void in a court of equity.	Legitimate	Nonage: within 1 year after attaining age of consent; otherwise, NSP.*

	Nonage (Underage at Time of Marriage)	Prior Existing Marriage	Prohibited Degree of Relation-ship	Violation of Mis-cegenation Statute[1]	Consent Obtained Under Fraud	Consent Obtained by Force or Duress
NEW HAMPSHIRE	Yes	Yes	Yes	No	No	No
NEW JERSEY	Yes	Yes	Yes	No	Lack of mutual assent.[15]	
NEW MEXICO	No statutory grounds.					
NEW YORK	Yes	Yes	Yes	No	Yes	Yes
NORTH CAROLINA	Yes[17]	Yes	Yes	Yes	Yes	Yes
NORTH DAKOTA	Yes	Yes	Yes	No	Yes	Yes
OHIO	Yes	Yes	Yes	No	Yes	Yes
OKLAHOMA	Yes	Yes	Yes	No	No	No
OREGON	Yes	Yes	Yes	No	Yes	Yes
PENNSYLVANIA	Yes	Yes	Yes	No	No	No
RHODE ISLAND	The courts have no power to annul marriages. The remedy is divorce. But the following marriages are void: incestuous marriages and marriages in which either party is an idiot or a lunatic. In the latter case, children born of such a marriage are considered illegitimate.					
SOUTH CAROLINA	A bigamous or incestuous marriage is void, but children are considered the legitimate children of the party who married in good faith. The court of common pleas may declare a marriage void for lack of consent or other cause showing that no real marriage contract was entered into, if there was no cohabitation.					
SOUTH DAKOTA	Yes	Yes	Yes	No	Yes	Yes
TENNESSEE	Yes	Yes	Yes	Yes	No	Yes
TEXAS[18]	Yes	Yes	Yes	No	[18]	[18]

CHART 30 (cont.)

Lack of Under-standing	Inability to Consummate Marriage	Other Grounds	Status of Children Born Before Annulment	Time Limit for Bringing Suit to Annul
No	No	Syphilis or gonorrhea.	Legitimate	NSP*
Yes	Yes		Legitimate[16]	NSP*
Yes	Yes	Either party has been incurably insane for 5 years.	Legitimate	5 years to lifetime of spouse, depending on ground.
Yes	Yes		Legitimate	NSP*
Yes	Yes		Legitimate	If ground is nonage, within 4 years of age of consent (18 M, 15 F); for fraud, force, nonconsummation, within 4 years of marriage; otherwise lifetime of spouse.
Yes	Yes		Legitimate	NSP*
Yes	No		Legitimate	NSP*
Yes	No		Legitimate	NSP*
Yes	No		NSP*	NSP*
Yes	Yes		Legitimate	If ground is nonage, within 4 years of reaching age of consent (18 M, 16 F); otherwise, NSP.*
Yes	No		Legitimate	NSP*
[18]	Yes		NSP*	If ground is nonage, 90 days after date of marriage; otherwise, NSP.*

CHART 30 (cont.)	Nonage (Underage at Time of Marriage)	Prior Existing Marriage	Prohibited Degree of Relation- ship	Violation of Mis- cegenation Statute[1]	Consent Obtained Under Fraud	Consent Obtained by Force or Duress
UTAH	Yes	Yes	Yes	No	Yes	Yes
VERMONT	Yes	Yes	Yes	No	Yes	Yes
VIRGINIA	Yes	Yes[8]	Yes	No	Yes	Yes
WASHINGTON	Yes	Yes	Yes	No	Yes	Yes
WEST VIRGINIA	Yes	Yes	Yes	No	No	No
WISCONSIN	Yes	Yes	Yes	No	Yes	Yes
WYOMING	Yes	Yes	Yes	No	Yes	Yes

* No statutory provision.

(1) Although miscegenation statutes are on the books in several states, they have all been held unconstitutional.

(2) A suit to annul on ground of nonage may be brought within 4 years of attaining the legal age of consent; a suit to annul on ground of fraud may be brought within 4 years of discovery; a suit to annul on ground that consent to marry was obtained by force or that the other party is physically incapable of consummating the marriage may be brought within 4 years of the marriage date; a suit to annul on ground of bigamy or lack of understanding may be brought at any time during the lifetime of either party.

(3) But children born of a bigamous marriage are considered the legitimate offspring only of the parent who entered into the marriage in good faith.

(4) An annulment will not be granted if chil-

dren have been born or are about to be born, nor will it be granted for any ground that is also a ground for divorce.

(5) But if the marriage was annulled on the ground that the wife concealed from her husband the fact that she was pregnant by another man at the time of the marriage, the child is considered illegitimate.

(6) Nonage is not a specific ground for annulment, but a marriage in which either party is below the age of consent may be annulled if the fact is made known within 6 months after the person attains legal age.

(7) Illegitimate if marriage is absolutely void, as in bigamous or incestuous marriage.

(8) But children born of an incestuous marriage are considered illegitimate.

(9) 1 year after petitioner obtains knowledge that marriage was prohibited; before party attains age of consent (18 M, 16 F); 90 days for all other conditions.

Lack of Under-standing	Inability to Consummate Marriage	Other Grounds	Status of Children Born Before Annulment	Time Limit for Bringing Suit to Annul
Yes	No	Syphilis or gonorrhea.	NSP*	NSP*
Yes	Yes		Legitimate	Inability to consummate, within 2 years of marriage. Nonage, before party reaches age of consent (16 years); cohabitation thereafter bars action. Otherwise, NSP.*
Yes	Yes	Wife prostitute prior to marriage, or pregnant by another man at marr.; husband fathered child of another woman within 10 mos. of marr.; either convicted of felony prior to marr. if other didn't know.	Legitimate	
Yes	No	_____19	Legitimate	If ground is nonage, within 2 years of reaching age of majority; otherwise, NSP.*
Yes	No	Epilepsy or venereal disease; husband licentious person, wife didn't know; wife prostitute or pregnant by another at marriage unknown to husband; pre-marriage felony conviction unknown to other party.	Legitimate	NSP*
Yes	Yes		Legitimate	NSP*
Yes	Yes		Legitimate[8]	If ground is nonage, before party reaches age of consent (18 M, 16 F). Otherwise, NSP.*

(10) Legitimacy depends on whether or not both parents were reasonably mistaken as to the validity of the marriage.

(11) Marriage of a male under 14 or a female under 12 is void without a court decree or legal proceeding unless the marriage is ratified by the underage party after reaching the age of consent. A marriage celebrated without parental consent is valid and not subject to annulment.

(12) But children born of a bigamous marriage are considered illegitimate.

(13) Such a marriage is void without a decree of annulment or other legal proceeding.

(14) If a woman is forced to marry against her will, the marriage is void if the husband is convicted of the act as a criminal offense.

(15) Fraud is not a statutory ground but, independent of statute, an annulment may be granted on the ground of fraud if the marriage has not been consummated; or, if the marriage has been consummated, an annulment may be granted if the nature of the fraud concerns the common-law essentials of marriage.

(16) But if the marriage was not ceremonial and is dissolved because either party had another spouse living at the time of the marriage, the children are considered to be illegitimate.

(17) Unless the female was pregnant at the time of marriage.

(18) Marriages may be annulled for impotency at the time of the marriage or for any other impediment which renders the marriage contract void.

(19) No woman under 45 nor man of any age (unless he marries a woman over 45) may marry if he (or she) is a drunkard, a habitual criminal, an idiot, feebleminded or an insane person, or afflicted with advanced tuberculosis or a contagious venereal disease.

(20) Available only as common-law grounds.

(21) Unless the court decrees otherwise.

LIABILITY OF LOCAL SCHOOL DISTRICTS FOR TORTS

CHART *31*

ALABAMA
The state constitution provides that the state is immune from liability for torts. This provision has been interpreted to include school districts.

ALASKA
Insofar as their duties are of a governmental nature, school districts are regarded as immune from liability.

ARIZONA
A decision by the Arizona Supreme Court abrogated the state's immunity from liability for torts. The state legislature subsequently passed a law establishing procedures for filing claims against the state.

ARKANSAS
State law permits school districts to buy general liability insurance & waives immunity up to the amount of the policy. A constitutional provision against liability is avoided by making the insurer, rather than the school district, liable.

CALIFORNIA
State law states that the governing board of a school district is liable for a judgment against the district arising from injury to person or property resulting from negligence of district, its officers or employes. The statute provides procedures for filing claims & limits amount recoverable.

COLORADO
Insofar as their duties are of a governmental nature, school districts are regarded as immune from liability.

CONNECTICUT
Governmental immunity from liability has been abrogated by the state courts. School districts may buy liability insurance, but no statute defines claims procedure or limits the amount of damages that may be recovered.

DELAWARE
Insofar as their duties are of a governmental nature, school districts are regarded as immune from liability.

D.C.
Insofar as their duties are of a governmental nature, school districts are regarded as immune from liability.

FLORIDA
The state constitution provides that the state is liable for torts as provided by general law.

GEORGIA
Insofar as their duties are of a governmental nature, school districts are regarded as immune from liability.

HAWAII
The state has waived its governmental immunity for the torts of its employes but is not liable for any interest prior to the judgment or for punitive damages.

IDAHO
A decision by the Idaho Supreme Court abrogated the state's immunity for liability for torts. School districts are subject to suit.

ILLINOIS
State law waives immunity of local school districts, establishes procedures for filing claims & limits the amount of damages that may be recovered. The state courts have ruled that limits on damages are unconstitutional.

INDIANA
State law waives immunity of school districts, with procedures for filing claims including a limit on recovery.

IOWA
State law waives immunity of school districts & establishes procedures for filing claims but does not limit the amount of damages that may be recovered.

*But school districts that do not buy general liability insurance cannot be held liable.

448

In many states, school districts are immune to tort suits under the theory of "sovereign immunity" (see sections 38, 333). The liability of school districts in your state is outlined on this chart.

KANSAS

State law permits school districts to waive immunity up to the amount covered by liability insurance for liability incurred by the negligent operation of motor vehicles, injury or death on school premises or in school activities & property damage.

KENTUCKY

Insofar as their duties are of a governmental nature, school districts are regarded as immune from liability.

LOUISIANA

State law waives immunity of school districts, but officials are immune from liability.

MAINE

State law waives immunity of school districts up to the amount covered by liability insurance for liability incurred by the negligent operation of motor vehicles.*

MARYLAND

Insofar as their duties are of a governmental nature, school districts are regarded as immune from liability.

MASSACHUSETTS

School districts are immune from liability to the same extent that towns are. Teachers, while acting in scope of employment, are liable only for their own acts of misfeasance.

MICHIGAN

Insofar as their duties are of a governmental nature, school districts are regarded as immune from liability except as to injury or damage resulting from a defect in school building of which the school district was aware.

MINNESOTA

State law waives immunity of school districts, limits the amount of damages that may be recovered & sets a time limit for bringing suit.

MISSISSIPPI

State law requires a school district to pay $10 annually per school bus into a state fund from which claims may be paid, not to exceed $5,000 per person or $50,000 per accident.

MISSOURI

Insofar as their duties are of a governmental nature, school districts are regarded as immune from liability.

MONTANA

State law permits school districts to buy general liability insurance & waives immunity up to the amount of the policy.

NEBRASKA

State law waives immunity of school districts excluding claims arising out of assault, battery, false arrest & certain other exceptions.

NEVADA

State law waives immunity of school districts, limits claims to $25,000 per claimant (award may not include exemplary or punitive damages or interest prior to judgment) & sets a 6-month statute of limitations. Certain actions are barred.

NEW HAMPSHIRE

State law waives immunity of school districts where liability insurance is purchased, but limits liability to the amount of the policy.

NEW JERSEY

State law waives immunity of school districts but sets no limit on the amount of damages that may be recovered or the time within which a suit must be brought.

NEW MEXICO

State law permits school districts to buy general liability insurance & waives immunity up to the amount of the policy.*

CHART 31 (cont.)

NEW YORK

State law waives immunity of school districts & permits school districts to insure pupils against accidents with accident insurance rather than liability insurance.

NORTH CAROLINA

State law permits school districts to buy general liability insurance & waives immunity up to the amount of the policy. School bus claims are exempted from the insurance & are paid from a state school bus fund.*

NORTH DAKOTA

Insofar as their duties are of a governmental nature, school districts are regarded as immune from liability.

OHIO

Insofar as their duties are of a governmental nature, school districts are regarded as immune from liability.

OKLAHOMA

Insofar as their duties are of a governmental nature, school districts are regarded as immune from liability.

OREGON

State law abolishes immunity of school districts & establishes claims procedures. Damages that may be recovered are limited to $25,000 for property, $100,000 per claimant for injury & $300,000 maximum per accident.

PENNSYLVANIA

Insofar as their duties are of a governmental nature, school districts are regarded as immune from liability.

RHODE ISLAND

State law waives immunity of political subdivisions of state & limits claims to $50,000 per action.

SOUTH CAROLINA

Insofar as their duties are of a governmental nature, school districts are regarded as immune from liability.

SOUTH DAKOTA

Insofar as their duties are of a governmental nature, school districts are regarded as immune from liability.

TENNESSEE

State law waives school district immunity but permits districts to obtain liability insurance.

TEXAS

State law provides that the waiver of sovereign immunity is inapplicable to school districts. School districts remain immune from liability.

UTAH

State law waives immunity of government employes for injury caused by negligence or omission. The amount of damages that may be recovered is not limited. Some situations are exempted.

VERMONT

State law permits school districts to buy general liability insurance & school bus liability insurance & waives immunity up to the amount of the policies.*

VIRGINIA

Insofar as their duties are of a governmental nature, school districts are regarded as immune from liability.

WASHINGTON

State law abrogates immunity of school districts & other governmental bodies.

WEST VIRGINIA

Insofar as their duties are of a governmental nature, school districts are regarded as immune from liability.

WISCONSIN

State law sets up procedures for filing claims against governmental bodies (including school districts). Damages that may be recovered are limited to $25,000.

WYOMING

State law permits school districts to buy general liability insurance & waives immunity up to the amount of the policy.*

*But school districts that do not buy general liability insurance cannot be held liable.

CHAPTER NINE

Your Job,
Profession or Business;
Your Social Security

The good of the people is the highest law.

—CICERO

9

Your Job, Profession or Business; Your Social Security

Your Job, Employer and Wages

370. Your Right to Work • The idea that you have certain rights with regard to getting or keeping a job is relatively recent. Historically, most private employment has been "employment at will," which meant that an employer could fire an employe for good cause, bad cause or no cause at all, and the employe had no recourse. While you still do not have a constitutional right to be employed or keep your employment, and the "employment at will" concept is still a very real one, both the federal and state legislatures have passed a number of laws designed to protect workers. One of the most important of these laws is the Civil Rights Act of 1964 as amended in 1972.

The Civil Rights Act, among its other provisions, forbids employers, labor organizations and employment agencies to practice discrimination in employment or membership on grounds of race, religion, national origin or sex. In 1965 the federal government banned discrimination in federal employment on grounds of race, color, creed or national origin. Older people have also received employment protection: the federal Age Discrimination in Employment Act of 1967 prohibits discrimination against the older worker solely because of his age. Most states have fair employment practice laws that parallel the protections granted in federal law.

The 1964 Civil Rights Act set up a five-member commission to administer it. This body, called the Equal Employment Opportunity Commission, is appointed by the President. The statute authorizes the commission to investigate complaints of discrimination in employment.

The statute provides for a number of exceptions. Religious organizations, for example, are not required to hire members of other religions. When there are bona fide qualifications for a job, the prohibitions of the law do not apply. A French restaurant, for example, has a right to hire a French chef. Certain jobs require men and others require women: a hotel is not required to hire a female attendant for the mens' bathroom and vice versa. Federal, state and local agencies are also required to follow the provisions of the Civil Rights Act of 1964.

The Civil Rights Act of 1964 relies heavily on persuasion for its enforcement. It leaves most of the initiative in the hands of the individual who has a complaint; many state agencies, however, will help the individual process the claim. If you think you have been discriminated against in a matter concerning hiring, wages or advancement in your job, you can

453

file a complaint with the Equal Employment Opportunity Commission within 180 days. However, if your state or city has a fair employment practices agency, the law gives precedence to that agency, to which you should submit a written complaint. Usually the agency is allowed sixty days to investigate the complaint and take action. After that period the commission can enter the case. The commission then investigates on its own, and may examine the records of the accused company.

If the commission finds that your complaint is justified, it tries informally to persuade the accused party to set things straight. If the commission is unsuccessful, you yourself must follow up by filing a civil suit against the employer within thirty days in a United States district court (in a limited number of cases the commission will file a suit on the complainant's behalf). The court can order the defendant to stop his discriminatory practice—to hire you or give you the back pay to which you are entitled—and oblige him to pay your attorney's fees. The defendant, if he is found guilty, has the right to appeal in the federal courts.

The legal process you must follow to obtain your rights is time-consuming, and the commission does not have significant powers of enforcement. However, in cases of "general public importance," if the commission determines that a practice or pattern of discrimination exists, it tries to obtain a court order compelling the accused employer to stop the discriminatory practice. The court can also order him to hire the people who have been discriminated against or to reinstate them with back pay.

You must be able to prove a specified act of discrimination. The mere statement that an employer has no blacks on his staff or that a union has no black members is not proof of discrimination. It is possible that no qualified blacks applied. However, the fact that there are no blacks may raise a strong inference that the employer or union is engaged in illegal conduct. Some large firms may hire a few blacks simply to create the impression that they are complying with the law, when their aim is actually to evade it through a show of compliance.

Employers may not discriminate on the basis of sex where either gender can perform the work required. Airlines must hire stewards as well as stewardesses; fine restaurants, which historically have hired all male staffs, must hire waitresses as well as waiters. Men and women must receive equal pay for equal work. However, under federal law employers can exclude pregnancy from disability coverage, although many state laws do cover pregnant women. Additionally, it is illegal to refuse to hire, or to fire, a woman because she is pregnant. Your local (state or city) Human Rights Commission is the best source for specific information.

454

The Civil Service Commission (see section 380) and the Secretary of Labor are responsible for enforcing the laws against discrimination in federal employment. Since 1972 federal employes have had the same rights under the Civil Rights Act of 1964 as private employes to seek relief in court. All executive departments and agencies must provide equal employment opportunity for civilian jobholders and applicants. Prompt hearings are required for all complaints of discrimination. Government contractors are also prohibited from engaging in discriminatory practices. Some states have similar rules regarding employment on public works or on other jobs financed by public funds.

Older employes, that is, those employes between the ages of forty and sixty-five, are protected against discrimination based on their age by the federal Age Discrimination in Employment Act of 1967. Responsibility for administration and enforcement of this law is in the hands of the Secretary of Labor. The act applies to employers, employment agencies and unions. As with other federal legislation, it covers only businesses engaged in interstate commerce.

Its provisions exempt jobs in which age is a bona fide occupational qualification. In some jobs, for instance, an employe must meet certain physical qualifications that an older person cannot satisfy. The law also states that an employer is not required to employ anyone who is not qualified to do a job, regardless of his age. Although aimed at protecting the employment rights of older people, the act declares specifically that it is legal to discharge them when there is a good cause. Many states also have laws protecting older workers. Additionally, many states have laws prohibiting job discrimination against handicapped or disabled persons. There is also some federal protection in this area for employes where an employer has contracts with the federal government.

371. Minimum Age Requirements for Employment • The federal Fair Labor Standards Act has laid down protective rules for the kinds of work children are allowed to do and how old they must be to do it. This act applies only to those who seek employment in interstate or foreign commerce or in the making of goods intended for that commerce.

The list of jobs forbidden to people under sixteen is long. Under sixteen you are not allowed to work as a public messenger or to tend power-driven machinery; you are also prohibited from jobs in construction, public utilities, transportation, mining, manufacturing and similar industries. If the law is disobeyed and people under sixteen help to produce manufactured or mined goods, these goods may not legally be shipped in in-

STATE LABOR LAWS

CHART 32	Fair Employment Practices Act	Civil or Human Rights Commission	Right-to-Work Law	Workmen's Compensation Act
ALABAMA	No	No	Yes	Yes
ALASKA	Yes	Yes	No	Yes
ARIZONA	Yes	Yes	Yes	Yes
ARKANSAS	No	No	Yes	Yes
CALIFORNIA	Yes	Yes	No	Yes
COLORADO	Yes	Yes	No	Yes
CONNECTICUT	Yes	Yes	No	Yes
DELAWARE	Yes	Yes	No	Yes
D.C.	Yes	Yes	No	Yes
FLORIDA	No	Yes	Yes	Yes
GEORGIA	Yes	No	Yes	Yes
HAWAII	Yes	No	No	Yes
IDAHO	Yes	Yes	No	Yes
ILLINOIS	Yes	Yes	No	Yes
INDIANA	Yes	Yes	No	Yes
IOWA	Yes	Yes	Yes	Yes
KANSAS	Yes	Yes	Yes	Yes
KENTUCKY	Yes	Yes	No	Yes
LOUISIANA	No	No	Yes	Yes[1]
MAINE	Yes[2]	Yes	No	Yes
MARYLAND	Yes	Yes	No	Yes
MASSACHUSETTS	Yes	Yes	No	Yes
MICHIGAN	Yes	Yes	No	Yes
MINNESOTA	Yes	Yes	No	Yes
MISSISSIPPI	No	No	Yes	Yes

[1] But workmen's compensation is not compulsory. Employers and employes may elect to be covered.

[2] The statute does not provide for enforcement, but discrimination in employment is a misdemeanor.

[3] A limited right-to-work law prevents union interference in the case of a sole proprietor or a partnership of 2 persons engaged in a retail business or an amusement activity.

[4] A limited antidiscrimination law applies only to state employes.

This chart shows which states have a fair employment practices act, civil or human rights commission, right-to-work law and workmen's compensation act, as described in sections 370, 383 and 430.

	Fair Employment Practices Act	Civil or Human Rights Commission	Right-to-Work Law	Workmen's Compensation Act
MISSOURI	Yes	Yes	No	Yes
MONTANA	Yes	Yes	No[3]	Yes
NEBRASKA	Yes	Yes	Yes	Yes
NEVADA	Yes	Yes	Yes	Yes
NEW HAMPSHIRE	Yes	Yes	No	Yes
NEW JERSEY	Yes	Yes	No	Yes
NEW MEXICO	Yes	Yes	No	Yes
NEW YORK	Yes	Yes	No	Yes
NORTH CAROLINA	No	Yes	Yes	Yes
NORTH DAKOTA	No	No	Yes	Yes
OHIO	Yes	Yes	No	Yes
OKLAHOMA	Yes	Yes	No	Yes
OREGON	Yes	Yes	No	Yes
PENNSYLVANIA	Yes	Yes	No	Yes
RHODE ISLAND	Yes	Yes	No	Yes
SOUTH CAROLINA	Yes[4]	Yes[5]	Yes	Yes
SOUTH DAKOTA	No	Yes	Yes	Yes
TENNESSEE	Yes	Yes	Yes	Yes
TEXAS	Yes[4]	Yes	Yes	Yes
UTAH	Yes	Yes	Yes	Yes
VERMONT	Yes	Yes	No	Yes
VIRGINIA	No	Yes	Yes	Yes
WASHINGTON	Yes	Yes	No[6]	Yes
WEST VIRGINIA	Yes	Yes	No	Yes
WISCONSIN	Yes	Yes	No	Yes
WYOMING	Yes	Yes	Yes	Yes[7]

(5) Human Affairs Commission limited to discrimination against state employes.

(6) But under state statute an agricultural laborer may not be denied work because of his membership or nonmembership in a labor union.

(7) For workers in extra-hazardous industries only.

terstate or foreign commerce. The federal government also regulates employment in firms that do business with it; in general, the employes must be sixteen years of age or older.

The states also play a significant part in the control of child labor, specifying the kinds of jobs young persons may or may not hold. Most states do not allow minors under fourteen to take jobs. Young people under sixteen are generally required to present work permits (working papers) to their employers. As many as half of the states require you to obtain a work permit until you have reached eighteen. Typically, the work permit shows your name, place of birth and home address. The employer has to keep this permit in his files and show it to government inspectors, which makes it difficult for him to evade the law by employing persons who have not reached the statutory age. You must also meet minimum standards of education to be granted working papers. All in all, the work permit is a most effective means of regulating child labor.

Statutes also regulate the number of hours that young people may work. In a great many states young people under sixteen are prohibited from working more than eight hours a day. Their workweek must not be longer than forty, forty-four or forty-eight hours, depending on the state. In some states persons under eighteen may not work between 10:00 p.m. and 6:00 a.m.; persons under sixteen are not allowed to do any night work at all in most states. Many states bar persons under eighteen from taking jobs in dangerous occupations, such as mining.

372. Wage and Hour Laws · The federal Fair Labor Standards Act (Wage and Hour Law) as amended in 1974 places a ceiling on hours and a floor on wages. It does not apply to all working people, however; like all federal legislation, it affects only those who work in interstate or foreign commerce or who help to produce the goods for that commerce. For example, if you are employed in a factory that manufactures goods that will be shipped out of your state, you are protected by the act. If you are a shipping clerk who packs the goods, you are also covered. But if the goods never leave town, you must look to your state and local laws for protection (see chart 33, page 466).

The minimum wage established by present law is $2.30 an hour. If you work more than forty hours in one week, your employer must pay, for the work hours over forty, at least one and a half times your regular hourly wage. It does not matter whether you do piecework or are paid on a commission basis; you must be compensated at one and a half times the regular rate for the extra hours you work.

There are certain exceptions to these provisions. Executives, administrative employes, outside salesmen and employes of certain types of transportation companies are not subject to the act. Some employes of airlines, service stations, railroads, shipping lines and other industries may be excluded from the overtime provision. Seasonal industries are also partly exempt from this provision. Certain types of employes, such as handicapped workers and students, may, with the government's permission, be paid a lower minimum rate.

The federal Fair Labor Standards Act is administered by the Wage and Hour Division of the U.S. Department of Labor. This division has field offices in most of the states to receive complaints and enforce the act. Businesses that come under the act must display posters that explain it in detail to their employes. The Department of Labor can sue to compel an employer to pay back wages or get a court injunction to stop him from violating the law. Serious offenders are subject to heavy fines and prison terms.

If an employe is not paid the legal minimum, he may sue for the wages owed him and, in addition, may request an equal amount as damages. He is also entitled to his court costs and his attorney's fee. His suit must be filed within two years of the employer's failure to pay. It is illegal to discharge an employe if he files a suit or lodges a complaint.

Some of the states have also established wage and hour laws of their own, which apply to all employes in the state. For details you should call your state department of labor or contact your state representative.

373. Laws Concerning Employe Safety and Working Conditions • Laws have been put into effect at every level of government to make working conditions safe. Without this government protection the toll paid by working people in death and injury, because of the increasing mechanization of industry, would be many times what it is today.

In 1970 the federal government enacted the Occupational Safety and Health Act (OSHA), which is administered by the Secretary of Labor. OSHA sets standards to ensure that workers are not unduly exposed to dangerous conditions. If you think your place of employment is unsafe you may make a complaint to the federal Department of Labor, and your employer can be compelled to correct a dangerous condition. It is a violation of the act for your employer to retaliate against you if you have filed a complaint.

All the states recognize that they have a responsibility to assure employes of a healthful, safe place in which to work, and their safety and

459

health laws and codes cover seven major areas: (a) buildings and their appurtenances; (b) construction; (c) equipment and machinery; (d) fire safety; (e) health; (f) industry safety; and (g) licensing and qualifications for various occupations. The states follow two fundamental procedures in writing safety regulations into the law. In the more usual procedure the state legislature draws up a bill with various safety or health provisions, and it is then voted on and signed by the governor. In the second procedure an agency in the state executive branch, such as the Department of Labor or Public Health, which has the authority to make rules, issues administrative codes or regulations which have the force of laws. For details, consult your state legislator.

374. Unfair Labor Practices • Labor legislation has established many ground rules for what management and labor may not do in dealing with each other. Particularly important are the laws regulating unfair labor practices.

The chief purpose of the National Labor Relations Act of 1935 was to aid workers in organizing labor unions that would not be dominated by employers. It was also intended to help unions get recognition from management as collective bargaining agencies. The act was not concerned with practices by unions that might be unfair to employers but only with employer actions that were prejudicial to labor. The major practices that the act declared unfair and prohibited to employers are:

a. Interfering with employes or restraining or coercing them in activities involving organizing a union or bargaining collectively.

b. Discriminating against employes by setting up hiring conditions that either promote or discourage membership in a union.

c. Dominating or interfering with any labor organization, either in its formation or administration, or making financial or other contributions to its support.

d. Refusing to enter into collective bargaining negotiations with representatives elected by the employes.

e. Discriminating against or firing any employe because he has filed a complaint against the employer under the National Labor Relations Act or has offered testimony under it.

The act set up the National Labor Relations Board to help employes select appropriate bargaining units and see that employers bargain in good faith; it gave the board power to look into charges of unfair practices by employers. It also authorized the board to order the employer to cease and desist from such practices where they were found to be present.

The Taft-Hartley Act, or Labor-Management Relations Act of 1947, listed the same unfair practices. In addition, it declared the following labor practices unfair and prohibited employes and unions from engaging in them:

a. Forcing or coercing workers into joining a union (unless there was a union shop) or coercing employers in their choice of representatives to deal with employe grievances or to speak for management in collective bargaining negotiations.

b. Compelling employers to discriminate against an employe, as, for example, by discharging him (this rule did not apply, however, to an employer with a union shop who had to take action against an employe for not paying union dues or initiation fee).

c. Refusing to enter into collective bargaining negotiations with an employer if the union had received certification as the employes' bargaining agent.

d. Taking part in jurisdictional work stoppages or secondary boycotts or forcing an employer to assign certain work to certain unions.

e. Compelling an employer to pay for labor that was not performed (the practice popularly referred to as featherbedding).

f. Charging excessive initiation fees or dues for employes working in plants with union-shop agreements.

The act thus outlawed discrimination, coercion and refusal to bargain by labor as well as management. It also made it permissible for an employer to give his employes his opinion about issues in a dispute with labor, as long as he did not offer a "promise of benefit" to those who would come over to his side or threat of reprisal to those who disagreed with him. In addition it banned "closed shop" agreements in companies engaged in interstate commerce (see section 383). A prospective employe does not have to be a member of a union to get the job.

Other aspects of labor and management relations are discussed in sections 382–388.

375. Insurance Required of Employers • One of the chief kinds of insurance that the law requires an employer to carry is workmen's compensation insurance. Each state has its own plan, and the coverage is variable. Every state requires that the disability for which the workman claims compensation must have occurred in the course of his employment. Injuries that are self-inflicted or that are the result of intoxication or willful misconduct are generally excluded from coverage. (For a more detailed discussion of workmen's compensation, see section 430.)

A few states have passed laws requiring that employers insure their workers against illness or injury that is not connected with their jobs. This insurance may be paid for by the employer alone or jointly by employer and employe (see section 431).

Employers must also contribute toward old-age, survivors and disability insurance, more popularly known as social security. (For a description of social security benefits and how to qualify for them, see sections 414–425.)

Another type of insurance that most employers must pay for is unemployment insurance (see section 432). The program is administered jointly by the federal government and the states. The employer finances the benefits in all but a few of the states; in those few the employe also contributes. Civilian employes of the federal government and members of the armed forces upon their discharge are also covered by unemployment insurance. Their coverage is financed by direct appropriations by the government, but benefits are paid under the unemployment programs of the individual states.

Anyone engaged in a business will find it to his advantage to carry a number of additional kinds of insurance that will protect him against loss or injury caused by his employes or suffered by them. Some of these are discussed in section 499. However, these types of insurance are usually not required by law.

376. The Law of Employer and Employe • Much of the law concerning the rights and obligations of employer and employe that developed in the nineteenth and twentieth centuries in England and the United States is based on old-fashioned theories of contract. This law means little in a highly industrialized society in which a large number of blue-collar workers belong to a union. If you work on an assembly line in an automobile or aircraft factory, you have no personal contract with your employer. The terms of your employment—the number of hours you work, the hourly wage you receive, the overtime pay you get, your fringe benefits, such as retirement and sick pay—all are stipulated in the contract your union negotiates with the management. What follows in the next two sections refers to nonunion employes, employes whose terms of employment really are separately negotiated with their employers.

377. The Employer's Rights and Duties • As an employer you should know that when you hire someone to work for you, you are making a contract with him. Usually your agreement is not in writing, but in the eyes of the law it is just as binding as if it were. In general, you will have an understanding with the employe that he is going to do his work at a specified wage for a given number of hours.

When a contract is signed, both you and the employe can be held to it. The employment contract should state whether the employe is to be paid by the hour, the week or the' month. It should give you the right to discharge him for cause. It should indicate the term of his employment and set forth his duties and obligations.

Even though the contract says nothing about termination of employment, you may, if you have good cause, fire an employe before the period of his employment is completed and not be responsible for any wages that he would have earned after the date of his termination. Acceptable causes include habitual disregard of your instructions, purposeful disobedience, dishonesty and immoral conduct. If your employe quits without good reason, you are generally required to pay his salary up to the time he leaves.

It sometimes happens that an employer hires someone to work for him without specifying the amount he will pay. In such cases the courts say that there is an implied understanding that the worker will receive the payment usual in that area for someone with his degree of skill. On the other hand, if a person says he will do some work for you free, he is not entitled to payment if he later decides to ask for it.

You must take all practical measures to ensure the safety of people who work for you. You have to provide them with safe working conditions, see to it that they have proper tools to do their work properly and make sure that they are warned about possible dangers that might be expected to occur. If they have to work with other people on whom their safety may depend, you must make certain that those others are reliable and competent in their duties.

The relationship of employer and employe closely resembles that of principal and agent (see section 393). You hire an employe to do a job under your direction. At certain times, however, he acts as your agent— for example, when he is authorized to make purchases for your business. When he acts in this authorized capacity, you are obligated by his action and are responsible for purchases or other commitments that he makes. If, in an emergency, he exceeds the authorized capacity but makes commitments or purchases in good faith, you are also obligated.

You are also liable to pay compensation if your employe, in the course of his work, is guilty of negligence, causing someone to sustain injury or loss. If, for instance, an employe negligently damages a tele-

463

vision set that he is repairing in your shop, you are liable to the owner for the amount of the damages. However, you are not responsible for acts that an employe commits outside the course of his employment. Suppose that you send your truck driver to make a pickup at a plant in the middle of town. Instead of proceeding there directly, the driver goes far out of his way to do an errand for his wife. On the way he collides with another vehicle and damages it. In this instance, because he was not following your instructions when the accident occurred, he, and not you, is liable. But if he had followed your directions and the accident had occurred as he was approaching the plant, the liability would be yours. (For a full discussion, see section 37.)

The question of rights to an invention or a profitable business idea developed by an employe is often a subject of controversy. If you are paying an employe to do research and development work for you, have him sign an agreement stating that anything he discovers or invents will belong to your business. Without such an agreement the invention or idea is the property of the employe. If the employe develops a new approach or a better method of working, using his own tools and his own time, it belongs to him exclusively.

Many statutes govern the relationship between the employer and the employe. As an employer you have to obey these statutes to the letter or be subject to a variety of penalties, some quite severe. Among other things you are obliged to: (a) withhold and deposit income taxes (see section 408); (b) withhold and deposit employes' social security payments and match them with an equal sum (see section 414) or, if you are self-employed, make a social security contribution to your own account (see section 416); (c) observe wage and hour laws (see section 372); (d) observe child labor laws (see section 371); (e) make contributions to the state unemployment compensation fund (see section 432); and (f) carry workmen's compensation insurance (see sections 67, 430).

378. The Employe's Rights and Duties • Your rights and duties as an employe complement those of your employer. When you agree to work for an employer, you enter into a contract with him. Usually wages, hours and working conditions are your main concern. But many items that you don't discuss may become an assumed part of your agreement, since they have been established by legal decisions and statutes.

In the language of the older law the employer was the "master" and the employe the "servant." Times have changed greatly, but these words in many ways still express the essence of the employer-employe relationship. When you accept a job, the law generally holds that you must obey the instructions your employer gives you. You are expected to be diligent in your work and also prudent and careful, so that your actions do not cause loss or injury to anyone.

When you apply for a job, you usually have to fill out a questionnaire. Some questionnaires require you to swear that all the information you provide is true to the best of your knowledge. But suppose that you neglect to mention a physical defect that you know is not likely to be detected in a physical examination. Does the firm have the right to discharge you if it later discovers that you held back this information? The answer is yes, if your physical defect is serious enough so that you would have been rejected for employment if the firm had known about it when you applied. But many companies will overlook a small omission if it does not relate significantly to your ability to do the job.

Group insurance interests most jobholders. Most companies inform their employes when changing or canceling insurance coverage, and some courts have held that employers who fail to give such notice are remiss in their duties. This is particularly likely if the employer pays for the insurance. Every employe should know exactly how much insurance his firm carries for him and should check it from time to time.

If you accept a salary from someone, you should show loyalty to him. In the course of your employment you may acquire an intimate knowledge of your employer's business practices and professional secrets. You must not reveal these to others who can use such secrets for their own profit. When you leave your job you are still under an obligation not to divulge these secrets.

Although you are not free to show your new employer how to use your former employer's secret processes or methods, you do have a right to exercise the technical knowledge you gained to develop different kinds of products. If you try to use your former employer's technical secrets to make products like those he manufactures, he probably could obtain a court order to stop you. But you have a right to exercise your unique talents in your work, so long as you do not infringe on the rights of others.

Your employer has the power to make reasonable rules regulating what you may or may not do in your job. These rules may even extend to "moonlighting," or work that you do for others after hours. He may forbid your taking an extra job that interferes with your giving him your best energies. He also has a legitimate complaint if you work for a client of his or for a competitor, and he can probably get a court order restraining you from such work.

465

MINIMUM WAGES AND MAXIMUM HOURS OF LABOR

NSP = No statutory provision

CHART 33	Basic Hourly Minimum Wage Rate Set by State Law[1]	Maximum Number of Hours You Can Work Per Day	
		Adults[3,4]	Children[5]
ALABAMA	NSP	NSP	8 (under 16)
ALASKA	$2.80	8	8
ARIZONA	NSP	NSP	8 (under 16)
ARKANSAS	$2.00	NSP	8 (under 16); 10 (under 18)
CALIFORNIA	$2.50	NSP	8 (under 18)
COLORADO	Minimum wages to be set by Director of Division of Labor	NSP	8 (under 18)
CONNECTICUT	$2.31 or ½ of 1% higher than federal minimum wage	NSP	8
DELAWARE	$2.00	NSP	8 (under 16)
D.C.	$2.46–$2.80	NSP	8 (under 18)
FLORIDA	NSP	NSP	10 (under 16)
GEORGIA	$1.25	NSP	8 (under 16)
HAWAII	$2.40	NSP	NSP
IDAHO	$2.30	NSP	9 (under 16)
ILLINOIS	$2.30	NSP	8 (under 16)
INDIANA	$1.25	8	8
IOWA	NSP	NSP	8 (under 16)
KANSAS	NSP	NSP	8 (under 16)
KENTUCKY	$1.60	NSP	See Commissioner of Labor's Regulations
LOUISIANA	NSP	NSP	8 (under 18)
MAINE	$2.30	NSP	8 (under 16)
MARYLAND	$2.30	NSP	8 (under 16); 9 (under 18)
MASSACHUSETTS	$2.10	NSP	8 (under 16); 9 (under 18)
MICHIGAN	$2.30	NSP	10 (under 18)
MINNESOTA	$2.10 $1.89 (under 18)	NSP	8 (under 16)
MISSISSIPPI	NSP	NSP	8 (14–16) 10 (over 16)
MISSOURI	NSP	NSP	8 (under 16)

This chart shows the provisions in each state regulating minimum wages, maximum hours and overtime (see section 372).

Maximum Number of Hours You Can Work Per Week		Increased Overtime Pay Required by Law[2]	
Adults[3,4]	Children[5]	Adults	Children
NSP	40 (under 16)	NSP	NSP
40	40	1½ times regular pay rate after 40 hours	
NSP	48 (16–18)	NSP	NSP
NSP	48 (under 16); 54 (under 18)	1½ times regular pay rate after 48 hours	NSP
NSP	48 (under 18)	1½ times regular pay rate after 8 hours per day and 40 hours per week	1½ times regular rate after 40 hours
NSP	40 (under 18)	NSP	NSP
NSP	48	1½ times regular pay rate after 40 hours	
NSP	48 (under 16)	NSP	NSP
NSP	48 (under 18)	1½ times regular pay rate after 40 hours	
NSP	40 (under 16)	Extra pay required for all work over 10 hours per day, unless contract to contrary	
NSP	40 (under 16)	NSP	NSP
40	40	1½ times regular pay rate after 40 hours	
NSP	54 (under 16)	NSP	NSP
NSP	48 (under 16)	1½ times regular pay rate after 40 hours, with some exceptions	
NSP	40 (under 18)	NSP	NSP
NSP	40 (under 16)	NSP	NSP
NSP	40 (under 16)	NSP	NSP
NSP	See Commissioner of Labor's Regulations	1½ times regular pay rate after 40 hours	
NSP	48 (under 18)	NSP	NSP
NSP	48 (under 16)	1½ times minimum wage after 48 hours	
NSP	40 (under 16); 48 (under 18)	1½ times hourly rate after 40 hours	
NSP	48 (under 18)	1½ times regular pay rate after 40 hours	
NSP	48 (under 18)	NSP	NSP
NSP	40 (under 16)	1½ times hourly rate after 48 hours	
NSP	44 (14–16)	NSP	NSP
NSP	40 (under 16)	NSP	NSP

	Basic Hourly Minimum Wage Rate Set by State Law[1]	Maximum Number of Hours You Can Work Per Day	
CHART 33 (cont.)		Adults[3,4]	Children[5]
MONTANA	$2.00	NSP	NSP
NEBRASKA	$1.60	NSP	8 (under 16)
NEVADA	$2.30 $2.15 (under 18)	NSP	8 (under 16)
NEW HAMPSHIRE	$2.30	NSP	8 (under 16); 10¼ (16–18)
NEW JERSEY	$2.20	NSP	8 (under 18)
NEW MEXICO	$2.30	16	8 (under 14)
NEW YORK	$2.30	8	8
NORTH CAROLINA	$2.00	10	8 (under 16); 9 (under 18)
NORTH DAKOTA	$2.10–$2.30	NSP	8 (under 16)
OHIO	$1.60	NSP	8 (under 18)
OKLAHOMA	$1.85	NSP	8 (under 16)
OREGON	$2.20	NSP	10 (under 16)
PENNSYLVANIA	$2.30	NSP	8 (under 18)
RHODE ISLAND	$2.30	NSP	8 (14–16); 9 (16–18)
SOUTH CAROLINA	NSP	NSP	NSP
SOUTH DAKOTA	$2.00	NSP	8 (under 16)
TENNESSEE	NSP	NSP	8 (14–15); 10 (16–17)
TEXAS	$1.40	NSP	8 (under 15)
UTAH	$1.70–$1.85	NSP	8 (under 18)
VERMONT	$2.30	NSP	8 (under 16); 9 (under 18)
VIRGINIA	$2.00	NSP	8 (under 18)
WASHINGTON	$2.30	NSP	8 (under 18)
WEST VIRGINIA	$2.20	NSP	8 (under 16)
WISCONSIN	Living wage	NSP	8 (under 18)
WYOMING	$1.60	NSP	8 (under 16)

[1] The federal minimum wage applies to all workers in interstate commerce.

[2] Most salaried executives, administrators or professionals are not eligible.

[3] The hours for working in certain hazardous occupations—such as mining, construction, public works and related industries—are restricted in some states.

468

Maximum Number of Hours You Can Work Per Week		Increased Overtime Pay Required by Law[2]	
Adults[3],[4]	Children[5]	Adults	Children
NSP	NSP	1½ times regular wage after 40 hours	
NSP	48 (under 16)	NSP	NSP
NSP	48 (under 16)	1½ times regular pay rate after 8 hours a day or 40 hours a week	
NSP	48 (under 16); 54 (16–18)	NSP	NSP
NSP	40 (under 18)	1½ times regular wage after 40 hours	
NSP	48 (under 14)	1½ times regular wage after 48 hours	
48	40 (under 16)	NSP	NSP
56	40 (under 16); 48 (under 18)	1½ times regular rate after 50 hours	NSP
NSP	48 (under 16)	1½ times regular rate after 40 hours	overtime illegal
NSP	48 (under 18)	1½ times regular rate after 40 hours	
NSP	48 (under 16)	NSP	NSP
NSP	44 (under 18)	1½ times minimum wage after 40 hours	1½ times minimum wage after 8-hour day or 40-hour week
NSP	44 (under 18)	1½ times regular rate after 40 hours	
NSP	40 (14–16); 48 (16–18)	1½ times regular rate after 40 hours	
NSP	NSP except maximum 10-hour day, 55-hour week in cotton & woolen manufacturing	NSP	NSP
NSP	40 (under 16)	NSP	NSP
NSP	40 (14–15); 48 (16–17)	NSP	NSP
NSP	48 (under 15)	NSP	NSP
NSP	44 (under 18)	NSP	NSP
NSP	48 (under 16); 50 (under 18)	1½ times regular rate after 40 hours	
NSP	40 (under 18)	NSP	NSP
NSP	40 (under 18)	1½ times regular rate after 40 hours	
42	40 (under 16)	1½ times regular rate after 42 hours	
NSP	24 (under 16); 40 (under 18)	NSP	NSP
NSP	NSP	NSP	NSP

(4) The hours for working in agricultural or domestic occupations in seasonal jobs or with perishable products are not subject to restriction in many states.

(5) The hours are further restricted for children of school age while school is in session. Children usually may not work at night. Work hours in certain industries may differ.

If you move on to another job you may not take with you lists of your former employer's customers to use for your own purposes. If you do, he can sue you for damages. However, you can visit customers you met while in your former job and invite them to do business with you.

Some businessmen require their employes to sign a statement that if they leave their jobs they will not go to work for a competing company. If you put your signature to such an agreement, you can be held to it.

If you are not eligible for workmen's compensation, it is your right to bring a suit for damages against your employer or any other person who may be responsible for an injury. However, if you are entitled to workmen's compensation, the state laws usually prohibit you from filing a suit (see section 430).

As a rule, your employer does not have to provide you with a reference when you leave your job. In some states, however, he may be required to give you a letter, at your request, saying that you have been in his employ. If he tells a prospective new employer that he does not want to say anything about the work you did for him, you have no recourse unless you establish that he acted out of malice. (For more information about your rights and duties, see section 377.)

There is no law requiring employers to provide pension and welfare benefits. If your employer does provide these benefits, your rights to them are governed both by the terms of the pension and welfare trust agreements and by the federal Employee Retirement Income Security Act of 1974, known as ERISA. ERISA requires employers with pension plans to allow employes to join the plan within a reasonable time after starting work. It ensures that the money will be there to pay pension benefits when due; that employes are informed of their rights under the plan; and that if an employe is denied a pension the denial can be reviewed. ERISA is a very complex law, administered by four separate government agencies (the Secretary of Labor has the major enforcement responsibility). If you want to know about your rights under ERISA or wish to file a complaint, you should contact the nearest regional office of the Department of Labor.

379. Who Has an Interest in Your Wages • The person with the primary interest in your wages is you. You are entitled to be paid promptly for any work you have performed. If your employer fails to pay you for a period of time, you have a right to sue him for the amount he owes you. Moreover, the statutes of your state may provide a criminal penalty for such an employer. If the company you work for goes bankrupt, the claim of its employes for payment of back wages takes precedence over the rights of all its other creditors (see section 411).

Anyone to whom you have a financial obligation also has an interest in your wages and may enter a claim against them, as well as against dividends or other income that is due you. Your husband or wife, present or past, may have a claim for support. Agencies of the government— federal, city or state—may make a claim, for instance, to collect past-due taxes or other obligations that you have to them. Other creditors may also look to your wages or other income for satisfaction of your debts.

If you are in debt and a judgment has been rendered against you (see section 86), it may happen that you do not have any personal property or real estate that can be seized to satisfy the judgment. If you have wages or other income coming due, in most states your employer can be compelled to pay out of them the amount that you owe. He does this by holding back part of your wages from every paycheck. Your employer is known as the garnishee, and the court order attaching your wages or warning your employer not to pay them to you but to hold them in trust is called a garnishment (see section 88 and chart 7, page 129).

380. Civil Service Jobs • The civil service, popularly speaking, is the merit system of public employment for which an applicant establishes his eligibility by passing a competitive examination or by submitting other demonstrations of his ability or proof of his qualifying experience. But it can also mean all the public employes of the government except members of the armed forces. In the United States there are two major types of civil service: (a) federal and (b) state and local. They have a great deal in common.

The federal government is the largest employer in the United States. It has several million people on its civilian payroll, most of them in the civil service merit system. These people staff the executive departments of the government, such as the Department of the Treasury and the Department of Commerce; over sixty major agencies; and hundreds of other boards, commissions, corporations and agencies. Approximately 11 percent are employed in Washington, D.C.; the rest are located throughout the United States and in foreign countries. Two out of three people employed in the federal civil service are white-collar workers.

People in a vast number of occupations are included in the civil service—not only janitors, clerks and stenographers but also teachers, dentists, botanists, historians, chemists, engineers and members of virtually all other professions.

471

The U.S. Civil Service Commission is a board of three commissioners. The board is bipartisan: no more than two of its members may belong to one political party.

Discrimination is one of the commission's major concerns. Discrimination on the basis of political opinions (except insofar as disloyalty to the United States is concerned), race, color, marital status, sex, age or religion is prohibited (see section 370).

The commission regulates examinations for civil service positions and also establishes personnel policies and standards. It supervises job classification, employe relations and other personnel activities.

The Bureau of Recruiting and Examining, an agency of the Civil Service Commission, publicizes the jobs that the commission wants to fill and conducts examinations for the candidates. Normally the tests are question-and-answer, but some applicants are graded on writing or drawings they present as proof of their skill, training or experience. The examination for more important positions frequently is made up of an evaluation of things that cannot be measured by a written test: judgment, personality, education and training, and experience in earlier positions.

The names of candidates who pass an examination are entered on a list in the order of their grades. However, the provisions of certain laws may affect someone's position on the list; for example, special preference is given to veterans, as we shall explain later. When the personnel officer of an agency has a vacancy to fill, he asks the Civil Service Commission for the names of those on the eligible list for the job he has open. The commission sends him the names at the top of the list. Usually this is done by the "rule of threes"—the top three who express interest in the job are invited to visit the agency. After one candidate has been accepted, the names of the remaining two are put back on the eligible list, to be considered again when the next vacancy occurs.

Not everyone is eligible for a federal civil service job. You must be a citizen of the United States or you must owe it your allegiance. When you apply for an examination, you have to fill out a detailed questionnaire, which asks you, among other things, about your loyalty to the American form of government.

Grounds for disqualification for federal employment include false statements in your application, various kinds of immoral conduct, excessive use of alcohol, evidence of disloyalty to the American form of government and mental or physical unfitness. You cannot be hired if two other members of your family living in your household work for the federal civil service. If you are an official or an employe of any state,

472

municipality or territory, you are, with few exceptions, barred from federal employment.

Appointment to a job in the civil service does not automatically bring lifetime tenure. As a new employe, you have to serve a probationary period. During this period you undergo, in a sense, additional testing of your qualifications for the job by the way you perform your duties. It is a basic rule that the head of a department makes the final judgment on the capability of his employes. The head of your department has the right to dismiss you if he decides that you are not doing your job well. No employe of the federal civil service can be removed except for such reasons as will "promote the efficiency of the service."

If a department wishes to remove an employe, he must be notified of the charges against him, and he must be granted a reasonable amount of time to prepare a reply to those charges before he can be removed. However, the employe does not have a right to a hearing or a trial. As a practical matter civil servants are seldom discharged except for flagrant misconduct.

The Hatch Act of 1939 prohibits almost all employes in the federal executive civil service from taking an active role in political management or in political campaigns. This prohibition now extends to state and local civil service employes who work for agencies that receive funds from the federal government. Anyone who violates the Hatch Act is subject to loss of his job, a fine and imprisonment.

Veterans receive preference for jobs in the civil service. To be eligible for these or other veterans' benefits, you must have been discharged under honorable conditions.

In examinations in which experience is required to establish that you are eligible, you may be credited with time spent in the armed forces. In most examinations height, weight and age requirements can be waived; physical requirements, too, can be waived for a job, provided you can perform it without endangering yourself and others. Moreover, examinations for certain jobs, such as custodian, elevator operator and guard, are available only to veterans as long as enough of them apply. For such jobs more than two members of an immediate family living under the same roof *may* be employed in the civil service, contrary to the general rule limiting the number to two.

If you are a veteran eligible for a job with a government agency and are passed over in favor of a nonveteran, the Civil Service Commission is required to review the agency's reason for its action. You are also accorded special treatment if you have completed your probationary period and the agency decides to discharge you, suspend you or demote you. The Veterans Preference Act states that you must be given written notice of the impending action, with the reasons for it, and that you have the right to reply within ten days after the action is taken or to appeal to the Civil Service Commission. If your agency is affected by an order reducing the number of workers, veterans get preference in keeping their jobs.

The federal civil service has an extensive plan of retirement benefits in the form of annuities. You are required to retire if you reach the age of seventy and have fifteen years or more of service. You may retire earlier if you have completed the periods of service specified (five years at age sixty-two; twenty years at age sixty; thirty years at age fifty-five). If you have had five years or more of service and suffer a total disability, you are eligible for retirement. The minor children or widow of a deceased employe may also be eligible for benefits. The fund from which annuities are paid is supported by contributions from the government plus deductions from the employe's salary.

Membership in the retirement system is automatic for most employes. Life insurance, health insurance, workmen's compensation and sick leave are also provided.

Federal employes are permitted to join labor organizations, and government agencies conduct collective bargaining negotiations with them. However, the government denies them the right to strike. The Taft-Hartley Act states the law and the penalties for failure to conform to it: "Any individual employed by the United States or by any . . . agency [thereof] who strikes shall be discharged immediately from his employment, and shall forfeit his civil service status, if any, and shall not be eligible for reemployment for three years by the United States or any such agency." Other legislation specifies additional penalties. (For other facets of labor relations between the U.S. government and employes of the federal civil service, see section 387.)

381. Household Help • Domestic workers—housemaids, chauffeurs, gardeners—are no different from other employes, and an employer stands in the same general relation to them, with the same responsibilities and claims, as he does to people who work for him in his factory or office. You are responsible for the acts of your servants when they act within the scope of the job you have assigned to them (see section 37).

A domestic worker is covered by social security if he is paid more than $50 in wages from one employer in a calendar quarter. As the employer, you are required to deduct a certain percentage of the employe's pay, match it with an equal amount and send this sum to the federal government at regular intervals with the employe's social security number. (If your employe does not have a social security card, he can obtain one from the local social security office.) You do not count room and board in calculating the employe's wage, but you do include carfare if you pay it in cash. The employe does not have to work for you regularly or full time. (For social security rules, see sections 414–428.)

You may be liable for injuries suffered by domestic workers, depending on the circumstances and the part your negligence may have played in the accident. In any event, you should carry liability insurance.

YOUR JOB AND LABOR UNIONS

382. The Role of the Labor Union • What is a labor union? It is an organization of working people who band together to obtain higher wages and better working conditions and to protect their rights and interests. In the United States today there are two major types of labor organization, the craft union and the industrial union.

The craft union is an association made up of workers in a certain craft, trade or occupation, such as carpenters. Often its members may be employed in different industries. The craft union reaches across these industries to include the workers in the same trade or on the same level of production, and so it is sometimes known as a horizontal union.

The second type is the industrial union. All the people who work in a particular industry can belong to an industrial union, no matter what their craft or occupation may be. For example, a single union might include secretaries, accountants, aircraft mechanics, test pilots and cleaning women.

In scope unions may be national or even international (which means they have locals in Canada as well as the United States) with a national executive board and a constitution that lays down rules and policies. The various union chapters or branches across the country are known as locals; they handle organizational activity and negotiations with management on a local level. Unions are supported by dues and special assessments paid by their members.

You will occasionally encounter a third type of labor organization, the union that exists independently within a single plant. As a rule this

475

kind of union was founded by the employes, or by one group of employes, and is not officially affiliated with a larger union. It should not be confused with the "company union," which is dominated by an employer and is illegal under our labor laws (see section 385).

Management and labor establish the terms on which they work together by a process known as collective bargaining. In the normal course of events the union draws up a detailed list of its demands and presents them to the representatives of management. The union's proposals cover such subjects as wages, hours, working conditions, employment of union members, vacations, seniority, safety measures, automation, pension or profit-sharing plans and a range of additional benefits.

Under the rules established by the National Labor Relations Board both the union and the employer are required to negotiate the union's demands—and management's—in good faith (see section 374). If the union's requests go beyond what management is willing to grant (and they often do, at least at the start of the bargaining), management must give its reasons for rejecting them and offer in their place proposals that it considers more reasonable. The union may counter by offering modifications of its own. If either side asks the other for information that may have bearing on the subjects under discussion, that information is supposed to be supplied unless there is a legitimate reason for withholding it. Meetings are held regularly at times convenient for both parties.

While negotiations are in progress, management is free to express its opinions to its employes on the proposals and counterproposals. Management must never present its point of view in such a way, however, that it appears to be threatening to discharge union members who do not see eye to eye with it or offering a reward to workers in order to win their support (see section 374). Labor is also required to avoid intimidating the management or employes who do not side with the union.

Generally, as the meetings and discussions continue, the representatives of the union and the employer eventually come closer together until they reach an agreement. The terms of this collective bargaining agreement or contract are then drawn up in a formal document and signed by the authorized representatives of both sides. Both must now abide by the terms of the agreement for the period of time it specifies, usually a year or longer. If, however, labor and management cannot reconcile their points of view, labor may decide to call a strike. Such a step requires the approval of the membership of the local (see section 386). No union in an industry engaging in interstate or foreign commerce can call a strike without giving its management sixty days' notice.

476

One of the major roles of the union is to protect employes from an unjust discharge or other unjust disciplinary action. Most collective bargaining agreements have a "just cause" for firing provision and a "grievance" provision. Under these provisions you can complain to the union about your unfair treatment, and if the claim appears to have some merit, the union will assist you in fighting your employer's disciplinary action. Unions are required by federal law to fairly represent you if you fall under the contract with your employer, even if you are not a union member.

383. Who Must Join a Union • Whether you must join a union very much depends on the industry or the state in which you are employed. The phrase *closed shop* describes a plant that is covered by an agreement between an employer and a union under which the employer can hire only members of that union. A federal law, the Taft-Hartley Act, outlaws the closed shop in industries making products for, or shipping them in, interstate or foreign commerce. About 80 percent of all businesses in the United States are in interstate commerce. So you don't have to join a union in order to obtain employment in any of these businesses.

On the other hand, the *union shop*—which is quite different from the closed shop—is entirely permissible under federal law. Most unions, when they negotiate a contract with an employer, include in it a clause establishing a union shop. Under a union shop the employer is free to hire a person who does not belong to the union, but that person must join it within a specified period of time, such as thirty days. If the employe fails to join, the employer must discharge him. A number of states have passed "right to work" laws, which make it illegal to fire an employe who refuses to join a union even though the contract contains a union-shop clause. Thus, you might work in a "right to work" state and not have to join a union, but if you moved to a state that did not have such a law and took a job in a union shop, you would be obliged to sign up with the union or lose your job. A "preferential shop" clause in a union contract requires the employer to show preference to union members when he hires new employes.

384. Getting into a Union—And Staying In • Unions have the right to make their own regulations for admitting new members or expelling old ones. As a rule, it is to a union's advantage to admit to membership all those who come within its jurisdiction, since its influence grows directly with the number of its members. Moreover, if the labor organization has a union-shop clause in its contract, it is committed to accept as

477

a member any applicant who has been placed on the company payroll.

Recruiting new members is the job of the union locals, and the general requirements for membership are laid down in the national constitution of the union. Usually the constitution provides for the admission of all persons who work in the trades covered by the union; sometimes it states that the candidates must be of industrious habits and good moral character. Since these last qualifications may be subject to interpretation, they can be used to bar some candidates from membership. Persons who belong to organizations opposed to the American form of government are sometimes specifically excluded from membership. Some of the constitutions provide that if a candidate is rejected, he may make an appeal to the national executive board of the union. In a union that has jurisdiction over only a small number of jobs, the local may have to submit details about the candidate to the national board and obtain its approval. Usually, however, the names of the candidates for membership are proposed at a meeting of the local, and in most cases the candidates are accepted without dissent.

Although unions have the right to establish their own rules for admitting new members, they cannot bar qualified workers from jobs in plants under their jurisdiction. Under the Taft-Hartley Act, if a union refuses to accept for membership anyone who works in the trades it represents, the union-shop clause in its contract with the employer cannot be enforced. The union-shop employer has to keep you in his employ if he has good reason to believe that you applied for membership in the union but were not accepted on the same terms as its other members. The same treatment is extended to workers in the opposite situation, those who are expelled from a union. If the union expels you for any reason except failure to pay your dues, an employer with a union shop must still keep you on.

The Taft-Hartley Act places a further restriction on unions; it prohibits them from charging excessive initiation fees and dues. The aim, in brief, is to stop unions from imposing unfair restrictions on membership, which some unions might do in order to limit the supply of qualified workers. The act also makes it an unfair practice for a union to discriminate against you or exert pressure on an employer to get him to discriminate against you in any way.

Both the federal government and a good number of states (see chart 32, page 456) have passed fair employment practices acts that have a bearing on membership in labor organizations. Generally speaking, these acts make it illegal for a union to discriminate in any manner against individuals because of race, sex, color, religion, national origin or ancestry. If you have convincing evidence that you have been discriminated against for any of these causes, you should get in touch with the Equal Employment Opportunity Commission.

Labor legislation gives protection to members of a union who may be treated unfairly in other ways. If the officials of your union want to discipline you or to subject you to a fine or expulsion, they are required, by the Landrum-Griffin Act of 1959, to give you a list of the charges against you in writing. Furthermore, they have to allow you sufficient time to prepare a reply to the charges and to give you a full and fair hearing. This also gives you the right to sue the union or its officials and forbids them to retaliate against you in the union. However, you must first make use of your union's machinery for settling your complaints. This act also requires that the union must provide you, or permit you to review, a copy of the company's collective bargaining agreement. If you are denied this opportunity you can file a complaint with the federal Department of Labor.

385. Management Actions That Affect Your Union • It is obviously to management's advantage, if it must deal with a union, to have one that is sympathetic. With this in mind, the head of a business might try to win the friendship of a union by extending valuable favors to it. If an employer does this for the purpose of controlling the union, so that in effect he, rather than its members, dictates the policies of the union, then he is in violation of the National Labor Relations Act, and a complaint to the National Labor Relations Board (NLRB) can bring an order for him to stop. He may not take any action against employes who lodge complaints against him because of this or other unfair practices.

A union that is dominated by management is often referred to as a company union. Such a union may be encouraged by an employer in an effort to keep a national union from gaining a foothold in his plant. If the NLRB investigates and finds that a labor organization is actually a company union, it has the power to dissolve the union.

Another restriction placed by Congress on the employer is that he must not engage in any activities that discriminate against a union. If there are two unions vying to represent the workers in a plant, management is not allowed to show a preference for one over the other by helping it or extending privileges or favors to its members.

The employer, then, can go so far and no further in attempting to win over or influence his personnel. If he addresses his workers on union matters while they are on his premises and does not allow them the privilege of leaving if they do not want to listen, he must grant union representatives equal time to present their point of view. If he talks to his employes about union matters within a day of an election to determine union representation and the union then loses the election, a second election may have to be held.

Just as labor can use the strike as a weapon to force its point of view on management, management can use a similar device against labor: He can resort to a lockout—that is, shut down his plant or refuse to give his employes work in order to compel them to agree to his terms. The lockout is in a sense the employer's strike against labor. The employer can also force the union to go on strike. If he offers the union terms that it considers unacceptable or if he insists on work rules that it views as unfair, the union may have no alternative but to call out its members.

386. Strikes and Other Union Actions That Affect You • Employes who take part in a legal strike continue to regard themselves as employes, and the law regards them in the same light. When the strike is settled, if the employer refuses to take an employe back simply because he took part in the work stoppage, the NLRB can compel the employer not only to rehire the striker but also to pay him for the time lost since the settlement of the dispute.

There is one important exception to this rule. The employer does not have to rehire his workers if he replaced them with others while they were on strike. If an employer engages new employes to keep his business in operation while a strike is in progress, he may not have many vacancies left when the dispute comes to an end. However, the workers who are not rehired still have the right to vote in an election to determine union representation if one is held during the one-year period after the beginning of the strike. In this way the law makes it difficult for an employer to try to break up a union by denying strikers the jobs they formerly held.

Quite another kind of treatment is in store for employes who take part in illegal strikes. The NLRB will order them to stop, and their employer will not be required to consider them as employes or to rehire them.

While the law frowns on some types of picketing as part of union activity, other types enjoy full legal sanction. If the picketing is being done only to bring certain facts to the attention of the public—if the picketing is purely informational—it is permissible. For instance, pickets are free to advise the general public that an employer has nonunion help working for him or that he has not signed a contract with a union. If,

THE GROWTH OF OUR LABOR UNIONS

The growth pattern of American labor unions over the past forty years shows their still-increasing importance in the country's life. After a spectacular rise between 1936 and 1944, total union membership has grown more slowly through the 1950s and 1960s, reaching a peak of over 21.6 million individual members in 1974.

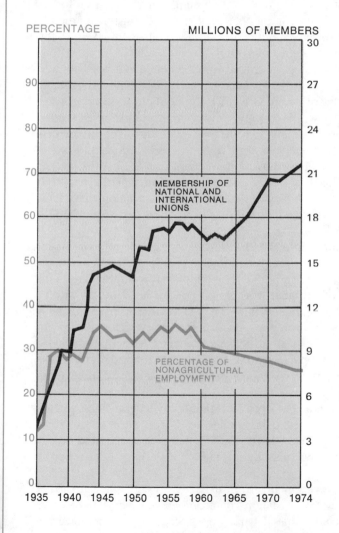

PERCENTAGE   MILLIONS OF MEMBERS

MEMBERSHIP OF NATIONAL AND INTERNATIONAL UNIONS

PERCENTAGE OF NONAGRICULTURAL EMPLOYMENT

1935 1940 1945 1950 1955 1960 1965 1970 1974

In contrast with the steady growth in total membership, the number of union members as a percentage of the total working population (with the exception of agricultural workers) has actually declined in recent years.

however, the aim of the pickets is to influence employes, then their activity is subject to restrictions.

Picketing for the purpose of persuading an employer to recognize a union is limited to a period of thirty days. By the end of that time the NLRB has to hold an election to establish whether a majority of the workers is in favor of having the union represent them. The law labels it an unfair practice for the union to picket an employer if a petition for an election has not been filed with the NLRB or the board has held an election within the past twelve months. Picketing is also outlawed if the employer has given valid recognition to a different union.

Naturally, when picketing is legal, it must be conducted honestly and peacefully. If the signs that the pickets are carrying contain statements that are inaccurate or are intended to give the public a false impression of the cause of the dispute, the employer may obtain a court order (called an injunction) from a judge obliging the pickets to desist. If the pickets threaten or interfere with people who want to pass through the picket line, the picketing can be halted by an injunction. It is against the law for pickets to parade in such a tightly packed formation that they make it hard for individuals to pass between them. (For court action that members of the public can take when injured by a strike, see section 388.)

387. Strikes by Public Workers • Employes of the federal government are not allowed to strike, and approximately three quarters of the states have also passed laws that prohibit their employes from striking. This does not mean that government workers do not go on strike, as witness the policemen's strike in Boston in 1919, the teachers' strikes in New York City in the 1960s, and the postal employes' strike of 1970. In recent years there has been an increasing tendency of public employes to take part in work stoppages as the number of unionized workers has risen. But they must pay the penalties provided by law, and often these are quite severe.

The Taft-Hartley Act of 1947 provides that if any federal employe goes on strike, he will be subject to immediate discharge. In addition, if he possesses civil service status (see section 380), it is forfeited, and he will not be eligible for reemployment by the federal government for a period of three years.

In 1962 the U.S. government, in an executive order, made a further statement of its policy toward labor organizations to which its employes might belong. It declared that it would not recognize any organization that asserted it had the right to strike. At the same time it granted employes of the federal government the right to join organizations of their own choice. It also gave, to any labor organization representing a majority of the employes in a given unit, exclusive recognition, as well as the right to enter into an agreement with a federal agency.

More than half of the states grant their employes the right to organize, but public employes are not given the right to strike in any state. Some states prohibit strikes but do not provide penalties for employes who go on strike. Some states that permit collective bargaining have set up state boards to assist in the bargaining. The principle of compulsory arbitration is also being widely accepted.

388. Court Action by the Public in Strikes • If you live close to a plant involved in a labor dispute and trouble breaks out, leaving you with a torn-down fence and a row of broken windows, you have a right to recover your damages. If strikers picketing a store threaten you or manhandle you when you pass by or try to enter the store, you are also entitled to compensation. A striker has no right to inflict injury or damage, and you are entitled to bring an action against him if you are able to identify him positively. If it is possible to establish that the striker was acting on instructions from the union, you can also bring a legal action for recovery against the union. For a detailed discussion of your right to recover damages, see chapter 3, page 81.

Your Job as a Self-Employed Artisan

389. Artisans Who Usually Require Licenses • An artisan is a workman or craftsman skilled in an art or trade. He may be a plumber, an electrician, a carpenter, a television repairman, an automobile mechanic, a barber, a beautician or a practitioner of some other skilled trade. Many artisans (see chart 34, page 492) are required to obtain licenses, usually for a fee, in order to practice their trades. A license is your permission from a governmental agency, generally on the city or the state level, to carry on your occupation. Artisans are licensed so that the interest of the public can be protected by providing official regulation and control.

If you carry on your business without the license that the law requires, you may be subject to a prison sentence or fine or both. Moreover, you will be unable to enter into an enforceable contract. In other words, if while unlicensed you make an agreement to do work for a customer and he refuses to pay you, you may not be able to collect from him (see section 172).

Requirements vary from state to state for different kinds of artisans. You may be required to take an examination to show that you have the skills needed in your trade. In addition, the licensing authority may require you to meet certain minimum standards of training and experience. You may be asked to give references from persons who will vouch that you are of good moral character. The equipment that you use in your business may also have to come up to certain standards.

The authority generally issues a license for a limited period, such as a year or two. When your license expires, you must apply to have it renewed and you must pay the required fee again. Often the law states that you have to display your license in a prominent spot in your place of business. If you fail to comply with the regulations established for your trade, you may be subject to a fine or imprisonment. In addition, your license may not be renewed, or it may be suspended or revoked.

390. The Artisan's Obligations to His Customers • If you are an artisan, you are a businessman and have the same obligations to your customers that any other businessman has. You must take prudent, diligent care of the people who enter your premises to do business with you. First of all, you must see to it that your place of business is safe for visitors and that they are not exposed to danger by any condition within your control. An exposed machine on which a customer may injure himself, a staircase with a defective step, a large crack in the linoleum—these and similar hazards must be guarded against. If there is a dangerous situation of a temporary nature, you have an obligation to warn the visitor about it and to remedy it as soon as possible. Unless there is contributory negligence (see section 64) on the part of the customer, the law is likely to hold you liable for any injury suffered by a customer. It is for this reason that businessmen carry accident and public liability insurance.

When you do business with a customer, you enter into a contract with him. That contract may not be in writing—usually it isn't—but it is just as binding upon you as though it were. Unless you and your customer agree otherwise, the law takes certain things for granted about your relationship with him. It assumes, for example, that when you take a job into your shop, you are saying that you can perform it in a satisfactory manner. Suppose you are a television repairman. If you fix a customer's television set and later the set causes a fire because of your negligence, you may be held liable (see sections 57, 58). In the same way, if you sell a product to your customer, you give him an implicit warranty that it is safe to use for the purpose intended. If he is injured as a result of using your merchandise, he can sue you for damages.

If a customer's property is left in your shop for you to work on, you have an obligation to take good care of it. The law expects you to take the same prudent care of it that you would of your own property. If an object is lost or damaged while it is in your place of business, the customer has a legitimate claim against you for compensation. Bailment insurance is carried by many businessmen as protection against such a contingency (see sections 197–206, 499).

Promptness in doing a job is often a cause of disagreement between an artisan and his customer. If your customer says he must have the job done by a specific date and you agree to that date, he may sue you for breach of contract if you are late. Generally the law allows you a certain amount of leeway. However, you are expected to complete your work within a reasonable time.

391. The Customer's Protection Against the Artisan • If an artisan who represents himself as knowing his trade does work for you that proves defective and you suffer injury or loss as a result, he has a liability to you. Suppose, for instance, that a mechanic repairs the steering mechanism of your car and guarantees it to be in good order, but the very next time you use your car the wheels fail to respond and you are involved in an accident. You have a clear-cut case against the mechanic, for breach of warranty.

On the other hand, you might not have such a case if you brought a complicated job to someone whom you knew to be a beginner in his trade. Because the job you entrusted to him required skill and knowledge, you may not reasonably expect him to perform it with the competence of an experienced mechanic, and thus you are unlikely to recover more than nominal damages if he does an inadequate job.

Much depends upon the understanding you have with an artisan. If you do not authorize him to spend extra time on the job and he does more than you ask for or want, you are under no obligation to pay him for his extra work. If, however, you know that he is doing more work than was originally arranged for and you do not object or you give your permission, you must make an additional payment at the usual rate or whatever rate you agree upon.

485

In certain circumstances you do not have to pay a workman with whom you enter into a spoken or written contract. If he fails to finish the job, so that the work is useless to you, you owe him nothing. This is also the case if he does a bad job because he did not follow the directions you gave him. If an artisan leaves a job unfinished, you are entitled to engage the services of somebody else to complete it. Should the hiring of the second artisan involve you in added costs, you may bring suit against the first one for compensation.

Naturally the great majority of artisans do a satisfactory job. When they do, you are under an obligation to pay them promptly, or they may take what is known as a mechanic's lien on the property you have entrusted to their care (see section 392).

392. The Artisan's Protection Against His Customers • Few legal devices are more effective for the protection of the artisan than the mechanic's, or artisan's, lien. Under the principle of the *mechanic's lien* you are not obliged to return to its owner an object you have worked on until your bill is paid. If the owner refuses to make payment, you may begin a legal proceeding to obtain the right to sell the object, as provided by state law. After the object has been disposed of, you are entitled to deduct the sum that is due you. Any excess has to be returned to the former owner.

But don't assume that a mechanic's lien automatically entitles an artisan to sell the property of another. It merely allows him to keep the object in his custody. The object may be sold only after the provisions of the law have been complied with. If he does not institute a proceeding to enforce the lien within a certain period of time, in some states the lien is *discharged,* or becomes invalid. If the owner pays his debt, the lien is also discharged.

The term *mechanic's lien* or *garageman's lien* is most frequently used in connection with automobiles that have been repaired. However, a mechanic's lien is often claimed by contractors such as electricians or plumbers against a building, a fence, a pier or some other structure on which they work. If the structure is sold to satisfy the claims of the various contractors and the proceeds are insufficient, the claimants are each entitled to a share in proportion to the amount that is due them, much as in the case of a bankruptcy.

An artisan usually has a property right in his work. If you find that a job you have contracted to do will cost more than the price agreed upon, you should notify the person you are working for before you proceed any further. If you put in extra work without his authorization, you are not entitled to additional payment. Silence on the part of the customer, after you have informed him of the need for more work, is interpreted by the courts as authorization to go ahead.

If the work is unsatisfactory or incomplete, the artisan may legally be denied payment (see section 391). However, there is one instance in which, even though the work is unfinished, you may have a right to payment: when the client requests you to stop working on the job he has given you. Such a request is completely within the customer's right, but he is under an obligation to compensate you for the amount of work you have completed. If you go on and finish the job in spite of instructions to stop work, you do not have a right to claim the full price that was agreed upon before you began.

Artisans who work on buildings are often asked by the builder to complete their work by a certain date. The terms of the contract usually govern the penalty, if any, for failure to finish the job by that time. The usual interpretation is that you must complete your work within a reasonable time.

If you substitute another material for one that is called for in your working arrangement, you will not be considered at fault, provided the substitute is of approximately the same character and worth. But if the material you substitute is not as good, you may face a penalty.

Your Job as a Salesman or Agent; Dealing with Agents

393. Agents and Principals • The law of agency, although few of us know it by that name, plays an important role in our lives. *Agency* is a legal relationship in which one person requests or authorizes another to act for him or do something for him. The person who makes the request is known as the *principal;* the person who acts for him is the *agent.* If you send your son downtown with the lawn mower to get it repaired, you are the principal and he is your agent. If you turn your car over to a garageman to sell it, he acts as your agent. There is usually a third party involved with whom the agent deals; in the first example it is the repairman, in the second the purchaser of the car. Generally speaking, the law says that the principal is responsible for what his agent does as part of his job, or—to use the precise legal term—within the scope of the authority granted him.

Commercial life makes extensive use of the principle of agency. Salesmen, advertising men, auctioneers, real estate brokers, insurance brokers, store managers, deliverymen and persons in hundreds of other essential occupations make their living in whole or in part acting as agents for other people.

You can create an agency in a formal way or in an informal one. An agency is a contract and, like other contracts, it may be written or simply a verbal agreement or understanding (see section 168). Both the agent and the principal must assent to the agency agreement, or there can be no contract between them.

If you have any doubts about how your agent will serve you or about problems that may arise in the course of his service, it is best to write down the details of your agreement, preferably with the help of your lawyer. One familiar legal document used for this purpose is a power of attorney, or letter of attorney. The *power of attorney* gives an agent the authority to act for you in a specific matter or in your general affairs. An agent to whom you give your power of attorney is called an *attorney-in-fact,* as opposed to an attorney-at-law. The document should be sworn to in the presence of a notary public and must conform to the statutes of your state. You might want to execute a power of attorney if you are going to be absent from your business for a while and want someone else to handle all of your affairs with your full authority. Obviously, you will entrust this power only to someone in whom you have complete confidence. A husband often gives his wife a power of attorney and vice versa.

All states have adopted one or another version of the old English law known as the *statute of frauds* (see chart 9, page 208), which requires that certain contracts be in writing in order to prevent fraud. Fraud is more possible with oral contracts. Agency agreements dealing with land, such as contracts with real estate brokers, are covered by this statute, as are contracts for the sale of goods above a given value. Also covered are contracts which cannot be performed within a year. In most simple transactions, however, a verbal agreement is sufficient, and verbal contracts of agency far outnumber written ones.

If you are qualified to make a legally binding contract, you have the right to serve as a principal or an agent. This means that you must be of sound mind—a feebleminded person or an insane one cannot make a contract (see section 176).

Certain kinds of agents (see chart 34, page 492) must be licensed, among them electricians, plumbers, insurance brokers and real estate brokers. Without a license they have no power to make a legal contract or to use the courts to collect money that is due them.

A member of a partnership acts as the agent of his partners in the ordinary conduct of its business unless the partners have made an agreement to the contrary (see section 404).

Corporations can serve as principals or agents in any type of business consistent with the purpose for which they were chartered.

You can engage a minor as your agent if you have confidence that he will be able to do the job you require. But he has the power to annul his agency agreement with you, since he is under legal age (see section 176).

As an agent you cannot serve two principals with conflicting interests. Suppose that someone hired you to auction off his property; you could not sell it to a company in which you had a financial interest unless you did so with the permission of your principal. Your principal must be made aware of any extra or special advantages you derive from the agency he has granted you.

As we have pointed out, when the principal authorizes an agent to do something for him, the acts of the agent are binding upon him. The contract of agency usually grants you a clearly stated authority to perform certain duties your principal wants you to do. But sometimes you cannot fulfill your specific duties without performing various acts incidental to them. Let's say that your principal authorizes you to sell his products throughout the world, knowing, however, that your own sales organization is limited to the United States and Canada. You then have an implied authority to make a marketing arrangement with organizations in Europe and elsewhere and pay them the commission that is customary in such circumstances. Your principal is bound by the acts you perform in his behalf under this implied authority.

The subject of how much authority an agent possesses has many aspects. Take the case of an emergency in which an agent has to go beyond his authority; he has to make a quick decision to protect his principal from a loss but cannot get in touch with him. The agent's decision will be binding on his principal, even though it has not been expressly authorized. If the action of the agent results in a loss to his principal, that is the principal's misfortune; so long as the agent acted in good faith, the principal bears the responsibility.

Sometimes an agent may perform an act that clearly goes beyond the

489

scope of his authority, and yet his principal may accept the act in one way or another. Once the principal indicates acceptance, he is bound by the agent's act. To illustrate: A used-car salesman is authorized to guarantee for thirty days the automobiles he sells. But business is slow, so he tells a hesitant prospect he will guarantee for six months a car that the prospect appears to be interested in. Result: the sale is made. The salesman's employer sees the bill of sale with the longer guarantee and doesn't complain. Because he does not reject his salesman's unauthorized act, the law assumes that he has approved it. The law also assumes that the agent now has authority to continue this practice in the future. If the employer later refuses to honor the guarantee, the court will side with the salesman, even though he acted without express authorization.

You can bring an agency to an end whenever you wish. If you are an agent and you no longer wish to continue in that role, you can terminate it by giving notice to your principal. The principal can terminate your agency in the same way. However, if an agency is terminated in violation of an agreement—for example, where it was originally stipulated that the agency would last for a longer period of time—a suit can be brought for breach of contract against the party that terminates the agency. Other circumstances, such as bankruptcy on the part of the principal or the insanity or death of either principal or agent, may also bring the agency to a conclusion.

394. Third Parties • The *third party* in the law of agency is the person who deals with an agent working for a principal. A typical third party is someone who buys a house through a real estate broker (the agent) who is acting for the owner (the principal). You are also a third party when you buy insurance from an insurance broker who represents an insurance company.

If you are dealing with someone you believe is acting as agent but you are not sure, you should find out how much authority he has to act for his principal. It's not enough for him simply to tell you that he has the authority; you need more substantial proof, such as a power of attorney or a letter of confirmation from the principal. If the agent exceeds his authority, his principal can safely ignore the contract you have made with the agent. In such a case you do have a right to sue the agent for the amount of damage that you suffer. Examine with care any papers you are asked to sign, or, better still, have your lawyer review them. Often the principal has made very precise statements about what he will or will not do for his part of the bargain. An overenthusiastic agent may promise you otherwise, but it is what is stated in black and white that the court will look at. If the agent acted without his principal's consent, you can hold only the agent liable.

Where you deal with an agent who does not tell you that he is acting for someone else (see section 393), you may hold the agent liable. If you subsequently discover the identity of his principal, you may have a choice as to whom you hold liable.

YOUR PROFESSION

395. The Special Status of Professionals · In general, a professional person must have a license to practice his profession, a license that is increasingly available only to someone with a graduate degree. Each state has its own system of qualifying men and women to practice in one of the several professions. (Chart 34, page 492, will show you what professions must be licensed in the various states.)

Lawyers, doctors, dentists, architects, engineers, certified public accountants, teachers, clergymen of the various religions—all must comply with a variety of regulations concerning their education and professional knowledge. Policing is done in great part by national, state and local professional associations, which have behind them the full power of the courts for serious violations.

One respect that distinguishes doctors, lawyers and clergymen from other professionals is that information confided to them by clients or persons under their care is *privileged:* no court can compel that they repeat or divulge such information. The reason is that doctors and clergymen are often the subject of confidences given in hours of physical or emotional strain. The nature of such information, like the nature of much that is revealed to a lawyer by his client, is confidential, because its disclosure might tend to incriminate the patient or client.

As the professions become more highly organized and controlled throughout the United States, it becomes increasingly difficult for the professional to practice outside the state which first issued him a license. State standards for obtaining licenses vary, and a doctor who was licensed in one state may not easily get a license in another. He may have to go before a board of examining physicians in the other state to get a new license. The same is even truer for a lawyer, because his knowledge

OCCUPATIONS AND PROFESSIONS REQUIRING LICENSES

CHART 34

C = certification required
L = license required
N = no license required
P = permit required
R = registration required

	ALABAMA	ALASKA	ARIZONA	ARKANSAS	CALIFORNIA	COLORADO	CONNECTICUT	DELAWARE	D.C.	FLORIDA	GEORGIA	HAWAII	IDAHO	ILLINOIS	INDIANA	IOWA	KANSAS	KENTUCKY	LOUISIANA	MAINE	MARYLAND	MASSACHUSETTS	MICHIGAN
Accountant	L	L	C/R	L	L	L	L	L	L	L	L	L	L	L	L	L	L	L	L	L	L	L	L
Architect	L	L	N	L	L	L	L	L	L	L	L	L	L	L	L	L	L	L	L	L	L	L	L
Attorney	L	L	L	L	L	L	L	L	L	L	L	L	L	L	L	L	L	L	L	L	L	L	L
Barber	L	L	L	L	L	L	L	L	L	L	L	L	L	L	L	L	L	L	L	L	L	L	L
Beautician	L	L	L	L	L	L	L	L	L	L	L	L	L	L	L	L	L	L	L	L	L	L	L
Chiropractor	L	L	L	L	L	L	L	L	L	L	L	L	L	L	L	L	L	L	L	L	L	L	L
Dental hygienist	L	L	L	L	L	L	L	L	L	L	L	L	L	L	L	L	L	L	L	L	L	L	L
Dentist	L	L	L	L	L	L	L	L	L	L	L	L	L	L	L	L	L	L	L	L	L	L	L
Electrician	N	N	N	N	L	L	L	L	L	N	L[2]	L	L	N	L	N	N	L	N	L	L	L	L
Embalmer	L	L	L	L	L	L	L	L	L	L	L	L	L	L	L	L	L	L	L	L	L	L	L
Engineer (professional)	L	L	N	L	L	L	L	L	L	L	L	L	L	L	L	L	L	L	L	L	L	L	L
Funeral director	N	L	L	L	L	L	L	L	L	L	L	L	L	L	L	L	L	L	L	L	L	L	L
Medical technician	L	N	N	N	N	N	N	N	L	L	L	N	N	N	N	N	N	N	N	L	N	N	N
Midwife	N	L	L/C	N	L	N	L	L	L	L	L	L	N	L	N	L	N	N	L	N	L	L	L
Motor vehicle dealer/salesman	N	R	L	N	L	L	L	N	L	L	L[5]	L	L	L	L/N	L	N	L	L	L/N	L	N	L
Nurse (practical)	L	L	L	L	L	L	L	L	L	L	L	L	L	L	L	L	L	L	L	L	L	L	L
Nurse (public health)	L	L	L/C	N	L	L	L	L	L	N	N	N	N	L	L	L	N	N	N	N	L	L	L
Nurse (registered)	L	L	L	L	L	L	L	L	L	L	L	L	L	L	L	L	L	L	L	L	L	L	L
Optician	N	L	L	L	L	N	L	N	N	L	L	L	L	L	L	N	L	N	N	N	L	L	L
Optometrist	L	L	L	L	L	L	L	L	L	L	L	L	L	L	L	L	L	L	L	L	L	L	L
Osteopath	L	L	L	L	L	L	L	L	L	L	L	L	L	L	L	L	L	L	L	L	L	L	L
Pharmacist	L	L	L	L	L	L	L	L	L	L	L	L	L	L	L	L	L	L	L	L	L	L	L
Physical therapist	L	L	L	L	L	L	L	L	L	L	L	L	L	L	L	L	L	L	L	L	L	L	L
Physician/surgeon	L	L	L	L	L	L	L	L	L	L	L	L	L	L	L	L	L	L	L	L	L	L	L
Plumber	N	N	N	L	L	L	L	N	L	N	L	L	L	L	N	L	N	L	L	L	L	L	L
Podiatrist (chiropodist)	L	L	L	L	L	L	L	L	L	L	L	L	L	L	L	L	L	L	L	L	L	L	L
Psychoanalyst	N	N	L	N	N	N	N	L	L	N	N	N	N	L	N	C	N	L	N	N	L	N	L
Psychologist	L	L	C/L	L	L	L	L	L	L	L	L	L	L	L	L	C	L	L	L	L	L	L	L
Real estate broker/salesman	L	L	L	L	L	L	L	L	L	L	L	L	L	L	L	L	L	L	L	L	L	L	L
Surveyor	L	L	N	L	L	L	L	L	L	L	L	L	L	L	L	L	L	L	L	L	L	L	L
Teacher	C	L	C	L	L	L	C	L	L	L	L	N	L	L	L	L	L	L	L	L	L	N	L
Veterinarian	L	L	L	L	L	L	L	L	L	L	L	L	L	L	L	L	L	L	L	L	L	L	L

(1) "Professional" nurse. (2) Electrical contractor.

The occupations and professions most commonly licensed in the states are listed here. The differences between licensing, certification, issuing of a permit and registration reflect the wording of the local statutes. In general, a higher standard of professional qualification is required for a license or certificate. All give permission to practice. (See sections 389, 395).

MINNESOTA	MISSISSIPPI	MISSOURI	MONTANA	NEBRASKA	NEVADA	NEW HAMPSHIRE	NEW JERSEY	NEW MEXICO	NEW YORK	NORTH CAROLINA	NORTH DAKOTA	OHIO	OKLAHOMA	OREGON	PENNSYLVANIA	RHODE ISLAND	SOUTH CAROLINA	SOUTH DAKOTA	TENNESSEE	TEXAS	UTAH	VERMONT	VIRGINIA	WASHINGTON	WEST VIRGINIA	WISCONSIN	WYOMING
L	L	L	L	L	L	L	L	L	L	L	L	L	C	L	L	L	L	L	L	L	L	L	C	L	L	L	L
L	L	L	L	L	L	L	L	L	L	L	L	L	L	L	L	L	L	L	L	L	L	L	L	L	L	L	L
L	L	L	L	L	L	L	L	L	L	L	L	L	L	L	L	L	L	L	L	L	L	L	L	L	L	L	L
L	L	L	L	L	L	L	L	L	L	L	L	L	L	L	L	L	L	L	L	L	L	L	L	L	L	L	L
L	L	L	L	L	L	L	L	L	L	L	L	L	L	L	L	L	L	L	L	L	L	L	L	L	L	L	L
L	L	L	L	L	L	L	L	L	L	L	L	L	L	L	L	L	L	L	L	L	L	L	L	L	L	L	L
L	L	L	L	L	L	L	L	L	L	L	L	C	L	L	L	L	L	L	L	L	L	L	L	L	L	L	L
L	N	N	L	N	L^2	L	L^2	L	N	L	L	N	N	L	N	L	N	L	L	N	L	N	N	L	L	N	L
L	L	L	L	L	L	L	L	L	L	L	L	L	L	L	N	L	L	L	L	L	L	L	L	L	L	L	L
I	N	L	L	L	L	L	L	L	L	L	L	L	L	L	L	L	L	L	L	L	L	L	L	L	L	L	L
N	N	N	N	L	L	N	L^3	N	N	N	N	N	N	C	N	L	L	L	N	N	N	L	N	L	N	L	L
L	P	L	L	N	N	N	L	L	N	L	N	L	N	N	L	L	L	N	N	N	L	N	L	L	L	N	L
L	N	N	L/N	L	L	N	N	L	L	N	N	L	L	N	L	L	N	L/N	L	N	L	N	N	L	L	L	N
L	L	L	L	L	L	L	L	L	L	L	L	L	L	L	L	L	L	L	L	L	L	L	L	L	L	L	L
L	L	N	L	L	N	L	N	L	L	N	L	N	N	L	N	L	L	L	L	N	L	N	L	L	N	L	L
L	L	L	L	L	L^1	L	L	L	L	L	L	L	L	L	L	L	L	L	L	L	L	L	L	L	L	L	L
N	N	N	N	N	L	N	L^4	N	L	L	L	N	N	N	R	L	L	L	N	L	N	L	N	L	L	N	N
L	L	L	L	L	L	L	L	L	L	L	L	L	L	L	L	L	L	L	L	L	L	L	L	L	L	L	L
L	L	L	L	L	L	L	L	L	L	L	L	L	L	L	L	L	L	L	L	L	L	L	L	L	L	L	L
L	L	L	L	L	L	L	L	L	L	L	L	L	L	C	L	L	L	L	L	L	L	L	L	L	L	L	L
L	L	L	L	L	L	L	L	L	L	L	L	L	L	L	L	L	L	L	L	L	L	L	L	L	L	L	L
L	L	L	L	L	L	L	L	L	L	L	L	L	L	L	L	L	L	L	L	L	L	L	L	L	L	L	L
L	N	N	L	N	N	N	N	L	N	L	L	N	L	L	R	L	L	L	L	L	L	L	N	L	L	L	N
L	L	L	L	L	L	L	L	L	L	L	L	L	L	L	L	L	L	L	L	L	L	L	L	L	L	L	L
N	N	N	L	N	L	N	N	N	N	N	L	N	L	N	L	N	L	N	N	L	N	N	L	L	N	L	N
L	L	N	L	L	L	L	L	L	L	L	L	N	L	L	L	L	L	L	L	L	L	N	L	L	L	N	L
L	L	L	L	L	L	L	L	L	L	L	L	L	L	L	L	L	L	L	L	L	L	L	L	L	L	L	L
L	L	L	L	L	L	L	L	L	L	L	L	L	L	N	L	L	L	L	L	L	L	L	N	L	C	L	L
L	C	L	C	L	L	L	L	L	C	L	L	C	L	C	L	L	L	L	L	L	L	L	C	L	L	L	L
L	L	L	L	L	L	L	L	L	L	L	L	L	L	L	L	L	L	L	L	L	L	L	L	L	L	L	L

(3) Public health laboratory technician.　(4) Ophthalmic technician.　(5) Used-car dealers only.

of various state laws and regulations is absolutely essential to his work.

Law and medicine are two professions in which it is becoming increasingly risky to make mistakes. The number of suits brought against lawyers and doctors for what is called malpractice is rising steadily. Neither the legal nor the medical profession is growing as fast as the country's population, and the demands on lawyers' and doctors' time are greater every year. Pressure too often means too little attention or not enough care, which in turn is likely to result in a mistake that may have a damaging effect on the client or the patient. Insufficient attention to a patient in the recovery room of a hospital may result in permanent brain damage. An honest but nevertheless important mistake in a lawyer's advice to a businessman about his rights under a contract or his duties under a statute may lose the client a good deal of money or subject him to a heavy fine or penalty.

The general public no longer has the awe of the professional men it once had, and judges and especially juries have been found very willing to award substantial damages when suits are brought by aggrieved patients and clients. To protect themselves, doctors purchase insurance policies to provide them with the funds needed for these damage awards, and medical societies are coming to their and the hospitals' help by retaining the services of lawyers to handle such suits. Lawyers are finding it increasingly possible—and desirable—to buy insurance against legal actions brought against them by clients.

396. Medicine and Related Professions · The legal regulation of medical practice is in the hands of the state. Each state has its own licensing law, or medical practice act, which sets forth the requirements that a physician must meet to be admitted to practice. These laws differ from one state to the next.

A license to practice medicine can be suspended or revoked if the physician fails to meet the standards set by the medical practice act of his state. Some of the reasons for revoking a license are advertising, conviction of a felony, mental incapacity, drug addiction, alcoholism and unprofessional conduct.

The states also give licenses to optometrists and podiatrists. Optometrists are licensed to dispense eyeglasses and to supervise exercises to strengthen the muscles of the eyes and their coordination, but they are not allowed to treat eye diseases or practice medicine or surgery. Their adherence to ethical standards is supervised by their professional association, the American Optometric Association.

Podiatrists, like optometrists, are specialists. They diagnose and treat ailments of the foot and perform minor surgery on the feet but are not allowed by law to treat other diseases. A national organization with affiliated state societies (to which most podiatrists belong) sees to it that practitioners conform to approved ethical policies.

Chiropractors and osteopaths are also licensed.

Registration or licensing is required for various specialties associated with medicine, such as nursing or therapy. To be allowed to use the word *registered* in connection with your occupation, as in the case of a nurse, you must have satisfied the requirements of the state body in charge of your specialty. However, in most cases you may practice your occupation even if you have not been registered, so long as you do not use that designation. If your occupation is subject to licensing, you cannot practice unless you have complied with the state licensing act.

The principal association establishing the code of medical standards is the American Medical Association (AMA). The association is made up of state associations, which in turn consist of county or local medical societies. Professional standards are also set by hospitals and clinics to provide for efficient administration and good patient care.

According to the AMA's Principles of Medical Ethics, every patient has the privilege of selecting his physician and of discharging him at will. He is also free to choose his pharmacist, optician or other medical auxiliary. By the same token, a doctor is free to choose his patients. However, he is expected to answer any call for help in an emergency. If he takes a case, he should not withdraw from it without making certain that the patient will continue to obtain adequate care.

The fee the doctor charges you should be in keeping with the kind of service he has given and the amount you can afford to pay. He is forbidden to receive a commission for referring a patient to another practitioner or to pay a commission when a patient has been referred to him.

If you are being treated by one doctor and another one has reports or other information that bears on your condition, he should send that information at once to the doctor handling your case, if you ask him to.

Since new medications and methods of treatment are continually being developed, special rules must be set for their use in experiments. Your doctor must obtain your consent before he performs an experiment on you, and you must be aware of the facts in the matter. The work must be done under careful medical supervision. Moreover, so far as is possible, any risk in the experiment should have been explored in experiments with animals.

Earlier we stated that the state can suspend or revoke a physician's license if he fails to meet the standards of the medical practice act. A hospital or a county medical society will also take steps against a physician charged with misconduct.

The standards that a medical society sets for its members are supervised by a committee on ethics. If you feel that a doctor has acted unethically, you should make your complaint to the appropriate committee in your state or locality. When a doctor is accused of violating the society's ethical code, he has a right to a hearing. The AMA requires that he be given a copy of the complaint and allowed sufficient time to prepare his defense. After all the evidence has been presented on both sides, the committee may decide to take disciplinary action. It can admonish, reprimand, suspend or expel the erring member. The member in turn has the right to appeal to a state committee for a review of the decision of the local committee. In certain circumstances he may carry his appeal to the Judicial Council of the AMA.

397. Law • Rules for admission of lawyers to practice in the courts of the United States are set by individual states. With few exceptions, applicants must pass an examination administered under the control of the state courts. To qualify for the examination the applicant must have received a college degree and the degree of Bachelor of Laws or Doctor of Laws upon completion of three years of daytime study or four years of evening study at an accredited law school.

Standards of professional ethics or behavior are set by the American Bar Association, which is the largest nationwide association of lawyers. These standards of ethics have been formally adopted by the courts of many states and are firmly enforced. Enforcement is in the hands of the courts, which usually act on the motion either of local bar associations within the courts' jurisdiction or of state prosecuting attorneys. Penalties for violation of these standards range from a reprimand to disbarment. An attorney who is disbarred in effect loses his license to practice law. If he practices despite having been disbarred, he is subject to prosecution for committing a crime and may be heavily fined or imprisoned or both. Complaints about unethical practices by a lawyer should be made to the local bar association (see sections 637–640).

An attorney who is admitted to practice law in one state has no right to practice in another without meeting that other state's requirements. Between some states there is an agreement of reciprocity, under which a lawyer who has practiced in one state for more than five years will be licensed to practice in another. These reciprocal agreements are not common. Where there is no such agreement, he may be allowed to appear for a client on an interim basis. In some states he must take the regular bar examination given all those who seek licenses for the first time.

Federal courts require lawyers to obtain permission to practice before them, but such permission is a matter of routine for lawyers of adequate legal education and good reputation. Several federal governmental agencies impose a further requirement that lawyers handling cases before them obtain specific approval before doing so.

For a complete discussion of your relationship with your lawyer, see chapter 14, page 719.

398. Architecture · Architects must be licensed or registered in order to practice their profession. All states, as well as the District of Columbia, have established qualifications for architects and give examinations to candidates. The major professional association in the field is the American Institute of Architects (AIA), whose ethical code is known as the Standards of Professional Practice.

The code points out that in rendering professional services to his client the architect acts as agent and adviser, and his advice must be sound and impartial. An architect, according to this code, must serve the interests of his client and the public with competence. Paid advertising or exaggerated publicity is prohibited to him. In addition he is forbidden to engage in building contracting.

Before beginning a project he must determine, together with his client, its scope, the services he is to perform and his compensation for them and must confirm the understanding in writing. He must keep his client informed of probable costs as they develop and must not give any guarantee about the total cost, since the actual figure is beyond his control. His compensation should be based on the value of his services.

Since the architect serves his client as an agent, the code emphasizes certain ethical facets of the law of agency (see sections 393, 394) that he must observe. He must keep his obligation to his client foremost and renounce any interests, personal or financial, that could compromise it. Thus, the only compensation he can accept is from his client.

If an institute member is disciplined by a state board of licensing or registration for infringing its rules or violating state law, the case must be reviewed by the National Judiciary Board of the AIA, which may also recommend action against him: censure, suspension or termination of membership. Censure is an official reprimand that is publicized among

497

the membership; it entails no loss of rights. Suspension means that the architect can no longer use the initials "AIA" after his name or represent himself as a member of the institute, since the institute, for the period of suspension, does not classify him as a member. When the suspension period comes to an end, the architect automatically regains his status as a member in good standing. If the judicial decision is termination, the member is expelled and loses all rights. However, after three years he may apply for readmission to the institute.

399. Professional Engineering · To practice, a professional engineer must be accepted for registration under the law of his state. This does not mean that anyone who does any kind of engineering work must be registered. But if a man calls himself an engineer or offers his services as an engineer, he must obtain a certificate of registration. The certificate tells the public that he is fully qualified to practice his profession.

State laws vary in their details, but by and large they follow the standards and procedures of the Model Law issued by the National Council of Engineering Examiners.

The state board has the power to administer a reprimand or to suspend, refuse to renew, or revoke a certificate of registration if its owner is guilty of various violations. Among these are gross neglect, incompetence and misconduct in the practice of engineering and any crime involving moral turpitude. A code of ethics or rules of professional conduct established by the state board must also be obeyed or the same penalties may be invoked.

At any hearing the accused person may be represented by counsel and has the right to cross-examine witnesses. He may also call witnesses in his defense. If he believes that the board's decision in his case is unjust, he is entitled to file an appeal with the proper court. A registrant whose certificate has been revoked may apply to the board to have it reissued.

State laws provide penalties for individuals or firms that practice engineering without being registered, pretend they are registered or give false information to the board in connection with an application for registration. The accused is charged with a misdemeanor and may be sentenced to pay a fine or suffer imprisonment or both.

There are a number of national engineering societies, such as the National Society of Professional Engineers, the American Society of Mechanical Engineers and the American Institute of Mining, Metallurgical and Petroleum Engineers. All of these have endorsed the Model Law and enforce standards of professional conduct among their mem-

498

bers. Individuals generally belong to state branches of these societies. When an accusation of failure to comply with the rules is brought against a member, the branch holds a formal hearing. If the accused is found guilty, the penalties may include a reprimand, suspension and expulsion. Thus a guilty person may be punished by his own professional society as well as by state law.

The code of ethics of the National Society of Professional Engineers requires an engineer to be honest in all estimates and reports. If a project looks as though it will be unsuccessful, he must tell this to his employer or client. In the performance of his duties, he must have proper regard for the safety of the public. If he observes conditions that may endanger public safety, he must notify the proper authority. He must also pledge not to prepare any plans of a design not consistent with accepted engineering standards.

As an agent, an engineer must try to avoid any conflict of interest. He must inform his employer of any business connections or interests that may influence his judgment or the quality of his services. An engineer must not accept compensation from more than one interested party for the same work unless he has the consent of all interested parties. Disclosure of confidential information about the technical processes or business affairs of his client or employer is forbidden.

400. Accounting · The certified public accountant's certificate is the mark that he is recognized as a professional in his field. You do not have to obtain a certificate to work as an accountant, and many competent people employed in that profession never qualify for one. However, the certificate, as an official acknowledgment of competence to practice in the principal areas of accounting, generally opens the door to advancement and to the more important, more demanding jobs in the field.

Every state varies somewhat in its procedures for issuing CPA certificates and licenses to practice. However, the certified public accountant title is unique in that it is based upon a uniform national examination that is prepared, administered and graded by the American Institute of Certified Public Accountants.

The Code of Professional Ethics of the American Institute of Certified Public Accountants states that its members shall hold the affairs of their clients in strict confidence, observe accepted standards of accounting, promote sound, informative reporting and maintain high standards.

As a member of the institute, an accountant must not express an opinion on the financial statements of a firm unless he is independent of

499

it—that is, he must not have a financial or other interest in the firm. He must not render professional services for which the fees will be dependent upon his findings.

Much of the code is concerned with technical standards. An accountant is prohibited from giving an opinion on a financial statement unless he or a member of his firm has in fact examined it. However, he may rely in part on the reports of other certified public accountants. If he knows of a material fact that is not disclosed in financial statements, which are misleading as a result of that omission, he is under an obligation to reveal that fact.

An accountant is not allowed to advertise his services or his professional attainments. Nor may he solicit clients. Competitive bidding for accounting jobs is also an improper practice. Standards for operating procedures and relations with fellow members are regulated by other provisions of the code.

When a member of the institute is charged with a violation of the Code of Professional Ethics, the ethics committee investigates the circumstances. If the facts warrant it, the member is summoned before the trial board. The member may be represented by an attorney if he wishes. If he is found guilty, he may be admonished, suspended or expelled.

The state board, being a governmental agency, may impose more severe penalties. A certified public accountant who has violated state regulations can have his certificate suspended or revoked.

401. Teaching · Millions of men and women are engaged in public education in elementary and secondary schools. If we add those who teach in private and parochial schools, the number is even bigger. Perhaps because of their large numbers and the differing requirements of the states, teachers are not as thoroughly unified or organized as members of other professions.

Most teachers are public or civil service employes, in contrast to other professions, and qualifications for employment vary somewhat with the local school boards or other employing agencies. However, the state department of education sets basic requirements for certification of teachers in public schools. The requirements for certification differ with the state, often to a considerable extent. In more than half the states teachers in private schools need not be certified.

In the majority of states a teacher must be a citizen of the United States or file a declaration of intent to become one. Another common requirement is that he sign an oath of allegiance to the United States and to the

YOUR JOB OR PROFESSION—
AND YOUR INCOME

Salaries vary considerably from one field of work to another, as the chart below demonstrates. Managers and executives are in the highest income bracket, closely followed by professionals. Lowest incomes are found among farm workers and the unemployed, although even in these areas the median income has increased significantly.

Median Money Income of Employed Civilians
by Sex and Occupation

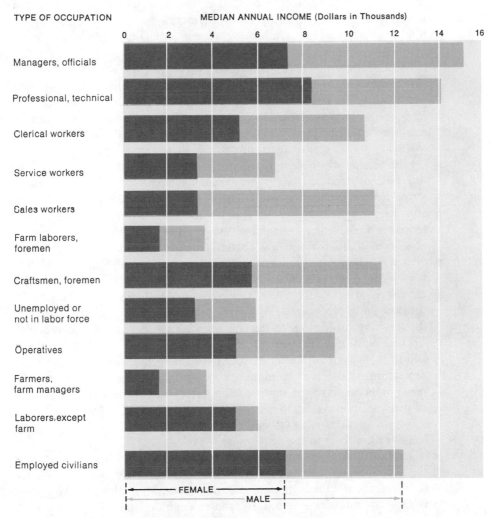

TYPE OF OCCUPATION

MEDIAN ANNUAL INCOME (Dollars in Thousands)

0 2 4 6 8 10 12 14 16

Managers, officials

Professional, technical

Clerical workers

Service workers

Sales workers

Farm laborers, foremen

Craftsmen, foremen

Unemployed or not in labor force

Operatives

Farmers, farm managers

Laborers, except farm

Employed civilians

FEMALE

MALE

The very considerable discrepancy between salaries paid to male workers and those paid to female workers in the same field is clearly shown by the overlying colored bars (female median income) on the graph above.

state. He may also be required to submit a certificate of good health.

Tenure is a term with special meaning in the teaching profession. *Tenure* is an assurance to certified employes that so long as they perform their services in a satisfactory manner, their contracts will remain in effect. Often a teacher has probationary status for the first two to five years of employment. Then when his contract is renewed for the following year he achieves tenure. If there are just grounds for dismissal of a teacher with tenure, the local board of education must follow a procedure that will guarantee him fair treatment. For example, the school board has to give the teacher with tenure a statement of the charges against him, and he has a right to a hearing. (Some typical grounds for discharge are discussed later.)

Most of the states (over 70 percent) have tenure laws. In some of the others the statute regarding discharge requires only that if a contract is not going to be renewed, the teacher must be given advance notice. If he is not notified by the date stipulated in the statute (during the spring semester), his contract is automatically renewed for the following year. With this type of continuing contract law, there are no provisions for telling the teacher why his contract is not being renewed.

In recent decades teacher organizations have been working hard to strengthen their claims to professional status. They are doing this at the state level by pressing for the enactment of professional practices legislation. In California, for example, the law now provides for enforcement of a code of ethics through a commission of the state educational association. If charges are brought to dismiss a teacher with tenure, a hearing must be held in superior court, and the local board may go ahead with the dismissal only if the court rules in favor of it. Legislation in Kentucky provides for a professional practices commission, which is nominated by the teaching profession, to develop standards for professional practice. The commission makes recommendations to the state board of education and to local boards of education that will help to improve the teaching profession. It also has the authority to reprimand teachers and to make recommendations to the state board of education in cases concerning the suspension and revocation of certificates. Such legislation has been passed in only a small number of states, but the movement is bound to make headway in others in the near future.

In the forefront of the movement to help the teaching profession in the United States assume responsibility for the conduct and performance of its members is the National Education Association (NEA). An organization of professional educators, the association traces its history back to 1857, when it was originally founded under the name of the National Teachers Association.

The Code of Ethics of the Education Profession adopted by the NEA is a model of codes of professional ethics that have been or are likely to be introduced into state law. There are four principles, or areas of commitment, in the code: the commitment of the educator to the student, to the public, to the profession and to professional employment practices. A teacher must pledge not to restrain a student from independent action in the pursuit of learning or deny him access to different points of view. Subject matter should not be distorted or suppressed. The teacher must protect students from conditions that may prejudice their safety or learning; he may not discriminate against them or in their favor because of race, color, creed or national origin. A teacher is prohibited from using for his private advantage his professional relationships with students. He cannot tutor for personal remuneration a student assigned to his class, unless there is no other teacher available. Also, unless he has a compelling reason for acting otherwise, he must not disclose any confidential information he acquires in the course of his work, just as doctors and lawyers are bound to respect their clients' confidences.

In dealing with the public, a teacher is forbidden by the code to misrepresent an institution with which he is affiliated. He must not use institutional privileges for personal gain or promote partisan political activities or political candidates. Furthermore, he must pledge that he will not interfere with a fellow educator's exercise of his political rights and responsibilities. Also on the forbidden list are the accepting of gifts or favors that might influence his judgment as an educator and the offering of services or gifts for special advantages to himself. Penalties for violation of these ethical principles vary depending on the area, the school system and whether or not they have been enacted into law in the particular state. They vary from reprimand to loss of the teacher's position.

The local school board, as we have seen, may discharge a teacher or fail to renew his contract. Typical grounds for terminating a teacher's contract are inefficiency, incompetence, failure to obey reasonable rules of the board, moral misconduct, disability as established by medical evidence and elimination of the teacher's position. States with tenure laws, in addition to providing for a hearing for the accused teacher, often specify that the discharged teacher may file an appeal, frequently in a court in the district where the school board is located. Teachers who have acquired tenure have greater protection against dismissal than new or probationary teachers.

503

402. The Three Basic Forms of Business • American society is a business society. All of us are involved with business in one way or another almost every day of our lives. Many of us make our living by working for some kind of business enterprise. We are dependent on the services of an endless variety of enterprises, large and small: banks, insurance companies, automobile salesrooms, service stations, fuel supply companies, real estate agencies, supermarkets and drugstores, among others. Some of us are the owners, or someday are likely to be the owners, of businesses. And an increasing number of us are part owners of American enterprise in the form of stocks and bonds that we have purchased. Because business plays so prominent a role in our lives, it is useful to have some knowledge of how it is organized.

Fundamentally, there are three major types of business organization. These are the individual proprietorship, the partnership and the corporation. Each type of organization has its strong or weak points that make it particularly suitable for certain specific purposes and unsuitable for others. If you are thinking about going into business or changing the form of your business, naturally your first move should be to consult with an attorney, preferably one well versed in business matters, to determine which type of organization is most appropriate to your needs, how to get started in business, and how to cope with problems. The following sections will help you to understand your attorney's legal advice.

403. The Individual Ownership • Individual ownership, known to lawyers as the sole proprietorship, is the simplest and most basic type of business structure. It is best suited to the small business that is just getting started. Setting up an individual proprietorship involves fewer legal procedures than either the corporation or the partnership. Usually you need only obtain a license to do business from your city or local government. In addition, the sole proprietorship is subject to the least amount of regulation by government agencies. Finally, this type of business is not taxed as a separate entitly; instead, the owner is simply taxed as an individual.

If you are the independent sort, with special skills or drive, this is the kind of business likely to appeal to you. As the sole proprietor of your own operation, you—and you alone—are in the driver's seat. You reap the complete rewards of your efforts and your business.

If there are no rewards but only losses, those are entirely yours, too. Legally you are responsible for the obligations or debts that you incur in the course of your business affairs. Your liability is limited not just to the amount of capital you invest in your business; your savings, your car and your other assets may be claimed by the people to whom you owe money. You have what lawyers call *unlimited liability*.

If you go into business as a sole owner, you have a choice of operating under your own name or under a company name. A person who plans to do business under a company name should check with his attorney for the state regulations in such a case. If you use anything but your own name for your business, the law calls the made-up name a *fictitious* or *assumed name*. (It's important, in selecting a fictitious name, that you do not choose one that is already being used by another company in your area. Such a name can confuse the public, and the first user can obtain a court order, under the law of unfair competition, to make you stop doing business under that name.) You may be required to file a certificate bearing the fictitious name and your own name and address in the office of the county clerk or a similar office.

Instead of setting up a business of your own, you may decide to buy one that is already established. This has several advantages. You can see the business in operation and examine its books; you can get the owner's help in learning how to deal with problems common to the business.

Although the business is a going concern, you need the advice of your attorney and accountant before you purchase, to be certain you are not making any serious mistakes. It takes experience in the buying and selling of businesses to avoid the traps that await an overoptimistic beginner. For example, the owner might give you an inflated picture of the prospects of the business and charge you too much for it. You should know whether there are any unpaid taxes or debts, or any unsatisfied judgments against the business for which you might be held responsible. The equipment should be examined closely. If the premises are held by a lease, you should find out when it expires; the landlord may be planning to increase the rent before granting a new lease. An aggressive, more up-to-date competitor may have opened up nearby, threatening the profits of the business you want to buy. In some states the law requires you to publish a notice of the transfer of the business in local newspapers, and you may face a penalty if you do not comply.

404. The Partnership • Partnership is a more complicated form of business organization than individual ownership. The law sets no limit on

505

how many people may enter into a partnership—there can be as many as 100 or more partners, but there must be at least two. They join together as co-owners of a business that they operate, hopefully for profit.

A partnership begins with an agreement, which can be spoken, written or simply a matter of understanding. Good friends who decide to form a partnership may not feel it necessary to reduce their arrangement to writing. Experience, however, proves that to avoid misunderstandings in the future, it makes sense to draw up an agreement, with the help of an attorney, outlining the basic features of the partnership. This document should describe the proposed business in detail. It usually deals with partnership name, names of partners, purposes of the partnership, location of the business and the investment or contribution of each partner (realty, equipment, cash, services). It also provides for the partners' sharing of losses and profits, the responsibilities and powers of each (particularly with regard to making purchases and disbursing the partnership's money), and voluntary or compulsory retirement. Finally, the agreement should provide for arbitration or other resolution of disputes among the partners, and for the dissolution of the partnership. (The dissolution of a partnership is discussed in section 412.)

Where a partnership agreement does not cover all these points or is not in written form, the law has established rules that cover the common problems that may arise. For example, unless the agreement provides otherwise, all the partners have a right to participate equally in running the business and all share equally its profits and losses, regardless of whether they invest capital and services or simply services. A partnership may be terminated at the request of any of the partners if no date is specified for bringing the arrangement to an end.

There are two chief kinds of partnership, the general partnership and the limited partnership. By far the more common is the *general partnership,* which has a good deal in common with an individually owned business. It is almost the same type of organization, but it has more than one owner. The number of partners (who are co-owners) gives the partnership one of its major advantages. Because the partners' combined resources are larger than those of a single person, more capital may be available to them, and it may also be possible for them to obtain more credit. In addition, the partners share the management of the business, which means that the burden of work and responsibility does not all fall on one pair of shoulders.

Like the individual proprietorship, the general partnership has unlimited liability. If the business is sued, the partners are all personally liable, and they may be obliged to satisfy judgments out of their personal property. Under the law, those provisions of the partnership agreement that deal with the sharing of losses between partners can have no effect on each partner's full liability to outsiders for debts and judgments.

If you are thinking of going into partnership, you should choose your partners carefully. They should be sound, conscientious money managers, because if they make mistakes you may have to pay for them; the law holds that each partner is responsible for the other partners' actions within the scope of the partnership business. But you do have certain built-in protections: all the partners must consent to any sale of the company's property, and the partnership agreement may require unanimous consent for other important decisions. If one partner makes an expensive mistake, however, all the partners have to share the cost—even if it means making it up out of their own bank accounts. If one co-owner commits a dishonest or harmful action in the conduct of the business, his partners are equally and individually responsible, even if they took no part in the action. The law considers every partner the agent of the other partners; they share a joint liability.

Accurate records of the business must be maintained and made available to all partners to inspect. The partnership's property should be used only in the interests of the business. Occasionally, however, if all partners agree, the property may be used for personal purposes. But in general you cannot draw on partnership funds to repay a personal debt or pledge the property of the partnership as security for a personal loan. If you lend money to the partnership after your original investment, you have a right to interest and also to its return.

So far we have been describing a general partnership. A *limited partnership* is quite a different arrangement. One or more limited partners may join a business with the general partners. However, there must always be at least one general partner. The term *limited* in the title of the limited partner refers to his liability, which will not exceed the amount of his original investment in the business, whether property or cash. He does not have a joint responsibility with the general partners. He is entitled to a share in the profits of the business, but he has little or no control over its management. His precise status should be spelled out in detail in the partnership agreement. A limited partnership is often created by a business when it wants to obtain additional funds. You cannot become a limited partner by contributing only your services.

Most states require that when a partnership includes a limited partner, a sworn document, called a *limited partnership certificate,* be filed with

507

the county clerk or some other state officer. This document states the amount of capital supplied by the limited partner and the percentage of profit he will be entitled to. The information in the certificate must also be published in two local newspapers. This makes it clear to the public that the liability of the limited partner extends so far and no further.

The rules for the use of a name for a partnership are much like those for an individual proprietorship. If you wish, you can string together the names of the individual general partners (names of limited partners may not be used), or you can make up a fictitious name. Again, you must take care not to use a name similar to one already in use in your locality. A fictitious name must be registered.

If your partnership brings a lawsuit against someone, the suit can usually be brought either in the names of all the partners or in the partnership name.

Subject to certain exceptions, the law does not regard a partnership as a legal entity. For example, the partnership *is* considered a legal entity in case of bankruptcy. However, like the sole proprietorship, the partnership is not taxed as a separate entity; instead, the individual partners are taxed on earnings that they derive from it. But the federal tax law does require that the partnership, as an entity, file an information return with the Internal Revenue Service. (For details about business taxes and insurance, see sections 408, 498, 499. For the termination of these businesses see sections 409, 410.)

405. The Corporation • The third major form of business, and by far the most important, is the corporation. Despite the impressive ring of the term and the fact that most major business enterprises in the United States are organized in this form, corporations may be small businesses.

A corporation is a group of people who obtain a charter from the state government that grants them, as a unit, some of the legal rights, powers and liabilities of an individual human being for conducting any lawful activities. Regarded by the law as a person, a corporation may sell, buy and inherit property in its own name; it may even commit crimes and be tried and punished for them.

Most corporations are businesses operated for profit: they obtain capital by selling *stock*—units or shares of ownership in the corporation that can be given or sold to others. Such shares are usually in the form of certificates bearing the name of the owner. But there are also nonprofit or nonstock corporations with different features. Counties and cities are municipal corporations. Religious, charitable and cooperative corporations are other types. We are concerned with business corporations.

The most striking advantage that the corporation offers to business-men is the limited liability of its owners. A corporation obtains its financing by selling stock, or shares of ownership, and the liability of a stockholder in almost all situations is limited to the cost of the stock for which he subscribes. The capital of the corporation may be seized and sold to pay debts or court judgments, but the personal property of its officers and shareholders, in most instances, may not be touched.

A corporation has perpetual existence. Its founders or owners may die or sell their interest in it, but the corporation does not come to an end until it is formally dissolved by legal procedure.

In a partnership all the partners are individually liable for the wrongful actions of one if the wrong is done in the course of business. In a corporation the situation is very different. The officers are not responsible for a wrongful action by one of them unless he acted with their knowledge and consent. Only the responsible officer or director and the corporation may be sued for such wrongful acts.

Another advantage of the corporate form is that in most cases a shareholder can transfer his ownership share to another person without any difficulty. All he has to do is sell his stock. Then the corporation will register the name of the new owner of that stock.

Probably the chief disadvantage of the corporation lies in the amount of income taxes it must pay. The tax rate is usually higher on corporate income than it is on individual income. Naturally, all the salaries paid to employes may be deducted in figuring net income; in a small corporation the actual owners are usually included in this category, and their salaries and other deductions may reduce the tax greatly. But the larger corporation may pay substantial federal tax on its earnings, and shareholders who subsequently receive income in the form of dividends must also pay a tax on them.

Forming a corporation is a relatively simple matter, although it involves more legal procedures than either the partnership or the sole proprietorship. It also generally requires the payment of certain organization fees and initial franchise taxes. You should seek the guidance of an attorney if you are planning such a move.

To begin with, the new corporation needs a charter, or certificate of incorporation, which is granted by the state. As a rule, the state in which you will do most of your business is the place in which to seek incorporation. The legal requirements differ from state to state in a variety of important matters, such as taxes, business fees, requirements as to number of directors and their liabilities for the debts of the corporation, limitations on the activities of the corporation and rules for the issuing of stock. Some states place relatively few restrictions on the organization and activity of corporations, and therefore large corporations tend to be incorporated in those states. Delaware is particularly well known as a state favorable to corporate organization. A corporation is called a domestic corporation in the state in which it is organized and a foreign corporation in other states. A corporation that wants to do business in another state usually has to apply for the permission of that state before it can proceed.

State regulations usually require a corporation to have a minimum of three incorporators to apply for a charter. The articles of incorporation must cover a number of basic points: the name of the corporation, its address, the purpose of the corporation, the different classes of stock that it can issue and the number of shares in each class, as well as their par value. The articles also state the amount of capital the corporation will have to conduct its business and how much indebtedness it is authorized to incur. The names and addresses of the incorporators are included. These papers, after being signed by the incorporators in the presence of a notary public, are filed in the office of the secretary of state, who then issues a charter. Some states also require that a certified copy of the articles be filed with a county or local office.

You may select any name you wish for a new corporation if it is not deceptively similar to a name already in use in your area or wherever you will be doing business. Your attorney will suggest having a national service verify that the name you have selected is not established in some other state. If you do not take this inexpensive precaution, you may later find yourself prevented from using your corporate name by a company that has a prior right. In such a case the cost and trouble of changing your corporate name and familiarizing your clients or customers with the new name can be considerable.

The name of the business must show clearly that it is a corporation. This is commonly done by adding after the name the word "Incorporated" or "Corporation" or the abbreviation "Inc." or "Corp." In most states the word "Company," by itself, is not a sign of a corporation and does not satisfy the requirement of the law.

When a corporation has received its charter from the state, the first order of business is for the incorporators to hold a meeting. At this meeting they take the necessary steps to get the corporation going. The most important items on the agenda are the election of directors and

510

THE THREE BASIC KINDS OF BUSINESS

There are three basic kinds of business in our society. The first is the individual proprietorship or ownership, the second is the partnership and the third is the corporation. Each of these types of business organization has unique characteristics that make it more or less suitable for a specific kind of operation. For more details, see sections 402–405.

The Individual Ownership

More than half the business concerns in this country are owned by a single person. This kind of business is known legally as an individual ownership or proprietorship. It may be small, like a newsstand or a candy store, or it may be a fairly large company. The individual owner has great flexibility; he is responsible only to himself and he alone reaps the rewards of a successful operation. By the same token, however, he is entirely responsible for any debts or losses his company incurs in the course of business. Many such businesses are started from scratch by the owner. Others are purchased from a previous owner. In either case, the individual owner may operate under his own name or under a company name.

The Partnership

A partnership is a more complicated form of business than an individual ownership. Any number of people may enter into a partnership (of course there must be at least two), investing their money or their services or both in the business of which they are co-owners. Usually there is a written partnership agreement between them that sets out their rights and duties under the partnership. Unless the agreement provides otherwise, the partners share equally in the profits or the losses of the company. In a general partnership all the partners are liable for any business debts, and they may be obliged to make up deficits out of their own personal property. A partnership may be for a limited or for an indefinite term.

The Corporation

While only a small percentage of American businesses are corporations, they are by far the largest and most important ones. The corporation is a group of people who have banded together to do business and who have been granted a charter by the government which gives them, as a unit, some of the legal rights and powers of an individual. In other words, the law regards a corporation as a person. A corporation may own, buy, sell and inherit property in its own name. It may even commit a crime and be tried and punished for it. Most corporations get the capital necessary for their operations by selling stock—units or shares in the ownership of the company. If the business is successful, the profits are distributed to the stockholders in the form of dividends.

the adoption of "by-laws," the rules by which the corporation is to be operated.

The next step is the first meeting of the directors. The directors, responsible for the overall management of the business, have as their first task the appointment of officers who will run the corporation. In small corporations, the incorporators, directors and officers are frequently the same persons. They have an obligation to exercise their office in the interest of the shareholders and to behave diligently and prudently. The shareholders, as the owners of the corporation, may vote to remove directors and officers from office.

Often, when a corporation is first formed, it is owned completely by its founder and his family and friends. The stock in such a business—which is frequently described as a closed corporation—is not available to the public. The owners will not sell it because they want to keep control of the corporation exclusively within their own hands. The closed corporation, because it is usually a small family-run business, also enjoys special tax advantages. However, as the business grows, the owners may want to raise more capital by selling some of their stock to others. In the case of a large corporation, such a sale would be done with the help of an *underwriter,* a financial firm that advertises the stock and sells it to interested buyers. In the case of a very large public sale of stock, the transaction must first be registered with and approved by a federal commission (see section 480) as well as a state agency. The proceeds of the sale are then paid to the corporation.

406. Your Rights as a Stockholder • Corporations issue two fundamental kind of stock, common and preferred. Ownership is shown by a stock certificate, usually bearing your name and the signatures of at least two officers of the corporation. Your name is also entered in the books of the corporation as a stockholder of record.

Common stock is the ordinary capital stock of the company. If you own common stock, you are entitled to vote at the annual and special meetings of the corporation. (Some common stock is issued in two classes, only one of which entitles the owner to vote.) At these meetings directors are elected and reelected, and major matters affecting the corporate business are decided upon. If you do not choose to attend an annual meeting, you can appoint someone else to act as your proxy, or representative, and cast your vote. Usually the management of the company solicits the votes of shareholders who will not be present at meetings. If the company is a large one with many shareholders, most do not attend, so that control of the meeting and the company is usually in the hands of its directors and officers.

Preferred stock usually entitles you to the same voting rights as common stock. The difference between the two is that preferred stock entitles you to a fixed dividend every year, regardless of how much the company earns. Common stock, on the other hand, entitles you only to such dividends as the company declares; in a year with high profits you may receive higher dividends than owners of preferred stock; in a bad year, however, you may receive small or even no dividends.

If the corporation issues new stock, the shareholder has a right to buy a proportionate number of the new shares so that he can preserve his relative interest in the company; often the company issues warrants to its old stockholders that allow them a certain reduction in the price of new stock. The shareholder also has a right to inspect the books of the corporation if he has convincing reason to believe that it is being mismanaged. He may even bring a suit against the officials of a corporation if he possesses evidence that their policies are doing it serious harm. (For information about how a corporation is terminated, see section 413.)

407. Your Business Records • Good records are indispensable in operating a business. Even in a very small enterprise, it is important to keep careful track of costs, income and profit and loss. Tax collectors of the federal government, the state and the city need information from the records of your business. If you borrow money or work with credit, your suppliers and creditors will want to see your records. And if the business should suffer a loss, it is essential to have accurate records to show to insurance adjusters. All this takes time, but in the long run it will save you money and spare you possible legal problems. Your banker, accountant and lawyer can advise you about the records you should keep.

Your financial reports must be prepared in keeping with tax laws and with accepted principles of accounting. They should be drawn up in a consistent method from one year to the next. Thus you or other interested parties, such as a bank from which you are seeking a loan, can compare the records for a number of years and quickly determine the overall trends of the business—whether its profits are increasing or decreasing, and why.

All of your records should be kept in an orderly, organized way and filed so that they will be accessible if you need to produce them. The *statute of limitations* (see section 185) of your state, which indicates the period of time in which a lawsuit can be brought, should help you decide how long to preserve records relating to matters that may come up in litigation. Do not throw out any letters or records that might be required in a suit for fraud.

Make certain that you don't throw away any records that establish your deductions, credits, gross income and related matters. They should be kept in their original condition, without changes, or the Internal Revenue Service may reject them. All records relating to your tax returns—including ledgers, journals, cashbooks and the like—should be kept for six years.

If your business comes under the Fair Labor Standards Act (see section 372), you should keep payroll records and union agreements, records of your personnel and their earnings, schedules of time worked and similar records. Records that prove that you have fulfilled your obligations under the unemployment insurance program, the Social Security Act, the Federal Trade Commission Act and other federal, state and city laws should also be kept.

408. Taxes on Your Business • Every businessman has to face the problem of preparing tax returns for the federal government, and often for the state and city as well. By keeping careful records all through the year and drawing up your statement of profit and loss at year's end, you will have all the information you need for your federal income tax form. It is to your advantage to pay particular attention to the deductions allowed for your business. The most common are business expenses, business losses and the depreciation of equipment. Be sure you know the due dates for your federal tax payments—and state and city as well.

The withholding tax is one that every businessman who has regular employes must be concerned with. This is the pay-as-you-go tax you withhold from the wages of your staff and forward to the Internal Revenue Service (IRS) on the required dates. (Many states and some cities also have a withholding tax.) The IRS supplies you with withholding tables that tell you how much must be withheld from each employe's pay. You are required, for the purpose of this tax, to be able to show how many persons you had on your payroll during the year, the periods they were employed, how much you paid to each that was subject to the withholding tax, the dates they were paid and the amounts, as well as each exemption and deduction claimed by each employe. You also have to keep on file your employes' withholding exemption certificates. These certificates remain in effect until you receive amended ones from your employes, if their circumstances should change (marriage, children, etc.).

The Internal Revenue Service requires you to file with it on specified dates a quarterly report of the income tax and the social security tax that you withheld from your employes' wages. Along with your quarterly return, you must remit the amounts withheld for tax and social security to the Internal Revenue district director. You must also file annual statements showing the total amount of wages paid each employe and the total income tax and social security tax withheld from him. Your employes, including those who have left you before the end of the year, must each receive two copies of the year's withholding form (W-2) from you no later than January 31 of the following year.

Severe penalties can be imposed on an employer who fails to pay the taxes or file the forms required by law or who makes out false returns, including fines and interest charges on the unpaid amounts.

Certain types of businesses, such as corporations, which pay $10 or more in interest or dividends, are required to furnish the Internal Revenue Service and the recipients with statements of the sums paid.

If your business has one or more employes or you paid out total wages of at least $1,500, you must pay a federal unemployment tax (see section 432). The return has to be filed no later than January 31, and the tax is paid with it. You are required to pay an unemployment tax to the state. In many states still another payroll tax must be paid for workmen's compensation (see section 526).

Some products, such as gasoline, liquor and cigarettes and a wide variety of manufactured items, are subject to a federal excise tax, and so are some transactions. The excise tax is not considered a part of the price, and the retailer is forbidden to lead his customers to believe that he is absorbing the tax himself. It is essential to keep exact records of items subject to excise taxes not only for the returns you must fill out but also to enable you to substantiate your returns if they are questioned later.

Sales and use taxes are other items as to which the businessman may be required to file a return and make payment, usually quarterly, but in some states on a monthly basis. These taxes are levied by states and cities in increasing numbers. Your state or city revenue office or your accountant can tell you what the sales and use taxes are in your business and when returns must be filed and the taxes paid. In many localities there are exemptions; for example, clothing for minors under sixteen or gasoline sold to farmers may not be subject to the tax. You must be careful to distinguish such tax-exempt sales in your records. Deductions from gross sales may also be allowed for bad debts, trade-ins and similar items, and every retailer should be aware of these.

409. Terminating a Business • Terminating a business may be a simple matter or a complex one, depending on the kind of business and why and how it is brought to an end. Let's look at the three types of business organizations we have been discussing—the individual ownership, the partnership and the corporation—for the legal problems involved in dissolving them or disposing of them.

If you are the sole owner of a business, you can dissolve it or stop it whenever you wish. You do this by going into *liquidation:* you satisfy any contracts you have, collect your accounts receivable, sell your equipment and stock, pay off your debts and taxes and lock the door. You can liquidate your business without any governmental permission.

A similar procedure might be followed if you were to die. In that case the money realized by the liquidation would become part of your estate and would be distributed by your executor as provided in your will (see sections 588–594). A business does not have to be liquidated if its owner dies; he may leave it to a relative, or he may in his will appoint a trustee to manage it and pay the income to his survivors. If you own a business, you should examine these various approaches with your attorney and make the most appropriate decision about how your property should be handled after your death.

410. Selling Your Business • When the owner of a business decides to retire from it, he often looks for a purchaser. Selling a business poses just about as many problems as buying one (see section 403), and he needs the advice of an attorney and an accountant. The details will vary, but here are some of the main points to bear in mind.

Before you agree to sell your business, it is essential, if the premises are not your own property, to study the lease and its provisions for subletting (see section 272). If the lease doesn't allow you to sublet, you should get in touch with the landlord and obtain his consent to a transfer of the lease to the new tenant. The prospective buyer of your business will also want to know whether, and on what conditions, he can renew the lease at the end of its term.

Besides such obvious items as equipment and inventory on hand, many other factors enter into the price you will set on your business. You may, for example, have bought new fuel and paid up your insurance policies and rent for a period of time beyond the date of the sale, and you should consider whether to add these and other prepaid charges to the sales price. You should itemize these expenses at the date of closing and obtain compensation for them (see section 288).

The goodwill of customers and suppliers is a valuable item in certain kinds of businesses, notably those in which the reputation of the owner is a major asset. If you have developed an extensive clientele on the strength of your services, as the owners of retail businesses often do, you can place a substantial price on your trade name and goodwill. If these are included in the sale, you may have to agree not to reestablish your business for a stated number of years in the same area as your old business, so that you will not compete with the new owner.

It often happens that not everything in a business has been fully paid for. You may have purchased equipment and obtained a chattel loan on it (see section 452) or bought it on the installment plan. All of your liabilities of this or any other type should be made known to the buyer and evaluated in establishing the sales price of the business. The purchaser may agree to assume your liabilities as part of the deal, or you yourself may prefer to satisfy them.

All states have passed laws, known as *bulk transfer laws,* to protect the rights of creditors. These laws regulate bulk transfers, sales of businesses in whole or in large part. Their aim is to furnish creditors with an opportunity to request payment of money owed them before a business is disposed of. If the provisions of the state's bulk transfer law are not complied with, the courts can, at the request of the creditors, set aside the sale of the business or make some other provision to assure that either you or your purchaser will pay the debts when due.

Under this regulation you have to give the purchaser a list of your creditors, with their addresses and the amount of money you owe to each one. Within a certain number of days before the sale takes place, the purchaser is required to give notice of the sale to your creditors. You must also supply the purchaser with a complete list of every item included in the sale, as well as the price you originally paid for it. The purchaser has to keep this list for a specified length of time so that your creditors can check it if they want to.

As an alternative, before the sale you can pay off all of your creditors and supply the purchaser with a sworn statement that you have done so. You can also give a written guarantee that you will satisfy all of your obligations. Another possibility is to deposit in escrow enough money to cover all of your debts. This sum may be subtracted from the amount you realize from the sale.

How the purchase price will be paid is a matter of paramount concern to you as the seller. The common practice is for a down payment to be made when you and the purchaser agree on the sale and its price.

Then you receive the balance in a certified check on the closing date, when you formally transfer the property. If the buyer is not prepared to complete the payment at that time, other arrangements are possible. You may agree to accept one or more promissory notes, falling due at various dates convenient to both parties. You might also arrange for a mortgage on the real estate, if there is any, or a chattel loan on some of the movable property, to secure the payments specified in the promissory notes. In return you must guarantee the buyer that the business is free of liens, mortgages or other debts (except those that he has agreed to take over as part of the deal) and that you have the full legal right to transfer it to him.

411. Bankruptcy • A business may also be dissolved by bankruptcy. Bankruptcy can be of either of two types, involuntary or voluntary. If a business cannot pay its debts, it can voluntarily petition the U.S. district court to declare it bankrupt. Detailed schedules listing the firm's assets, liabilities and creditors must be filed with the petition. In an involuntary bankruptcy the creditors file the petition. If there are fewer than twelve of them, any one creditor who has a claim of $500 or more can file; if there are twelve or more creditors, at least three must file. To be adjudged bankrupt the debtor must owe at least $1,000 and must have committed an "act of bankruptcy" within the previous four months, such as transferring property in an attempt to defraud his creditors or stating in writing that he is willing to be declared bankrupt. A trustee is appointed by the creditors or the court, and he collects the assets, sells them and distributes the proceeds among the creditors, usually paying them a certain number of cents on each dollar owed them.

The same general procedure is followed whether the business is an individual proprietorship, a partnership or a corporation. In a partnership the assets of the individual partners may be seized as well as the property of the business. (For more information about the procedures in bankruptcy, see sections 463–468.)

You do not necessarily have to go into bankruptcy if your business is in financial difficulty. You can file in court a petition to reorganize your business or make an arrangement with your creditors that will enable you to continue in business and gradually repay them. Both your creditors and the court must approve of your "plan of arrangement." Such an arrangement ordinarily extends your credit, provides for a committee or trustee to oversee your business and may require certain managerial changes in your business.

412. Dissolving a Partnership • Partnerships, like individual owner-ships, may be dissolved by death. If one of the partners goes into bank-ruptcy, the partnership is also dissolved. But there are many more rea-sons for dissolution.

A partnership may be formed for a special business venture or with a date of termination specified in the original partnership agreement. When its venture has been completed or the date has been reached, the partner-ship automatically comes to an end, unless there is an agreement to extend it. The essence of the organization of a partnership lies in the special qualities that each partner brings to it, so when one partner de-cides to withdraw, the partnership may be dissolved unless the remaining partners agree otherwise.

A partnership can also be dissolved by court decree. There are a num-ber of well-established grounds for such a decree. For example, a partner may act fraudulently or otherwise injure the reputation of the business. He might also fail to live up to the terms of the partnership agreement or become unable to fulfill them as a result of physical or mental illness. A court decree may also be sought if the business itself becomes unlawful. Such a decree may be applied for by any partner.

If you sell or assign your interest in a partnership to another person, your partners may terminate the partnership if they desire. If they de-cide to accept him, a new partnership can be formed. But you, the for-mer partner, retain your liability for the debts of the old firm unless the new partner agrees to assume your liability and the firm's creditors accept him as a substitute for you. An announcement to creditors and others stating that you have withdrawn from the firm is required; without it you can even be held liable for the debts of the new organization.

Suppose that instead of selling your interest you withdraw from the business or die. Your remaining partners, if they agree to remain in business as a new partnership, are still responsible for the obligations of the old business. In addition, you or your estate can be held liable for the obligations of both the old partnership and the new one if notice is not given to creditors and others doing business with the firm when the law so requires. As you can see, notice of a change in the composition of a partnership is important for the protection of all concerned.

A partnership does not cease to exist legally when you decide to dis-solve it; it terminates only when its affairs have been wound up. During the winding-up period the partners have no authority to enter into new business. Their role is that of trustees. Their job now is to see that un-finished business is completed, the accounts are audited, accounts receivable are collected, the inventory, fixtures and other property are liquidated and the proceeds are properly distributed to the creditors and among the partners.

Not every partnership is solvent upon dissolution. If your partnership has failed, you and your partners must draw on your personal resources to pay debts of the firm.

413. Dissolving a Corporation • Like a partnership, a corporation does not go out of existence as soon as its owners decide to terminate it. The law usually provides that it will continue for the time it takes to wind up its business. This includes collecting its assets, satisfying the creditors' claims and distributing whatever is left to the shareholders in proportion to the number of shares they own. Depending on the state of incorporation, trustees or "liquidators" may be appointed to liquidate the corporation, or the board of directors may be charged with this responsibility.

Corporations have a perpetual existence—that is, they may continue for an indefinite period of time. However, if the charter provides that the corporation will exist for a specific period, when that period expires, the corporation does too. But if the directors and shareholders want the business to continue beyond that date or event, it is usually a simple matter to have the state renew the charter or to apply for a new one.

Frequently the owners of a corporation dissolve it voluntarily. To do this they must comply with the requirements of the state in which they are incorporated. As a rule, a certain percentage of the shareholders must vote for the dissolution—typically, the state requires two thirds or three quarters of the shareholders to vote in favor. The directors then file a certificate of dissolution with the secretary of state or another authorized state officer. Usually dissolution takes place automatically, provided the corporation has paid the taxes it owes the state.

A corporation may also be dissolved for bankruptcy on a petition of the creditors or the company itself; sometimes it may be reorganized in the interests of its creditors without actually undergoing dissolution. In case of bankruptcy the stockholders are usually not liable for the debts of the corporation. In some states, however, shareholders are personally liable for debts and back wages due employes of the corporation, and they may also be personally liable if they personally participated in mismanaging the corporation.

Minority stockholders may bring about dissolution by petitioning the court when the directors of the corporation have gone beyond their authorized powers and are guilty of improper management of the business or wasting its resources. If the stockholders' suit is successful, the court will appoint a trustee to supervise the business and property of the company for its owners. The state itself may also move against a corporation and cause its charter to be canceled. If the corporation abuses the powers granted by the charter, if it never becomes operative as a business or if it fails to pay its taxes to the state or comply with state statutes, the attorney general of the state may start a suit for revocation.

Your Social Security and Financial Protection

414. How the Government Protects Your Social Welfare • To provide for the social welfare and financial security of all citizens, the federal government and the states have enacted legislation that not only aids those in need but also makes a substantial contribution to the economic stability of the nation.

The Social Security Act is the cornerstone of national social welfare legislation, providing a variety of benefits. Benefits are financed in some cases by general tax revenues; in others by the social security trust fund, which is maintained by the Social Security Administration and into which both the employe and the employer regularly pay money. Self-employed persons pay for themselves (see section 416).

Anyone who is sixty-five or over is also eligible to register for Medicare, which provides two types of health insurance, hospital and medical (see section 426). Individuals eligible for social security disability benefits for at least 24 months are now also eligible for Medicare, as are certain individuals with chronic kidney disease. Most states also have established Medicaid programs, which provide for the health care of persons of any age if their incomes fall below a minimum level (see section 429).

Unemployment insurance is another program that has yielded great social benefits. Under this program qualified unemployed workers receive benefits from a fund financed mainly by their employers. The program also helps workers to find new jobs (see section 432).

Workers' disability insurance is provided for, to some degree, by social security and is also covered under workmen's compensation, now available in every state. The program varies from state to state but in general provides medical payments and income for employes who are injured in connection with their employment. A number of the states also

521

require benefits to be paid to workers who contract diseases as a result of their employment (see section 430). Several states (California, Hawaii, New Jersey, New York and Rhode Island) also provide benefits to workers unemployed because of nonoccupational illness or injury (see section 431).

The number of military veterans has reached an all-time high because the United States has been involved in four wars in this century and maintains large armed forces. Many services and benefits are supplied to qualified applicants by the Veterans Administration. The law requires that the veteran, to qualify, have a discharge other than dishonorable (see section 433).

415. Who Is Covered by Social Security • Almost everyone who works in a job or profession is covered by social security. This coverage includes self-employed persons (see section 416) and men and women on active duty in the armed forces.

The main group of people not included under social security are those employes of the federal government who are covered under a federal retirement system (see section 380). But a majority of the federal workers who do not participate in such a system are covered by social security. Employes of local—town, city and county—and state governments are eligible for coverage if the state enters into an agreement with the federal government. Not all states have such agreements, so a teacher or sanitation worker might be covered in one town but not in another town just over the state line.

Service in the armed forces is credited toward social security, but the way it is credited varies with the dates of service. If you were on active duty between mid-September 1940 and the end of 1956, deductions were not made from your pay, but you can receive a credit of $160 a month. This credit should be requested if you need it when you make application for your social security benefits, since it is not included in your social security record. However, if you served after 1956, deductions were made, and the amount of your base pay is part of your record.

If you work on a farm or a ranch, you are entitled to social security benefits provided your annual earnings are at least $150 in cash from one employer. You also qualify if you are employed for twenty days or longer within one year and are paid in cash on a time basis. But if you are a citizen of a foreign country and were allowed to enter the United States to perform agricultural labor, you do not qualify for coverage.

Household workers, such as maids, chauffeurs and gardeners, may also

522

qualify. If your pay amounts to $50 or more from any one employer in a three-month period, you are covered by social security. This sum must be in cash, and it may include carfare, but room and board are not counted. A regular domestic worker should have a social security card and present it to the employer when reporting for work.

A close relationship between employer and employe may interfere with eligibility for coverage. For example, work for your husband or wife will not entitle you to benefits. If you employ your minor child as a domestic or in any other type of work, that child does not qualify. In some limited situations, though, work of a parent for his or her son or daughter is covered, if there is a genuine employment relationship.

Employes of nonprofit organizations—organizations engaged in educational, charitable, religious, humanitarian or similar activities—may or may not be covered. The law leaves the decision up to the individual employer and his employes. It's a good idea, before you take a job with an organization of this kind, to find out whether it provides social security coverage for you or has a pension plan of its own.

If your income is under $50 in a calendar quarter, you are not covered under any circumstances. Also excluded from coverage are students, such as student nurses or college students, who do certain types of work for the institution in which they are enrolled.

Railroad workers are treated in a special way. They are not under the jurisdiction of the Social Security Administration; instead, the Railroad Retirement Board administers their pensions and disability benefits.

416. Social Security and the Self-Employed • Most self-employed people now enjoy the protection of social security. You're covered if you're in business for yourself in a trade or a profession or if you're a partner or a contractor. If you have a net income of $400 or more a year, the law expects you to report your income and pay a social security tax. (You are not allowed, by the way, to deduct your social security tax from your income tax.) The Social Security Administration keeps an individual account for you, just as it does for people who work for others, and it records your earnings in this account. The tax for the self-employed is lower than the total of the sums paid by an employe and his employer.

417. When You Are "Fully Insured" Under Social Security • Being *fully insured* means that you can collect benefits when you reach retirement age or become disabled and that your dependents can also collect.

To be fully insured you most have the required number of quarters of coverage. You are considered to have a quarter of coverage for every quarter (three months) of a calendar year that you work at a job covered by social security and earn $50 or more—$100 if you are self-employed (see section 416).

You must have either one quarter of coverage for every year after 1950 and before the year you reach sixty-two or die or one quarter of coverage for every year after the year you turn twenty-one if that occurred after 1950. A person who has forty quarters of coverage is fully insured for life. There are special provisions for individuals who are disabled.

In some cases your dependents may be entitled to survivors' benefits (see section 425) although you do not have enough quarters of social security credit to be fully insured. All that you need is six quarters of credit in the three years preceding your death. In other words, if you have worked for one and a half years during those three years, your survivors may collect benefits just as though you had been fully insured.

418. Checking Your Social Security Account • Your earnings must be correctly reported to the Social Security Administration and credited to your account if you are to receive your full benefits. Unfortunately, sometimes mistakes occur, particularly if you keep moving from one job to another, or if you are a household employe. These mistakes may be hard to correct if more than three years have passed after the year you received the earnings. So it makes sense, every couple of years, to write to the administration and ask for a statement of the earnings they have recorded for you. You may do this by sending a postcard to the Social Security Administration, P.O. Box 57, Baltimore, Maryland 21203 (be sure to include your social security number and to sign your request). Or you can get a form from your local social security office to fill out and send in for this information. Their statement normally shows the maximum sum that may be credited to your account, not the actual amount you were paid (if the latter was greater). If there are any errors in your earnings record, you should notify the administration at once.

419. How to Claim Your Social Security Benefits • To obtain your benefits, you must apply for them at your local social security office. Visit it at least a few months before you reach retirement age (see section 420) or get in touch with it as soon as possible after a death or disability occurs. Some benefits may be lost if you put off your application. The Social Security Administration requires proof of your age to establish your eligibility for old-age benefits. The best proof is a copy of your birth certificate; take it with you when you go to the office. If you want to claim benefits for your wife and dependent children, you must also take documents along to prove that they are eligible. Copies of the birth certificates of your wife and children and your marriage certificate are all that you require for this purpose. Your social security office will tell you what other types of proof are acceptable if you do not have these documents.

420. Your Old-Age Benefits • A worker is entitled to a monthly old-age insurance benefit if he or she is fully insured (see section 417) and has reached age sixty-two. You must file an application for the benefits. The amount you will get depends on your average monthly earnings in the past, and the age you choose to begin getting benefits. Between the ages of sixty-two and sixty-five you may choose to receive a reduced benefit, or you may wait until you are sixty-five and receive your full benefit amount. If you wait until you are older than sixty-five to receive your benefits, your benefits will be increased for each month between the ages of sixty-five and seventy-two in which you do not receive benefits. Benefits are also available to your dependents when you reach retirement age (see sections 422, 424).

Although old-age benefits are often called retirement benefits, you do not have to stop working entirely to collect them. Benefits are, however, reduced in proportion to the amount earned. The amount you are allowed to earn without reduction in your benefits has changed a number of times over the years, and in 1972 the law was changed to adjust the amount for increases in the cost of living. In 1977 the amount you can earn without losing benefits is $3,000 a year (or $250 in any month, even if you earn more than $3,000 annually). It is expected that this amount you can earn without loss of benefits will increase each year, so check with your social security office for latest figures. If you earn more than the exempt amount, $1 in benefits is withheld for every $2 earned. Obviously, if you have substantial earnings you won't get any social security benefits at all. Seventy-two is the magic number; once you reach the age of seventy-two you may earn any amount and still continue to receive full benefits.

In calculating your earnings you must include everything you earn from work of any type. Net earnings from self-employment as well as wages have to be counted. But you do not include gifts, inheritances, pensions, dividends, interest on savings accounts, royalties, annuities or rent that is paid you. Remember that you may be eligible for benefits in any month in which your income is below the limit, even if you earn more than the limit annually. When you are formulating financial plans for your retirement, you should take all of these facts and conditions into account if you want to make the most of the social security benefits you have paid for.

421. Disability Benefits Under Social Security • If you work in employment covered by social security and you become disabled, you may qualify for benefits no matter what your age is. If you are eligible as described below, get in touch with your local social security office at once. There is a waiting period of five months· before you can collect. If you qualify, not only you, but your dependents as well, may be eligible to receive monthly disability payments.

What does "disabled" mean? Under social security regulations, you must be unable to engage in any substantial gainful activity. In other words, your disability must be so severe that you can't do any kind of work that will provide you with a livelihood. Another requirement is that the condition must have lasted, or be expected to last, for at least a year or must be expected to result in death. The disability may be mental or physical. Your social security office will provide you with forms to be filled out by any physicians who have treated you. If you have been hospitalized, you should tell your social security office so they can help you get your hospital records.

You need to have sufficient social security credit to be eligible for disability insurance. You will be able to meet the requirement if you are fully insured (see section 417) and have social security credit for five of the ten years or twenty out of forty quarters preceding your disablement. If you are denied benefits you think you are entitled to, you can appeal. The amount you collect as a disability benefit each month is the same amount you would receive as an old-age benefit at age sixty-five. This benefit may, however, be reduced if you are under sixty-two and are getting workmen's compensation (see section 430).

422. Your Wife's (or Husband's) Benefits • If a husband is eligible for social security retirement or disability benefits, his wife may also be entitled to payments. If she has reached age sixty-five, she can collect a benefit equal to one half of the sum that you receive. She may elect to receive a benefit earlier, at age sixty-two, but her payment will be reduced proportionately. A wife who is caring for a dependent child (see section 424) is eligible for a monthly payment at any age. The wife must sub-

526

mit proof of her eligibility in the form of a marriage certificate, a birth certificate or similar documents.

A divorced wife is eligible for social security retirement or disability benefits provided she was married to you for twenty years or longer.

The husband of a disabled or retired woman worker is entitled to the same benefits as the wife of a male worker. (For a discussion of survivors' benefits, see section 425.)

423. Collecting on Separate Accounts • If a husband and wife both worked in covered employment, at retirement age each may collect benefits under a single account, but they cannot collect double benefits. Social security will select the account that gives each person the higher payment. For example, if a wife would collect more on her own account than as the wife of a retired worker, she will be given the larger sum. If the wife becomes eligible before the husband, benefits may be collected on her account.

424. Your Children's Benefits • If you receive benefits because of disability or old age, a child of yours under eighteen is entitled to a monthly payment of about half the amount you receive unless the "family maximum" rule applies. In that case the benefit rate per child is reduced. This benefit continues until the child is eighteen, with exceptions. If a child is seriously disabled before he is twenty-two, benefits may be reinstated and he may collect the benefit as long as his disability lasts. A child who is attending school full time may receive payments until he is twenty-two.

425. Your Survivors' Benefits • If you have an adequate number of social security credits (see section 417), your survivors may be eligible for benefits, including burial expenses.

A lump-sum payment for the cost of burial is made to the widow or widower, or to anyone who supplies proof that he bore that cost. The sum is now $255. Payment must be applied for no later than two years after the death of the insured.

If you have children under eighteen, or under twenty-two and attending school full time, or disabled children over eighteen (known as dependent children), your wife or husband is entitled to a benefit for taking care of them. This amounts to three quarters of the sum you would have received had you retired. The benefit comes to an end when the youngest child is no longer eligible for children's benefits.

527

Your surviving wife or husband is also entitled to benefits at age sixty (or age fifty, if disabled). But if benefits are collected before age sixty-five, they are reduced, and they stop if your spouse remarries.

If your spouse has worked in covered employment and is entitled to a benefit in his or her own right, he or she will receive a payment based on his or her own earnings if this will yield a larger sum.

Your dependent children, who would be eligible for a 50 percent benefit if you retired (see section 424), will receive 75 percent of your monthly benefit in case of your death. If you are survived by parents who depended on you for support and they are over sixty-two, the law provides for them, too. Two parents may each collect 75 percent of your benefit; if only one survives, the benefit is 82½ percent. However, there is a maximum sum that can be paid a single family, so these benefits may have to be reduced.

426. Medicare—What It Is · Medicare is a broad program of health insurance established by the federal government in 1965. The program is primarily for those aged sixty-five and older, but has been extended also to younger individuals eligible for disability insurance benefits for at least two years, and to spouses and children of insured individuals who suffer from chronic kidney disease so severe that they require hemo-dialysis or a kidney transplant. The program includes two kinds of insurance, hospital insurance and medical insurance.

Medicare hospital insurance is financed by the payments made by you and your employer under the social security program, or by you as an individual if you are self-employed. Everyone who is entitled to monthly old-age benefits under the social security or railroad insurance programs gets hospital insurance automatically (see sections 427, 525). Even if you are working and do not plan to retire, you can still have hospital insurance protection as long as you are eligible for social security monthly cash benefits.

The medical insurance, by contrast, is voluntary; you pay a sum each month in advance (this sum may be deducted from your social security benefits) and the government contributes an equal amount.

To make certain you get the full protection of Medicare the month you reach sixty-five, check with your social security office three months before that date. You. can apply for your monthly cash benefits and sign up for medical insurance at the same time.

Medicare should not be confused with Medicaid, a publicly financed program of medical assistance for the needly of all ages (see section 429).

427. Your Hospital Insurance Benefits Under Medicare • Medicare hospital insurance helps pay the bills for hospitalization and for care after you leave the hospital. It covers up to ninety days of inpatient care in any participating hospital during a period of illness. You have to pay a deductible, and there is a fixed charge for every day over sixty.

If you spend at least three days in a hospital, most of the cost for up to 100 days of care in an extended care facility such as a skilled nursing home is paid for in each benefit period. For details of the coverage, contact your social security office.

Certain health-care costs are not covered by your hospital insurance. Among these are bills for your doctor's care (which is paid for by your medical insurance, if you obtain it), private-duty nursing or care in a nursing home that does not meet strict requirements to qualify as a so-called skilled nursing facility. Also not covered are items not essential to health, such as a television set or a telephone.

428. Your Medical Insurance Benefits Under Medicare • Medical insurance under Medicare is entirely voluntary; benefits are available only if you sign up and pay a premium (as described in section 426). Almost everyone is eligible for medical insurance at sixty-five. It doesn't matter whether you have ever worked under social security or whether you intend to retire. However, the premium rises if you wait longer than a year to apply and after three years you are no longer eligible. So the sooner you apply the better.

Like the hospital insurance, Medicare medical insurance begins to compensate you only after you have paid the deductible amount. You have to pay this deductible only once in a calendar year. After that, the program takes care of 80 percent of reasonable charges for covered services. Your social security office has a list of services covered. Services and supplies not covered include prescription drugs, eyeglasses, hearing aids, dentures, routine dental care and orthopedic shoes. Also excluded are routine physical checkups and eye examinations for the purpose of fitting glasses.

429. Medicaid • Medicaid is a government-financed welfare program offering medical aid to the needy of all ages. It is financed in part by the federal government and in part by the states. Each participating state has its own program, which it administers in its own way; thus the programs vary. Only the minimum services that must be provided are specified by the federal legislation that established Medicaid.

529

Every state Medicaid program must cover all persons who receive federal welfare assistance. It must make available to them a minimum of six services: inpatient hospital care, outpatient care, doctors' services, laboratory and X-ray services, screening and diagnostic services and corrective treatment for minors, and nursing home care. Each state is free to add other services and to include in its program its own welfare clients as well as medically needy people who can otherwise support themselves but do not have enough money to meet their medical expenses.

Since 1974 Supplemental Security Income (SSI), a federal program administered by social security, has replaced state-run programs for the blind, aged and disabled.

430. Workmen's Compensation · All the states of the Union, as well as the federal government, have adopted workmen's compensation programs, administered by workmen's compensation agencies or by the courts. These programs differ considerably from state to state. However, every program provides compensation for injuries that are suffered in connection with employment. It doesn't matter who is responsible for the injury; you are eligible for benefits even if it occurred through your own fault (unless you were drunk or injured yourself deliberately).

A number of states limit the payments to injuries suffered in certain occupations that are recognized as particularly hazardous. Some states are also restrictive when it comes to occupational diseases, diseases that you may contract on the job. These states list the disorders that entitle a worker to compensation. In general, you are not covered unless your employer has three or more people on his payroll.

If you suffer a disability, the law expects you to notify your employer as quickly as possible. The worker who neglects to notify him or waits too long may lose his right to make a claim. If you need medical treatment and your employer doesn't provide it when asked, you can get it on your own. The medical bills can then be included in your request for compensation. A lawyer would be of considerable help in this case.

If you accept compensation from your employer, you may not bring an action against him for your injuries. But if you are ineligible for compensation under the law of your state, it is possible to start a legal action (see sections 67, 378).

Benefits are of two types, medical and income. A brief waiting period is generally called for before you can collect. Many states provide complete medical payments; others place limits on your medical benefits. All have provisions for rehabilitation training to make you fit to earn a living again, and surgery and prosthetic appliances may also be included.

The laws usually place disabilities in a number of classes. Some typical ones are permanent total disability, temporary total disability and permanent partial disability. Compensation may amount to as much as two thirds of your average earnings, up to a specified maximum. The payment for a partial disability varies with the type of disability. In some states benefits are provided for dependents.

If the worker dies, his dependents are also eligible for benefits. As a rule, a pension for the death of a worker varies with his average wage but is usually not more than two thirds of that amount.

431. Nonoccupational Disability Insurance • Only a few states—New York, New Jersey, Rhode Island and California—have established plans to protect employes against loss of income from nonoccupational disabilities. These are the medical problems that have no connection with your job (approximately 90 percent of all illness) and that may make it impossible for you to earn a living for a long period of time. Railroad workers are covered under a plan of their own. These plans, not related in any way to workmen's compensation or social security, are administered by the unemployment insurance system of each state.

Each of the states mentioned has its own nonoccupational disability insurance program. In general, both employer and employe contribute to the plan. The sum you receive will depend on your regular weekly earnings, but there are fixed minimum and maximum benefits. Payments begin after a waiting period of a week and continue for up to half a year. Your right to benefits depends upon the type of disability you have and whether you have worked a sufficient number of weeks or earned the minimum amount required to satisfy the state law.

432. Collecting Unemployment Insurance • Unemployment compensation is administered by each state, as well as by the District of Columbia, in its own way and is supported by taxes paid exclusively by employers in most of the states. The federal government also supplies some funds.

Unemployment compensation was set up to tide you over during periods of joblessness. If you lose a position that was covered by unemployment insurance, you should apply at once to your local state unemployment insurance office and file your claim for benefits. File as promptly as you can, because you may not receive benefits for weeks of unemployment before you make your first claim. You'll save time if you take with you your social security card and the notice of discharge given

531

you by your employer. But don't put off filing if you do not have these.

Your state employment service generally shares the same quarters as the state unemployment insurance office. You have to report to the former, too, and register for work. Then you report back regularly at the time you are told to. You must appear in person every week to receive your check. At the same time you must affirm that you are still out of a job. If you are doing any work at all, you must report it, as the wages you receive are deductible from your benefits.

You don't have to be completely unemployed to receive benefits. If you earn less than your usual full-time weekly pay, you may be entitled to partial benefits. To establish eligibility for partial benefits, bring with you to the unemployment insurance office a payroll voucher or any other form stating the gross amount of your pay. The amount of benefits you receive is based on the wages that you earned in covered employment. However, a minimum and a maximum benefit are fixed by the state.

To be eligible for benefits you must be ready, willing and able to take any suitable full-time job that is offered. If the state employment office sends you out on such a job and you refuse to accept it, you may be disqualified for benefits.

You may also be considered ineligible if you are receiving workmen's compensation, dismissal payments, a pension or other remuneration. If you left work in order to attend school or because of pregnancy, you will be refused benefits. If a woman is fired because she is pregnant, however, she should be entitled to unemployment benefits if she is willing and able to work (see section 370). If your claim for benefits is turned down for any reason, you have the right to file an appeal. Your state unemployment insurance office will give you full information about how to do this.

Your Veterans' Rights

433. Veterans' Rights Under the GI Bill • If you have served on active duty for more than 180 days or were discharged for service-connected disabilities, you are entitled to educational assistance under the GI Bill of Rights. You must have been discharged under conditions other than dishonorable. Meet these qualifications and you may receive one and a half months of schooling for each month you served in the armed forces. Your educational benefits are limited to a maximum of forty-five months.

You may apply for instruction at any of a wide range of educational institutions: a college or university; a technical, scientific or professional institution; a junior or teachers college or normal school; a correspondence, business or vocational school; or a secondary school.

If you qualify, the Veterans Administration gives you a monthly allowance that varies with the number of dependents you have. Out of this allowance you pay for your tuition, subsistence and books. Widows of veterans and wives of disabled veterans are also eligible for these benefits.

To establish your eligibility, you need your discharge papers and, where relevant, your marriage certificate and children's birth certificates. Your Veterans Administration regional office will guide you in choosing an appropriate program of schooling. You are allowed ten years after your discharge to complete your education.

434. Veterans' Rights to Their Former Jobs • If you are a serviceman who was drafted, enlisted or was recalled to active duty, you are legally entitled to get your former job back after your discharge. Moreover, you acquire seniority for the time you spent in the service. It is important to apply for your preservice job promptly—you must do so within ninety days after your discharge. If you encounter any difficulty in regaining your position, contact the nearest Veterans Reemployment Rights Office of the U.S. Department of Labor and give them the facts.

435. Your GI Home Loan Guarantee • For qualified veterans the government offers to guarantee a loan obtained to buy a home, mobile home, condominium or farm. You can apply for a loan any time after your discharge. The Veterans Administration can't guarantee the entire price of the property; the law places a limit on the size of the mortgage the government will insure for you. To get a certificate of eligibility for a loan guarantee, you should apply to your regional Veterans Administration for approval. If the bank or agency to which you apply for a loan turns you down, you must shop around to see if you can find another lender. This may be impossible in parts of the country where there is a great demand for mortgage money. For more details on different types of home mortgages see section 291.

In certain rural areas if there is no lender available, the Veterans Administration will make the loan directly to you.

436. Veterans' Hospital and Medical Care • The Veterans Administration maintains hospitals throughout the United States at which medical

533

care may be obtained by qualified veterans. If you suffer from a service-connected disability, this care is available without charge. But even if your disability is not service connected, you may be admitted to one of these hospitals if a bed is available and you certify that you cannot pay elsewhere. This benefit is available to you at any time.

If you have a service-connected disability, you may also receive treatment at a Veterans Administration clinic. If necessary, you may ask the administration for authorization to be treated by your own physician.

437. Compensation and Pensions for Disabled Veterans • If you fall victim to a disability or disease while you're on active service, or if you already have one and it is made more serious as a result of your active service, you may qualify for disability compensation. The amount of compensation you get will vary with the type of disability you suffer from. If you are 50 percent or more disabled and you have a wife and children or other dependents, you may be eligible for an additional payment to help cover the cost of their support.

Suppose you have a disability that can't be traced to your military service. If the disability is total and permanent, you may also be entitled to benefits. To be eligible, however, you must have served at least ninety days in the armed forces and received an honorable discharge (a basic requirement for most service benefits).

438. Social Security and Other Benefits and the Income Tax • Are social security benefits subject to income tax? No, the payments that you and your family receive under social security are tax-free. This is equally true of railroad retirement benefits. If you are sixty-five or older, you don't file a federal income tax return unless your gross income from other sources amounts to at least $3,200. If you have other income and are required to file a return, you simply do not include your social security benefits as part of your gross income.

If you are self-employed and have a net income of $400 or more from your self-employment, you have to file a federal income tax return and pay a self-employment tax even if you are sixty-five and are collecting social security retirement benefits.

Some of the other types of benefits discussed in this chapter are also not subject to taxes: workmen's compensation payments for physical disability, state unemployment insurance and state disability insurance benefits. Disability pay received by a veteran of the armed forces is also tax-free.

CHAPTER TEN

Your Money,
Credit and Investments

---

*The law, in its majestic equality, forbids the rich
as well as the poor to sleep under bridges.*

—ANATOLE FRANCE

10

Your Money, Credit and Investments

Some Key Points in This Chapter—
Consult these sections for information on:

Charts in This Chapter

Your Money, Bank Accounts and Checks

439. What Money Is • Love of money may be the root of all evil, but money is essential to any economy, and laws are required to control its use. There has to be some common measure that you can use when you exchange things: your labor for the means of buying food and clothing, your painting for someone else's work of art, your manuscript for a piece of furniture. There was a time when many things were directly exchanged, or bartered, as is still true in some isolated communities. But barter is too cumbersome and time-consuming and raises too many questions as to the relative value of the items being bartered. If you are a farmer and take a sack of potatoes to market, should you swap it for a tube of toothpaste or a hairbrush? Your decision would probably rest on your need of a hairbrush and the need of the owner of the hairbrush for potatoes. The respective needs of the parties often result in very unfair exchange.

The function of money is to give you an objective basis for knowing the value of what you are offering (your potatoes) and what is being offered to you (the hairbrush). Because their intrinsic value was well known, gold and silver were among the earliest kinds of money, and they still are the basis of our monetary system.

Gradually it became necessary, for the vast majority of transactions, to use pieces of gold or silver of different sizes and therefore of different values. A large piece of solid silver or gold was useful only for transactions involving articles of considerable value; it would not help in most cases, where the value was relatively small.

The next step in the history of money was the development of what we call *coins:* pieces of metal containing varying amounts of gold or silver, on which were impressed a word or figure expressing the coins' worth. For a great many years man's addiction to gold and silver as the only metals of universal value meant that a coin's value was expressed in terms of its gold or silver content: the greater the gold or silver content, the greater the value.

It was not long before governments asserted the sole right to coin money and to issue paper currency. By Article I, Section 8, of the United States Constitution, the states yielded to Congress the right to "coin money" and "regulate the value thereof." Supreme Court decisions have affirmed the exclusive right of Congress in all matters affecting what is sometimes called *legal tender,* whatever currency may be lawfully offered as payment of a debt or obligation. Although the states have wide taxing powers and may borrow money, they may not issue money.

The intrinsic value of your money is determined by Congress. The dollar is defined by law as being worth a specified amount of gold. Putting it the other way around, every ounce of gold is worth a set number of U.S. dollars. The government keeps a reserve of gold that it sells to other countries in exchange for dollars. The United States also buys gold on the world market at a specified price per ounce. This willingness to buy and sell gold internationally makes the dollar one of the stablest currencies —perhaps the most stable—in the world.

440. Your Checking Account • Most persons in the United States whose income exceeds their everyday needs keep at least some of their money in checking accounts in banks. As the owner of a checking account you deposit money in your bank. The bank is allowed to use your money—it mingles yours with the money of other depositors—but commits itself to making payments from your account as you direct. Your order takes the form of a check. So long as you have funds in your account to cover the amount of your check, the bank must honor your check; failure to do so would be a breach of contract with you, and you could sue the bank to recover damages.

If, either by oversight or deliberately, you have *overdrawn* your account (meaning that the total amount of checks you have written on your account is larger than the amount of money in your account), your bank may not honor the checks. One bank wrote a courteous letter to a depositor saying that her account was overdrawn in the amount of $5.85. She wrote out a check for $5.85 to the bank as payee and mailed it in with a covering letter saying, "Don't let this happen again!" The bank's decision whether or not to honor your check will depend on your previous history as a depositor and what it believes is likely to be your future performance. But it has no obligation to honor a check drawn on nonexistent funds. You should keep careful track of the size of your account, lest you find yourself prosecuted for the criminal offense of drawing checks on a bank when you know you have no funds with which to pay them (see section 136).

From time to time after you have paid for something by check you will want to call back the check. You may find that the book you ordered by mail is one you already have or that the salesman who came to your door selling vacuum cleaners was a crook wanted in five counties for misrepresenting himself as a vacuum cleaner salesman. In such cases and others, when you have mailed or delivered your check but don't want your bank to cash it, you can write or call your bank to *stop payment* on the check. If the check has already been presented for payment, it is of course too late for payment to be stopped. If it has not, however, the bank will, for a small charge, agree not to make payment on it. If by mistake the bank does make payment, you may be able to collect the amount of the check from the bank.

If a check you write is lost by the payee, you should also have payment stopped. Similarly, if you lose a check made out to you, you should ask the drawer (the person who wrote the check) to send you another; he will ask his bank to issue a stop-payment order on his first check to you. He may reduce the amount of the second check to pass on to you the bank's charge for the stop-payment order, particularly if the loss of the check was clearly your fault.

A *joint checking account* is an account in the names of two persons, either of whom may draw checks on it. Most often such an account is established by a husband and wife, who are issued a single checkbook, usually with both their names printed on the checks. A joint checking account should not be confused with the checking account established by two or more partners in a business: the account is in the name of the partnership—the Magnificent Manicurers Company or the law firm of Edwards and Edwards. Partnership accounts may require the signatures of two partners on each check, whereas the joint account usually requires the signature of only one of the owners of the account. Obviously, joint accounts should be established only by persons whose interests are identical and whose trust in each other is complete.

There are several kinds of checks that are widely used today. We have been discussing personal checks, the rules for which are pretty much the same for individuals, partnerships and corporations: when the bank account is established, forms are filled out that authorize the bank to honor the signatures of one or more specified persons. If it is a joint account, the authorized signatures are most often those of a man and his wife. If it is a partnership or a corporate account, the authorized signers are usually several named partners or officials. The partnership or corporation is required to adopt a resolution authorizing the establishment of an account in a specific bank and listing the names of the partners or officers authorized to sign checks drawn on that account; these partners or officers place their signatures on file with the bank, which is then responsible for honoring only those checks signed by them.

441. Cashier's Checks • Every now and then the person or company from which you're buying something expensive may demand proof that you have enough money in your bank to meet the amount of the check. If you inherit $5,000 from your Aunt Maud and decide to use $3,000 of it to pay cash for a new car, the car dealer may not believe you have $3,000 in the bank. He may not like your looks, or he may just have had another buyer's personal check returned and marked "no funds"—meaning that it bounced. You have a choice of two ways of handling the problem. One is to go to your bank and have it make out a *cashier's check* to you for the $3,000: Either the bank transfers $3,000 from your account to its own, or you write a check to the bank's order for $3,000. With that $3,000 now in its control, the bank issues its $3,000 check to your order or to the order of the car dealer. If the check is made out to your order, you endorse it to the car dealer; if it is made out to the dealer, the result is the same: he has the bank's official undertaking to pay him $3,000.

442. Certified Checks • The other choice, *a certified check,* is identical in effect: You write out a $3,000 check to the order of the car dealer and take the check to an official of the bank saying you want it certified. The official then stamps "certified" across the face of your check, that is, the bank certifies that you have $3,000 in your account. Immediately upon certification it freezes that amount in your balance and holds it until the certified check is presented for payment.

443. Check Clearance • Your check has *cleared* when it has been presented to your bank and payment has been made for the amount indicated on it. Clearance takes from one to three days if the payee is in the same city as your bank. Your check to your local drugstore, if deposited by the store owner in his bank, will probably be presented by his bank to yours within twenty-four hours of deposit. More time is involved if the check passes through several hands or if the payee lives in a different area from your bank's. Banks have an efficient, nationwide clearing system, however, and you are running a considerable risk if you write a check for a larger amount than is in your checking account, expecting to be able to cover your check before it clears.

If you don't have enough money in your bank account to cover a check, but you know you will have in a day or so when you get your salary, you can protect yourself by *postdating* your own check, that is, by writing on it a date later than the present. The dealer from whom you are buying an antique chair may accept your postdated check and agree not to sell the chair to anyone else even though he cannot cash the check until the date you write on it. But you should not postdate checks in most cases. You can never be sure that the payee won't deposit it at once, and with the tremendous volume of checking activity these days the clerk at your bank may not notice that your check presented for payment on June 1 is actually dated June 5.

444. Endorsements • So far we have discussed transactions among three parties only: the drawer of a check, the bank on which the check is drawn and the payee, the person or company or organization to whom the check is drawn. But several others may also be involved. Your check, that little piece of paper you put into circulation by signing it and turning it over to someone else, often goes through several hands before it gets to your bank. The process by which the payee you have named designates another payee or other payees is called *endorsement,* of which two kinds are most commonly used.

One is called an *endorsement in full.* Your $25 check made out to the order of your drugstore owner is almost as good as cash if properly endorsed. If he owes $25 to one of his suppliers, he may pay his supplier simply by writing on the back of your check "Pay to the order of Famous Drug Supply Company" and signing his name. By so doing, he has endorsed your check, which means that if your bank should for any reason not honor your check, he must pay the drug supply company for the full amount of your check. But Famous Drug Supply Company may owe $25 to one of its delivery men and decide to use your endorsed check to pay him. It does so by writing on the back of the check "pay to the order of" followed by the name of the delivery man, signed by one of the supply company's officials. Of course, the supply company becomes liable to the delivery man if your check is not honored when it finally gets to your bank for payment.

If the drugstore wants to keep your check from going into wider circulation, it may endorse it "for deposit only to the account of Neighborhood Drug Store." This would prevent anyone else from endorsing the check to any payee other than its bank.

Another kind of endorsement, the *blank endorsement,* results in an even less restricted use of your check. The payee writes only his name on the back of your check. Such a check, once endorsed, can be cashed by anyone who gets possession of it.

The law is not very precise regarding the length of time you may hold on to a check before cashing it. The drawer is not liable indefinitely. As a general rule you need not cash a check for three to four weeks after the date appearing on the check. If you wait any longer, however, the drawer or maker of the check may refuse to accept liability, and many banks will not, as a matter of practice, honor it. Rules regarding time for presentation of checks have unquestionably become more liberal as the volume of checks in circulation has increased.

445. Forgery • It is a crime to forge a check. The forgery may be one of several kinds. The man who steals your checkbook and signs your name to one of the checks has committed the offense of *forgery,* for which he may be penalized by fine and imprisonment (see section 104). The man who sees someone else forge your name to a check, and then snatches the forged check, takes it to a bank and cashes it has *uttered a forged document,* which is also a criminal offense (see section 104). It is a crime to *kite* a check: to change the figures so that a $10 check appears as one for $100, or a $50 one becomes one for $55. The only way to protect yourself against having your checks kited is to write the dollar amount out in such a way that it cannot be altered or added to.

446. Savings Accounts • Savings accounts differ from checking accounts in several ways. As the name of the account suggests, its purpose is to handle your savings rather than to give you the opportunity to use your current income to pay for rent, utilities, clothing and so forth. The laws of most states today permit banks to offer savings as well as checking accounts. The word *national* in a bank's name means that it is licensed by and operates under the federal government, whereas all other banks are licensed and supervised by state banking departments. The federal government permits national banks to offer both savings and checking accounts, and it regulates the rate of interest that may be paid on savings accounts. Savings banks as such—banks that offer only savings facilities—are chartered by state governments. Savings and loan associations may be chartered by either the national or a state government.

Interest is what the bank pays you for the use of your money. When you deposit money in a savings account, both you and the bank understand that you expect to leave it there for at least a longer period of time than the money you deposit in your checking account. Although you are free to withdraw your money from your savings account, it is not worthwhile until the money has been in the savings bank long enough—usually three months—to earn interest. The bank agrees to pay you in-

TIPS TO PROTECT YOU
WHEN YOU WRITE OR CASH CHECKS

The physical alteration of legitimate checks for dishonest ends is one of the most widespread crimes. A clever forger can easily change the name of the payee and the amount of the check with a few strokes of a pen. The success of this kind of forgery is in large part the result of our own negligence in writing, safeguarding and cashing checks.

Typically, in this example the forger has changed the name of the payee from that of a store (The Toggery) to that of an individual (Theo. Foggerty).

Here the Davis Co has become David Cox, and $3 has become $30. Tracing over the colored changes in black ink would show a convincing result.

Space to the left of both the numerals and the written figure allowed a door-to-door salesman to increase the amount of this check by $30.

Surprisingly convincing alterations in written amounts and in numerals can be made, unless lines are tightly filled and letters and numbers are clearly written.

Ten Points for Check Cashers to Observe

• Don't be afraid to ask questions about a check and its passer. • Never cash a check that shows any sign of alteration. • Always demand that a check be endorsed in your presence. If it is already endorsed, make the endorser sign again, then compare the writing. • Make sure that a check is drawn by an existing concern or individual on an actual bank. • Be just as wary of certified checks or cashier's checks as of ordinary ones. • Never cash checks for juveniles. • Never endorse a check for anyone you don't *know* to be reliable. • If you are a merchant, beware of any unknown customer who offers you a check for more than the amount of his or her purchase. • If a bankbook is offered as identification, phone the bank named to check the account. • *Know your endorser.* Bear in mind that the successful forger rarely fits the Hollywood version of the criminal type.

terest at certain regular intervals, usually every three months too. Some banks pay interest from the day you open your account and from the day of deposit for subsequent deposits. Others pay interest starting with the beginning of the three-month, or quarterly, period on all sums deposited in the first ten days: your deposit of January 10 will draw interest from January 1.

Simple interest is calculated at a fixed rate for a specific period of time, usually a year. It is credited by the bank each year on the amount in your account at the start of the year. Compound interest is computed, usually quarterly, on the amount in your account as increased by the interest earned. If on January 1 you deposit $1,000 in a simple interest account paying 5 percent and leave it there for a year, by the next January 1 you will have $1,050. If you deposit $1,000 in an account that pays 5 percent interest compounded quarterly, by the next January 1 you will have slightly more than $1,050 because each quarter's interest is added to the principal and the 5 percent is computed each time on the increased size of the account.

Remember that savings banks use your money just as do commercial banks. The things savings banks and savings and loan associations can do with your money are different from and more limited than what commercial banks can do. By statutes in all states, savings banks are usually limited to making loans on real estate—called *mortgages*—and to investing in various kinds of high-grade bonds and governmental securities. Commercial banks, on the other hand, may make a much wider use of your money: they make loans to individuals, to partnerships and to corporations, and they lend to all kinds of businesses. But the savings bank was created for a much more limited purpose: a place where you may leave your money and have every confidence that it will be there when you want it, increased by the interest it has earned during the time you have left it in the savings bank.

447. Federal Deposit Insurance • Money you deposit in both commercial and savings accounts is protected by the federal government through the Federal Deposit Insurance Corporation if your bank is insured by the FDIC, as the vast majority of banks are. That corporation now assures each depositor that his deposit up to the amount of $40,000 is guaranteed by the corporation. If, for any reason whatever, your bank should run into financial difficulties and be unable to pay you the amount you have deposited in either a checking or a savings account, the Federal Deposit Insurance Corporation will pay you that amount, up to $40,000. Similarly, if your savings and loan association is insured by the Federal Savings & Loan Insurance Corporation, then your account will also be insured up to $40,000. Do not just assume that your bank or savings and loan association is federally insured—ask.

YOUR CREDIT AND PERSONAL LOANS

448. How the Law Affects Credit • The American economic system is built on credit. Both businesses and individuals borrow money in a variety of ways. The function of the law is to protect both the borrower and the lender. It protects the borrower by setting limits on the amount of interest he can be charged for borrowing and by requiring the lender to make clear exactly how much he is charging. The law provides the lender with various remedies if the borrower doesn't pay his debts.

When you borrow money you enter into a contract with the lender. It is unwise to borrow any large amount of money without having something in writing as to when, where and in what manner you are to pay the money back. Because the terms of that contract are important to you, you should read the contract carefully. Although the laws today are far less harsh against debtors in default than they used to be (not long ago you could be jailed for failure to pay your debts when due), you can experience embarrassment and suffering if you don't meet your obligations.

The amount of your loan is called the *principal*. The amount you pay the lender for the use of his money is *interest*. An *unsecured loan* is supported only by your promise to pay the lender. In a *secured loan* there is more than your promise; the lender is given rights to some of your property if you fail to pay as agreed. There are many kinds of secured loans, as you will see from the following paragraphs.

449. Unsecured Loans • A *promissory note,* or IOU, is the simplest and most widely used way of formalizing an unsecured loan. You may write it out yourself, or get a printed form at a stationery store and fill in the blanks with the name of the lender, the amount you are borrowing, the date on which you are to pay the lender and the amount or rate of interest you agree to pay him. Occasionally, it may be necessary to have someone else's signature on the note along with your own, if your credit is not particularly strong. Such a *co-maker* would be as responsible as you to the promisee. Or you may strengthen your own note by getting someone else to sign on the back as an endorser or guarantor. If you fail to pay the note when due, he would have to pay, and he would then have a right to collect the amount from you.

450. Pawnbroker's Loans • A good example of a secured loan that once was very common but is relatively rare today is the loan made by a pawnbroker. In return for your depositing with him your watch, a ring or something else valuable, he lends you an amount of money based on the value of what you *pawned,* or left as security for the loan. For him it is a perfect loan: he has physical possession of the security for the loan, and he collects interest from you in advance, by reducing the amount of the loan to reflect the interest. (This practice is called *discounting*, and it is widely used by banks and finance companies, as we shall see.) The pawnbroker becomes a bailee of the property you leave with him: he has to take good care of it and return it to you in the same condition as when you delivered it to him (see sections 197, 206). If, contrary to his agreement with you, he converts the property to his own use or sells it to someone else, you can sue him for its value (see section 198).

451. Mortgage Loans • Other kinds of secured loans that are widely used are mortgage loans, known generally as mortgages. When you want to borrow money using your real estate as security, you execute a real property mortgage (see section 290). You go to a bank, insurance company or savings and loan association, and in return for its making you a loan you *mortgage* your property; that is, you (the mortgagor) sign a paper that gives the lender (the mortgagee) the right to sell your property if you don't make the required payments on your loan. Sometimes the mortgage will be differently worded: you surrender legal title to your property to the mortgagee with the understanding, as expressed in the mortgage, that legal title returns to you when you have completed the payments on your loan. The former kind of mortgage, however, is the much more common one today in most states.

Most modern mortgage loans set out a schedule of payments that include both interest and principal. These are called *constant payments* and are so calculated that at the end of a specified time you have paid off the entire loan. The early payments consist largely of interest, but the balance shifts with the passage of time until, at the end of the term of the mortgage, your payments are applied almost entirely to principal (see section 292).

You are not legally limited to one mortgage on your property. Many businesses, especially railroads, make it a practice to execute two or more mortgages on their property. If the value of your property is appraised at $50,000, and you have given a mortgage on it in the amount of $10,000 as security for a loan, you should be able to borrow a great deal more on the property and execute a second mortgage. The only difficulty is that many lenders don't like second mortgages, because their rights as second mortgagees come after the rights of the first mortgagee: if your property is sold because you can't keep up your payments, the second mortgagee gets what he is owed only after the first mortgagee has been paid. What you should do if you need to raise more money and cannot get a second mortgage is to refinance your property: arrange with either the first mortgagee or a new lender for a new loan in the amount you need (and can get), pay off the $10,000 first-mortgage loan, thus canceling that mortgage, and execute a new "first" mortgage for the larger loan. For more about mortgages see sections 290–293. Years ago people often tried very hard to pay off their mortgages early to be free of debt. However, this is no longer always advantageous. If you have an old mortgage, representing a loan made to you when interest rates were much lower than they now are, you may be better advised to use your excess money to avoid interest charges on charge accounts or simply to deposit the excess money in a savings account. For example, if your bank or savings bank is paying 5½ percent interest on deposits, it would not normally be advantageous for you to use your excess money to pay off a 4½ percent mortgage.

452. Chattel Loans • Even though you own no real estate, there are plenty of ways of borrowing money through a secured loan. The most common is the loan in which the lender is given a security interest in a chattel (formerly called a *chattel mortgage*), some item of personal property. You borrow money and give the lender the right to repossess and sell your personal property if you don't meet your loan payments. If you suddenly need $1,000, you might borrow it from your bank and give it a security interest in the car you've already paid for: the bank lends you $1,000; you give it a note for $1,000 and a security interest in the car; the bank is entitled to move in, seize and sell your car unless you meet your payments on the loan when they are due. You retain title to the car if you meet your payments. A financing statement, identifying you, the lender and the property covered by the lender's security interest, will be recorded in a state or county office by the lender.

453. Life Insurance Loans • Another very common type of secured loan is the one you take out from your life insurance company, which will lend you an amount up to the cash value of your insurance policy. That value reflects the total amount of premiums you have paid on your policy, plus whatever dividends the company has paid and you have left with it. The insurance loan is so cheap (usually only 5 percent) and easy to obtain that it's hard to remember that the unpaid balance of your loan is, on your death, deducted from the amount that is paid to your beneficiary. For more detail, see section 508.

454. Interest • Borrowing money is an American habit—and an expensive one. Until recently many borrowers didn't realize how expensive. An interest charge of 1½ percent per month amounts to 18 percent a year. Lenders of all kinds—banks, stores, finance companies and credit card companies—are now required by federal law to explain to you exactly what your loan is going to cost you. This is the so-called Truth-in-Lending law. Under the Truth-in-Lending Act there are different disclosure requirements for different kinds of transactions. However, in practically all credit or loan transactions with someone regularly in the business of lending or furnishing credit, there is a requirement that you be furnished a disclosure statement. Among other things, the disclosure statement must tell you the effective annual interest rate and explain how any penalties (for late payment, for example) will be computed and how any discounts (for early payment, for example) can be earned. You should read this disclosure statement and the underlying loan or credit agreement very carefully.

Ask your lender exactly what he is charging you. Keep in mind that many bank loans are *discounted in advance:* your $1,000 loan for twelve months produces considerably less in cash because the interest is deducted from the $1,000 before you get the money. Note that the interest rate on a discounted loan is effectively higher than the discount rate.

Be very careful of the loan shark or any other person who offers you a loan, with "no questions asked," at high or extortionate rates of interest. A common underworld trick is to make loans to persons in financial trouble, repayable in short periods of time at interest rates that may seem justified by the ease of the loan but that can quickly bankrupt you. If you borrow $1,000 for a month at 6 percent, you are being charged interest at the annual rate of 72 percent.

The law tries to protect borrowers against such loans by setting limits on what interest rate may legally be charged. Check chart 35, page 549,

LEGAL LIMITS ON INTEREST RATES

The legal limit on annual interest rates in your state (except for interest on small loans and corporate loans) is shown in the chart below. Most states set 2 separate rates: one for loans made without a written contract and another for loans agreed upon in writing. Loans made at a higher rate of interest are *usurious* (see section 454).

CHART 35	Non-contract Rate	Contract Rate	Can Debtor Recover Interest on Usurious Loans?
ALABAMA	6%	8%[1]	Yes
ALASKA	6%	8%[22]	Yes[2,3]
ARIZONA	6%	10%	Yes
ARKANSAS	6%	10%	Yes: both principal & interest
CALIFORNIA	7%	10%	Yes[4]
COLORADO	6%	12%[5]	Yes
CONNECTICUT	6%	12%	No
DELAWARE	6%	9%	Yes: interest above statutory rate[6]
D.C.	6%	8%	Yes
FLORIDA	6%	10%	Yes
GEORGIA	7%	9%[7]	Yes
HAWAII	6%	12%	No
IDAHO	6%	10%[5]	Yes[2]
ILLINOIS	5%	8%[23]	Yes[2]
INDIANA	8%	8%[5]	Yes[8]
IOWA	5%	9%	No
KANSAS	6%	10%	Yes: interest above statutory rate[2]
KENTUCKY	6%	8½%[9]	Yes: interest above statutory rate[2,3]
LOUISIANA	7%	8%	Yes[3]
MAINE	6%	No statutory limit[10]	No[11]
MARYLAND	6%	8%[12]	Yes: interest above statutory rate[6]
MASSACHUSETTS	6%	No statutory limit	No[11]
MICHIGAN	5%	7%	Yes
MINNESOTA	6%	8%	Yes[3]
MISSISSIPPI	6%	10%[24]	Yes. If interest is over 20%, principal is also forfeited.
MISSOURI	6%	10%	Yes: interest above statutory rate[2]
MONTANA	6%	10%	Yes[2]
NEBRASKA	6%	9%	Yes
NEVADA	7%	12%	No
NEW HAMPSHIRE	6%	No statutory limit	No

CHART 35 (cont.)	Non-contract Rate	Contract Rate	Can Debtor Recover Interest on Usurious Loans?
NEW JERSEY	7½%	8%	Yes
NEW MEXICO	6%	[13]	Yes[2,3]
NEW YORK	6%[14]	6%[14]	Yes: interest above statutory rate
NORTH CAROLINA	6%	[15]	Yes[2,3]
NORTH DAKOTA	4%	9%[9]	Yes[16]
OHIO	6%	8%	Yes[8]
OKLAHOMA	6%	10%[5]	No
OREGON	6%	10%	[17]
PENNSYLVANIA	6%	6%	Yes: interest above statutory rate[18]
RHODE ISLAND	6%	21%	Yes: both principal & interest
SOUTH CAROLINA	6%	8%[19]	Yes
SOUTH DAKOTA	6%	10%	Yes
TENNESSEE	6%	10%	Yes[3]
TEXAS	6%	10%	Yes: twice the amount of interest[20]
UTAH	6%	10%[5]	Yes[4]
VERMONT	7½%	7½%[21]	Yes: interest plus ½ principal
VIRGINIA	6%	8%	Yes[2,3]
WASHINGTON	6%	12%	Yes[2]
WEST VIRGINIA	6%	8%	Yes: interest above statutory rate
WISCONSIN	5%	12%	Yes[3]
WYOMING	7%	10%[5]	Yes[3]

(1) 15% on $100,000 and over.
(2) Up to twice the amount of interest paid.
(3) If suit is brought within 2 years.
(4) Up to 3 times the amount of interest paid over 10%.
(5) Has Uniform Consumer Credit Code. Rate ceilings are imposed, in general, at 18% per year on consumer transactions coming under provisions of the Act.
(6) Three times the amount of excess interest or $500, whichever is greater.
(7) 7% add-on interest is maximum for installment loans generally; no limit over $100,000.
(8) If interest charged is over 8%, all interest paid over 6% may be recovered.
(9) No limit on business loans over $25,000.
(10) No limit if in writing but 16% on personal loans over $2,000.
(11) But usurious loans are void.
(12) No limit on business loans over $5,000.
(13) Rate is 10% on secured contracts; 12% on unsecured contracts.
(14) The state banking board sets the maximum, from 5%-7½%. If no rate is set, the maximum is 6%.

(15) Rate is 8% on secured contracts; on unsecured contracts, 9% for less than $100,000; 12% for $100,000-$300,000; no limit for over $300,000.
(16) One fourth of the principal and up to twice the amount of interest paid if suit is brought within 4 years.
(17) The entire debt is forfeited to the school fund of county where suit is brought.
(18) Triple the excess of the lawful rate if suit is brought within 4 years.
(19) 10% for $50,000-$100,000; 12% for $100,000-$500,000; no limit over $500,000.
(20) If interest exceeds twice the statutory rate, principal is also forfeited.
(21) 12% on loans for income-producing business or activity.
(22) No more than 5 percentage points above current Federal Reserve discount rate. No limit over $100,000.
(23) 9½% where security is residential real estate on loans made after 7/12/74.
(24) 15% on $2,500 and over.

to see what that interest rate is in your state. Bear in mind, however, that since lenders may compound their interest rates, these figures do not show the real annual ceiling on interest for a loan. On small loans you may legally pay the equivalent of 25 percent or more of the principal amount. Interest rates higher than the legal limit are called *usurious*. The making of a usurious loan is an offense for which the lender can be fined and may be required to forfeit the interest on the loan and sometimes the principal amount as well. The legal rates have gone up substantially in recent years, but there will always be legal limits and you should be aware of them to protect yourself.

455. Charge Accounts and Credit Cards · Even the charge account you establish at a department store is just another kind of loan. Most such accounts give you thirty days after your bill is mailed to you to pay the amount of the bill: this is an interest-free loan for thirty days. From the end of the thirty-day period most stores and other sellers who extend you credit charge you 1½ percent interest per month on the unpaid balance of your bill. The credit card company—whether a bank or a nationwide lender—operates the same way. You have a certain period within which to pay what you owe, during which no interest is charged; thereafter you pay 1½ percent interest monthly on what you owe.

If you own and use credit cards, you should keep a list of the card numbers and of the issuers, so as to be able to notify the issuer at once if your card is lost or stolen. Otherwise you may find yourself charged— up to a statutory limit of $50 per card—for purchases you never made. You are not obliged to keep a credit card that is sent to you in the mail. If you don't want it, return it or destroy it. But don't just toss it out without mutilating it, or someone may pick it out of the trash and use it. Several states have now passed statutes prohibiting the mailing of unsolicited credit cards.

WHEN YOU CAN'T PAY: INSOLVENCY AND BANKRUPTCY

456. Your Duty to Pay · Your obligation to pay your bills may be expressed as your obligation to perform your part of a contract that you entered into voluntarily. Obviously, you need not pay a bill for something you didn't buy. The bill you get for something you ordered but canceled can also be ignored unless there is a question whether your cancellation became known to the seller or whether the seller misunderstood you. In either case, you would have a defense to an action he might bring against you for breach of contract. These defenses are discussed in section 185.

457. Insolvency • If you fall on really hard times and find that you can't pay your bills as they come due, you are said to be *insolvent*. What you should do depends on how serious your situation is.

Practically all your creditors (the people and companies you owe money to) will extend you at least one month's extra credit. These so-called *grace periods* are so common in some industries that you are not even expected to pay your bill until thirty days after it is due. Your life insurance company sends you a premium notice, or bill, saying that the annual (or semiannual or quarterly) premium on your insurance policy is due and payable July 1. You may put off paying the premium until the end of the grace period, or July 31, without fear of your policy's being canceled or the company's charging your policy with a loan in the amount of the premium payable July 1.

Not all creditors behave the same way. Their action in most cases will depend on your previous record of paying your bills, and, especially with small creditors, on their knowledge of your particular situation and of how much business they can expect from you in the future. Almost all creditors will be willing to wait for their money, as an alternative to suing, if they are convinced you plan to pay. The most common mistake of debtors who get behind in payments is to stop communicating with the creditor: because this is frequently the conduct of people who have decided not to pay at all, it is very likely to convince the creditor that he must sue for any money he will get. If you fall on hard times and get more than a month behind on your bills, you will usually be much better off if you communicate with your creditors and tell them about your situation. Generally, you will find that a creditor's attitude toward a delinquent debtor who frankly explains his situation will be completely different from his attitude toward a debtor whom he has to chase. The extraordinary growth of credit in recent years, with all kinds of business owners in effect making loans through credit cards, has certainly led to a more lenient or tolerant attitude toward the late payment of bills by anyone.

For one thing, statistics alone have produced an easier attitude: they establish that in reasonably prosperous times the percentage of persons who do not pay their bills, and who must be sued for the creditor to collect, is remarkably low. For another thing, the credit card has a built-in device that protects the creditor: If you don't pay your Sears Roebuck bill within thirty days, your account is automatically charged with interest at the rate of 1½ percent a month. That's interest at the rate of 18 percent a year. The same is true of virtually all your other "credit card accounts." It is scarcely worthwhile for the department store to cancel your credit if you don't pay, because the store can let the interest mount up at a much higher rate than it has to pay on the money it borrows, and it is reasonably sure of eventual payment from you.

Finally, as you'll see shortly (section 460), going to court is likely to cost your creditor more than he can collect from you. A variety of steps are available to you as debtor to enable you to put off having to pay. And the legislature and the courts are taking an increasingly tolerant view of your situation as an insolvent person.

458. Legal Proceedings Against a Debtor • But today's more relaxed attitude will not protect you from legal proceedings by your creditor if he decides you are acting in bad faith toward him. First he goes to court and gets a judgment against you establishing that you owe him a certain amount of money. Then he tries to collect the money, usually by an *execution:* a court order directing the sheriff to seize your personal property, sell it and pay him the amount of your debt from the proceeds of the sale. If you haven't much property, your creditor may try to get a court order directing your employer to set aside part of your wages or salary every pay period and turn the amount over to him. Called a *garnishment,* such an order can be a source of embarrassment to you, and it is an annoyance to your employer. Federal and state statutes now provide that part of your salary is exempt from garnishment, in order that you may have enough money to meet your necessary living expenses (see chart 7, page 131).

The creditor who is convinced that a debtor is about to leave the state or the country, taking all his possessions with him, may go to court and ask for a *writ of attachment*, which directs the sheriff to attach, or seize, enough personal property to protect and compensate the creditor if he later succeeds in getting a judgment for the amount that he claims is owed him.

459. Favored Creditors • Some of your creditors are in a stronger position than others to make life miserable for you. The automobile or refrigerator or other appliance you have bought on a conditional sale contract, although in your possession, is not legally yours until you've made your last payment on it. If you continually fail to make your payments, the seller is entitled to *repossess* the appliance without going to court. In most states you have ten days in which you may get the appliance back by making the payments you owe and by compensating the seller for his expenses in the repossession. If you don't redeem the appliance, the creditor may sell it to someone else, paying you any excess he receives over and above his expenses and the amount you owe him.

Your personal property in which you have given the lender a security interest (see section 452) is almost as vulnerable as property you are purchasing on time payments. You own the property, but the terms of the security agreement authorize your creditor to foreclose if you don't meet your payments. The creditor goes into court and establishes the fact of your default in your payments. If you have no legal defense, the court issues an order certifying the creditor as the owner of the property covered by the security interest and giving him permission to sell it.

Another group of favored creditors consists of *lienors*, persons who by statute in most states come ahead of others in the right to collect what is owed to them. The owner of the warehouse where you have stored some furniture has a lien on that furniture if you don't pay the storage bill. The dry cleaner has a lien on the suits you left to be cleaned; the garageman has a lien on the car you left to be repaired (see section 392). The meaning of the *lien* is that the property in question can be held until you pay for the services rendered to you.

In view of all the unpleasant things your creditors can do, when your debts have come to more than you can pay, you should consult a lawyer and go over with him the several steps you can take.

460. Steps a Debtor Can Take • Basically, there are two things to do if you find that you can't pay your bills. One is to try to enter into a voluntary agreement with one or more of your creditors either to reduce the amount of your indebtedness or to stretch out the period of time allowed for your repayment. The other is to use the federal bankruptcy laws and have yourself declared bankrupt by a federal court, which means that most of your debts are discharged (see section 467).

No creditor can reach certain kinds of your property. Although the laws of the states vary widely, your real property or part of it may be *exempt from execution;* that is, it cannot be sold to satisfy your creditors. So is much of your life insurance and some of your clothing, books, tools and other things you need for carrying on your business.

One creditor may be willing simply to reduce the debt, if you can find the money to pay him the smaller amount now. You should get from him a statement in writing to that effect. In some states you will have to give him something as consideration for his agreement (see section 175); otherwise his agreement does not bind him. In other states a written release is binding, even without consideration. However, if there is confusion or disagreement about how much you owe him, your payment to him of a specific amount and his agreement not to claim any more from you is binding on him.

Sometimes a creditor will agree to substitute a new debtor. Knowing your financial troubles, he may be willing to have your debt assumed by one of your relatives or friends. Such a substitution is called a *novation:* it is a new contract between the creditor and your relative or friend and discharges your obligation.

461. Assignment for the Benefit of Creditors • Statutes in a great many states permit you as an insolvent person to make an assignment for the benefit of creditors: You draw up an inventory of all your property and turn it over to an assignee who becomes a trustee. He files a bond in an amount equal to the value of your property and undertakes to handle the claims of your creditors. You assign your property to him, and he publishes a notice of the assignment so that they can file their claims with him. He then sells your property and pays your various creditors with the proceeds from the sale.

The trouble with this arrangement is that your debts are discharged *only* in the amount paid to the creditors. If you owe $100,000 and your trustee or assignee receives only $75,000 on the sale of your property, your creditors are only going to receive $75,000 less your assignee's expenses. You still owe at least $25,000. The assignment for the benefit of creditors, therefore, is much less advantageous to you than bankruptcy, as we'll soon explain (see section 463).

462. Composition with Creditors • On the other hand, a composition with creditors, like bankruptcy, does operate to discharge your debts entirely. Your assignee or trustee might persuade your creditors, in the example just mentioned, that there is no possibility of your ever being able to pay the whole $100,000 you owe and that, all things considered, they should settle for $75,000 and forget the extra $25,000. If he succeeds in doing so, you and your creditors enter into a contract whereby you spread the $75,000 among them as they agree, and they jointly discharge you from the remaining $25,000 obligation.

463. Bankruptcy • Far more common than an assignment or a composition is the use of procedures established by the federal government in the Bankruptcy Act and carried out under the supervision of the U.S. district courts by special bankruptcy judges. The Bankruptcy Act says you are an *insolvent* when your property, appraised at a fair valuation, is insufficient to pay your debts. You are a *bankrupt* when you have been declared a bankrupt under the Act. You may take the initiative yourself and file a petition in bankruptcy (this situation is called *voluntary bankruptcy*) or your creditors may file a petition against you (this is called *involuntary bankruptcy*).

To make the decision whether to file your own petition or wait until a petition is filed against you, you should consult a lawyer. Your experience in getting to the point of bankruptcy is likely to have been painful, and you need legal advice, if only to be warned against doing things that may cause you trouble in the bankruptcy proceedings, such as transferring your property or some of it to someone else in the mistaken belief that it can escape the claims of your creditors.

If you can see no reasonable prospect of paying your bills, you should not regard bankruptcy as dishonorable or immoral. Bankruptcy proceedings are authorized by Congress; they were established to enable you to receive a full discharge from all but certain debts (see section 467). The expenses of going through a bankruptcy proceeding are prescribed by the Bankruptcy Act. There is a $50 fee for filing a petition. In a special category of bankruptcy proceeding called wage-earner cases the initial fee is only $15. You will aso be responsible for paying your own attorney's fees, although any legal aid society will furnish counsel to you without charge if you are unable to cover this. There may, depending upon the nature of your assets, be other costs of the bankruptcy proceeding—some of them substantial. These other costs, however, will be paid out of the property you have turned over to the trustee and are, therefore, realistically expenses of your creditors.

464. Filing the Petition in Bankruptcy • A bankruptcy proceeding begins with the filing of a petition in the office of the clerk of the U.S. district court where the debtor resides. A voluntary petition may be filed by any debtor, except a municipality or an insurance or banking company, who is sane and who has not filed a petition within the past six years. An involuntary petition may be filed against any person except a wage earner or a farmer and against most business corporations. When the debtor has fewer than twelve creditors, any one of them may file an involuntary petition of bankruptcy against him. If the creditors number twelve or more, three must sign the petition. But the involuntary petition can be filed only when: (a) the debtor owes $1,000 or more, (b) the petitioning creditors are owed at least $500 and (c) the debtor has committed an "act of bankruptcy" within four months of the day the petition is filed.

The National Bankruptcy Act mentions six *acts of bankruptcy,* on the basis of which you may be declared bankrupt.

The first is a *fraudulent transfer* of property, that is, a transfer designed to defraud your creditors. You would be guilty of fraudulent transfer if you gave or sold your house to your son for less than its value when you realized your creditors were after you or if you sold all your stocks and bonds and left the country taking the cash with you.

The second is a *preferential transfer* of your property, within four months before filing of the petition. If you are insolvent and pay off some of your creditors in full, with the result that there's nothing left over for the others, or at least not enough to go around, you have made a preferential transfer.

The third is the situation in which one of your creditors sues you for the amount you owe him and gets a judgment against you in that amount and that judgment then becomes a lien, or legally enforceable claim, against any of your property.

The fourth act of bankruptcy arises when you make a general assignment for the benefit of your creditors (see section 461).

The fifth occurs when a receiver or trustee has been appointed, for the benefit of all your creditors, to take charge of all your property while you are insolvent or unable to pay your debts.

The sixth and last act of bankruptcy is one in which you admit in writing that you are unable to pay your debts and are willing to be adjudged or declared a bankrupt by a court.

When an involuntary petition in bankruptcy is brought against you and you believe you are solvent and are unwilling to be declared a bankrupt, you are entitled to a trial by jury as to your financial condition.

Although bankruptcy petitions are filed in the U.S. district court, they are actually handled by bankruptcy judges.

When a bankruptcy petition is filed against you, whether it is voluntary or involuntary, you must file *schedules,* listing all your creditors and all details of your property and assets, and a *statement of affairs,* which sets forth all necessary information regarding your financial condition. These are required in order to avoid the expense of lengthy examinations. It

557

is a criminal offense for you to conceal your assets, unless the property is exempted from the proceeding by statute (see sections 301, 460). Any debts you fail to list will not be discharged by the bankruptcy proceeding.

Not more than a month after the petition of bankruptcy has been filed, the referee notifies all the creditors listed in your schedules of the first meeting, at which you must be present. The creditors may request the court to appoint a *receiver* of your property until the petition is heard or a trustee is appointed.

For more information on business bankruptcy, see section 411.

465. Rights and Duties of the Creditors • It is the responsibility of the creditors to file written *proofs of claim* if they want to receive any payment from the bankrupt estate. A proof of claim must state: (a) the nature of the claim, (b) what it is based on (services rendered or goods sold to the bankrupt), (c) whether the creditor has any of the debtor's property to be credited against the claim, (d) any payments the debtor may already have made to reduce the amount of the claim and (e) that the claim is due and owed by the debtor to the creditor. Proofs of claim must be filed with the bankruptcy court within six months of the date set by the referee for the first meeting of creditors.

Secured creditors are ones who have property pledged for the debt: the holder of a security interest in your refrigerator would be a secured creditor. *General creditors* are those who have no security or property pledged. The friend who loaned you $1,000, taking only your promissory note in that amount, would be a general creditor.

466. Role of the Trustee in Bankruptcy • A trustee in bankruptcy is usually appointed by the referee at the first meeting. The trustee is responsible for administering your estate as a bankrupt. He takes over all your assets. He examines you and anyone who has any knowledge of your affairs. He must uncover any irregular dealings that violate the bankruptcy act, such as fraudulent and preferential transfers, and locate any concealed property. The trustee's job is to see to it that all creditors are treated fairly and equally.

When the trustee has found out all he needs to know about your property and has got control of all of it, and when at the end of the six-month period he has received all your creditors' claims, he will get permission of the referee to liquidate, or sell, your assets to raise the money to pay off your creditors. The order in which your creditors are paid off may be hard to decide if your debts are of various kinds. As a general rule, your secured creditors come first: the holder of a security interest, for example, or the bank that has possession of $1,000 in common stocks that you put up as collateral for a $500 loan. Also, certain other types of creditors have a prior claim; that is, they are entitled under the bankruptcy act to be paid before any of your general creditors. These prior claimants are workmen, servants, clerks or salesmen to whom you owe less than $300 each. Taxes and rent you owe also come ahead of general creditors, and the various administrative expenses of the bankruptcy must be paid before any general creditor receives anything.

467. The Discharge in Bankruptcy • When your trustee has distributed your assets as fairly as he can, the bankruptcy court issues an order discharging you as a bankrupt. The order means that you are free from any further obligation to pay your debts, except for those that by law are not discharged by the bankruptcy.

These nondischarged debts include: (a) taxes you owe of all kinds— federal, state, county or municipal; (b) liability for any money obtained fraudulently; (c) liability for any willful and malicious injury to anyone or to his property; (d) liability for alimony or for nonsupport of a wife or child; (e) any debts you failed to list in the bankruptcy schedules (see section 464); (f) wages you owe for services performed for you within three months of the date of the start of the bankruptcy proceeding.

For any one of several reasons your creditors may object to your being discharged. Most of them have to do with your withholding information regarding your affairs, making false statements during the proceedings or removing some of your property from the court's jurisdiction in order to defraud your creditors.

468. Advantages of the Bankruptcy Laws • As recently as 100 years ago you might well have gone to prison for failing to pay your debts. The whole philosophy of today's bankruptcy law is to give you an opportunity to throw in the sponge when your debts get unbearable (and unpayable) and to make a new financial start. But you must be willing to surrender very nearly everything you own.

Congress has established a carefully spelled-out procedure for you to follow; the United States courts are there to help you. The district courts are not overcrowded. The costs of a bankruptcy proceeding are easy to find out and are much less than the costs of most litigation. One might say that bankruptcy is a form of legal surgery, to be used only when necessary, and far from pleasant in that you are required to disclose your whole financial picture to public view. But bankruptcy is a form of surgery that is widely used and very successful. Perhaps 100,000 petitions in bankruptcy are filed each year, the great majority of them voluntary. If you feel that bankruptcy might be the answer to a personal financial dilemma, obtain the advice of an experienced lawyer and co-operate with him. Your greatest loss may be to your pride. But that loss is a small price to pay for a discharge from the burden of most of your debts and an opportunity for a completely new financial beginning. (For information on business bankruptcy, see section 411.)

IF YOU INVEST YOUR MONEY

469. Protecting the Value of Your Money • There are all kinds of people who will offer you ways of using your savings or your inheritance. Laws exist to protect you from the unscrupulous, but to make the most of their protection you should have some basic understanding of what these laws are and of the various things you can do with your money.

Perhaps the safest thing to do with your extra money is put it in a safe-deposit box. For hundreds of years the people of France are said to have hidden their savings in their mattresses because they didn't trust their government not to waste their money if they bought government bonds. If you could be sure that the dollar would be worth more, that you could buy more with it a year from now than you can today, then a safe-deposit box would be a very safe place indeed. Unfortunately, recent history proves rather convincingly that the value of the dollar goes down, not up. The dollars you put into the safe-deposit box will in all likelihood be worth less a year from now than they are today, so that you actually lose money by putting it in a safe-deposit box or other safe place. Also, of course, you get no interest on your money.

470. Savings Accounts as an Investment • If you put your money in a savings account (see section 446), the bank will pay you interest, at a rate that today will almost compensate for the shrinkage in the value of your dollar because of inflation. Inflation has been running at the rate of about 7 percent a year. Most savings banks pay from 5 to 6 percent interest a year, so that you would not quite keep up with inflation by depositing your savings in a savings account. But at least you'd be getting something back on it. Your savings account is insured by the federal government, which, with the state governments, closely regulates the activities of banks and savings and loan associations.

471. Certificates of Deposit • You may also go to a bank and invest your money in what are called certificates of deposit. The most important thing about an ordinary savings account is that you may withdraw your money at any time. But the key to a certificate of deposit is that you agree to leave the money in the bank for a specified period. The longer the period, the higher the interest the bank will pay on your certificate. Because the bank knows it will not have to pay back the amount of your certificate for the time agreed upon, it has more freedom to invest your money in a variety of loans. Therefore, it can afford to pay you a larger amount of interest. The rates banks may pay on certificates are controlled by the Federal Reserve Board.

But even certificates of deposit will barely make it possible for you to keep the value of your savings up with the inflation of recent years. Another disadvantage of the certificate is that you may find it difficult to sell your certificate if you need the money before the period of time agreed upon by you (three, six, nine, twelve or twenty-four months) has passed, or you may have to sell it at a lower interest return than you would otherwise be entitled to. A third and serious disadvantage is that banks are not always willing to issue them in "small" amounts, such as $1,000.

472. Federal Bonds • To invest your money with maximum safety and get a return that will keep you at least even with inflationary trends, you may need to look beyond bank savings plans. One area to investigate is obligations of the United States government. These come in several forms. *Savings bonds* are long-range obligations· you lend the government your money for, say, twenty-five years; the government promises to repay you at the end of that time, and, like the bank or savings and loan association, to pay you interest for the use of your money. Unfortunately, long-range government bonds carry relatively low interest rates. They are backed by the credit of the U.S. government and are an absolutely safe investment. United States government notes and Treasury bills are also obligations of the government itself, but they carry interest at a much higher rate than long-term bonds. Obligations issued by certain governmental agencies, such as the Federal National Mortgage Association and the Federal Home Loan Bank Board, are partially backed by the U.S. government itself; it could not afford to have these agencies default on their obligations, which are very similar to U.S. Treasury bills. They are quite safe, relatively short term and pay interest.

473. State and Municipal Bonds • You may also lend your money to a state or one of its agencies, a county or a municipality. All these have the legal power to borrow money by issuing bonds (for long-term borrowing, one year or more) or notes (for short-term borrowing, usually less than a year). These state and local governments and state agencies offer you two different kinds of bonds in return for your loan. One type of bond is a general obligation of the state, county, city or one of their agencies. It has behind it the issuer's taxing power.

The other type of bond issued by state and local governments is a *revenue bond:* the state or city or agency selling it to you promises to pay you back from one specific source of revenue only. If you buy a bond sold to finance construction of a sewer, for example, you should ask your banker or adviser to make sure that enough money can be raised from charges made to the users of the sewer to pay you and other bondholders back both the amount of your bond (loan) and the interest on it. In other words, make sure the proposed investment is a sound one.

The bonds sold by state and local governments and agencies have one distinct advantage: the interest on them is exempt from federal income taxation. If you have considerable other income, the effect of the tax-exempt aspect of the state and local bonds is to increase the net (after-tax) income in your hands by 25 to 50 percent.

Until very recently, state and municipal bonds were regarded as extremely safe investments. The recent experience of New York City in defaulting on billions of dollars of its obligations has occasioned a new look. The bonds and notes of state and local governments, unlike the securities of private businesses, are not subject to SEC disclosure requirements (see section 480). This means that the financial statements of governmental issuers have not normally been reviewed by any outside auditor. Therefore, it is important to familiarize yourself with the rating services, notably Moody's and Standard & Poor's, which evaluate such securities from the point of view of their safety. The services are generally conservative in giving good ratings, and their historic record on foreseeing trouble has been good.

474. Bonds, Debentures and Common Stocks • If you decide that you want to invest your money privately, you have many choices. One of the most important things to ask yourself is how safe you want your money to be—how sure you want to be of getting it back. The safer the investment, the lower the interest rate. The riskier or more speculative the investment, the greater your possible gain. As we move into the area of private investing, it is vital that you understand the difference between a bond (or debenture), which is an evidence of debt, and stock, which is an evidence of partial ownership. Debt obligations that are secured in some way, as by a mortgage on land, are usually called bonds. Unsecured obligations, which represent a simple promise to pay, are usually called debentures. Debentures typically command a higher interest rate than bonds of the same issuer because of the absence of security.

The utility company that sells you a $1,000 bond payable ten years hence with interest at 6 percent is promising only to pay you $1,000 ten years from now and to pay you 6 percent, or $60, a year for each of the next ten years.

The company meets its entire obligation to you by paying the interest on schedule and the principal when due. It's much the same as with government bonds, savings accounts and certificates of deposit. You get back only what you loan the government, bank or utility company, plus the agreed interest on your money.

You can share in a private company's growth only by becoming a part owner of the company through the purchase of its common stock. What you receive for your $1,000 investment in the common stock of, say, the Magic Multiplier Company is a piece of paper, called a stock certificate, which says you are the owner of 100 shares of its common stock (meaning each share cost you $10). You are promised nothing.

You buy or sell common stock through a stockbroker: all he does is find you a seller when you want to buy and a buyer when you want to sell. The price in each case is determined by supply and demand: if more people want to buy than to sell, the price will rise, as it will fall if more want to sell than to buy. Neither Magic Multiplier Company nor your broker makes you any promise or guarantees any return on your investment.

Nothing is said, either, about you right to "interest" on your investment, in this case your right to dividends. The directors of Magic Multiplier annually declare the dividend, if any, that is payable on its common stock. Some companies pay no dividend. Others pay high dividends. But you are legally entitled only to the dividend declared on the common stock, when it is declared. If the dividend is ten cents a share, you are entitled to $10 for your 100 shares. If Magic Multiplier Company prospers and its profits rise, in all likelihood the price of its common stock will

563

rise: more and more people will want to buy; fewer and fewer people will want to sell.

Should Magic Multiplier succeed, the price might rise in ten years from the $10 per share you paid for your common stock to $100 per share. You would then make a handsome profit if you sold at $100, a profit of 1,000 percent. This investment, at least, would have kept you far ahead of the inflation in the economy, or the decline in the value of the dollar. You would also have received dividends every year, probably each somewhat larger than the previous one, so that all in all—despite no legal protection such as the bondholder has—you end up far ahead of him in your profit on your investment.

On the other hand, it may happen that after you buy your 100 shares of Magic Multiplier at $10 per share and have received your portion of a ten-cent dividend, or $10, another company brings to market a similar product, better made and priced lower. It sells so many of its products that Magic Multiplier's sales and earnings go down instead of up, and to save the company's cash, the directors declare no dividend. Next year Magic Multiplier goes into bankruptcy and is liquidated. After the creditors are paid off, there are no assets left. You are out of luck and out of $1,000. You have nothing to complain about, provided the directors and officers of Magic Multiplier acted in good faith, were honest and used the best known methods of business management. You were promised nothing, and you got nothing. Therein lies the risk of common stock as an investment. As an owner of part of the company's assets, you prosper with it if it succeeds and fall with it if business is bad or it becomes bankrupt.

475. Preferred and Convertible Preferred Stock • A kind of stock that gives you slightly greater protection than common stock is called preferred stock. As the holder of preferred stock you get dividend preference over the common-stock holder. Also, most preferred stock issues give you the right to a dividend of a stated amount, usually $5 or $6 per share, if the company's earnings permit. As a common-stock holder you get dividends only when the directors declare them after all the company's other, prior obligations have been met. First comes the interest on the company's bonds (long-term debt), then the interest on any short-term loans the company may have, then the dividend per share on the preferred stock. Last of all comes the dividend per share on the common stock.

Because preferred stock has so many similarities to bonds, corporations often issue convertible preferred stock. Because convertible stock can be converted into common stock in certain circumstances, its price

HOW HISTORY AFFECTS THE STOCK MARKET

News headlines often influence stock market prices: bad news, such as the Japanese attack on Pearl Harbor in 1941, sends prices downward; good news, such as the end of the Korean War in 1953, drives prices upward. The highs and lows of the Dow Jones industrial average over the last 45 years, as shown below, reflect history's impact on stock prices.

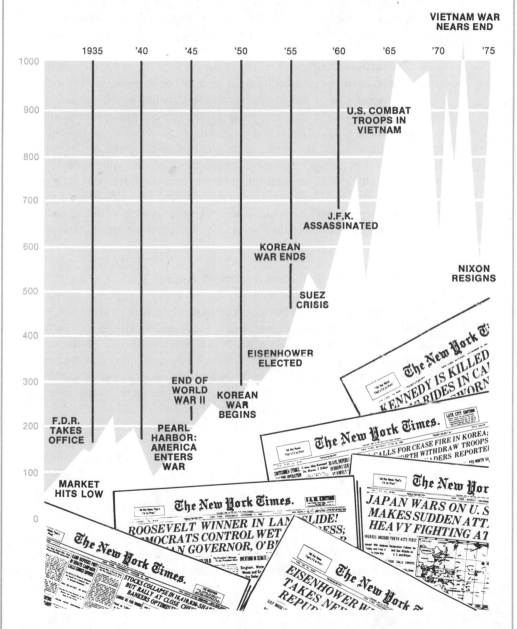

VIETNAM WAR NEARS END

1935   '40   '45   '50   '55   '60   '65   '70   '75

1000
900
800
700
600
500
400
300
200
100
0

U.S. COMBAT TROOPS IN VIETNAM

J.F.K. ASSASSINATED

NIXON RESIGNS

KOREAN WAR ENDS

SUEZ CRISIS

EISENHOWER ELECTED

END OF WORLD WAR II

KOREAN WAR BEGINS

F.D.R. TAKES OFFICE

PEARL HARBOR: AMERICA ENTERS WAR

MARKET HITS LOW

will rise with the price of the common stock in a favorable market. But if the price of the common stock goes down, the preferred falls less sharply because its minimum dividend is guaranteed. The holder of convertible preferred stock is thus in a stronger position than the holder of common stock because (a) his dividend rights come ahead of the common-stock holder's and (b) he comes ahead of the common-stock holder (but behind the bondholder) if the company goes out of business.

476. Convertible Debentures • In recent years many corporations have tried to attract investors who hesitate to buy bonds because of the low return with something called a convertible debenture. The word *convertible* means that the debenture can be converted into common stock at certain prices and under certain conditions spelled out in the debenture itself. The price of the debenture then gets tied to the price of the stock. If the price of the stock rises, so does the price of the debenture. If the price of the stock falls, so does the price of the debenture, although, according to experts, it will not fall so rapidly. As the holder of a convertible debenture, you have the added protection of a claim ahead of stockholders on the company's assets if the company is dissolved or goes into bankruptcy.

477. Voting Rights of Common-Stock Holders • Besides the right of common-stock holders to share in the growth of the company's earnings, they have an even more important right: the right to exercise their part ownership by participating in and voting at annual meetings. The significance of this right obviously varies, depending on the size of the company. If you own even 1,000 shares, there's not much you can do about the management of a company with over 100 million shares of common stock, but your voting right becomes very meaningful in the case of small companies whose shares are in the hundreds of thousands.

But even though you may own only a small number of shares of common stock, you should exercise your voting rights. Every year, before the annual meeting—and more often, if special meetings are called by the directors—you will get in the mail a proxy form. If you are not going to the meeting you can sign the form, giving your proxy to an official of the company to vote your stock as you direct at the meeting.

478. Mutual Funds • If you decide to invest in securities that involve some level of risk, you must first decide whether to put your eggs in one or in many baskets. In general, your chances of gain and your risk of loss are both greater if you invest directly in specific securities. If you are willing to accept more limited gains, you can reduce your risk of loss substantially by investing through a mutual fund.

A mutual fund is simply a fund of money owned by many persons, each of whom receives shares or units representing his or her share of the total. The investment of the money in the fund is managed by professionals. Diversification is the great advantage of such funds. Your modest contributions are pooled with those of hundreds or thousands of other shareholders or purchasers of the fund. The management invests these assets in many different companies and many different industries. Losses that may be experienced by one company or industry are evened out by the gains experienced by others.

The mutual fund management declares dividends as they are received from companies in which the fund has invested. You may instruct the management to pay you your share of the dividends, or you may authorize it to use your share of the dividends to purchase additional units of the fund for you.

Some mutual fund organizations charge the buyer what is known as a sales load. This means that in addition to the price of the share or unit, you pay another 6 to 8 percent to cover the company's sales expenses. Other funds, including some of the best managed and most successful, charge you no sales load. When you sell your shares or units, you pay 1 percent to cover the management's expenses in setting up your account, issuing and redeeming your shares, and managing the fund.

Under both types of fund the management agrees to redeem your shares at any time. The amount you receive is their value (based on the market value of all the shares owned by the fund) on the day you order that they be redeemed.

479. How You Buy Securities • If you decide to invest in the stock or debt securities of a particular company, you will have to find someone to sell you the security. You might ask friends if anyone owns the security and wishes to sell it, or run a classified ad. These are likely to be slow and inconvenient ways to purchase, and for that reason you will wish to deal with a securities industry professional, called a broker or dealer. How your order is filled will depend importantly on whether the security you wish to purchase is traded on a stock exchange. An exchange is essentially a continuous public auction in which at various points on the trading floor simultaneous auctions are being conducted in every security traded on that exchange. Your order to purchase a security traded on an exchange is filed by a broker who is physically present at the appropriate auction, offering to buy or sell as various orders reach him.

If the security you wish to buy is not traded on an exchange— and the vast majority of securities are not—it is said to be traded over the counter (OTC). Buying securities in the OTC market is very much like buying merchandise from a catalog company. Because there is no auction market, you must buy from a dealer who holds an inventory of the security for sale. There are about 20,000 companies whose securities are traded OTC; obviously, no broker could have more than a few of them in inventory. When you place an order for an OTC security, it is unlikely that your broker will own it. He will use a national system of quotations, now partially computerized, to find dealers who own that security and the prices at which they respectively are offering it for sale. Such dealers are said to be "making a market" in the security.

If you are selling a security, the process is reversed. If the security is traded on an exchange, your broker will arrange for it to be sold at the exchange auction; if the security is traded OTC, your broker will either buy the security for his own inventory or use the quotation system to find a dealer who makes a market in the security.

Brokerage firms handle state and municipal bonds like other OTC securities, and there are some firms that specialize in these bonds. Alternatively, you can probably buy or sell the bonds through your bank.

How you go about buying a mutual fund will depend on how the fund markets its shares. If it charges a sales load (see section 478), its shares will be sold through brokers. If it is a no-load fund, it will not pay any commission to brokers to handle sales of its shares. Therefore you will have to deal directly with the fund. Many no-load funds advertise in the newspapers and will send you a prospectus on request.

480. Legal Protection for Investors • Both federal and state governments have departments to protect investors by requiring corporations to disclose all necessary information to help investors decide whether to buy proposed bonds, notes and stocks. These governmental departments and agencies were created because of lessons learned over many years. People in general are gullible. We all want to make money the easy way and tend to forget that the easy way is almost always the riskiest. When you want to invest you should go to one of the offices of an established brokerage company. Such companies are registered with the appropriate state agency, if there is one (see chart 36, page 571 for your state's agency), and with the Securities and Exchange Commission (SEC) in

Washington, D.C. Almost all brokerage houses also have departments for handling their customers' orders for buying and selling the several kinds of bonds discussed earlier. You can also get help from your local banker in handling municipal bond orders, if you decide on bonds.

Before the creation of the SEC in 1934, protection of the investor was done by the states. Many of the states adopted blue-sky laws requiring registration and approval by state agencies of the sale of securities (stocks and bonds) in certain industries—largely mining and oil—where the individual investor had no way of checking on the truth or accuracy of the statements made in the literature promoting the stock issue.

Even today these state agencies are actively at work in areas that the SEC doesn't try to cover. The New York State attorney general's office, for example, is the only governmental department that requires the filing of full information regarding the sale to residents of New York of land in other states. Many people had lost money because of misleading literature promoting these land sales—and the SEC has nothing to do with sales of real estate. Moreover, the SEC has no jurisdiction over the sale of securities in one state only. The family business operated as a corporation, which decides to raise $100,000 by selling $10,000 worth of common stock each to ten family friends, does not come under the SEC.

The SEC comes in when the company needs more money than it can raise locally and will have to go to an underwriter for professional assistance. An underwriter, for these purposes, is a company that agrees to buy an issue of bonds or stock at the end of a certain time; the underwriter sells the bonds or stock to the public at a slightly higher price; the difference is his profit. The underwriter may be able to raise the money from a few friends within the state, and the SEC is not involved. But if the stock is to be sold to the public, requiring advertising in the press or a mailing of promotional literature (called a prospectus) to potential buyers, the proposed stock issue must be registered and approved by the SEC. In the registration process the issuer furnishes the SEC with copies of the proposed prospectus and certain additional information. The SEC reviews the documents to make sure investors will be adequately informed of any risks. The SEC must make its judgment on the basis of information the company has provided, but it does not ordinarily investigate this information. What makes the system work is that the penalties to which the company becomes subject by failing to make adequate disclosure are extremely serious.

The SEC also supervises the daily operations of the securities markets.

569

It tries to investigate unusual market performance. If the common stock of one or another corporation suddenly rises or falls for no apparent reason, the SEC (and the stock exchanges) may issue an order stopping all transactions in the stock pending the results of full investigation.

Most companies whose securities are traded on an exchange or OTC are subject to a continuous disclosure system administered by the SEC. Companies must publish an annual report to stockholders with detailed financial information; copies are available in libraries and from brokers.

All these areas of governmental concern with and protection of you as an investor exist alongside your right to assert your legal claim against a company or its officers or directors if you believe they are guilty of fraud or mismanagement. In consultation with your lawyer you should decide how, when and where to proceed. Generally speaking, you will find it difficult to hold directors or officers liable for errors of judgment as long as they acted in good faith. Their failure to act or their action that results in loss to the company which they knew would occur or should have known would occur, is something else again.

As a stockholder, then, you do have the right to demand conscientious, intelligent and honest performance by your company's directors and officers, and you have the right to take legal action if you have reason to believe that their performance hasn't met those standards. But litigation, as we have said, is prolonged and expensive, and the scales are uneven: because it has one or more lawyers on retainer (see section 619), the corporation can afford its defense much more easily than you can afford to start and prosecute a lawsuit. Precisely for this reason the federal and state governments created the SEC and similar agencies, to assert your rights, at public expense.

Almost all brokers must be licensed by the SEC and be members of an industry self-regulatory organization, the National Association of Securities Dealers (NASD). SEC and NASD rules require brokers to observe fair standards in making recommendations to clients. Your broker's violation of these rules could cause you serious losses. If he recommends excessive trading for the purpose of generating commission he is engaging in "churning," and if you believe this is happening you should see your lawyer. Don't pick a broker at random; ask your accountant, lawyer or banker for recommendations. Be sure your broker understands your situation. A young person with few responsibilities and cash to spare might well be interested in speculative securities. Older people with heavy responsibilities and limited resources should usually be interested in less dramatic but safer investments.

STATES WITH BLUE-SKY LAWS

The so-called blue-sky laws are designed to regulate the sale and promotion of securities and to protect the public against fraudulent stock offerings (see section 480). This chart shows the nature of your state's blue-sky law and what agency administers it.

CHART 36	Does State Have Blue-Sky Law?	Who Administers It?
ALABAMA	Yes: Securities Act of Alabama	Alabama Securities Commission, Birmingham
ALASKA	Yes: Uniform Securities Act	Alaska Securities Commission, Department of Commerce, Juneau
ARIZONA	Yes: Securities Act of Arizona	Arizona Corporation Commissioner, Phoenix
ARKANSAS	Yes: Uniform Securities Act	Securities Commissioner, Arkansas Securities Dept., Little Rock
CALIFORNIA	Yes: California Corporate Securities Law	Commissioner, Dept. of Corporations, Sacramento
COLORADO	Yes: Uniform Securities Act	Securities Commissioner, Denver
CONNECTICUT	Yes: Connecticut Securities Act	Bank Commissioner, Hartford
DELAWARE	Yes: Delaware Blue-Sky Law	Securities Commissioner, Dover
D.C.	Yes: District of Columbia Securities Act	Public Service Commission, Washington, D.C.
FLORIDA	Yes: Florida Sale of Securities Law	Division of Securities, Department of Banking and Finance, Tallahassee
GEORGIA	Yes: Georgia Securities Act	Secretary of State, Atlanta
HAWAII	Yes: Uniform Securities Act	Director of Regulatory Agencies (ex-officio Commissioner of Securities), Honolulu
IDAHO	Yes: Idaho Securities Act	Director of Finance, Boise
ILLINOIS	Yes: Illinois Securities Law	Secretary of State through Securities Commissioner, Springfield
INDIANA	Yes: Indiana Securities Act	Secretary of State through Securities Commissioner, Indianapolis
IOWA	Yes: Iowa Securities Law	Commissioner of Insurance through Superintendent of Securities Department, Des Moines
KANSAS	Yes: Speculative Securities Act	Securities Commission of Kansas, Topeka
KENTUCKY	Yes: Uniform Securities Act	Division of Securities, Department of Banking and Securities, Frankfort
LOUISIANA	Yes	State Bank Examiner (ex-officio Commissioner of Securities), New Orleans
MAINE	Yes	Director of Securities Division, Bureau of Banking, Augusta
MARYLAND	Yes: Maryland Securities Act	Securities Commissioner, Department of Securities, Baltimore
MASSACHUSETTS	Yes: Uniform Securities Act	The Secretary of the Commonwealth, Boston
MICHIGAN	Yes: Michigan Uniform Securities Act	Corporation & Securities Bureau, Lansing
MINNESOTA	Yes: Minnesota Blue-Sky Law	Commissioner of Securities, Securities Division, Department of Commerce, St. Paul
MISSISSIPPI	Yes: Mississippi Securities Act	Secretary of State, Jackson

CHART
36
(cont.)

	Does State Have Blue-Sky Law?	Who Administers It?
MISSOURI	Yes: Missouri Uniform Securities Act	Securities Commissioner, Office of Secretary of State, Jefferson City
MONTANA	Yes: Securities Act of Montana	State Auditor, Helena
NEBRASKA	Yes: Securities Act of Nebraska	Director of Banking, Lincoln
NEVADA	Yes: Nevada Securities Act	Secretary of State, Carson City
NEW HAMPSHIRE	Yes	Insurance Commission, Concord
NEW JERSEY	Yes: New Jersey Securities Law	Bureau of Securities, Department of Law and Public Safety, Newark
NEW MEXICO	Yes: Securities Act of New Mexico	Commissioner of Securities, Santa Fe
NEW YORK	Yes: Martin Act	Attorney General, Albany
NORTH CAROLINA	Yes: North Carolina Securities Act	Secretary of State, Raleigh
NORTH DAKOTA	Yes: North Dakota Securities Act	Securities Commissioner, Bismarck
OHIO	Yes: Ohio Securities Act	Division of Securities, Columbus
OKLAHOMA	Yes: Oklahoma Securities Act	Administrator appointed by Oklahoma Securities Commission, Oklahoma City
OREGON	Yes: Oregon Securities Law	Corporation Commissioner, Salem
PENNSYLVANIA	Yes: Pennsylvania Securities Act	Securities Commission, Harrisburg
RHODE ISLAND	Yes	Director of Business Regulation, Providence
SOUTH CAROLINA	Yes: South Carolina Securities Act	Secretary of State, Columbia
SOUTH DAKOTA	Yes: South Dakota Securities Law	Commissioner of Securities, Pierre
TENNESSEE	Yes: Securities Law of 1955	Commissioner of Insurance and Banking, Memphis
TEXAS	Yes: The Securities Act	Securities Commissioner of State Securities Board, Austin
UTAH	Yes: Utah Uniform Securities Act	State Securities Commissioner, Salt Lake City
VERMONT	Yes: Securities Act of Vermont	Commissioner of Banking and Insurance, Montpelier
VIRGINIA	Yes: Virginia Securities Act	State Corporation Commission, Richmond
WASHINGTON	Yes: Security Act of Washington	Administrator of Securities, Department of Licenses, Olympia
WEST VIRGINIA	Yes	State Auditor, Commissioner of Securities, Charleston
WISCONSIN	Yes: Uniform Securities Act	Commissioner of Securities, Madison
WYOMING	Yes: Uniform Securities Act	Secretary of State, Securities Division, Cheyenne

CHAPTER ELEVEN

Your Insurance

The law is not a machine and the judges not machine-tenders. There never was and there never will be a body of fixed and predetermined rules alike for all.

—JEROME FRANK

11

Your Insurance

Some Key Points in This Chapter—
Consult these sections for information on:

THE NATURE OF INSURANCE

481. What Insurance Is • Man is constantly in search of security, but life is full of uncertainties. Although you may follow all the rules of proverbial wisdom, never leaving for tomorrow what you can do today and applying ounces of prevention endlessly, you will still be exposed to the risk of accident and disaster. A fire may break out in your house and leave it a charred, smoking ruin. A sudden, unforeseeable illness may smother you with doctor and hospital bills. A thief may break into your home and walk off with your most valued possessions. Your minor son may ram your car into a neighbor's, causing an accident that can cost you a small fortune in damages. If you are in business, you face as many risks as a porcupine has quills.

It is difficult for the average man to bear the cost of serious damage to his property or injury to his person. Liability for injury to others can be even more costly. It was precisely for these reasons that insurance was developed. Insurance offers a method to share the perils of life and business with other people so that the consequences will not fall too heavily upon you if you experience a severe loss. The principle is an extremely simple one. People who are exposed to the same kinds of hazards pay set sums of money (called *premiums*) into a general fund. When one of them suffers a misfortune of the kind insured against, money is drawn from the fund to indemnify him. Since a large number of people contribute to the fund and only a relatively small number suffer the loss within a given period, the cost of the premium is not great.

Insurance, essentially, is a cooperative plan for sharing risks with a group. To join the group you must make a contract with it. Under this contract, or *policy,* you agree to make payments to the plan at regular intervals. In exchange, the plan promises to make payments to you up to a specified sum if you suffer any of the misfortunes or meet the other conditions covered by the policy.

482. Roles of Insurance Agents and Brokers • Generally speaking, an *insurance agent* is employed by an insurance company to sell policies for it. He works for the company, not for the insured, and has authority to act for it in its dealings with the policyholder. The agent may work for a salary as an employe, or he may be an exclusive company agent working for a commission. (See also sections 393, 394.)

The *insurance broker,* by contrast, represents the man or woman to whom he sells insurance. Basically he is a middleman who will get you the kind of insurance you want from any one of a number of companies. He is normally not authorized to act for these companies or to make a commitment in their name, as an agent is.

There are two special situations in which your broker acts as an agent for the company whose policy he sells you. One is when the company turns over your policy to him for delivery to you. The other is when he collects a premium from you at the time he gives you the policy. If, for example, he forgot to forward the premium to the company and you died after giving it to him, the company would still be obliged to pay the insurance benefit.

Whether he is a broker or an agent, you should call on your insurance salesman for counsel on your insurance problems. He can advise you whether you should change your policy when your risk increases or your family grows larger. He will help you file a claim, tell you how you can borrow against the cash value of your policy and assist you in protecting your interests in other ways.

All of the states require an insurance agent to obtain a license in order to sell insurance. Insurance brokers also must be licensed in many of the states. Frequently the applicant is required to pass an examination.

483. When Your Protection Starts • When an insurance policy goes into force depends largely on the kind of insurance and on the provisions it contains. With casualty or fire insurance the insurance company or its agent may give you a memorandum, or *binder,* summing up the coverage you have agreed to purchase. This insurance is effective immediately; it gives you protection while the company checks on your insurability and issues your policy. Often you may be issued a binder even before you have made a payment. Sometimes an agent will give you an oral acceptance that is effective at once and may be as binding as a written receipt.

A life insurance company may also give you a binder, which may place your insurance in force either immediately or as of the date you pass a medical examination. As a rule, however, you are expected to pay your first premium at the time the binder is written up. If your binder is effective at once and you should die before the policy is issued, the company must pay the insurance benefits if you were insurable on the day the binder was issued.

If the insurance company doesn't give you a binder or issue an oral acceptance saying that you have temporary protection, your insurance generally doesn't go into effect until the policy has been delivered to you. With life insurance a common stipulation is that you must also pay the first premium or part of it on receipt of the policy.

A policy does not necessarily have to be in your hands for it to be considered "delivered" to you. The moment the policy is dropped into the mail, addressed either to you or to the insurance agent for forwarding to you, it is generally regarded as having been *constructively* (that is, in effect) delivered.

484. Dealing with the Insurance Claim Adjuster • When you give notice of a claim to your insurance company, its first step must be to look into the circumstances of your loss and to determine whether it is liable under the terms of your policy. The person charged with looking into your claim is variously known as an adjuster, investigator or examiner. The company's agent often acts as an adjuster on small claims, say up to $250.

You are unlikely to experience any difficulty in obtaining a settlement from the company if the claim is a minor one and the cause and value of the loss are easy to ascertain. But if the loss amounts to a large sum, if there is a possibility of contributory negligence as in an automobile accident case (see section 249) or if there is a question as to whether the loss really falls under the provisions of your policy, you may be in for protracted negotiations.

If your claim is a simple one, as for minor damage under your homeowners policy, then you are safe in dealing directly with the adjuster, or your broker can make the settlement for you. On the other hand, if you have suffered personal injury or have a substantial claim, or if you have a complicated claim involving other parties, you will be wise to talk the matter over with your attorney. Insurance claims often have more ins and outs than the layman can anticipate, and the guidance of a seasoned attorney may save you a considerable amount of money. It may even be to your advantage to have him handle the negotiations with the insurance adjuster.

The procedure in adjusting, or settling, a claim varies somewhat with the kind of insurance and the type of claim. All adjusters, however, have to perform certain basic functions: they investigate the claim, establish the value of the loss and negotiate a settlement with you. The first requirement is that the adjuster must satisfy himself that the loss actually occurred and is covered by the provisions of your insurance contract.

When you reach a settlement with the insurance company, you will often be asked to sign a release. By putting your name to this paper, you indicate that you are satisfied with the settlement and that you will not bring a suit against the insurer. With a small claim the company includes a release statement on the back of the check it gives you, and your endorsement serves as the signature. If the claim of a minor is being settled, the parents or guardian may be asked to sign the release, and if the settlement is large it will probably require court approval. When the claimant is a married woman, the company may want not only her signature but her husband's as well. If you have any doubts about signing, consult your attorney.

If another party is legally liable for the loss, the insurer may want to proceed against him and get back the money it has paid to you. This is called *subrogation*. In such an event, the adjuster will ask you to sign a paper giving the company your authorization.

485. Your Recourse Against the Insurance Company • Because an insurance policy is a contract like any other contract, if the insurance company refuses to pay your claim, it has breached the contract. Under these circumstances you have a right to bring a legal action to compel the company to meet its obligations. (See section 500.)

Most insurance companies have been in business for a long time. They are interested in their good names. Moreover, the structure of the insurance system provides insurers with the funds they need to meet claims. Accordingly, an insurance company will not capriciously turn down a claim; however, it may reject a claim if it thinks it has sufficient legal grounds for refusing to pay. Sometimes, of course, what are sufficient legal grounds can be a matter of interpretation. If you feel that the company is offering you less than you are entitled to or is not meeting its obligations in some other way, your first step, after discussing the matter in depth with the insurance agent, should be to consult your attorney. It is important to take along copies of any correspondence you have had with the insurance company.

486. Government-Administered Insurance • Government has been playing an increasingly important role in the insurance business. When risks are too costly or unprofitable for private insurance companies to bear, government often steps in and takes up the burden; in some cases it makes protection available at premiums within the reach of almost everyone. Federal, state and local governments all are involved in underwriting or administering a multitude of different kinds of insurance. Here we shall look at the most important of these. If you want more detailed information, you can obtain it from the appropriate government agency.

a. *Social security.* The range of coverage afforded by the social security program is suggested by its more formal designation: Old-Age, Survivors and Disability Insurance. Medicare, which provides hospitalization and medical service benefits, is part of social security. (See sections 414–428.)

b. *National Service Life Insurance.* (See section 504.)

c. *Veterans' benefits.* The Veterans Administration pays benefits to qualified veterans with service-connected disability, provided they are totally and permanently disabled and served in wartime.

d. *Federal Deposit Insurance Corporation.* This corporation insures depositors against loss up to $40,000 on each account as a result of bank failure. Most banks of deposit in the United States are insured. The corporation supervises them to see that sound practices are followed. When an insured bank fails, the corporation pays the depositor his loss up to $40,000 or arranges for another insured bank to take over the liabilities of the insolvent one. (See section 447.)

e. *Federal Savings and Loan Corporation.* Depositors in federal savings and loan associations are afforded the same protection by this corporation as other depositors are by the Federal Deposit Insurance Corporation. Savings and loan associations with state charters can also be insured if they belong to the Federal Home Loan Bank System.

f. *National Insurance Development Fund.* In 1968 the federal government established the fund to reinsure private insurance companies against major loss as a result of riots. The state where the loss occurs must agree to bear some of the cost.

g. *Federal Crop Insurance Corporation.* This agency makes available crop insurance against losses from natural causes like hail, drought, flood, freezing, plant disease and insects. A fixed number of pounds or bushels of many farm products are guaranteed per acre. You can also collect on your private policy for the same loss.

h. *Flood insurance.* The secretary of Housing and Urban Development was authorized in 1968 to set up a program making this insurance available on personal and real property in states with approved land control programs. Small commercial properties and residential properties receive preference.

i. *Loan insurance.* Various types of loans are guaranteed by the federal government. Loans to veterans for buying a home or farm are insured up to a given sum (see section 291). Also guaranteed are loans for the improvement of property and construction of cooperative housing and loans to students for college tuition.

j. *Workmen's compensation.* All the states administer programs that provide compensation for employes who are injured in the course of their work. The cost is borne by the employer. (See section 430.)

k. *Unemployment insurance.* This type of insurance provides benefits for qualified workers when they lose their jobs. Most, but not all, workers are covered, as are members of the armed forces after discharge. The cost is paid by the employer. (See section 432.)

l. *Postal insurance.* (See section 494.)

INSURANCE ON HOMES AND PROPERTY

487. Fire Insurance • You have a choice of different types of fire insurance policies to suit your needs. If you are an apartment dweller, the building you live in is your landlord's worry; your main concern is with the contents of your apartment. You may want to buy a *blanket policy* that covers your furnishings and other belongings up to a given sum. No value is stated for particular articles, and you are compensated for the actual cash value at the time your loss occurs. If you have articles of considerable value, such as antiques and paintings, you can take out a policy that describes these possessions and states the value for each. (Standard fire policies do not provide coverage for securities, money, bills, deeds or evidence of debt.) If you have manuscripts in your possession, these must be listed individually in your policy. In case of loss you would be indemnified for the stated value of these articles. If you own your own home, you will want a policy that protects you against fire damage to both your dwelling and its contents.

To take out any insurance policy you must have an *insurable interest* in the property. You must actually own the property in question or have some other right to it. If you own an interest in the building, have a lien on it or are an executor for an estate of which the building forms a part, you possess an insurable interest. You do not have an insurable interest if you simply have expectations of inheriting property; wills can be changed and often are.

Furthermore, your insurable interest must still exist at the time of the loss if you are to make a valid claim. Your interest automatically expires

580

when you transfer the property to someone else. (This rule applies not just to fire insurance but to every other type of insurance.) If you sell your house and a loss occurs, neither you nor the new owner is entitled to collect if the fire insurance policy is still in your name. However, you can arrange to transfer your policy to the new owner at the time of the sale, if the insurance company consents.

For some fires you can collect, for others you cannot. The basic requirement under the law is that the fire must be *accidental and unfriendly:* it either starts by accident or gets out of control. If you set a fire on purpose or engage someone else to set it, that is not an accidental fire, and you have no right to compensation. But if another person starts the fire without your knowledge, the law regards that as an accidental fire. If a fire is caused through negligence by you or an employe of yours, it is also an accidental fire.

Is there such a thing as a "friendly" fire? Yes, when the fire exists in the container intended for it, such as a fireplace, oven, burner or furnace, and you have started it intentionally, for the customary purpose. Thus, if you have an expensive piece of furniture next to your fireplace and you stoke the fire up so hot that it melts the finish on the piece, you cannot collect. The fire remained in the fireplace, and the cause of the damage was the heat from it. But if glowing cinders popped out and set the rug on fire, you would be entitled to compensation for the loss caused by the unfriendly fire on the rug.

The distinction between a friendly and an unfriendly fire is extremely important. If you unconsciously threw a valuable object into the incinerator, you could not collect for the loss. The fire, being in its usual place, was friendly and therefore excluded as a basis for a claim.

The standard fire insurance policy offers protection against certain kinds of loss incidental to a fire. If, for instance, firemen drench your belongings with water or chemicals in order to put out a fire, your loss is covered. It is covered, likewise, if heat or smoke produced by an unfriendly fire causes damage. (Smoke caused by a friendly fire is not covered, however.) If the firemen have to break your windows or batter down your doors, you are also covered. If the fire doesn't occur in your own home, but in your next-door neighbor's, and yet you suffer losses from smoke, heat, water or chemicals, you will be reimbursed.

Sometimes a roof is damaged in a fire and, before you can have it repaired, rain or snow damages the contents of the exposed rooms. Your insurance will compensate you in this case too, since the original cause of the trouble was the fire. If your possessions were carried outside the

581

house to save them from the fire, but then were harmed by a downpour before you could get them to a secure place, the loss is also covered.

Lightning is another peril that the standard fire policy takes account of. The coverage applies even if the damage is inflicted by the lightning itself, without accompanying fire. The standard policy does not cover a loss caused by electricity; however, if electrical trouble with your wiring or fixtures is responsible for a fire you can collect as for any other hostile fire. Losses caused by explosions or riots are excluded, unless a fire results from them and produces the damage.

Nobody likes a fire, least of all the insurance companies. That is why your policy provides that you must take all reasonable precautions to avoid a fire. When a fire occurs, you are under an obligation to protect the insured property from additional damage. For instance, if the fire fighters had used water extensively to put out a fire on the second floor of your home, you would be expected to remove any insured belongings on the floor below if you saw water dripping through the ceiling. You must also use "all reasonable means" to preserve your property if it is imperiled by a fire in a neighbor's dwelling.

There are some additional desirable features that are included in fire insurance policies or may be added to them. One is a *floater* that gives you coverage on your property or that of your immediate family when the property is away from home. This property is protected only against the risks named in your basic policy. Another popular feature is the *extended coverage endorsement*. This protects you against damage by windstorm and damage to the interior of your home from hail, snow, rain and dust if these get into the house as a result of wind damage to the exterior. You can also be compensated for damage caused by explosions, vehicles and airplanes; losses from smoke caused by defective operation of certain heating or cooking units; water damage from heating systems or plumbing; and a variety of other hazards.

A typical fire insurance policy is issued for one year or three years. The three-year policy is the more advantageous one. It is sold to you at a discount, usually 10 percent, and purchasing it protects you against increases in the cost of insurance for the term of your contract. Upon renewal or at other regular intervals it is a good practice to reexamine the amount of insurance you carry. Property values keep going up, and you should be sure that any increase in the worth of your house and other possessions is accurately reflected in the face amount of your insurance. You may suffer a severe loss if your property is underinsured and you have to replace it.

582

FIRE AND YOUR FAMILY

If a fire breaks out in your office or home, fire insurance should cover most or all of the property damage. The best way to insure your family's safety is to stay calm and remember these important rules.

If a fire breaks out in your home, get out fast—with your family. A fire can spread faster than you can run. Even if you just smell smoke, get out. If you escape through smoke, stay near the floor where the air is better. Take short breaths, breathe through your nose. If you are trapped in a room, follow the tips on the right side of this page.

Make sure children can open doors, windows and screens to escape routes.

If a fire breaks out in your office or apartment, get out fast. Many people are killed because they don't realize how fast a small fire can spread.

If you are caught in smoke, take short breaths, breathe through your nose and crawl to escape.

Head for stairs—not the elevator. A bad fire can cut off the power to elevators. Close all doors behind you.

If you are trapped in a smoke-filled room, stay near the floor, where the air is better. If possible, sit by a window where you can call for help.

Feel every door with your hand. If it's hot, don't open. If it's cool, make this test: Open slowly and stay behind the door. If you feel heat or pressure coming through the open door, slam it shut.

If you can't get out, stay behind a closed door. Any door serves as a shield. Pick a room with a window. Open the window at the top *and* bottom. Heat and smoke will go out the top. You can breathe out the bottom.

DON'T fight a fire yourself.

If you find smoke in an open stairway or open hall, use another preplanned way out. Teach your children how to use the phone to report a fire if they are trapped. They should also know where the alarm box is in the neighborhood.

Make sure your family knows the quickest and safest ways to escape from every room in the house. Close doors behind you. Keep a flashlight in every room to help escape at night.

DON'T jump. Many people have jumped and died—without realizing rescue was on the way.

If there is a panic for the main exit, get away from the mob. Try to find another way out. Once you are safely out, DON'T go back in. Call the fire department immediately.

488. Burglary, Robbery and Theft Insurance • There is no question that this is a good type of insurance to have—crime has been on the rise for decades. In recent years it has gone up five times as rapidly as the population. If you live in a city, you have to pay a steeper premium than in the country, for the crime rate is considerably higher in urban areas. In some sections of America's cities the rate is so high that premiums on personal theft policies are almost prohibitively expensive.

The standard policy spells out the meaning it gives to the words "burglary" and "robbery," since the statutes of the various states define these terms somewhat differently. In the typical policy *burglary* is defined as the theft of property from your house by a person who breaks in by force. *Robbery,* by contrast, is the taking of your possessions from you by violence either inside or outside the premises. Theft is a general-purpose term that covers any form of stealing. (See sections 131–133.)

Theft insurance usually provides blanket coverage for your belongings. It may also be written to provide coverage of your property in two groups: your furs and jewels form the first, all your other belongings the second. If you have valuable items such as rare books, a stamp collection or paintings, or if you want increased coverage on money, securities or other property, these can be listed and valued separately. You also have the option of insuring against loss when the property is away from your premises.

Under the standard policy you are indemnified not only for the stolen property but for any damage done to your dwelling or its contents by the thieves. Vandalism and malicious mischief are likewise covered.

Policies generally do not provide compensation for losses suffered by guests who are staying with you. If you have a tenant living in your house, your insurance will not protect him. Only your own losses and those of members of your family who live with you are eligible.

You should discuss your particular situation or requirements in detail with your insurance salesman so that he can provide the right kind of policy for you. Before accepting the policy, unless you are an expert in the legal language that such a contract usually abounds in, you may want to have your attorney scan it to make certain that it really gives you the protection that you are looking for.

489. Floaters—All-Risk Policies for Personal Property • You can obtain a policy to cover all your personal property or certain valuable items against most of the risks you are likely to encounter. This kind of policy is called a *floater:* it protects your property not merely at home but wherever you take it or send it—either in the United States and Canada or anywhere in the world. (You generally pay a higher premium for the wider coverage.) Thus your goods are covered when they are in transit or in storage—when they "float."

The comprehensive personal property floater gives you all the insurance you will ordinarily need for your own possessions and those of members of your family who live with you. It can also provide coverage for the belongings of others on your premises, including servants. The policy covers every category of belongings, including furniture, appliances, silverware, rugs, clothing, books and other personal property. These possessions are covered by a blanket amount of insurance. Then articles of particular value—paintings, antiques, jewelry, furs, stamps, securities—are listed separately, with the amount of insurance you want for each. Unless such articles are listed this way, there are limitations on the amounts you can collect for each under the ordinary blanket coverage of the comprehensive personal property floater.

You can, if you wish, obtain property floaters on individual types of valuable articles. These can be combined in a single policy, or you may take out individual policies. Some of the types of possessions commonly insured by individual floaters are works of art, furs, jewelry, musical instruments, cameras and other photographic equipment, stamp and coin collections and sports equipment. Floaters to protect wedding presents are also available at low cost; these expire ninety days after the wedding. Salesmen can take out floater insurance on their merchandise samples and physicians on the instruments they usually carry with them.

490. Floater Insurance on Personal Effects • The articles that you usually carry with you when you travel are *personal effects*. Insurance is ordinarily written to provide protection for property while it is at the place described in the policy. But many policies include a floater clause that gives your property coverage while it is in transit from one place to another. In other words, your personal property or that of a member of your family who lives with you is covered away from home just as it is when you are at home. This coverage may apply only to property in the United States and Canada or throughout the world, depending upon the wording of the clause in your policy.

Homeowners policies (see section 493) and fire insurance policies (see section 487) usually include a floater that covers personal property, but the compensation is limited. As a rule the floater will reimburse you for losses up to 10 percent of the amount of insurance you carry on the

585

contents of your house. The perils you are insured against in your basic policy are the only ones that apply under this limited floater.

Homeowners policies, for example, do not provide coverage for property losses due to floods, so if you are unlucky enough to lose your baggage in one, you can't collect. On the other hand, you are protected against losses caused by smoke from an unfriendly fire (see section 487). If you are staying at a resort and your personal effects are ruined by smoke, you are entitled to compensation for your loss. But if you carry just $10,000 worth of insurance on the contents of your dwelling, you will not be reimbursed for losses in excess of $1,000, under the 10 percent coverage afforded by most such policies.

Suppose you travel frequently and usually carry with you property worth more than $1,000. Then you will want to obtain a personal effects floater to insure you for the actual value of your possessions. Such a policy gives you blanket coverage for a wide range of articles, from baggage to tennis rackets. It protects your property against "all risks," but only while it is away from your usual residence. If someone steals your binoculars at a racetrack, if your bags are damaged on an airplane or if you lose your briefcase on a train, you can be compensated.

Two common types of loss are excluded from floaters. One is the theft of property from an unoccupied private car if it is not completely enclosed or if the doors and windows have not been locked. A limit is usually placed on the amount that can be recovered. The other exclusion is loss of the property of a student from the premises of a school, dormitory or fraternity or sorority house, unless the loss is due to fire. Coverage for these can be obtained by paying additional premiums.

It's important to remember that a personal effects floater, although it covers many different objects, is restricted to those generally carried by a tourist or a traveler. It won't compensate you for a punchbowl that you lend to the ladies' auxiliary, which damages it. If the cleaner loses your handsome Persian carpet, you cannot collect, either, except from the cleaner (see sections 201, 390). Furs and jewelry are covered only for 10 percent of the face amount of the policy, and there is a limit on any single piece.

491. Making a Claim for Property Insurance • Your policy usually states that you must give the insurance company immediate notice in case of loss. Be sure to give this notice in writing even if you have orally notified the company or your insurance man. Within a specified number of days you have to provide the company with a sworn statement of your loss. The company needs an inventory of the items included in the loss, with their actual cash value at the time. The agent or an adjuster employed by the company will give you help in preparing the inventory.

Insurance companies often advise that you prepare an inventory of the contents of your home before you have occasion to make a claim, with the cost of each important item and the date of purchase. Later, when many of the items may have been destroyed, it may prove impossible to gauge your losses accurately.

Suppose you and the company can't agree on the dollar value of various articles lost by fire or theft. Usually you can iron out your disagreement in a conference with the adjuster. If you still disagree, the policy spells out a procedure by which the value of the loss shall be appraised. The company also has the alternative of repairing or replacing the loss.

Most insurance companies pay promptly, usually well before the time limit that the policy mentions. If you run into a snag, however, it's a good idea to discuss your problem with the agent who sold you the policy. He wants to keep your goodwill and may be able to present your point of view to the company more effectively. If this does not overcome the difficulty, it's time to talk with your attorney. If he thinks that the company is withholding payment on questionable legal grounds, he may be successful in getting them to make a settlement. If persuasion fails, he can bring a suit against the company to enforce your rights.

Damage to your insured property may be caused by someone else. For example, your neighbor's carelessness in the use of a powerful insecticide may result in damage to valuable plantings on your property. Get in touch with your insurance salesman at once and give him the facts. He will advise you whether your company will cover your losses or whether you should get in touch with the other party's insurance company or whether you should consult an attorney.

492. How Much You Can Recover from the Insurance Company • You can never recover more than the actual amount of your loss up to the face value of your insurance policy. The principle of insurance is to restore your property to you in its condition at the time of the loss. In fact, the insurance company has the option of repairing or replacing the loss with material of the same type and quality, although it seldom finds it worthwhile to do so.

To restore your property to you in the condition it was in when the loss occurred, the company pays you the actual cash value of the property that was lost, damaged or stolen, less depreciation. This principle applies to fire and theft insurance and to most personal property floaters. Suppose your fur coat is stolen. It cost you $1,000, but because you had owned it for several years its value had depreciated to $600. That would be the maximum sum you could collect.

Some floater policies, on the other hand, are written on a *valued* basis. Such a floater states the value of the article and provides for full payment of that value without any adjustment for depreciation. Naturally, if there is only a partial loss, then a proportionate amount is paid.

Many fire insurance and homeowners policies carry a coinsurance clause. This clause provides that if you are to receive full payment for any partial damage or loss, you must insure your property for at least 80 percent of what it would cost you to replace it. If you insure for less than 80 percent of the value and you suffer a partial loss, then you must bear a proportionate amount of the loss. You yourself, in the language of insurance men, *coinsure* (or are responsible for) the difference between the amount of insurance you carry and 80 percent of the value of the property.

Let's say that you own a cottage that is valued at $10,000. To be fully protected against partial damage to the property under a homeowners or fire insurance policy that includes the coinsurance clause, you must carry insurance for at least 80 percent of $10,000, or $8,000. Now suppose that you carry only $6,000 worth of insurance. The company will pay the proportion of the loss that the actual amount of insurance bears to 80 percent of the value of the property. The proportion here is $6,000/$8,000, or three fourths. If you have a $1,000 loss, your proceeds from the company will be three fourths of this sum, or $750. The balance of $250 must come from your own pocket.

We can express this principle in a simple formula:

$$\frac{\text{Policy's face amount}}{80\% \text{ of property value}} \times \text{amount of loss} = \text{recovery}$$

Filling in the figures of our previous example, we get:

$$\frac{\$6,000}{\$8,000} \times \$1,000 = \$750$$

The coinsurance clause doesn't apply if you suffer a loss of 80 percent or more. In such a case you collect the full amount of the loss, up to the face value of your policy.

Many policies have a *deductible* of $50 or $100: you are responsible for all losses up to that sum. The typical homeowners policy has a deductible of $50. If you have a loss between $50 and $500, you pay a gradually reduced part of the loss as the loss rises, and the company pays the rest. If your loss is over $500, the company will pay you the actual cash value of the loss up to the amount of the policy.

Pro rata liability is a term that may crop up when you apply to collect an insurance loss. This simply means that an insurance company's liability for a loss can be no greater than the proportion of its policy to the total amount of applicable insurance you carry, whether you are entitled to collect that total or not. If you have two policies, one for $5,000 and another for $10,000, and you suffer a loss, you can collect one third of your loss from the first company and two thirds from the second—not the entire amount from each. The controlling principle of indemnity insurance is that the cost of indemnification must be shared fairly by the insurers and that you cannot recover more than the actual amount of the loss you incurred.

We have mentioned insurable interest (see section 487) as a requirement for taking out an insurance policy; this term has a particular bearing when you come to collect on a policy. The company is liable to you only in proportion to your insurable interest in the property. Suppose, for example, that you and your brother are co-owners of a house on a fifty-fifty basis. The fire insurance policy covers the full value of the property, but only your brother is named on the policy, since he was sole owner at the time the policy was taken out. If a loss occurs, the company pays out only half of the proceeds since your brother had only a 50 percent interest at the time of loss. This example underlines the importance of seeing to it that everyone with an insurable interest is named in a policy to be sure of full recovery.

Many policies set limits on the amount you can collect for various losses. For example, the maximum paid for a loss of personal effects while away from home is usually 10 percent of the face value of your insurance on the contents of your home. Other types of losses are excluded altogether. Read your policy carefully both when you buy it and when you make a claim so that you will know what you are entitled to.

493. Comprehensive Home Insurance Policies • A comprehensive home insurance policy provides the person who owns or rents a one- or two-family dwelling with protection against a whole range of perils involving his property and personal liability. Instead of buying a number of policies you buy a package of protection in just one policy. You have only one premium to pay and it costs you less than if you had bought the various

589

kinds of coverage separately. Farm owners may purchase insurance with many of the same features as homeowners insurance.

The *homeowners policy,* as it is commonly called, covers your living quarters, an attached garage and any other structures attached to your house. Also included are what the policy refers to as *appurtenant private structures:* a detached garage, a guest cottage, a tool shed and other structures on your property. However, the policy excludes any building used for commercial purposes.

The policy includes your personal property, too. All of the contents of your house as well as your personal belongings and those of your family are protected. Loss of your personal property is covered even if it occurs away from home. You can have personal property coverage written to protect the belongings of guests who are staying with you. A cat, dog or other pet is not covered. Neither is a car; for this you must obtain automobile insurance (see chapter 6, "Your Automobile," page 237).

What if your home burns down and you have no place to live? The homeowners contract provides for this emergency by allowing you *additional living expense*—money to defray the increase in your living costs made necessary by the situation. To the extent stated in your policy, the insurance company will compensate you for expenses you incur while living in a hotel and eating out in restaurants, over and above your normal expenditures for food and shelter, until your home has been repaired.

There are several types of homeowners policies. The principal difference between them is in the perils they protect you against.

The *basic, or standard, form* insures you against loss by fire, lightning, windstorm, hail, explosion, riot, vehicles, aircraft, smoke, vandalism, theft, breakage of glass and loss of your property when it is removed from premises made unsafe by fire or other dangers.

The *broad form,* which is more widely used, insures you against these perils and many more. The additional risks covered include: falling objects; weight of ice or snow; collapse of buildings; sudden cracking, burning or bulging of a hot-water or steam system; accidental discharge of steam or water from a heating, plumbing or air-conditioning system or household appliance; the freezing of such a system or appliance; accidental damage from artificially generated currents to electrical appliances, devices, fixtures and wiring (excluding television and radio tubes).

The *comprehensive form* is known as an all-risk policy because of its extensive coverage. It protects you not only against all the perils that the broad form does but also against a multitude of others. In fact, it gives you coverage against all perils except earthquake, landslide, flood, surface water, waves, tidal water or waves, the backing up of sewers, seepage, war and nuclear radiation.

If you rent your home or apartment you can obtain comprehensive protection with the tenant's form or contents broad form. Your dwelling and appurtenant private structures are not insured (they are not your property), but all of your personal belongings are protected against most of the risks covered by the broad form.

Most homeowners favor still another form—the *special form*. This provides them with the thorough protection of the comprehensive form on their dwelling and private structures. It also insures their personal property against almost all of the perils covered by the terms of the contents broad form.

The other major feature of the homeowners policy is personal liability coverage. If you, someone in your family or one of your pets causes injury or damage—whether on your own property or anywhere else—the policy gives you protection in case of a lawsuit or a claim.

Suppose you are spraying weeds on your property. A wind springs up and carries the spray into your neighbor's yard, where it settles on his expensive ornamental shrubs and kills them. Or a member of your wife's sewing circle slips in your living room and breaks her ankle. If you are sued, the insurance company will hire a lawyer to defend you; if you are found to be at fault, it will pay the damages up to the amount specified in your policy.

The liability part of your homeowners policy provides a small medical payment for someone who is injured on your premises or elsewhere, whether it is your fault or theirs. The cost of first aid and bail bonds is also covered.

The premium for a homeowners policy varies with the type of material your house is made of, the distance from water suitable for fire fighting and the equipment and adequacy of your local fire department. (These are basic considerations with any fire insurance.) It also varies with the amount you insure the house for and the type of coverage you select: the broad form costs more than the basic because it protects you against more perils, and the comprehensive form costs more than either for the same reason.

494. Postal Insurance • The United States Post Office offers insurance that will compensate you if domestic mail is lost, rifled or damaged. This insurance is limited to third-class mail (which includes bulk material such as books, bulbs or seeds) and fourth-class mail (parcel post). You

591

can also insure airmail that contains third- or fourth-class mail. Parcels containing material offered for sale to people who have not requested it cannot be insured. Neither can articles so fragile that there is a risk of breakage regardless of how you package them or articles that are packed so that they will not withstand normal handling. The fee, which you pay in addition to postage, varies with the amount of insurance you purchase; the maximum liability for insured mail is $200.

495. Insurance Rights and Obligations Under a Mortgage • When you take out a mortgage on real estate, the lender (the mortgagee) usually insists that you (the mortgagor) carry a fire insurance policy or home-owners policy. In addition he requires you to include in your policy a standard mortgagee clause to protect his interests in case of damage to the property. This clause, which we will explain in a moment, in effect creates a separate contract between the insurance company and the lender. But you pay the premiums.

Under the standard mortgagee clause the insurance company agrees to make any payment for loss to the lender who is named in the policy, up to the amount of the mortgage. Your rights as the owner of the mort-gaged property, obviously, are secondary to the lender's. Even if after a fire you make the repairs at your own expense, compensation for the damage is payable to the mortgagee. (As a matter of practice the check is usually made out to you and him, but he can request that it be paid to him exclusively.)

As a rule, of course, the lender is glad to have the money used to repair the damage to the property. Sometimes, however, the mortgagee clause can lead to difficulties. If the lender is short of cash or if you and he have had difficulties, he might decide to pocket the payment and leave you with the bills. However, the amount of your mortgage would be reduced by the sum paid to the mortgagee under your insurance policy. If, for example, you had a $10,000 mortgage and a $9,000 loss covered by insurance was paid to the mortgagee, you would henceforth owe him only $1,000.

The standard policy requires you to take reasonable precautions to prevent damage to your property and lists various conditions under which you are not entitled to payment—for example, if you fail to ob-serve the requirements of the local fire safety code. If you have a fire and are not entitled to compensation because you have not lived up to the conditions in your policy, the lender still has a legal right to pay-ment for the damage to the property. Even if you intentionally started the fire, he may collect from the insurance company up to the amount of the mortgage. But the insurance company, because of your omission, now has a claim against you for the money it paid the holder of the mortgage. It even has an option to take over your mortgage by paying the mortgagee the balance of your debt. On the other hand, you are not completely defenseless: you have a right to bring a suit against the company if you believe that you met the conditions for payment described in the policy.

A mortgagee has obligations as well as rights. If you neglect to pay the premiums on your policy, the company may ask him to make the payment if he wants to keep the policy in force. If you sell the house or rent it, or if you do something to increase the hazard of fire and he learns about this condition, he can protect himself by notifying the company and paying any increase in premium that the changed status makes necessary, if you are unable to pay. If you have a fire and do not give the company the inventory of loss specified in your contract, the mortgagee must assume this and other obligations that are normally the responsibility of the homeowner. As already mentioned, the company can also oblige the mortgagee to assign to it the mortgage and the balance of the mortgage debt if it exercises its option to take over the mortgage.

A mortgagee has an insurable interest (see section 487) in your property by virtue of the fact that he holds a mortgage on it. He can, if he wishes, insure the property on his own account. If he does so and a loss occurs, the payment that the insurance company makes to him does not reduce the amount of your mortgage. If you insure the property for your own benefit and are not required to include the standard mortgagee clause, any payment you receive is yours alone.

Normally, the mortgagee makes you take out insurance as a condition for lending you the mortgage money. In some instances a lender may even ask you to take out a policy with an agency in which he has a financial interest. In a number of states, but by no means all, this is illegal. If you are arranging for a mortgage and you have your own insurance agent or a company whose services or rates you are satisfied with, you should bring this matter up before concluding the transaction. If you have a policy that insures the contents of your home as well as the dwelling itself, have your attorney arrange that any insurance proceeds for damage to personal property be paid directly to you—not lumped together with payments for damage to the house, which go directly to the mortgagee. (For more details on your mortgage, see sections 290–293.)

593

496. Personal Liability Insurance • The comprehensive personal liability insurance policy provides you, as a private individual, with extensive protection if you or members of your family are responsible for bodily injury or property damage. Basically, liability insurance provides two kinds of protection. One is legal defense. If someone brings a liability suit against you, the insurance company will supply or pay for attorneys and also bear any other costs incurred in your defense. It will assume this expense whether or not the court finds that you were to blame. The second kind of protection is the payment of damages for which the court finds you responsible, up to the value of the policy. Any act of negligence is covered unless specifically excluded. The policy applies to accidents for which you are liable, on your own premises and elsewhere. If you own more than one residence, however, you must pay an additional premium.

Your comprehensive liability insurance gives you protection against claims from people who do work for you in connection with your residence, unless the injury they sustain should be covered by workmen's compensation insurance (see section 430). This policy excludes your use of the premises for business unless you are employed by someone else and this business use is brought to the attention of the insurance company. Owners of businesses or shopkeepers need a different kind of policy to cover their liability. You aren't covered for liability arising from the use of an automobile (see sections 261–268, 501). There are special requirements for boats and swimming pools.

You must have committed some act of negligence to be liable under this insurance (see sections 57, 58). But what if someone suffers a bodily injury or loss while on your premises or as a result of your activities elsewhere, or those of an employe, and you and your employe are not at fault? Say, a child falls from a swing in your backyard and breaks his arm or a tooth. The comprehensive policy provides a specified sum for medical or dental expenses. This provision also applies if an accident is caused by an animal that belongs to you or that you are taking care of for someone else. However, you can't claim payment for an accident of which you or a member of your household is the victim.

Comprehensive personal liability insurance gives you broad coverage at a reasonable price. A policy of this type is to your advantage whether you own or rent. You can also purchase the same coverage in the home-owners policy. (See section 493.)

497. General Liability Insurance · This kind of insurance protects you against liability for physical injury and property damage to which you may be exposed in the operation of a business. As with personal liability insurance, it provides you with legal representation in the event of a law-suit, plus the payment of such damages as the court finds you responsible for, provided they are covered by the terms of the policy. If you own an apartment house or a business building as an investment, you will want a general liability policy to cover you against claims from your tenants or from visitors in the building.

There are two basic forms: (a) the owners', landlords' and tenants' form, and (b) the manufacturers' and contractors' form. Under the first form you can insure a store, hotel, theater, office building or similar structure. You use the second form if you are engaged in manufacturing, contracting or a similar business. Coverage is basically much the same under each form, but is designed to satisfy the needs of the specific group. Various kinds of risks are excluded: for example, accidents that occur on elevators or escalators or that are caused by the use of your products once they pass out of your control. You can buy coverage against these and other common risks by adding them to your policy.

The comprehensive general liability policy wraps up basic coverage and all the individual coverages in one package; you do not have to apply for them individually. It gives you protection against risks to which you might not expect to be exposed but that might someday bring a process server to your door. All locations are covered that you rent, own or control; all the equipment that you use and all the operations that you engage in are insured. As usual there are some exclusions. Typical ones are obligations under workmen's compensation insurance, liability agree-ments not described in the policy and loss from the operation of automo-biles, airplanes and boats.

You can also take out an *umbrella liability policy*. This coverage (sub-ject to a deductible) protects you against risks for which you have no other liability insurance. You also get coverage for risks already insured, providing you with added protection when your existing insurance is ex-hausted. For example, you could carry several million dollars of addi-tional insurance to protect you in case of a catastrophe. Naturally you must have adequate general liability insurance before an insurance com-pany will issue you an umbrella liability policy.

595

Liability policies are also available to afford professional men protection against liability suits, including suits for malpractice. Doctors, dentists, optometrists, accountants and others find this kind of policy a necessity in their professions. (See section 395.)

498. Types of Business Insurance Required by Law • In certain circumstances, the federal, state and local governments may require businesses to carry or contribute to various types of insurance. The aim is to protect the public from loss or provide benefits for employes who are deprived of income. Here we list the most common kinds of compulsory insurance that may be required. Some of these are carried by almost every organization or individual doing business; others are designed for particular industries, occupations or states. In most instances the purpose of the insurance will be self-evident from its name.

Federal deposit insurance (see section 447)
Federal savings and loan insurance (see section 486)
Nuclear energy liability insurance
Public vehicle insurance
Social security (see sections 414–428)
  Disability insurance
  Medicare
  Retirement benefits
  Survivors' insurance
Unemployment insurance (see section 432)
Workmen's compensation (see section 430)

499. Other Insurance That Businesses Should Have • There are policies to cover almost every risk that a businessman may have to face. The catalog of optional policies—policies that are available but not required by law—seems just about endless. Here we show you some of the commoner types—aside from fire, theft, general liability and automobile insurance—so that you may know the coverages that typical businessmen with whom you deal are likely to carry. There are many more.

Bailment insurance
Bonding, fidelity and guarantee insurance
Builder's risk insurance
Business interruption insurance
Contractors' equipment insurance
Credit insurance
Crop insurance for farmers

Forgery insurance
Installment sales floater
Insurance on goods in transit or storage
Insurance on lives of partners or key executives
Insurance on special events
Insurance to protect passengers
Livestock floater
Marine insurance
Parcel post insurance
Physicians' instrument floater
Products liability floater
Rent and rental value insurance
Salesman's samples floater
Sprinkler leakage insurance
Use and occupancy insurance
Water damage insurance
Professional liability (malpractice) insurance
   Accountants' policy
   Beauty parlor policy
   Druggists' policy
   Hospital policy
   Insurance agents' policy
   Lawyers' policy
   Optometrists' policy
   Physicians', surgeons' and dentists' policy

500. Rights and Responsibilities Under Liability Insurance • If someone brings a suit against you for loss or injury, under what circumstances will a court find you liable? You will be held responsible if you caused the accident on purpose or if you conducted yourself in a negligent way that led to the loss or injury. The law views both types of actions as torts (see chapter 3, "Your Protection Against Wrongs," page 79); here we shall see how they are treated in liability insurance cases.

Criminal acts committed by the insured party are not covered under the typical liability insurance policy. However, you can obtain coverage for the intentional torts (see sections 39–49) of people who work for you. This will give you protection if, for example, your employe intentionally strikes a third party and you are held liable for his act. (Assault and battery by an employe—an intentional tort—is described as an "accident" in liability insurance policies.)

597

If you conduct yourself in such a negligent way that you cause harm to another person, you and your insurance company must be ready to compensate him for that harm. The courts interpret negligence as carelessness. It doesn't matter if you had no intention of injuring the victim or causing him a loss. To be free of responsibility, the law holds, you must conduct yourself with the care and prudence of a reasonable man.

You can be guilty of negligence and still not be liable or completely liable. Let's say that you fail to remove a patch of frozen snow from the sidewalk outside your house. A woman who is wearing high heels and no boots slips on it and falls. She may be guilty of *contributory negligence,* and so under the law in some states she might not be able to collect. In others, however, the law is based upon the principle of *comparative negligence.* Here, if the injured party contributed to the accident but wasn't fundamentally responsible for it, you may be held liable for damages in proportion to your share of the liability.

The duties of the insurance company are spelled out in your insurance contract. The company undertakes to defend you when you are sued, and you have no right to assume liability or settle a claim yourself, except at your own expense. The insurer has complete control if a lawsuit is brought against you, except in some malpractice cases; it is free to settle the case out of court or bring it to trial, if it so decides.

Your insurance company has to defend you no matter what the kind of suit, whether it is well grounded or not, as long as it falls within the liabilities covered by your policy. Sometimes, a suit may not appear to be covered and the company may decline to defend you; however, in the course of the trial, facts may be brought out that show the complaint actually came under the terms of your contract. Suppose you supplied your own attorney in such a case. If you were found liable, you would be able to sue the company for breach of its contract with you, and the amount of your recovery from the insurer would be what you had to pay in defending yourself and the damages for which you were liable.

As with other kinds of insurance, the insured party has to fulfill certain duties; if you fail to satisfy these obligations, the company is relieved of its liability under your policy. You are required, as soon as practicable, to notify the insurance company in writing of any accident you've had. Your notice should include details about the accident, its time and place, the names and addresses of the injured and of any witnesses. It is unwise to accept any assurances from the other party that he really has not suffered any loss or injury and does not intend to make a claim. Any incident that could possibly give rise to a claim must be reported. Only if you are certain that the incident is a trivial one and will not result in a claim are you free from the responsibility of making a report. The information should be forwarded to the insurance company or its authorized agent. Sending it to your broker may not be sufficient, as he is not usually considered the company's agent but your own (see section 482).

A second requirement is that you forward any notice of a claim or a lawsuit to the insurance company at once.

A third standard requirement is that you assist the company and cooperate with it. You are obliged to attend hearings and trials when the company so requests, to give evidence and to help in making settlements, in getting witnesses to attend and in conducting the lawsuit. You are forbidden, except at your own cost, voluntarily to make any payment or assume any obligations or incur expenses except for immediate medical treatment that is necessary at the time the accident occurs.

501. Automobile Liability Insurance • Automobile liability insurance is extremely important and is required by law in a number of states. For complete details see sections 261–268.

LIFE AND RETIREMENT INSURANCE

502. Whose Life May Be Insured • A *life insurance policy* is a contract under which you pay in a lump sum or promise to pay at regular intervals an amount of money, known as a *premium,* to an insurance company, in return for which the company insures your life: it agrees to pay the face amount of the policy, less the amount of any outstanding loans, to the person or persons you name as beneficiaries on your death. You can also take out a policy on someone else's life, naming yourself as beneficiary and paying the premiums.

Planning for the future is an important prelude to buying life insurance. You should discuss with your broker all your present and anticipated future needs, as well as present and possible future sources of income, such as dividends, pensions and social security. Savings and investment plans should also be considered. Then you should decide which life insurance plan is best for you. After choosing a base plan, you should consider buying the appropriate riders: family income, term insurance, family insurance, etc. It is more economical to buy one policy with riders

599

to take care of your particular needs than several different policies.

The law requires that you have an insurable interest in anyone whose life you insure, at the time you take out the policy. You have such an interest if you can be expected to benefit from the continued life of the person insured and will suffer a loss if he dies. The insurable interest may be based on a bond of love and affection to the insured party or on a pecuniary interest in his continued survival. The reason for this requirement of insurable interest is to reduce the likelihood that a beneficiary will try to bring about the death of the insured person.

Obviously, you have an interest in your own life, so you have a complete right to insure it. You have the same right to take out a policy on your wife's life, just as she has a right to take out a policy on yours, while you are married. Neither of you needs to obtain the other's consent for this purpose. The insurable interest comes to an end if you obtain a divorce. (But your spouse does not automatically cease to be your beneficiary; you have to change the beneficiary in your policy to achieve that purpose; see section 506.) After a divorce a wife can take out a policy on her former husband's life with herself as beneficiary if he has to pay her alimony—her claim to alimony gives her an insurable interest.

The close relationship of children and parents also creates an insurable interest. Children have a right to take out insurance on the lives of their father and mother. The parents may also insure the lives of their minor children, but the amount of insurance is frequently limited by state statute. If a child plans to take out a policy on a parent and name himself as beneficiary, he must first get the parent's consent. In virtually all the other instances we shall discuss, you must get the permission of the person whose life you insure if you are the beneficiary.

Other relatives, such as brothers and sisters, do not necessarily have an insurable interest in each other's lives. Normally, they must have some expectation of pecuniary benefit from the person they insure. In some states, however, the courts have held that certain relatives can insure each other without any such expectation. A dependent may insure the life of the person who supports him even if they are unrelated.

There are many other situations in which an insurable interest exists. If someone owes you money, you have an insurable interest in his continued existence to the extent of the debt and may take out a policy on his life, naming yourself as beneficiary to make certain that you are repaid. An employer has an insurable interest in his key employes (but not his ordinary employes) and may insure their lives in his own behalf. Key employes have the same interest in their employer. Partners in a business have an insurable interest in each other (see section 404).

Before we leave the subject of insurable interest, one fact must be emphasized. In this discussion we have been mainly concerned with policies that are taken out by someone who insures the life of another person but names himself as the beneficiary. However, in the typical policy you insure your own life and name someone else as beneficiary. Such a beneficiary is not required to have an insurable interest. You may designate anyone you wish as the beneficiary of your policy (see section 506). You may also designate your own estate as the beneficiary and in your will provide for the disposition of the proceeds (see section 513).

Almost everyone is eligible for insurance. Usually the insurance company requires you to take a physical examination and meet certain health standards. If you are applying for a large amount of insurance, your examination will be much more thorough than usual. If the company does not find you to be a good risk, it may reject your application or require you to pay a higher premium. You may be denied standard insurance if you are seriously overweight, if you have high blood pressure or some other disorder or if your family has a history of early deaths. Some companies will turn you down if you are over sixty-five.

Your occupation, hobby, habits or other factors may also make you a bad risk for insurance. If you work in a hazardous industry where you are exposed to accidents or conditions dangerous to health, you may be rejected or required to pay a higher premium. Commercial pilots are accepted as standard risks, but military fliers usually are not. Persons who have a history of addiction to drugs or alcohol are generally considered poor risks. In time of war companies insert war clauses in their policies that relieve them of liability if the insured is killed while in the armed forces. If you drive a racing car as a hobby or go skin diving in your spare time, this activity is also considered by the insurance company in evaluating you as a risk. However, over 90 percent of all people who apply are able to meet the overall standards for acceptance.

We have said that almost everyone is eligible for insurance. An insurance policy is a contract, however, and the law places restrictions on contracts entered into by children and incompetents (see section 176).

If a minor repudiates the contract, the company is obliged to pay back the premiums it has received. The company obviously is in a risky position when it sells to minors. To make the sale of insurance to minors a less onesided proposition, many states have passed laws giving minors the right to enter into binding insurance contracts if they have reached the age of fifteen or sixteen.

The law of contracts applying to the incompetent or insane applies with equal force to insurance policies that they take out. An incompetent has a right to make a contract for insurance if he has not been declared insane by due process of law. He may be medically insane—insane in the opinion of doctors—but that will not invalidate his contract unless a court has held him to be incompetent. But the insane person may have a right to repudiate the policy even if he has not been legally declared insane. If he has been, his guardian can void the policy.

503. Types of Life Insurance · Americans own an almost unbelievable amount of life insurance—over a trillion (1,000 billion) dollars' worth. In a recent typical year they purchased $50 billion worth. Their chief aim is to provide financial protection for their loved ones in case they themselves should die, but a large number of people take out insurance to assure themselves of financial security when they get on in years. The kinds of policies you can buy vary greatly and are offered singly or, often, in combination. Here and in the sections that follow we shall look briefly at the most important types being purchased by Americans today.

Term life insurance gives you protection for a stated number of years, usually one, five, ten or more. The policy expires at the end of the term and it usually has no cash value, as other kinds of life insurance do (see below). Like your automobile insurance policy, it gives you insurance for the term stated in the policy and nothing more.

One of the most popular types is *renewable term insurance.* When this policy expires, you can renew it without taking another medical examination. However, when you renew, you have to pay a larger premium, depending upon your age at the time. This is because the risk of death goes up with advancing age (see section 507). You can also obtain term insurance with a convertible feature: you may convert it later to a permanent plan that accumulates cash value, without taking a physical examination. For example, you might have a five-year renewable term policy that allows you to convert at any time during the life of the policy. Since other types of insurance are more expensive, this is a desirable feature for the young family man who expects his income to increase or who might not be able to pass a medical examination later.

Decreasing term insurance is another type that many people buy. The term may run for twenty-five years or longer. It provides large benefits at the start of the period, but these gradually decrease to nothing by the end. You pay the same premium throughout. This policy provides a maximum amount of benefits when your children are young and you may be carrying a large mortgage. You can buy decreasing term or other types of term insurance in combination with permanent (whole) life insurance (see below).

Term insurance has the lowest premiums of all insurance since it normally does not have a cash or loan value. On the other hand, the premium increases with your age whenever you renew the policy, in contrast to permanent insurance.

Whole life insurance is the oldest and most popular form of insurance in the United States. It is also called ordinary or straight life insurance. It provides protection for as long as you live. You pay a *level premium;* that is, the premium remains the same for the life of the policy. Your premium is lower than it is for any other type of permanent insurance, but you go on paying it for most of your life.

With whole life insurance you accumulate *cash value,* the money that you would get back if you gave up, or "surrendered," the policy—also called cash surrender value. Cash value is low when the policy is new but builds up with the years. You can borrow against the cash value of your policy (see section 508).

Limited payment life insurance has most of the features of whole life; the only difference is that you pay premiums for a limited number of years. The protection lasts for your entire life. The premiums are higher than for whole life since there are fewer of them. Advantages of this policy are that you accumulate a large cash value more rapidly, and you can limit the payment of premiums to the earlier years of life. However, dollar for dollar, you are paying more for the same face value than you would with a whole life policy. You can also obtain a paid-up policy for just a single payment; this is practical if you come into a large sum of money or wish to make a gift of a policy to someone.

Endowment policy benefits, in contrast to benefits of the other types of insurance we have been discussing, can be collected while you are still alive. However, if you die before the policy matures, the proceeds are paid to the secondary beneficiary you name. As with the limited payment life policy, you can take out an endowment policy requiring payments for twenty or thirty years or until you reach a specified age, sixty-five for example.

The premiums you pay for an endowment policy are higher than for other types of life insurance since the insurance company must accumulate the entire amount of the policy by the maturity date. In the other types you usually do not pay in more than 60 percent of the face value; here you have to supply most of the face amount yourself. The endowment policy, obviously, is a means of forcing you to save. If you are more interested in insurance than in building a savings fund, any of the kinds of policies we talked about earlier will give your beneficiary the same protection for much less money.

You can obtain endowment policies in special forms for special purposes. One particularly useful type provides funds for a child's education. The policy can be on your own life or the child's and arranged to mature when the child is ready to go to college. If the policy is on your child's life, you can have a clause that provides that no more premiums will be due if you die or become disabled before the policy matures.

You can take the proceeds of your endowment policy in a lump sum or, if you choose, in monthly installments.

Family policies insure the entire family—father, mother and children. The policy usually starts at $5,000. The father is insured for the entire amount and the wife and children for lesser sums. Children are covered automatically shortly after birth. Such a policy may have much to recommend it if you plan to have a large family. You can also get family insurance as a rider in combination with your ordinary life insurance policy.

The family income policy is a widely used type of combination policy. It allows for increased benefits during the years your financial needs may be greatest—when you have a growing family. The policy combines decreasing term insurance with a whole life policy. You can provide for a substantial cash payment on death, plus monthly payments.

A *preferred risk policy* is available if you work in a job where you are exposed to a minimum of risk and if you are in excellent physical condition and have a good health history. A physical examination is usually required for this type of policy.

Mortgage insurance is a decreasing term insurance that insures the payment of the mortgage on your house. The policy runs for the term of your mortgage, but the coverage gets smaller as your mortgage does. Usually you pay a level premium throughout. If you should die, the proceeds may be paid in a lump sum to the beneficiary you name or in monthly benefits the same size as the mortgage payments that fall due.

Credit life insurance is a widely used type of life insurance. It is taken out to cover a personal debt should you die before you complete your payments. Finance companies, banks and other lenders extend this insurance to you when you make a loan, adding its cost to your charges. As you pay back the loan, the amount of insurance usually decreases.

Group life insurance is offered by many business concerns to employes and by trade unions and other associations to their members. The face

LIFE INSURANCE IN THE UNITED STATES

Most American families today own at least one life insurance policy, as illustrated in the chart below. This is a direct reflection of the tremendous growth in the number of policies purchased, shown in the middle chart, as well as the increase in life expectancy, depicted at the bottom.

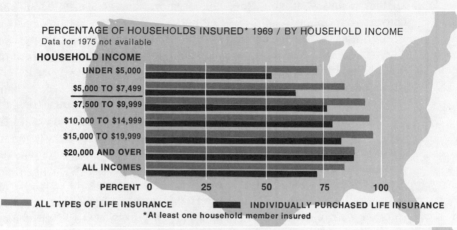

PERCENTAGE OF HOUSEHOLDS INSURED* 1969 / BY HOUSEHOLD INCOME
Data for 1975 not available

HOUSEHOLD INCOME
- UNDER $5,000
- $5,000 TO $7,499
- $7,500 TO $9,999
- $10,000 TO $14,999
- $15,000 TO $19,999
- $20,000 AND OVER
- ALL INCOMES

PERCENT 0   25   50   75   100

ALL TYPES OF LIFE INSURANCE   INDIVIDUALLY PURCHASED LIFE INSURANCE
*At least one household member insured

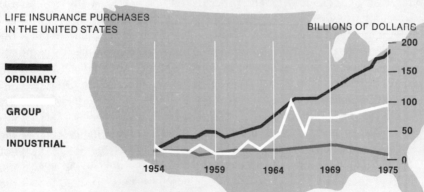

LIFE INSURANCE PURCHASES IN THE UNITED STATES

BILLIONS OF DOLLARS

ORDINARY

GROUP

INDUSTRIAL

— 200
— 150
— 100
— 50
— 0

1954   1959   1964   1969   1975

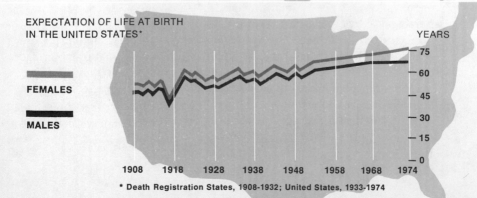

EXPECTATION OF LIFE AT BIRTH IN THE UNITED STATES*

YEARS

FEMALES

MALES

— 75
— 60
— 45
— 30
— 15
— 0

1908   1918   1928   1938   1948   1958   1968   1974

* Death Registration States, 1908-1932; United States, 1933-1974

amount often equals a year's earnings. The employer or other sponsor may pay the entire cost, or he may share it with those who are covered. The premium as a rule is the same for all members of the plan, and medical examinations are not required. The cost is lower than for other types of insurance since the sponsor of the plan makes one payment for all the members. If you leave the organization, you may be able to convert your policy to an individual policy.

Split-dollar insurance enables two people to share the cost of a policy. These plans are often set up to enable employes to bear the cost of large policies with the help of their employers. However, any two parties can share the premiums of a split-dollar policy.

There are many forms of the split-dollar plan. In a typical one the employer pays a part of the premium proportionate to the increase in the cash value of the policy. The employe pays the balance. In case of death, the employer gets part of the policy proceeds—the amount that he has paid in. Thus the only cost to him of the insurance that he has helped his employe purchase is the lost interest he might have earned on the premiums he has paid. The Internal Revenue Service does not consider the part of the premium paid by the employer each year as income received by the employe. The proceeds on death are usually not taxable to either party.

Annual term insurance is often coupled with this plan to keep the death benefit of the insured employe level as the cash value of the policy rises. Dividends may be drawn upon to help pay for the term insurance. In a typical example, an insured person might be able to carry a $100,000 policy to age sixty-five at a yearly cost of only a few dollars for each $1,000 of insurance.

Industrial insurance, as its name implies, was originally created for industrial workers. It is issued in low amounts, generally not above $1000. The premiums are collected weekly or monthly by an agent who calls at the home. The proceeds are generally used to provide a fund to take care of the immediate expenses connected with a burial. Fraternal organizations also issue small policies that are widely used for the same purpose (see section 512).

Accidental death and dismemberment benefits are a common feature of industrial life insurance and do not require an additional premium, as a rule. You can in most instances obtain this insurance without a medical examination. The policy has cash value only after three years. Settlement is generally in a lump sum.

With most industrial policies the proceeds are needed quickly when a death occurs. Accordingly, these policies include a *facility of payment clause*. It provides that if the named beneficiary is not available, the insurance company can pay the benefits to any relative it believes entitled to receive them, especially the one who takes charge of the burial. This provision is also found in some fraternal insurance contracts. However, it is not included in standard life insurance policies.

Flight insurance may be purchased by travelers when they are about to make a trip by air. These policies, which are often sold by vending machine at airports, provide a substantial face amount of coverage for a single premium of usually no more than a few dollars. Accidental death and dismemberment benefits are provided, as well as a blanket medical reimbursement of 5 percent of the death benefit. You can also collect benefits if you are injured at the airport or in a vehicle controlled by the airport or airline. You are protected for a continuous round trip on a scheduled airline provided you complete the trip within a year.

504. Life Insurance for Veterans and GIs • Men and women who served in the armed forces of the United States during World War I and afterward and during World War II and the Korean War were offered an opportunity to purchase attractively priced insurance, and government-sponsored insurance is still available to the services. If you bought GI insurance and have not converted it to a permanent policy, you should get in touch with the Veterans Administration. If your policy has lapsed, you may still be able to have it reinstated.

United States government life insurance was available to members of the armed forces who served on active duty from 1917 to 1921. The government offered it for sale until 1951 under a number of different plans, much like those available under National Service Life Insurance.

National Service Life Insurance (NSLI) was issued by the government to people in the armed forces between October 8, 1940, and April 25, 1951. The maximum amount of insurance sold was $10,000. It was originally sold as five-year term insurance, renewable indefinitely, but it can be converted to any of six plans: whole life, twenty-payment life, thirty-payment life, twenty-year endowment, endowment at sixty and endowment at sixty-five. Conversion is possible even if you are totally disabled. You can convert as of your present age, or you can date it back to your age when you took out the term insurance; naturally, you have to pay the difference in reserves. You can change from one plan to another if you satisfy the conditions set by the Veterans Administration.

Nonforfeiture options (see section 509) resemble those of commer-

607

cial life insurance. You have the option of surrendering your policy for cash, extended term insurance or a paid-up policy for a lower sum. If you need money, you can borrow up to 94 percent of your policy's cash value. Reinstatement provisions are highly favorable. If your policy lapses, you can reinstate it within three months, provided you submit a statement of good health. Beyond three months you are required to provide medical proof of good health. In general you can reinstate a permanent policy anytime within the extended term period, provided you pay all premiums owing, as well as interest on them.

You can name anyone you wish as a beneficiary or provide for the payment of benefits to your estate. A choice of payments is available to you, ranging from a lump sum to monthly installments.

If you served in the Korean War or for a minimum of 31 days between June 25, 1950, and January 1, 1957, the government insured you for $10,000 free of cost. After discharge you could apply for five-year term insurance; you have a choice of converting this into any of the permanent policies available under National Service Life Insurance. No medical examination is required.

In 1965 the government established Servicemen's Group Life Insurance for people on active duty. Under this program you can take out $5,000 or $10,000 of group life insurance if you wish. The insurance is underwritten by private companies but supervised by the Veterans Administration. It may be converted after you leave the service.

Since 1957 GIs have been covered under the social security program; contributions are deducted from their pay, as they are for civilians in covered employment, and they collect the same benefits when they become eligible (see section 415).

505. Life Insurance Policies Issued by Banks • Mutual savings banks sell life insurance in three states—Massachusetts, New York and Connecticut. Under these programs the bank sets up its own insurance department, which is distinct from its other activities. You can buy the insurance at your bank from this department and are spared the usual broker's commission, which immediately results in a saving. The issuing bank arranges for your medical examination, keeps records, collects premiums and invests the funds. Other mutual banks may work as agents for the issuing banks for a small commission.

The three state systems make the standard types of life insurance coverage available to you: whole life, endowment policies, group insurance, term insurance, family plan policies and others. A savings-insurance plan combines life insurance with a savings account; premiums, when they fall due, are automatically drawn from your savings account. Individual state systems have special policies; for example, Connecticut offers a home mortgage security plan, which meets monthly payments on your mortgage if you become disabled or die prematurely. Massachusetts is the only state selling annuity contracts. Inquire about the different types of policies your bank has available, if you live in one of the states in which banks issue insurance.

Policy provisions are much the same as those in policies sold by regular insurance companies. However, you will find some provisions more to your advantage. For example, favorable nonforfeiture values (see section 509) start in the first year; extended term insurance may be available when your policy has been in effect for only a month. You also receive a dividend at the end of the first year even if you drop out of the program.

A possible disadvantage is that the amount of insurance you can buy on an individual life in any one bank is limited. The total amount that you can buy on one life from all banks is $38,000 in Massachusetts, $30,000 in New York and $5,000 in Connecticut. Settlement options are different from state to state, depending upon the amount of insurance you are allowed to carry. Accidental death benefits are not included, but there is a provision for waiver of premium should disability occur.

506. Ownership and Beneficiary Provisions · As a rule, if you take out insurance on your own life, pay the premium and have a right to change the *beneficiary*—the person to whom benefits will be paid—you are the owner of the policy. The beneficiary's vested rights come into existence only after you have passed away. However, in some cases you might give up the right to change the beneficiary. Generally there is a special reason for such a step; for example, the face value of the policy may be a factor in a divorce settlement or the beneficiary may be paying the premiums. Here, the beneficiary automatically has a vested interest in the policy, and you can't make changes in it unless you obtain his permission. In fact he usually can assign his interest in the policy to a third party while you are still alive. Obviously, if you do not want to give up control of your insurance, you should be careful not to name a permanent, or irrevocable, beneficiary.

Usually the policyholder keeps all of his rights to his insurance: he can change the beneficiary, increase or decrease the face value or turn the policy in for its cash value. However, in states with community property laws (see section 317), special rules prevail. Husband and wife have an equal interest in all the assets they acquire after they marry. If you pay the premiums on your policy with community property funds, you need your wife's permission if you want to change the beneficiary.

Under most circumstances a husband names his wife as his beneficiary. To provide against the contingency that your wife may not survive you, you should name alternate beneficiaries to receive the proceeds of your insurance. Generally these will be your children, if you have any. You may designate your estate as the beneficiary, but this is usually not a wise move as the money then may become subject to the taxes and expenses involved in settling the estate (see section 550).

If you have children who are minors, you should name a trustee to receive payments for them. Many insurance companies require you to do so, because a minor is not considered legally capable of handling his own assets (see section 337). But if the benefits are small, the company may not enforce this requirement. It's a good idea to designate an alternate trustee in case the first one should not be available. When you draw up your will, you should talk over with your attorney the general problem of selecting trustees for your minor children.

If you and your wife obtain a divorce, her interest is not affected as the beneficiary of your insurance. If you do not want her to collect the proceeds, you must exercise your right to change the beneficiary.

In mystery novels when someone is murdered the police usually focus their suspicions on the person who stands to gain most from the death. However, the beneficiary of life insurance who is found guilty of having murdered an insured person automatically loses his right to any share in the proceeds. If no other beneficiary is named, the money is paid into the policyholder's estate. On the other hand, if the beneficiary kills the insured party while defending his life against him, he is still entitled to benefits. If the beneficiary is accidentally responsible for the death of the policyholder, he is allowed to collect.

It makes sense to review, from time to time, the beneficiaries you have designated in your policies. Children may be born or grow up and become independent, or your aging parents may need to be provided for. Consider making changes as your family situation changes.

It is usually a simple procedure to change the beneficiary of your life insurance policy. Generally the policy tells you how to proceed. You are commonly required to fill out a form provided by the company and file it with them. The company also endorses the change on the policy. Sometimes the former beneficiary may have the policy in his hands and refuse

610

to make it available to you for the change. The courts have generally ruled that if you do everything you can to indicate you intend to name a different beneficiary, they consider the change to have been made. The case is different, however, if you try to make the change by naming the new beneficiary in your will. Usually the courts have refused to recognize the new designation.

How the proceeds of your policy should be paid out is a question that calls for serious thought. The variety of methods and combinations of payment is great, and they can be adjusted to meet almost every requirement. Many policyholders consider it advisable to provide for the payment of a lump sum to take care of the costs of the funeral and burial. Some people have a special policy for this purpose (see section 503). If most of your assets are in insurance, you may want to have monthly payments made to your widow for the support of her and your children. You can also provide that she may draw on the balance in case of special needs. If the proceeds are substantial, it might be possible to earn significantly more by skillful investment and management than an insurance company would pay. In this situation, setting up a life insurance trust to handle the funds might be the wisest course (see sections 545, 550). A trust also protects against the dissipation of the proceeds by beneficiaries who are not used to handling money.

Most Americans are entitled to social security benefits. You should consider fitting these benefits into your insurance program. Social security makes payments for dependent children and your widow who takes care of them. If you have no children, your widow will not be entitled to benefits until she reaches retirement age herself. A small sum is also available as a burial benefit under social security and also for veterans (see section 425).

Ask your insurance salesman's advice on how you can set up a combination program that will provide most adequately for the changing needs of your dependents, including their educational expenses (see section 503).

Frequently, if a widow is dissatisfied with the method of settlement that her husband has chosen, the insurance company will permit her to alter it.

As the owner of a life insurance policy, you have a legal right to *assign* a policy, or transfer its ownership to someone else. Assignments are usually made in repayment of a debt or in return for some other benefit you have received. You can transfer the policy absolutely, giving the other party (the *assignee* or *transferee*) complete right to the proceeds,

611

or only partly, assigning to him merely the amount that you owe him. A typical policy states that the beneficiary's interest is subordinate to any assignment and that "the assignee shall receive any sum payable to the extent of his interest." If you have given up the right to change the beneficiary, you need the beneficiary's consent before you can assign a policy in which he is named.

If you assign a policy, you have to notify the company that issued it. Usually this is done by filing a certified copy of the assignment with the company at its home office. Any assignment is subject to your indebtedness to the company on the policy.

Many states will not recognize that the transfer of a policy is valid unless it can be shown that the transferee has an insurable interest (see section 487). Even if an absolute assignment has been made to repay a debt, the assignee in these states can collect no more than the amount that is owed him. Because of the possible complications it is a sensible step to consult with your attorney before undertaking the assignment of so valuable an asset as an insurance policy.

507. Premium and Dividend Options on Life Insurance • Most life insurance policies are based on the level premium system. Under this system you pay the same premium every year for your insurance. Obviously, the risk that you will die is much less when you are young than when you are older. The company is able to meet its costs for older people because of the sums they paid in when younger. Moreover, the money is invested all through the years and earns interest, which also helps to pay the increased costs later on. Thus your insurance costs don't go up when you are older and possibly less able to bear them.

The sum charged as a premium is based upon the *mortality table.* This is a statistical table showing the death rate at each age. The *actuaries,* or statisticians of the insurance industry, have been keeping careful records for many years of the number of policyholders of every age who die in a given year and thus can predict fairly accurately how much money the company will have to pay out each year for the number of deaths likely to occur among its policyholders of all ages. They also calculate the amounts that will be required for policy reserves, nonforfeiture values (see section 509) and other expenses. Working with these and similar figures, the actuaries figure out how much to charge policyholders of different ages so that the premiums and investment earnings will meet the company's needs each year. Since women are longer-lived than men, they are charged a lower premium rate. People who are poor health risks or work in hazardous occupations are charged more, if they are accepted at all.

A choice is offered you in the payment of premiums. You can pay them monthly, every six months or once a year. It is to your advantage to pay a premium only once a year, as a service charge is added for each payment if you pay more frequently. This charge, in total, may be higher than 10 percent of the yearly premium. You can save yourself the service charge by putting away the installments for your annual premium on a regular schedule until you have the entire sum. You might also take out a number of small policies instead of a big one and stagger the dates of the premiums over the year so you can pay them conveniently when due.

Essentially, there are two types of life insurance policies, participating and nonparticipating. The insurance company that issues the *participating policy* pays you a *dividend,* or a partial refund, of the premium you have paid. It can afford to do this because it sets its premium somewhat higher than it has to. When the company figures out its costs at the end of the year—the sums it has paid to beneficiaries, its costs of operation and the amounts it expects it will require to meet future needs—it usually finds itself with a surplus. This surplus is returned to you in the form of the dividend. You generally receive dividends after your policy has been in force for a year or two. This type of insurance policy harks back to the early days of the industry, before the development of accurate mortality tables.

By contrast, if you buy a *nonparticipating policy,* you receive no dividends. The insurance company fixes its premium rate as accurately as possible to provide the sums it will need to meet all its expenses.

You have a number of options available for taking your dividends. You can have them paid to you in cash; you can request the company to apply them to future premiums; you can leave them with the company to build up with interest; you can use them to buy extra paid-up insurance. Most policyholders follow the first two courses.

Basically, there are two types of company in the life insurance business, the mutual company and the stock company. The *mutual life insurance company* is a nonprofit company owned by its policyholders, who elect the board of directors that manage it. It is not owned by stockholders. Usually it is the mutual company that issues participating insurance. The *stock life insurance company,* on the other hand, belongs to the people who own stock in it. Nonparticipating insurance is commonly sold by stock companies; however, they also issue the dividend-paying participating insurance.

Is nonparticipating insurance cheaper than participating insurance? There is no simple, general answer to the question. Policies vary from company to company, and you have to consider the provisions of a given policy in evaluating the cost of its participating insurance by subtracting the dividends paid from the premiums charged over a period of years.

508. Borrowing Against Life Insurance · You can borrow up to the cash value of most kinds of life insurance policies, except term insurance, from the company that issued them, and you can borrow on some annuity contracts. Naturally, you must pay interest on your loan. The amount you can be charged is fixed by statute, usually at 5 or 6 percent, which is deducted in advance for the balance of the policy year. Thus, you get up to 95 or 94 percent of the amount of your loan. You can find the cash value at the end of every year listed in a table in your policy. To borrow from your insurance company, get in touch with the company or its local agent and fill out a loan application.

If you prefer, you can take your policy to a bank and use it as collateral for a loan. However, with the typical bank loan you pay back the principal in installments, so that the amount you have at your disposal for a year or longer is much less than the amount you borrowed. Thus the true rate of interest can be considerably higher than it may at first appear. Another drawback is that the bank loan is for a limited period.

By contrast, the insurance company places no time limit on your loan. You can make payments of interest and principal at your convenience. The company will routinely keep adding to the amount of the loan the interest that falls due. When you owe the company a sum equal to the policy's cash value, it will send you a notice. At this time you can make a payment to keep the policy in force. If you fail to do so, your policy can be terminated.

You still have insurance protection when you borrow against your policy. But if you die before you pay back the loan, the company deducts the amount you owe from the proceeds it pays to your beneficiary. In effect, the amount of insurance you carry is reduced by your loan.

Your policy, incidentally, continues to increase in cash value during the course of the loan. The money you have paid the company keeps on earning interest and growing. The company merely uses it as collateral, which it can lay claim to if you fail to pay the loan. Bear in mind, however, that the interest you owe the company also continues to accumulate during the life of the loan unless you pay it when billed, and after a while you are being charged interest on the interest.

In many policies there is provision for another kind of loan—the automatic premium loan. Under this system, if you do not pay a premium before the end of the grace period—the period after the due date of the premium during which the policy remains in force—the company advances the premium in your behalf and charges it as a loan against your cash reserve. The positive feature of this system is that your policy stays in force if you are sick or away from your usual residence or cannot pay the premiums when they are due. All the provisions of your policy continue to be operative during this period, and you receive any dividends due you. But as we have seen in the case of an insurance loan, the benefits are reduced in case of death by the amount of your loan.

You can also borrow against your cash reserves if you own GI insurance. The procedure is much the same, except that you obtain the loan from the Veterans Administration. Applications are available from the branch to which you pay your premiums or from the local offices of the Veterans Administration.

509. Cancellation, Lapse, Surrender and Reinstatement of Life Insurance • A life insurance company can move to cancel a policy if it believes the applicant was guilty of fraud, misrepresentation or concealment of material facts (see section 514). However, the company's right to challenge the applicant's statements is limited to a period of two years from the date the policy was issued, except in case of gross fraud. The company also does not need to pay the full benefits if the applicant commits suicide within a specified period—one or two years—after the issue of the policy (see sections 123, 515).

If you fail to pay your premium after the grace period, as spelled out in your policy, it lapses. And when automatic premium loans exceed the cash value of your policy, the policy may be terminated and you will have no further right in it.

The law provides you with three options, known as *nonforfeiture values,* if you decide to discontinue your policy. (These options do not apply to term insurance.) The options are (1) cash value, (2) extended term insurance and (3) reduced paid-up insurance. You must send a written request for the option you choose to the home office of the company along with your policy. If you fail to select an option, your policy states that one will be selected, usually extended term insurance.

Cash value is the amount of money the insurance company will pay you upon the surrender of your policy. It is guaranteed in your policy. Because their needs change over the years, many people decide to turn in their policies for the cash value rather than keep the protection.

Extended term insurance is an option that allows you to have the cash value of your policy applied to the purchase of term insurance (see section 503) for the full face value of the policy. The number of years of coverage you will get is usually shown in a table in your policy. However, you lose any additional benefits under your original policy, such as accidental death or disability benefits. With an endowment policy there is usually enough cash value for you to buy term insurance to the maturity date of the original policy, plus a smaller endowment policy. You do not have to pay any further premiums.

Reduced paid-up insurance is a plan under which the company applies the cash value of your policy to buy fully paid-up insurance in a smaller amount. The date of maturity will be the same as on your original policy and so will the basic terms.

If your policy has lapsed, you can have it *reinstated,* or put back in force, if you have not surrendered it for its cash value. Generally the insurance company allows you up to five years to reinstate your policy. You have to pay all overdue premiums at a specified rate of interest from the due date of each one. You must also provide "evidence of insurability satisfactory to the company." As a rule, no proof is needed if you reinstate the policy within a month after the grace period. If you apply for reinstatement within half a year, the company frequently will not insist on more than a statement that you are in good health. If the period of lapse is longer, you will probably be required to pass a physical examination. The company will also want to know, among other things, if you have a more dangerous job and if your habits are the same.

510. Life Insurance Trusts • When you set up a trust, you create an arrangement by which assets you intend for the benefit of one person are entrusted to another, known as the *trustee,* whose responsibility is to manage them in a skilled and prudent way. Trusts are widely used in estate planning (see section 545). They may be revocable (you have the right to cancel them) or irrevocable (you give up that right for certain tax advantages). Life insurance is one of the most important assets that many of us possess, and a life insurance trust provides a means for protecting the proceeds of your policies.

In establishing a life insurance trust, you usually name as trustee a bank, trust company or similar organization expert in the handling and investment of money. In your policies you designate the trustee as the beneficiary of your insurance proceeds. In keeping with the trust agree-

616

ment, the trustee will invest the proceeds and pay them out in install-ments to your widow, children or other heirs. In this way you can pro-vide for the financial security of your survivors for a long period of time. If the money were paid to them in a lump sum or over a few years, it might quickly slip through their fingers because of carelessness or inex-perience.

Obviously it does not pay to set up an insurance trust if the amount of insurance is fairly insignificant. If you have policies that add up to $15,000, for example, a trustee who invested it at 6 percent could only show an annual yield of $900. From this he would be entitled to deduct his fee, and whatever is left over would hardly go far to support a family. It would clearly make more sense to have the benefits paid to your heirs by the insurance company. On the other hand, if you carry a substantial amount of insurance, it could be profitable to have the pro-ceeds professionally invested and managed.

There are a number of common types of life insurance trusts. One is the *unfunded trust*. With this, you yourself pay the premiums and have the right to collect dividends. When you die, the trust instantly becomes active, and the provisions you have made for the proceeds of your insur-ance are carried out. Under a second type, the *funded trust,* you place in the hands of your trustee sufficient assets to provide funds for the pay-ment of the premiums due on your policy. These assets can be money, securities, real estate or other property that yields income. You can also arrange for the trustee to handle all of your financial affairs.

If you do not have sufficient assets to place in trust to supply your premiums, you can establish a *cumulative trust fund.* Here you give the trustee whatever assets you can set aside to yield money for the pre-miums, and you pay the balance out of your own pocket.

Business insurance trusts are sometimes established to provide for the continuance of a business if a principal should become disabled or die (see section 513). The trustee may be relied upon to purchase the share of the deceased member as promptly as possible, so that the business can continue to function smoothly.

511. Retirement Insurance • Gains made in medical science have added years to the life expectancy of almost everyone. As a result, more and more of us are concerned with providing for our later years, and so is the government. Aside from the personal savings and investments he makes, the average person is likely to rely on one or more of the follow-ing sources to provide him with income when he reaches retirement age:

social security (see sections 414–423), a company pension plan, a tax-sheltered retirement plan, a retirement endowment policy, an annuity. If by combining your anticipated income from various sources you can count on having approximately 50 percent of your average salary, you should be able to take care of your later years. If not, it might be wise to discuss the problem with your insurance salesman and other experts in financial planning.

More and more companies are establishing *pension plans* to provide retirement income for their employes. These plans differ widely. In some, the employer bears the entire cost; in others, the employe also contributes. Usually the plan is supervised by a bank or an insurance company, which invests the contributions. The plan sets a minimum length of service to qualify for benefits. Your benefit will vary with your annual salary when working and your length of service. Age at time of retirement is also a factor; your pension may be reduced if you retire early, or you may be able to receive a higher pension at first and then have it lowered proportionately when you begin to receive social security benefits. Usually the pension stops when you die. However, various options may be available, as they are for annuities (which are discussed later in this section), so that you may be entitled to a guaranteed minimum of payments, which will be paid to your beneficiary if you die. If you leave your employer, you are entitled to a refund of the premiums you have paid, plus interest.

Because of the great differences in pension plans, it is best to find out from your personnel department the exact details of the one your company offers and how you can take best advantage of its specific features in combination with your other sources of retirement income.

Tax-sheltered retirement plans, also known as the Keogh plans, offer self-employed persons, such as doctors, lawyers and sole proprietors, a method of setting up a retirement program with certain tax advantages. If you have a full-time job but earn income from self-employment on the side you may also be eligible. Retirement programs that you may participate in include mutual fund shares that are held by banks, trust accounts with banks, special U.S. Treasury savings bonds and annuity contracts issued by life insurance companies.

Under these plans, you are allowed to contribute to your retirement fund up to 15 percent of the net income from your work or business with a yearly maximum of $7,500. All of your contributions are deductible from your income in the year they are made, and you pay no taxes on the earnings of your pension fund until you retire. Of course,

WHAT'S IN YOUR LIFE INSURANCE POLICY

Some of the most common provisions of a typical life insurance contract are outlined below. These include the name of the insured and the beneficiary, the amount of insurance, the terms of the contract, definitions of the owner and beneficiary and a statement of their rights, a schedule of premium payments and the settlement options available.

Type of Policy

Vital Statistics Concerning Policy and Contract

Terms of the Contract Between the Company and the Insured

Definition of the Owner and Rights of Ownership

Definition of the Beneficiary and Statement of His Rights

Schedule for the Payment of Premiums Generally, an individualized program of payment is arranged between the Insured and the Company, and is attached to the policy itself.

Options for Settlement A table of Installments is attached to the policy. This will vary according to the type of insurance and the form of settlement arranged between the Owner and the Company.

Settlement Options

1. DEPOSIT OPTION: Left on deposit with the Company with interest payable at a rate of 2½% per year.

2. INSTALLMENT OPTION, FIXED PERIOD: Payable in equal installments for the number of years elected (not more than thirty) in an amount determined by the table of installments.

3. LIFE INCOME OPTIONS:
   a. *Ten or twenty years certain.* Payable in installments for the certain period elected.
   b. *Refund certain.* Payable in installments until the total amount paid (exclusive of dividends) equals the proceeds applied under this option.

4. INSTALLMENT OPTION, FIXED AMOUNT: Payable in installments until the proceeds applied, together with interest on the unpaid balance at the effective rate of 2½% per year, are exhausted.

5. JOINT AND SURVIVOR OPTIONS, TEN YEARS CERTAIN: Payable in installments for ten years, and continuing thereafter while either of two persons upon whose lives the income depends is surviving.

ORDINARY LIFE POLICY

Insurance Payable in Event of Death. Annual Dividends. Premiums Payable For Life.

The Insured RICHARD ROE
Register Date JANUARY 1, 1965
Face Amount $10,000
Policy Number SPECIMEN
Beneficiary M. H. ROE, WIFE

The Contract. This insurance is granted in consideration of payment of the required premiums. This policy and the application constitute the entire contract.

All statements made in the application shall be deemed representations, not warranties.

This policy may not be modified, nor may any of the Company's rights or requirements be waived, except in writing and by a duly authorized officer of the Company.

Owner. The Owner is the Insured unless otherwise specified in the application or endorsed on this policy by the Company. While the Insured is living, the Owner may exercise all rights and take any other action agreed to by the Company in connection with this policy.

Beneficiary. The Beneficiary is as designated in the application unless changed. The Owner may change the Beneficiary from time to time during the lifetime of the Insured, by written notice to the Company, but any change will be effective only if it is endorsed on this policy by the Company. Upon endorsement, the change will take effect as of the date the written notice was signed, whether or not the Insured is living, but without further liability as to any payment or other settlement made by the Company before endorsing the change.

Premiums. Premiums are payable for the premium period indicated elsewhere but no premium will fall due after the death of the Insured. The premium period is measured from the register date.

A premium not paid on or before its due date will be in default, and its due date will be the date of default. Upon default this policy will lapse and the insurance will cease as of the date of default, except as stated in the grace and options-on-lapse provisions.

the tax you pay when you draw the funds after retirement is usually much lower than it is when you are actively earning a living. You become eligible to draw on your retirement fund at age fifty-nine and a half, but may put off your retirement till seventy and a half.

You may also deposit an equal amount annually into other private plans. This sum is included in your income each year for tax purposes, but you aren't taxed on the dividends until retirement.

The Internal Revenue Service will give you information about how to set up a tax-sheltered retirement plan; so will various banks, insurance companies and mutual funds. However, you should discuss your situation thoroughly with your attorney or accountant before going ahead.

The *retirement-income policy* is a form of endowment policy (see section 503), that provides death benefits if you should die before the maturity date. After that date you receive the benefits in monthly payments, as a rule.

Annuities are often confused with retirement-income policies. The confusion arises because the same companies sell both, and both are based upon mortality tables. Moreover, both are frequently paid out in monthly installments for the rest of the annuitant's life, if not for a specified number of years.

For a typical annuity you make payments to the insurance company annually over a period of years. (You can also make a single lump-sum payment.) The annuity matures when you reach the age at which you wish to retire. The money the company pays you consists of a repayment of the principal plus interest. The payments may stop when you die, with no refund of the balance, or if you have arranged otherwise, the balance may be paid to a beneficiary. You can take out a plan in which you are guaranteed a minimum number of payments and then an income for life; if your death occurs during the minimum guarantee period, the remaining payments are made to your beneficiary. Other arrangements, including one that provides for a husband and wife, are possible.

If you are concerned with the effect of inflation, you can take out a special type of annuity known as a *variable annuity*. Here the payments you receive are determined by the value and earnings of securities in which the company invests. If the securities earn more or less within a given period, your annuity is proportionately larger or smaller. Your income varies much as it would if you had invested in mutual funds.

512. Fraternal Insurance Contracts and Burial Insurance • Many fraternal organizations have their own insurance companies for the benefit of their members. They offer much the same line of life insurance policies as private insurance companies. Small policies are also available to defray the costs of a member's funeral and burial.

The provisions of fraternal policies closely resemble those of policies issued by commercial companies, but there is one major difference. With the private company, the application for insurance and the policy make up the contract between you and the company. With a fraternal order policy, the order's charter and constitution also become part of the contract. In addition, if the organization's financial reserves are diminished because of a large number of deaths or other causes, you can be required to contribute an extra payment to bring the reserves up to the necessary strength. If you fail to pay, the amount you owe is considered a lien against your policy.

To provide funds for burial, many people carry small policies known as industrial life insurance (see section 503).

513. Life Insurance in Business Situations · Businesses often find it to their advantage to take out insurance on the lives of key members of the firm. The person insured might be the sole owner, a partner, a shareholder in a closed corporation or a key executive. Insuring the life of such a person can save the business from severe loss, dissolution or a forced sale in the event of his death.

A *sole proprietorship* is a business owned by one person (see section 403). These individual ownerships outnumber every other form of enterprise in the United States, making up about 70 percent of all business establishments. If you are the sole owner of a business, its assets are included in your estate on your death. So, unfortunately, are its debts, which are a charge against the estate. If you die without having arranged for someone to take over the business, it usually has to be sold, often at a price well below its value. Insurance, however, can offer a remedy. If you buy a life insurance policy in a sufficient amount and name your estate as the beneficiary, the proceeds can protect your heirs against some of the loss involved in a forced sale. The insurance will also help to build up your estate if the business is saddled with debts. Another possibility is to arrange for the sale of your business to key employes in the event of your death. They can buy a policy on your life to finance the purchase.

You can also use life insurance to give a partnership stability. In most of the states a partnership is dissolved when one of the partners dies (see chapter 9, "Your Job, Profession or Business; Your Social Security," page 451), unless the partnership agreement provides otherwise. It might

621

contain a provision, for example, that the remaining partners have the right to buy the deceased partner's share in the business. To provide the necessary funds, the business can take out policies on the lives of all the partners. The firm itself can be named as the beneficiary, and the insurance proceeds used to purchase the interest of the deceased partner. If there are only two partners, each could take out a policy on the other.

A large number of corporations employ insurance for much the same purpose. Most corporations are small and closely held—they are the property of a family or a few closely associated individuals who own a controlling amount, if not all, of the company's stock. If one dies, his executor could decide to sell the stock to outsiders, who might have an influence on the operation of the firm. To keep the control in the original hands, the members of a closely held corporation often arrange that the shares of any of their number who dies be sold only to those who survive. Policies are bought on the lives of all to provide the purchase price of these shares.

Nowadays, more and more companies take out policies on the lives of officers or key employes. The beneficiaries are the companies themselves. If the dynamic founder of a company dies, its credit may be shaken or it may suffer other losses. It may cost a company considerable sums to find and compensate replacements in the event of the death of the skilled executives who guide its operations. Benefits from policies on these men's lives help the company to make up any financial loss it may suffer.

Disability insurance also can play a useful role in cushioning the sole proprietorship, partnership and closed corporation against losses that may be caused by serious illness. Income from a disability policy gives the sole owner the time he needs to dispose of his business on favorable terms, without having to face a forced sale. Another possibility is that he can use the benefits to hire a replacement until he is well enough to take up the reins of management again. Partners can take out disability insurance on one another to provide the funds needed to acquire a permanently disabled partner's interest. The members of a closed corporation can make a similar arrangement to purchase the shares of a disabled major stockholder or key executive.

514. If You Misrepresent Your Age or State of Health in Your Life Insurance Application · Some people are tempted to understate their age when they apply for insurance in order to pay a lower premium. Others may misstate their age because they have no birth certificate or other record of their birth date and honestly do not know how old they are. To protect themselves against misrepresentations or misstatements of age, most insurance companies include in their contracts a clause like this: "If the age or sex of the insured has been misstated, the amount payable shall be such as the premium paid would have purchased on the basis of the correct age and sex."

In other words, if the insurance company discovers the misstatement, it will pay no more than you are actually entitled to. The amount of insurance will be adjusted to the amount your beneficiary would have received for the same premiums if you had declared your true age. Your beneficiary thus might collect thousands of dollars less than the face amount of the policy. A reverse situation can also occur. If you stated on your application that you were older than your actual age and paid a higher premium than necessary, the company would pay your beneficiary a sum proportionately greater than the face amount. If the error were discovered while you were still alive, the company would pay back the excess.

No doubt you were struck by the reference to sex in the insurance policy clause that we quoted above. Some people purposely misrepresent their sex in applications. Many insurance companies charge a lower premium for women since they tend to be longer-lived than men and so are better risks.

If you have no proof of your age when you apply for insurance, you can bring this fact to the company's attention. You can then get an agreement in writing from the company that it recognizes your presumed age as your actual one for the purpose of the policy. Such an agreement may spare your beneficiary needless difficulty when the policy falls due.

Life insurance policies include another standard provision called the *incontestability clause*. In contrast to the misstatement-of-age provision, this clause exists for the protection of the insured and is frequently required by state law. Here's what the clause says in a typical insurance contract: "This policy shall be incontestable after it has been in force during the lifetime of the insured for two years from the date of issue except for nonpayment of premiums."

What does this provision mean? Briefly, that after the policy has been running for two years, the company cannot turn down a claim for payment because you made a misstatement on your application or concealed an important fact about your health. (This clause does not apply to misstatements about age or sex, of course.) If you die before the end of the two-year period, the company can contest the policy at any time. Otherwise, the only ground on which the company can void the life insurance provisions of your policy is that you failed to pay your premiums when they were due.

It has been said that the incontestability clause obliges the company to treat as binding a contract that the applicant has entered into fraudulently. Suppose, for example, that a person has suffered from a serious ailment and has been treated for it by a doctor. Later, in his application for insurance, he states that he has never had such an illness. His statement is a material misrepresentation; if the company knew the truth, it would not enter into a contract with the applicant. A misrepresentation of this type voids an ordinary contract. But with a life insurance contract, if the company does not challenge the statement within the period specified, it has to pay the beneficiary when the policyholder dies—even if his death is caused by that same ailment.

The law, of course, does not sanction fraud. But it must protect the policyholder and his beneficiary. Otherwise the insurance company could contest the policyholder's statements in his application after his death. At that time, no one might know the actual facts. So the company is given a reasonable period of time to raise questions. If it fails to do so, it must take the consequences.

The incontestability clause does not excuse every type of misrepresentation. The courts have held that the insurance company does not have to pay in case of a gross fraud, for example, if the applicant got someone else to take his medical examination for him. Double indemnity and disability benefits generally do not come under the incontestability clause (see sections 518, 522).

515. Suicide · Sometimes people buy life insurance policies for substantial sums with the idea of killing themselves to provide an estate for their beneficiaries. To guard against this possibility, the typical policy contains a suicide clause. Under this clause, if the insured person commits suicide within a specified period after the policy is issued—usually one or two years—all that the company has to pay to his beneficiaries is the amount of the premiums paid up to then. The insurance companies have wisely concluded that a person eager to depart this life may wait a week or two, but a year or two will be too long for him.

516. Making a Claim on Life Insurance · In order to collect life insurance benefits you must furnish the insurance company with proof that the insured person has died. Usually you do this by submitting a copy of the death certificate, signed by the examining physician (see section 598).

624

Sometimes it may not be possible to obtain a death certificate. The body of the insured person might be lost, or he might have disappeared mysteriously. The courts are practical and will be satisfied with convincing circumstantial evidence or a reasonable explanation of the death. Witnesses may have seen the insured person at work in a place where an explosion occurred shortly afterward, or his name might be on the passenger list of an airplane that disappeared without a trace. In cases like these the insurance company would have little reason to contest a claim for benefits.

Once in a while it happens that the insured person simply disappears. Does the insurance company have to pay benefits if there is no evidence of death? The courts will presume that if the vanished person is not heard from for seven years, he is indeed dead (see section 584 and chart 39, page 677). But the company may fight this presumption if it can present a plausible reason for the disappearance. For example, it might be able to show that the person liquidated his assets shortly before he disappeared or that he had left home for long periods on several previous occasions without announcing his departure. In the face of such evidence a court might hold that he was very likely still alive and that the beneficiary had no right to the proceeds of the policy.

If a claim is made under a double-indemnity accidental-death clause, an autopsy may be required.

INSURANCE AGAINST SICKNESS AND ACCIDENT

517. Understanding Your Health or Accident Insurance Policy • A health or accident insurance policy, like other contracts, at first glance may seem to be a complicated document. This is only because it has to explain in detail all of your benefits and the conditions you must meet to receive them. The policy is worded with extreme care, to rule out the possibility of misunderstanding.

a. *The insuring clause.* If one part of your policy can be said to be more important than the rest, that part is the insuring clause. The insuring clause describes the risks against which the policy insures you. Generally it provides you with coverage against a loss that occurs *while the policy is in force.* In other words, you are not eligible to obtain compensation for a disorder you already had when you took out the policy. The

625

clause may also say that the policy is not effective until you have passed a probationary period (fifteen or thirty days as a rule).

The insuring clause defines the loss you must suffer to be entitled to benefits. Under a medical expense policy, for example, the loss must be from sickness or bodily injury that causes you to incur medical and surgical bills. Your confinement in a hospital must be prescribed by a licensed physician, and so must all the medical services and supplies you receive.

Under a disability income policy, you must suffer from a disease or accidental bodily injury that causes you to be totally or partially disabled. *Total disability* exists when you are judged unable to perform the normal duties of your job for a year or longer, or the duties of any job you are fitted for by your experience and training. Sometimes it is defined as inability to perform the work required for any gainful employment. *Partial disability* means that you are unable to perform one or more of the basic duties of your job.

Some policies insure only the policyholder; others insure his dependents as well. The insuring clause tells you exactly who is protected. Under policies for hospitalization, medical and surgical expenses and major medical expenses, both you and your dependents are covered as a rule. Under a disability income policy only the policyholder is protected. The meaning of *dependents* is fairly limited: it is your husband or wife and your unmarried children up to a certain age.

b. *The benefit clause.* A list of the benefits generally follows the insuring clause. In a medical and surgical policy, for example, the benefit clause lists the common operations and the payment allowed for each. In a hospitalization policy, you are told the benefit for room, board and general care, as well as other services and supplies. The benefit clause must include or be followed by a description of the "exceptions, limitations and reductions" that affect the benefits.

c. *"Exceptions, limitations and reductions."* Under this heading your policy lists the limitations on your coverage. For example, many hospitalization and medical and surgical policies will not allow benefits for injuries or sicknesses covered by workmen's compensation. Most health insurance policies also exclude compensation for disabilities treated in government hospitals (such as those maintained by the Veterans Administration) or in public programs. The purpose of this exclusion is to avoid duplication of benefits; thus it serves to keep down the premiums that you or the sponsor of your group insurance program has to pay. Many policies exclude payments for hearing aids, eyeglasses and dental work.

626

Generally injuries and sickness suffered while you are a member of the armed forces are also not covered.

The typical health insurance policy provides coverage only for a sickness or accident that occurs after the date the policy becomes effective. This provision automatically rules out any condition already present when you apply for the insurance. On the other hand, if you have a physical impairment, you may be able to obtain a policy that will exclude that condition, but provide benefits for all other disabilities. It may also be possible to get a policy covering your impairment if you pay a higher premium or accept a longer waiting period. This kind of arrangement may be made with a person who has suffered a heart attack, for example.

Some policies call for a waiting period before you can apply for benefits for certain conditions or operations such as childbirth or the removal of tonsils.

Group plans (see section 518) usually accept you automatically, without an examination, so that preexisting conditions do not affect your right to benefits. Although other types of health insurance exclude a variety of conditions—like drug addiction, mental disorders, alcoholism —as a basis for a claim, group plans frequently do not. On the other hand, they generally will not pay benefits for injury or illness that occurs outside the United States. Self-inflicted injuries are excluded.

Most Blue Cross policies (hospitalization policies) will not compensate you for treatment you obtain from veterans' hospitals. They also exclude on-the-job injuries that are covered by workmen's compensation or other benefits. However, group disability policies will sometimes allow benefits for such injuries, particularly for a resulting long-term disability, but they deduct from the benefit the amount you receive from a governmental agency.

Blue Shield (a nationwide medical and surgical plan) has exclusions similar to those of Blue Cross. Reduced benefits may be paid for the treatment of nervous conditions, alcoholism, drug addiction and other disorders potentially of long duration.

d. *Time limit on certain defenses.* This provision limits the time a company is allowed to contest a claim on the ground that the condition existed when the policy was taken out. After a two- or three-year period (depending on the state) the condition is considered not to have existed at the time the policy was bought. In some policies—those that are guaranteed renewable or are not cancelable—instead of the time limit clause there is an incontestability clause (see section 514).

627

e. *Grace period*. This clause provides that the insurance will remain in force for a period ranging from seven to thirty-one days after you fail to pay a premium. After expiration of the grace period the policy lapses. If you want to reinstate the policy, the insurance company may require you to make a new application and take a medical examination. If you become ill less than ten days after your policy is reinstated or have an accident during the period of lapse, you are usually not entitled to benefits.

518. Group Insurance Plans • Group health insurance—insurance that is made available through an employer, professional organization, labor union or similar association—is growing at a rapid rate in the United States. More than 75 million people are protected for a portion or all of their hospital and medical expenses under group health plans.

Often group insurance plans are paid for entirely or in part by your employer and form an important part of collective bargaining agreements. However, even if you have to bear the cost of the premium yourself, it is to your advantage, since a group policy invariably costs less than one that you buy as an individual. In a group plan many people are insured under a single contract, and the savings in sales and administrative costs are passed along to you. There are other advantages. As a rule you do not have to pass a physical examination to establish your eligibility. The insurance company is usually concerned with the group average and can accept the risk that is poorer than average. Thus, as a member of a group you are automatically eligible for coverage that you might not qualify for as an individual. (However, there are some grounds for denial of benefits.) An additional advantage is that the company cannot cancel your policy. It comes to an end only when you leave the company or association (and even then you can generally convert to an individual policy) or the entire group plan is terminated.

Group plans, by and large, are renewed on an annual basis. At the time of renewal the insurance company can make adjustments in premiums or the terms of coverage. Your group can also arrange for changes in coverage at the same time, to keep pace with changing conditions.

A number of different types of health insurance plans are available. The most important of these are hospitalization insurance, medical and surgical insurance, major medical insurance, dental insurance, disability income insurance, group life insurance and accidental death and dismemberment insurance.

a. *Hospitalization insurance*. This type of insurance, of which Blue

Cross is a familiar example, provides benefits to meet the cost of confinement in a hospital. Room and board and general nursing care in a semi-private room are covered up to the number of days specified in the policy. Necessary medical services and supplies are provided. If you require a private room, the plan pays a set amount toward its cost and you pay the balance. You also pay for nonmedical services, such as the use of a telephone and a television set. Commonly, all you need do is show the hospital your plan membership card; the hospital bills the plan directly and receives payment from it for all covered services.

Hospitalization plans generally require you to be a member for a certain number of months before you are eligible for childbirth benefits. It usually places a limit on the number of days for which you can receive benefits, and often you have to pay a deductible—$25 to $50 or the first day's hospital costs.

b. *Medical and surgical insurance.* When illness strikes, the fees of the physician and surgeon are another important consideration. Medical and surgical insurance, which many people carry in the form of the Blue Shield plan, provides for these charges. In many plans provision is made for the full payment of the doctor's fees if you belong to a low-income group. If your earnings are above a certain figure, the surgical plan pays the sum that is specified in its schedule and you pay the rest. There is seldom any provision for nursing care.

A typical policy places limitations on certain types of treatment as well as medical conditions that you already have at the time you apply for insurance. With some conditions, such as pregnancy or hernia, you must have the policy a stated number of months before you are eligible for benefits. The company includes this provision to remove the risk that you might apply for the policy with a specific operation in mind.

An optional feature that may be added to hospital-surgical insurance is regular medical expense benefits, or general medical insurance. This insurance provides benefits for visits by your doctor when you are in the hospital for a condition that does not require surgery. You may also be able to bill the insurance company for visits to or from your physician for treatment. Benefits generally start at once if the condition is caused by an accident. In case of disability due to illness, you cannot collect until the third or fourth visit.

Examine a medical and surgical policy carefully before you sign on the dotted line. Pay attention to the schedule of benefits and see how close they come to typical surgical fees charged in your vicinity. Look for limitations and exclusions; some policies are definitely more stringent than

629

others. If you are in doubt, a brief discussion with your family physician will prove helpful. The purchase of a major medical policy (discussed below) is a sensible measure to provide for extraordinary expenses not covered by these policies.

c. *Major medical insurance.* Major medical insurance provides you with protection to meet the heavy charges caused by serious or chronic illness. In most group plans it picks up when the cost exceeds the maximum paid by group hospitalization and group surgical insurance benefits.

This kind of insurance has two significant features. One is the deductible. As with automobile insurance or a homeowners policy, you must contribute a specified sum toward the total amount of your claim. The deductible makes it possible for you to obtain your insurance at a lower rate, since the company does not have to pay the multitude of smaller claims. The amount of the deductible varies with the individual policy. It usually ranges from $100 to $1,000.

The second important feature is that you pay a percentage of the medical costs above the deductible. Frequently your share amounts to 20 or 25 percent. Suppose, for instance, that you have a policy with a $100 deductible and have to pay 20 percent of the cost above that amount. On a medical bill for $1,000 the company pays $720, after it subtracts your $100 deductible plus $180, or 20 percent of the remaining $900. Obviously, if the bill were ten times as large—as it easily could be with today's high cost of medical care—you would have to pay several thousand dollars. However, the lion's share of the cost would be borne by the company.

Your policy describes the services for which you will be compensated. These usually include bed, board and care in a general hospital; treatment by a physician or a surgeon; services of a registered nurse; and local ambulance service. If you use a private room, a limit may be set on the daily charges for bed and board that will be paid. Medical and surgical services and supplies are covered, such as X rays, laboratory tests, transfusions, prosthetic appliances, the use of medical equipment and drugs and medicines prescribed by a physician.

Your policy also specifies certain services that are excluded from coverage. Among these are expenses for dental work or cosmetic surgery (plastic surgery undertaken to improve the appearance), unless made necessary by an accident while you are insured. Expenses for eyeglasses and hearing aids are not covered. Special terms apply to compensation for psychiatric care; it may be required that you be a patient in a general hospital, or a smaller proportion of the expenses may be covered than for

630

NATIONAL HEALTH EXPENDITURES
1965–1975

The price of medical care has risen sharply in the last
several years. Overall medical services cost the consumer
almost 47 percent more in 1975 than they did in 1965.
Medical spending has increased at much the same rate.

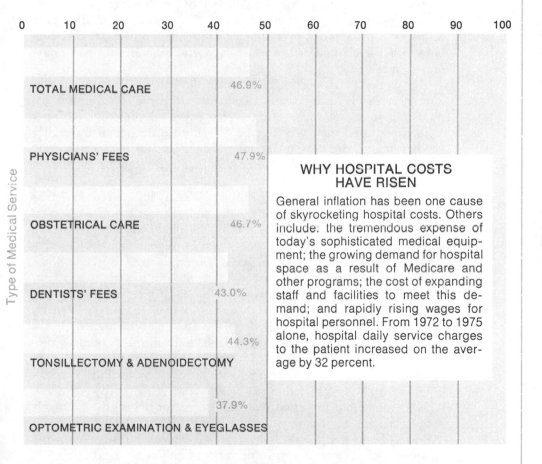

PERCENTAGE OF INCREASE

Type of Medical Service

	0	10	20	30	40	50	60	70	80	90	100
TOTAL MEDICAL CARE						46.9%					
PHYSICIANS' FEES						47.9%					
OBSTETRICAL CARE						46.7%					
DENTISTS' FEES					43.0%						
TONSILLECTOMY & ADENOIDECTOMY					44.3%						
OPTOMETRIC EXAMINATION & EYEGLASSES					37.9%						

WHY HOSPITAL COSTS HAVE RISEN

General inflation has been one cause
of skyrocketing hospital costs. Others
include: the tremendous expense of
today's sophisticated medical equipment; the growing demand for hospital
space as a result of Medicare and
other programs; the cost of expanding
staff and facilities to meet this demand; and rapidly rising wages for
hospital personnel. From 1972 to 1975
alone, hospital daily service charges
to the patient increased on the average by 32 percent.

The graph above illustrates the increase in medical costs from 1965 to
1975. Figures are based on Bureau of Labor Statistics calculations of the
Consumer Price Index for that period.

other medical treatment, depending on the policy. No payments are made if you are confined or treated at a hospital operated by the U.S. government or for treatment received through a public program. If your sickness is covered by workmen's compensation (see section 430), you are not entitled to major medical benefits.

A typical policy covers not only you but your dependents as well. Frequently your unmarried dependent children are insured to their nineteenth birthday or, if they are full-time students at an accredited college, to their twenty-third birthday.

d. *Dental insurance.* A fairly recent development in the group health field, dental insurance provides a schedule of benefits for various kinds of work, much as surgical insurance does. You can receive most types of dental care, including X rays, fillings, extractions, bridges, inlays, dentures, oral surgery and orthodontia. Even oral examinations and cleanings are included.

The system of payments is built along the pattern of major medical insurance. You begin by paying a deductible of perhaps $25 or $50 toward your yearly cost. After that the plan pays from 50 to 80 percent of the charge. In addition you may be limited to a maximum benefit for any one year. Schedules are variable. You might, for instance, have to pay half the cost of dentures but contribute nothing toward less expensive procedures.

e. *Disability income insurance.* Group disability insurance covers both partial and total disability. (For a definition of these terms, see section 517a.) Partial disability benefits usually are payable if the disability is due to sickness or injury that occurs apart from your job, since on-the-job disability is covered by workmen's compensation (see section 430). Some plans provide one half or two thirds of your average weekly pay up to a certain maximum; others give a specified amount for each pay range. In cases of total disability due to occupational causes, benefits may be paid to supplement those from workmen's compensation.

Group professional policies are available to the members of many professional societies such as the American Bar Association and the American Medical Association. These policies provide for monthly payments of up to $1,000 for a period of two to five years. Their purpose is not to replace income but to permit the disabled person to exist comfortably until he can find another way to make a living.

f. *Accidental death and dismemberment insurance.* This group plan provides a schedule of payments for various kinds of losses as a result of an accident. The losses include life, both hands, both feet, sight in both

632

eyes, one hand and sight in one eye, one foot and sight in one eye, one hand and one foot. If a single hand or foot is lost, or the vision in one eye, half of the benefit is paid. Depending on the plan, the benefit may be paid for occupational or nonoccupational injury or both.

g. *Other plans.* A number of other types of health insurance are used by special groups, and new ones are constantly being developed. Many firms have programs that provide supplemental assistance for retired employes on Medicare (see sections 426–428). Lending institutions often take out health insurance on debtors, to protect loans that they have made to them. *Dread disease insurance* covers the extraordinarily high expenses you may incur with certain serious diseases such as poliomyelitis, leukemia and spinal meningitis. (This coverage may be added to a Blue Shield or Blue Cross contract.) *Physicians' attendance insurance* reimburses you for medical treatment other than surgery, such as visits from or to physicians. *Travel accident insurance* is often taken out by companies to protect their employes from injury while traveling; it is a limited form of accidental death and dismemberment insurance.

519. Making a Claim on Your Group Insurance • If you belong to a group hospitalization plan such as Blue Cross, you usually have a membership card supplied by the insurance company. This card shows the number of your group policy. The hospital admissions office will take down this number when you are admitted and send its bill to the insurance company, with a copy to you.

If you have a claim under a medical and surgical policy, such as Blue Shield or a major medical policy, you file this separately. You will be given forms to have filled out by the surgeon or attending physician. Copies of bills for medicines and other medical supplies are also required for a major medical claim.

Some companies do not give you a group membership card. If this is your case, get the appropriate claim forms from your personnel office before you are admitted to the hospital. These forms may provide for the assignment of benefits directly to the hospital or doctor. The forms point out that you are responsible for expenses not included in your insurance coverage. If you prefer, you can pay the bills yourself and fill out the forms and send them to the company for reimbursement, with the bills. It is important that the bills should state exactly to whom the service or treatment was supplied, the date and the nature of the medical treatment. Otherwise they may be returned to you with a request for clarification or additional information.

633

If you make a claim under a disability income policy, your doctor has to indicate how long he expects you to be disabled. With a long-term disability, he may be required to file periodic reports. You should complete your proof-of-loss form for disability benefits as soon as possible and send it to the insurance company. Be sure to do this within ninety days of your recovery or your claim may be contested or refused.

520. Private Health Insurance Policies • You can obtain individual hospitalization and surgical insurance policies fairly similar to those available from an employer under a group plan. In fact, if you leave your employer, you usually have the privilege of converting your company insurance to private policies, at an additional charge, and maintaining them on an individual basis.

To obtain an individual medical care or hospitalization policy, you must generally complete an application. If the company agent fills out the application for you, read it over carefully before you sign, and make sure he wrote in the correct information. You may be refused benefits if there is an erroneous answer to a material question about your health. For a description of benefits, see section 518.

521. Major Medical Insurance • Major medical insurance provides you with financial help in case you fall victim to a costly illness or an accident. The benefits are substantial; for a single occurrence of illness, you may be entitled to $15,000, $25,000 or more toward your medical expenses. For a description of benefits see section 518.

522. Private Accident Insurance Policies • For a description of benefits see section 518.

Accident policies usually provide that they will make payments for injury or death caused by an accident or by a disease or infection resulting from an accident or by drowning. They frequently state that the insurance company does not accept liability if there is no external or visible sign to prove the accidental injury. Depending on the policy, the company may exclude claims for benefits that arise from infections and disease, mental illness, self-inflicted injury, taking poison or a drug, inhaling gas (whether on purpose or by accident), intoxication, suicide, committing a crime, medical treatment, military service and certain kinds of aviation risks. The company does not, as a rule, have to pay benefits if the insured person's death is caused by a disease that he already had and that was aggravated by an accident.

Many accident policies contain a *double indemnity clause,* which provides that you will be paid two (or three times) the specified indemnity if you sustain injuries under certain special circumstances. Typical ones listed are injuries caused by lightning, hurricane, tornado, boiler explosion, collapse of the outer walls of a building, fire or an elevator car accident.

Some policies make provision for medical care. Under these, the company agrees to pay expenses incurred within a certain number of weeks after an accident. Hospital care, treatment by physicians and surgeons and care by a trained nurse may be provided up to a specified maximum.

The chance that you will suffer an accident often has a close relationship to the kind of work you do. The insurance company considers the kinds of risks you face in your occupation when it sets your premium. If you change your occupation to a more dangerous one and you are injured, the company will pay you only the amount of benefits your payments would have entitled you to at the higher rate of the more hazardous job.

The insurance company, when presented with a claim, has a right to give you one or more physical examinations. If it is not prohibited by law, the company may, in cases of death, have an autopsy made within thirty days after it receives notice of death.

The question of whether an injury or death is accidental or not is frequently a difficult one; it has led to numerous lawsuits and occasionally to conflicting court decisions. Basically, an accident means an unforeseen happening that is not intended by the victim.

Some policies, however, state that they will pay benefits only if there are bodily injuries "effected solely through accidental means." Courts occasionally interpret this to mean that if you perform an act intentionally and you suffer an accident as a result of it, you are not entitled to benefits; the means were not accidental. On this principle, if you lifted a weighty packing case and suffered a back injury, you might be denied benefits since your act was intentional. But the courts tend more and more to take the part of the insured and interpret "accidental means" simply as "accident."

If you suffer injury as a result of someone else's intentional act, that is an accident in the eyes of the law, unless your policy specifically excludes such coverage. On the other hand, if you egg the other person on until he assaults and injures you, the responsibility may be yours; the happening could have been foreseen.

523. Private Disability Income Insurance · For a description of benefits see the discussion of group disability insurance you will find under section 518.

524. Making a Claim on Your Private Health Insurance Policies · Your first step should be to get in touch with the insurance company and ask them for a claims form. Get this form filled out and signed by the hospital or the physician and mail it to the company with the bills you received from the hospital, the doctor, the pharmacist or others, as provided in your policy.

525. Social Security and Medicare · Most people think of retirement benefits at age sixty-five as the main content of the social security program, but it has many other provisions. One of the most important of these concerns disability benefits, which are described in greater detail in section 421.

Medicare, which is also a part of the social security program, provides for hospital care for most people aged sixty-five and over. In addition, for a small monthly payment you can obtain coverage for 80 percent of your physician's fees and other medical health charges, after paying a fixed deductible sum. (See sections 426–428.)

Many persons on social security carry private insurance to supplement their Medicare benefits. Some policies, known as hospital income policies, provide benefits for up to one year in a hospital. Frequently, supplementary policies cover charges for private nurses or care in a nursing home, as well as other medical expenses not provided by Medicare. Employers sometimes provide for their retired employes with group plans that pay their deductibles and other charges not met by social security.

526. Workmen's Compensation Laws · If you are injured on your job or contract a disease as a result of your employment, you may be eligible for workmen's compensation. All the states have laws that call for benefits, but the provisions vary greatly. For a detailed discussion of workmen's compensation and the major provisions of the various state laws, see chapter 9, "Your Job, Profession or Business; Your Social Security," page 451. If you have health insurance coverage, many policies provide that they will deduct from your benefits the payments you receive from workmen's compensation, so that you do not receive what is in effect a double payment (see sections 430, 517).

CHAPTER TWELVE

Your Estate, Will and Death

The law is not concerned with trifles.

—ANONYMOUS

12

Your Estate, Will and Death

Some Key Points in This Chapter—
Consult these sections for information on:

Charts in This Chapter

527. The Importance of Your Will · Your will may be the most important paper you ever sign. It is one of your few opportunities to direct the distribution of your property among your survivors. Its significance depends less on the size of your estate than on the kind of assets you leave and on matters you want taken care of after your death. It tells your family, business associates and the state, whom you want to administer your property and other assets, to whom you want to leave them and the conditions under which the people you name are to receive them. It also concerns such vital family matters as who will be the guardian of your minor children.

If you die without a will you may saddle your family with needless work and trouble, heavy administrative expenses that a will may prevent and, very likely, estate tax liabilities that eat up much of the money otherwise available for your family's support. For example, if you or your wife fails to execute a will, the survivor might be deprived of the estate tax advantage of a full marital deduction (see section 576).

You are said to die *testate* if you have left a valid will and *intestate* if you have not. A *testator* is a man who leaves a will; a *testatrix* is a woman who leaves a will. All your assets, including money owed you at your death—less your debts and expenses—constitute your estate. (See section 573 for a fuller explanation.) If you die intestate, your assets must be distributed according to the intestate distribution laws of the state where you live, and these laws may in no way conform to your wishes: Under the laws of one state your wife would get only one third of your assets and your infant child two thirds. Another state's laws would divide your property equally between your wife (who might have nothing else to live on) and your parents (who might have ample means). The best way to make sure that your wishes are carried out and that each of your loved ones is fairly protected is to leave a will stating exactly who is to get what, when. (For the laws governing the distribution of your estate if there is no will, see sections 555–570 and chart 42, page 696.)

528. When to Make Your Will · Make your will immediately. Accidents strike down young and old indiscriminately. What's more, your will should be drawn as though you *expect* to die tomorrow. And you should review it whenever there is an important change in your finances, your family situation, your state's laws concerning wills or the federal estate tax laws. Your lawyer can advise you.

Experts in many fields besides the law can help you draw documents with legal significance. But you are inviting trouble for your family if you fail to consult your lawyer in drafting your will.

529. A Wife's Duty to Make a Will • Should you, as a wife, have your own will? Absolutely. Statistics indicate that you will probably outlive your husband and therefore you presumably have time to make a will after his death. But if you die without leaving a will, the laws of intestacy operate without regard to sex. In these days when well over half the country's wealth is owned by women, you should regard your duty to make a will exactly as seriously as you doubtless expect your husband to regard his. To be sure your property ends up where you and your husband want it to, you should make a will designed to achieve the same ultimate goals as your husband's—goals on which you have both agreed. For example, if a childless couple were killed in an accident, but the intestate wife survived her husband even by seconds, all of the property he left her might go to her relatives, and none to his. To avoid such possibilities, husbands and wives should be aware of, and agree to, the terms of each other's wills. Sometimes a wife and a husband make what are called reciprocal, or interlocking, wills, to ensure that their respective wishes are carried out under all foreseeable circumstances. You don't have to go that far, however. What is important is to learn the provisions of your husband's will and have your lawyer prepare for you one that fits, or at the least doesn't conflict with, those provisions.

530. Types of Wills • The law recognizes several different types of wills. Much the most common, and valid throughout the United States, is the *witnessed will*. Whether handwritten or typewritten, it must be signed by you and should bear the signatures of two adults who saw you sign the will, whom you advised that the document you were signing was your will and whom you asked to act as witnesses to that signing. Numerous instances of attempted fraud against estates, particularly large ones, have made courts eager to protect the true wishes of testators. The purpose of having witnesses is to enable the probate court (see section 585 and chart 43, page 704) to be sure that the document presented to it after your death is in fact your will. Therefore, witnesses should be people likely to be available when your will is offered for *probate,* or proof; they should be residents of your home state or live nearby. But they may not be people who will benefit from the provisions of your will, because the testimony of such persons is naturally suspect. A properly witnessed will, drawn by, or with the assistance of, a lawyer, is your best assurance that your estate will be distributed according to your wishes and with the least delay.

A *holographic* will is one you write, date and sign in your own handwriting. If it is properly witnessed it falls under the category of witnessed wills and will likely be validated by the probate court. But if you write your will in solitude, in circumstances of stress—like those of a trapper freezing in the wilderness or a castaway at sea—the problem of proving your will becomes more difficult.

It may be impossible to establish that the document presented for probate is in fact your will. No witnesses can come forward to testify that you intended the document to be your will—or that you were in full possession of your faculties when you signed it. For these reasons, several states, by statute, do not recognize holographic, or unwitnessed handwritten, wills at all. And in all states probate courts are most reluctant to accept them.

A *nuncupative* will is your oral declaration, in critical circumstances, before one or more witnesses, of what you want to do with your estate. Even though it may later be transcribed, some states will not accept a will of this kind at all, some will accept it if properly proved by the witnesses and some will weigh the circumstances under which it was made. In weighing the circumstances, the court must consider that the maker may have found himself in such an extreme situation that it was impossible for him to make any other kind of will. Because such a will is most frequently made under the fear or expectation of imminent death, with attendant emotional stress and pain, courts examine it especially carefully and suspiciously. For information on the status of oral wills in your state, see chart 41, page 692.

A *joint will* is one that husband and wife make together. It is infrequently used today, for it is relatively inflexible as a means of disposing of different parts of your estate.

However, *mutual,* or *reciprocal,* wills present a couple with greater flexibility. They are separate documents, drawn separately, but in reliance upon each other's terms. You should discuss with your lawyer whether such wills may meet your needs—particularly if your requirements are at all unusual in terms of family relationships or your mutual business interests. Such wills may also include clauses providing for presumption of survivorship (see section 544).

531. Restrictions on Your Right to Make a Will • Almost any adult may make a will. The significant question before the probate court to which your will is offered is whether testimony about your health, state of mind or the circumstances under which the will was drawn should induce the court to uphold the document as your will or to set it aside. Generally speaking, the court is likely to uphold your will if: (a) it was properly executed and witnessed and (b) at the time you signed it you were (1) of age, (2) of sound mind and (3) free from undue influence.

Be careful: *of age* means eighteen or twenty-one in most states and even younger in a few (see chart 37, page 643).

You must have a certain level of mental competence at the time you sign your will if it is to meet the *sound mind* test: the court must be satisfied that you knew what you were doing and intended to do it. Although many testators are elderly and many more on the ragged edge of mental competence, their wills are more likely than not to be honored by the court. Persons with an abysmally low IQ, alcoholics who sign their wills while on the wagon, narcotic addicts taking a cure, even persons institutionalized for senility or mental illness—all may have moments of lucidity and clarity in which the wills they sign will stand up in court.

In general, the probate court, in examining the document presented to it as your will, tries to ascertain whether, when you signed it—assuming that it was properly executed and witnessed—(a) you were lucid enough to know what you were doing, (b) you could recognize or remember members of your immediate family (as lawyers say, "the natural objects of your bounty") and (c) you understood the nature and extent of your assets. Unless the court can be persuaded that one of these essential criteria is lacking, the court will almost surely sustain it.

Courts don't want to interfere with your disposal of your property. They dislike declaring invalid any document that has the essential characteristics of a valid will. In the absence of overwhelming evidence of mental incompetence, their strong preference is to uphold a will.

The charge that when you signed your will you were subject to *undue influence* will get equally tough scrutiny from the courts that review your will. The mere fact that you are a bedridden woman who leaves the bulk of her estate to her handsome doctor, or that you are an elderly tycoon who leaves almost everything to his beautiful, buxom secretary, will not invalidate your will unless it can be established that helplessness or infatuation rendered you a powerless puppet.

Requirements for a valid will in your state are summarized in chart 37, page 643.

REQUIREMENTS FOR A VALID WILL

If your will is to be accepted as valid by a probate court, it must meet the legal requirements outlined in this chart (see section 531).

CHART 37

	At What Age May You Make a Will Disposing of Real Property?	At What Age May You Make a Will Disposing of Personal Property?	How Many Persons Must Witness Your Will?	Are Holographic Wills Recognized?		At What Age May You Make a Will Disposing of Real Property?	At What Age May You Make a Will Disposing of Personal Property?	How Many Persons Must Witness Your Will?	Are Holographic Wills Recognized?
					MISSOURI	18	18	2	No
ALABAMA	21	18	2	No	MONTANA	18	18	2	Yes
ALASKA	19	19	2	Yes	NEBRASKA	18	18	2	Yes
ARIZONA	18	18	2	Yes	NEVADA	18	18	2	Yes
ARKANSAS	18	18	2	Yes	NEW HAMPSHIRE	18	18	3	No
CALIFORNIA	18	18	2	Yes	NEW JERSEY	18	18	2	No
COLORADO	18	18	2	Yes	NEW MEXICO	18	18	2	No
CONNECTICUT	18	18	2	No	NEW YORK	18	18	2	No
DELAWARE	18	18	2	No	NORTH CAROLINA	18	18	2	Yes
D.C.	18	18	2	No	NORTH DAKOTA	18	18	2	Yes
FLORIDA	18	18	2	No	OHIO	18	18	2	No
GEORGIA	14	14	2	No	OKLAHOMA	18	18	2	Yes
HAWAII	18	18	2	Yes	OREGON	18	18	2	No
IDAHO	18	18	2	Yes	PENNSYLVANIA	18	18	2	Yes
ILLINOIS	18	18	2	No	RHODE ISLAND	18	18	2	No
INDIANA	18	18	2	No	SOUTH CAROLINA	18	18	3	No
IOWA	19	19	2	No	SOUTH DAKOTA	18	18	2	Yes
KANSAS	18	18	2	No	TENNESSEE	18	18	2	Yes
KENTUCKY	18	18	2	Yes	TEXAS	18	18	2	Yes
LOUISIANA	16	16	2	Yes	UTAH	18	18	2	Yes
MAINE	18	18	3	No	VERMONT	18	18	3	No
MARYLAND	18	18	2	No	VIRGINIA	18	18	2	Yes
MASSACHUSETTS	18	18	3*	No	WASHINGTON	18	18	2	No
MICHIGAN	18	18	2	No	WEST VIRGINIA	18	18	2	Yes
MINNESOTA	18	18	2	No	WISCONSIN	18	18	2	No
MISSISSIPPI	18	18	2	Yes	WYOMING	21	21	2	Yes

* After January 1, 1978, only 2 witnesses required.

532. Making Sure Your Will Really Says What You Mean It To ·
When you discusss your will with a lawyer, be certain that he understands
just what you want it to say. When he has drawn your will, go over it
carefully with him to be sure you understand the meaning of the legal
language. If you don't, have him explain it to you. There should be no
chance for error, because if the phrases used in your will do not precisely
express your intentions, the law may require courts and executors or
administrators to distribute your property in a manner you never intended.

A man who was a millionaire when he made his will left $100,000 to
a university and the "residue of the estate" to his children. Unintentionally he cut them off with nothing when it was discovered after his death
that the value of his assets had fallen below $100,000. Another man left
a yearly income to his married niece "as long as she is above ground."
When she died her husband installed her in a mausoleum above ground
and collected the money for the rest of his life.

Leaving out details can lead to other pitfalls. You give most of your
property to your only son while you are alive and therefore provide in
your will that the rest of your assets go to others, without mentioning
your son or stating the reasons for leaving him out. Depending on the
law of the state in which the will is probated, he may be able to collect
all or part of the remaining estate on the ground that you had forgotten
about him. In preparing a will it is vital that you spell out your desires
specifically and unmistakably, leaving nothing to chance.

533. Disinheriting Members of Your Family · Up to a point you can
disinherit members of your family. You may be able to disinherit your
children and other relatives, but not, in most states, your wife or husband.
As a rule your widow is entitled to one third or more of your estate, and
if you leave her less than that in your will, the court may grant it to her
anyway—and possibly more.

In some states, however, you may satisfy the law by leaving your
widow one third of your estate in trust. She enjoys the income from the
trust during her lifetime, but when she dies the principal passes to someone else you have named in your will—perhaps a son, daughter or
grandchild, perhaps an institution that you would like to help. (For more
detail see section 545.)

Widowers have much the same rights, but most states do not treat them
quite as generously as they do widows. If you disinherit any of your children, it is wise to refer to them by name in your will and to give your

reasons for cutting them off (see section 543). The laws vary from state to state, however. Your lawyer will know the inheritance provisions, and the many exceptions to them, in your own state.

534. Property You Cannot Dispose of in Your Will • You cannot dispose of life insurance benefits, pensions or U.S. government savings bonds in your will, since you have already designated beneficiaries for them. An exception to the rule governing the proceeds of a life insurance policy occurs when you name your estate as the beneficiary, in which case the proceeds would be distributed under the terms of your will. You can of course change the beneficiaries at any time before your death by making proper arrangements with the organizations that issue the policies, pensions or bonds.

Other assets that you cannot dispose of by will include: (a) jointly owned property with the right of survivorship, which automatically goes to the surviving owners upon your death (see section 306); (b) exempt property, which must by law go to your widow and surviving children; and (c) property that you expect to inherit but have not actually received before your death. Nor can you bequeath any assets over which you have no control after your death, like the income from a trust that you receive only during your lifetime or a house in which you have a "life tenancy" (see section 306). If you try to bequeath any of these assets in your will, the court will simply ignore your wishes.

535. The Importance of Consulting a Lawyer When You Make a Will • Writing a will is a tricky business, fraught with pitfalls for the unwary and the untrained. To be certain that your will stands up legally and that your property is disposed of in accordance with your wishes, it is essential to have an attorney prepare the document.

A good lawyer will do far more than simply write out the will, as if taking dictation with embellishments. He will help you prepare an itemized list of your real and personal property and other assets, so that you know just what your estate amounts to. He will advise you about legal requirements of which you are probably unaware. He will explain the dangers of certain provisions you may want to include. He will help you plan your estate for the greatest benefit to your family. He will help shape the will in a manner that takes advantage of the current estate-tax provisions, so that your estate will not find that because of oversights it has to pay more than the minimum amount of taxes required by law (see sections 571–583).

645

The lawyer's fee for this service is usually modest, particularly when you consider the importance of having a clear and valid will.

536. Information Your Lawyer Needs in Drawing Up Your Will · When you visit a lawyer to discuss your will, you should have with you the following information and documents:

a. A complete list of all your assets, including bank accounts, stocks, bonds, business ownership and money owed to you, as well as your more valuable personal effects, such as jewelry, furs, art objects and the like.

b. An itemization of all of your real estate, together with its value and location, including property you own jointly with your wife or others.

c. A list of your obligations, including mortgages on your house or business, leases and debts.

d. Any inheritances you expect to receive before your death (your lawyer will want to take these into account in planning your estate).

e. A statement of any instruments, such as trusts or wills of others, under which you are given a *power to appoint*—that is, the power to designate to whom certain assets will go upon your death.

f. A statement of your approximate income and general standard of living for the past several years.

g. Records on insurance of all kinds, including numbers and face amounts of the policies, their premiums and any outstanding loans that have been made against them.

h. Family information, such as the ages and the state of health of its members, adopted children, marital problems, family feuds and black sheep, if any.

537. Format and Contents of Your Will · Your will may contain all the following clauses. As you can see, some of them are absolutely necessary, while the inclusion of others is dictated by your circumstances.

a. The first sentence or opening statement identifies you by name, gives your residence and states that you are knowingly making your will.

b. Make it clear that you are revoking any previous wills or codicils you may have made (see section 551).

c. Direct the prompt payment of your burial expenses, debts and taxes (see section 546).

d. Next, provide for the distribution of your estate (see sections 538–545).

e. If you are leaving any of your estate in trust, specify the trustees (see section 548).

f. If you have minor children, specify who, if your spouse is not living at your death, is to be the guardian of their persons until they reach their majority and who is to be the guardian of their property (see section 549).

g. It is most important that you designate an executor: he has the job of carrying out your wishes (see section 547).

h. Finally comes your closing statement, which contains your signature; the date of your signature; and then the signatures and addresses of your witnesses, including a statement by them that they saw you sign the document you acknowledge as your will and that they have signed as witnesses, at your request, in your presence and in the presence of each other (see section 531).

You may be reasonably sure that such a document thus signed will be upheld by almost any probate court in the United States—unless doubts can be cast upon it on the ground that you lacked mental competence or were subject to undue influence when you signed. And to attack a properly drawn will on these grounds is extremely difficult because the court will require affirmative proof of your alleged incompetence from some source beyond the document itself.

The statutory requirements for a valid will in your state are summarized in chart 37, page 643.

538. Disposing of Your Property in Your Will · Generally speaking, you may leave your property to anyone you please. (The disposition of property you own jointly with someone else, however, is seldom governed by your will; your interest automatically passes to the surviving owner upon your death; see also sections 159 and 306.) You may direct that your entire estate go to one person (most commonly, your wife, if she survives you) or that it be divided among several persons. A common division is one half to your wife and one half to your children.

You may want to follow the example of most testators, which is to make several specific bequests of parts of your estate; that is, to stipulate that certain specific assets in your estate are to be distributed to specific legatees or individuals named by you: your house to your wife, your automobile to your eldest daughter, your stamp collection to your younger son and $5,000 each to your older son and to your godson. Then you would customarily go on to direct the distribution of your assets remaining after these specific bequests, or legacies.

Such assets are called your *residuary estate*—the residue, or remainder —and are generally directed to be distributed among all your survivors, some of whom may have received specific bequests but many of whom may not. You should inquire of your lawyer how long the laws of your state may permit you to delay such distribution, especially among your younger children or grandchildren. Substantial tax savings may result from putting off final distribution as long as possible.

539. Disposing of Real Estate in Your Will • With the exceptions noted in section 534, buildings and land may be given to anyone you please.

You may, if you wish, give your wife (or someone else) "beneficial use" of your home or other real property or the income from it either for her life or for a period of years, specifying that when such use has ended the property will go to your son or some other person or will become part of your residuary estate. *Beneficial use* means that the person you name may live on the property or receive a benefit from it.

But it is your will that determines what will happen to the property after that person dies or ceases to use it. Such a direction for the use and ultimate disposal of real estate is similar in principle to putting personal property, like securities, in trust. The person who receives the income from the entrusted property is called the beneficiary of the trust estate: he or she is enjoying the beneficial use of the trust property. If you make no provision for your real property, it too becomes part of your residuary estate and may have to be sold to assure the proper division of your assets among the legatees you have designated in your will.

540. Bequeathing Legacies in Your Will • If you leave a relative or friend some of your personal property, like one of your paintings, an article of furniture or 100 shares of the stock of XYZ Company, you have made a *specific legacy*. But if you leave him $1,000 with no indication where that amount is to come from, it is a *general legacy*. If your relative or friend predeceases you, the legacy is said to *lapse;* he of course receives nothing and the legacy falls into your residuary estate. If the specific item you bequeath has been sold, lost or destroyed by the time of your death, the person to whom you left the specific legacy has no claim against the estate. Most legacies have priority over other bequests. They are paid before the rest (or *residue*) of your estate is distributed. You must take care, therefore, that legacies to others are not so large in proportion to the value of your estate as to deprive your family and other beneficiaries of what you want them to have. The safest way to avoid this danger is to describe your general legacies as percentages of the value of your total estate. As in all such complicated matters involving your will, you should discuss this question at length and frankly with your lawyer.

541. Making Charitable and Educational Bequests • The whole field of so-called eleemosynary, or charitable, bequests is so controlled by state and federal laws that you must consult a lawyer before deciding whether to make such bequests and how to make them. Although you may not disinherit your family entirely (see section 533), you are legally free to leave substantial amounts of your estate to a church, charity or college—but both federal and state estate tax laws are placing increasingly severe limits on how much you may thus leave free of estate or inheritance tax. Moreover, the purpose for which you direct your money to be used must be reasonable. A bequest to the Society for the Propagation of Two-Headed Calves is not likely to stand up against attack by one of your aggrieved relatives whom you cut off without a penny. But some odd bequests have been sustained, such as a fund for maintaining the grave of the testatrix's departed cat.

542. Providing for Your Wife or Husband in Your Will • The right of your surviving wife or husband to share in your estate is outlined in section 533. Many states still recognize the old common law right of *dower*, which entitles a widow to an interest in one third of her husband's real property. Fewer states still accord widowers a similar right of *curtesy*. Increasingly, states have recognized, instead of the rights of dower and curtesy, the right of widow and widower to "elect to take against the will" the amount that they would have been entitled to receive had the deceased spouse died intestate. The principle in such cases is that a man who has taken on the responsibility of marriage should not be allowed to leave his wife to be supported by the state. For example, if a man's estate amounted to $120,000 at his death, and he left his wife only $25,000 in his will, she could, under the laws of many states, choose to reject the $25,000 and elect her one third intestate share, or $40,000. In some states, however, her husband might be able to satisfy the statute by leaving her the minimum share of $40,000 in trust, in which case she would enjoy only the income on that amount, with the principal, at her death, going to any other persons he chose to name in his will, whether they were relatives or not.

For more details on dower and curtesy rights see section 306 and chart 20, page 353. For state laws governing the right of election see chart 38, page 650.

649

LAWS GOVERNING YOUR RIGHT OF ELECTION
IF YOU DON'T LIKE YOUR SPOUSE'S WILL

CHART 38	Does Husband Have Right of Election?	Does Wife Have Right of Election?	If So, What Share of the Estate Is He (She) Entitled To?	Where Is Election Filed?	What Is the Time Limit for Filing?
ALABAMA	No	Yes	Dower plus intestate share of personal property[1]	Probate office	Within 6 months of admission of will to probate
ALASKA	Yes	Yes	⅓ of net estate	Superior court	Within 6 months of admission of will to probate
ARIZONA	No	No	Spouse cannot choose between the terms of the will and the share allowed him under state intestacy laws, but the will does not affect his right to community property.		
ARKANSAS	Yes (if will executed prior to marriage)	Yes	Intestate share	Probate clerk	Within 1 month of expiration of time for filing claims
CALIFORNIA	No	No	Spouse may not will away more than ½ of community property. Unless the terms of the will show contrary intent, the surviving spouse may take his share of community property as well as property under the will.		
COLORADO	Yes	Yes	½ of net estate	District court; in Denver, probate court	Within 6 months of notice to creditors or 1 year after death, whichever expires first
CONNECTICUT	Yes	Yes	Life estate in ⅓ of entire estate	Probate court	Within 2 months of expiration of time for filing claims
DELAWARE	Yes	Yes	$20,000 or ⅓ of elective estate, whichever is less	Court of Chancery	Within 6 months of issuance of letters testamentary
DISTRICT OF COLUMBIA	Yes	Yes	Dower plus ½ of net personal estate or intestate share of net personal estate	Probate court	Within 6 months of admission of will to probate
FLORIDA	Yes	Yes	30% of net estate	Court where estate is administered	Within 5 months of first notice to creditors
GEORGIA	No	No[2]			

(1) Where there are no children or issue and personal estate exceeds $50,000, widow may elect to receive $50,000 and balance will be distributed according to will.

(2) Widows may seek 1 year's support from husband's estate unless will negates it.

(3) If deceased had children by earlier marriage and none by this, spouse may elect to receive ⅓ personal estate and life estate in ⅓ real estate.

650

In many states, rather than to accept the terms of your spouse's will, you may choose, or "elect," to follow the state laws that normally come into play if your husband or wife has died without a will (see chart 42, page 696). This statutory privilege is called your right of election. It applies in the various states as shown in this chart. The dower and curtesy laws of your state are explained in chart 20, page 353.

	Does Husband Have Right of Election?	Does Wife Have Right of Election?	If So, What Share of the Estate Is He (She) Entitled To?	Where Is Election Filed?	What Is the Time Limit for Filing?
HAWAII	Yes	Yes	⅓ of augmented estate	Probate court	Within 6 months of notice to creditors of deceased
IDAHO	Yes	Yes	⅓ of augmented estate	District court	Within 6 months of notice to creditors of deceased
ILLINOIS	No	No			
INDIANA	Yes	Yes	⅓ of entire estate[3]	Office of clerk of court where will is probated	Within 10 days of expiration of time for filing claims or within 30 days of pending litigation
IOWA	Yes	Yes	Intestate share	District court	Within 6 months of second publication of notice of admission of will to probate
KANSAS	Yes	Yes	Intestate share	District court	Within 6 months of admission of will to probate
KENTUCKY	Yes	Yes	Dower plus intestate share of personal property	Office of clerk of court where will is probated	Within 6 months of admission of will to probate
LOUISIANA	No	No	Spouse may not will away more than ½ of community property.		
MAINE	Yes	Yes	Intestate share limited to ½ of entire estate	Probate court	Within 6 months of admission of will to probate
MARYLAND	Yes	Yes	Statutory share	Orphans' court	Within 30 days of expiration of time for filing claims, unless extended by court order
MASSACHUSETTS	Yes[4]	Yes[4]	Intestate share, limited to $25,000 plus income of balance for life[5]	Registry of probate court	Within 6 months of admission of will to probate
MICHIGAN	No	Yes	Personal property: up to $5,000 plus ½ of intestate share; real property: intestate share or dower & homestead[6]	Probate court	60 days from entry of order closing estate to claims

(4) Spouse may choose between dower/curtesy and intestate share; or between testamentary share and statutory share; or between testamentary share and dower/curtesy.

(5) There are 3 possible statutory shares depending on whether decedent leaves kindred or issue.

(6) But if election gives widow all the real

CHART 38 (cont.)	Does Husband Have Right of Election?	Does Wife Have Right of Election?	If So, What Share of the Estate Is He (She) Entitled To?	Where Is Election Filed?	What Is the Time Limit for Filing?
MINNESOTA	Yes	Yes	Intestate share, limited to ½ of entire estate if decedent left no issue	Probate court	Within 9 months of death or within 6 months of admission of will to probate
MISSISSIPPI	Yes	Yes	Intestate share, limited to ½ of entire estate[7]	Chancery court	Within 3 months of admission of will to probate
MISSOURI	Yes	Yes	If issue survive, ⅓ of estate; otherwise, ½	Probate court	Within 10 days of expiration of time for contesting will or 90 days after final determination of litigation
MONTANA	Yes	Yes	Dower plus intestate share of personal estate (not to exceed ⅔ of net estate after payment of debts)	District court	Within 6 months of admission of will to probate
NEBRASKA	Yes	Yes	⅓ of augmented estate	County court	Within 1 year of issuance of letters testamentary
NEVADA	No	No	But spouse may not will away more than ½ of community property.		
NEW HAMPSHIRE	Yes	Yes	Distributive share of estate	Probate office	Within 6 months after appointment of executor or administrator
NEW JERSEY	Yes	Yes	Dower or curtesy	Surrogate court	Within 6 months of admission of will to probate
NEW MEXICO	No	No			
NEW YORK	Yes	Yes	If issue survive, ⅓ of net estate; otherwise, ½[8]	Surrogate court	Within 6 months of issuance of letters testamentary
NORTH CAROLINA	Yes	Yes	Intestate share, limited to ½ of estate	Superior court	Within 6 months of issuance of letters testamentary
NORTH DAKOTA	Yes	Yes	⅓ of augmented estate	Office of clerk of superior court	Within 6 months of notice to creditors of deceased
OHIO	Yes	Yes	Intestate share, limited to ½ of estate	Probate court	Within 1 month of date of notice to elect or 7 months of appointment of executor
OKLAHOMA	Yes	Yes	Intestate share	District court	Before final settlement of estate

estate, she may take only ½ absolutely and other ½ subject to devises and legacies.

(7) No right of election if surviving spouse has separate property equal in value to his intestate share. If he has separate property worth less than his intestate share, he may elect to make up the difference. If his separate property equals ⅛ or less of intestate share,

652

	Does Husband Have Right of Election?	Does Wife Have Right of Election?	If So, What Share of the Estate Is He (She) Entitled To?	Where Is Election Filed?	What Is the Time Limit for Filing?
OREGON	Yes	Yes	¼ of net estate[9]	Probate court	Whichever is later: 90 days after will is admitted to probate or 30 days after filing of inventory
PENNSYLVANIA	Yes	Yes	If issue survive, ⅓ of estate; otherwise, ½	Register of wills	Within 1 year of issuance of letters testamentary
RHODE ISLAND	Yes	Yes	Dower or curtesy[10]	Probate court	Within 6 months of admission of will to probate
SOUTH CAROLINA	No	Yes	Dower	Probate court	At the time of or before distribution of estate
SOUTH DAKOTA	No	No			
TENNESSEE	Yes	Yes	Dower or curtesy plus: ⅓ of personal estate if 2 or less children survive; a child's share of personal estate if more	Probate court or county court	Within 6 months of admission of will to probate
TEXAS	No	No			
UTAH	No	Yes	Dower	District court	Within 4 months of admission of will to probate
VERMONT	Yes	Yes	Dower or curtesy	Probate court	Within 8 months of admission of will to probate or issuance of letters testamentary
VIRGINIA	Yes	Yes	Dower or curtesy plus either: ⅓ of personal property if issue survive; if not, ½ of personal property	Court with probate jurisdiction	1 year from admission of will to probate or 1½ years if provision of will is doubtful
WASHINGTON	No	No			
WEST VIRGINIA	Yes	Yes	Dower or curtesy plus up to ⅓ of personal property	Office of clerk of county court	Within 8 months of admission of will to probate
WISCONSIN	Yes	Yes	⅓ of net estate	County court	Within 6 months of decedent's death, unless extended by court order
WYOMING	Yes	Yes	Intestate share of estate, limited to ¼ of estate if issue survive & ½ if not	Probate court	Within 3 months of admission of will to probate

he may take entire intestate share.

(8) Certain provisions in will defeat right of election.

(9) But share of the estate may be reduced in the event of certain transactions.

(10) Unless will specifically forbids it, surviving spouse may elect to take dower or curtesy in addition to testamentary share.

543. Providing for Your Children, Grandchildren and Other Relatives in Your Will • Only in Louisiana are you required to provide in your will for your offspring. But note two things. First, courts assume parents intend to care for their young children. If in your will you provide for your wife and for only three of your four children, and the fourth has been a close member of the family and a faithful son, he may be able to persuade the court that your omission was an oversight. In this case the court might both sustain the will and direct the executor to set aside part of your estate for your apparently overlooked child. You may effectively disinherit a child, if you wish, by stating that you are intentionally making no provision for him. Second, be sure you understand the difference between your broad rights to dispose of your property *by will* (including the right to disinherit) and the formal pattern of inheritance contained in the *intestacy statutes* of all states. These statutes stipulate who among your survivors gets what part of your property if you die without a will. Your children come high on the list. In other words, if you are determined to disinherit your children, you must make a will.

Assuming you want to follow the more normal pattern of dividing your estate among all your descendants, there are two methods to consider: *per stirpes* and *per capita distribution*. Under per stirpes distribution, if your children die before you, their shares of your estate are divided equally among their surviving children (your grandchildren)—a child's only child will receive his parent's full share; each of a child's three children will receive one third of his parent's share. Per capita distribution means that, if your children die before you, your estate will be distributed equally among your surviving grandchildren. Under either arrangement, a child or grandchild born after you drew your will, but before your death, would receive the same share as the others, even though not specifically mentioned in the will.

Intestate distribution laws direct that if you die without a will your parents and even your *collaterals* (brothers and sisters) may share in your estate if you leave neither a wife nor children. But you have no obligation to provide for parents or collaterals in your will, and a valid will that makes no provision for them cannot be effectively attacked.

544. What Happens to Your Estate If You and Your Wife Die Simultaneously • Modern high-speed transportation has increased the chances of a tragedy that until recent years was rare: your and your wife's simultaneous death, as in an automobile accident or a plane crash. Such accidents may produce inequities in distributing your estate.

If you and she die childless and neither of you leaves a will the laws of intestacy may force a sharing of your estate between her children by an earlier marriage and your surviving parents. That could be unfair. If your parents are getting along adequately on retirement pay and social security, while the children are young or struggling to get started in life, you might want those children to receive all your property.

If only the husband has a will, in which he leaves his estate to his wife, the estates of both will be distributed according to the state intestacy laws if it can be proved that he died first. This, too, may result in a sharing of the estate that is contary to the couple's wishes. The same thing would be true if only the wife had a will, in which she left everything to her husband.

Even if both you and your wife have wills, however, the matter of survivorship may become crucial. This is especially true if one of you has substantially more assets than the other, but the respective relatives for whom you wish to provide are very different. Suppose you have $1 million in stocks, and your wife owns a summer cottage worth $25,000. You have a few close relatives, but she has children by a prior marriage, and both her parents are alive and prosperous. Presumably your will leaves everything to her, and it is her will that directs the distribution, among her children only, of the million she receives from you, after taxes. Your simultaneous death with her creates the same kind of complications. How can it be established that she survived you—even for a matter of minutes—so that your million will flow into her estate and be distributed according to her will?

To meet these and other similar situations, lawyers have increasingly inserted in wills clauses providing for a *presumption of survivorship*. Such a clause enables the probate court, in the situation described above, to carry out your and your wife's clear intentions by indulging in the presumption, should you and your wife die as a result of a fatal accident and it is difficult or impossible to determine which of you died first, that she in fact survived you. Thereby, her will would control, and the intestacy statutes would not come into play.

545. The Advantages of Leaving Your Estate in Trust • As often happens, when you draw your will you may become hesitant about giving the full control of part or all of your estate to your wife, child or other relatives to whom you are making a bequest. You may then want to put the property *in trust*; that is, direct your executor to turn over the property to a *trustee*, to invest and manage it for the benefit of your wife or

655

child or invalid parent (the beneficiary), paying the beneficiary the income and perhaps part of the principal as you direct in your will.

The trustee can be an individual or a bank with powers to act as trustee. You may want to name both a person in whom you have confidence and who knows your family and a bank or trust company. Your trustee (or trustees) has legal title to the property in the trust, must manage it as a prudent man would manage it if it were his own and must ultimately distribute the property as directed by you on the death of the beneficiary or at the time specified is your will. A trust for the benefit of a minor child, for example, might terminate on his twenty-first birthday. (All states limit the time that property may be tied up in trust, and this area of the law is full of schemes by ingenious testators carefully designed to extend these limitations as long as possible.) Trustees are entitled to remuneration for all their expenses as trustees and to fees (commissions) for their services as set forth in state statutes.

If a trustee violates his obligations by failing to act prudently, the beneficiary may go to court to seek restitution and to *surcharge* the trustee for the loss he caused the trust property, that is, force him to pay the amount of the loss to the trust. If the trustee converts the trust funds for his own use he may be prosecuted by the local district or state attorney's office for the crime of theft or sued by the beneficiaries for the civil wrong of conversion (see also section 47) or both.

The trusts you set up in your will are called *testamentary trusts* and, of course, come into being only after your death. But you may, for a variety of reasons, want to put part or all of your property in trust while you are still alive. A *living trust, or inter vivos trust,* is just such a device. If you believe that your present property is substantially what you will have at the time of your death and are willing to have it managed by trustees for the benefit of yourself, your wife, your children or your parents, you simply execute a trust agreement. Such a trust may be either *revocable,* one that you 'may amend or revoke at any time, or *irrevocable,* one that you cannot legally amend or revoke except with the consent of all the people mentioned in the original trust instrument.

If the terms of the trust agreement cover almost all your property, by signing it you put into effect the distribution of your assets and provide for the enjoyment of your property by others now instead of after your death. Or you could name yourself as life beneficiary of the trust. Because the time and expense involved in probating a will and settling an estate can be reduced through the use of the inter vivos trust, it has become increasingly popular. You can, of course, provide in the trust agreement that all or part of the income from the principal of the trust be paid to you during your lifetime, and afterward to other beneficiaries named in the agreement, in the amounts you designate.

You will occasionally see references to other kinds of trust agreements that testators insert in their wills from time to time. In a *life insurance trust* agreement you direct that your trustee distribute the proceeds of the policy or policies as you provide in the trust agreement. (Similar trusts are often set up as living trusts.) *Accumulation trusts* are ones in which you seek to increase the amount of the trust property by instructing the trustee to add the yearly income to the principal for a designated period of time, usually the minority of a child beneficiary. A *spendthrift trust* agreement is one in which you authorize payment to the beneficiary of the income only, but stipulate that the principal is under no circumstances to be touched, no matter how great the need of the beneficiary. If you want a large part of your estate to be used for charitable or other purposes, you may do so by preparing a *charitable trust*.

Except for charitable trusts, which may be of indefinite duration, all trusts have termination dates, which may range from the death of the beneficiary, in the case of marital trusts, to the time a child reaches the age of twenty-one or any other specific age (depending on the law of your state) in the case of accumulation trusts and life insurance trusts. The laws of the states differ widely in this respect. When the trust terminates all funds are disposed of in accordance with the instructions made in the trust provisions of your will or in the separate trust instrument.

Setting up a trust of any kind is a highly complicated matter and should never be undertaken without the aid of a lawyer, who can advise you as to the many laws concerning the organization, purposes, administration, duration and eventual disposition of the principal of the trust.

546. Providing for Payment of Burial Expenses, Taxes and Debts · Burial expenses, taxes and debts are a first charge against your estate. They must be paid before your beneficiaries get anything. You and your lawyer should estimate the amount of these first charges and make sure the money is at hand to pay them. Unless you provide otherwise, all the assets in your estate are regarded as one pool of money from which these expenses are to be paid, and your executor must charge each beneficiary with a proportionate share of them. Suppose, for example, that you underestimate the estate tax on your estate or overestimate the amount of your assets at the time of your death. Conceivably the bequest of your automobile to your favorite niece couldn't be carried out: your executor might have to sell the car to raise the money to pay the proportionate share of your estate tax applicable to that bequest, unless your niece herself paid that part of the tax.

You can avoid this situation by directing that your estate tax, debts and expenses of administration be paid from a specific fund you set aside for these expenses. You can't beat the tax collectors. One way or another, from one fund or another, the taxes must be paid first. Your executor can exercise the discretion or instructions you give him only if there are enough liquid assets at the time of your death both to meet these prior demands and to carry out your wishes.

547. Appointing Executors of Your Will · Unless your estate is valued at less than $500, you will need at least one executor to carry out the terms of your will and to manage your property until all its provisions have been carried out. If you don't name an executor in your will, the court must appoint one, called an administrator, to handle the job. (The duties and rights of executors are described in sections 587–592.) Generally, your executor can be any U.S. citizen over the age of twenty-one who is mentally competent and has never been convicted of a felony. Your executor should be someone whose judgment and integrity you trust, who knows your affairs and has the interests of your family at heart and who lives near you, so that he will not be required to travel long distances to make court appearances, consult with lawyers and sign papers. The most common practice is to appoint your wife, husband or a close relative or friend as your executor. You should designate someone else to act as a substitute executor, in case the person you have named dies or becomes incapacitated. You may also want to name a co-executor to assist the executor in the performance of his duties, particularly if your estate includes a going business. In choosing a co-executor you may want to consider a partner or close business associate, your accountant or your lawyer. In some instances it may be desirable to name your bank or trust company as co-executor. Many banks have a separate department set up to perform such services. Banks have the advantages that they are impartial, stay in one place, are sure to outlive you, can carry on any business and fully understand the tax requirements.

Most states insist that your executor post a bond in order to assure faithful performance of his duties unless your will includes a specific provision exempting him from the requirement. The executor has whatever authority you give him, plus those powers granted him by state statute even though you may not have mentioned them in your will. The laws of the several states are so different, however, that only an attorney can analyze and explain them, especially if the circumstances in your particular case are unusual.

The fees and commissions paid to executors are set by state statute and are usually based on the value of the estate. Some states also allow executors additional compensation for unusual extra time, work or responsibility required to administer the estate (see chart 44, page 706).

548. Appointing Trustees in Your Will • The requirements and laws governing the conduct of the trustee, who administers the trust property turned over to him by the executor, are similar to those that apply to executors, who administer and settle the entire estate. You may name the same person as both executor and trustee, but this is not always advisable. The executor's job is over when the provisions of the will have been faithfully carried out, but a trustee must continue to function as long as the part of your estate for which he serves as trustee remains in trust (see sections 545 and 594). In the case of a trust set up for a minor, for example, an older person—quite able to fulfill the role of executor— might not live or remain able to carry out his duties until the child reaches his majority.

549. Appointing Guardians in Your Will • One of the most important reasons for having a will is to name guardians for your children. If you die leaving children below the age of eighteen (twenty-one in some states), guardians must be appointed to take care of them and their property. If you have not named a guardian in your will, the responsibility for choosing one falls on the courts, which will almost always recognize the right of the remaining natural parent to continue as guardian of the children even if the two of you are no longer married at the time of your death. Although you may have specifically stated otherwise in your will, the courts are likely to honor the natural parent's right to act as guardian unless he or she is mentally incompetent or otherwise unfit or ineligible to serve or has deserted you and the children. But if both parents are dead, the guardianship must of course go to another person. Therefore, you should be sure to designate someone for this role —usually a close relative—when you draw your will. The guardians you name are not required to serve, if they do not choose to, so it is wise to be sure before you make your will that they are willing to undertake the responsibility and to provide for alternative guardians in case they change their minds or die before you do.

There are two types of guardianship: *guardians of the person*, who physically take the place of the dead parent or parents, raising and caring for the children in their own homes; and *guardians of the property*, who manage the property left to the children until they are old enough to manage it themselves. If you want the same person to act in both capacities, you should say so in your will. However, if you do not trust the ability of your wife (or any other person you choose) to manage the property, you may designate her guardian of the person only, naming another person or a bank to act as guardian of the property. Neither of these types of guardians should be confused with the *guardian ad litem*, appointed to represent an underage child who is involved or has an interest in a lawsuit (see section 336). The expenses of raising the children, as well as a reasonable fee for the guardian's services, may be drawn from the estate according to the terms of the will. If the will makes no provision for these expenses, the amount allowed will be determined according to the laws of the state.

550. Disposition of Your Life Insurance Proceeds • For a great many people life insurance makes up all or most of their estate. For such a person, therefore, the terms of his life insurance policy in effect constitute his will, directing the insurance company to distribute the proceeds of the policy, just as his will directs his executor to distribute other assets such as his cash and the contents of his house. If you do not own a home and have few assets, the proceeds of your life insurance might well be the major part of your estate.

You should read most carefully those clauses in your policy covering the disposition of the proceeds on your death (the "beneficiary" clauses). Be sure that they do not conflict with the terms of your will. (You may of course make your policy payable to your estate, but this will increase the size of the estate and the legal fees and commissions to be paid when your assets are distributed.) You may want to leave the proceeds with the company, directing it to pay only the income to your wife and children; this, in effect, makes the insurer your trustee. Or you may authorize the company to make your wife a specific number of *payments certain;* that is, you direct the company to pay her both the income and part of the principal for a specified period of time. Bear in mind that if you direct your insurer to pay part or all the proceeds of your insurance to your children, and you should die while they are minors, a guardian may have to be appointed by a probate court to receive these proceeds on their behalf and to manage them for their benefit. You can avoid this by including in your will a *power in trust* provision, authorizing an executor or trustee you name to receive the proceeds and handle them on behalf of the children. For more details see section 506.

Discuss any proposed large life insurance policy with your lawyer. Like a will, an insurance policy is a testamentary document, and you owe it to your family to make sure that the disposition of the proceeds of your life insurance is arranged to their advantage.

551. How to Change or Revoke Your Will • Your will is automatically revoked if you destroy it or make a new will which specifically states that you are revoking the old one (see section 537). You may change your will at any time by writing a new one or by adding a *codicil*— a separate document that changes certain provisions of the existing will or adds new provisions to it. You can add any number of codicils. But you cannot change a written will orally or by simply scratching out and rewriting on the original document. Codicils must be executed with the same legal formalities required in making the original will. The tests of validity are the same as for the will (see section 585 and chart 37, page 643).

552. If All or Part of Your Will Is Held Invalid • Under some circumstances your entire will may be declared invalid. If it is not signed or witnessed or if it can be established that you were not of sound mind or were under physical compulsion or under the influence of a designing charlatan when you signed it, the probate court may set it aside entirely. In this event one of two things happens: A prior will properly executed by you that contains the provisions for your family that you might reasonably be expected to have made, might be accepted for probate. But if the prior will is not accepted, the court will declare that you died intestate, just as if you had never made a will at all (see section 555). Your assets will be distributed according to the intestacy laws of your state, by a court-appointed administrator instead of by the executor you named.

If your will is admitted to probate, but one of your provisions fails to conform to state law—if, for example, you leave your wife less than state law allows her—that provision may be set aside. The court will direct your executor to follow state law in carrying out that clause and to follow your will in other respects.

553. Safeguarding Your Will and Other Important Papers • Be sure to inform your lawyer, executor or one of your family—and preferably all three—where your will is kept. If it cannot be found the court must con-

661

clude that you died without a will, even if it is positively known that you made one. Only the original document—no copies—should be *executed,* that is, signed and witnessed. If you later execute another, different will it may be difficult to establish, should an extra, signed copy of the old will be found, which document is actually your "last will and testament." But there is no harm in having other unsigned copies available for you or your wife to refer to or for the information of your executor. The best way to safeguard the executed document and still keep it readily accessible is to give it to your lawyer for his safekeeping. Do not put the original in your safe-deposit box, because many states require your executor or your family to obtain a court order to have the box opened after your death, with a representatives of the state tax commission standing by to make sure nothing is removed but the will.

In addition to the will, there are other documents and records your family, lawyer and executor will need when you die. Somewhere, in a safe, but accessible, place known to them, keep a notebook or sheet of paper containing the information in the following checklist:

Name and address of:	*Location of:*
Your lawyer	Your will
Accountant	Recent income tax returns
Employer	Social security card and pension and group insurance policies
Insurance companies and agents	Insurance policies (list their face values and loans against them)
Stockbrokers	Stocks, bonds and other securities
Banks	Accounts and passbooks
	Safe-deposit vault (give branch, box number and location of key)
	Military service discharge certificate
Real estate	Deeds, surveys, title reports and tax receipts
Mortgagee	Mortgage documents and amounts of loan outstanding
Businesses owned, in whole or in part	Partnership agreements, contracts and similar documents
Debtors	Notes payable to you
Creditors	Copies of notes you signed
Burial society	Membership certificates or policy, cemetery plot certificates or contracts

662

In addition, give the description, purchase price, date of purchase and location of any valuables, or other personal property you own, such as cars, boats, jewelry and valuable art objects or antiques, with a description of the insurance policies covering them and their locations. Without such a record money, property or benefits may be lost if your family is unaware of their existence. Moreover, under the tax law amendment effective January 1, 1977, the capital-gains tax basis for some inherited assets is no longer computed from the assets' value on the decedent's date of death. The executor needs these records in order to tell the heirs the tax basis of what they have inherited (see section 590).

554. Keeping Your Will Up to Date • This matter is important enough to stress again. Ask yourself the following questions, which you may use as a checklist:

Has the value of your estate gone up or down sufficiently to make the provisions of your present will either impractical or inappropriate?

Has there been a change in the tax laws sufficient to affect the security of your family and dependents?

Has your marital status altered because of marriage, separation, divorce, remarriage or death?

Has the status of your children and grandchildren changed as the result of new births, adoptions, illness, deaths, growing up, their marriages or their acquisition of income and property?

Has the status of your other dependents, including parents, brothers, sisters, other relatives and friends, been altered by illness, death or financial reverses or gains?

Has there been a change in your love and affection for members of your family, dependents or friends, for any reason?

Have you acquired any new philanthropic interests or abandoned old ones?

Have the executors, trustees or guardians named in your will died, moved away or otherwise become unable to serve?

Have witnesses to your will died or become inaccessible? If so it will be difficult or impossible to locate them to appear for probate.

Should the terms of the trusts established by your will be altered to meet any of the above situations?

If your answer to any of these questions is yes, then you will needs changing. In any event, you should review it periodically with your lawyer because laws affecting the terms or wording of wills change from time to time.

555. The Meaning and Dangers of Intestacy · If you die without leaving a will you are said to have died *intestate*. You may also be declared intestate if your will cannot be found after a certain period of time or if your will is declared invalid for any of the reasons cited in section 585. Intestacy may cause your family many injustices and hardships. It can result in a distribution of your assets different from what you would want (see section 558). If you do not leave a will the court can exercise little discretion in disposing of your property, but must operate under the limits set by law, which are fixed and do not allow for unusual situations. The court cannot give a larger share of your estate to the physically handicapped son or to the widowed daughter whom you had been supporting, for example, than to any of your other children. Nor can it appoint a trustee for your twenty-two-year-old child who is too flighty and inexperienced to manage the money. Intestacy may also increase the administrative costs of the estate (see section 595). It also heightens the likelihood of litigation, which can eat up the assets at an alarming rate and may deprive your family and dependents of needed income for months or years while the legal wrangling goes on.

556. Court Appointment of an Administrator · If you die intestate, the court of the state in which you legally reside will take over your entire estate and appoint an *administrator* to gather all the assets you have left; pay all debts, taxes and expenses; and then distribute the residue according to state law. While the administrator fulfills the same role as the executor (see sections 587–592), he does not have the wide, flexible powers you may grant your executor. He must operate as the law dictates. He may have to sell the business or heirloom you expected your son to inherit, in order to make a proper distribution to the other heirs. If it becomes necessary to dispose of property to pay off debts or taxes, or to do anything else that is not strictly within his legal powers, the administrator must go to court to obtain permission. Each court appearance may add to the administrative cost and cut down the amount that will eventually go to your family.

In selecting an administrator, the court will usually choose a member of the family in this order: husband or wife, children, grandchildren, father or mother, brother or sister, the nearest next to kin. Whether the administrator is a relative or a stranger, he must be bonded. The administrator is entitled to compensation based on the value of the property placed in his hands, plus—in some states—extra compensation for any unusual amount of additional work or time required to administer the estate (see chart 44, page 706). The administrator is subject to the same penalties that apply to an executor for failure to manage the estate prudently and honestly (see section 588).

557. Court Appointment of Guardians · If you die intestate, leaving minor children, the court must appoint a guardian or guardians to raise them and to manage any property distributed to them by the laws of intestacy. The court will usually appoint as guardian of the child's person the surviving spouse if he or she is the child's natural parent. The court may also appoint a guardian of the child's property. Court-appointed guardians have the same rights, duties and functions as guardians appointed by your will (see section 549)—except that they have much less discretion in making investments.

558. The Laws of Intestate Distribution · Who inherits your property if you die without leaving a will? The answer is to be found in your state's laws of succession, often referred to as the *laws of intestate distribution*. These laws, all of which are carefully written statutes with histories going back hundreds of years, are based on the assumption that most persons intend their property to pass on to members of their immediate family: wife or husband, children, parents and collaterals (brothers and sisters). Within this general framework, the intestacy laws of the states vary widely. For exact information regarding the laws in your state, you should consult a lawyer. Remember that if you want any of your property to go to anyone outside your immediate family, or to those within it but in shares different from those the intestacy laws provide, you must say so in a will.

What happens in the differing intestate situations is controlled by statutes in the fifty states and the District of Columbia. These are summarized for you in chart 42, page 696. In reviewing these tables to answer any specific question that interests you, keep a few fundamental considerations in mind.

The state's primary concern is the protection of the financial needs of your immediate family. If you fail to express your wishes in a will, the state steps in and establishes a *testamentary pattern*. It requires the probate court to appoint an administrator whose responsibility it is to

665

distribute your property following the principles of the state's laws of inheritance. Your wife or husband is always given the use of a share of your estate (in some states the share is given outright), whether your estate consists of real or personal property or both. The size of the share, usually one third to one half, varies from state to state and depends on whether you are also survived by children and by parents.

If you have children and parents, but no spouse, your children inherit to the exclusion of your parents. If you leave neither a spouse nor children, chances are your estate will be distributed among your parents and your brothers and sisters.

559. When Husband and Wife Are Separated or Divorced · If you and your wife have separated, both of you have the same rights of intestate inheritance as though you had not separated—unless you have entered into a separation agreement specifically relinquishing your mutual rights of inheritance (see section 361). But if you have been divorced, by a court decree that is final and valid, you have no rights to each other's estate. However, if the divorce decree is *interlocutory,* meaning that some time must elapse before it becomes final, your inheritance rights are not terminated until such time has in fact elapsed (see chart 26, page 415). Of course you may leave property to your divorced spouse if you want to but you must make a will to that effect. If your marriage has been annulled all mutual inheritance rights ceased the date the decree was issued. The laws with respect to the effect of abandonment or desertion on the spouse's inheritance rights vary widely from state to state. In some the deserting spouse may still inherit, in others he may not.

560. Inheritance Rights of Legitimate Children · Children born in wedlock who are the offspring of both parents are entitled to all of the property if both parents die intestate. If one parent is still alive, the children may receive one half, one third or none of the property of the dead parent, depending on state law (see chart 42, page 696). In all cases the property that descends to the children must be divided equally among them; and if one child dies before his parent or parents, his share is apportioned equally among his own surviving children, if he has any. Posthumous children, born after the death of the father, are entitled to the same share as those children born before his death.

561. Inheritance Rights of Stepchildren · Those children related by blood to only one of the parents who raised them (for example, your

666

wife's children by a former marriage) are treated differently by different states. In some states they receive the same share as the children born to the marriage, other states give them half shares and two states exclude them from any right to inherit.

562. Inheritance Rights of Adopted Children • Adopted children (see section 346 and chart 24, page 394) are entitled to the same share of their foster parents' property as are the natural offspring, although some states make exception. But only a few states give adopted children the right to inherit the property of their foster parents' relatives if any of them should die without a will. Adopted children sometimes have the right to inherit the property of their real, or natural, parents as well as that of their foster parents.

563. Inheritance Rights of Illegitimate Children • The right of children born out of wedlock to inherit the property of the mother if she dies without a will varies widely from state to state. Some states give them the same shares as the mother's legitimate children; others grant them lesser shares; still others allow them to inherit only if the mother has no legitimate children. But illegitimate children almost never have any right to the property of the mother's relatives who may have died intestate As to property of the father, an illegitimate child has the right to inherit only if the father has acknowledged the child to be his own. Some states require only that the acknowledgment be in writing, while others insist that the parents be married after the child has been born as well. Once legally acknowledged, however, the illegitimate child has the same inheritance rights as the father's legitimate children.

564. Inheritance Rights of Grandchildren • Grandchildren do not necessarily receive equal shares of their grandparents' property in case of intestacy, since the inheritance descends to them through their parents, as explained in section 560. If you have two children, John and Mary, and no other claimants, each is entitled to 50 percent of your estate. If they die before you do, their shares are divided equally, or *per stirpes,* among their children. Thus, your two grandchildren by John will each receive 25 percent of your estate, while the five grandchildren by Mary will end up with only 10 percent apiece.

565. Inheritance Rights of Parents, Brothers and Sisters • If the intestate deceased leaves children or grandchildren, no other relative except

667

his surviving spouse may share in the estate. If the deceased leaves a spouse, but no children, his parents, brothers and sisters may or may not share his property with his spouse, depending on the state law. In some states surviving parents, and sometimes brothers and sisters as well, may receive up to half of the property, to be shared among them in the proportions specified by state law. If the deceased leaves neither spouse nor children, all of the property goes to his surviving parents; or to his brothers and sisters if no parent survives; or may be shared among the surviving parent, brothers and sisters, in the proportions fixed by state law. If both the parents and the brothers and sisters of the deceased are dead, his nieces and nephews may inherit.

566. Inheritance Rights of Other Relatives · Relatives by marriage, including daughters-in-law and sons-in-law, are excluded from any right to inheritance. Uncles, aunts and cousins of the deceased share in the estate only if there are no closer surviving kinsmen. More distant relatives come into the picture only if there are no surviving uncles, aunts or cousins either. Their right to inherit, and the shares of the estate they receive, are governed largely by their degree of blood relationship to the deceased and by the law of the applicable state.

567. Inheritance of Intestate's Share of Joint Property and Community Property · The laws differ depending on the state and the type of property involved. In most states if a person dies intestate his share of real estate owned jointly with his wife (or husband) automatically goes to her at the time of his death. His share of real estate jointly owned with others may or may not go to them when he dies, depending on the wording in the deed. His jointly owned personal property and household effects do not automatically go to his wife. His children or other heirs may be entitled to a share of these belongings or their value. In most states the intestate's share of jointly held bank accounts goes to the surviving owner in the case of savings accounts, but not always in the case of checking or commercial accounts. Joint ownership of a safe-deposit box does not necessarily create joint ownership of its contents.

In a few states, known as community property states, the laws dictate that at least half of all property owned by either husband or wife automatically goes to the surviving spouse, whether there is a will or not. The only assets not considered community property in these states are property the husband or wife already owned before marriage or inherited after marriage.

568. Inheritance in the Case of Simultaneous Death • If a childless couple dies in a single accident or disaster, neither partner leaving a will, the laws of inheritance decree that the entire estate passes to the heirs of the one that outlived the other, even if only for seconds (see section 544). The heirs of the other spouse receive nothing. If it is impossible to tell which of the two persons died first, the estate of the husband goes to his heirs, and the wife's estate to hers. The same rule applies to the simultaneous death of other members of the family, but the intricacies of inheritance in such cases can be so complicated that only a lawyer can untangle them.

569. Inheritance in Case of Murder or Manslaughter • A murderer may not inherit from his victim, will or no will. But the mere accusation of murder or verdict of a coroner's jury (see section 121) is not sufficient to disinherit him; he must have been convicted of the crime. In some states the perpetrator of manslaughter (see section 122) may inherit from his victim. Accidental death, if not adjudged manslaughter, does not affect the right to inherit of the person who caused it.

570. When the State May Inherit Property • If no will is left, and no legal heirs can be found, the estate is said to *escheat* to, that is, become the property of, the state. The time allowed to search for heirs or to make claims against the estate varies from three to seven years, depending on the applicable state laws.

Taxes on Your Estate

In 1976 Congress passed the Tax Reform Act (TRA), which differs drastically from the previous tax law in several areas. In this chapter we are concerned with (1) estate and gift taxes and (2) capital-gains taxes paid when legatees sell inherited assets. For estate-tax purposes, TRA, which went into effect on January 1, 1977, combines the former exemption on certain lifetime gifts made by the decedent and the personal exemption subtracted before his taxable estate was computed (see section 574). For computing capital gains when selling inherited assets, TRA provides a new formula, designed to collect certain capital-gains taxes previously inapplicable when the decedent did not sell assets during his

669

lifetime. Although a discussion of income taxes is beyond the scope of this book, the new capital-gains basis is noted because of new duties it imposes on executors (see section 590).

571. The Tax Bite on Estates • All estates are subject to both federal and state taxes. State "death taxes" (levied everywhere except in Nevada) vary widely. The tax rate depends on various facts, such as the size of the estate or inheritance, the type of property involved and sometimes the closeness of the heir's blood relationship to the person who has died. In one state, for example, inheritance tax rates start at 2 percent of the value of money or property left to a spouse or minor child, 6 percent for brothers and sisters and 10 percent for nonrelatives. The federal estate tax is a graduated assessment based on the size of the estate after deductions (see section 576), without regard to the blood relationship of beneficiaries. It ranges from a minimum of 18 percent for the smallest taxable estates to 70 percent of anything over $5 million.

Some states have both an estate tax and an inheritance tax. The *estate tax* is directed at the taxable assets of the estate only and is levied on the gross estate (see section 573). The *inheritance tax* is levied on the person who is inheriting the property, and depends on the person's relationship to the deceased and the amount and kind of his inheritance.

Besides these taxes, federal and state income taxes must be paid on the salary or other income earned or received by the deceased during the portion of his taxable year prior to his death.

572. Death Tax Rate and Regulation Changes • Not all of the information in this chapter may be accurate at the time your estate is administered, since both federal and state tax rates and regulations are subject to frequent change. For the most up-to-date information, consult your lawyer or accountant, the U.S. Internal Revenue Service in Washington, D.C., or the appropriate tax authority in your state capital.

573. Computing Your Gross Estate • Your *gross estate* is made up of all the assets and property you own at the time of your death, less your debts and other obligations. It includes cash on hand in banks (including, more often than not, the entire amount of joint accounts); personal effects (such as automobiles, jewelry, art objects and the like); the face value of life insurance policies you own, less outstanding loans against them; real estate; securities of all kinds; business interests (including partnership interests, stock in closed corporations, contracts, franchises and so on); miscellaneous assets (such as money owed to you, commissions and salary due, pension fund payments); and jointly owned property (except for the amount paid in by the other owners). However, for some property jointly owned by a husband and wife, if the joint tenancy was created after December 31, 1976, TRA says that only one half of the value will be included in the gross estate of the first spouse to die, no matter how much of the consideration he or she provided therefor.

In addition, for tax purposes your executor must report as part of your gross estate the following gifts you made while still alive: outright gifts made after January 1, 1977; gifts over which you have retained or controlled the income for life, or as to which you reserved the right to designate the ultimate donee; and gifts that you retained the power to amend or revoke during your lifetime. All such gifts (except those referred to in the next sentence of this paragraph) must be included in your gross estate because under TRA gifts made after December 31, 1976, are taxed at the same rate as estates (see section 574). Not usually included in your taxable estate, however, are the tax-free gifts of up to $3,000 per year ($6,000 if given jointly by husband and wife) that you made to various individuals.

574. The Unified Tax Credit • Under the pre-1976 federal tax law amendment, lifetime gifts were taxed at a lower rate than estates. TRA taxes them equally. In addition, before January 1, 1977, each person was allowed to make tax-free gifts (over and above the annual $3,000 exclusions referred to above) totaling $30,000 before death, and he was given a personal estate exemption of $60,000. An adjusted gross estate of less than $60,000 was not taxed. Now that gift taxes and estate taxes are combined, the federal government allows what it calls a unified tax credit. This takes the place of the old specific exemption for lifetime gifts and the old personal exemption. This tax credit is being phased in gradually between 1977 and 1981 as follows:

Year	Credit	Equivalent exemption
1977	$30,000	$120,667
1978	34,000	134,000
1979	38,000	147,333
1980	42,500	161,563
1981	47,000	175,625

575. Federal and State Estate Tax Returns • If the value of your gross estate (see section 573) qualifies it for a federal tax (see section 574), a

671

federal estate tax return must be filed with the U.S. Internal Revenue Service. The return (Form 706) is due nine months after the date of death. It is a complicated document that sets forth in complete detail all required information about your real estate, stocks and securities, mortgages, notes, contracts, cash and insurance; your business interests; jointly owned and miscellaneous property; gifts you made both before and after you made your will, whether to individuals or to a charity, church or other public institution; funeral and administration expenses; debts and claims against the estate; and the proposed distribution of property to beneficiaries.

State inheritance tax returns usually require the same information and procedures as the federal, although the time intervals allowed for filing may be different. All estate and inheritance taxes are payable when the final returns are filed. The preparation of these returns may be difficult unless the executor obtains the assistance of a lawyer.

576. Exemptions and Deductions from Federal Estate Taxes • You can determine your personal estate exemption by consulting the table in section 574. If your gross estate is worth less than the equivalent exemption indicated there, no estate taxes are payable and no return need be filed. (For nonresident aliens the exemption is only $60,000.) There is also a military exemption applicable to members of the U.S. armed forces who are killed or die of wounds or disease while on active service.

Deductions that may be allowed from the gross estate include: burial expenses; expenses of administering the estate, including commissions (see section 595); claims against the estate, including any debts you owe; unpaid mortgages on your property; losses due to casualty or theft that have not previously been compensated; and charitable bequests up to a certain limit (see section 541).

Most important of all is the *marital deduction.* You may leave tax free to your wife (or husband) up to 50 percent of your adjusted gross estate (the gross estate minus the deductions described above) or $250,000, whichever is greater, provided that she survives you and that by the terms of your will she either takes the property outright or is given unlimited authority, in a trust for her benefit, to dispose of it upon her death. This means that if you die in 1981 with an adjusted gross estate worth $425,000, leaving $250,000 to your wife, no federal estate taxes need be paid on your estate (assuming you made no taxable gifts during your lifetime), since your personal exemption, via the credit, is $175,000 (see section 574) and the rest is covered by the marital deduction. If you fail to make a will and your estate passes under the laws of intestacy, however, your wife will not get the full $250,000, and she may even get less than $212,500 (50 percent of your estate in the example above), which means that your estate will lose the full advantage of the marital deduction. Assuring the benefit of the full marital deduction can be an important reason for making a will.

577. Credits Allowed Against Federal Estate Taxes • The estate tax is assessed against the *net estate,* or the part that remains after subtracting the marital and other deductions and the exemption equivalent to your unified tax credit (see section 574). Once the tax has been computed, credit is allowed for a portion of the following taxes: "death" (estate and inheritance) taxes payable to state governments, death taxes paid to foreign governments; taxes paid by the deceased on gifts made before December 31, 1976, that are counted as part of his gross estate (see section 573); and taxes paid on legacies and gifts the deceased received within ten years of his death. The percentage of credit allowed for each payment can be learned from the Internal Revenue Service.

578. State Taxes on Estates • Death levies imposed by the states are called by different names inheritance tax, transfer tax, estate tax, gift tax or legacy tax. As a general rule, states allow about the same kinds of exemptions and deductions as the federal government, but not necessarily in the same amounts. Thus, since the state exemption may be lower, you may have to pay state taxes even though you are not required to pay a federal tax. In addition, some states impose different tax rates for various types of property and classes of heirs.

If an estate tax is paid, a large amount of your state tax may be deductible from your federal tax, if any (see section 576). State tax laws are many, varied and complicated. You should discuss your state's laws with your lawyer or accountant.

579. Which State Collects the Tax • If you live in more than one place, which state collects the estate tax? Inheritance taxes and state estate taxes are payable to the state in which you legally reside—meaning where you own property and pay taxes; where you vote, send your children to school and take part in community activities. But if you have a second house in another state—a farm, perhaps, or a summer cottage or retirement home in which you spend a large part of your time—that state may also claim inheritance taxes that can add greatly to the tax

673

burden. To avoid double death taxes you should make clear now, by word and deed, which is the "home" in which you legally reside and which the temporary residence that you merely visit. If you are contemplating a move, upon retirement or otherwise, be sure to consider its effects on the tax aspects of your estate plan. Discuss all these matters with your lawyer when you make your will, and regularly thereafter, because estate taxes are not only certain but certain to change, and your will should take advantage of these changes.

580. The Importance of Estate Planning • The cost of dying is high. Taxes can eat up the accumulation of a lifetime. If you die without a will or without having made proper arrangements beforehand, you run the risk that your property will be taxed far more than is necessary or that it will be taxed several times as it passes successively to your wife, then from her to your child and finally to your grandchild. To minimize this danger you should organize your financial and property matters now. You should consult a lawyer, insurance man, accountant or financial counselor, and sometimes all four. A good estate plan—a better name might be family plan—will not only safeguard the security of your family after you are gone, but should provide for your own security today and in your retirement years.

581. The Right to Minimize Estate Taxes • In a famous decision Judge Learned Hand once stated: "Anyone may so arrange his affairs that taxes shall be as low as possible; he is not bound to choose that pattern which will best pay the treasury; it is not even a patriotic duty to increase one's taxes." The United States Supreme Court agrees that "the legal right of a taxpayer to decrease the amount of what otherwise would be his taxes, or to altogether avoid them by means which the law permits, cannot be doubted."

This is not to suggest that you should ever falsify or hold back any information on any tax return. Tell all. You may win or lose your point with the tax authorities, but be honest about it.

582. Ways to Protect Your Estate from Death Taxes and Other Expenses • Here are some tax-saving and expense-saving devices:

a. *The marital deduction.* The *marital deduction* allows you to leave to your spouse, outright or in trust with unlimited power of disposition, but tax free in either case, one half of your adjusted gross estate or $250,000, whichever is greater (see section 576).

674

b. *Trusts.* Your use of one or another type of trust, either testamentary or inter vivos (see section 545), enables you to postpone final distribution by as much as an entire generation, thus in effect often skipping a second estate tax bite on the property you leave at your death.

c. *Life insurance.* To keep life insurance from becoming part of your estate, during your lifetime you can transfer ownership of the policy to another (either the named beneficiary or another person). Having done this, you will avoid having the policy proceeds taxable in your estate, upon your death, as long as you are careful *not* to designate your estate or your executors as beneficiary under the policy.

d. *Joint ownership of property.* Jointly held property between husband and wife or parent and child may also materially reduce the administration costs of the estate (see section 538).

583. Money for Taxes and Immediate Expenses After Death • You should leave enough cash or other liquid assets on hand to pay taxes, debts, burial costs and the living expenses of your family until the estate is settled. Otherwise the executor or administrator may be forced to sell your business, real estate or personal property in order to get the funds. Perhaps the best way of meeting the problem is to take out a life insurance policy large enough to meet the anticipated taxes and expenses. Since proceeds of the policy are paid directly to the designated beneficiary, life insurance provides immediate cash for these emergency needs. You should be wary of any possibility that the claim to the proceeds of your life insurance policy might be contested by the company, though, because this could delay payment or stop it completely (see section 514). Your widow will usually be able to draw on the funds in a joint account, or part of them. But since these funds are probably includable in your taxable estate, they may be blocked, at least temporarily; separate accounts are safer.

THE DISPOSITION OF YOUR ESTATE

584. "Proving" Your Death • Distribution of your estate must be made after your death, either as you have directed in your will or as the laws of inheritance direct if you leave no will. The first step to be taken in either case is establishing the fact of your death with the appropriate court in your state. The name of this court varies from state to state (see chart 43, page 704). As common a name as any is the probate court.

In the typical situation, all that is needed to establish the fact of your death is the filing of a copy of your death certificate with the clerk of the probate court. The certificate itself is issued by a public department; it should be checked for accuracy as to time, place and cause.

In these turbulent times, however, situations that are far from typical often occur. "Proof of death" sufficient to bring probate machinery into operation varies. If you are killed serving in the armed forces, their official notification is all that is necessary. If you are the victim of a catastrophe under such circumstances that your body is not recovered—an earthquake, a ship that goes down at sea with no apparent survivors or an airplane crash in which no bodies can be identified, the probate court may take judicial notice of the disaster and issue a declaration of death. But if you simply disappear and all efforts to find you fail, you may be declared legally dead at the expiration of a considerable time—usually seven years. These provisions are known as Enoch Arden laws, after Tennyson's poem about a sailor who returns home after a seven years' absence to find his "widow" happily remarried.

For details of the laws that govern the presumption of death in your state, see chart 39, page 677.

585. Proving Your Will • Once your executor has obtained proof of your death he must present your will to the probate court to be *probated*, or proved as your last will and testament. He signs a petition for probate; that is, he presents the document purporting to be your will and requests a date for a hearing to establish its validity. When this petition has been filed the court will issue a notice to all the parties interested in the estate (their names are usually taken from a list drawn up by the executor), setting a date for the probate hearing. The date is usually set far enough ahead so that interested parties can request a copy of the will to study, decide whether they want to contest any of its provisions and make preparations for their opposition. Minor children must in many states be represented by a guardian to ensure that their interests are protected at the hearing. Your executor or his attorney will then arrange to have the witnesses to your will appear before the probate court or its clerk and affirm that they witnessed your signature to your will and one another's signatures as witnesses.

The probate hearing is the first chance anyone who thinks the will invalid has to contest its validity. The only grounds for contesting it are statutory—for example, that you did not sign it, that the witnesses did not actually watch you sign it, that the signaure is not yours but some-

WHEN YOUR HUSBAND OR WIFE MAY LEGALLY BE PRESUMED DEAD

The laws of the various states provide that a person missing for the number of years shown here may legally be presumed dead and that his or her estate may be distributed according to a will or the state laws of descent and distribution (see chart 42, page 696).

CHART 39

State	5 Years	6 Years	7 Years	30 Years
ALABAMA			■	
ALASKA	■			
ARIZONA	■			
ARKANSAS	■			
CALIFORNIA			■	
COLORADO			■ [1]	
CONNECTICUT			■ [2]	
DELAWARE			■	
D.C.			■	
FLORIDA	■			
GEORGIA			■ [1]	
HAWAII	No statutory presumption			
IDAHO	■ [1]			
ILLINOIS			■	
INDIANA			■	
IOWA	■ [1]			
KANSAS			■ [1]	
KENTUCKY			■	
LOUISIANA				■
MAINE			■	
MARYLAND			■ [3]	
MASSACHUSETTS			■	
MICHIGAN			■	
MINNESOTA			■	
MISSISSIPPI			■	
MISSOURI			■	
MONTANA			■	
NEBRASKA			■	
NEVADA			■	
NEW HAMPSHIRE		■ [4]		
NEW JERSEY			■ [1]	
NEW MEXICO	■			
NEW YORK		■ [1]		
NORTH CAROLINA			■	
NORTH DAKOTA			■	
OHIO	■			
OKLAHOMA			■	
OREGON			■	
PENNSYLVANIA			■ [1]	
RHODE ISLAND			■	
SOUTH CAROLINA			■	
SOUTH DAKOTA			■	
TENNESSEE			■ [3]	
TEXAS			■	
UTAH	No statutory presumption			
VERMONT	■ [5]			
VIRGINIA			■	
WASHINGTON			■	
WEST VIRGINIA			■	
WISCONSIN			■ [3]	
WYOMING			■	

(1) The presumption of death arises only after a diligent search for the missing person.

(2) 7 years if bond posted; otherwise 12 years.

(3) The presumption is not mandatory, but court may decide if such presumption is justified.

(4) Court may appoint administrator of missing person's estate after 1 year of absence, but estate may not be distributed until 5 years after appointment of administrator.

(5) Court will permit administration after 5 years but will only distribute estate 5 years from date of administration, provided bond is posted. If no bond posted, distribution 7 years after administration.

677

one else's or that you didn't know what you were doing when you signed it, either because of illness or duress. If, as frequently happens, one or both of the witnesses to your will is dead or cannot be located, the court may still admit the document to probate in the absence of strong evidence casting doubt on the technical validity of the will. But it is still wise to choose witnesses who are likely to be available when needed.

Do not confuse these fairly routine hearings admitting your will to probate with attacks on the validity of the document as a whole or on one of its key provisions. If your wife feels aggrieved that what you have left her is less than her intestate share of your estate, she may choose to *elect against your will*—to have the court ignore your bequest to her and order your executor to turn over to her what would have been her share had you died without a will (see section 542 and chart 38, page 650). Or one of your legatees may have died before your death; that legacy lapses and must be distributed to others. Such attacks are not necessarily part of the probate proceedings; they are not challenges to the will itself and will not delay the probate of the will.

Similarly, suppose that the person you named as executor of your will is dead or too ill to serve and that you named no one to serve in his place. Although this matter would doubtless come up at the probate hearing—because the provisions of your will cannot be carried out without an executor—it would not affect probate as such. Your will is valid, even though your named executor is dead or absent. Under such conditions the court accepts your will for probate and after consulting with your heirs appoints an *administrator with the will annexed*. This administrator, unlike the court-appointed administrator of your estate if you die intestate (see section 586), follows the provisions of your will rather than the inheritance laws in distributing your estate, but he is a person named by the court rather than by the testator.

586. What Happens to Your Estate If You Die Intestate • If you leave no will, if your will cannot be located or if for any one of a variety of reasons it is declared invalid, you are declared to have died intestate. Upon receiving proof of your death the probate court, usually on petition of your wife or one of your heirs, designates an *administrator without a will*. He must strictly follow the inheritance statutes and conduct all his operations under close court supervision.

587. What Is Required of Executors and Administrators • Your will is merely a piece of paper telling what you want done with whatever property you possess at the time of your death. Someone is required to execute the purposes of your will if there is one, to administer your estate if there isn't. It is quite possible that during your lifetime you may be asked to serve as the executor or administrator of someone else's estate. Knowledge of what is expected of an executor or administrator should be useful.

588. What the Executor Does • Briefly, the executor or the administrator takes over all your property and assets; he makes a detailed inventory of them and has them appraised; he pays your funeral expenses, settles debts and claims against your estate including any unpaid portion of your current income taxes. (All states limit the period of time during which claims may be made against an estate. For details see chart 40, page 680.) He prepares and submits the federal and state estate tax returns and pays those taxes. Then he pays the specific bequests and legacies to the persons you named; he turns over to trustees you named any property you left in trust; and finally he distributes your residuary estate according to your instructions. Once the executor or administrator has carried out his functions he files with the court an accounting of everything he has done, and is then discharged by it.

Your trustee's responsibility will, of course, carry on into the future as prescribed in your will.

The executor derives his authority from what are called *letters testamentary*, that is, the provisions of the will, and the administrator from *letters of administration* issued by the probate court to someone it selects. Usually the court will give preference to close relatives of the deceased. But unusual circumstances might influence the court's choice: if the estate includes a particular kind of business, for example a motel, the court might choose someone with experience in that business.

As you may imagine, both executors and administrators must be over twenty-one, must be mentally competent and must have no criminal record. They must take an oath promising the faithful performance of their duties, and they can be surcharged (see sections 545, 594) for breach of that oath. Unless relieved of the responsibility by the testator, the executor—and always the administrator—must post a bond, which will be forfeited if the estate suffers from mismanagement or dishonest administration. On the death of either the executor or administrator before his duties are completed and he is formally discharged by the court, a successor is appointed by the court, which of course follows the testator's designation if there is one in the will.

CHART
40

ALABAMA	4 months after first publication of notice to creditors; if no publication, 3 years after decedent's death[1]
ALASKA	4 months after first publication of notice to creditors; if no publication, 3 years after decedent's death[2]
ARIZONA	4 months after first publication of notice to creditors; if no publication, 3 years after decedent's death[1,2,3]
ARKANSAS	6 months after first publication of notice to creditors[1]
CALIFORNIA	4 months after first publication of notice to creditors[1,4]
COLORADO	4 months after first publication of notice to creditors; if no publication, 1 year after decedent's death[1,2,3]
CONNECTICUT	Not less than 6 nor more than 12 months after appointment of executor or administrator[3,5,6]
DELAWARE	6 months after first publication of notice to creditors[1,7]
D.C.	No statutory provision, but distribution begins 13 months after issuance of letters; time limit may be extended 4 months
FLORIDA	3 months after first publication of notice to creditors[1]
GEORGIA	6 months after issuance of letters testamentary or letters of administration, but exceptions may be made
HAWAII	4 months after first publication of notice to creditors[1]
IDAHO	4 months after first publication of notice to creditors; if no publication, 3 years after decedent's death[1,2]
ILLINOIS	6 months after issuance of letters testamentary or letters of administration[1]
INDIANA	5 months after first publication of notice to creditors[1]
IOWA	6 months after first publication of notice to creditors[1]
KANSAS	6 months after first publication of notice to creditors[1]
KENTUCKY	No statutory limit, but notice to creditors must urge creditors to present claims within 3 months
LOUISIANA	No statutory limit
MAINE	6 months after qualification of representative or his appointment[1]
MARYLAND	6 months after appointment of administrator[2]
MASSACHUSETTS	Generally, not less than 3 nor more than 9 months after giving bond, but exceptions may be made[8]
MICHIGAN	18 months after hearing for proving claims (hearing takes place no more than 4 months from first publication of notice to creditors)
MINNESOTA	4 months after clerk's notice to creditors; if no publication, within 3 years of decedent's death[1,2,3]
MISSISSIPPI	3 months after first publication of notice to creditors[1,9]

(1) All claims are barred after date specified.
(2) The time limit does not apply to certain insurance claims or the foreclosure of lien claims.
(3) Claims arising at or after death generally must be presented within 4 months after they arise.
(4) But if the claimant was out of state at time of notice, he may present his claim any time before final distribution of the estate.

(5) Time limit may be extended if merited.
(6) Probate court sets the exact time limit.
(7) Mortgages and judgments that were liens at the time of decedent's death are not subject to the time limit.
(8) After January 1, 1978: claims must be brought within 2 months of notice of impending bar to claims or within 9 months of giving bond. The probate court may extend the time limit.

Creditors' claims against the estate of a deceased person must be filed with the executor or administrator within the time allowed by law, as shown below.

MISSOURI	6 months after first published notice of administration[1]
MONTANA	4 months after first publication of notice to creditors; if no publication, within 3 years of decedent's death[1,2,3]
NEBRASKA	2 months after first publication of notice to creditors[1]
NEVADA	3 months after first publication of notice to creditors[1]
NEW HAMPSHIRE	6 months after issuance of letters testamentary or letters of administration[1]
NEW JERSEY	6 months after court order to publish notice to creditors[10,11]
NEW MEXICO	6 months after first publication of notice to creditors; if no publication, within 3 years of decedent's death[1,2,3]
NEW YORK	Date specified in public notice to creditors, or, if none is published, 7 months after issuance of letters testamentary or letters of administration[10]
NORTH CAROLINA	6 months after first publication of notice to creditors[12,13,14]
NORTH DAKOTA	4 months after first publication of notice to creditors; if no publication, within 3 years of decedent's death[1,2,3]
OHIO	3 months after appointment of executor or administrator[15]
OKLAHOMA	2 months after first publication of notice to creditors[1,4]
OREGON	4 months after first publication of notice to creditors[12,16]
PENNSYLVANIA	No statutory time limit, but all claims must be presented in court at the audit of the executor's or administrator's account[1]
RHODE ISLAND	6 months after first publication of notice to creditors
SOUTH CAROLINA	5 months after first publication of notice to creditors[1,7]
SOUTH DAKOTA	2 months after first publication of notice to creditors[1,4]
TENNESSEE	6 months after first publication of notice to creditors[1]
TEXAS	6 months after issuance of letters testamentary or letters of administration[12]
UTAH	3 months after first publication of notice to creditors[1,4,7]
VERMONT	(For most claims arising before decedent's death) 4 months after publication of notice to creditors; if no publication, within 3 years of decedent's death
VIRGINIA	No statutory limit
WASHINGTON	4 months after first publication of notice to creditors[1,17]
WEST VIRGINIA	Not less than 4 nor more than 6 months after first publication of notice to creditors; time limit specified in notice
WISCONSIN	3 months after application for administration; notice must be given within 15 days after order of court[1,6]
WYOMING	3 months after first publication of notice to creditors[1,4]

(9) If the estate is insolvent, all claims must be filed at the time specified in the notice.

(10) But creditors of a solvent estate may present claims any time before final distribution.

(11) The probate court may order the executor or administrator to publish notice to creditors within 20 days of that court order.

(12) Claims are not necessarily barred after that date, but payment is delayed until claims presented within set time limit are paid.

(13) If creditors are personally served with notice, their claims must be presented within 3 months of the date they received notice.

(14) Claims arising at or after death generally must be presented within 6 months.

(15) Except for contingent claims, a claim not presented within 4 months of appointment of the executor or administrator is barred.

(16) All claims not presented within 12 months of first notice to creditors are barred.

(17) Certain liability or casualty insurance claims are not subject to the time limit.

589. Rights of Executors and Administrators • Executors and administrators are entitled to commissions for managing the estate. The amount of the commissions is set by statute in almost all states. Separate commissions are payable, at different times, on estate principle and estate income during the period between the court's designation of the administrator and his ultimate discharge. The executor may also, with the court's approval, retain legal and other professional assistance and charge the cost against the estate. Individual executors who may not need any fee, or who may also be beneficiaries under the will, may waive their commissions. For the executor's and administrator's fees allowed by the various states, see chart 44, page 706.

590. Duties of Executors and Administrators • The duties are clear: to take title to all the deceased's property, wherever located (except for property that does not pass under the will; see section 534), and to distribute it either as directed in the will or as provided by statute. The executor must submit the will for probate and notify all persons whose interests might be affected by the will. He must see that all assets of the estate are inventoried and appraised; that all funds due the deceased are collected, by legal action if necessary; that any apparently unjustified or unenforceable claim against the estate is rejected and any suit against it defended; that unpaid income taxes of the deceased are paid; that estate tax returns are filed with both federal and state authorities; that heirs of the estate are informed of the tax basis of each asset they receive.

Before the passage of the Tax Reform Act of 1976, the tax basis for all inherited assets was their value on the date of the deceased's death. Now, however, for all assets acquired by the deceased before December 31, 1976, the tax basis for the heirs becomes the assets' value as computed for December 31, 1976. For purposes of computation (except in the case of marketable stocks and bonds, whose value on that date is a matter of record), it is assumed that the rate of appreciation between the date the deceased acquired the asset and the date of his death is constant. The proportion of growth by December 31, therefore, is a fraction of the overall growth. This fraction is: the number of years and days between the purchase and December 31, 1976, divided by the number of years and days between the purchase and deceased's death. This computation itself is subject to further adjustments, defined in the new law, which are too numerous and too complicated to present here.

Here is an example of the computation called for in the preceding paragraph, omitting the extra adjustments.

A man buys an oil painting on December 31, 1966, for $60,000. He dies on December 31, 1986, at which time his painting is worth $100,000. He has owned the painting for ten years up to December 31, 1976, and twenty years overall. The fraction is 10/20 or 1/2. The value of the painting on December 31, 1976, therefore, is calculated at $80,000 (the original purchase price plus one half of the overall appreciation of $40,000). The heir assumes this figure as the basis for computing his capital gain when he sells the painting, and it is one of the duties of the executor to inform him of it.

The executor or administrator will occasionally need court approval of actions he thinks advisable, such as the sale of an unprofitable business venture carried on by the deceased or the settlement of a debt owed to the estate for less than the face amount of the debt. Courts are accustomed to issuing interim rulings under such circumstances, approving or disapproving what the executor wants to do.

When all these duties have been fulfilled, the executor files a motion that he be discharged. He files an accounting of his actions and informs all parties interested in the estate of what he has done. If the court is satisfied, it discharges him. Any objections to his actions filed by any of the beneficiaries, or by guardians representing them, are of course heard and reviewed by the court in this final proceeding.

If the estate is small and no questions have arisen during its administration, or if no minor children are involved, a formal accounting may not be called for. The executor or administrator can simply have the interested parties sign an agreement, often called an informal release and account, that discharges him and waives any claims against him for his conduct during administration.

591. What to Consider in Choosing Your Executor • You will have noted from this discussion of the duties and functions of executors and administrators the importance of naming an executor who is close to the family, familiar with its problems, sensitive to its needs. As you survey the future of your family, with you absent, you will appreciate the desirability of having someone close to all of you as executor in handling your estate. If you don't want to leave this selection up to a court, you yourself must draw a will and name the person and an alternate.

Another essential, if the estate is large, is to get the help of experienced persons in such areas as the sale of your property and the handling of your investments. Most individuals lack the time and the know-how to deal with these business affairs effectively. What testators may do, therefore, is to appoint two executors, one a close relative or a family friend, the other a professional man, a bank or a trust company. The former supplies the human and humane element and the personal interpretation of your wishes. The latter supplies the indispensable facilities for bookkeeping, accounting, clerical work and business advice when needed.

Finally, note that there will be innumerable occasions after your death when a lawyer must be consulted. The need for a lawyer arises the moment your death becomes known. He can be extremely helpful immediately after the death of a loved one in advising the family about burial and funeral arrangements, explaining which expenses should be paid immediately and which deferred, making funds available from joint bank accounts and other estate sources and petitioning the court for a family allowance from the tied-up estate pending its settlement. He must be there to advise your family what should be done with your files. He must be on hand to advise your executor how to proceed to probate your will. He will have to prepare the petition for probate and the *citations,* which tell persons mentioned in your will to appear at the probate hearing. He will have to arrange for the witnesses to your will, if available, to give testimony regarding its execution. His assistance will be needed in prosecuting claims against those who owe the estate money and in defending the estate against lawsuits if they arise.

If anyone challenges the will, or any part of it, your executor must have a lawyer to help him answer the challenge and defend the will. The executor will need a lawyer, and often an accountant, to help him prepare your estate tax returns. No large estate can be effectively administered without a lawyer's constant advice and assistance. In many cases the lawyer your executor retains is the one who prepared your will (and this is true in virtually every case where a bank is the executor), for the obvious reason that he is likely to be the person most familiar with your personal and business affairs. The amount of the lawyer's fees for representing the executor, incidentally, must be approved as a charge against the estate by the probate court.

592. If You Are Named Executor • In the laws governing the management of estates, words such as *honesty, diligence* and *vigilance* are used repeatedly in connection with the functions to be carried out. If you are called upon to serve as executor or administrator of an estate, observe these standards strictly. Handle the estate's property with even greater care and circumspection than you do your own, for the penalties for carelessness or inefficiency are more severe. Here are some guidelines:

a. In inventorying the property of the deceased, examine all of his belongings, not only his account books and the contents of his safe-deposit box, but every scrap of paper in his possession. You may discover assets that he had forgotten about!

b. Unless you are looking for trouble, never deposit estate funds in your own bank account, even if the entire estate has been left to you. In the estate's name, open a bank account in which to deposit the deceased's cash and the proceeds of liquidated assets and from which to pay taxes, debts, claims and family living allowances.

c. Don't be a "good guy" by acceding to the wishes of other relatives and heirs, no matter how legitimate and urgent their needs may seem. Lend them money out of your own pocket, if you like, but never out of estate funds, unless you have obtained a court order to do so.

d. Seek expert professional assistance in areas in which you have little experience, particularly when it comes to disposing of real estate or running, selling or liquidating a business. Ask a lawyer or the court beforehand whether the fees, commissions and expenses of accountants, agents, appraisers or other specialists are payable from estate funds.

e. When necessary, take whatever time the law allows before settling all assets. But if stock and securities are involved, consider the possibility of selling them earlier to obtain a better price. You may also want to consider selling enough stock to meet the cash needs of the estate, thus avoiding the risk of a falling market.

f. Above all, keep an accurate record of receipts and disbursements of estate funds and property so that the accounts you render to the court will reflect all your transactions. Thus, even if the wisdom or prudence of something you have done as executor may be questioned, your accuracy and probity cannot be attacked.

593. When and How the Heirs Get What's Coming to Them · How long the heirs may have to wait before receiving their legacies or property depends to a considerable degree on the nature of the estate.

If the estate is large or complicated, it may be that no estate property except for court-approved family living allowances will be distributed to anyone until authorized expenses, debts and claims have been paid and the federal and state tax authorities have taken their cuts. But if the estate is very simple or unquestionably sound, the executor may make a partial distribution of the assets right after probate, asking each heir to file a bond guaranteeing that he will refund the money if necessary. Factors other than the size or complexity of the estate may also affect timing.

The amount of time allowed for creditors to enter claims against an estate is shown in chart 40, page 680.

Although in some states estate property may be distributed within six or seven months of the appointment of the executor or administrator, this is unlikely to happen unless the estate is not subject to federal taxes. One reason the executor may want to delay distribution is to take advantage of the law allowing *alternate valuation* of the assets of the estate if it contains a large proportion of stocks or other securities. This provision allows him to evaluate the assets on the basis of prices either on the date of death or six months from that date, and if the stock market has gone down during this period there may be a substantial tax saving. In any case, it usually takes the Internal Revenue Service a year or more to audit an estate tax return. Add this year to the nine months allowed for preparation and filing, and it is likely to be two years, at least, before the heirs receive all their inheritances.

Provided the estate is not in litigation when expenses, claims and taxes have been paid, the executor or administrator is required to distribute the property within the time period specified by state law. Whether he makes the payments in lump sums or in installments as estate assets are liquidated is usually left to his judgment. However, if an heir feels the executor or administrator is being unnecessarily slow in making the distribution, he can apply to the court for earlier payment.

594. When and How Inheritance Trusts Are Paid • If while he was alive the deceased entered into a trust agreement covering part or all of his assets, the assets that made up the trust fund were turned over to the trustees when it was set up (see section 545). If he established a life insurance trust the proceeds of his policies would be paid directly into the hands of the designated trustee by the insurance company immediately after his death (see section 506). So although the executor lists these trusts in the estate tax return and pays taxes on them as necessary, he does not receive as assets of the estate any of the assets of trusts established while the deceased lived or any of the insurance proceeds, and he has no responsibility for administering them. However, the executor does receive the moneys that make up the principal of any trusts that the testator establishes in his will. After the expenses and taxes are paid and claims against the estate have been settled, he turns these moneys over to the designated trustees at the same time that he distributes all other property to other legatees and heirs.

The person who gets the income from a trust, called the income beneficiary, is entitled to receive from the trustee the periodic payments provided for by the terms of the trust itself. When the trust terminates (see section 545), all moneys remaining in it are disposed of according to the terms of the will or trust instrument. Before the trustee is discharged, however, he is usually required to render an *account of his proceedings* to the probate court, including a record of all receipts, disbursements, expenses incurred and fees or commissions he received or paid. If the court does not approve the accounting, the trustee may be found guilty of malfeasance and *surcharged,* that is, required to pay to the estate the amount of any losses for which he is responsible. If the beneficiary, or the guardian of an underage child, believes the trust has been mismanaged, either while it is still in effect or when it expires, he can go to the court to seek satisfaction, as described in section 545. In some states a formal accounting can be waived by mutual agreement of the interested parties if no minors are involved (see also section 590).

595. What It Costs to Administer the Estate • The commissions of persons serving the estate are fixed by state statute and vary widely. The fees set by law in the various states are shown in chart 44, page 706.

However, there are many additional costs that are chargeable to the estate, including: (a) additional compensation to executors, administrators and trustees, allowed in many states for extra work they may be required to perform; (b) business expenses of administration, such as travel, telephone, stenographic assistance; (c) fees or commissions of lawyers, accountants, brokers, agents, appraisers and other experts whose services may be required; and (d) potentially the most expensive of all, the costs of litigation involved in defending the estate against lawsuits by disgruntled heirs or by others.

If the additional compensation and expenses charged by the executor or administrator and others appear unduly high, the heirs may go to court to have them reduced. The executor also has the right to challenge fees that seem exorbitant.

When Death Occurs

596. Keeping Your Head in Time of Sorrow • A death in the family is a deeply painful experience. The grief and sense of loss you feel may

687

be enormous. Yet it is precisely during the time of suffering that you must enter into complex and frequently expensive business arrangements, calmly and with presence of mind. Unfortunately, mistakes made at this time are likely to be costly and can seldom be corrected. If you are too emotionally upset to exercise good judgment, it would be wise to call on a close relative, a trusted friend or, better still, your family lawyer to do the things that must be done.

597. First Things to Do After a Death—A Checklist

a. Obtain a death certificate from the physician attending at the time of death or from the coroner or other doctor who examines the body.

b. Find out whether the deceased has expressed any specific wishes about the disposal of his body, including the possible donation of organs for medical purposes (see section 601). If you can find no other record of the dead person's wishes, call the lawyer who drew the will to see if it contains any reference to the method of disposal.

c. Engage a mortician to handle the body or notify the burial society if the deceased belonged to one.

d. Notify the insurance company or agent if the deceased had burial insurance. Make a list of the burial allowances that may be available from social security, Veterans Administration, labor union, fraternal bodies and other sources and make applications for them.

e. Obtain a burial plot, unless the deceased already had one.

f. Arrange for the funeral and interment.

g. Inform friends and relatives of the date, time and place of the funeral and interment.

h. Locate the deceased's will and turn it over to the executor to start probate proceedings. Ideally, the will should be in the lawyer's vault and the executor may already have a copy (see section 553).

i. With the executor and his lawyer go over the documents left by the deceased (see section 553 for a checklist), and hand over to them the ones they will need to set in motion the settlement of the estate.

598. Death Certificates • All states require that a physician or coroner examine the dead body, issue a certificate stating the time, place and cause of death and file the document with the county registrar or other designated public official of the place in which the death occurred. The mortician you have engaged will normally supply you with copies of the death certificate. You will need several, since a copy of the certificate is generally required as proof of death in arranging probate of the will and

securing social security benefits, life insurance payments, pensions and the like. You can obtain extra copies at any time by writing the appropriate authorities in your locality.

It is important that you check the certificate for cause of death as soon as you receive it. Insurance recovery may depend on accurate recording of the cause, and you will need to catch errors quickly if, for example, you need to line up witnesses who may later be needed to prove that death was accidental.

599. Filing the Death Certificate • If death was due to natural causes, the certificate must be filed within a few days of death, depending on state laws. If death was due to accident or other unnatural causes (for example, murder or suicide), an official medical examiner or coroner, sometimes with the aid of a coroner's jury, must determine the date and probable cause of death. If the cause of death is doubtful, an autopsy may be performed. The consent of surviving relatives is required for all autopsies, except those performed by the coroner. (Procedures for obtaining a death declaration where the body cannot be found are described in section 584.)

600. Disposal of the Body • A dead body must be buried, or otherwise legally disposed of, within the number of days specified by the law of your state. Any desires a person expresses in his will as to who should prepare his body after death, where it should be buried, or the nature, size and cost of the funeral he prefers are wishes that are not legally binding on his family or executor. However, the law usually does honor his right to donate his body's organs to hospitals, eye banks and the like, for transplantation to living patients (see section 601). If the deceased leaves no instructions in his will his spouse or next of kin has the right to make the decisions, including the right to donate his body's organs to medicine. If a body is unclaimed for a specified period of time after death, the state must bury it or it may donate the body to a medical school. The unclaimed bodies of people who die in common disasters—such as floods, hurricanes, earthquakes and plagues—where the risk of contamination is great, may be cremated or buried by local authorities without delay and without identification or notification of next of kin.

601. Disposal of Organs for Medical Purposes • A new body of law is growing up around the increasingly common practice of leaving all or part of one's body to a medical institution for research or transplantation.

689

Generally speaking, such a donation, properly signed and witnessed, is legally binding on the heirs of the deceased. In practice, however, hospitals, medical schools and research foundations are reluctant to go to court to enforce such a gift if squeamish relatives object—as often happens. Besides, any delay the dispute causes will probably render the organ useless for transplantation. If you want to leave your body for scientific or medical purposes, therefore, it is best to sit down with your family, discuss your wishes with them, seek their agreement and be sure they understand the procedures to be followed after your death.

602. Cemetery Plots • Except when special permission is granted, which is rare, no state permits a human body to be buried anywhere but in an officially designated cemetery or graveyard. All cemeteries are regulated and supervised by government bodies—local, state or federal. They may be operated by public authority, supported by tax funds; or by religious, fraternal and philanthropic organizations, maintained by private funds and endowments; or by private corporations, for profit, which must set aside 10 percent of their revenues to assure perpetual care. (Private family cemeteries may no longer be established in most states, although this does not affect the status of those that already exist.)

If you do not foresee moving from your community to another before your death, you should consider the advisability of buying a burial plot while you are still alive. This will save your bereaved family the pain and inconvenience of choosing a plot quickly after your death.

603. The Laws of Cremation • Once a body has been reduced to ashes, an autopsy is of course impossible, and virtually no evidence remains regarding the cause of death. The regulations governing cremation, therefore, are often more stringent than those that cover burial. Many states and counties require a longer waiting period, and sometimes the permission of an official medical examiner or health authority before the body may be cremated. Although no state law requires that a body to be cremated must be embalmed or burned in a casket, many undertakers and crematory establishments insist on it, which adds to the expense. In many localities cremated remains may not be scattered, but must be placed in a niche in a *columbarium,* an enclosed structure maintained at a cemetery or elsewhere. The laws governing columbaria are similar to those that apply to cemeteries, and the cost of a niche may be as high as that of a burial plot. In many places a box or urn containing the ashes of the deceased may be buried in the family plot.

604. Costs of Private Burial or Cremation • The undertaker is in a more favorable position than any other businessman imaginable. He knows that the bereaved family rarely has the time, inclination or experience to shop around and compare prices, and that he is practically certain to receive his money, since the estate of the deceased must pay burial, funeral and cremation expenses first—even before taxes. The high-pressure tactics of some unscrupulous undertakers have led to national scandal.

Few burial expenses are actually necessary. The law requires that the body be buried in a cemetery in a casket, but the casket need not be of metal or expensive hardwoods; it can be made of pine or even cardboard. Unless burial is delayed and the family wishes the remains to be viewed, there may be no necessity for embalming, or preserving the body. To keep the funeral within reasonable—and tasteful—bounds, the family must steel itself against the blandishments of the mortician who insists that expensive services and trappings are the proper way to "honor the loved one," and that they are "customary" and "expected" of a family in its social and economic position.

There is no "best" way to find an ethical or reasonably priced funeral home, although the advice of your minister, priest or rabbi, or of friends who have been through the experience, can be helpful. You are probably safer with an undertaker who is a member of the National Funeral Directors Association or National Selected Morticians, organizations that police their members to some extent. It is unwise to have anything to do with mortuaries that solicit your business by telephone after reading of the death. The practice is unethical. At your first meeting with the funeral director, inquire frankly about the costs and exact nature of the services to be performed, being careful to find out also what is not included in the "complete services" package he offers. The practice of adding extras is all too common. Do not accept the first package the mortician offers if it is more than you want to spend. He probably has less expensive ones. Above all, insist on a written itemized list of the services and merchandise the undertaker will provide, the exact cost of each, the amount of money that must be paid in advance and the balance to be paid later, including any interest charges.

605. Burial of Veterans and Members of the Armed Forces • The family of a wartime veteran or of a peacetime veteran who has been receiving compensation for a service-connected disability is entitled to a payment of up to $250 for burial expenses.

691

NUNCUPATIVE (ORAL) WILLS

CHART 41

	Is an Oral Will Valid?	If So, Who May Make One?	What Can Be Willed Orally?	Must There Be Witnesses? If So, How Many?	How Soon After Declaration Must Will Be Written Down?	How Soon Must Will Be Admitted to Probate?
ALABAMA	Yes	Anyone during his last illness[1]; soldiers in actual service & mariners at sea	Up to $500 of personal property[2]	Yes[3]	Within 6 days	Within 6 months of declaration
ALASKA	Yes	Soldiers in actual service & mariners at sea	Personal property plus wages	NSP*	Within 30 days	Within 6 months of declaration
ARIZONA	No					
ARKANSAS	No					
CALIFORNIA	Yes	Soldiers in actual service & mariners at sea[4]	Up to $1,000 of personal property	Yes: 2[3]	Within 30 days	Within 6 months of declaration
COLORADO	No					
CONNECTICUT	No					
DELAWARE	No					
DISTRICT OF COLUMBIA	Yes	Soldiers in actual service & mariners at sea, during last illness	Personal property	Yes: 2	Within 10 days	NSP*
FLORIDA	No					
GEORGIA	Yes	Anyone during his last illness	No limitation	Yes: 2	Within 30 days	NSP*
HAWAII	No					

*No statutory provision.

(1) Will is valid only if made at testator's home or where he resided for 10 days, unless he became ill and died away from home.

(2) But a person in active military service or a mariner at sea may dispose of his personal estate as he might have at common law.

(3) It must be proved that testator called upon at least one of the persons present to bear

Probate courts in many states do not accept oral wills under any circumstances. In other states such wills are accepted subject to the restrictions shown on this chart. (See also section 530.)

	Is an Oral Will Valid?	If So, Who May Make One?	What Can Be Willed Orally?	Must There Be Witnesses? If So, How Many?	How Soon After Declaration Must Will Be Written Down?	How Soon Must Will Be Admitted to Probate?
IDAHO	No					
ILLINOIS	No					
INDIANA	Yes	Someone in imminent peril of death who dies from that peril	Up to $1,000 of personal property[5]	Yes: 2	Within 30 days	Within 6 months of death
IOWA	No					
KANSAS	Yes	Anyone during his last illness	Personal property	Yes: 2[3]	Within 30 days	NSP*
KENTUCKY	No					
LOUISIANA	Yes	Anyone, if will is written in presence of testator & signed by him	NSP*	Yes[6]	Immediately	NSP*
MAINE	Yes	Anyone during his last illness[1]; soldiers in actual service & mariners at sea	Personal property: up to $100 without witnesses & any amount if proved by 3 witnesses[2]		Within 6 days[7]	NSP*
MARYLAND	No					
MASSACHUSETTS	Yes	Soldiers in actual service & mariners at sea	Personal property	NSP*	NSP*	NSP*
MICHIGAN	Yes	Anyone; soldiers in actual service & mariners at sea	Up to $300 of personal property[2]	Yes: 2	NSP*	NSP*
MINNESOTA	No					
MISSISSIPPI	Yes	Anyone during his last illness[1]	Personal property: up to $100 without witnesses & any amount if proved by 2 witnesses[3]		Within 6 days[7]	NSP*

witness that such was his will.

(4) And in actual contemplation, fear or peril of death; or in expectation of immediate death from injuries sustained the same day.

(5) But a soldier in active military service in time of war may orally dispose of up to $10,000 of personal property.

(6) The will must be received and written down

CHART 41 (cont.)	Is an Oral Will Valid?	If So, Who May Make One?	What Can Be Willed Orally?	Must There Be Witnesses? If So, How Many?	How Soon After Declaration Must Will Be Written Down?	How Soon Must Will Be Admitted to Probate?
MISSOURI	Yes	Someone in imminent peril of death who dies from that peril	Up to $500 of personal property	Yes: 2	Within 30 days	Within 6 months of death
MONTANA	No					
NEBRASKA	No					
NEVADA	Yes	Anyone during his last illness	Up to $1,000	Yes: 2[3]	Within 30 days	NSP*
NEW HAMPSHIRE	Yes	Anyone during his last illness[1]	Personal property: up to $100 without witnesses & any amount if proved by 3 witnesses[1,3,7]		Within 6 days	Within 6 months of declaration
NEW JERSEY	No					
NEW MEXICO	No					
NEW YORK	Yes	Soldiers during war or other armed conflict & mariners at sea[8]	NSP*	Yes: 2	NSP*	NSP*
NORTH CAROLINA	Yes	Anyone during his last illness	NSP*	Yes: 2[3]	Within 10 days[7]	NSP*
NORTH DAKOTA	No					
OHIO	Yes	Anyone during his last illness	Personal property	Yes: 2[3]	Within 10 days	Within 6 months of death
OKLAHOMA	Yes	Soldiers in actual service & mariners at sea[4]	Up to $1,000	Yes: 2[3]	NSP*	NSP*
OREGON	No					

by a notary public in the presence of 3 witnesses who are residents of place of execution (or 5 nonresidents). If the will is not notarized, there must be 5 resident witnesses (or 7 nonresidents).

(7) A will cannot be admitted to probate more than 6 months after speaking unless it was written down within 6 days of declaration.

694

	Is an Oral Will Valid?	If So, Who May Make One?	What Can Be Willed Orally?	Must There Be Witnesses? If So, How Many?	How Soon After Declaration Must Will Be Written Down?	How Soon Must Will Be Admitted to Probate?
PENNSYLVANIA	No					
RHODE ISLAND	Yes	Soldiers in actual service & mariners at sea	[2]	NSP*	NSP*	NSP*
SOUTH CAROLINA	Yes	Anyone during his last illness[1]	Up to $50 without witnesses & any amount if proved by 3 witnesses[2,3]		Within 6 days[7]	NSP*
SOUTH DAKOTA	Yes	Soldiers in actual service & mariners at sea[4]	Up to $1,000	Yes: 2[3]	Within 30 days	Within 6 months of declaration
TENNESSEE	Yes	Someone in imminent peril of death who dies from that peril	Personal property up to $1,000[5]	Yes: 2	Within 30 days	Within 6 months of death
TEXAS	Yes	Anyone during his last illness[1]; soldiers in actual service & mariners at sea	Up to $30 without witnesses & any amount if proved by 3 witnesses[2,3]		Within 6 days[7]	NSP*
UTAH	Yes	Someone in expectation of death from injury within 24 hours of making will	Up to $1,000	Yes: 2[3]	Within 30 days	Within 6 months of declaration
VERMONT	Yes	NSP* except soldiers in actual service & mariners at sea	Up to $200 personal property[2]	Yes: 1	Within 6 days	Within 6 months of death
VIRGINIA	Yes	Soldiers in actual service & mariners at sea	Personal property	NSP*	NSP*	NSP*
WASHINGTON	Yes	Anyone during his last illness; soldiers in actual service & mariners at sea	Up to $1,000 personal property[9]	Yes: 2[3]	Before admission to probate	NSP*
WEST VIRGINIA	Yes	Soldiers in actual service & mariners at sea	Personal property	NSP*	NSP*	NSP*
WISCONSIN	No					
WYOMING	No					

(8) And persons with such armed forces.
(9) Persons in active military service and mariners at sea may dispose of their wages and personal estate.

695

And Your Closest Surviving Relative Is

CHART 42

	Your Wife or Husband & Children or Their Issue[1]:		Your Wife or Husband (But No Children or Their Issue Survive):	
	What Share of Your Real Property Does Each Receive?	What Share of Your Personal Property Does Each Receive?	Does Your Wife or Husband Take All, Whether or Not Your Parent(s) Still Live?	If Not, Does Your Wife or Husband Share with Your Surviving Parent(s)?
ALABAMA	Spouse, life estate in 1/3; children, remainder	If husband survives, 1/2; children, 1/2. If wife survives with (1) one child: wife, 1/2; child, 1/2 (2) 2-4 children: wife & children share equally per capita (3) more than 4 children: wife, 1/5; children, 4/5	Yes	Not applicable
ALASKA	Spouse, $50,000 plus 1/2 balance; children, residue	Same	No	Yes: spouse takes $50,000 plus 1/2; parents, residue.
ARIZONA	Spouse, all[2]	Same	Yes	Not applicable
ARKANSAS	Spouse, life estate in 1/3; children, remainder	Spouse, 1/3; children, 2/3	Yes: if spouse was married to you at least 3 years (otherwise see next column)	Yes: if married less than 3 years, spouse takes 1/2; parent(s), 1/2.
CALIFORNIA	Separate property: (1) with 1 child: spouse, 1/2; child, 1/2 (2) with more than 1 child: spouse, 1/3; children, 2/3. Community property: all to spouse	Same	Separate property: no. Community property: yes	Yes: spouse takes 1/2 separately owned property; parent(s), 1/2.
COLORADO	Spouse, $25,000 plus 1/2 balance; children, residue[4]	Same	Yes	Not applicable
CONNECTICUT	Spouse, $50,000 plus 1/2 balance; children, residue[4]	Same	No	Yes: spouse takes $5,000 plus 3/4 of residue; parent(s), other 1/4.
DELAWARE	Spouse, life estate; children, remainder	Spouse, $50,000 plus 1/2 balance; children, residue[4]	No	Yes: spouse takes $50,000 plus 1/2 balance personal estate, life estate, real estate; parent(s), residue personal estate, real estate.
DISTRICT OF COLUMBIA	Spouse, life estate in 1/3; children, remainder	Spouse, 1/3; children, 2/3	No	Yes: spouse takes 1/2; parent(s), 1/2.
FLORIDA	Spouse, $20,000 plus 1/2 balance; children, residue[4]	Same	Yes	Not applicable
GEORGIA	Wife, equal shares with children but never less than 1/5; husband, equal shares with children regardless of number	Same	Yes	Not applicable
HAWAII	Spouse, 1/2; children, 1/2	Same	No	Spouse takes 1/2; parent(s), 1/2.
IDAHO	Separate property: spouse, $50,000 plus 1/2 balance; children, residue[4] Community property: all to spouse	Same	Separate property: no. Community property: yes	Yes: spouse takes 1/2 of separate property; parent(s), 1/2.

[1] In every state, if only your children or their issue survive, your estate is divided per capita among your children and per stirpes among the issue of any deceased children.

[2] If 1 or more of the living children are not the issue of the surviving spouse: spouse, 1/2 separate property; children, 1/2 community property of decedent.

If you die without leaving a valid will, your property will be distributed to your heirs according to the laws of the state in which you live, as explained in sections 543, 555-567. This chart outlines the so-called laws of descent and distribution of the various states.

If Your Parents Are Not Alive, Does Your Wife or Husband Share with Your Brothers & Sisters & Their Issue?	Your Parent(s) (i.e. Neither Wife or Husband nor Children nor Their Issue Survive): What Share Does Each Receive?	Your Brothers & Sisters & Their Issue (i.e. Neither Parents nor Wife or Husband nor Children nor Issue Survive): What Share Does Each Receive?
Not applicable	1. If both parents survive, ½ to each 2. If 1 parent, ½ to parent; ½ to brothers & sisters or issue per stirpes 3. If 1 parent & no brothers & sisters or their issue, all to parent	Equal shares to brothers & sisters or their issue per stirpes
No	½ to each parent or all to surviving parent	Equal shares to brothers & sisters or their issue per stirpes
No	½ to each parent or all to surviving parent	Equal shares to brothers & sisters or their issue per stirpes
Yes: if married less than 3 years, spouse takes ½; brothers & sisters or their issue take ½.	½ to each parent or all to surviving parent	None[3]
Yes: spouse takes ½ separately owned property; brothers & sisters or their issue take ½.	½ to each parent or all to surviving parent	Equal shares to brothers & sisters or their issue per stirpes
Not applicable	½ to each parent or all to surviving parent	Equal shares to brothers & sisters or their issue per stirpes
No	½ to each parent or all to surviving parent	1. Equal shares to brothers & sisters or their issue per stirpes 2. Equal shares to half brothers & half sisters or their issue per stirpes
Not applicable	½ to each parent or all to surviving parent	Equal shares to brothers & sisters or their issue per stirpes
Yes: spouse takes ½; brothers & sisters or their issue take ½.	½ to each parent or all to surviving parent	Equal shares to brothers & sisters or their issue per stirpes
Not applicable	½ to each parent or all to surviving parent	Equal shares to brothers & sisters or their issue per stirpes
Not applicable	Equal shares to parents, brothers & sisters (whether whole or half blood) or their issue per stirpes	
Yes: spouse takes ½; brothers & sisters or their issue take ½.	½ to each parent or all to surviving parent	Equal shares to brothers & sisters or their issue per stirpes
No	½ to each parent or all to surviving parent	Equal shares to brothers & sisters or their issue per stirpes

(3) Equal shares go to the heirs (determined at the time of your death) of a deceased spouse who was married to you when he (she) died.

(4) If surviving children of the decedent are not issue of the surviving spouse: spouse, ½ estate; decedent's issue, residue.

CHART 42 (cont.)	Your Wife or Husband & Children or Their Issue[1]:		Your Wife or Husband (But No Children or Their Issue Survive):	
	What Share of Your Real Property Does Each Receive?	What Share of Your Personal Property Does Each Receive?	Does Your Wife or Husband Take All, Whether or Not Your Parent(s) Still Live?	If Not, Does Your Wife or Husband Share with Your Surviving Parent(s)?
ILLINOIS	Spouse, life estate in ⅓; children, remainder	Spouse, ⅓; children, ⅔	Yes	Not applicable
INDIANA	1. With 1 child or issue: spouse, ½; child, ½ 2. With more than 1 child or issue: spouse, ⅓; children, ⅔	Same	No	Yes: spouse takes ¾; parent(s), ¼.
IOWA	Spouse, ⅓; children, ⅔	Same	No	Yes: spouse takes first $15,000 of nonexempt property plus ½ of residue; parents(s), other ½ of residue.
KANSAS	Spouse, ½; children, ½	Same	Yes	Not applicable
KENTUCKY	Spouse, ½; children, ½	Same	Yes	Yes: spouse takes ½; parent(s), ½.
LOUISIANA	Spouse, life estate; children, remainder	Same	No	Yes: spouse takes ½; parent(s), ½.
MAINE	Spouse, ⅓; children, ⅔	Same	No, unless personal property is less than $10,000	Yes: spouse takes $10,000 plus ½ remaining personal property & ⅔ remaining real property; parent(s), residue.
MARYLAND	Spouse, ⅓; children, ⅔	Same	No	Yes: spouse takes ½; parent(s), ½.
MASSACHUSETTS	Through 1977: spouse, ⅓; children, ⅔. After Jan. 1, 1978: spouse, ½; children, ½	Same	No	Yes: spouse takes $50,000 plus ½ of residue; parent(s), other ½ of residue.
MICHIGAN	Spouse, ⅓; children, ⅔	1. With 1 child or issue: spouse, ½; child, ½ 2. With more than 1 child or issue: spouse, ⅓; children, ⅔	No	Yes: surviving husband takes ½ & parent(s) ½; surviving wife takes $3,000 plus ½ of residue & parent(s) other ½ of residue.
MINNESOTA	1. With 1 child or issue: spouse, ½; child, ½ 2. With more than 1 child or issue: spouse, ⅓; children, ⅔	Same	Yes	Not applicable
MISSISSIPPI	Equal shares to spouse & children or their issue per stirpes	Same	Yes	Not applicable
MISSOURI	Spouse, ½; children, ½	Same	No	Yes: spouse takes to parent(s),

If Your Parents Are Not Alive, Does Your Wife or Husband Share with Your Brothers & Sisters & Their Issue?	Your Parent(s) (i.e. Neither Wife or Husband nor Children nor Their Issue Survive):	Your Brothers & Sisters & Their Issue (i.e. Neither Parents nor Wife or Husband nor Children nor Issue Survive):
	What Share Does Each Receive?	What Share Does Each Receive?
Not applicable	Equal shares to parents, brothers & sisters or their issue; but if 1 parent is dead, surviving parent takes a double share.	
No	¼ to each surviving parent & the rest equally to brothers & sisters or their issue per stirpes	Equal shares to brothers & sisters or their issue per stirpes
Yes: spouse takes first $25,000 of nonexempt property plus ½ of residue; brothers & sisters or their issue, residue.	½ to each parent or all to surviving parent	To brothers & sisters & their issue per stirpes as though through the estates of the parents
Not applicable	½ to each parent or all to surviving parent	To brothers & sisters & their issue per stirpes as though through the estates of the parents
Not applicable	½ to each parent or all to surviving parent	Equal shares to brothers & sisters or their issue per stirpes
No	¼ to each parent & remainder in equal shares to brothers & sisters or their issue per stirpes	
Yes: spouse takes $10,000 plus ½ remaining personal property & ⅔ remaining real property; brothers & sisters or their issue take residue.	½ to each parent or all to surviving parent	Equal shares to brothers & sisters or their issue per stirpes
Yes: spouse takes $4,000 plus ½ of residue; brothers & sisters or their issue take other ½ of residue.	½ to each parent or all to surviving parent	Equal shares to brothers & sisters or their issue per stirpes
Yes	½ to each parent or all to surviving parent	Equal shares to brothers & sisters or their issue per stirpes
Yes: surviving husband takes ½; brothers & sisters take ½. Surviving wife takes $3,000 plus ½ of residue; brothers & sisters or their issue take other ½ of residue.	½ to each parent or all to surviving parent	Equal shares to brothers & sisters or their issue per stirpes
Not applicable	½ to each parent or all to surviving parent	Equal shares to brothers & sisters or their issue per stirpes
No	Equal shares to parents, brothers & sisters or their issue per stirpes	
½; other ½ goes in equal shares ...rothers & sisters or their issue.	Equal shares to parents, brothers & sisters or their issue per stirpes	

CHART 42 (cont.)	Your Wife or Husband & Children or Their Issue[1]:		Your Wife or Husband (But No Children or Their Issue Survive):	
	What Share of Your Real Property Does Each Receive?	What Share of Your Personal Property Does Each Receive?	Does Your Wife or Husband Take All, Whether or Not Your Parent(s) Still Live?	If Not, Does Your Wife or Husband Share with Your Surviving Parent(s)?
MONTANA	1. With 1 child or issue: spouse, ½; child, ½ 2. With more than 1 child or issue: spouse, ⅓; children, ⅔	Same	Yes	Not applicable
NEBRASKA	Spouse, $35,000 plus ½ balance; children, residue[4]	Same	No	Spouse, $35,000 plus ½ balance; parent(s), residue
NEVADA	Separate property: (1) with 1 child or issue: spouse, ½; child, ½; (2) with more than 1 child or issue: spouse, ⅓; children, ⅔. Community property: all to wife (husband)	Same	Separate property: no. Community property: yes	Yes: spouse takes ½ of separately owned property; parent(s), other ½.
NEW HAMPSHIRE	Spouse, $50,000 plus ½ balance; children, residue[4]	Same	No	Yes: spouse takes $50,000 plus ½ of residue; parent(s), other ½ of residue.
NEW JERSEY	Spouse, life estate in ½; children, remainder	Spouse, ⅓; children, residue	Yes	Not applicable
NEW MEXICO	Separate property: spouse, ¼; children, ¾. Community property: all to spouse	Same	Yes	Not applicable
NEW YORK	1. With 1 child or issue: spouse, $2,000 plus ½ of residue; child, ½ of residue 2. With more than 1 child or issue: spouse, $2,000 plus ⅓ of residue; children, ⅔ of residue	Same	No	Yes: spouse takes $25,000 plus ½ of residue; parent(s), other ½ of residue.
NORTH CAROLINA	1. With 1 child or issue: spouse, ½; child, ½ 2. With more than 1 child or issue: spouse, ⅓; children, ⅔	Same	No	Yes: spouse takes ½ real property & $10,000 of personal property plus ½ of excess; parent(s), residue.
NORTH DAKOTA	Spouse, $50,000 plus ½ balance; children, residue[4]	Same	No	Yes: spouse takes $50,000 plus ½ of residue; parent(s), other ½ of residue.
OHIO	1. With 1 child or issue: spouse, $30,000 plus ½ balance; child, residue[5] 2. With more than 1 child or issue: spouse, $30,000 plus ⅓ balance; children, residue[6]	Same	Yes	Not applicable
OKLAHOMA	1. With 1 child or issue: spouse, ½; child, ½ 2. With more than 1 child or issue: spouse, ⅓; children, ⅔	Same	No	Yes: spouse takes ½; parent(s), ½.
OREGON	Spouse, ½; children, ½	Same	Yes	Not applicable
PENNSYLVANIA	1. With 1 child or issue: spouse, ½; child, ½ 2. With more than 1 child or issue: spouse, ⅓; children, ⅔	Same	No	Yes: spouse takes $20,000 plus ½ of residue; parent(s), ½ of residue.

(5) If surviving child or issue is not the natural or adopted child or issue of the surviving spouse: spouse, $10,000 plus ½ balance; child, residue.

If Your Parents Are Not Alive, Does Your Wife or Husband Share with Your Brothers & Sisters & Their Issue?	Your Parent(s) (i.e. Neither Wife or Husband nor Children nor Their Issue Survive): What Share Does Each Receive?	Your Brothers & Sisters & Their Issue (i.e. Neither Parents nor Wife or Husband nor Children nor Issue Survive): What Share Does Each Receive?
Not applicable	½ to each parent or all to surviving parent	Equal shares to brothers & sisters or their issue per stirpes
No	½ to each parent or all to surviving parent	To brothers & sisters per stirpes
Yes: spouse takes ½ of separately owned property; brothers & sisters or their issue take ½.	½ to each parent or all to surviving parent	Equal shares to brothers & sisters or their issue per stirpes
Yes: spouse takes $50,000 plus ½ of residue; brothers & sisters or their issue take other ½ of residue.	½ to each parent or all to surviving parent	Equal shares to brothers & sisters or their issue per stirpes
Not applicable	Equal shares to parents, brothers & sisters (whether whole or half blood) or their issue per stirpes	
Not applicable	½ to each parent or all to surviving parent	To brothers & sisters & their issue per stirpes as though through the estates of the parents
No	½ to each parent or all to surviving parent	Equal shares to brothers & sisters or their issue per stirpes
No	All to parents or surviving parent	Equal shares to brothers & sisters or their issue per stirpes
No	½ to each parent or all to surviving parent	Equal shares to brothers & sisters or their issue per stirpes
No	½ to each parent or all to surviving parent	Equal shares to brothers & sisters or their issue per stirpes
Yes: spouse takes ½; brothers & sisters or their issue take ½.	½ to each parent or all to surviving parent	Equal shares to brothers & sisters or their issue per stirpes
Not applicable	½ to each parent or all to surviving parent	Equal shares to brothers & sisters or their issue per stirpes
Yes: spouse takes $20,000 plus ½ of residue; brothers & sisters or their issue take other ½ of residue.	½ to each parent or all to surviving parent	Equal shares to brothers & sisters or their issue per stirpes

(6) If the surviving children or issue are not the natural or adopted children or issue of surviving spouse: spouse, $10,000 plus ⅓ balance; children, residue.

CHART 42 (cont.)	Your Wife or Husband & Children or Their Issue[1]:		Your Wife or Husband (But No Children or Their Issue Survive):	
	What Share of Your Real Property Does Each Receive?	What Share of Your Personal Property Does Each Receive?	Does Your Wife or Husband Take All, Whether or Not Your Parent(s) Still Live?	If Not, Does Your Wife or Husband Share with Your Surviving Parent(s)?
RHODE ISLAND	Husband, life estate in all; wife, life estate in ⅓; children, remainder	Spouse, ½; children, ½	No	Yes: spouse takes life estate in all real property & first $50,000 of personal property plus ½ of residue; parent(s), any remaining personal property.
SOUTH CAROLINA	1. With 1 child or issue: spouse, ½; child, ½ 2. With more than 1 child or issue: spouse, ⅓; children, ⅔	Same	No	Yes: spouse takes to parent(s), brothers
SOUTH DAKOTA	1. With 1 child or issue: spouse, ½; child, ½ 2. With more than 1 child or issue: spouse, ⅓; children, ⅔	Same	No	Yes: spouse takes $100,000 plus ½ of residue; parent(s), other ½ of residue.
TENNESSEE	Husband, life estate in all; wife, life estate in ⅓; children, remainder	1. With 1 child or issue: spouse, ½; child, ½ 2. With more than 1 child or issue: spouse, ⅓; children, ⅔	Yes	Not applicable
TEXAS	Separate property: spouse, life estate in ⅓; children, remainder. Community property: spouse, ½; children, ½	Separate property: spouse, ⅓; children, ⅔. Community property: spouse, ½; children, ½	Separate property: no. Community property: yes	Yes: spouse takes separately owned & sisters or their
UTAH	1. With 1 child or issue: spouse, ½; child, ½ 2. With more than 1 child or issue: spouse, ⅓; children, ⅔	Same	No	Yes: spouse takes $100,000 plus ½ of residue; parent(s), ½ of residue.
VERMONT	1. With 1 child or issue: spouse, ½; child, ½ 2. With more than 1 child or issue: spouse, ⅓; children, ⅔	Spouse, all clothing & ornaments & ⅓ other; children, residue	No	Yes: spouse takes $25,000 plus ½ of residue; parent(s), remainder equally.
VIRGINIA	Spouse, life estate in ⅓; children, remainder	Spouse, ⅓; children, ⅔	Yes	Not applicable
WASHINGTON	Spouse: all of community property, ½ other property; children, residue	Same	No	Yes: spouse takes ½ community property plus ¾ of other; parent(s), residue.
WEST VIRGINIA	Spouse, life estate in ⅓; children, remainder	Spouse, ⅓; children, ⅔	Yes	Not applicable
WISCONSIN	1. With 1 child or issue: spouse, $25,000 plus ½ balance; child, residue 2. With more than 1 child or issue: spouse, ⅓; children, residue	Same	Yes	Not applicable
WYOMING	Spouse, ½; children, ½	Same	No	Yes: spouse takes $20,000 plus ¾ balance; parent(s) residue.

If Your Parents Are Not Alive, Does Your Wife or Husband Share with Your Brothers & Sisters & Their Issue?	Your Parent(s) (i.e. Neither Wife or Husband nor Children nor Their Issue Survive): What Share Does Each Receive?	Your Brothers & Sisters & Their Issue (i.e. Neither Parents nor Wife or Husband nor Children nor Issue Survive): What Share Does Each Receive?
Yes: spouse takes life estate in all real property & $50,000 of personal property plus ½ of residue; brothers & sisters or issue take remaining personal property.	½ to each parent or all to surviving parent	Equal shares to brothers & sisters or their issue per stirpes
½; other ½ goes in equal shares & sisters or their issue.	Equal shares to parent(s), brothers & sisters or their issue per stirpes, descendants of the whole blood preferred	
Yes: spouse takes $100,000 plus ½ of residue; brothers & sisters or their issue take ½ of residue.	½ to each parent or all to surviving parent	Equal shares to brothers & sisters or their issue per stirpes
Not applicable	½ to each parent or all to surviving parent	Equal shares to brothers & sisters or their issue per stirpes
all personal property plus ½ real property; parent(s), brothers issue take ½ of residue.	1. If both parents surivive, ½ to each 2. If 1 survives, ½ to parent & ½ to brothers & sisters or their issue	Equal shares to brothers & sisters or their issue per stirpes
Yes: spouse takes $100,000 plus ½ of residue; brothers & sisters or their issue take ½ of residue.	½ to each parent or all to surviving parent	Equal shares to brothers & sisters or their issue per stirpes
Yes: spouse takes $25,000 plus ½ of residue; brothers & sisters or their issue take remainder per stirpes.	½ to each parent or all to surviving parent	Equal shares to brothers & sisters or their issue per stirpes
Not applicable	½ to each parent or all to surviving parent	Equal shares to brothers & sisters or their issue per stirpes
Yes: spouse takes all community property plus ¾ of other; brothers & sisters or their issue take residue.	½ to each parent or all to surviving parent	Equal shares to brothers & sisters or their issue per stirpes
Not applicable	½ to each parent or all to surviving parent	Equal shares to brothers & sisters or their issue per stirpes
Not applicable	Statute does not specify	Equal shares to brothers & sisters or their issue per stirpes
Yes: spouse takes $20,000 plus ¾ balance; brothers & sisters or their issue take residue.	Equal shares to parent(s), brothers & sisters or their issue per stirpes	

COURTS THAT HANDLE PROBATE, WILLS AND ADMINISTRATION

CHART 43

	Circuit Court	County Court	District Court	Orphans' Court	Probate Court	Register's Court	Superior Court
ALABAMA					■		
ALASKA							■
ARIZONA							■
ARKANSAS							■
CALIFORNIA							■
COLORADO			■ [1]				
CONNECTICUT					■		
DELAWARE						■ [2]	
D.C.			■				
FLORIDA		■					
GEORGIA					■		
HAWAII							
IDAHO			■				
ILLINOIS	■						
INDIANA	■ [3]						
IOWA			■				
KANSAS			■				
KENTUCKY		■					
LOUISIANA			■				
MAINE					■		
MARYLAND				■			
MASSACHUSETTS					■ [4]		
MICHIGAN					■		
MINNESOTA					■ [5]		
MISSISSIPPI	Chancery court						

(1) Probate court in city and county of Denver. Circuit and/or superior courts have jurisdiction in other counties.
(2) Presided over by the register of wills.
(3) But jurisdiction is exercised by probate courts in Marion and St. Joseph counties.
(4) Superior courts may hear issues relating to wills.

The name of the court that deals with wills and the distribution of estates varies from state to state (see section 584). This chart shows the name of the appropriate court in your state.

	Circuit Court	County Court	District Court	Orphans' Court	Probate Court	Register's Court	Superior Court
MISSOURI					▓		
MONTANA			▓				
NEBRASKA		▓					
NEVADA			▓				
NEW HAMPSHIRE					▓		
NEW JERSEY	Surrogate's court						
NEW MEXICO					▓		
NEW YORK	Surrogate's court						
NORTH CAROLINA							▓
NORTH DAKOTA		▓					
OHIO	Probate division of court of common pleas						
OKLAHOMA			▓				
OREGON	▓ 6						
PENNSYLVANIA	Orphans' court division of court of common pleas						
RHODE ISLAND					▓		
SOUTH CAROLINA					▓		
SOUTH DAKOTA		▓					
TENNESSEE		▓ 7					
TEXAS		▓					
UTAH			▓				
VERMONT					▓		
VIRGINIA	▓						
WASHINGTON							▓
WEST VIRGINIA		▓					
WISCONSIN		▓					
WYOMING			▓				

(5) Probate courts are also county courts except in Hennepin and Ramsey counties.

(6) But jurisdiction is exercised by county courts in Gilliam, Grant, Harney, Malheur, Sherman and Wheeler counties.

(7) But jurisdiction is exercised by: (a) probate court, Shelby County; (b) law and equity court, Dyer County; (c) chancery court, Hamilton County.

CHART *44*

ALABAMA
Such commission as court may deem just and fair, not to exceed 2½% of monies received plus 2½% of monies paid out (plus expenses)[1]

CONNECTICUT
No statutory rate. Commission is set by the probate court.

IDAHO
No statutory rate. A reasonable commission is permitted.

ALASKA
A reasonable commission is permitted.

DELAWARE
A reasonable commission is permitted.

ILLINOIS
No statutory rate. Commission is set by the probate court.

ARIZONA
A reasonable commission is permitted.

DISTRICT OF COLUMBIA
1%–10% of the appraised value of the estate; commission is set by the probate court.

INDIANA
No statutory rate. Commission is set by the probate court.

ARKANSAS
10% on first $1,000 of personal property; 5% on next $4,000; 3% on balance over $5,000[2]

FLORIDA
A reasonable commission is permitted.[4]

IOWA
6% on first $1,000 of estate value; 4% on next $4,000; 2% on balance over $5,000[3]

CALIFORNIA
7% on first $1,000 of estate value; 4% on next $9,000; 3% on next $40,000; 2% on next $100,000; 1½% on next $350,000; 1% on balance over $500,000[3]

GEORGIA
2½% on monies received plus 2½% on monies paid out (plus expenses)[2]

KANSAS
A reasonable commission is permitted.

COLORADO
A reasonable commission is permitted, not to exceed 6% on first $25,000 of estate value; 4% on next $75,000; 3% on balance over $100,000 (plus expenses).

HAWAII
After July 1, 1977, no statutory rate. A reasonable commission is permitted.[5]

KENTUCKY
5% of value of personal property plus 5% of income received thereon[2]

(1) 2½% of value of lands sold for division, but no more than $100, unless the lands are sold under terms of the will.

(2) Probate court may permit additional compensation for extraordinary services or for services in connection with real estate.

(3) Probate court may permit additional compensation for extraordinary services.

(4) If there is more than one fiduciary, total compensation is set by the probate court.

The executor you appoint in your will or the court-appointed administrator is entitled to the fees set forth by state law as shown below (see sections 547, 556).

LOUISIANA
2½% of appraised value of estate[1,4]

MISSISSIPPI
Commission is set by the probate court, but in no case may it exceed 7% of value of entire estate.

NEW JERSEY
Principal of estate: 5% on first $100,000; & on the balance such percentage as set by probate court, but in no case more than 5%. Income from estate: 6%[8]

MAINE
Commission is set by court, not to exceed 5% of estate value (plus expenses).[1]

MISSOURI
5% on first $5,000 of estate value; 4% on next $20,000; 3% on next $75,000; 2¾% on next $300,000; 2½% on next $600,000; 2% on balance over $1 million

NEW MEXICO
A reasonable commission is permitted.[9]

MARYLAND
Such commission as court may deem appropriate, not to exceed 10% on first $20,000 of personal property; 4% on balance[6]

MONTANA
A reasonable commission is permitted, not to exceed 3% on first $40,000 of estate value; 2% on balance.[3,7]

NEW YORK
For receiving and paying first $25,000, 4%; next $125,000, 3½%; next $150,000, 3%; sums over $300,000, 2%[10]

MASSACHUSETTS
No statutory rate, but 2½%–3% on personal property up to $500,000 & 1% on balance is usually considered not unreasonable.

NEBRASKA
A reasonable commission is permitted.

NORTH CAROLINA
Commission is within discretion of clerk of court and may not exceed 5% on monies received and paid out.[11]

MICHIGAN
5% on first $1,000 of estate value; 2½% on next $4,000; 2% on balance over $5,000 (plus expenses)[3]

NEVADA
6% on first $1,000 of estate value; 4% on next $4,000; 2% on balance over $5,000[3,7]

NORTH DAKOTA
A reasonable commission is permitted

MINNESOTA
A reasonable commission is permitted.

NEW HAMPSHIRE
No statutory rate. If claim for compensation is deemed reasonable, court directs payment from the estate.

OHIO
6% on first $1,000 of estate value; 4% on next $4,000; 2% on balance over $5,000

(5) No commission is permitted on real estate sold during administration of estate.

(6) Unless the will provides for a larger commission. No commission is permitted on real estate or income from real estate.

(7) If there is more than one fiduciary, one commission is divided equally among them.

(8) If there is more than one fiduciary, commission may be increased by no more than 1% for each additional fiduciary. If administra-

CHART 44
(cont.)

OKLAHOMA

5% on first $1,000 of estate value; 4% on next $4,000; 2½% on balance over $5,000[3]

SOUTH DAKOTA

5% on first $1,000 of personal property; 4% on next $4,000; 2½% on balance over $5,000[9]

VIRGINIA

A reasonable commission is permitted, usually 5% of estate value.

OREGON

7% on first $1,000 of estate value; 4% on next $9,000; 3% on next $40,000; 2% on balance over $50,000[3]

TENNESSEE

A reasonable commission is set by the probate court.

WASHINGTON

No statutory rate. Commission is set by probate court.

PENNSYLVANIA

No statutory rate but usually 5% of principal and income on small estates; 3% of principal and income on large estates

TEXAS

5% of all monies received in cash plus 5% of all monies paid out in cash[12]

WEST VIRGINIA

A reasonable commission is permitted, usually 5% on monies received.

RHODE ISLAND

No statutory rate. Commission is set by probate court.

UTAH

Commission may not exceed 5% on first $1,000 of estate value; 4% on next $4,000; 3% on next $5,000; 2% on next $40,000; 1½% on next $50,000; 1% on excess over $100,000.

WISCONSIN

2% of inventory value of property[3]

SOUTH CAROLINA

2½% on appraised value of personal assets received and 2½% on personal assets paid out plus 10% of interest on money loaned[3]

VERMONT

$4 a day[3]

WYOMING

10% on first $1,000 of estate value; 5% on next $4,000; 3% on next $15,000; 2% on balance over $20,000[3]

tion of the estate lasts more than 25 years, additional compensation may be granted, up to ⅕ of 1% for each additional year.

(9) Probate court sets the commission on real estate.

(10) If there is more than one fiduciary, commission is divided among the fiduciaries as follows: (a) if the value of the estate is $100,000 or less, the commission is divided equally among the fiduciaries; (b) if the estate is over $100,000 but less than $200,000, each gets a full commission unless there are more than 2 fiduciaries; in the latter case, the total of 2 full commissions is divided equally among the fiduciaries; (c) if the estate is $200,000 or more, each fiduciary gets a full commission unless there are more than 3 fiduciaries. In such case, 3 full commissions are divided equally among the fiduciaries.

(11) The clerk of the probate court may set the commission if the estate is $2,000 or less.

(12) Total commission can never be more than 5% of the gross fair market value of the estate.

CHAPTER THIRTEEN

Environmental Law

Six hours in sleep, in law's grave study six,
Four spend in prayer, the rest on Nature fix.

—Translation of lines quoted by
SIR EDWARD COKE

13

Environmental Law

Key Points in This Chapter—

Consult these sections for information on:

Chart in This Chapter

THE ISSUES INVOLVED

As recently as the early 1960s, the phrase "environmental law" would probably have produced little more than a puzzled look, even from many lawyers. Such issues as clean air, pure water and freedom from noise pollution were not important public concerns. There were, of course, numerous state and some federal laws intended to protect America's rivers and streams from excessive industrial pollution and to guard wildlife from the depredations of man. But these regulations were generally ignored. With enforcement power dispersed among many federal, state and local agencies, most of which were seriously undermanned, and with noncompliance penalties so slight as to have little more than harassment value, there were few incentives to obey the laws. Indeed, many environmental statutes were so little publicized and so vaguely worded that their existence was hardly known and their meaning was scarcely understood.

Then, in 1962, came a book called *Silent Spring* by Rachel Carson. A powerful indictment of America's disregard of ecology, *Silent Spring* was aimed chiefly at the wholesale use of chemical pesticides, especially DDT. The book's grim vision of an earth denuded of much of its wildlife, of fields and streams laid waste by man's misapplication of the fruits of his own technology, touched off a nationwide controversy that brought environmental concerns into the foreground.

In 1965 a court action took place that ranks in environmental importance with the publication of *Silent Spring*. That was the reversal by a court of appeals of a Federal Power Commission decision to grant a license for a Consolidated Edison power plant at Storm King Mountain on the Hudson River in New York. The court ordered new proceedings that were to "include as a basic concern the preservation of natural beauty and of national historic shrines."

Today concern for the environment extends into such areas as chemical pollution of the air we breathe and the water we drink, strip mining, dam and road building, noise pollution, offshore oil drilling, nuclear energy, waste disposal, the use of aerosol cans and nonreturnable beverage containers and a host of other issues. In fact, there is hardly a realm of national life that is not touched by the controversy that often pits those who style themselves environmentalists against proponents of economic growth in our energy-consuming society.

606. The Issues • Too often the debate is cast in terms of today's jobs and comforts against tomorrow's need for clean air, pure waters and an abundance of wildlife. The energy crisis and recession of the mid-1970s put these issues into sharper focus than ever before. Typical is the nationwide dispute over the burning of soft coal, an energy source that America has in abundance. On one side are those who contend that the use of this resource will ease America's energy problems and, by lowering the cost of power, put hundreds of thousands of the unemployed back to work. With these goals in mind they recommend the temporary lowering of air quality standards to permit the use of soft coal. Their opponents are equally adamant, holding that any relaxation of state and federal clean air standards will open the way to a new and damaging wave of air pollution. And these environmentalists believe that increased use of coal will lead to a rash of strip mining that will turn some of our most majestic scenery into a scarred wasteland.

The debate over coal is only one of many. Should the Tennessee Valley Authority be allowed to build a much-needed dam that will destroy the feeding grounds of a relatively rare type of fish? Should tuna fishermen be forced to adopt new and expensive techniques to avoid entangling porpoises in their nets? Should a local real estate group be permitted to build lakeside condominiums and perhaps cause increased sewage disposal problems? These are questions that affect us all, whether as citizens concerned about the environment, workers hoping for a strong economy or consumers trying to cope with the high cost of living. The problem is to balance the needs of the environment against those of the economy, to find new means of maintaining a high standard of living without destroying the earth on which we all depend.

607. Early Governmental Actions • In the late 1960s both state and federal governments began enacting legislation and establishing new agencies to set and enforce standards of clean air and water and to protect America's remaining open land from abuse by overzealous developers. The federal Clean Air Act of 1967, the Clean Air Act Amendment of 1970 and the 1972 amendments to the federal Water Pollution Control Act set new high standards for environmental quality. In many cases states have followed suit by setting their own tough standards of air, water and land use. At every session of Congress and at most sessions of state legislatures new bills are brought forth, either to strengthen or weaken environmental standards, and hearings are held in which groups with different interests battle through private lobbies, industrial associations, labor unions and citizens' organizations to effect the legislation to their liking. Inevitably, trade-offs are made—such as a lowering of mandated auto pollution standards for the immediate future against a raising of overall air quality requirements—and the degree to which long-term environmental considerations are taken into account usually depends upon the ability of environmental groups to bring their pressure to bear in the hearings.

608. The National Environmental Policy Act • In 1969 Congress, noting the lack of a comprehensive national environmental policy, passed the National Environmental Policy Act (NEPA). Its purpose: "To declare a national policy which will encourage protective and enjoyable harmony between man and his environment; to promote efforts which will prevent or eliminate damage to the environment . . . and stimulate the health and welfare of man. . . ." One section of the NEPA, designed to put this policy into action, requires that all federal agencies prepare detailed descriptions of the environmental changes that would result from any proposed programs in which the federal government has a jurisdictional or financial role. Moreover, this report—called an environmental impact statement—must also include alternatives to the proposed action, together with their environmental impacts, and must accompany the proposed program wherever it is reviewed. (It must be reviewed—the NEPA states this explicitly—by all federal and state agencies with some expertise in the environmental impact involved.) Only after this impact statement and the relevant comments have been filed with the Council on Environmental Quality—a body in the Executive Office of the President, created by the NEPA—and studied and approved by its staff, can the project itself be approved. Given the pervasiveness of federal influence throughout all 50 states, there is hardly a project of even moderate dimensions, whether initiated by government or private actions, that does not require NEPA approval. And even many of these that do not need federal support will probably have to meet state standards, because more than 20 states have adopted their own environmental impact statements. Thus, in matters as seemingly disparate as determining the site of the Kennedy Library in Cambridge, Massachusetts, the construction of the Alaskan oil pipeline and the channeling of an Alabama stream, environmental impact statements were required, and drastic modifications of the original plans were ordered. On the federal level alone, hundreds of major and minor projects have been abandoned or altered as a result of the environmental impact statements, and many important environmental laws have arisen from challenges to agencies for filing insufficient statements. As these statements are a matter of public record, citizen groups can challenge them.

609. Environmental Protection Agencies • In 1970 the federal Environmental Protection Agency (EPA) was established as a high command for the national campaign to ensure clean air and pure water and a host of other environmental requirements that Congress had mandated. During the years since, most states have also created their own regulatory agencies to define and enforce statewide standards (see chart 45, page 716). Many cities and towns now also have offices to pass on projects that may affect the environment. All of these agencies—whether federal, state or local—operate within the guidelines set by Congress, the legislature or the city council, whichever created them. These guidelines merely set the limits and the goals that these agencies, through their interpretation of the law and enforcement powers, must attempt to meet. The actual day-to-day activities—the review of projects, the granting of licenses, the setting of specific standards—are the work of the regulatory agencies. The federal EPA, for example, in carrying out its diverse tasks, has created a large body of administrative regulations, which themselves have the force of law. True, these regulations may be challenged in the courts or overridden by Congress, but barring such lengthy and expensive tactics, the rules set forth by the agency are as much a part of the legal code as those passed by Congress.

The federal EPA (as well as its state counterparts) has acted on literally thousands of projects and passed on thousands of requests for variances from mandated standards. In the matter of automobile emissions alone, the EPA has required manufacturers to install antipollution devices but, when it felt it necessary, has also ordered delays in the implementation of some standards to permit the car makers additional time for research and development. Similarly, it was the federal EPA that banned the use of DDT in 1972 and has since forced the abandonment or chemical modification of other pesticides. It has also banned the manufacture of contaminating chemicals that have been found in some of the nation's waterways and are dangerous to fish, plant life and human health.

Like other governmental agencies, the EPA and state environmental commissions often hold public hearings before setting standards or passing on a project.

The Role of the Private Citizen

There is, perhaps, no realm of public policy more susceptible to citizen action than questions affecting the environment. Either acting alone or with other concerned citizens, the individual is in a position to influence policy. Indeed, the whole environmental movement is, in large measure, the result of an aroused public's demands for change. Although much has already been done, still more remains to be accomplished on local, state and federal levels.

610. Private Pressure Groups • That old saying "In union there is strength" is wise advice for the environmentally concerned citizen. There are dozens of nationwide organizations, many with state and local chapters, that the individual can join. Some, like the Defenders of Wildlife, address themselves to a narrow range of issues; others, like the Sierra Club, provide information and lobby on a broad range of topics from air pollution to nuclear energy to conservation. Still others, like the Environmental Defense Fund and the National Resources Defense Council, are court oriented and bring environmental suits against both private interests and government agencies. Before joining a national organization, read its literature carefully to make sure its views coincide with your own. If you are primarily interested in state or local environmental issues, attend a few meetings of the local chapters of these groups so that you can be certain that they are organized in such a way as to have an impact in your area.

611. Forming Your Own Committee • If you are concerned about a local environmental question—something as simple as an ordinance permitting open leaf burning, for example—you can rally your friends and neighbors into your own pressure group. Try to get as broad a representation of people as possible, but be particularly careful to include persons who might qualify as "experts." It always helps to have a sprinkling of doctors, lawyers, engineers and the like on a committee concerned with the environment.

612. Keeping Yourself Informed • If your organization is concerned with a wide range of environmental issues, appoint a small group within it to keep track of relevant legislative or agency hearings. Your local

STATE ENVIRONMENTAL AGENCIES

ABBREVIATIONS: Bd., Board; Bur., Bureau; Comm., Commission; Conserv., Conservation; Eng., Engineering; Environ., Environmental; Nat., Natural; Pub., Public; Res., Resources; Sec., Section; Serv., Service(s).

CHART 45	Air Pollution Agencies	Water Pollution Agencies
ALABAMA	Dept. of Pub. Health, State Office Bldg., Montgomery 36104	Water Improvement Comm., State Office Bldg., Montgomery 36104
ALASKA	Dept. of Environ. Conserv., Pouch O, Juneau 99801	
ARIZONA	Div. of Air Pollution Control, 4019 N. 33rd Ave., Phoenix 85017	Environ. Health Serv., Health Dept., 1624 W. Adams St., Phoenix 85507
ARKANSAS	Dept. of Pollution Control and Ecology, 8001 National Dr., Little Rock 72209	
CALIFORNIA	Air Res. Bd., P.O. Box 2815, Sacramento 95812	Water Res. Control Bd., 1416 Ninth St., Sacramento 95814
COLORADO	Dept. of Health, 4210 E. 11th Ave., Denver 80220	
CONNECTICUT	Dept. of Environ. Protection, 165 Capitol Ave., Hartford 06115	
DELAWARE	Div. of Environ. Control, Tatnall Bldg., Capitol Complex, Dover 19901	
D. C.	Bur. of Air & Water Pollution Control, 25 K St. N.E., Washington 20002	Water Res. Management Admin., 415 12 St. N.W., Washington 20004
FLORIDA	Dept. of Pollution Control, 315 S. Calhoun St., Suite 300, Tallahassee 32301	
GEORGIA	Environ. Protection Div., 47 Trinity Ave. S.W., Altanta 30334	Water Quality Control Bd., 47 Trinity Ave. S.W., Atlanta 30334
HAWAII	Air Sanitation Branch, Environ. Health Div., 1250 Punchbowl St., Honolulu 96813	Dept. of Health, P.O. Box 3378, Honolulu 96801
IDAHO	Dept. of Environ. Protection & Health, Air Pollution Control, State House, Boise 83707	Environ. Improvement Div., Dept. of Health, State House, Boise 83707
ILLINOIS	Environ. Protection Agency, 2200 Churchill Rd., Springfield 62706	
INDIANA	Bd. of Health, 1330 W. Michigan St., Indianapolis 46206	Stream Pollution Control Bd., 1330 W. Michigan St., Indianapolis 46206
IOWA	Environ. Eng. Serv., Dept. of Health, Lucas State Office Bldg., Des Moines 50319	Water Pollution Div., Dept. of Health, Lucas State Office Bldg., Des Moines 50319
KANSAS	Dept. of Health and Environment, Topeka 66620	
KENTUCKY	Air and Water Pollution Control Comm., 275 E. Main St., Frankfort 40601	
LOUISIANA	Air Control Sec., Bur. of Environ. Health, P.O. Box 60630, New Orleans 70160	Water Pollution Control Div., P.O. Box FC, University Sta., Baton Rouge 70830
MAINE	Dept. of Environ. Protection, Bur. Air Pollution Control, State House, Augusta 04330	Environ. Improvement Comm., State House, Augusta 04330
MARYLAND	Bur. Air Quality Control, Dept. of Health, 610 N. Howard St., Baltimore 21201	Dept. of Nat. Res., Water Res. Admin., Tawes Bldg., Annapolis 21401
MASSACHUSETTS	Bur. of Air Quality Control, Pub. Health Dept., 600 Washington St., Boston 02111	Div. Water Pollution Control, Dept. Nat. Res., Saltonstall Bldg., Govt. Center, Boston 02202
MICHIGAN	Div. Air Pollution Control, Pub. Health Dept., 3500 N. Logan St., Lansing 48194	Water Res. Comm., Dept. of Nat. Res., Stevens Mason Bldg., Lansing 48926
MINNESOTA	Pollution Control Agency, 717 Delaware St. S.E., Minneapolis 55440	
MISSISSIPPI	Air and Water Pollution Control Comm., Robert E. Lee Bldg., Jackson 39205	

If you have a question or a complaint about air or water pollution, you may write to the appropriate agency in your state. In some cases one agency handles both air and water pollution.

	Air Pollution Agencies	Water Pollution Agencies
MISSOURI	Air Conserv. Comm., P.O. Box 1062, Jefferson City 65101	Water Pollution Bd., P.O. Box 154, Jefferson City 65101
MONTANA	Dept. of Health & Environ. Sciences, Cogswell Bldg., Helena 59601	
NEBRASKA	Dept. of Environ. Control, P.O. Box 94653, State House, Lincoln 68509	
NEVADA	Bur. of Environ. Health, 201 S. Fall St., Carson City 89701	Comm. of Environ. Protection, 201 S. Fall St., Carson City 89701
NEW HAMPSHIRE	Air Pollution Control Agency, 61 S. Spring St., Concord 03301	Water Supply & Pollution Control Comm., 105 Loudon Rd., Prescott Pk., Concord 03301
NEW JERSEY	Dept. of Environ. Protection, P.O. Box 1390, Trenton 08625	
NEW MEXICO	Environ. Improvement Agency, 725 St. Michael's Dr., Santa Fe 87501	
NEW YORK	Dept. of Environ. Conserv., 50 Wolf Rd., Albany 12233	
NORTH CAROLINA	Office of Water and Air Res., P.O. Box 27687, Raleigh 27611	
NORTH DAKOTA	Environ. Eng. Div., Health Dept., 1200 Missouri Ave., Bismarck 58505	Water Supply & Pollution Control Div., Health Dept., 1200 Missouri Ave., Bismarck 58505
OHIO	Air Pollution Unit, Health Dept., 450 E. Town St., Columbus 43216	Water Pollution Control Bd., Health Dept., 450 E. Town St., Columbus 43216
OKLAHOMA	Air Pollution Control Div., Health Dept., 3400 N. Eastern Ave., Oklahoma City 73105	Environ. Improvement Agency, Health Dept., 3400 N. Eastern Ave., Oklahoma City 73105
OREGON	Dept. of Environ. Quality, 1234 S.W. Morrison St., Portland 97205	
PENNSYLVANIA	Dept. of Environ. Res., P.O. Box 2063, Harrisburg 17120	
RHODE ISLAND	Div. Air Pollution Control, 204 Health Bldg., Davis St., Providence 02908	Div. Water Supply & Pollution Control, 335 State Office Bldg., Providence 02903
SOUTH CAROLINA	Dept. of Health & Environ. Control, Environ. Quality Control, 2600 Bull St., Columbia 29201	
SOUTH DAKOTA	Air Quality Control Program, Dept. of Health, Bldg. #2, Pierre 57501	Committee on Water Pollution, Dept. of Health, Pierre 57501
TENNESSEE	Div. Air Pollution Control, Pub. Health Dept., C2-212 Hull Bldg., Nashville 37219	Water Quality Control Bd., Hull Bldg., Room 621, Nashville 37219
TEXAS	Air Pollution Control Serv., Dept. of Health, 1100 W. 49th St., Austin 78756	Water Quality Bd., 1108 Lavaca St., Austin 78701
UTAH	Div. of Health, 44 Medical Dr., Salt Lake City 84113	Water Pollution Committee, Soc. Serv. Dept., 44 Medical Dr., Salt Lake City 84113
VERMONT	Agency of Environ. Conserv., Air Pollution Control, P.O. Box 489, Montpelier 05602	Agency of Environ. Conserv., Water Res. Dept., 5 Court St., Montpelier 05602
VIRGINIA	Air Pollution Control Bd., Rm. 1106, 9th St. Office Bldg., Richmond 23219	Water Control Bd., P.O. Box 11143, Richmond 23230
WASHINGTON	Dept. of Ecology, P.O. Box 829, Olympia 98504	
WEST VIRGINIA	Air Pollution Control Comm., 1558 Washington St. E., Charleston 25311	Water Res. Div., Nat. Res. Dept., 1201 Greenbrier St., Charleston 25311
WISCONSIN	Dept. of Nat. Res., Div. of Environ. Standards, P.O. Box 7921, Madison 53707	
WYOMING	Div. of Health and Medical Serv., State Office Bldg., Cheyenne 82001	

newspaper will announce some. Ask your state legislators and city councilmen to put your organization on their mailing lists to receive notification of hearings. Check all pending bills on both the state and local level for proposals that might have an environmental impact. Write to your elected representatives when such a bill is introduced. Often in the rush of legislative business a lawmaker may not notice the environmental aspects of a seemingly minor bill. If you help keep him informed, he cannot plead ignorance.

613. Attending Hearings • You should prepare yourself to testify before governmental bodies on legislation or projects affecting the environment. Bring the most knowledgeable members of your group along to add weight to your testimony. Draw up a position paper outlining the reasons for your organization's stand and distribute it widely, both to the general public and to legislators and agency personnel.

614. The Wisdom of Compromise • Law, like politics, is the art of compromise. Your organization may, for example, want a complete ban on open leaf burning, but your fellow citizens may not be willing to shoulder an additional tax burden to have the leaves carted away. You may have to accept a compromise limiting leaf burning to certain hours of certain days.

615. Seeking Judicial Relief • In general, this should be a last resort. The time-consuming nature of litigation and the great costs involved make it advisable that every other avenue of agreement be explored first. However, hundreds of environmental issues must finally be decided in the courts. If your organization has reason to believe a particular project or practice may violate federal, state or local environmental standards, by all means, sue. In recent years both federal and state courts have become much more receptive to suits by private citizens or organizations on environmental issues. In addition, there are now hundreds of law firms that specialize in these matters, and if the issue transcends the purely local (and sometimes even if it does not), financial and legal support may be obtained from well-endowed national organizations.

We now have a legal structure through which environmental concerns may be adjudicated. It is up to the citizen, both as an individual and as a member of the community, to see to it that the legal structure is an effective weapon for the preservation of nature's heritage.

CHAPTER FOURTEEN

Your Lawyer

*Although the law is a highly learned profession,
we are well aware that it is an intensely practical one.*

—FREDERICK M. VINSON

14

Your Lawyer

Some Key Points in This Chapter—
Consult these sections for information on:

A LITTLE ABOUT YOUR LAWYER

Throughout this book we have discussed many of the points of law you may encounter in your daily life. In many cases we have pointed out that the advice and assistance of a lawyer are either desirable or necessary. This chapter will tell you a little about lawyers: what they do, how they are trained, how you can find a lawyer when you need one and how you can work with your lawyer to your mutual advantage.

Unfortunately, for reasons we discuss below, some people are vaguely distrustful of lawyers and are reluctant to seek out legal advice when they need it. This is unfortunate, because your lawyer can be a real friend in need—as helpful and important to you and your family as a doctor or a clergyman. He is a specially trained man whose purpose in life is to serve his clients and the community in which he lives and to give you the best advice he can about some of the most complex problems of modern life. By describing what the lawyer does, we hope to make it easier for you to see him as a human being whom you can confide in and trust and who may be of enormous help to you in ordinary transactions and in time of trouble.

616. Historical Role of the Lawyer • Lawyers are involved in so many vital aspects of modern American life that it is easy to forget that they once were very much on the outside. The early colonists, especially in New England, were strongly opposed to lawyers. The colonists believed each man should be able to assert and protect his individual rights, and because all the early settlers were—or thought they were—like-minded, having left England for the same reasons, they did not expect any conflicts to arise among themselves or between them and the colonial governments that would require the help of lawyers to resolve.

Human nature being what it is, however, the colonists soon learned that they had to establish a method of handling disputes between individuals as well as a method of reviewing and prescribing punishment for the commission of crime and violations of governmental orders. Courts were established in the colonies well before there were lawyers to appear before them.

The conscious effort to conduct a system of courts without lawyers was unsuccessful. The judges found that issues were not being clearly framed, that the people appearing before them were unable to assert their rights effectively. It was not long, therefore, before individual courts began authorizing men well read in government and law to appear in the courts to represent other persons not so well educated. In the middle Atlantic and southern colonies sons of wealthier colonists went to England, studied law in the English Inns of Court (which compare loosely to our law schools) and returned to America to become lawyers and practice law.

Because the very nature of their legal studies (even the informal sort that long prevailed in New England) gave the lawyers an understanding of governmental operations and society in general that most of the colonists lacked, the lawyers moved into positions of influence in the colonial governments and took prominent parts in the movements and organizations that led to the establishment of a new nation—the United States. Thomas Jefferson made an observation that is perhaps even more apt today than it was at the end of the eighteenth century: the legal profession is the "nursery of the legislature."

So, by the time of the adoption of the United States Constitution, lawyers had become an essential part of the government of our country. It took somewhat longer for them to win acceptance in the states, such as Massachusetts, which had traditionally distrusted them. But during the early 1800s the legal profession took shape pretty much as it is today. Lawyers are called different things in different parts of the country, but the verbal distinctions mean little.

617. Kinds of Lawyers • *Attorney-at-law* is perhaps the most common term for a lawyer. As distinguished from an attorney-in-fact, who is authorized to act for another person in a specific situation (for example, the person to whom you give a power of attorney to sign a contract in your absence), an attorney-at-law represents you in lawsuits and other legal matters. *Counselor-at-law* means the same thing as attorney-at-law: a person trained and qualified to give you counsel or advice on legal matters.

A trial lawyer is a lawyer who tries cases in court. In the United States, all lawyers are presumed qualified to try cases in court and before various administrative agencies. But in England a trial lawyer, called a *barrister*, is sharply distinguished from a lawyer called a *solicitor*, who may not appear in court. The British barrister is prohibited from seeking or even having his own clients; all his cases are referred to him by a solicitor. The solicitor "briefs" the barrister on what the case is all about, frequently just a short time before the case comes up in court. The barrister

THREE KINDS OF LAWYERS

Lawyers fill many roles. Some are primarily advisers to private individuals managing their personal affairs; others develop expertise in specialized fields; still others concentrate on trial work. Three of the most familiar kinds of lawyers are described below.

The Family Lawyer

The so-called family lawyer is a generalist in much the same sense as the old family doctor. Usually active in the affairs of his community, he advises his clients on matters such as leases, contracts, wills, estate planning, the purchase and sale of real estate, divorce and separation proceedings, adoption and hundreds of other problems that arise in an ordinary lifetime. He is a friend and a counselor in time of trouble. One of his most important functions is to keep you out of litigation unless it is clearly necessary.

The Trial Lawyer

Although some successful lawyers never appear in court, many individuals and firms make a specialty of representing parties in litigation. The trial lawyer does not necessarily limit himself to courtroom work, but his greater experience in it makes him alert to procedural points and nuances in the presentation of evidence that might escape a competent attorney whose major interests lie elsewhere. Some courtroom experience is valuable to any lawyer, regardless of his special field of competence.

The Corporation Lawyer

The corporation lawyer is a salaried employe of a company for which he has gone to work either right after passing his bar examination or, more likely, after a period of employment with a large law firm. He specializes in whatever fields of law are of particular importance to his company. A lawyer in a publishing company, for example, might be particularly strong in areas such as copyright law, libel, plagiarism and the interpretation of royalty contracts. He may or may not be involved in courtroom work.

handles all aspects of the court proceeding, including the appeal if one is indicated, and then bows out while the solicitor takes over again.

This British line between barrister and solicitor exists in fact in parts of the American legal profession: Hundreds of our lawyers, perhaps the most influential ones, seldom if ever appear in court. They regard their role as counseling, and they are most likely to counsel that every effort be made to keep their clients from the risks of unnecessary litigation. If they conclude that litigation is unavoidable, or even desirable, they may in a big or complicated case turn to an outstanding trial lawyer, just as the British solicitor turns to the barrister.

The criminal lawyer is a legal specialist of great importance to our society, because everyone accused of a crime has a right to representation in the courts. Criminal laws are complex and vary considerably from state to state, and the average "family lawyer" or general adviser is seldom familiar with them in enough detail to make the best possible defense of a person charged with a crime. If anyone in your family is ever charged with a serious crime, your lawyer will probably recommend that the case be handled by a specialist in criminal law. (For a full discussion of criminal law, see chapter 4, "Your Protection Against Crime and Criminal Charges," page 133.)

Another specialty in U.S. legal practice should be mentioned: the patent lawyer, who spends his entire professional life advising about patent matters (see section 161). Most American lawyers' early education is in the social sciences or humanities. Consequently, these lawyers carefully avoid patent matters because they involve technical and scientific areas of knowledge of which the average lawyer is usually ignorant. The patent lawyers, who are trained in engineering or some other scientific specialty, have the whole patent field to themselves. They are much in demand by patent law firms, corporations and the government.

When Jefferson called law the "nursery of the legislature," he recognized a duality in the U.S. legal profession that remains strikingly true today. American lawyers are both counselors and activists, to an extent unknown in any other country. The reason, perhaps, is the scope of their education, which we will elaborate upon later. But whatever the reason, you as a citizen may look to lawyers either for counseling on your personal problems or for leadership in coping with society's problems. You probably would be unwise to look to one lawyer for both, if only because no lawyer has time to do both well.

A counselor must retain some degree of objectivity to be able to give good advice. Many people believe that a lawyer has no business being an activist, that he is abandoning his historical role as advocate for individual clients if he becomes too wound up in political and social affairs, that he should remain above the battle—or at least a good distance from it. You must decide what kind of service you are after when you consult a lawyer. If you want dispassionate advice on what the law is in the situation confronting you, make sure (as we shall tell you how) to find a lawyer who knows what the law *is*, not one whose consuming interest is what the law should be. The latter lawyer is necessary to keep the country's policies up to date and to make essential improvements, but the former is the one you want in a personal crisis.

When to Consult a Lawyer

618. When a Lawyer Is Essential • There is a difference between when you *should* and when you *must* consult a lawyer. However, the line between these situations is not always clear. Some general rules should be helpful in guiding you.

As far as civil actions are concerned—such as damage suits, suits for breach of contract and the like—it is essential that you have a lawyer if you are sued for a substantial amount, and all the more so if the person suing you has a lawyer working for him. You also need a lawyer if you want to sue for more than can be recovered through an action in small claims court (see section 620). It is more than an untrained person can do to follow the twistings and turnings of a damage suit or to argue the meaning of a complicated contract before a court. It is also advisable to have a lawyer when a written contract is to be drawn up between you and another person or a business concern.

In criminal cases you must have a lawyer. Even a glance at chapter 4 should convince you of the folly of trying to represent yourself when charged with the commission of a felony or misdemeanor. The seriousness of the penalties if you are found guilty, in some cases depriving you of basic civil rights; the fact that the criminal courts are so congested you may be held in jail for weeks or even months without a hearing; the risk that bail may be set at a figure you cannot afford to pay; the intricacies of criminal procedure—all argue the wisdom of consulting a lawyer at once should you run afoul of the police or the public prosecutor in your area.

Federal law now requires that you have the benefit of legal counsel.

State laws differ, but the United States Supreme Court recently ruled that the states must require legal counsel for persons accused of the more serious offenses. You should do everything possible to avoid a "criminal record"—particularly in these days when your credit is so important in making essential contracts, and so many governmental and private agencies are keeping files on all of us. Doing everything possible means finding a lawyer to represent you. How to find one when you need him is described in sections 622–625.

619. Why a Family Lawyer Is Desirable • As to when you *should* consult a lawyer—as compared to *must*—our suggestion is that you read over the part of this book that deals with your particular problem before making up your mind. If your tendency is to base your decision on your finances, you are likely to postpone getting legal advice. Few of us have extra money, and we are inclined to regard a lawyer as a luxury we can postpone until a crisis comes up.

This attitude is unfortunate. If you and your family can possibly manage to do so, you should at the least find a lawyer on whom you can call in emergencies. The pressures of modern life; its impersonality, especially in large cities; the astonishing mobility of modern Americans, with one out of very five families moving homes every year—all have tended to cut us loose from moorings that in the recent past gave us a sense of security. All the more reason for the family to establish an association of some sort with a minister, a doctor and a lawyer. A lawyer should be an identifiable person on your horizon, someone you can consult whenever you believe you have legal problems requiring action of one sort or another. This book should help you identify such problems.

620. When You May Not Need a Lawyer • If you have no lawyer and don't know one, you'll have to be your own best judge as to whether the problem before you requires one. Clearly, not all problems require legal help. If you need money for an emergency, you should consult your local bank. If you are having trouble with an income tax matter, you should first consult an accountant. If you are buying a house in a routine situation from a well-known builder with a fine reputation, you may decide to rely on a real estate agent, or on the title company that insures your title to the property, or on the attorney for the bank or other institution that is lending you part of the money in return for your mortgage. If you are not receiving social security or unemployment compensation checks to which you believe you are entitled, government officials stand ready and have a

SMALL CLAIMS COURT

A cheap and effective way of getting fast justice without the help of a lawyer is by using one of the many small claims courts that exist in most urban areas. The general procedures are outlined below.

If you want to make a claim for an amount below the statutory limit—usually from $200 to $500—you may be able to handle the case yourself through a local small claims court. The normal steps in such a proceeding are these:

1. You go to the clerk of court in the defendant's borough or county and tell him your story—briefly. He will give you forms to fill out, including a formal complaint, and will charge you a modest filing fee. The clerk may assist you in drawing up the legal papers.

2. The clerk will assign a date for the hearing of your case and will arrange for the delivery of your complaint to the defendant, usually by mailing it to his legal address.

3. Either you or the defendant may request a postponement of the hearing if the date is inconvenient or does not give you enough time to prepare your case.

4. On the appointed day you both appear before the magistrate for an informal recital of the facts in your case. Failure to appear will result in a judgment against you. Bring with you any evidence or any witnesses you need to prove your side of the story. Hearings are often held in an ordinary office before a judge dressed simply in a business suit. Concentrate on making your case clear to him, not on arguing with the other party.

5. After listening to the testimony for both sides and examining whatever evidence is presented, the judge will frequently render a decision on the spot. If you are successful, he will then issue an order that the defendant pay your claim or a sum the court considers fair.

duty to help you. In these and similar situations, if you are dealing with honest and reputable people, you will be alerted by them to any unusual aspects of your situation requiring the services of a lawyer.

Another situation in which you may not need a lawyer is when you have a claim for a small amount of money. If the amount is under the limit set by state or local law, you simply swear out a complaint before the clerk of the small claims court. He then notifies the person against whom you have the claim, and the case is tried before a judge of the small claims court. If you are successful, judgment will be entered in your favor. Your only dealings with your lawyer in this case might be a phone call to find out the statutory limit on small claims and the procedure to be followed with the clerk of court.

621. When You Should Consult a Lawyer • Situations where you clearly should get a lawyer are probably obvious: when you are making a will or revising one (see sections 527–554); when you receive notice, called a citation, that you have been named as a legatee in the will of a recently deceased friend or relative and a contest seems to be developing over the validity of the will (see section 585); when you are involved in an automobile accident and are sued for an amount of money larger than your insurance protection (see section 241); when you want to adopt a child (see sections 346–352); when someone with whom you do business has broken his contract with you, causing substantial damages. In all such cases and a host of others you need the services of a lawyer to be as certain as possible that your interests will be fully protected. In the last analysis, common sense should be your guide.

How to Find a Lawyer

There is no reason why you cannot find a lawyer if you use common sense and make the most of your associations in whatever circumstances you live. This statement can be made with assurance even though in an absolute sense there are not enough lawyers in the United States at the present time.

622. If You Can't Afford a Lawyer • Even if your income is very modest, you should not hesitate to look for legal help, because today, more than ever in the country's history, legal services are being made available to persons of limited means, or of no means at all.

If you find yourself in jail, charged with a serious offense, and have no money, the court will assign you a lawyer who will represent you free of charge. The system varies from state to state and is different in federal and state courts. In some metropolitan areas there are *legal aid societies,* staffed by lawyers with varying degrees of experience: some are permanent members of the society's staff, whereas others are young lawyers associated with large law firms in the area and loaned to the society for six months to a year. In other areas there are newly formed groups of *public defenders:* lawyers who handle criminal cases for persons having little or no funds of their own—all with the approval of local bar associations and of the local criminal court judges.

If your legal troubles are civil rather than criminal, lawyers can be found, although not by assignment by the court. Neighborhood legal offices are being established in city after city, staffed by young men and women lawyers eager to obtain the experience of dealing directly with clients like you, for a variety of reasons. First, in the larger law offices such face-to-face contact with the client may not come for two to three years. Second, these young lawyers believe strongly that you should have legal advice whether or not you can pay for it. Third, they are eager to correct social ills—as epitomized by landlords who demand excessive rents and furnish inferior services—by representing you with all their enthusiasm and newly acquired skills and compelling others to behave decently and responsibly toward you.

These neighborhood legal offices take many forms. Some are financed by grants from the U.S. government; there are hundreds of these across the country. Others are both financed and staffed by law firms who assign partners and associates to them for varying periods of time. More and more frequently these firms are also taking on as regular clients persons with real legal complaints, however small may be the amount of money involved and however little the client can afford to pay. Suffice it to say that if you will look and ask around you, you can get a lawyer for both civil and criminal matters that you may face from time to time.

623. Finding a Lawyer—Sources of Information • What has happened in many parts of American life is that persons on the middle-income level are finding services of all kinds increasingly hard to finance. Legal services are no exception. We have already described what services are available to the poor. The rich are sure to associate with lawyers either in making or preserving their money. The rest of this discussion will therefore be directed toward the millions of Americans whose income is well above the poverty level but who have had no firsthand contact with members of the legal profession.

Let's assume you are faced with one of the many situations described throughout this book in which you must or should obtain a lawyer. Analyzing your problem is the first step toward selecting one. If you need to make or revise a will or if you receive legal papers in connection with a probate proceeding, several possibilities come to mind. An official of the bank where you keep a checking account, or which holds the mortgage on your home, is sure to know several lawyers in your area. He will give you their names and outline their experience in the field of estates. The clerk of the local court with jurisdiction over wills and trusts, usually called the probate court (see section 585), knows all the local lawyers who come before his court and will give you guidance among them.

If you have questions about the language in a contract for sale (see section 281) that you've been given to sign when you're about to buy a house, you would again get help in locating a lawyer from your bank, or from the real estate agent who is negotiating the sale of the house to you.

Apart from these obvious sources of information about lawyers, you should consult your friends, your insurance salesman or your accountant. Another place to turn, especially in a small community, is to the librarian. Chances are he knows the various lawyers in town or can easily find out for you. Nor should you forget that you can get suggestions from the fraternal or benevolent association you may belong to, or from your doctor, because as a professional man he has his own lawyer or, if he doesn't, his local medical association has one. If you are a churchgoer, you might even ask the minister, priest or rabbi for a recommendation.

If none of these sources is available to you, there are two other places to go. One is the local bar association, which exists both to serve the interests of the lawyers in your community and, where necessary, to discipline them. Many bar associations throughout the United States now maintain lawyers' referral services. They were created for the very purpose you have in mind: to give you an opportunity, at a minimum fee, to explain your legal problem and get advice as to how to handle it.

Lastly, bear in mind that American political life is dominated by lawyers. If you belong to a political party and have done any work for it, you have a claim on your party's local leadership for help in finding you a lawyer suited to your needs. You should take as much care making up your mind about the referrals you get from the political leader as about the referrals you get from others. But his referrals are likely to be extremely helpful and well adapted to your ability to pay.

624. Choosing Your Lawyer · If you have followed any one of these suggested methods of finding a lawyer, you have probably received several names. Your problem now becomes one of selection, and again your only guide is your common sense. You should not hesitate to request an interview with one or more of the persons on the list. You are, hopefully, entering into a longtime association with the lawyer you select —unless you want advice in a highly specialized area and are unlikely to need it again. You should feel that your lawyer is someone with whom you can easily discuss any problem you may confront. You should not settle on someone you do not like or trust.

625. Lawyers Who Are Specialists · There is considerable specialization within the practice of law. It is clearly impossible for any lawyer to become or remain an authority on all fields of law. If there were a great need for such an authority, the lawyer in greatest demand would be the recent law school graduate who has just successfully passed an examination for admission to the bar of his state after a thorough review of all or a great part of the laws in his state. But he can't use any of that knowledge unless he has a chance to put it to work for a client. At that point, his future is decided for him. If he goes to work by himself or with a few other lawyers in a small office, the chances are he will continue to have a very general practice. If he goes to work for the government, a corporation or a large metropolitan law firm, he will inevitably spend much of his time in one or a few areas of law. As he becomes known as an expert, and if his areas are broad ones, such as corporation law in all its aspects, clients are likely to consult him as a wise man. He is then in a position to broaden out again and spend his career as a generalist, referring specific matters to specialists. The fields of law that occupy most American lawyers are: corporate law; real estate or property (including zoning); condemnation; patent; copyright and trademark; negligence or torts; taxation; wills, trusts and estates; labor law; and criminal law.

For the average reader of this book, our suggestion is that you look for a lawyer who shares his workload with a few partners and associates, whose time is spent on a variety of matters and who therefore will be able to direct you to, or himself take up your problem with, a specialist as seems necessary. Things may work out differently for you, however. You may go to a condemnation expert because the state is about to condemn for a ridiculously low price the small house that you bought with your life's savings—and the condemnation lawyer may so win your confidence that from then on you go to him first for help with a host of other problems. If so, he is *your* legal general practitioner and only proves the point we are making. Find a lawyer you trust and let him guide you through any legal wilderness you may encounter.

How to Arrange Fees with Your Lawyer

626. The Sensitive Subject of Fees • Perhaps the most delicate—and difficult—aspect of the legal profession's relations with nonlawyers centers on the subject of fees. There are many reasons.

First, the amount of time and effort a lawyer spends on a particular problem or case is not always apparent. It does not seem possible to many people that a five-page brief could be the end result of many hours' work or that the numerous papers involved in even simple litigation serve an indispensable purpose for the courts in framing the issues. Nor do the lawyer's concerns in protecting his client always seem worthwhile to the client. Sometimes, for example, a person who is in the process of buying a house can't understand why his lawyer gets concerned over a "defect in title" (see section 284), and so perhaps thinks that he is deliberately building up a fee.

In addition, for a great many years, and especially in the cities, there were too many lawyers and too few good ones. The result was that poor and uneducated people were often victimized by lawyers who were guilty of ambulance chasing, inciting litigation or exaggerating their clients' problems in order to increase the size of their fees.

Perhaps hypersensitive to the layman's resentment over legal fees, lawyers have too often sought to duck the issue by failing to discuss fees frankly with prospective clients. Granted that the lawyer who is asked what he would charge for drawing "a simple will" never knows what complications may arise—particularly in these days of multiple marriages for many—and that the lawyer who is asked what is the fair fee for an "uncomplicated matrimonial action" knows there is no such thing. Nevertheless, many lawyers are reluctant to give an estimate, just because they fear that subsequent talks with the client will turn up unforeseen complications in what at first seemed a simple matter, and they will have to put in many hours more work than they had originally expected to—at a greatly increased cost to the client.

627. Basic Fees and Expenses • Because of all the considerations discussed in the previous section, the *only* way to minimize misunderstandings with your lawyer about the fee he is going to charge you is to discuss it with him at the start. To get an idea of what lawyers in your community are likely to charge for various routine services, ask friends what they have been charged and consult local banks and real estate brokers.

You should keep in mind that lawyers are entitled to and do charge you for expenses (called *disbursements*) they may have in handling your problems. Suppose your husband deserts you and you get a judgment ordering him to pay you so much a month for your and your children's support. But he has fled to another state. Your lawyer will have to get in touch with a lawyer in that state and have him go to court there to get the order enforced. Several telephone calls may be necessary. Travel costs, meals away from the office and special postage payments may also be needed. These are typical disbursements, the total amount of which he will list on his bill. The same, of course, is true regarding fees he has to pay the court on your behalf; these fees are prescribed by law and are properly charged to you.

628. Paying by the Hour • If your legal problem is unusual or will require a large amount of your lawyer's time, a minimum fee schedule will not help you or him in reaching an understanding on how his fee is to be determined. Sometimes you and he may find it mutually agreeable for his charge to be based on a stated dollar amount for each hour he devotes to your affairs. Lawyers keep careful track of their time, and this method of charging is a relatively simple one to use.

But you should be sophisticated about it. You may end up paying the lawyer who will charge you only $25 an hour a great deal more than the one who charges $50 an hour. Inexperience or lack of competence in the area of your particular legal difficulty may require the former to spend much more than twice as many hours as the latter. A lawyer who is a well-known expert in income tax matters will charge much more than the lawyer who does tax work along with other kinds of law, but the expert may save you money by a quicker analysis of your problem and a more ingenious solution. The size of the fee will in each case reflect the nature or difficulty of your legal problem, the lawyer's reputation and experience, his overhead in running his office and the result achieved.

629. The Retainer • Some lawyers will ask you to make a small "down payment" toward the fee when you and he agree that he is to represent you. You are retaining him as your lawyer, which means he agrees to work exclusively for you in the matter for which you consulted him—drawing a will or a contract, examining the lease you are about to sign, suing someone who has injured or wronged you—and you pay him a *retainer* as proof of your own good faith and willingness and ability to pay him for his services to you. The word *retainer* is also used to describe the method of payment to a lawyer by a company or a corporation that knows it will have frequent occasion to use him over a period of time. The company agrees to pay the lawyer a fixed amount on a regular basis, such as every month or every three months, so as to be able to consult him—to the exclusion of others—whenever it wants to.

630. Contingent Fees • It often happens, particularly when court action or litigation is involved, that you don't have the money to pay your lawyer in advance for the time he must spend in preparing your case for trial and in conducting the trial. Also, litigation is always something of a gamble; the law is seldom black or white, and juries are unpredictable. What seems an ironclad case in your favor when you discuss it in the calm of your lawyer's office may turn out to be something very different when it gets into the court. There is a method of paying your lawyer under these circumstances, called a *contingent fee:* your lawyer gets all or part of his fee only if his efforts on your behalf are successful.

Contingent fee arrangements have caused much discussion in the legal profession. Many lawyers frown on them because they are likely to encourage litigation rather than to discourage it. A lawyer will be severely censured and may even be disbarred (see section 637) if he is found guilty of *champerty* and *maintenance,* which mean stirring up and sometimes actually financing litigation himself. It is unethical and illegal for a lawyer to indulge in such practices.

Despite the misgivings of some lawyers, much litigation in the United States is conducted on a contingent fee basis, especially in the accident or negligence field. The situation in which you are injured in an automobile accident and have to pay $5,000 for medical and hospital bills, with little, if any, money left over to pay a lawyer, is fairly typical. When you locate a lawyer and discuss your case with him and he says he thinks the law is on your side, you may want to pay him something then and there—a retainer—and agree to pay him the balance from the amount he recovers for you from the person who injured you. This retainer should also include a part of the anticipated costs of the lawsuit, such as court fees. The balance is often one third of the amount recovered. If he recovers $5,000 you will keep two thirds of $5,000 less the amount of your lawyer's expenses and court costs. Under these circumstances the contingent fee arrangement is perfectly proper. You sought out your lawyer after the injury; you obtained his professional advice and paid him a small part of the larger fee he was to receive if the litigation was successful.

Contingent fee arrangements are approved by courts and by bar associations so long as everything is made clear at the start and so long as the percentage your lawyer is to receive from the amount recovered is reasonable: one third is a common arrangement that is widely used and approved, whereas a higher percentage is not only frowned upon but is illegal in some states.

631. If You Are Not Satisfied • Clients will occasionally try to avoid paying their lawyers, usually because of dissatisfaction with their services. Such efforts are generally unsuccessful. The lawyer has an *attorney's lien* on his client's property in his possession, for the amount owed him by the client. Until you pay him for his services, your lawyer has a lien or claim on any papers you left with him, on any money you gave him to finance your litigation and on any money he received by way of settlement. To obtain the return of your papers, you must go to court and establish that the fee your lawyer wants to charge, or has charged, is excessive or unfair in view of the services he has rendered.

WORKING WITH YOUR LAWYER

632. Your Confidential Relationship with Your Lawyer • Once you have determined that you need a lawyer to handle your general interests or a particular matter, made your choice of the lawyer whom you wish to represent you and discussed with him and agreed on his fee and the method of payment, you must keep in mind one more very important concern. That is the quality of the working relationship between you and your lawyer—how best you and he can function together and establish the degree of harmony that is most profitable to you.

The general principles that should always govern your lawyer in the practice of his profession are clearly set forth in section 637. The most important obligation that he takes on with his representation of you, in addition to listening carefully to your requirements and giving you his full time and attention when he is working with you or for you, is to keep secret and inviolate anything and everything that he learns about your private affairs while he represents you. This includes information you give him not only during face-to-face consultations but also in telephone conferences and by correspondence and information that he derives from projects that he undertakes on your behalf, such as the results of research or the investigation of witnesses.

This confidential relationship applies not only to your lawyer personally but to others in his firm, whether they are his partners or his secretaries or stenographic help. In other words, you have the right to assume, if you are represented by a competent and reputable attorney, that anything and everything that you tell him or ask him to do is absolutely confidential unless you authorize him to disclose it to somebody else. It is the same kind of relationship that you have with your doctor.

633. Giving Your Lawyer the Facts • How can you cooperate with your lawyer in order to achieve the best working relationship with him? For one thing, you should at all times be completely honest and open with him and disclose to him every fact that is relevant to the situation you are discussing. You should not be the one to judge whether a fact is legally significant or whether your interests will be better served by concealing it from your lawyer. He cannot do a thorough job for you unless he knows everything you know that bears on the situation. You must then have confidence in his ability to do two things: to screen what is relevant from what is not relevant and to keep in confidence everything that you have told him. This applies whether you are talking about a contract or a lease negotiation, the defense of a criminal or tort suit or any other problem about which you are consulting him. To the extent that you fail to disclose information to your lawyer, you are acting as your own attorney—a grave mistake—and you may be damaging your own position in the matter he is handling for you.

634. Taking Your Lawyer's Advice • A second principle for working well with your lawyer is to follow his advice. You shouldn't go to a lawyer in the first place unless you believe that you need his special knowledge and skills and unless he has been recommended to you. This principle carries even more weight when your relationship with your lawyer has become well established over a period of time. When you go to your family doctor to be treated, you would feel rather foolish if you didn't follow whatever advice he gave you. You would have wasted his time and your money. The same is true of a lawyer.

Only in unusual instances would it be a better course not to follow a lawyer's advice: if, for example, you had spoken to four lawyers and three had recommended one course of action and the fourth another; or if a friend of yours in a similar situation has been given advice that is diametrically opposed to the advice your lawyer gave you. But in most situations you should either stay with your lawyer and take his advice or find another lawyer.

A strong temptation to ignore your lawyer's advice might arise if he advised you not to discuss a specific legal problem with anybody but him. If the matter involved is a marital problem where the husband and wife feud, for example, it is quite likely that the client would be advised not to discuss it at all with his spouse, not to conduct his own negotiations and not to engage in any conflict until the lawyers have settled the matter. This might be true whether the parties were still living together or had already separated. If the client should reject this advice and continue to negotiate or to get into lengthy arguments with his wife, he might increase the bad feeling between the parties, creating more work for his lawyer over a longer period of time and resulting in higher fees and a postponement of the final settlement.

635. Respecting Your Lawyer's Time • Be considerate of your lawyer. Realize that all he has to sell is time. Avoid telephoning him unnecessarily or about trivial matters. Don't try to second-guess him and don't fall into the habit of rearguing points with him. When you make dates with him keep them, and be on time. If you are late for an appointment, he might not be able to fill that time at a last minute's notice. In this respect his situation is different from a doctor's. The doctor will often have a waiting room full of patients, so that several people are ready to follow in turn after the previous patient has finished his business.

But a lawyer usually doesn't operate that way. He may have reserved a half hour or an hour for you, and no other client will be waiting at that time to see him. His situation is like that of a music teacher who has spaced his pupils at half-hour or hour intervals. If the pupil does not appear or arrives late, there is nothing that the teacher can do to make up for the lost time. Yet if he were then to bill the pupil for this time, some resentment would arise. In the same way you put the lawyer on the spot if you are careless of his time.

636. When You Don't Understand Something • Don't hesitate to ask your lawyer for a complete and detailed discussion of the matter at hand.

You may not understand the language of certain legal pleadings or of wills, leases and contracts. These instruments are not written primarily for the comprehension of the client himself, but rather so their meaning will be unmistakably clear to other lawyers and to the courts. Even though a contract might be technical in its wording, if it expresses what you want and what is in your best interest, the lawyer has done a good job. Similarly, the two lawyers on opposite sides of the negotiation are primarily concerned with expressing exactly what has been agreed upon.

Since it is not to be expected that you understand this technical language, you shouldn't be shy about asking the lawyer what the words mean. You need not accept an explanation such as "Well, this is a standard form," or "This is what we always do," without receiving the lawyer's explanation of the meaning of the words so that you can judge for yourself whether they are applicable to the situation. Conversely, don't be picayune and insist on an explanation of every sentence in every paragraph on every page.

The important thing is the maintenance of this delicate balance. You want reasonable assurance as to what has been stated without feeling that you are making too much of a nuisance of yourself. From the lawyer's point of view, he should always feel that his client is pleased with the work that has been done and he should not resent your desire to get a reasonable interpretation of the work product.

637. Legal Ethics and Disbarment • If you should have the rare and unpleasant experience in which you believe you are not being properly treated or represented by your lawyer, you may of course change to another one—as you may change your doctor or accountant. You will probably have to pay your original lawyer what you owe him for the services he has rendered to you, however unsatisfactory you may think them to be (see section 631).

If you believe your lawyer's conduct has been improper, unethical or illegal, you are entitled to complain. As a guide to you in deciding whether you want to complain, the canons of the Code of Professional Responsibility adopted by the American Bar Association are printed here.

Canon 1. A lawyer should assist in maintaining the integrity and competence of the legal profession.
Canon 2. A lawyer should assist the legal profession in fulfilling its duty to make legal counsel available.

Canon 3. A lawyer should assist in preventing the unauthorized practice of law.

Canon 4. A lawyer should preserve the confidences and secrets of a client.

Canon 5. A lawyer should exercise independent professional judgment on behalf of a client.

Canon 6. A lawyer should represent a client competently.

Canon 7. A lawyer should represent a client zealously within the bounds of the law.

Canon 8. A lawyer should assist in improving the legal system.

Canon 9. A lawyer should avoid even the appearance of professional impropriety.

Here are some of the basic principles of legal ethics: An attorney should never take advantage of his client's confidence in order to realize some personal benefit or gain. He should promptly account for any money or property or funds belonging to the client that come into his possession. He must not mingle his client's funds with his own money. Of course, he may never disclose any information about his client's affairs that he learned in confidence while working with the client. He should accept no compensation of any kind from others involved in a case without telling his own client, nor should he do so without his client's consent if that compensation is related to the case in any way that would be hostile to his client's interests. He should never buy an interest in the subject matter of any litigation that he is conducting or in which he is advising. He always has a duty, if it is possible, to seek a fair settlement of a case rather than to promote litigation to the end. When he is retained by a client, or if the situation should arise at a later date, he has a duty to tell the client of any relationship he may have to other parties involved in a case and of any possible conflict of interest that he senses may have arisen or may arise in the future.

Generally speaking, an attorney should never be a witness for his own client, on any matter which is material to the case. If he finds it necessary to do so, he should turn over the case to some other counsel so that he can be free to act just as a witness. The lawyer should use his best efforts to prevent his client from doing things of which the lawyer does not approve or which the lawyer knows the client ought not to do—particularly with reference to the client's conduct toward the court, jurors, witnesses or opposing parties.

This code is enforced by local bar associations around the country; they receive complaints about the conduct of lawyers in their area and conduct hearings if they believe the facts justify doing so. The vast majority of lawyers will do everything possible to avoid unfavorable publicity or censure by their fellow lawyers. In the rare case in which a lawyer's conduct is a clear violation of professional ethics, the bar association will go to court to seek an order censuring the lawyer or even disbarring him. A lawyer who has been disbarred can no longer practice before the court. He has lost his principal means of making a living, and the courts are understandably reluctant to punish him so severely unless there is no justification for his conduct.

638. Practicing Law Without a License • There is a difference between the unethical or unprofessional conduct we discussed in the previous section and what is called the unlawful practice of law. Simply stated, unlawful practice is practice by persons who are not licensed to practice, that is, who are not lawyers. A person who has not been licensed to practice law is guilty of unlawful practice if he gives legal advice or prepares legal documents and charges for these services.

Persons who are most likely to slip into unlawful practice are accountants and others who advise people about income tax matters. Preparing an income tax return is not practicing law. But advising someone about his income tax liability under one or more provisions of the Internal Revenue Code may be, and some courts have held it to be illegal. Again, as in the case of unethical conduct, it is the local bar association that takes responsibility for proceeding against the accountant who oversteps the boundary between his and the legal profession and that monitors others who from time to time spill over into the legal field—such as banks and trust companies that occasionally prepare clauses for inclusion in their customers' wills. The decision as to whether an unauthorized person is actually practicing law is one that the court must decide on the basis of the facts in each case.

639. When a Lawyer Breaks the Law • A lawyer whose conduct is illegal, as distinguished from unethical, is liable to prosecution like any other person accused of breaking the law. Champerty and maintenance (see section 630) are criminal offenses, which the local district attorney or public prosecutor will take action to stop if the offenses can be proved. The lawyer who extorts money from his client by blackmail or any other kind of duress or who fails properly to account to his client for money the client paid him or for money received for the client is equally subject to prosecution. A license to practice law is no cloak of immunity from violation of any law.

740

640. Legal Malpractice Suits • Recent years have seen the increase in another sort of control over lawyers, a control exercised by clients in the form of malpractice suits. Doctors have been the subject of these suits more than lawyers. Nevertheless, many lawyers now take out insurance against loss to their clients from a variety of causes: loss of important documents, perhaps because a secretary carelessly threw them in the wastebasket; failure to appear in court on the right day, resulting in loss of a lawsuit; and losses caused by the lawyer's malpractice—that is, by his failure to exercise the standard of care common among lawyers of his stature in the community where he practices.

But you should think carefully before making public charges against a lawyer. His reputation is vital to his professional life, and he is entitled to protect himself when he is slandered. Your best course if you feel aggrieved by his conduct is to have your differences out with him. If you get no satisfaction, then discuss your complaint with the local bar association or the public prosecutor. They will tell you whether your complaint is well founded and give you guidance as to how to proceed.

How to Become a Lawyer

641. Preparing for a Legal Education • These sections of You and the Law are written primarily for the guidance of the younger reader who may be thinking about becoming a lawyer. But we hope they will also interest those who wonder about how lawyers are trained.

The time to start thinking seriously about law is during your college years. On most college campuses you will find prelaw counselors who can advise you what courses to take before going to law school and tell you something about different law schools. As to college courses, your best procedure is to take as many so-called liberal arts courses as possible: courses in English, literature, history, philosophy, government, politics and economics. You should try to obtain some familiarity with the arts. A broad range of knowledge should be your stock in trade: as a lawyer you never know what sort of problem in what sort of field you will encounter through your clients. It will help if you can find summer employment as a trainee or an intern in one of the many governmental agencies that now employ students on a temporary basis—in Washington, D.C., or with your state, municipal or county government.

642. Applying to a Law School • Toward the end of your college career you should file applications for admission to several law schools. The reason more than one application is necessary is that the competition for admission is already severe, and it is growing, because the applicants include not only future practicing lawyers but young people who plan to enter other fields such as social service or government. There are some 150 accredited law schools in the United States. The great majority of them require you to obtain a college degree before entering law school, although some permit you to combine your last year of college with your first year of law school.

Two categories of schools exist side by side: law schools attached to state universities and schools that are part of private universities. Two distinguishing characteristics—but not the only ones—are the size of the student body and the faculty-student ratio. In general the state schools are the larger ones. Publicly supported, they are required to accept many more students than are private schools. Ask yourself whether you prefer a large academic community or a relatively small one. The larger law schools will have several hundred students in each year's class; smaller schools range in size from 125 to 175 per class.

643. What Our Law Schools Teach • State university law schools tend to concentrate on the traditional law courses: contracts, torts, constitutional law, procedure, property, wills, trust and estates, corporation, partnerships, agency, international law, maritime law, labor law, administrative law. Private law schools, since they are somewhat smaller and generally enjoy a higher proportion of faculty to students, can afford to offer a wider variety of courses, particularly in new, developing fields. The catalogs of these schools list courses or seminars in such areas as psychiatry and law, law and sociology, urban law, poverty law, environmental law, urban finance, land planning, and so on. The titles of the courses are often misleading, because much of the material covered in them was previously covered in other courses with less glamorous titles. Inquire, to be sure the material covered is what you want.

Whether the law school you choose is public or private, large or small, traditional or novel in its approach to law, there is no other program of graduate study that is so sweeping in the range of subjects covered. One reason lawyers are found in so many of the most sensitive spots in American political and economic life is simply that their legal education has exposed them to a broader range of public problems than any other graduate program.

644. Practical Experience While You Are in Law School • More than ever before, law schools today offer you an opportunity to apply your legal skills as you acquire them, to use what you learn as you learn it. Schools all over the country now have programs under which you can spend time while in law school working for the city's legal aid department or the public defender organization. You are also given opportunities to work with governmental agencies in drafting legislation, codes and regulations. During the summertime you will find many jobs available in government offices. The summer after your second year at law school—or perhaps even after the first year—you may have the chance to go to work in a law firm, to see at first hand what these firms do and how they do it. Some of these firms use summer employment as an opportunity to look over promising newcomers to the profession. By the time you graduate from law school, at the end of three years' study, you will have been exposed to the practical side of the legal profession far more than any students have been since law schools, as we now know them, developed toward the end of the last century. Then you sat in a chair and listened to lectures and took examinations. You'll still listen to lectures—but in addition you have the opportunity for a great deal of practical experience that will make you a better, more knowledgeable lawyer.

645. State Bar Examinations • Most of our law schools do not try to teach you the "law" of one state or another; they concentrate on teaching you legal principles, legal reasoning and something of the philosophy of law. When you graduate, you must take a bar examination given by public authorities of the state you expect to live in and where you intend to practice the law you have learned. In almost every state there are lawyers who offer cram courses in the law of that state. These lay down the law for you, with no ifs or buts. Law school courses are general; the cram courses are detailed and specific. Also, the cram course teaches you the procedures to be followed in using the state courts—something many of the better law schools do not try to cover. The length of the course is usually about six weeks.

You must then take the state bar examination, which is usually given to large groups two or three times a year. If you pass it (about 50 percent succeed on the first try), you must appear before a committee that examines your character and fitness to become a member of the bar. Your record will be examined at length. You must reveal any legal troubles you have encountered at any time in your life. Minor troubles such as traffic violations or fines for breaking windows during a spree at college will not be held against you. But a conviction for having committed a felony will in all likelihood prevent your being admitted to practice, as will membership in any subversive group or organization, unless you can explain it away as something you did when you were young and foolish and show that you have long since resigned.

646. Getting Started in Private Practice · The number of ways in which you can, directly or indirectly, put your legal education to use is large. The most obvious is to practice law in the traditional sense, either by yourself or with one or more other lawyers. If you want to make as much money as possible, you should go to work in a large law firm. The figures are unanswerable: the larger the law office, the higher the income of the lawyers in the office. Large firms, with from 100 to 200 lawyers, are found in the country's major cities with populations of over a million. But if you neither need nor want the maximum possible income, smaller firms offer many advantages. You are your own boss to a greater extent and can engage in outside or community activities somewhat more easily. To try to practice by yourself is extremely difficult unless the community is very small. You cannot be an expert in all branches of the law; you cannot be in your office all day long every day of the year. It is enormously helpful to have at least a few fellow lawyers to help you handle your clients when you're ill or on vacation, and simply to exhange ideas with. Also, there is unquestioned benefit in having the advice and assistance of an older lawyer as you start your career.

If traditional legal practice doesn't appeal to you, consider the alternatives. One is to go to work for the legal department of a corporation. A corporation offers you about as much money as you might expect from a large law firm, quite a variety of commercial and real estate work, and financial security with pensions and other fringe benefits.

647. Legal Jobs with Government · Another alternative is government work—whether federal, state or local. The number of governmental jobs is enormous and their variety great. Practically every department and agency of the federal government has its own legal division or general counsel. The work is more of an advisory and policy-making kind than it is in actual practice. Very few governmental agencies actually litigate, that is, go to court. The "lawyer" for the U.S. government is the attorney general of the United States and his assistants around the country, called U.S. attorneys. The U.S. attorneys are the ones who prosecute civil and criminal cases for the government and who defend the government in lawsuits brought against it. A few years' service in one of these U.S. attorneys' offices will be of great help to you, particularly if you plan to be a litigating lawyer.

Because the structure of state government closely resembles that of the U.S. government, you will find similar openings for lawyers in state government departments and agencies. Because state governments are smaller, the openings are fewer. And salaries are lower. But legal positions are available in a variety of state offices, although political party membership is likely to be a factor in obtaining the most challenging positions. The "lawyer" for the state government is, again, the attorney general of the state. But in most states the public prosecutor, who handles violations of state criminal laws, is a local official and not directly responsible to the attorney general.

Local governments also use the services of lawyers in all sorts of positions—in the corporation counsel's office, which is the mayor's legal adviser, and in agencies such as the board of education, the welfare department, the housing and urban renewal departments. Excellent trial experience may be obtained in the county and municipal prosecutors' offices, at salaries that are gradually becoming more competitive with legal jobs in law firms, corporations and with the various agencies and departments of the federal government.

648. Clerking for a State or Federal Judge • As you approach graduation from law school, you may be unsure about which of the many available career opportunities you'd like to choose. If your law school record has been strong, you may qualify for a position for a year or two as clerk to a federal or state judge. Judges are so busy, and the volume of litigation has grown so fast, that they are increasingly resorting to the use of young law school graduates to do their legal research for them and to draft analyses and memorandums of the legal points in the cases that come before them. All federal judges now are entitled to two law clerks, and many states are now according the same privilege to state court judges. These clerkships offer an excellent opportunity for the student to acquire experience from a seasoned lawyer. State court jobs, though, tend to go to students with good political connections.

Clerkship is well regarded throughout the profession. The large law firms that you may want to enter after a year of clerking will pay you the same salary as if you had entered the firm directly from law school and had done well and received a bonus or salary increase at the end of your first year. Many lawyers believe that if on graduation you know you want

745

to practice you would be well advised to start off at once. But for the present, the judicial clerkship with a fine judge is much to be desired and the competition is increasingly stiff, for understandable reasons. Your law school experience, even today, is mainly theoretical, and in great part your law teachers are not practicing lawyers. To combine your formal legal education with apprenticeship under a leader of the bar is in many cases most worthwhile.

649. Teaching Law • A clerkship with an appellate court judge will help if your legal career goal is to teach law. Much of the instructional material used in law schools consists of decisions by judges in appellate courts. Law schools believe the clerkship experience with such a judge gives you the kind of training that is particularly helpful in teaching law. They also like you to have some experience as a practicing lawyer.

The academic side of the legal profession has much to recommend it. As a law professor you have considerable freedom of action. You can engage in a variety of activities apart from teaching, including giving advice to public and private agencies and companies, serving on public commissions and working with practicing lawyers on problems that come within the area in which you specialize.

650. Public Service Jobs • You have probably read in the papers of the many ways that younger lawyers in particular are trying to serve persons who are too poor to afford their own lawyers. Earlier in this chapter, in section 622, we indicated the kinds of public legal services that are now available to the very poor, such as legal aid and public defender offices.

Young lawyers are also providing free counsel to persons who are accused of narcotics law violations, whose defense is not only unpopular but requires knowledge of technical statutes and procedures with which many lawyers are unfamiliar. But not all such offenders are unable to afford legal services, and law offices are being established by younger lawyers to serve these clients.

651. Where You May Practice • Remember that your admission to the bar—your license to practice—in one state does not entitle you to practice in another state. Some states have reciprocal arrangements permitting lawyers who have practiced in one state for a specified number of years to be admitted to practice in the other by making a request or motion to the appropriate court. But these arrangements are few in number and growing fewer. However, the rules are somewhat more relaxed if you are a trial lawyer and your client sues in another state. What usually happens is that you retain a lawyer in that state to work with you as co-counsel. He then asks the court to give you permission to work with him on the case, and you appear in court with him. How much of the court case each of you handles is decided by the two of you.

Your admission to practice in the courts of your own state does not automatically entitle you to practice in the United States courts, even in your own state. However, such permission is granted upon your request so long as your reputation and character are satisfactory. Similarly, to practice or appear before the U.S. Supreme Court, you must make a special application, often through the office of your representative in Congress, if he is a lawyer, or through any other lawyer who already practices before it. These applications are as a rule granted routinely.

In Closing: The Lawyer in Our Society

We hope this book has persuaded you that the law is, in the words of one of our greatest judges, Oliver Wendell Holmes, "not a brooding omnipresence in the sky," but rather an ever-present force for order that holds the innumerable parts of society together.

No society can function without rules, nor does any society run smoothly all the time. There are bound to be frictions and difficulties between neighbors, between businessmen and their competitors, between husbands and wives and employers and employes. It is the lawyer's job to help us to apply the rules in these situations: to avoid trouble where we can and to resolve conflicts fairly where we cannot.

Because our society is complex and gives rise to many intricate problems, the lawyer with his special training is essential to its continuing operation and to our own well-being. Most lawyers spend most of their time helping with our everyday problems, counseling us on business or personal matters, drawing documents like contracts, wills, deeds and leases. In contributing to the orderly conduct of our affairs and the orderly solution of our problems, they are in a real sense the glue that holds society together. They put the rules of law to work. They are the referees who prevent the game from degenerating into a brawl.

In addition to smoothing the progress of our personal and business dealings, lawyers have another important role in the control of crime.

Men and women are not tranquil and peace-loving by nature. Even in an organized, "civilized" society they lie and cheat, steal and fight and all too often kill. Laws are written to provide penalties for these acts. Courts are established to hear charges of such conduct and impose the penalties if the charges are proved. Lawyers are trained and licensed to help you obtain the full protection of the laws, on the one hand, and, on the other to make sure that if you do violate the law, you are convicted only of the offense you actually committed and that the penalty imposed on you is no greater than the law provides.

It is the duty of your lawyer to employ every proper method of asserting your rights. Every person accused of having committed a crime, every person whose civil rights have been violated, is entitled to legal advice and representation. Hopefully, the legal profession in the United States will some day provide legal services to all who need them.

The demand for lawyers' services is steadily growing. Tensions among various groups in society result in lawlessness that requires more lawyers than ever in the criminal courts. Governmental programs in areas where there were none a few years ago—such as the protection of consumers against fraud and the control of pollution of the environment (see chapter 13, "Environmental Law," page 709)—also require new lawyers.

The increasing concentration of the country's population in and around cities has created a host of urban problems where lawyers are required to help both in devising solutions and in advising people affected by the problems. These people are often at or near the poverty level, yet their need of legal services is constant and great. New and imaginative programs are being developed to make legal services available to them. These programs of course require lawyers, who until recently have not been available.

The growing complexity of the income and estate tax laws (see sections 571–83) makes it increasingly difficult for persons who have the gift of making money to hold on to it and to pass it on to their families. Lawyers are more in demand here than ever before.

There is scarcely an area of American life in the last third of this century in which social and political and economic developments are not increasing the demand for lawyers. We hope we have helped you to get a sense of the many problems in which you need a lawyer and of how to go about finding one. If your problem is outside his area of direct knowledge or experience, he knows better than anyone where to send you for advice. Find a lawyer whom you trust, and consult him when you see trouble approaching that you probably will be unable to handle yourself.

Glossary

GLOSSARY

This glossary contains definitions of some of the legal terms you are most likely to encounter. For more detail or background information about an expression, refer to the numbered section or sections of *You and the Law* indicated in the definition. Key words that appear in SMALL CAPITAL LETTERS are defined elsewhere in the glossary.

abandonment (1) The giving up of property or of a right, with the intent of never reclaiming it. (2) In divorce or family law, willfully leaving children or a spouse without intending to return (see sections 327, 361).

abate To decrease, reduce, remove or destroy. For example, *to abate* a legacy is to decrease or reduce it because of a deficiency in the funds out of which it is to be paid; *to abate* a nuisance is to remove or destroy the thing that causes it.

abdication The act of a person who voluntarily gives up or renounces a throne, an office, a function or a trust.

abduction (1) The carrying away, by force or fraudulent persuasion, of a wife, child or ward. (2) The unlawful taking away or detention of a female, in most cases one under a prescribed minimum age, for purposes of prostitution or marriage.

abet To incite or encourage someone to commit a crime.

ab initio A Latin phrase meaning "from the beginning." To say that a marriage was unlawful *ab initio,* or a contract void *ab initio,* means that the marriage or the contract never had any validity.

abortion The expulsion of a human fetus before the time when the fetus is capable of sustaining an independent life. In many states abortion is a crime. Specific conditions for legal abortion are established by state law (see section 125).

abrogate To repeal, annul or abolish. A law, for example, is *abrogated* by legislative action, constitutional authority or usage.

abscond To go secretly out of a court's jurisdiction or to hide within the jurisdiction in order to avoid legal proceedings.

abstract of title An abridged history of the title to a piece of land, recording all the conveyances, transfers, liabilities, covenants against or burdens upon the land and other facts pertinent to such title that would be of interest to a prospective purchaser (see section 284).

abuse (1) The destruction of the substance of something in using it, as by misuse, injury, wearing away or lessening in value. (2) Any act of a corporation that is in violation of its charter and detracts from the public right. (3) Sometimes used as equivalent to rape.

Abuse of discretion refers to a legal conclusion by a judge that is not justified by reason, evidence or legal precedent and is clearly against them.

Abuse of process refers to the malicious use of a regular legal proceeding for a purpose which it is not intended to effect (see section 40).

abut To touch, border upon, be contiguous to. For example, one might say that "two estates *abut*," that "a bridge *abuts* against a pier," that "a lot *abuts* an improvement." Although the word usually refers to things that actually adjoin, it is not an inflexible term and sometimes is used more loosely to imply close proximity.

abutting owner An owner of property that touches, is contiguous to or, more loosely, is in close proximity to other property.

acceptance The receiving of something offered with the intention of keeping it, such receipt generally being considered an unspoken agreement to some earlier act or understanding. For example, *acceptance* of a delivery of furniture means that the person who accepts it makes himself liable to pay the price that had been agreed upon with the furniture store. *Acceptance* of an offer is essential to the existence of a contract (see section 174).

access In real property law, the legal right of a landowner whose land adjoins a road to go to and return from his land to the road without being obstructed.

accession (1) Coming into possession of an office or right. (2) Acquisition by a property owner of something added to that property, by growth, labor or the like. Shrubs planted by a tenant become the property of the owner of the land by *accession*.

accessory A person who, although not necessarily present, is involved, either before or after, in the commission of a felony (see section 91).

An *accessory before the fact* is one who incites, advises or encourages another to commit a felony.

An *accessory after the fact* is one who knows that a crime has been committed but conceals his knowledge and protects or assists the person who is accused of it.

accommodation An arrangement, such as a loan, made by one person as a favor to another.

An *accommodation paper* is a note or bill endorsed, drawn or accepted by one person, not for any CONSIDERATION, but as an act of friendship toward the person who wishes to raise money on it.

accomplice A person who participates in the commission of a crime, either as a PRINCIPAL or as an ACCESSORY (see section 91).

accord and satisfaction An agreement between two persons for the delivery and acceptance of something, usually worth less than the amount legally owed or enforceable, in settlement of a debt or as damages for a wrong (see section 182).

account stated An account rendered by a creditor and acknowledged as correct by his debtor.

accused A person charged with a crime or misdemeanor; the defendant in a criminal case.

acknowledgment The formal declaration by a person, before a competent authority such as a notary, that his signature on a legal document is his free act and deed.

acquit (1) To release or discharge from a liability, obligation or engagement. (2) To release from a criminal charge by judicial action.

act (1) An enactment passed by a legislative body; a law or statute. (2) A determination or decision, as a decree or award, made in writing by a court.

action A judicial proceeding to enforce or protect a right, to redress or prevent a wrong or to punish a public offense. An action can be a civil lawsuit or a criminal prosecution (see section 35).

An *action in personam* is against a specific person, arising out of an obligation owed by him personally.

An *action in rem* asserts a right in a specific thing.

actionable Giving legal grounds for an action, as trespass, slander, breach of contract.

act of God An event that happens purely through the operation of nature unmixed with any human agency or human negligence (see section 244).

ad damnum A Latin phrase meaning "to the damage." It refers to that clause in a declaration, writ or pleading which states the damages demanded by the plaintiff.

ademption An act by which a testator, during his lifetime, satisfies or revokes a legacy that had been set forth in his will. The testator, while he is still alive, may give to a legatee whatever he has provided for him in his will, or he may dispose of the legacy in such a manner as to make impossible the carrying out of the legacy provision.

ad hoc A Latin phrase meaning "for this," that is, for a particular purpose. An attorney *ad hoc* or an *ad hoc* committee is one appointed for a particular purpose.

ad interim A Latin phrase meaning "in the meantime." When an official is temporarily absent or incapacitated, an officer *ad interim* may be appointed to discharge his duties until the official returns.

adjective law That branch of the law which deals with rules of practice or procedure, providing a method to enforce or maintain rights and to obtain redress if they are violated.

adjournment The act of putting off, postponing or suspending business or a session, either temporarily or indefinitely. An indefinite or final adjournment is said to be *sine die,* from Latin "without a (set) day."

adjudication (1) The pronouncement of a judgment or decree by a court. (2) The judgment so given.

adjuster A person whose job is to set right, arrange or settle a matter; especially, a person employed by an insurance company who investigates and settles claims for personal injury or property damage (see section 484).

753

administration (1) The direction or management of any office, business, institution or the like; also, in public law, the direction and management of the executive department of the government. (2) The legal management and settlement of the estate of a deceased person, as by an executor (see section 590). (3) The management of the estate of a minor, lunatic or someone legally incompetent for other reasons, by an appointed trustee, guardian or committee (see sections 345, 356).

administrative law That branch of the law which deals with various agencies of the government, prescribing what they are supposed to do and how they are supposed to do it (see section 9).

administrator (*m.*) or **administratrix** (*f.*) A person granted authority by a proper court to administer the estate of a deceased person (see section 556).

admiralty law That branch of the law which deals with maritime affairs, civil and criminal. Admiralty law is the law of the sea and is handled by the federal courts.

admissible Of such a nature that the court or judge must allow it to be introduced, as certain evidence or testimony.

admission In criminal law, the acknowledgment of a fact or circumstance that may tend to prove the offense charged, but that does not involve criminal intent and therefore is not considered a confession of guilt.

adoption Voluntarily taking a child of other parents into one's family and giving him or her all the rights, privileges and duties of one's own child. An adoption must be authorized by a court according to state law (see sections 346–354 and chart 24, page 394).

adult In common law, a person who has attained his or her age of majority, usually twenty-one years, although in some states a woman attains her majority at eighteen. In most states you must be an adult to enter into a contract or to start or defend a legal action. See also AGE OF CONSENT. (See sections 137, 176 and chart 28, page 428.)

adultery Voluntary sexual intercourse between a married person and someone who is not that person's spouse (see section 117).

advancement An irrevocable gift of money or property, either made by a parent to his child or used by the parent for the child's benefit, in anticipation of the share that the child will inherit in the parent's estate and with the intention that the amount of the gift will be deducted from that share. For details on inheritance, see chapter 12, page 637.

adversary proceeding An action at law that involves opposing parties; a contested action. Because each side can present its version of the facts and the law for impartial consideration, the adversary proceeding—or trial—is considered the foundation of our system of justice (see section 13).

adverse possession Occupancy of real property to which the occupier has no title, in continuous, open defiance of another person's legal title to it.

If adverse possession continues for a specified period set forth by law (see chart 19, page 346), title to the property may pass from the original owner to the person occupying it without the original owner having an opportunity for legal recourse (see section 302).

advisory opinion An opinion given by a judge or law officer (such as an attorney general) or by a court on a legal question that has been submitted by a government official or a legislative body. This function is non-judicial or extrajudicial because the question is not presented in a concrete case at law.

advocate A person who gives legal advice and aid, and pleads the cause of another person in a tribunal or court; a counselor; a lawyer.

affected with a public interest A phrase used to describe a business or property of such a kind or so employed that it is clearly devoted to the public use or interest.

affiant A person who makes and swears to an affidavit—a statement of fact for a legal purpose.

affidavit A voluntary statement or declaration of facts, written or printed and sworn to by the person making it before an officer authorized to administer oaths.

affirm To confirm, or ratify, or approve. An appellate court (one to which appeals are taken) may *affirm* a judgment or decree of a lower court.

aforesaid Mentioned before; already said.

a fortiori A Latin phrase meaning "by a stronger reason; all the more," used to make the argument that because one known fact exists, another less improbable fact, analogous to the first, must also exist.

age of consent (1) The age, varying in different states, when a person may legally enter into a marriage contract without the consent of parent or guardian. (2) The age, fixed by statute, at which a woman may consent to sexual intercourse and before which such intercourse constitutes the crime of statutory rape (see sections 307, 312 and chart 28, page 428).

age of majority Generally, the legal age when a person achieves the capacity for independent action and responsibility in personal affairs (see chart 28, page 428). See also ADULT, SUI JURIS.

agency The relationship of one person acting for or representing another, called the PRINCIPAL, by the latter's authority (see section 393).

agent Someone authorized by another person to act for him, as in the transaction of business or the management of property or the performance of miscellaneous tasks (see section 393).

aggravated assault A term used to describe (1) assault committed with the object of committing another crime beyond the assault itself, as, for example, assault with intent to commit robbery (see section 126), or (2) a particularly atrocious or heinous assault.

agreement (1) A "meeting of the minds," the understanding between

755

two or more parties in respect to some common purpose, such as the transfer from one to another of property, a right or a benefit. (2) A CONTRACT (see sections 166–185).

alderman In many U.S. cities, a member of a board of municipal officers, ranking below the mayor, or of the city's legislative body.

alibi A Latin word meaning "elsewhere." In criminal prosecution, an *alibi* is a defense by which the accused establishes or attempts to establish his innocence by showing that he was elsewhere than at the scene of the crime when it was committed.

alien In the United States, a foreign-born person who has not been naturalized under our Constitution and laws.

alienation of affections The act of intentionally causing a wife to withdraw her affection, society and comfort from her husband, or vice versa.

alimony The money allowance made to a woman from her husband's estate or income by court order to support her after her divorce or legal separation from him or while a divorce action is pending. The allowance provided for during the action is called *alimony pendente lite;* that provided for after judgment is called *permanent alimony.*

allegation The formal written statement by a party to a legal action, telling what he expects to prove in the case, whether for the plaintiff or for the defense.

allocate To apportion, allot, assign or set aside according to a predeter-

mined schedule or with some particular purpose in mind.

allotment A distribution, as of shares in a corporation to purchasers of such shares; apportionment; division.

allow (1) To grant as a right, privilege or share; give; allot. (2) To give consent to; approve; permit; sanction. (3) To make provision for; grant as a deduction or addition; abate; deduct.

ambulance chaser A lawyer or lawyer's agent who approaches victims of street accidents and tries to persuade them to institute lawsuits for damages. The term sometimes denotes anyone who solicits personal injury cases for an attorney or who directs injured persons to an attorney for a percentage of the recovery.

amendment (1) The act of altering or modifying a law, bill, motion or resolution; also, the alteration or modification so made. (2) The correction of an error or defect in any process, pleading or proceeding at law.

amicus curiae A Latin expression meaning "friend of the court." It designates (1) a person, usually an attorney, who volunteers information for the assistance of the court in regard to some matter of law of which the judge is doubtful or in error; or (2) a person who, although he has no legal standing in an action, is permitted to introduce evidence, authority or arguments to protect his interests.

amnesty A general pardon granted by a government to all or certain persons guilty of an offense (generally a political offense such as treason or rebellion) often before trial or conviction.

amortization The payment of an indebtedness, such as bonds or a mortgage, by installments or by a sinking fund (see section 292).

anarchy The absence of government; a condition of society in which there is neither law nor supreme power.

ancillary Subsidiary; auxiliary: used to describe a legal proceeding that depends upon or is auxiliary to another, principal proceeding.

Ancillary administration is the administration of a deceased person's estate in a state where he had property but which was not his fixed permanent residence.

annexation (1) The addition of new territory into a nation's boundaries. (2) The attachment of something to real property so that it becomes a part of it. If a tenant builds bookshelves in a house, they are *annexed* to it.

annuity A fixed amount of money, granted or bequeathed or contracted for, payable periodically for life or for a specified period.

annulment The act of making something legally void in respect to the past as well as to the future. When a marriage is *annulled,* the law considers that it never existed (see section 362).

answer (*n.*) A pleading by a defendant in a lawsuit that usually denies allegations of the plaintiff's complaint or admits them and states new matter in defense. (*v.*) To respond or reply to in defense. If a defendant fails to answer a summons or complaint, he may be found liable by default for damage claimed in it.

antenuptial settlement An agreement or contract made by a man and woman before their marriage, in which the interests and property rights of either or both of them are determined, or in which property is set aside for the benefit of the prospective husband or wife or both of them or for some other person, such as their children (see section 317).

antitrust acts Federal and state laws protecting commerce and trade from monopolies and illegal restraints.

appeal The taking of a case from a lower to a higher court for a review of the lower court's decision. An appeal is usually based on a claimed error of law by the lower court judge. In a civil case either party can appeal; in a criminal case only the convicted defendant can appeal (see sections 87, 156).

appearance The coming into court, in person or by a proper representative (usually the party's lawyer), of a party to a lawsuit, either as plaintiff or defendant.

appellant A person involved in a litigation who appeals a decision from a lower to a higher, or appellate, court for review.

appellate court A court that has the jurisdiction of reviewing appeals from lower courts and of affirming, reversing or modifying the lower court's decisions (see sections 7, 8).

appellee The party in a litigation against whom an appeal is taken; also called RESPONDENT.

757

apportionment The proportional assignment of rights or liabilities to several persons according to their respective interests in the subject matter involved; for example, the division of rent among a number of owners of a building.

appraisal An estimated value set on property by two qualified persons. It may not have the legal weight of an APPRAISEMENT.

appraisement A true valuation of property given by a qualified person or persons under the authority of a court or legislature.

apprehension The taking into custody of a person for the purpose of holding him to answer a criminal charge. The term is synonymous with ARREST in reference to criminal cases, but is not used, as arrest is, in reference to civil cases.

appurtenant Belonging, attached, annexed, incident, accessory, subsidiary or appended to something else more important. A right of way to a piece of land, for example, is *appurtenant* to the land in question.

a priori A Latin expression meaning "from what is before." The term is used in logic to describe a type of argument that proceeds from cause to effect or from an assumption to its logical conclusion.

arbitration The hearing and settlement of a dispute between opposing parties by a third party whose decision in the matter the contestants have agreed to accept. Statutory provisions sometimes permit court enforcement of arbitration awards (see section 78).

arraign To call into court a person indicted for crime, read the information, or INDICTMENT, to him and instruct him to plead guilty or not guilty. (For details on arraignment see section 152.)

arrangement The settlement of a dispute or matter of mutual concern; adjustment by agreement; a compromise between a debtor and his creditors that modifies his obligation to them—he might, for example, pay part of the debt or receive an extension of time in which to pay (see sections 460–462).

arrears An overdue and unpaid debt or liability; especially, a remainder after part of a debt has been paid.

arrest To seize a person and hold him by legal authority so that he may answer a criminal charge or civil demand (see sections 39, 152).

arrest of judgment The act of suspending or refusing to render judgment in an action at law or in a criminal case, after the court or the jury has given its verdict. An arrest of judgment is based on a defect in the trial record or in the pleadings that would render a judgment, if given, either erroneous or reversible.

arson At common law, the malicious burning of another person's occupied house or of a building adjacent to the house. Statutes in many states extend the crime of arson to the malicious burning of your own house or of anyone's commercial or industrial property (see section 129).

articles of agreement A written memorandum of the terms of an understanding between two or more people.

assault An unlawful, intentional threat or attempt, with force, to do physical harm to another person (see sections 41 and 126).

assessment (1) The valuation of property in order to apportion a tax on it, according to its value or in relation to the benefit received from it (see section 305). (2) An installment of the money subscribed by stockholders for shares in the corporation, called for from time to time as the company requires. (3) The act of fixing the amount of damages to which the successful party in a suit is entitled.

assets All the property of any kind that a person has, as contrasted with his liabilities or debts.

assign (1) To transfer or sign over property or an interest in property. (2) To transfer title or ownership of something not yet owned, but to which one has a right under a claim or contract.

assignment (1) The act of transferring property or an interest in property. (2) The instrument by which such property or such an interest is transferred.

assured That person in whose favor an insurance policy is issued. The *assured* is not necessarily the person on whose life or property a policy is written. For example, if a woman insures her father's life for her benefit and he has no interest in the policy, the woman is the *assured* and her father the "insured." But she must have an "insurable interest" (see section 502).

asylum (1) In former times, a place of refuge in which criminals and debtors found shelter and protection and out of which they could not be taken without sacrilege. (2) Refuge given by a state to a fugitive from another land. A state has the right to grant asylum by virtue of its territorial sovereignty; the fugitive, however, has no right to demand asylum from that state. (3) An institution for the care of the mentally ill, the aged, the destitute, etc.

at issue (1) A phrase used to refer to a specific point or question in pleading which is affirmed by one side and denied by the other. (2) A phrase meaning "on calendar" or "ready for adjudication."

attachment (1) The act of taking persons or property into the custody of the law. Its purpose may be to bring before the court someone who is guilty of contempt of court, or, in the seizure of property, to provide security for payment of the judgment that the plaintiff expects to recover (see section 88). (2) A writ or other judicial order used to accomplish this act. A writ of attachment may be issued before a case has been tried and a judgment entered.

attainder The loss of all civil rights and capacities as a result of being sentenced to death for treason or a felony.

A *bill of attainder* is a special act of a legislature that passes a sentence of capital punishment upon a person supposed to be guilty of an alleged crime (especially treason), without having been convicted as the result of an ordinary trial.

attempt The intent to commit a crime together with an open endeavor to commit it, which, if it had not been prevented, would have resulted in the successful commission of the crime. Such an attempt may, in itself, constitute a criminal offense (see section 90).

attestation The act of bearing witness to the execution of a document and the writing down of his name by the witness in testimony of such fact.

attorney-at-law A person who has been formally trained and licensed by special examination to be a member of the legal profession. An attorney-at-law is qualified to give legal advice, to act in legal formalities and negotiations and to prepare, manage and try cases in court; a lawyer (see chapter 14, page 719).

attorney-in-fact A person chosen by another and given authority by him to act in his place in a situation that is not legal in character. The authority is given by a written instrument called a *letter of attorney* or, more commonly, a POWER OF ATTORNEY.

attractive nuisance A condition, machine or other thing that is dangerous to young children and that may attract them onto the owner's property and expose them to risks for which the owner may be held responsible (see section 61).

audit An official examination and verification of an account.

averment A positive statement of facts in a pleading, without argument or inference.

award (*n.*) (1) A decision, judgment or sentence given by arbitrators on a controversy that has been submitted to them. (2) The amount of money awarded by such a decision. (3) A document embodying such a decision. (*v.*) To grant or assign, as damages or an injunction, by judicial determination.

bail (*n.*) (1) The security, either in cash or in the form of a promise, given to procure the release from custody of a person under arrest and to assure that he will appear at an agreed-on time and place. (2) A person (called a surety) who procures the release of a suspect under arrest by assuming responsibility for this promise. (*v.*) To furnish or act as bail (see sections 26, 27, 152).

bail bond The instrument that a defendant executes with a surety or sureties to guarantee his appearance in court when his presence is required to answer to a charge.

bailee A person who receives personal property of another person with the understanding that he will do something with the property. For example, a mover who receives goods for transportation or a tailor who receives clothes for alteration is a *bailee* (see section 197).

bailiff A court attendant whose duties include keeping order in the court, seating witnesses and guarding the jury.

bailment The delivery of personal property by one person (a BAILOR) to another (a BAILEE) in trust for a special purpose, with a contract that the trust shall be performed and the property returned or accounted for when the special purpose is accomplished (see sections 197–206).

bailor The person who transfers property to another under the contract of BAILMENT.

bankruptcy The condition of being a bankrupt, that is, being one who has been declared judicially insolvent and whose property is subject to seizure and distribution among his creditors under a federal statute commonly referred to as the bankruptcy law (see sections 411, 463–468).

bar (1) A particular place in a courtroom, the spot where a prisoner stands to plead. (2) The court sitting in full term. (3) All the members of the legal profession, referred to as the *bar* because of the place they usually occupy in court. (4) In litigation, a special plea that, if valid, defeats the plaintiff's action altogether, called a *plea in bar*.

barratry (1) In criminal law, the offense of frequently provoking suits and quarrels, either at law or otherwise. (2) In maritime law, any willful and unlawful act by the master or crew of a ship, whereby the owners sustain injury.

bastard (1) A child born out of wedlock; an illegitimate child (see section 326). (2) A child born to a married woman whose husband, for some particular reason (such as absence at the time of conception), could not possibly be the father of the child.

battery The unlawful use of force by one person upon another: commonly used in the term "assault and battery," ASSAULT being the offer or threat to use force and *battery* being the actual use of force. A battery can be either a civil or a criminal offense or in some circumstances both (see sections 41 and 126).

bearer A person who is in possession of a bill, note, check, draft or any negotiable instrument that is payable to *bearer,* and who presents it for payment.

bench (1) The judge or judges who make up a court; also the court itself. (2) The court, as distinguished from the BAR. (3) The judges' seat in court.

bench warrant A warrant issued by a court in session for the arrest of someone guilty of contempt, someone against whom an indictment has been filed or someone who has not obeyed a SUBPOENA served upon him.

beneficial use A right to the occupancy and use of property, including the enjoyment of any benefits or profits that may be derived from such property. A person does not have to own property in order to have the beneficial use of it. (see section 539).

beneficiary (1) Someone who may receive and use the profits and proceeds of an estate or property, even though the legal title is vested in another person, as in a trustee. (2) The person to whom the proceeds of an insurance policy are paid or payable (see section 506).

bequest A gift of personal property that is made in a will; a LEGACY. The term is often used synonymously with DEVISE, although the latter more strictly applies only to the disposition of real estate in a person's will (see section 541).

bicameral Consisting of two chambers, houses or branches: used to describe a legislative body, as in the U.S. Congress.

bigamy The crime of a person who contracts a second marriage when his or her first marriage has never been dissolved (see section 116).

bill (1) A formal written statement or complaint, as one filed in a court calling for some specific action on grounds given or alleged. (2) The draft of a proposed law submitted to a legislature for enactment: sometimes loosely extended to the law or statute enacted.

bill of attainder See ATTAINDER.

bill of rights (1) A formal summary and declaration of the fundamental principles and rights of individuals, as for example the one enacted by the British Parliament in 1689. (2) The name given to the first ten amendments to the United States Constitution (see section 15).

binder (1) In insurance, a memorandum of a verbal contract, given by the company to the insured, which provides for temporary protection until a formal policy is issued. (2) In real estate, a written agreement signed by the buyer and seller and covering the purchaser's initial payment toward purchase, often to show his good faith: at times the initial payment itself is referred to as a *binder* (see section 280).

blacklist A list of persons under suspicion or censure, or refused approval or employment for any cause.

blackmail (1) The extortion of money or something else of value by means of intimidation, such as threats of criminal prosecution or injury to a person's reputation. (2) The money so extorted.

blue law Any of a number of strict statutes or ordinances for the regulation of personal conduct on Sundays. Blue laws have to do with such things as gambling and the sale of liquor.

blue ribbon jury A jury selected for its special qualifications (for example, superior education) to try cases of greater importance or intricacy than those submitted to ordinary juries.

blue-sky law A law enacted to regulate the sale of stocks and bonds, intended to protect inexperienced investors from fraudulent exploitation (see section 480).

bona fide A Latin phrase meaning "in or with good faith." It is often used in combination with other terms, such as *bona fide purchaser*, which denotes a person who has bought property in good faith for good consideration.

bond (1) A written promise to pay to another a certain sum of money at a specified time; evidence of a debt. (2) An interest-bearing certificate of debt issued usually by a corporation, municipality or government, and often designed to cover a particular financial need. (3) An insurance agreement by which a person or a corporation becomes surety to pay, within certain defined limits, for a financial loss suffered by a second person as the result of an act or a failure to act by a third person or of a contingent circumstance over which the third person has no control. See also BAIL BOND.

bondsman A person who assumes the responsibility of a bond; a SURETY.

book value (1) The value of a business, an item of property or the like, as shown on the balance sheet of the owner. (2) In reference to stock in a corporation that has only one kind of stock outstanding, the net worth of the corporation divided by the number of shares of stock outstanding.

boycott A form of coercion directed against an individual, corporation or group, especially used in labor disputes. A *primary boycott* occurs when employes of an organized union, acting in concert, refuse to have anything to do with the products or services of an employer in order to force that employer to accept certain conditions desired by the union. A *secondary boycott* occurs when pressure is applied on customers, actual or prospective, to coerce them to withhold or withdraw patronage from a particular business (see section 374).

breach of contract A violation of or a failure to perform any or all of the terms of an agreement (see section 183).

breach of the peace Unlawful disturbance of the public tranquility, as by violent or disorderly behavior (see section 110).

breach of promise Failure to fulfill a promise, especially a promise of marriage (see section 308).

breach of warranty The violation of a contract of warranty. For example, the failure of a manufacturer to make his product safe for the intended use is a breach of warranty (see section 190).

breaking and entering Exerting force, however slight, to enter a dwelling place with intent to commit a crime (see section 131).

bribery The crime of giving or offering something of value in an attempt to influence the action of a person in some official public position (see section 106).

brief (1) In American law practice, a written statement prepared by the counsel arguing a case in an APPELLATE COURT, embodying the points of law that counsel intends to establish, along with the arguments, facts, precedents upon which he rests his contention. (2) An abstract of all the documents, such as liens and court proceedings, affecting the title of a piece of real property: also called ABSTRACT OF TITLE.

broker A person employed as an agent to negotiate sales or contracts, or to make sales and purchases, for an agreed-upon commission (see sections 278, 482).

burden of proof The obligation to prove affirmatively a disputed fact or facts related to or bearing upon an issue that is raised between the parties in a case being tried before a court (see section 84).

burglary The unlawful, intentional breaking in and entering of a dwelling, at night, with intent to commit a felony, extended by statute in some states to the breaking in and entering of any building at any time with intent to commit a crime (see section 131).

by-laws A set of rules adopted by an association, a corporation or the like, and subordinate to its constitution or charter. By-laws govern the internal, mechanical procedures of a corporation and regulate its dealings with others.

763

calendar A schedule or list of things or events arranged in a particular way, as a list of cases set down for hearing, trial or argument in some particular court.

calumny A false and malicious accusation of some offense or crime; slander; defamation.

canon The name for a rule, law or ordinance, now used in two major areas: (a) Ecclesiastical: *canon law* is the set of rules and doctrines adopted by church authorities for governing the church. (b) Legal: *canons of judicial ethics* are rules for the conduct of judicial behavior; *canons of professional ethics* (now called the Code of Professional Responsibility) are rules for the conduct of the legal profession as a whole.

capacity The status or attributes necessary for a person in order that his acts may be legally allowed and recognized; legal qualification. *Testamentary capacity*, for example, means legal ability to make a will (see sections 176, 177).

capital (1) The total amount of money or property owned or used by an individual or corporation. (2) The amount of property owned by an individual or corporation at a specified time, as distinct from the income received during a specified time. (3) Wealth in any form employed in or available for the production of more wealth or of income. (4) *Capital stock*, that is, the amount of stock a corporation is authorized to issue; also, its total face value.

capital gain Profit from the sale of certain property for more than its original cost.

carrier A person or company that transports persons or goods for hire.

case (1) An action or suit at law or in equity. (2) The set of facts offered in support of a claim.

casualty An accident, an event that cannot be guarded against.

cause of action The grounds of an action; those facts which if alleged and proved in a suit would, in the absence of an effective defense, enable the plaintiff to obtain judgment.

caveat emptor A Latin phrase meaning "let the buyer beware." It is a legal doctrine which warns that in the absence of a warranty a purchaser must make sure that goods which he purchases are what they purport to be, the purchase being made at his risk. Recent consumer laws have considerably weakened the doctrine (see sections 68, 69, 190).

cease and desist order An order issued by an administrative agency directing a person (or corporation) to refrain from some proscribed business practice (see section 9).

certiorari A writ from a superior to an inferior court, directing that a certified record of its proceedings in a designated case be sent up for review. Cases are frequently brought up for review by the U.S. Supreme Court through a *writ of certiorari.*

chain of title The succession of conveyances or other forms of transfer relevant to a particular piece of land, commencing with the government or original source of title and ending with the present holder (see section 283).

champerty A bargain, illegal in many jurisdictions, made by an outsider with the plaintiff in a lawsuit, whereby the outside party agrees to bear the expense of the suit or to render services in consideration of receiving a share of the matter sued for, if the plaintiff is successful (see section 630).

change of venue The change of the place of a trial, for good cause, from one county or district to another; sometimes the change of the place of a trial from one court to another court in the same county or district.

charge (1) An address given by a judge to a jury at the end of a trial. In it, the judge sums up the case and instructs the jury as to which rules of law are applicable to the issues involved (see section 155). (2) An accusation, allegation or imputation; also, its subject matter. (3) Any burden or encumbrance upon a person, upon public or private property or upon resources. A tax upon property is an example of such a *charge*.

charitable trust A trust set up for the benefit of the public or of some part of the public.

charter (1) A formal document by which a sovereign or government grants special rights or privileges to a person or company or to the people. (2) A document of incorporation of a municipality, institution or corporation, specifying its privileges and purposes.

chattel An article of personal property.

chattel loan A secured loan on a chattel or chattels; the conditional transfer of a legal interest in personal property as security for a debt or obligation (see sections 193, 452); formerly called a *chattel mortgage.*

check A draft for payment of money; an order, in writing, upon a bank or banker, for payment on demand of a specified sum of money to a certain person or to his order or to BEARER (see section 440).

c.i.f. or **C.I.F.** Abbreviation of "cost, insurance and freight," used in sales contracts to indicate that the price of the goods covers the cost of insurance and freight (see section 188).

circuit court A court that sits in various counties or districts over which its jurisdiction extends.

circumstantial evidence Evidence consisting of facts and circumstances that furnish reasonable ground for inferring the existence of some other connected fact or facts.

citation (1) A summons by a court, ordering a person to appear on a particular day and do something specified, or to show cause why he should not so appear and act. (2) A lawyer's formal reference to published court decisions, statutes or legal authorities in order to establish or support his argument.

civil action A lawsuit brought by a private individual or group to recover money or property, to enforce or protect a civil right, to prevent or redress a civil wrong. It differs from a criminal action in which the state prosecutes an individual for committing an offense against all the people (see sections 79–86).

765

claim (1) A request or demand, as for some right or supposed right. (2) The thing that is requested, such as a piece of land or an insurance payment or a tax refund.

claimant One who makes a claim.

class action An action brought by one or more plaintiffs on behalf of other persons who are similarly situated or have suffered a similar wrong. For example, a group of stockholders in a corporation may bring a *class action* on behalf of all other stockholders who have a similar grievance.

close corporation (Frequently referred to as a *closed corporation*.) (1) A business enterprise whose directors and officers are empowered to fill vacancies in their number, the general body of stockholders being allowed no choice or vote in the election. (2) A business enterprise in which the stock is owned by only a few persons as distinguished from one in which the stock is available to the general public (see section 405).

closed shop A business whose employes must be members of a union as a condition of their employment (see section 383).

cloud on title An outstanding claim or incumbrance upon property that, if not proved to be invalid or inapplicable, renders the owner's title to the property defective (see section 284).

codicil A supplement to a will that alters, modifies or explains the original document (see section 551).

codification The act or process of collecting and arranging the laws of a state or country into a systematically arranged, unified body called a code.

co-executor A person named with one or more persons in a will to perform the duties of executor (see section 547).

cohabitation The act or state of living together as husband and wife.

coinsurance A system of insurance in which there is a relative division of risk between the insurer and the insured. In such a system the insured must buy coverage up to a stipulated percentage of the total value of the property insured, or, in the event of partial loss, share in that loss by having his claim reduced in proportion to the deficiency in coverage (see section 492).

collateral (1) Not directly connected with; outside of; accompanying; subsidiary. (2) Additional, supplementary or supporting. *Collateral security*, for example, is given in addition to a direct security as additional protection to the lender. (3) Descended from a common ancestor, but in a different line. *Collateral descendants* are those not directly related as are ascendants or descendants (such as parent and child), but related in the sense of common descent from the same ancestor. Brothers are *collateral descendants* from their parents.

collective bargaining Negotiations between the representatives of an employer or an employers' association and the representatives of a trade union or organization of trade unions. Such negotiations concern wages, hours, fringe benefits and other conditions of employment (see sections 382, 387).

collusion A secret agreement or action of two or more persons (sometimes persons whose interests are apparently conflicting), made or performed for a fraudulent or deceitful purpose as (a) the deprivation of a person's rights, often by lawful means, or (b) the obtaining of some object or committing some act forbidden by law (see section 367).

combination in restraint of trade Any combination of two or more individuals or corporations having as its purpose the illegal restraint of trade or commerce in some particular commodity, as by the regulation of production, restriction of sales, establishment and maintenance of prices or the stifling or the exclusion of free competition.

comity Courteous behavior: used primarily in the phrases *judicial comity* and *comity of nations.*

Judicial comity refers to the principle that the courts of one state or jurisdiction should give full effect to the laws and judicial decisions of another state.

Comity of nations refers to the recognition granted by one nation, out of courtesy or convenience, to the laws of another nation, even though such recognition is not required by international law.

commit (1) To do, perform or perpetrate, as a crime. (2) To lawfully deliver, send or consign for custody, as to commit a person to a prison or mental institution. (For details on commitment, see section 357.)

common law (1) In a wide sense, that system of law generally in force in a nation or state, as distinguished from regulations of local or specific application. (2) A system of jurisprudence based on custom, traditional usage and precedent, rather than on codified written laws; especially, the ancient unwritten law of England (see section 2).

common-law marriage An agreement between a man and woman to live together as husband and wife, followed by their cohabitation. Such an agreement is not solemnized by a conventional marriage ceremony (see section 310).

community property That property which is owned in common by a husband and wife, generally considered to be all that is acquired by either or both after marriage, with the exception of those things gained by gift, devise, legacy or descent. Property owned by either spouse at the time of marriage is not considered community property (see sections 306, 317, 567).

commutation (1) A reduction of the penalty imposed by a judicial sentence, as from hanging to life imprisonment. (2) The substitution of one kind of payment for another, as a lump sum for installments.

company union A union composed of workers within one company and having no outside affiliation, usually considered to be dominated by the employer. Under the National Labor Relations Act, company unions are illegal (see section 385).

comparative negligence A legal doctrine applicable in negligence suits according to which the negligence of the plaintiff as well as that of the defendant is taken into account, the two being compared in the degrees of

767

"slight," "ordinary" and "gross." Damages are based upon the outcome of such a comparison and are apportioned (see sections 64, 242).

competent (1) Legally qualified, as a competent witness. (2) Having legal authority and jurisdiction, as a court or public officer. (3) Having the mental capacity to understand the nature of an act, as a maker of a will (see section 531). (4) Legally valid, as evidence.

competitive bidding Bidding that is free of the presence of monopoly or collusion; it requires that everyone, equally, be given the opportunity to bid upon the same conditions and terms.

complainant A person who files a bill of complaint; the party who starts a legal action; also called PLAINTIFF.

complaint (1) In civil practice, the document setting forth the plaintiff's cause of action (see section 80). (2) In criminal law, the formal presentation or INFORMATION stating the commission of an offense, made before a magistrate, grand jury or other tribunal (see section 152).

composition A settlement between an insolvent debtor and his creditors in which the creditors, in order to obtain immediate payment or payment earlier than when due, agree to accept less than the total amount of their claims as satisfaction for the whole. The amount settled upon is distributed among the creditors on a pro rata basis (see section 462).

compound interest Interest computed on the original principal together with its accrued interest.

compound a felony To agree not to prosecute a criminal in return for a consideration. For example, a person who has been robbed would *compound a felony* if he took back the property that had been stolen from him or accepted other reparation in return for an agreement not to prosecute (see section 101).

comptroller See CONTROLLER.

compulsory arbitration ARBITRATION that takes place when statutory power is invoked to enforce the consent of one or both parties involved. Compulsory arbitration is binding on the parties (see section 378).

concealment The act of hiding or withholding something; especially, the intentional suppression or nondisclosure by a party to an insurance contract of facts that he was bound to know and duty-bound to reveal (see section 514).

conciliation The intervention in a labor dispute of a private or governmental mediator who, since he is without power to force a settlement of the dispute, relies instead on persuasive methods of suggestion.

concur To agree or approve, as in an opinion. Thus, a *concurring opinion*, in appellate courts, is one rendered by a judge or justice agreeing with the conclusions of another opinion filed in the case, either the prevailing one or a dissenting one.

concurrent jurisdiction A situation in which each of a number of different judicial bodies has the authority to deal with the same subject matter at the discretion of the person starting a legal action.

condemnation (1) In real property law, the proceeding by which private property is taken for public use without the consent of the property's owner but upon payment of a just compensation to be established by the court (see sections 23, 299). (2) In admiralty law, the judgment of a court having appropriate jurisdiction that (a) a vessel captured at sea and claimed as the property of the belligerent that captures it is liable to be treated as prize; or (b) property seized for the alleged violation of a revenue law or navigation law is lawfully forfeited to the government that seizes it; or (c) the ship that is the subject of investigation is unsafe and unfit for navigation.

conditional sale A sale in which transfer of title to the purchaser is contingent upon his fulfilling a certain condition or conditions, usually the full payment of the purchase price.

condominium An apartment house in which the units are owned separately by individuals and not by a corporation or cooperative.

condonation The conditional forgiveness on the part of a husband or wife of a breach of marital duty by the other, the condition being that there will be no repetition of the offense. Cohabitation with the guilty party after the offense is known as evidence of condonation (see section 366).

confession and avoidance The setting up of new matter in a defendant's plea that, without denying the facts in a plaintiff's charges, destroys the legal effect of the facts admitted.

confidential communication A special kind of communication that, as a matter of public policy, the law will not permit to be divulged and that may not be investigated by the courts. Such communications pass between persons whose relationship is confidential or fiduciary, as a husband and wife or an attorney and his client (see section 632).

confiscate To appropriate for public use private property that the owner has forfeited.

conflict of laws (1) The disagreement between the laws of different states or nations as it affects the rights of persons acting under the laws of more than one jurisdiction. (2) That branch of jurisprudence, sometimes called private international law, which determines what laws should be given effect or enforced in legal relations between citizens of different countries.

confrontation In criminal law, the bringing of an accusing witness face to face with the person accused. This is done so that the accused or his lawyer may cross-examine and object to the witness, or to enable the witness to make positive identification of the accused.

connivance The guilty or corrupt consent of one person to another's wrongful or criminal act.

consanguinity The relationship that proceeds from a common ancestry, as distinguished from affinity, or relationship by marriage. *Lineal consanguinity* is kinship between persons of whom one is descended in a direct line from the other, as the son, the father, the grandfather. *Collateral consanguinity* is the kinship of those who descend from one and the same

769

common ancestor, but do not descend one from the other, as brother and sister, nephew and uncle, and cousins.

conscientious objection Opposition to participation in war on the basis of religious or moral scruples.

consideration An inducement offered and accepted in the formation of a CONTRACT; a thing given or done, or to be given or done or abstained from, by one party to a contract, which is accepted by the other party as an inducement to him to perform his part of the agreement (see section 175).

consignment (1) The act of forwarding or delivering something to be sold, disposed of or cared for, as merchandise or movable property. (2) The thing that is forwarded or delivered.

consortium The right of a husband or wife to the care, affection, company and cooperation of the other spouse in every aspect of the marriage relationship.

conspiracy In criminal law, a combination or agreement between two or more persons to commit an act punishable by law or to effect a legal purpose by criminal or unlawful means (see section 94).

constitution (1) The organic law of any organized body or association. (2) The fundamental laws and principles (written or unwritten) that normally govern the operation of a nation or state; also, a document recording such laws and principles. (3) The Constitution of the United States, written and signed in 1787, went into effect March 4, 1789.

constructive Assumed or inferred by legal interpretation: used to describe an act or condition that is not the thing named but that acquires the character of the thing named because of the way it is regarded by the law. For example, a landlord's failure to maintain a tenant's apartment in livable condition would constitute *constructive eviction* of the tenant (see section 274).

consul An officer residing in a foreign country who has been appointed to protect the commercial interests there of his own country and of its citizens.

contemplation of death A phrase used where expectation of impending death influences someone to make a gift (see section 573).

contempt of court Willful disregard of the authority or dignity of a court, as the disobeying of its orders or the disruption of its proceedings. Contempt may be direct or constructive (indirect). *Direct contempt* is that which is committed in the immediate presence of the court (such as insult or violence) or near enough to the court to obstruct its proceedings. *Constructive contempt* usually refers to the failure or refusal to obey a lawful order, injunction or court decree (see section 96).

contingent Possible; questionable; dependent upon some uncertain future event. A *contingent liability,* thus, is one that will come into being only upon the occurrence of some uncertain future event.

contingent fee A fee payable to an attorney representing a client only in the event that a certain result is achieved (see section 630).

continuance (1) Adjournment of the proceedings in a case from one day or term to another. (2) The entry made for such a purpose in the court record.

contraband Goods that, by law or treaty, may not be imported into or exported from a country. *Contraband of war* is merchandise that, by international law, a neutral may not furnish to either one of two belligerents and that may be seized and confiscated.

contract A legally enforceable agreement between two or more parties to do or not to do a particular thing, upon sufficient CONSIDERATION (see section 167).

contribution In common law, the reimbursement of one person who has paid a debt or suffered a liability that was the responsibility of several persons. Such reimbursement is normally made by each of the co-debtors, co-sureties or the like, in proportion to his share of the obligation.

controller A person who checks expenditures, finances and so forth; especially, an officer appointed by a state, by a municipal or other public corporation or by a private corporation to examine and audit the accounts of collectors of the public or private money, as the case may be. Also written *comptroller*.

conversion (1) The exchange of real to personal property, or the reverse, that is considered to have taken place where no actual exchange has been effected, as in settling the affairs of an estate. (2) The wrongful appropriation to one's own use of the goods or personal property of another (see section 47). (3) Wrongful keeping or use of property originally legitimately received.

convey To transfer or pass, as property or the title to property, from one to another.

convict To find a person guilty of a criminal charge after a judicial trial.

conviction The act of convicting, or the state of being convicted, by judicial process.

cooperative association A jointly owned union, as of laborers, farmers or consumers, operated for the mutual benefit of all the persons making up the union; its profits, if any, being shared by all according to the capital or labor they contribute.

copyright (1) An author's right of literary property, recognized by common law, in unpublished literary and artistic productions. (2) The statutory protection of the author's exclusive privilege of multiplying, publishing and selling copies of his production, for a specified period of time (see section 164).

coram nobis A Latin phrase meaning "before us ourselves." For example, a *writ of error coram nobis* is one that, on the ground of an error in the proceedings, seeks the review of a judgment by the same court where it was rendered.

corespondent A joint respondent; especially, in a suit for divorce, a person charged with having committed adultery with the defendant spouse.

coroner A public officer whose principal duty is the investigation, with

771

the aid of a jury, of the cause and circumstances of any death that occurs suddenly or through violence and with any suspicion attached to it.

corporate bond A written promise under seal, according to which a corporation pledges to pay a sum of money at a specified future time with interest thereon set to be paid on a fixed date or at fixed intervals.

corporate franchise The right granted by a government to a private corporation to exist and do business.

corporation An entity or artificial person created by law, consisting of one or more natural persons united in a body bearing a distinctive name. A corporation is endowed by the law with the capacity of perpetual succession—that is, it remains the same though its members may die or change—and is empowered to act as a unit or as a single individual (see section 405).

corpus delicti A Latin phrase meaning "the body of the crime," used in reference to the essential fact necessary to the commission of a crime, as, in a case of murder, the death of the victim. The term has come to refer, loosely, to the body of the victim in a murder case.

corroborate To strengthen; to give increased support or credibility to something, as evidence, by furnishing additional or different evidence, confirming facts or the like.

costs An award to the successful party in a lawsuit (payable by the losing party) for the expense incurred in prosecuting or defending the suit (for example, the expense incurred

in attaching property). Such awards are relatively small and strictly limited by statute. Usually, in the United States, attorneys' fees are not included (see section 75).

counsel A person who gives legal advice and who prepares and manages cases and tries them in court; a lawyer. The term may also refer to a team of lawyers engaged to conduct a case in court.

counselor or **counsellor** Another name for COUNSEL.

counterclaim A claim alleged by a defendant that seeks to reduce the plaintiff's claim or provide grounds for a judgment in favor of the defendant to whatever extent the counterclaim exceeds plaintiff's claim. If the plaintiff's claim is defeated, judgment may be given on the counterclaim as if it were an entirely new suit. See also OFFSET.

counterfeit To copy, imitate or forge; especially, in criminal law, to make something in imitation of something else with the intent to defraud by passing the imitation for the genuine: commonly used in reference to the fraudulent imitation of money (see section 105).

court (1) A government body or organ whose function is the administration of justice. (2) The persons, elected or appointed under the Constitution and laws of the United States or of a state, who make up this body. (3) One or more members of this body, sitting in an authorized place at an authorized time, engaged in the performance of judicial functions (for example, a judge at the trial of a case). (4) A place where justice is administered (see sections 7, 8).

court-martial A court of military or naval officers that is convened under the authority of government and the Uniform Code of Military Justice in order to try offenses against military or naval law.

court of last resort A tribunal from which there is no appeal.

court of record A court whose acts and judicial proceedings are recorded for a perpetual memorial and testimony. Courts of record have the power to imprison or fine for contempt of court.

covenant (1) A written agreement by parties under seal. (2) A specific stipulation or agreement within a contract or deed. (3) An action to recover damages for breach of contract. See also RUNNING WITH THE LAND.

creditor (1) A person to whom money is owed as the result of a financial or business transaction. (2) A person who has the legal right to demand and recover money from another for any reason. (3) A person who has the right to require the performance of any legal obligation.

credit union A cooperative group that makes loans to its members at low rates of interest.

crime An act or omission in violation of a public law either forbidding or commanding it, for which a punishment is prescribed and which is prosecuted by the state in its own name or in the name of the people or the sovereign (see chapter 4, page 133).

criminal insanity A deranged mental condition that deprives a person of the capacity to comprehend the nature and consequences of a particular act or to distinguish right from wrong (see section 144).

cross-action An action brought by a defendant in a suit against a plaintiff in the same suit. Such an action is brought upon a cause growing out of or related to the original controversy that prompted the suit.

cross-claim A claim brought by a defendant in an action against a plaintiff or a codefendant or both in the same action. Such a claim concerns matters in question in the original complaint.

cross-examination The examination of a witness by or on behalf of the party against whom he is called, usually to test the accuracy and credibility of his first testimony (see sections 85, 154).

cumulative Increased in volume, strength or value; additional.
Cumulative evidence is additional evidence that reinforces or proves something that has been established by other evidence.
A *cumulative legacy* is one bequeathed in a will to a legatee to whom the testator has made a previous bequest in the same will.
Cumulative punishment is greater punishment imposed for a person's second or third conviction of the same offense.
Cumulative sentences are separate sentences imposed on a defendant convicted of several distinct offenses. Each sentence is imposed as an addition to the others, and each is made to begin at the expiration of another.

773

curfew A regulation issued by public authority, requiring persons to keep off the streets between designated hours (see section 30).

curtesy The right by which, according to common law, a man is entitled to enjoy his dead wife's estate, or part of it, during his lifetime (see section 306 and chart 20, page 353).

custody (1) The care and keeping of property. (2) The legal detention of a person, as by imprisonment.

custom duties Tariffs or taxes assessed upon merchandise imported or exported.

cy pres A French expression meaning "as nearly as possible." It refers to the doctrine whereby a gift or trust impossible to administer as the testator directed may be used or administered as nearly as possible in accordance with his intentions.

damages The indemnity or reparation in money that may be recovered by a person who has suffered an injury to his person, property or rights by the unlawful act or default or negligence of another (see sections 35, 71).

days of grace The days (usually three) allowed for payment of a note or bill after its stated due date. Once a matter of favor, the grace period is now regarded as a legal right.

debenture (1) Any writing that acknowledges a debt. (2) A bond secured only by the credit and financial reputation of the issuer rather than by a lien upon any specific property. (3) A customhouse certificate providing for a refund of money paid on duties for imported goods when the importer, instead of selling the goods in the United States, reexports them.

debt (1) A specified sum of money owed by one person to another because of an express or implied contract. (2) Something other than money that is owed by one person to another, as goods or services.

debtor A person from whom something is due to another, as money, goods or services.

decedent A deceased person.

deceit A trick, false statement, secret device or pretense by which one person misleads another who, being ignorant of the fraud, suffers injury or damage as a result.

decision The judgment of a court, often in writing, on a dispute tried before it or submitted to it for review.

declaratory judgment A judgment that declares the status, rights or duties of the parties involved, or that does not order any action to be taken.

decoy To lure or inveigle someone by fraud, trickery or temptation, but not by force.

decree The decision of a court of equity, admiralty, divorce or probate. A *decree* corresponds to a JUDGMENT; the terms are often used synonymously.

dedication In real property law, the act of setting aside private property for public use. Such an act is done by the property's owner with the consent and agreement of the public authority involved.

774

deduction Something that is subtracted; a reduction. A business expense, for example, may be a *deduction* from one's taxable income.

deed A written instrument, signed, usually sealed, and delivered, that contains some contract, bargain or transfer. The term usually refers to such an instrument by which land or an interest in land is conveyed from one person to another (see section 283).

de facto A Latin expression meaning "in fact." It is often used to describe a government that has seized power by violent and unlawful means from a rightful, legally constituted government.

defamation The act of maliciously injuring the reputation or good name of another person. The term includes both LIBEL and SLANDER (see section 44).

default The failure or neglect to fulfill a legal obligation or requirement, such as the failure to pay money due or to appear in court to answer a summons.

defendant A person against whom a claim or charge is brought; the party defending or denying a claim in an action or suit (see section 50).

defraud To cheat, trick or swindle; to deprive a person of property, an estate or the like by fraud but not by intimidation or force (see section 49).

de jure A Latin expression meaning "by right" or "by law." It is used in reference to something, such as a corporation or government, that exists or functions in accordance with the requirements of law.

delinquent (*n.*) A person who commits some offense or crime or who fails to perform some duty. (*adj.*) (1) Due and unpaid, as a debt or a tax. (2) Neglectful of or failing in a duty or obligation; guilty of an offense: said of a person.

demand note A note payable on demand.

demise (1) A conveyance of an estate for life or (the usual sense) for a term of years or at will. (2) Death; decease.

demurrer (1) In a lawsuit, a statement by one party that, even if the facts stated by the other party are true, they do not constitute an effective or enforceable claim and do not require an answer. (2) Any objection or exception taken by one party to evidence introduced by the other.

denial In pleading, a contradiction by one party of a statement or charge by the opposite party.

dependent A person who depends on another for support or favor, as a wife or child. Often used in tax law to denote a person whose relationship to a taxpayer is such that the latter, in the determining of his income tax, is granted an exemption for said person.

deponent A person under oath who gives testimony that is set down in writing.

deportation The sending back to the country from which he came of an alien whose presence is deemed incompatible with the public interest of the country sending him back (see section 14).

deposition Testimony of a witness taken outside a court and set down in writing for use as evidence in court.

depreciation A loss in value or efficiency resulting from deterioration, usage or age.

deputy A person duly authorized to act for or in place of another. A person who acts under your POWER OF ATTORNEY is acting as your *deputy*.

derivative action A suit brought by one or more shareholders of a corporation on behalf of the corporation.

descend To pass or be transmitted by succession, as when an estate becomes the property of an heir as an immediate result of the death of his ancestor.

descendant A person who is descended from another; one who proceeds from the body of another, however remotely, as a child, grandchild or great-grandchild.

descent The transmission of an estate by inheritance or by law.

desertion The willful abandonment, without legal justification or authorization, of a person, obligation or post of duty (see section 361).

devise (*v.*) To give or transmit real estate by will. (*n.*) A gift of real property by a last will and testament. The term sometimes is used loosely to refer to any testamentary disposi-tion of property; however, *devise* commonly applies to a gift of realty, whereas a testamentary disposition of personal property is called a BEQUEST or LEGACY.

dictum A remark or observation: used often as shortened form of OBITER DICTUM, an incidental remark or observation made by a judge on some point not necessarily involved in or essential to the determination of the case or the issue in question.

diligence The degree of personal care, attention or effort given by a person to his affairs. The law recognizes three degrees of diligence and three corresponding degrees of negligence: (a) common or ordinary; (b) high or great; (c) low or slight.

direct examination The first examina-tion of a witness by the party who has called him to testify in a trial: also called examination in chief (see section 85).

disability (1) Legal incapacity or in-ability to act, as that of infants or lunatics. (2) The state of being phys-ically disabled, as from an accident.

disbar To expel from the bar; to take back an attorney's license to practice law (see section 637).

discharge (1) To pay a debt or satisfy a claim or obligation. (2) To release a bankrupt from the obligations of his debts, following adjudication of bankruptcy and the administration of the bankrupt's estate (see section 467). (3) To revoke, annul, cancel or refuse to confirm the original pro-visional force of an injunction, an order, a rule, a certificate, a process of execution or a proceeding in court.

776

(4) To free (a prisoner) from confinement or restraint. (5) To relieve (a jury) of further consideration of a case. (6) To release a member of the armed forces from further service.

discount (1) An allowance or deduction from a gross sum for a particular reason, such as to encourage immediate cash payment. (2) The interest deducted beforehand from an advance or loan of money.

discovery In legal or court practice, the disclosure of facts, documents and the like by one party at the request of the other for use by the latter as material evidence in a case that is being prepared for trial or expected to be tried.

discrimination (1) The failure to treat all persons equally. Discrimination between individuals on the basis of race, religion, sex or country of national origin is illegal under a variety of state and federal laws. (2) In reference to a common carrier, the failure to treat passengers or shippers alike under similar conditions. An example of such *discrimination* would be the charging of different rates to two shippers who receive the same service.

disfranchise (1) To deprive a person of the rights and privileges of a free citizen, especially the right to vote. (2) To deprive (as a corporation) of a franchise, privilege or right.

disinherit To prevent an heir from coming into possession of any property or right that, by law or custom, would become his in the course of descent; to deprive of an inheritance (see section 533).

dismissal An order or judgment terminating a case without a complete trial of the issues involved.

dismissal without prejudice The dismissal of an action or proceeding in a way that does not prevent the plaintiff from bringing another suit based on the same cause of action.

disorderly conduct A somewhat indefinite term that generally refers to any of a wide range of petty violations of public order or decency (see section 110).

dispossession The ejecting of a person from the occupancy of real property by legal process (see sections 298–301).

dissent The disagreement of one or more judges on a court with the decision of a majority of judges in a case before that court. Such a disagreement is often set forth in a written OPINION.

dissolution A breaking up or separation, as (a) the cancellation of a contract; (b) the termination of the existence of a corporation; (c) the ending of a marriage by divorce.

distribution The act of parceling out, apportioning; especially, in probate practice, the apportionment of the remainder of an intestate's estate after payment of the decedent's debts and claims against the estate.

dividend (1) A share in a fund set aside out of a corporation's profits; also, the fund out of which distribution to shareholders is made. (2) In bankruptcy or insolvency proceedings, a proportional payment made to a creditor out of an insolvent's estate.

(3) A sum of money paid by an insurance company from its surplus to a policyholder in a participatory insurance policy.

divorce Judicial dissolution of a marriage contract (see section 363).

divorce decree A court order dissolving a marriage.

docket The list of cases to be tried before a court at a specified term; the court calendar.

Doe, John A fictitious name used to identify a party in a legal action whose true name is unknown or who wishes to remain anonymous. Additional unknown or anonymous parties are sometimes known as *Richard Roe* and *Peter Poe.*

domicile A person's fixed permanent dwelling, the place to which he intends to return whenever he is absent from it (see section 314).

double indemnity A provision in a life insurance policy by which a payment of double the face value of the policy is to be made in the event of the accidental death of the insured in circumstances covered by the policy (see section 522).

double jeopardy The subjection of a person to trial for the same offense for which he has already been tried under a valid charge. The Fifth Amendment to the Constitution protects citizens against double jeopardy (see section 28).

dower That share of or interest in a deceased husband's real estate that is assigned by law to his widow for life (see section 306).

draft (1) An order drawn by one person on another for the payment of money to a third. A check is a common form of draft. (2) A preliminary or rough version of a writing, as a contract, lease, will or the like.

drawee A person on whom an order for the payment of money is drawn. In the case of a check, the bank.

drawer A person who draws a bill of exchange and addresses it to a drawee. In the case of a check, the person who writes it.

dual nationality A status arising from the fact that two states claim the allegiance of a person at the same time.

duces tecum A Latin expression meaning "you will bring with you." It is the name of a variety of writs or legal orders, a common example being the SUBPOENA DUCES TECUM, which requires someone ordered into court to bring with him papers mentioned in the order.

due process of law A phrase used in reference to certain fundamental rights or principles of justice that limit the government's power to deprive a person of his life, liberty or property. Its definition by Daniel Webster remains a classic. He said that *due process* denotes "law which hears before it condemns; which proceeds upon inquiry; and which renders judgment only after trial." (See sections 15, 26.)

duplicate (1) A document substantially the same as another and having the validity of the original. (2) A new original of an instrument or document made to replace one lost or destroyed and having the same validity.

duress (1) Compulsion or constraint, as by force or threat, exercised to make a person do or say something against his will or judgment. (2) Imprisonment without legal sanction; also, legal imprisonment for an illegal purpose.

earnest Something given or done in advance as a pledge or an indication of good faith; a partial payment of the purchase price of goods sold or a delivery of part of the goods themselves, for the purpose of binding an agreement.

easement A liberty, privilege or advantage obtained by will, deed, prescription or necessary implication that the owner of one parcel of land holds or enjoys in the land of another. It entitles the holder to some limited use of the other's land, such as the right to cross it in order to reach a highway (see section 284).

ejectment The common-law action now brought in the United States to determine who has title to or ownership of land.

election In the law of wills, the choice by a widow either to accept the provision made for her in her husband's will or to disregard that provision and claim what she is entitled to by her state's laws of descent and distribution (see section 542 and chart 38, page 650).

eleemosynary Having to do with, derived from or dependent on charity. An *eleemosynary corporation* is one created for and having to do with charitable purposes.

elopement (1) The act of a married woman who voluntarily leaves her husband to go away and cohabit with another man. (2) More popularly, the act of an unmarried woman who runs away from her home to get married, especially without her parents' consent. (3) The act of a couple who run off secretly to marry.

emancipation (1) The act of releasing from bondage, oppression or authority. (2) The surrender by a parent of authority and control over his minor child and also of his right to the child's earnings. An emancipated minor has certain rights that a minor does not usually have because of his legal independence of parental control (see section 176).

embargo An order by a government restraining merchant vessels from leaving or entering its ports. Embargoes are often imposed in time of war or threatened hostilities, but are also used merely to control trade.

embezzlement The fraudulent taking of money or goods for his own use by a person to whom they have been entrusted, such as an agent, a public officer or any other person who acts in a fiduciary capacity.

eminent domain The inherent sovereign power of the state to take private property for public use (see section 299).

encumbrance Another spelling of INCUMBRANCE.

endorse To write one's name on the back of a document.

endowment (1) The assignment of a woman's dower. (2) The bestowal of

779

money, income from a fund, use of property, etc., to some person or institution.

enjoin To direct, command, forbid, or prohibit some act by court order (called an INJUNCTION).

entirety Something that is complete; a whole as opposed to a part. An *estate in entirety* is created by conveying land to a husband and wife. Being one person in law, both own the entire estate (the *entirety*), so that neither can sell without the consent of the other, and, in the event of the death of one partner, the entire estate belongs to the survivor.

entrapment The act of an officer of the government in inducing a person to commit a crime he had not contemplated so that the person may be prosecuted for the offense.

equal protection of the laws A phrase in the Fourteenth Amendment to the Constitution of the United States that requires every state to extend to all persons within its jurisdiction equal treatment and protection under the laws of that state. This guarantee applies both to privileges conferred and liabilities imposed. Unequal treatment is unconstitutional (see section 24).

equity (1) Justice administered between two persons that is based on the concepts of natural reason, ethics and fairness independent of any formulated body of law. (2) A system of jurisprudence administered by courts of equity, designed primarily to soften the rigors or inadequacies of common law by administering *equity* in the sense given above. In the United States, the distinction between law and equity has lost much of its meaning (see section 2).

escheat The reversion of property to the state; in the United States, when no legal heir or other qualified claimant can be found.

escrow (1) A deed, bond or other legal instrument delivered by a grantor to a third person, who in turn delivers it later to the grantee upon proof of the performance or fulfillment by the grantee of some condition stated by the grantor. (2) A fund of money (called *escrow fund*) similarly delivered by a grantor (see section 282).

estate (1) The amount, degree, nature and extent of interest to which a person is lawfully entitled with regard to the ownership or use of real or personal property. (2) The property in which a person has a right or interest. (3) The property and possessions of a deceased person or a bankrupt (see sections 464, 527).

estate tax A tax not upon property but upon the privilege of transmitting or transferring property by reason of death (see section 571).

estoppel A condition in which a person is prevented by law either from contradicting what he has previously stated or from stating or claiming what he has previously denied. Estoppel can arise from a person's conduct as well as from his oral or written statements.

et al An abbreviation for the Latin phrase *et alii,* "and others."

eviction (1) The recovery of property by legal process or by virtue of a

PARAMOUNT TITLE. (2) The dispossession of a person from property he has held, either pursuant to a court judgment or by virtue of a paramount title. (3) Popularly, the dispossession of a tenant, either by reentry or by legal proceedings according to statute (see section 275).

evidence Anything that furnishes or tends to furnish proof at the trial of an issue, such as the testimony of witnesses, documents and objects.

exception (1) In litigation, a formal objection to the decision of a court during trial, implying that the objection may be used in a motion for a new trial or on an appeal. (2) In more general use, that which is separated from a list or a description.

excise tax (1) A tax imposed on certain commodities, as liquor and tobacco, that are produced, sold, used or transported within a country. (2) A tax imposed on licenses to pursue certain trades or occupations.

execution (1) The act of carrying out or enforcing a legislative or judicial act or decree. (2) A judicial writ for carrying into effect a judgment or decree of a court. (3) The act of completing a written instrument, as a contract or will, by signing, sealing and delivering it, or by the fulfillment of any other legal requirements necessary to render it valid.

executor (*m.*) or **executrix** (*f.*) A person who is appointed by a TESTATOR to carry out the terms of the testator's will after his death (see section 547).

executory Designed to be executed or put into effect at some future time; becoming operative on the happening of some future event. For example, an agreement between two parties that requires one party to perform a service for the other at some future date is an *executory* contract.

exempt To free or excuse from some obligation to which others are subjected as, for example, military service, taxes, jury duty.

exemption (1) Freedom or immunity, as from a tax or obligation. (2) In the computation of income or estate tax, an amount allowed as a deduction from one's gross income or estate before arriving at the amount upon which the tax is computed. (3) A privilege allowed to a debtor by law which permits him to retain a portion of his property free from the claims of his creditors.

exhibit (*v.*) (1) To present formally or officially. (2) To file as part of the record. (*n.*) A document or written instrument, marked for identification and attached to or filed with the papers it refers to for future use as evidence, formally submitted to a court or officer.

ex officio A Latin phrase meaning "from or by virtue of the office." For example, a corporate president is often an *ex officio* member of several committees of the corporation because of his position.

ex parte A Latin phrase meaning "from or in the interest of one side only." An *ex parte* order is an order granted by a court at the request of one party to a judicial proceeding without prior notification to the other party involved.

expatriation The voluntary giving up

781

of citizenship in one's native country to take up citizenship in another.

expert witness A witness, usually well informed about science or some other specialized field beyond the competence of a layman, whose factual testimony and opinions relating to that field are received in evidence.

ex post facto A Latin phrase meaning "after the fact." An *ex post facto* law makes punishable as a crime, or increases the punishment for, an act that was not punishable at the time it was committed, or for which the penalty was then less severe.

express Explicitly set forth in words; stated, not implied.

extortion The act of unlawfully obtaining money or something else of value from a person by violence, threat, oppression or abuse of authority (see section 102). See BLACKMAIL.

extradition The surrender by one government of a person accused or convicted of a crime to the government within whose jurisdiction the crime was committed. Usually, extradition is arranged between sovereign states by means of treaties. Between the states of the United States, it is authorized under Article IV, Section 2, Clause 2, of the Constitution.

extreme cruelty Grave and serious misconduct by one spouse toward the other—such as physical violence, threats of violence, abuse that impairs mental health—that defeats the marital relationship (see section 363).

face amount The amount indicated by the actual language of an instrument, without taking into consideration any accrued interest, dividends or discounts.

factor A person or company employed by a principal to sell merchandise for and in behalf of the principal. Usually the factor is given possession and control of the merchandise, which he then sells in his own name, for which he receives a commission on the sale, called *factorage*.

failure of consideration A term used in the law of contracts to describe a situation in which the event or thing upon which the contract was based (the CONSIDERATION) failed to take place or ceased to exist (see sections 175, 185).

fair comment In the law of libel, a writer's statement on matters of public interest, made in the belief that they are true even if, in fact, they are not (see section 44).

fair market value The price a willing buyer would pay and a willing seller would accept for a piece of property in ordinary circumstances.

false arrest or **false imprisonment** The unlawful restraint or detention of one person by another; any use or threat of force that makes someone stay where he does not want to stay or go where he does not want to go (see section 39).

false pretenses Willful misrepresentation made by one person in order to cheat and defraud another.

false representation A representation deliberately made by a person who knows it to be untrue and who makes it in order to deceive, thereby injuring another (see section 49).

family car doctrine A doctrine that rests on the theory that since a parent furnishes a car for the use of his family, any member of the family who drives the car does so as the parent's agent in pursuance of the parent's "business." According to this doctrine, if a family member inflicts injury by negligent operation of the car, the parent is held responsible for the negligence (see section 254 and chart 15, page 275).

f.a.s. Abbreviation of "free alongside ship," a term used to specify delivery of merchandise to the dock from which it is to be shipped, the shipping and insurance costs to be borne by the buyer from the time of such delivery (see section 188).

fee simple Absolute ownership of property, meaning that the owner has unconditional power to dispose of the property during his lifetime and to pass such absolute ownership to whomever he wishes upon his death.

felonious (1) Of, pertaining to, or involving a felony, as *felonious intent.* (2) Constituting or resembling a felony, as *felonious assault.*

felony One of a number of grave crimes, as murder, rape, arson, burglary, etc., considered more serious than a MISDEMEANOR and punishable by fine and imprisonment or, in some cases, by death (see section 90).

fidelity bond A contract by which the insurer undertakes to indemnify or pay the insured for losses caused by the dishonesty of an officer, employe or agent of the insured.

fiduciary (*n.*) A person who acts for another or handles his money or property in a capacity that involves a confidence or trust. Examples of such *fiduciaries* are executors, guardians and the trust departments of banks. (*adj.*) Like, having to do with or founded upon a trust or confidence. A person who acts in a *fiduciary* capacity, for example, acts for the benefit of another person in a relationship involving confidence and trust.

fine A sum of money required or paid as the penalty for an offense.

fixture Any chattel or article of personal property annexed or affixed to real property with the intention that it become a part thereof (see sections 273, 276).

f.o.b. Abbreviation of "free on board," a phrase indicating that the seller or consignor of goods will place them on board a carrier at a designated place from which they are to be shipped to their destination, the expenses of shipping and insurance from that point to the final destination of the goods to be paid by the buyer (see section 188).

forcible entry and detainer A legal action brought to recover possession of real property that has been forcibly or wrongfully taken by another.

foreclosure Any one of several methods used in various states to enforce payment of a debt secured by a mortgage, by taking and selling the mortgaged property (see section 298).

foreman A member of a grand or petit jury, appointed by the jury or

783

by the court to speak for the jury, preside over its deliberations and communicate with the court.

forensic medicine The science that deals with the application of medical knowledge to the law, as when doctors testify regarding the nature of relatively rare illnesses. Also called *medical jurisprudence.*

forfeit To surrender to an individual or the state money, property, a right or a privilege because of a fault, omission, misconduct or crime.

forgery The act of falsely making or materially altering, with fraudulent intent, any writing that, if genuine, would have legal effect or be the foundation of a legal liability (see section 104).

franchise (1) Rights of a citizen, especially the right to vote. (2) A special privilege, such as the right to operate a bus line, granted an individual or corporation by the government. (3) Permission granted by an individual or corporation to sell his or its product or service under conditions set forth in a contract.

fraud Any act of trickery, deceit or misrepresentation, deliberately performed to deprive someone of a right, to do him harm or to induce him to part with something of value (see sections 49, 185).

full age The age at which a person reaches the period of independent action and responsibility in personal affairs; legal majority, usually twenty-one years (see chart 28, page 428).

full faith and credit A phrase from the United States Constitution, Article IV, Section 1, which provides that "Full faith and credit shall be given in each State to the public acts, records and judicial proceedings of every other State."

fungible Of such a nature as to be easily replaced by another equivalent thing of the same kind, such as grain, wheat, coal or gravel (see section 197).

garnishee (*v.*) To serve a notice of garnishment upon someone. (*n.*) A person upon whom a notice of garnishment has been served.

garnishment A notice to a person holding money or property belonging to a defendant not to turn over the money or property to the defendant but to appear and answer the plaintiff's suit. Many states still permit creditors of wage earners to obtain an order of garnishment requiring the debtor's employer to deduct a specified amount from each paycheck and to pay that amount to the creditor until the debt is paid off (see section 458).

gift (1) The voluntary transfer of property without any CONSIDERATION. (2) The property so transferred.

gift tax A tax on gifts of money or property levied in the United States by the federal government.

goods and chattels A general term denoting personal property as distinguished from real property.

grand jury A jury of from six to twenty-three persons called to hear complaints and accusations of the commission of crimes, to hear evidence produced by the state and to file indictments when it believes from such evidence that a crime has been committed (see section 153).

grant (1) The formal transfer or conveyance of real property. (2) The instrument by means of which such a transfer is made. (3) The property transferred.

grantee The person to whom a grant is made.

grantor The person by whom a grant is made.

gross estate The total value of all the property left by a deceased person (see section 573).

gross income (1) The entire receipts or revenue of a business before any expenditure, such as payment of wages or payment for materials. (2) The total income of a taxpayer from all sources before deductions or exemptions.

group insurance Any of various systems of life, accident or health insurance covering members of a group, as the employes in a business organization, under a single contract (see section 518).

guarantor A person who makes or gives a guaranty.

guaranty A pledge or promise to be responsible for the contract, debt or duty of another person in case of his default or miscarriage.

guardian One who is legally assigned care of the person or property of an individual not competent to act for himself, as an infant or minor (see sections 343, 356).

guardian ad litem A person appointed by a court to represent, in a particular litigation or proceeding, someone who is considered incompetent because of age or mental condition (see section 336).

guardianship (1) The office, obligations or authority of a guardian. (2) The relationship existing between a guardian and his ward (see section 344).

habeas corpus A Latin phrase meaning "you have the body," the name of a number of writs designed to compel the bringing of the "body," or person before a court or judge; especially, the *writ of habeas corpus ad subjiciendum* (Latin for "you should have the body for submitting"), which directs a person having another in custody to produce the person detained in order to enable the court to review the legality of his detention (see section 27).

hearing In criminal law, a preliminary examination by a magistrate or judge of a person accused of a crime to determine whether there is sufficient evidence to warrant holding the accused in jail pending a trial (see section 152).

hearsay Secondhand evidence; evidence derived from something a witness has heard others say; evidence depending on the veracity of some person other than the witness.

heir A person who inherits property, either real or personal, whether by will or by operation of the law from someone who dies without a will.

holder The person who has legal possession of a check, promissory note

785

or bill of exchange and who is entitled to receive payment.

holding company A corporation organized and authorized to hold common stock in one or more other corporations.

hold over To remain in possession after the end of the term, as an office-holder or a tenant (see section 270).

holographic will A will entirely written and signed by the testator or maker with his own hand (see section 530).

homestead Under modern homestead statutes, real property exempt from attachment or sale by a creditor for the homeowner's general debts.

homicide The killing of any human being by another person (see section 120).

hostile witness A witness who, under direct examination, displays such prejudice or hostility toward the party that called him to the stand that such party is permitted to cross-examine him.

hung jury A jury that is so divided in opinion that it is unable to agree upon a verdict.

hypothecate To pledge property as security without the actual transfer of possession.

idiot A person who is born abnormally defective in intellectual capacity and who the law assumes is never likely to attain understanding.

i.e. Abbrevation of the Latin phrase *id est*, which means "that is."

illegitimate child A child whose parents were not married at the time of his or her birth (see section 326).

illicit Forbidden by law; unlawful.

imminent danger A term used in reference to self-defense. It denotes danger of such immediacy that it must be instantly met and cannot wait upon the assistance of others or the protection of the law (see section 149).

immunity Freedom from duty or penalty; exemption, as from tax.

impanel To list the names of persons summoned for jury duty.

impeach (1) To charge a public official before a legally constituted tribunal with crime in office. (2) To discredit or question the veracity of a witness. (3) To challenge the authenticity or accuracy of a document, decree, judgment or something of a similar nature.

implied Intended but not directly or explicitly stated; deduced from circumstances, conduct or language; suggested or understood: contrasted with EXPRESS.

impotence Incapacity for sexual intercourse.

inalienable Not capable of being bought, sold, transferred or taken away.

in camera A Latin phrase meaning "in a room." It is used to describe a case which is heard in a judge's chambers or in a private courtroom from which all spectators are excluded.

incest The crime of sexual intercourse or cohabitation between a man and a woman so closely related that marriage between them is forbidden by law (see section 118).

inchoate Begun but not finished; incomplete or imperfect, as a contract that has not been executed by all parties involved.

incite To urge on to some action; stir up; instigate; more specifically, in criminal law, to urge or instigate another to commit a crime. In this sense, to ABET.

income (1) The return on one's invested capital. (2) The money received from one's labor or business.

in common Owned, used or enjoyed by several persons without division into individual parts.

incompatibility Inability to exist together in harmony. As ground for a divorce, *incompatibility* denotes such deep conflicts in personality as would make it impossible for a husband and wife to continue a normal marital relationship with any degree of success (see section 363).

Incompetence A lack of ability or fitness or of some legal qualification necessary for the performance of an act or the discharge of a responsibility (see section 356).

incorporate To form a legal corporation.

incriminate (1) To charge with a crime or fault. (2) To expose oneself or another to an accusation or a charge of crime. A witness cannot be forced to give testimony that would incriminate himself.

incumbrance Any charge, claim or liability attached to property (see section 284). Also spelled *encumbrance*.

indemnify (1) To compensate for loss or damage that has already occurred. (2) To give security against future loss or damage.

indemnity (1) A contract or agreement by which one party agrees to pay another for an anticipated loss, or to protect him from the legal consequences of the act or omission of one of the parties or of a third person or from the consequences of a condition beyond the control of any of the contracting parties. (2) Compensation given for loss or damage already sustained.

indenture A legal document, such as a deed or contract, to which two or more persons are parties and which is executed by all parties involved.

independent contractor A person who contracts to do certain work according to his own methods without control by his employer except as to the result or product of his work.

indictment A formal written charge of crime presented by a grand jury on oath to the court in which it is impaneled, as the basis for trial of the accused. The indictment is usually prepared by the prosecuting attorney for the government (see section 153).

indorse. See ENDORSE.

infant One who has not attained the age of legal majority, usually twenty-one years (see sections 137, 176 and chart 28, page 428). See also ADULT; AGE OF CONSENT.

787

information An accusation similar to an indictment but presented by a prosecuting or arresting officer on his oath instead of by a grand jury.

infraction A violaton, breach or infringement, as of a law, obligation or contract.

infringement Any breaking in upon, or violation of, a right, privilege, regulation, law or contract: used particularly in reference to the violation of rights secured by copyrights, patents and trademarks (see sections 161, 163, 164).

inheritance In its strictest sense *inheritance* refers only to the passing of real property by descent. More broadly, however, an *inheritance* may be either real or personal property passed by will or through the intestacy of the former owner to heirs designated in his will or by law (see sections 538–540, 555).

inheritance tax A tax on the passing of property (not on the property itself) by descent or will (see section 571).

injunction An order, writ or process issued by a court of equity directing the person named therein to take, or more commonly to refrain from taking, some specified action.

in lieu of In place of; instead of.

in loco parentis A Latin phrase meaning "in the place of a parent." A person *in loco parentis* is one who takes on parental obligations toward a child who is not his own.

innocent purchaser A person who purchases or acquires an interest in property without knowledge (or without sufficient means of knowledge to be charged in law with knowledge) of any defect in the seller's title (see section 189).

in pari delicto A Latin phrase meaning "in equal fault" or "equal in guilt."

in personam A Latin phrase meaning "against the person," used to describe an act or proceeding against or in reference to a specific person. (See also IN REM.)

inquest (1) A judicial inquiry into a special matter by a jury impaneled for that purpose. (2) The investigation by a coroner of the cause or manner of death of anyone who is found dead, dies suddenly, is slain or dies in prison.

in re A Latin phrase meaning "in the case or matter of," used in the title of certain law cases in which there are not opposing parties.

in rem A Latin phrase meaning "against the thing," used to describe an act or proceeding against or in reference to a specific thing rather than its owner.

insane Unsound in mind; deranged; diseased in mind.

insanity Such a total lack of reason, memory and intelligence as prevents a person from understanding the nature and consequences of his or her acts or from distinguishing between right and wrong conduct or from being able to refrain from doing what he or she knows to be wrong (see section 144).

instrument A formal written document with legal effect, such as a contract, a will, a lease or a promissory note.

insurrection A revolt of citizens or subjects against their government.

insolvency The financial condition of an individual or a partnership or a corporation that is unable to pay its debts as they fall due (see section 457).

insurable interest An interest in property (such as the likelihood of financial damage at its loss) or in person (as one based on a blood tie) sufficient to prevent an insurance contract taken out by the interested person from being a mere wager policy (see section 487).

intent The state of mind in which, or the purpose with which, one acts (see sections 36, 37, 121, 122).

inter alia A Latin phrase meaning "among other things."

interest (1) A share in the ownership of property or in a commercial or financial undertaking or enterprise. (2) The price paid for borrowing money, usually a percentage of the amount lent (see section 454).

interim For or during an intervening period of time; in the meantime. A temporary injunction, for example, is an *interim* order.

interlocutory Temporary or provisional. An *interlocutory divorce decree,* for example, is one that does not become final until the passage of the time mentioned in the decree: thirty, sixty or ninety days or more

(see section 365 and chart 26, page 415).

international law The system of laws that regulates the relations among nations.

interpleader A proceeding by which a person who has money or goods claimed by two or more other persons may, for his own protection, ask that the claimants be required to litigate their title between themselves instead of litigating it with him.

interrogatories A series of questions in writing used in the judicial examination of a party or of a witness.

inter vivos A Latin phrase meaning "between the living." An *inter vivos trust,* for example, is one set up by one living person for the benefit of another and becomes operative during the donor's lifetime (see section 545).

intestate A person is said to die *intestate* when he dies without having made a valid will (see sections 555–570).

in transitu A Latin phrase meaning "in transit," used in reference to goods in the course of transportation.

invalid Of no binding force; having no legal efficacy; without authority.

involuntary manslaughter The unintentional killing of one person by another who was engaged in an act that was unlawful but did not amount to a felony (see section 122).

ipso facto A Latin phrase meaning "by the fact itself" or "by the mere effect of an act or fact."

789

issue (1) In a legal action, a single, certain, material point, affirmed by one side and denied by the other, which is to be decided at the conclusion of the pleadings or of the trial. (2) A direct descendant: a child, grandchild, great-grandchild, etc.

jeopardy The danger of conviction and punishment in which a person is put when he is placed on trial upon a valid indictment before a competent court and a jury duly sworn. See also DOUBLE JEOPARDY.

joinder (1) The joining of two or more legal proceedings. (2) The uniting of two or more persons as plaintiffs or defendants in one suit.

joint and several Binding two or more persons both collectively and individually. In a suit against *joint and several* tort feasors (persons who have committed TORTS), a successful plaintiff could recover his damages from any defendant or from all of them.

jointly owned property Property that is owned by two or more persons without regard to the nature of their relationship or how that relationship came into being.

judgment The final determination or adjudication by a court of the rights and claims of the parties to an action; the sentence or final order of a court in a civil or criminal proceeding (see sections 86, 155).

judiciary (1) The department of government in which judicial power is concentrated. (2) The system of courts set up to administer the law. (3) The judges of the courts considered as a body (see sections 7, 8).

jurat The clause in an affidavit attesting that it was duly sworn to at a stated time before competent authority.

jurisdiction A comprehensive term, widely used, which denotes the legal right by which courts and judicial officers exercise their authority; the right or authority by which courts and judicial officers interpret and administer the law, whether in a general sense or in respect to some particular matter (see sections 7, 8, 79). It may refer to (a) the power of a court to render judgment against a specific person (*jurisdiction* "in personam"); (b) the power of a court to hear and determine a particular type of action (*jurisdiction* over the subject matter); or (c) the power to determine the rights of a person regarding property or a status or relation (*jurisdiction* "in rem").

jurisprudence The science or philosophy of law, treating the principles of positive law and legal relations.

jury A body of qualified men and women (usually twelve) selected and sworn in by a local court to try and determine any question of fact, in any civil or criminal proceeding, according to the law and the evidence given (see sections 83, 155).

kidnapping The unlawful seizure and detention of a person by force or fraud; the unlawful carrying off of a person from his residence, his state or his country, usually for the purpose of obtaining ransom.

kin Those related by blood as distinguished from those related only by marriage. NEXT OF KIN are one's closest blood relations (see section 311).

kleptomania An irresistible impulse bordering on insanity, in a person who is otherwise sane, to steal goods of any description.

laches Such neglect, omission or unreasonable delay in asserting a right or claiming a privilege as to warrant or justify the withholding of relief. Laches is a defense against various kinds of suits (see section 81).

landlord The owner of an estate in land who has leased it for an agreed period at a specific rental to another person called the TENANT or LESSEE (see section 270).

lapse The termination of some right or privilege; forfeiture caused by the failure to perform some act or by the failure of some contingency. A *lapse* of legacy, for example, may occur if the person to whom the property is left dies before the death of the person bequeathing it.

larceny The unlawful removal of the personal property of another with the intention of converting it to the taker's own use (see section 132).

last clear chance A doctrine in the law of negligence according to which a person who has the last obvious opportunity to avoid injury to another person is liable if he does not do so (see section 65).

latent Not visible or apparent; hidden; concealed. A *latent defect,* for example, is one so concealed as to be undetectable by a reasonably careful inspection.

lateral support The right of a landowner to have his land supported by the land adjoining it.

law (1) A rule of conduct, recognized by custom or decreed by formal enactment. (2) A body of such rules, considered by men or nations as binding and enforced in any given community by courts, administrative agencies or some authorized official. (3) The profession of a lawyer, attorney, counsel; the legal profession.

lawyer A person licensed to practice law (see chapter 14, page 719).

leading question A question intended to suggest or elicit the reply desired by the questioner.

lease A contract for the use and enjoyment of property, at an agreed rental, for a specific period or during the pleasure of the parties. The landlord is the "lessor" and the tenant is the "lessee" (see section 272).

leasehold Land held by lease.

legacy A gift of personal property in a will; a BEQUEST (see section 540).

legal aid society An organization providing free advice and representation in court to persons who are unable to afford the services of a lawyer. Also called legal aid association. (see section 622).

legislation (1) The act or procedures of making and enacting laws. (2) An officially enacted law or laws.

legitimate In accordance with law; authorized or sanctioned by law; lawful; legal.

legitimate child One born in wedlock; also, one made legitimate by the legal process called legitimation (see section 322).

legitimation The process of making lawful or legitimate something that was not originally so; especially, changing the status of an illegitimate child to that of a legitimate one (see section 322).

lessee One to whom a lease is granted; a tenant holding property by lease.

lessor One who grants a lease; a landlord letting property under a lease.

letters of administration A document issued by a probate court authorizing a specified person or persons to administer the estate of a person who dies INTESTATE (see section 588).

letters testamentary A document issued by a probate court authorizing the executor of a will to act as such (see section 588).

levy (1) To impose or collect; exact, as a tax or fine. (2) To collect money by the seizure of property in satisfaction of a legal claim or judgment.

lex The Latin word for "law," used often in combination with other Latin words to denote a particular kind of law.

liability The condition of being liable or responsible, either for damages resulting from an intentional tort or a negligent act, or for the discharging of an obligation or the payment of some indebtedness (see section 70).

liable (1) Bound or obliged; chargeable; accountable for; responsible. (2) Subject or exposed to some probable event, damage, penalty or burden.

libel (1) A form of defamation, expressed in published writing, printing or other graphic representation, that damages a person's reputation or exposes him to public ridicule (see section 44). (2) In an admiralty court, the written statement by the plaintiff of his cause of action and the relief he seeks.

license (1) Permission granted by an authorized official to perform some act or engage in some business activity (see sections 389, 396). (2) The document that grants such permission. (3) Written authorization by the owner of a patent empowering another person to make or use the patented article or process for a limited period of time in a limited area (see section 161).

licensee (1) A person who enters another's premises with the owner's permission or toleration but without invitation. (2) A person who has been granted a license in order to perform some act or engage in some business activity.

lien A legal claim on property as security for a debt or charge, under which the property may be seized and sold to satisfy the debt (see section 459).

life estate An estate held by a tenant for the duration of his life or the life of some other person or persons.

life insurance trust An agreement between an insured person and a trustee according to which, upon the death of the former, the trustee is to be paid the insurance policy's proceeds for investment and distribution to beneficiaries named by the insured (see section 510).

life interest An interest or claim that does not amount to ownership and which is held only for the duration of the life of the person to whom the interest is given or for the duration of the life of another person, as a widow's life interest in part of her husband's estate (see sections 306, 533, 545).

liquid assets Assets that can be readily converted into cash.

liquidated Settled or satisfied; determined; paid; discharged.

literary property The natural right of an author or his assigns to the exclusive use of and profit from his work (see section 164).

litigation A judicial contest; lawsuit.

living trust A trust created by a grantor during his lifetime: distinguished from a TESTAMENTARY TRUST, which is created by will. Also called INTER VIVOS trust (see section 545).

lobbying The act or practice of attempting to influence a member or members of a legislative body, usually in connection with the passage of a particular bill or resolution affecting the lobbyist's interests.

locus A place; location; area.

lunacy INSANITY. Lunacy was once considered different from other forms of insanity because it was believed to be distinguished by lucid intervals; today the terms are synonymous.

magistrate A judge of a court of limited jurisdiction, as a justice of the peace or a judge in a police court.

maim To injure seriously, as by mutilating or crippling.

majority The age when full civil and personal rights may be legally exercised; also, the condition or status of a person who has reached this age (see section 321 and chart 28, page 428).

malfeasance The commission of an unlawful act, or an act one has no right to commit: used most often to describe official misconduct.

malice The intention or desire to injure another by deliberately doing some wrongful act without legal justification or excuse; also, the wrongful act itself. *Implied malice* is that which is inferred from a deliberate act of cruelty, however sudden, as when a man kills another without provocation. *Express malice* is the deliberate intention to injure another, indicated by external circumstances. *Malice aforethought* is the premeditated intention to do something unlawful, especially the intention to injure another, as by the infliction of serious bodily harm or by the act of murder (see sections 121, 122).

malicious Characterized by, prompted by, resulting from, or involving malice. *Malicious injury,* for example, is injury that is wrongful, intentional and without legal justification or excuse. *Malicious mischief* is the willful, unlawful damaging or destruction of another's property, done with ill will toward the property's owner or possessor. *Malicious prosecution* is a civil or criminal prosecution that is begun with the intention of injuring the defendant, without probable cause to believe the charges can be sustained, and which is terminated in

793

favor of the defendant (see section 40). *Malicious abuse of process* is the willful misapplication or misuse of process to accomplish an unlawful purpose (see section 40).

malpractice Improper, injurious, negligent or immoral conduct in the performance of professional or fiduciary duties; the failure of a lawyer, doctor or other professional man to exercise, on behalf of a client or patient, the knowledge, ability and skill and standard of care commonly applied by similar members of the profession in the area (see sections 395, 640).

malum in se A wrong in itself; an act that is wrong or evil by its very nature, whether or not it is punishable by law, as opposed to *malum prohibitum.*

malum prohibitum An act that is prohibited by law even though it may not be inherently wrong or immoral, as opposed to *malum in se.*

mandamus A Latin word meaning "we command." A *writ of mandamus* is an order issued by courts of superior jurisdiction and directed to public officials, subordinate courts, etc., commanding them to do or not to do something specified in the order that is within the scope of their office or duties.

mandate (1) A judicial command directed to an officer of the court to enforce an order of that court. (2) An order from an appellate court directing certain action to be taken by the lower court from which the appeal was taken. (3) A contract by which one individual acts for another gratuitously.

manslaughter The unlawful taking of human life without malice either expressed or implied. It may be *voluntary,* as a killing that is the result of sudden passion, or *involuntary,* as a death caused by criminal carelessness or as an incident in the commission of some wrongful act (see section 122).

marital deduction For purposes of the federal estate tax, a deduction in computing the taxable estate of property passing to the surviving spouse. Such deduction is limited to one half of the decedent's adjusted gross estate (see section 574).

maritime law That system of laws pertaining to commerce and navigation on the high seas, harbors and coastal waters.

martial law Temporary jurisdiction or rule by military forces in an area where civil law and order do not exist or have broken down. It is really no law, because it suspends existing laws and procedures for administering justice (see section 31).

mayhem The offense of violently injuring or maiming a person's body so as to render him less able to defend himself.

mechanic's lien A statutory lien securing a priority of payment for work performed and the materials furnished by an artisan in constructing or repairing a building. Such a lien attaches to the land as well as the buildings constructed thereon (see sections 296, 392).

mediator A person who tries to bring about an agreement between two parties by reconciling their differences.

merger (1) The absorption of one thing, such as an estate, right or liability, into another thing of greater importance or dignity. (2) The combining of two or more commercial interests or corporations into one, by which procedure all the properties are transferred to the surviving corporation.

metes and bounds The boundary lines of a tract of land, with their angles and terminal points.

military law The branch of law that concerns military discipline and the government of persons employed in the armed forces. Not to be confused with MARTIAL LAW (see section 31).

militia A body of citizens enrolled and trained in military organizations other than the regular military forces and called out only in emergencies.

minor A person who is below that age, usually twenty-one years, when civil and personal rights may be legally exercised (see section 321 and chart 28, page 428).

misdemeanor An offense less serious than a FELONY, but nevertheless a crime, generally punishable by fine or by imprisonment elsewhere than in a state prison or penitentiary (see section 90).

misfeasance The doing of a lawful act in an unlawful or improper way.

misrepresentation Any representation by words or conduct that misleads the party to whom it is made; especially, in a contract or other document, a statement made that is not in accordance with fact.

mistake An act or omission caused by a misunderstanding of law or fact (see sections 139, 140).

mistrial (1) A trial ending without a conclusion on the merits because of some error in its conduct or because of disruptive conduct by either party or by counsel. (2) A trial that is inconclusive because of the jury's inability to agree on a verdict.

mitigate To make less severe; lessen. Circumstances that do not justify or excuse an unlawful act but may be properly considered in reducing punishment for it are called *mitigating circumstances.* The circumstances may also *mitigate* damages in a civil lawsuit (see section 195).

monopoly The exclusive right or power to carry on trade or a business, manufacture a product or control the total sale of a particular commodity. Such right (or power) is vested in one or more persons or companies by privilege (as a government grant) or peculiar advantage (as a corner on a market).

moot Open to discussion; not yet settled; undecided; debatable. A *moot point* is one that has not been settled by judicial decisions. A *moot case* involves an abstract question not arising from existing facts or rights.

moral turpitude Action or behavior contrary to the accepted rules of right and duty between a man and his fellowman or man and society. *Moral turpitude* is characterized by baseness, immorality or depravity.

mortgage A lien upon land or other property as security for the perform-

795

ance of some obligation, usually the repayment of a loan, to become void upon such performance (see section 290).

mortgagee A person to whom a mortgage is given as security for the money he has lent; the holder of a mortgage.

mortgagor A person who mortgages his property to another as security for a loan.

motion An application to a court or judge to obtain an order or rule directing some act to be done.

motive The cause or reason for a person's behavior.

municipal (1) Of or pertaining to a town or city; more generally, pertaining to any local governmental unit. (2) Of or pertaining to the internal government of a state or nation.

municipal corporation A public corporation formed by a charter from a sovereign government for purposes of local civil government.

murder The unlawful, intentional killing of one person by another with malice aforethought, either implied or express (see section 121). See also HOMICIDE; MANSLAUGHTER.

mutiny A revolt by members of the armed forces against their commanders, or by merchant seamen against their captain.

mutuality The state or quality of being mutual; reciprocity. *Mutuality of contract* means that an obligation rests on each party to a contract to do (permit, promise) something in consideration of another party's action or promise (see section 174).

N.B. Abbreviation of *nota bene*, a Latin phrase meaning "note well."

nationality The fact, state or quality of being a member of a nation or state, by birth or by naturalization.

native (1) A person born in a specified country. (2) A person born outside a specified country of parents who were then citizens of that country and not permanently residing abroad.

naturalization The act or process of admitting an alien to citizenship.

necessaries Those things that are indispensable, proper or useful for the sustenance and reasonable enjoyment of life. The term is flexible and has relation in each case to the person's financial and social condition (see sections 176, 336).

negligence The failure to exercise the standard of care that would be expected of a normally reasonable and prudent person in a particular set of circumstances. If the prudent man would act, failure to act is negligence; if the prudent man would not act, to act is negligence. In a suit to recover damages resulting from an unintentional TORT, the plaintiff must prove negligence (see sections 57, 58).

negotiable instrument A check, note, bill of exchange or any other written security that can be transferred by endorsement and delivery, or by delivery only, which gives to the person to whom it is transferred the legal ownership, enabling him to demand the full amount called for on the face of the instrument (see section 440).

negotiate (1) To discuss, arrange or conduct a business transaction, sale or contract. (2) To transfer (a note, bond or the like) so as to make the person to whom it is transferred the legal owner of the instrument.

net (*n.*) The portion of original gross income or assets that remains after the deduction of expenses or losses. (*adj.*) Remaining after the deduction of expenses or losses.

neutrality The status of a nation that does not interfere or side with any belligerent in a war.

next of kin In the law of descent, the person or persons most nearly related to a decedent by blood; also, sometimes, those entitled to share in the decedent's estate according to the applicable laws of distribution (see section 558 and chart 42, page 696).

nolle prosequi An entry of record by the plaintiff in a civil case or the prosecutor in a criminal case by which he signifies that he will not proceed any further in a suit or action.

nolo contendere A Latin phrase meaning "I will not contest it," used to denote a plea by a defendant in a criminal action that has the same legal effect as a plea of guilty. Such a plea does not prevent a defendant from denying the truth of the charges in any other proceedings arising out of the same matter.

nominal Existing in name only; connected with something in name but not in interest; inconsiderable; trivial. *Nominal damages,* for example, are trivial in amount, indicating the violation of a legal right without any important loss or damage to the plaintiff (see section 39).

nominate To propose someone for an elective or appointive office.

nonage Lack of the required legal age to do something (see chart 28, page 428).

non compos mentis Not of sound mind or discretion; insane: a general phrase used to refer to all varieties of mental incapacity.

nonfeasance The failure to perform some act that one ought or is required to perform.

nonsuit (1) Termination of a lawsuit without any judgment on the issues involved. (2) A judgment against the plaintiff in a lawsuit because he cannot prove his case or does not proceed to a trial.

notary public An officer, commissioned and holding a seal of office, who is empowered by state law to administer oaths, to witness signatures or otherwise certify or attest deeds and other documents (or copies of them). Many common documents must be witnessed and stamped by a notary public to be legally valid.

note A signed promise by one party to another to pay a certain sum of money at a specified time and place.

notice Information about or knowledge of the existence of some fact or condition. *Actual notice* is knowledge that may be positively proved to have

797

been communicated to a person directly and personally or that he is presumed to have received personally. *Constructive notice* is knowledge imputed to a person by law, regardless of his actual knowledge, because he could have obtained such knowledge and should have done so because of his particular situation.

novation (1) A substitution of a new debt or obligation for an old one. (2) Substitution by agreement of one debtor for another or of one creditor for another.

nuisance Any thing or practice that by its existence or use causes annoyance, harm, inconvenience or damage. A nuisance is often a valid basis for a civil suit (see section 45).

null Of no legal force or effect; invalid.

nullity An act or proceeding that has no legal effect.

nunc pro tunc A Latin phrase meaning "now for then," used in reference to an act that is allowed to be performed after the time when it should have been performed, with a retroactive effect.

nuncupative will An oral will made by a person in his last illness or extremity before witnesses, sometimes later put in writing (see section 530). Many states do not honor a nuncupative will and instead regard the maker as having died INTESTATE; others will honor it only in specific situations (see chart 41, page 692).

oath A solemn affirmation by which an individual certifies that he is bound in conscience to do something in good faith. An oath often contains an appeal to a personage or object regarded by the person swearing as high or holy, to witness the truth of the affirmation.

obiter dictum An opinion expressed by a judge that is incidental or collateral rather than essential to the main issue before him. See DICTUM.

object To make or raise an objection.

objection The act of calling the court's attention to something that counsel to one of the parties in a lawsuit considers improper or illegal.

obligate To bind in a legal or moral sense or by a legal or moral tie.

occupancy (1) Actual possession of real property without implication of ownership, as in the case of a tenant's *occupancy* of a rented apartment (see section 273). (2) The act of taking possession of something unowned so as to become its owner.

of counsel A term used to describe an attorney who is not the principal attorney, but who is retained or employed as an expert or specialist to assist the principal attorney in the preparation or management of a case or matter where his special knowledge applies.

offense A breach of law; used to refer to both crimes and misdemeanors (see section 89).

offer A proposal to make a contract, containing within itself all the terms of the contract. Acceptance of such a proposal creates the contract (see section 174).

office (1) A position of trust and authority in government or business. (2) A legal right to exercise a public function or employment and to receive compensation.

offset A legal claim that balances, diminishes or cancels another claim. See also COUNTERCLAIM.

ombudsman A government official appointed to receive, investigate and report upon grievances of private citizens against the government.

open shop An establishment employing both union and nonunion labor.

opinion A formal statement by a judge or court; the decision reached in a case tried or argued before him. An *opinion* is an expression of the reasons and principles upon which such a decision has been based.

option The privilege, for which one usually pays, of either buying or selling something at a specified price within a specified time.

oral Uttered through the mouth; consisting of spoken, not written, words, as *oral testimony*.

order (1) A direction, command or regulation. (2) In court practice, any direction of a judge made or entered in writing and not included in the final judgment. (3) A written instrument, drawn by one person and addressed to another, directing the latter to make payment of money or to deliver something to a person named in the instrument. An ordinary personal check is an example.

ordinance A law or statute; specifically, an enactment of the law-making body of a municipal corporation.

orphan A person, especially a minor or infant, who has lost both or sometimes only one of his parents.

overt Open to view; observable; manifest.

owner A person who has the legal or rightful title to property.

ownership The right of a person to possess, enjoy and dispose of property to the exclusion of all other persons; legal claim or title (see sections 158, 159).

pact An agreement; covenant; compact; bargain.

paramount title (1) A title that is superior to another to which it is being compared, in that the latter is derived from the former. (2) Less strictly, a title that is stronger or better than another, or one that will prevail over another when tested in a court of law.

pardon To release a person who has committed a crime from the entire punishment for the crime, even after conviction.

parol A word; something spoken or said. Thus, *parol evidence* is oral evidence.

parole The release of a convict from part of his sentence under certain conditions. If these conditions are not met, the convict must return to prison to serve the rest of his sentence.

parol evidence rule A rule that prohibits the change or modification of

799

a written agreement by any oral agreements made by the parties or their agents prior to the writing, in the absence of a plea of mistake, ambiguity or fraud in the writing (see sections 175, 180).

particulars Details of a claim: used often in the phrase *bill of particulars,* a written statement of the details in the claim of a plaintiff or the counterclaim of a defendant.

partition (1) The dividing of property between co-owners or coproprietors. (2) More specifically, the dividing of lands held by tenants in common, or joint tenants, into separate parcels, so that they may be held individually.

partner A person who has joined with another or others to form a partnership (see section 404).

partnership An association formed by contract between two or more competent persons to combine their money, capital, effects, labor and skill, or any or all of them, in lawful business or commerce and to share the profit and bear the loss in certain proportions (see section 404).

party wall A wall common to two adjoining buildings, built partly on the land of one owner and partly on the other's, for the benefit of both.

par value The nominal or stated value of stock, bonds or other financial instruments.

passport (1) In United States law, a document issued to a person by the government, certifying to his citizenship and requesting foreign governments to grant him safe and free passage and all lawful aid and protec-tion while within their jurisdiction. (2) In maritime law, a document issued by a neutral state to a merchant vessel during wartime, which document is to be carried on voyages as evidence of the vessel's nationality and protection against the cruisers of belligerents.

patent (1) A government grant to an inventor, securing to him for a limited time the exclusive right to make, use, sell and license his invention (see section 161). (2) The instrument by which title to public lands in the United States is conveyed to individual holders.

pauper (1) A person so poor that he is entitled to receive public charity. (2) A person who, because of poverty, is permitted to prosecute or defend a suit without being charged with costs (see section 87).

penal (1) Having to do with punishment. (2) Relating to or containing a penalty.

penalty (1) The punishment set by statute for the commission of some offense. (2) A sum of money stipulated to be forfeited and paid in case of the nonperformance of the conditions or obligations of a contract. (3) A sum of money fixed by statute to be forfeited as a punishment.

pendente lite A Latin phrase meaning "pending or during suit," that is, while litigation is in progress.

pending Begun but unfinished; during the process or continuance of; before the conclusion of. A *pending action,* for example, is one that has commenced but has not been terminated by final judgment.

per capita A Latin phrase meaning "by heads; for each person; share and share alike." It is used often in the law of wills and of descent and distribution to denote a method of dividing an estate by giving an equal share to each of a number of persons (see section 543).

per curiam A Latin phrase meaning "by the court," used to describe an opinion rendered by the whole court rather than by any one judge.

per diem A Latin expression meaning "by the day," used generally in relation to pay for a day's service.

peremptory Not subject to question, debate, delay or reconsideration; final; absolute; arbitrary.

peremptory challenge An objection to a juror made without giving any reason. In selecting a jury each of the parties to a suit is entitled to a certain number of peremptory challenges as well as to challenges for good cause (see sections 83, 154).

perjury The willful giving of false testimony by a witness under oath in a judicial proceeding about some matter material to the issue or point of inquiry. Such testimony may be given in open court or in an affidavit or otherwise (see section 97).

perpetuities, rule against A rule that full ownership of property cannot be postponed longer than a life or lives in being plus twenty-one years.

per se A Latin phrase meaning "by itself; intrinsically; inherently."

per stirpes A Latin phrase meaning "by stock or roots," used often in the law of wills and of descent and distribution to denote a method of dividing an estate by which a deceased person's descendants share as a group in the portion to which their deceased ancestor was entitled (see section 543).

petition A formal application in writing made to a court requesting judicial action concerning the matter set forth in the application.

petit jury The jury that sits at a trial in civil and criminal cases.

pilfer To steal, especially something of small value.

piracy (1) Robbery on the high seas. (2) The unauthorized publication, reproduction or use of another's copyrighted artistic work.

plagiarism The act of appropriating the ideas, writings, musical or artistic work of another without due acknowledgment; especially, the stealing of passages, either word for word or in substance, from the writings of another and publishing them as one's own.

plaintiff The person who begins an action at law, the complaining party in an action.

plea (1) A pleading; also, more specifically, a defendant's first pleading. (2) An ANSWER (n.). (3) In criminal practice, the answer of the accused to the charge made against him.

pleading (1) The art, science or system of preparing the formal written statements of a party to a legal action. (2) Any one of these statements, the aggregate of which are termed "the pleadings." (3) Oral advocacy of a cause in court.

plebiscite A vote by all the enfranchised persons in a state or nation on a matter of great importance to the public interest, such as a proposed change in its constitution.

pledge A security consisting of personal property for some debt or other obligation.

plenary Full in all respects; entire; absolute; complete; unqualified, as certain confessions.

police (1) That department of government whose responsibility it is to maintain order, promote safety, enforce the law and prevent and detect crime. (2) The members of such a department.

police power The power of government to make and enforce all laws and regulations necessary for the good and welfare of the state and its citizens.

poll a jury To examine all the members of a jury individually in order to determine whether or not they have assented, and still do assent, to the verdict.

poll tax A tax on a person as distinguished from a tax on property, especially as a prerequisite for voting.

polygamy The offense of having more than one wife or husband at the same time (see section 116).

possession (1) The having, holding or detention of property in one's power or command; the detention or enjoy-

ment of property by a person himself or by another in his name; the condition under which one may exercise power over a thing at one's pleasure, to the exclusion of all others. (2) Something that a person owns, controls or occupies; property.

posthumous child. A child born after the death of its father (see section 320).

post mortem Happening or performed after death: said especially of an autopsy or examination of a human body made by medical authorities after death to determine the cause of death (see section 599).

power of appointment The authority conferred by one person to a second person, in a will or deed, to name the third person or persons who will receive an interest in an estate of the first person (see section 536).

power of attorney The legal document that grants the authority for one person to act as another's agent or attorney-in-fact (see section 393).

preamble An introductory clause in a constitution, statute or resolution, explaining its intent and the reason for its adoption.

precatory Expressing advice or recommendation rather than command or direction.

precedent An adjudged case or judicial decision that furnishes a rule or model for deciding a subsequent case that presents the same or a similar legal problem (see section 2).

preemption In the United States, a privilege accorded by law to an actual settler upon public lands to purchase the tract settled upon at a fixed price, in preference to all other applicants.

preliminary hearing The hearing given by a judge or magistrate to an accused person to determine whether or not there is sufficient evidence to require the commitment and holding to bail of the accused (see section 152).

premeditation Prior consideration of an act, for no matter how short a period of time, and determination to do it.

preponderance of evidence In a case of contested facts, superiority in weight (determined by value and not by amount) of the evidence presented by one side over that of the other (see section 84).

prerogative An exclusive and unquestionable right belonging to a person or body of persons.

prescription In real property law, a method of acquiring an interest in land or a right in respect to land by using and enjoying it for a period set by statute.

presentment A statement made by a grand jury concerning some wrongdoing, based on the jury's own investigation and knowledge and presented to the court but not accompanied by an indictment.

presumption of fact An inference that affirms or denies the existence of some unknown fact, based on the existence of some fact that is already known or that has already been proved.

presumption of law An inference based on the rule of law that courts and judges are compelled to draw a particular inference from a particular fact or from particular evidence, unless and until contrary evidence is offered that disproves the truth of such inference.

prima facie A Latin phrase meaning "at first view; on first appearance." Something that is assumed to be true or factual in the absence of evidence to the contrary.

A *prima facie case* is a case strong enough that it can be overthrown only by contradicting or rebutting evidence.

Prima facie evidence is evidence that, if unexplained or uncontradicted, would establish the fact alleged.

primogeniture (1) The state of being the first-born child among several children of the same parents. (2) The right of the eldest son to inherit the property or title of a parent, to the exclusion of all other children.

principal (1) Property or capital, as distinguished from interest or income. (2) The employer of an agent (see section 393). (3) A chief actor in a crime, or one who is present at its commission, as distinguished from an accessory. (4) The person primarily liable on a note or a debt for whom another has become surety.

privacy, right of The right of an individual (or corporation) to be let alone, free from public scrutiny and unwarranted publicity (see section 22).

privilege (1) A particular benefit, favor or advantage not enjoyed by all or enjoyed only under special conditions. (2) An exemption, resulting from one's office or position, from a burden or liability to which others are subject.

privity (1) A mutual or successive relationship to the same property rights. An heir is in *privity* with his ancestor. (2) The relationship of mutual interest existing between parties to a contract (see section 173). (3) Private or secret knowledge shared with another or others and usually implying consent or concurrence by those who share it.

prize In admiralty law, property, such as a vessel and its cargo, captured at sea by a belligerent in conformity with the laws of war.

probable cause In a criminal case, a state of facts that would lead a man of ordinary intelligence and prudence to believe that the accused person committed the crime with which he is charged (see section 152).

probate (1) The act or process by which a will is proved and legally established. (2) The act or determination of a competent court that establishes the validity of a will (see section 585).

probation A method of allowing a person convicted of a minor offense to go free under suspension of sentence, but usually under supervision (see section 341).

procedure The established methods of conducting judicial proceedings or hearings.

proceeding The manner and form of conducting business before a court or other legally established bodies.

proceeds Whatever is derived from, or obtained as a result of, the sale of property.

process (1) Any writ or order issued at the start or during the progress of a legal proceeding; especially, a writ issued to bring a defendant into court (see section 80). (2) The whole course of proceedings in a case, civil or criminal, from beginning to end. (3) In patent law, a means or method of effecting a useful result other than by a machine or mechanical device.

proclamation (1) A formal declaration. (2) That which is proclaimed; especially, a matter of great public interest made known by an authoritative official.

pro forma A Latin expression meaning "as a matter of form," used in relation to certain decisions rendered to facilitate further proceedings.

prohibition The name of a writ issued by a superior court commanding an inferior court to desist from proceeding in a matter not within its jurisdiction.

promissory note A written promise by one person to pay, unconditionally, to another person named therein, or to his order or to the bearer, a certain sum of money at a specified time or on demand.

proof Anything that serves to convince the mind of the truth or falsity of a fact or proposition, including evidence for or against it, presumptions either of fact or of law and citations of law.

property (1) The legal right to the possession, use, enjoyment and disposal of a thing; an unrestricted and exclusive right or interest in or to a thing. (2) Anything that may be owned or possessed.

proprietary Having to do with or belonging to an owner. *Proprietary rights* are the rights that go with ownership.

proprietor A person having the exclusive title or legal right to something; an owner.

pro rata In proportion; proportionately; according to a given proportion, rate or percentage.

prosecute To institute and carry forward an action or other judicial proceeding.

prosecutor (1) A person who institutes and carries forward a suit, especially a criminal suit, against another person in a court of justice. (2) A public officer who conducts criminal proceedings on behalf of the state or the public.

protest (1) A formal declaration of dissent by a person who has done or is about to do some act, made to prevent the inference that by such act the protester has relinquished a right or accepted a liability. (2) A formal notarial certificate attesting the fact that a note or bill of exchange has been presented for acceptance or for payment and that it has been refused. (3) A formal statement in writing made by a person called upon to pay a sum of money, as an import duty or a tax, in which he declares that he does not concede the legality of the claim.

prove (1) To establish or make clear and certain, as a fact or hypothesis, by argument or evidence. (2) To establish the authenticity or validity of, as a will.

proviso A stipulation or clause, as in a contract or statute, limiting, modifying or rendering conditional its operation.

provocation Action or behavior by one person toward another that incites the latter to do a particular deed.

proximate cause The direct, immediate cause to which an injury or loss can be attributed and without which the injury or loss would not have occurred (see section 57).

proxy A person empowered by another to represent him, act or vote for him, especially at a meeting (see section 479).

publication In the law of libel and slander, the making of a libelous or defamatory statement to a person or persons other than the one who is defamed (see section 44).

punitive damages Damages awarded to a plaintiff over and above those to which he is entitled, because the defendant has violated one of his legal rights. Such damages are awarded because of the special character of the wrong done to the plaintiff (violent, malicious, fraudulent or the like) or to punish and thereby make an example of the defendant to deter others from acting in the same way (see section 39).

purchase (1) The act of acquiring property by payment of a price of any kind. (2) Any lawful mode of acquiring property other than by inheritance or descent or the mere operation of law.

purchase money mortgage A mortgage given, concurrently with a sale of land, by the buyer to the seller, on the same land, to secure all or part of the purchase price.

putative Supposed; reported; reputed.

quarantine That period of time (originally forty days) during which a vessel arriving from a port or place infected with contagious disease is detained, without being allowed to discharge her passengers or crew or to unload her cargo.

quash To make void or set aside; abate; annul, as an indictment.

quasi Appearing as if; simulating in appearance: often used in combination with English words to suggest a lack of reality. A *quasi corporation,* for example, is a body that exercises certain corporate functions but is not expressly incorporated by statute.

quid pro quo A Latin phrase meaning "something for something," used to describe the CONSIDERATION that passes between parties to a contract, rendering it valid and binding (see section 175).

quorum The number of members of any deliberative or corporate body necessary for the legal transaction of business; a majority of the body.

ransom (1) The amount asked or paid for the return or release of a person held in captivity. (2) The amount paid to an enemy for the redemption of captured or detained property.

rape In criminal law, the forcible and unlawful carnal knowledge of a woman against her will. Compare STATUTORY RAPE (see section 124).

ratification (1) The act of approving, confirming or sanctioning. (2) The acceptance or adoption of that which has been done by another acting as representative or agent, especially where the other did not have original authority.

ratify To approve, sanction, confirm, validate or make legally operative.

re Concerning; about; in the matter of.

real property or **realty** Land and generally whatever is erected on it, growing upon it or affixed to it.

reasonable doubt A degree of doubt that would make a reasonable and prudent person hesitate to accept the truth of a charge. Proof "beyond a reasonable doubt" must satisfy the judgment and conscience of the jury as to the guilt of the accused.

rebate A discount, deduction or refund, as from some stipulated payment, charge or rate.

rebut To contradict, refute, oppose or deny; to defeat a charge or accusation, as by opposing evidence.

rebuttal (1) The act of disproving or refuting something. (2) The introduction by one party of evidence that refutes testimony previously introduced by the opposing party in a trial.

receiver A person appointed by a court to take into his custody, control and management the property or funds of another pending judicial action concerning them (see section 464).

receiving stolen goods The acceptance of property with the knowledge that such property has been feloniously or unlawfully obtained, as by theft, extortion, embezzlement or the like. Receiving stolen goods is a crime (see section 134).

recidivist A person who persistently lapses into crime; an habitual criminal.

recognizance An undertaking or agreement entered into before a magistrate. An accused person is released "on his own *recognizance*" when he is set free, without bail, on his undertaking to return to the court at its direction.

recovery Restoration of a person's right or property, or the obtaining of some right or property taken from him. Recovery is effected by formal judgment in a competent court, at the aggrieved or injured person's instance and suit.

redeem To regain possession of something by paying a price; to repurchase.

redemption The act of redeeming, as the recovery of property that has been mortgaged or pledged.

referee A court officer to whom a pending case is referred by the court. A referee takes testimony relative to the case, investigates it and reports on this testimony to the court, but he does not make the final ruling in the case.

referendum The submission of a proposed public measure or law, which has been passed upon by a legislature or convention, to a vote of the people for ratification or rejection.

register or **registrar** A legally authorized officer whose job is to keep official records, such as the *register of deeds.*

regulate To adjust, order or govern by rule, method or established mode; direct or manage according to certain standards or laws; subject to rules, restrictions or governing principles.

rehabilitate To restore to a former status, capacity, right, rank or privilege; reinstate.

reinsurance Insurance procured by an insurer, from another person or company, against a risk that he has previously assumed.

relation A person connected by blood or marriage; relative; kinsman.

release (1) The act of surrendering or relinquishing some claim, privilege or right to the person against whom such claim may have been exercised or enforced. (2) The conveyance of one person's right in property to another person who is actually in possession of the property.

remainder That part or residue of an estate which is left after all the other provisions of a will have been satisfied (see section 538).

remand To send back; especially, (1) to send a case back to the court from which it came for some further action or (2) to recommit an accused person to custody after a preliminary examination.

remedy A legal method for enforcing a right or for redressing, compensating or preventing a wrong, including money damages, restitution, injunction and performance (see sections 71–75).

rent Money paid for the possession, use and enjoyment of another person's property for a period of time and according to the terms of a lease (see section 270).

renunciation The act of surrendering or disclaiming a right or privilege without transferring it to another.

repeal The revocation of a law previously passed, by the passage of a new law.

replevin A legal action to regain possession of specific personal property alleged to have been unlawfully taken or detained.

reply The answer by a plaintiff to the original plea or response of the defense (see section 81).

representation A statement of fact, incidental or collateral to a contract, made in writing or orally and on the basis of which the contract is entered into (see section 185).

reprimand An official reproof administered by someone in authority.

reprisal The forcible seizure of something from an enemy by way of retaliation or indemnity.

repudiate To renounce or disavow, as a right, privilege or duty.

repugnancy (1) A disagreement or inconsistency between two or more clauses of the same legal instrument. (2) A disagreement or inconsistency between two or more statements of material facts in a declaration or other pleading or in any two writings.

requisition (1) An authoritative, formal request or demand. (2) The seizure of property by a government.

res A thing; an object, subject matter or status concerning or against which a suit is brought.

rescind To make void; abrogate; annul; cancel; especially, to abrogate a contract from its beginning, restoring the parties to the positions they occupied before the contract was made (see section 182).

reservation A clause in an instrument of conveyance whereby the grantor or seller reserves some right or interest out of the thing granted.

residence One's place of abode at any given time, whether it is temporary or permanent.

residuary Pertaining to or constituting the residue or remainder. The part of your estate left after the distribution of specific legacies is your *residuary estate* (see section 538).

residue That portion of an estate which remains after all charges, debts and particular bequests have been paid.

res ipsa loquitur A Latin phrase meaning "the thing speaks for itself," used in reference to a negligence case where a defendant's negligence is inferred from proof that the thing which caused injury was under the exclusive control of the defendant and, further, that the accident was of a kind that does not ordinarily occur in the absence of negligence (see section 62).

res judicata A Latin phrase meaning "a matter decided," used in reference to an issue or point of law that has been previously decided in respect to the parties involved by a court of authoritative or competent jurisdiction. Once decided, the point is not to be decided again.

respondent The party called upon to answer an appeal. If the defendant appeals the decision of a lower court, the original plaintiff becomes the *respondent* in the appellate court (see section 87).

restitution (1) Restoration of the parties to a rescinded contract to the positions they occupied before making the contract (see section 184). (2) Restoration of property to the person entitled to it after the reversal of a judgment under which the property was taken.

restraint of trade Agreements or understandings between companies that are designed to stifle competition, fix prices or otherwise obstruct the natural course of commercial and business activity.

retainer (1) The act of employing an attorney or counsel. (2) The fee which a client pays an attorney to act for him and to prevent the attorney from acting for the client's adversary (see section 619). (3) The right of an executor or administrator to retain from the assets of an

estate enough to pay a debt due to himself before other debts of equal degree.

retroactive law or **retrospective law** A law that relates to and affects actions that occurred before the law came into effect. See also EX POST FACTO.

return (1) The bringing back by a court officer of an instrument to the court from which it was issued. (2) The endorsement made by the officer on such an instrument, reporting what he has done under it. (3) A formal document filed with the Internal Revenue Service for tax purposes.

reverse To annul, vacate, set aside or revoke, as a judgment or decree. An APPELLATE COURT may *reverse* the decision of a trial court (see section 87).

reversion (1) The return of an estate to the grantor or his heirs after the expiration of the term of the grant. (2) The estate so returned to its original owner.

revocation Annulment; cancellation; repeal; reversal; rescission (see section 182).

rider An addition or amendment, as to an insurance policy, contract or legislative bill.

right of way (1) The right to pass over another person's ground. (2) The ground over which a right of way exists, as the strip of land over which a railway lays its tracks. (3) The legal or customary right of the operator of one vehicle or vessel to cross in front of another.

809

riot A tumultuous disturbance of the public peace by three or more assembled persons in a manner calculated to terrorize the people (see section 112).

riparian rights The rights of a person whose property borders on a watercourse, relating to the use of the water.

risk (1) The hazard of a loss of the property covered by an insurance contract; also, the degree of hazard of such a loss. (2) A person or thing considered as a hazard to an insurer. (3) A danger to which a person knowingly assents, thus barring recovery for injuries he may suffer as a result, as in *assumption of risk* (see section 63).

robbery The felonious act of taking the personal property of another from his person or in his presence against his will and under constraint of fear or force (see section 133).

running with the land A phrase used to describe a covenant or undertaking that goes with the land, that is, one that passes to each successive owner of the land, thus making the purchaser subject to whatever contractual obligation the former owner had (see section 284).

sabotage The malicious damaging of property or a deliberate slowdown of work, either to interfere with or to halt industrial production.

sale A contract under which property is transferred from one person (called the seller or vendor) to another (called the buyer or purchaser) in return for the latter's payment or promise of payment of a fixed price of money or property (see section 186).

salvage The compensation allowed to persons whose voluntary efforts save a vessel or its cargo from danger or loss in case of wreck, capture or other marine disaster.

sanction The penalty or punishment for violating a law.

sanctuary A place to which a fugitive from the law might go to avoid arrest and punishment.

sanity Soundness of mind; the reverse of INSANITY; in criminal law, the ability to distinguish right from wrong (see section 144).

satisfaction The extinguishment of a claim or obligation, as by payment, performance, restitution or the rendering of an equivalent.

scandal Defamatory rumors or reports.

sealed verdict A signed verdict placed in an envelope that is sealed and delivered by a judge's order to a court official, usually the clerk of the court, and retained by him until the judge calls the jurors to declare it themselves. Its object is to allow jurors who have reached a verdict to separate temporarily if the court is not in session.

search and seizure The examination of a person's premises or of his person in an effort to find stolen or illicit property or contraband, or to discover evidence of his guilt that may be used in prosecuting a crime with which the person is charged (see section 22).

search warrant A judicial order in writing, directing an officer to search a house or other specified place for things alleged to be unlawfully concealed there (see section 22).

secured creditor A creditor who holds a mortgage or lien upon property of his debtor as security for payment of the debt (see sections 459, 466).

security (1) Something deposited or pledged as a guarantee of payment, performance or appearance. (2) A person who guarantees such payment, performance or appearance; a guarantor. (3) *pl.* Stocks, bonds or notes.

sedition Conduct or language directed against public order and the tranquility of the state; disorder or commotion in a state, not reaching the point of insurrection; also, the stirring up of such disorder, tending toward treason but lacking an overt act (see section 95).

seduction The act of inducing a woman to consent to unlawful sexual intercourse by enticement, persuasion or bribery, but without use of force.

seizure The act of forcibly taking real or personal property into legal possession.

self-defense The defense (or the right to such defense) of oneself or one's family from personal assault or of one's property from destructive violence (see sections 53, 149).

senility Mental and physical infirmity due to old age, often characterized by total incompetence to enter into a binding contract or to execute a will (see sections 356, 531).

sentence The penalty pronounced upon a person who has been convicted by due process of law in a criminal prosecution.

separate but equal A phrase that denotes the doctrine used to justify separation of the white and black races, as in public schools or public transportation where segregated accommodations and facilities are supposed to be equal in quality (see section 24).

separation A stopping of cohabitation (or living together) between husband and wife by mutual consent (see section 361).

separation agreement An agreement entered into by a husband and wife who have stopped or are about to stop cohabiting, providing among other things for support of the wife and children and for the distribution of property (see section 361).

service of process The legal communication of a judicial process to the designated person. Such communication may be made by personal or constructive service. *Personal service* is made by personally delivering a copy of the process to the person concerned. *Constructive service* is made by sending the process through the mails, delivering it to an authorized representative or publishing it in a newspaper.

set off A counterdemand that is made by the defendant to reduce or defeat the plantiff's demand and that is unconnected with the plaintiff's cause of action.

sheriff The chief administrative officer of a county, charged with exec-

811

utive duties in criminal courts and civil courts of record.

shifting the burden of proof A phrase used in litigation wherein the party having the original burden of proof has presented a PRIMA FACIE case or defense so that the other party must rebut it with contradictory evidence. See also BURDEN OF PROOF.

simultaneous Occurring, done or existing at the same time. Thus, *simultaneous death* denotes the death of two or more persons in the same calamity under circumstances that render it impossible to determine who was the first to die or the last to survive (see section 568).

sinecure An office or position for which compensation is received but which involves few or no duties.

sine die A Latin phrase meaning "without a (set) day." Thus, *adjournment sine die* is a final adjournment, without a day set for reassembly.

sine qua non A Latin phrase meaning "without which not," used to describe a thing or a condition that is essential or indispensable.

situs Place; location: the place where a crime or accident occurred.

slander An oral statement of a false, malicious or defamatory nature, tending to damage another's reputation or means of livelihood (see section 44).

solicitor A person who represents a client in a court of justice; an attorney.

solvency The condition of being able to pay all debts or just claims of one's creditors.

sound mind The condition of the human mind in which its faculties are developed to a normal extent and not impaired by a severe mental illness. In the law of wills, a degree of mind and memory that allows for a clear understanding, a recollection or realization of the property to be devised or bequeathed, of the persons who are to receive the bequests and of the manner in which the property is to be distributed among them (see sections 531, 552).

sovereign immunity The immunity of a government from being sued in its own courts except with its consent (see section 37).

specialty A legal instrument or writing, sealed and delivered.

specific performance The actual carrying out, or a proceeding to compel the actual carrying out, of an agreement, as, for example, the purchase and sale of real estate. A plaintiff may often wish to sue for *specific performance* rather than for damages (see section 184).

spendthrift trust A trust created to provide a fund for the maintenance of an incapable or an improvident person. The trustee of such a fund is given the power to distribute only the income to the beneficiary; thus, the principal is kept free from the reach of creditors (see section 545).

squatter A person who settles on land without permission or right.

star chamber (1) Formerly, in England, a secret court held by members

812

of the Privy Council with judges of the courts of common law and no jury. It was abolished by Parliament in 1641 because of abuses. (2) Any court engaged in arbitrary or illegal procedures.

stare decisis A Latin phrase meaning "to stand by decided matters." It refers to the judicial policy of following legal principles established by previous court decisions.

state's evidence The evidence of a person who is an accomplice or participant in a crime, tending to incriminate others and given in the hope of pardon or a lighter sentence.

states' rights Those rights and powers not delegated to the federal government by the United States Constitution nor prohibited by it to the respective states (see section 3).

status quo The condition in which a person or thing is or has been; the existing situation at any given time.

statute A legislative body's written enactment, expressed in the form necessary to make it the law of the governmental unit concerned.

statute of frauds A statute requiring that certain classes of contracts and engagements, and certain memoranda of sales, be in writing and signed by the party to be charged or by his agent (see section 180).

statute of limitations A statute that imposes time limits upon the right to sue in certain cases, such as the requirement that the victim in an automobile accident sue to collect damages within a specified time after the accident (see sections 81, 185).

statutory rape The crime of having sexual relations with a female who is under the age of consent, whether or not she is willing to have such relations (see sections 124, 307).

stay A stopping or suspension of judicial proceedings or the execution of a judgment.

steal To commit a theft; to unlawfully take away another person's property without his consent, secretly and without the use of threat or violence (see section 132).

stepchild The child of one's husband or wife by a former marriage.

sterility The state of being incapable of producing offspring.

stipulation An agreement between the parties to an action or between their attorneys. They may, for example, *stipulate* that certain facts are accepted as true by both sides.

stock (1) The capital or principal fund raised by a corporation through the contribution of subscribers or the sale of shares (see sections 475–477). (2) The proportional part of this capital credited to an individual stockholder and represented by the number of shares he owns. (3) The total merchandise or goods that a merchant or other commercial establishment has on hand.

strike The quitting of work by a body of workers in order to force their employer to comply with a demand for higher wages or better working conditions (see section 386).

subcontractor A person who enters into a contract with a principal contractor to do work specified in the latter's contract.

subdivide To divide land into lots for sale or improvement.

sublease A lease granted by a lessee to another person of all or part of the leased premises for a term no longer than that for which the lessee holds it (see section 272).

subornation of perjury The offense of persuading another person to commit perjury (see section 97).

subpoena A writ commanding a person to appear in court to give testimony.

subpoena duces tecum A writ commanding a person to appear in court with a particular document or paper pertinent to a pending controversy.

subrogation The placing of a person who, acting as a surety, has paid the debt of another in the same legal position as the original creditor, thus giving him the same right to collect on the debt (see section 484).

subscribe To write or inscribe something, such as a name, below or underneath; especially, to write one's signature at the end of a written or printed instrument.

subsidiary A corporation controlled by another corporation that owns the greater part of its shares and thus has control. Also called *subsidiary corporation*.

subsidy Financial aid granted by the government to an individual or private enterprise deemed beneficial to the public.

succession (1) The acquiring of property from the estate of a decedent by will, inheritance or operation of the law. (2) The act or right of legally or officially coming into a predecessor's office, dignity, possessions or functions.

suffrage The right or privilege of voting (see section 19).

suicide The voluntary, intentional taking of one's own life.

sui juris (1) Having the legal capacity to act for oneself. (2) Having full social and civil rights.

suit A proceeding in a court of justice in which a plaintiff demands the recovery of a right or the redress of a wrong (see sections 76–88).

summary Immediate; speedily effected without ceremony or delay. A *summary proceeding* is one in which certain minor causes are handled by a judge without jury and without adherence to conventional trial procedure.

summons A writ directing a sheriff or other public officer to notify some specified person to appear in court and answer the complaint in an action that has been commenced against him.

supplementary proceedings A legal procedure designed to discover the extent of a debtor's property and to apply it to the execution or carrying out of a judgment that has been entered against him by a court (see section 88).

Supreme Court (1) In the United States and in various states, a court of appellate jurisdiction and, in most cases, of last resort. (2) In some states, such as New York, the highest trial court of general jurisdiction though not of last resort.

surcharge To show that an item is missing from a supposedly complete accounting presented to a court for approval, as by the executor of an estate, and that the item should be included to the credit of the party surcharging (see sections 545, 594).

surety A person who agrees to be responsible for the obligation, default or wrongdoing of another.

surname The name of a person's family; the last name of a person.

surrogate A judge or judicial officer who has jurisdiction of the probate or proving of wills, administration of estates and guardianship.

survivor A person who lives on after the death of another.

survivorship (1) The state or condition of being the one person out of two or more who remains alive after the death of the other or others. (2) The right of a surviving party having a joint interest with others in an estate to take the whole estate.

syndicate An association of individuals united to negotiate some business or prosecute some enterprise.

talesman A person summoned as a juror to complete a panel when a regular panel is exhausted by means of challenges or any other cause.

tariff (1) A list or schedule of merchandise with the rates of duty to be paid to the government upon their importation into the United States. (2) A duty levied according to such a schedule. (3) Any list or schedule of charges.

taxable income For income tax purposes, a person's gross income less a standard deduction or itemized deductions plus exemptions for the taxpayer and his dependents.

tax court A federal court with jurisdiction over appeals from tax decisions by the commissioner of Internal Revenue.

tax sale The sale of a delinquent taxpayer's property to collect payment of a tax due from the owner.

tenancy (1) The holding or possession of lands or buildings by any kind of right or title; for example, the temporary occupancy of a house or property under the terms of a lease (see section 270). (2) The period during which a tenant holds or possesses land or a building.

tenant A person who has temporary occupation and use of another person's real property, usually under terms fixed by an instrument called a lease (see section 270).

tenants in common Tenants who have, together, an undivided possession of land, but who hold it by several and distinct titles.

tender A person's formal offer, of money or property, in satisfaction of some claim or demand held against him.

tenure (1) The fact or manner or term of holding or occupying some

815

particular office. (2) Permanent status granted to an employe after a specified trial period of employment (see section 401).

term (1) An interval allowed a debtor to meet his obligation. (2) One of the prescribed periods of the year during which a court may hold a session. (3) The specific extent of time (as a year or a definite number of years) for which an estate is granted; also, an estate or interest held for such a time.

testament A written instrument by means of which a person disposes of his estate, such disposition to take effect after his death. In modern usage, *testament* is synonymous with WILL and last will and testament; strictly speaking, however, the terms are different in that a testament bequeaths personal property only (see sections 527–543).

testamentary (1) Of or pertaining to a will or testament, as a document. (2) Provided or appointed by a will, as a guardian. (3) Founded on, derived from or created by a will, as a *testamentary trust*.

testator (*m.*) or **testatrix** (*f.*) (1) A person who makes or has made a will or testament. (2) A person who dies leaving a will or testament (see section 527).

testify To give evidence or testimony; to state or declare on oath or affirmation before a judicial officer or tribunal; to bear witness.

testimony The statements of a competent witness, on oath or affirmation, before a judicial officer or before a tribunal.

theft (1) In ordinary usage, an act of stealing. (2) More specifically, the crime of larceny (see section 132).

tithe A tax or assessment of a tenth part; formerly, in England, a tenth part of the yearly profits arising from lands, the stock on lands and the personal industry of the inhabitants for the support of the church and the clergy.

title (1) The right to or ownership of property. (2) The grounds whereby the owner of lands has the just possession of them. (3) The union of those elements that constitute legal ownership, divided at common law into possession, the right of possession and the right of property (the last two being to all intents and purposes interchangeable terms). (4) The legal evidence of a person's right of property; also, the means by which or the source from which a person has accrued his right of property.

toll A sum of money paid for some privilege, as the use of a road or bridge.

tort Any private or civil wrong by act or omission, but not including breach of contract (see sections 35–38). Some tortious acts may also be crimes.

trademark A distinctive name, mark or other symbol, often officially registered, which is affixed by a manufacturer to his goods to identify them and to distinguish them from those made by other manufacturers (see section 163).

trade name The name used in trade to identify a particular business, its products or the place where the business is located. A trade name differs from a trademark (1) in that it is not affixed to merchandise or (2) because it is incapable of exclusive appropriation by anyone as a trademark (see section 163).

trade union An organization of people from the same trade or several allied trades, the purpose of which is the protection and promotion of the members' common interests, especially the increase of wages, better conditions or shorter hours of labor, mutual insurance or fringe benefits (see section 382). See also UNION.

transfer The act by which a right, title or interest in real or personal property is conveyed from one person to another. A *transfer tax* is a tax upon a transfer made out of or from a decedent's estate by inheritance, bequest or devise.

treason An overt attempt to overthrow the government to which one owes allegiance (see section 93).

treaty A formal agreement, league or contract, duly concluded and ratified, between two or more nations or sovereigns.

trespass (1) Broadly, any voluntary transgression of law or rule of duty; any offense done to another's person or property. (2) More specifically, any unlawful act accompanied by force, either actual or implied, such as unauthorized entry on another person's land either intentionally or unintentionally (see section 46).

trial The judicial examination of the issues, whether of law or of fact, between the parties to a civil or criminal action, such examination being conducted by a competent tribunal (either a judge alone or a judge and jury) in accordance with the law of the land (see sections 82–86, 154, 155).

tribunal (1) A court of justice. (2) The seat, bench or place set apart for judges.

true bill The endorsement by a grand jury on a bill of indictment that the jurors find the same to be sustained by the evidence.

trust (1) A right of property held by one person (called a TRUSTEE) for the benefit of another (called a BENEFICIARY). (2) The confidence placed in a trustee that he will faithfully apply the property for the benefit of the beneficiary. (3) The property so held; also, the relationship between the holder of the property and the property so held (see section 545).

trustee A person in whom an estate, interest or power is vested under an agreement to manage it for the benefit of another; one who is appointed, or legally required, to carry out a trust.

trustor A person who creates a trust, either by his will or by another trust instrument; often called a grantor.

turpitude Behavior that is contrary to justice, honesty or morality.

tyranny Absolute power arbitrarily or unjustly administered; the exercise of sovereignty in a manner contrary to law or justice; despotism.

ultra vires A Latin phrase meaning "beyond the powers," often used in reference to a corporation's acts or

817

contracts that are beyond the powers defined by the corporation's charter or act of incorporation (see section 405).

unconstitutional Contrary to or in violation of a constitution and therefore void and legally inoperative.

undertaking A promise, engagement, obligation or guaranty.

underwrite (1) To assume a risk by way of insurance; insure life or property (see chapter 11, page 573). (2) To agree to purchase the unsold shares of a certain number of securities to be offered for sale to the public (see sections 405, 480).

undue influence Improper influence exerted upon a person so as to overpower his will and induce him to perform an action he would not freely have performed or not to perform an action that he would otherwise freely have performed (see section 531).

uniform laws Laws approved by the National Conference of Commissioners on Uniform State Laws and adopted by one or more jurisdictions in the United States and its possessions. Their aim is to make laws consistent from state to state.

unilateral Binding or obligatory on one party only, as certain contracts (see section 171).

union An association, as of persons, parties, states or nations, combined for some mutual interest or purpose (see section 382). See TRADE UNION.

unlawful assembly The coming together of three or more persons with a mutual intent to assist one another

in the execution of some unlawful act using force and violence (see section 111).

unlawful detainer The unlawful retention of possession of real property by a person whose right to such possession has terminated and who refuses to quit the property.

unliquidated Unascertained as to amount; undetermined or not settled or liquidated.

unsound mind Incapability of managing oneself or one's affairs; infirmity of mind; INSANITY (see sections 356, 531).

upset price A price at which property is offered at an auction or foreclosure sale, such price being the lowest at which the property may be sold.

usage A customary or habitual practice that is lawful, reasonable and either known to the involved parties or so well established that it is presumed that the parties have acted in accordance with it: evidence of an existing standard of practice.

use The right of one person (called the beneficiary) to the enjoyment of the rents and profits of lands and buildings, the legal title to and the possession of which are vested in another in trust for the beneficiary.

usury (1) The demanding and taking (or contracting to receive) for a loan of money a rate of interest beyond what is allowed by law. (2) Interest beyond what is allowed by law charged to a person who borrows money (see section 454 and chart 35, page 549).

vacancy An unfilled or unoccupied position, post or office; a position, post or office without an incumbent.

vacate (1) To set aside; annul; declare void; rescind or cancel, as a judgment or entry of record. (2) To make vacant; move out; surrender possession of by removal.

vagrancy The condition of a person with no visible means of support who wanders about without a fixed home and who, although able to work, lives without labor on the charity of others.

valid Legally binding; sound, as to form and substance; sufficient or effective in law; that which will be upheld by the courts.

valuable consideration See CONSIDERATION.

variance (1) A disagreement between two steps or two instruments in the same proceeding, which ought by law to agree, as (a) a disagreement between the allegations in the pleadings and the proof in an essential matter or (b) a material disagreement between the writ beginning an action and the declaration or complaint. (2) A waiver of or exemption from a provision of a zoning law.

vendee The person to whom something is sold.

vendor A person who sells something.

vendor's lien An implied lien the law allows a vendor for the purchase price of property for which the vendee has not paid.

venire facias A Latin phrase meaning "that you cause to come." A

writ of venire facias is issued to a sheriff directing him to summon a jury. Also called *venire*.

venireman A person summoned under a writ of VENIRE FACIAS to serve on a panel of jurors.

venue (1) The place where a crime is committed or a cause of action arises. (2) The county or other geographical or political division from which the jury must be summoned and in which the trial must be held.

verdict The final decision or finding by a jury, if there is one, or by the judge if there is no jury, upon the matters or questions submitted for deliberation and determination (see sections 86, 155).

verification A sworn statement attesting to the truth of a pleading, petition, account or any other document.

vest (1) To confer ownership of, as property, upon a person; invest a person with the full title to property. (2) To give a person an immediate fixed right of present or future enjoyment.

vested interest A fixed and present right to the present or future enjoyment of property; the right may be sold or otherwise disposed of.

vested right An immediate fixed right to present or future enjoyment, held by a tenure that is subject to no condition or contingency.

void Having no force or validity; invalid; null; nugatory; ineffectual; incapable of confirmation or ratification.

voidable Capable of being made void, although not necessarily void in itself.

voir dire A preliminary examination of a person, especially of a proposed witness or juror, as to his qualifications for the function or duty in question.

voting trust A trust created by the agreement of a number of shareholders to deposit their stock in the hands of a trustee or trustees. Under such an agreement the shareholders retain ownership of the stock but delegate their power of voting it to the trustee or trustees.

waiver (1) The voluntary relinquishment or abandonment of a right, privilege, claim or advantage, as in a *waiver of immunity* (see section 153). (2) The instrument that evidences such relinquishment.

ward (1) A territorial division of most American cities, made for convenience of management and government. (2) A person, usually a minor, who is in the charge or under the protection of a guardian (see section 344).

warrant (*n.*) (1) A writ directing the doing of an act; especially, a writ issued by a competent authority, directing a sheriff, constable or other officer to make an arrest, a search or a seizure or to do any other designated act in aid of the administration of justice. (2) A document giving a certain authority; especially, a document authorizing payment or receipt of money. (*v.*) (1) To pledge that a fact or facts in relation to the subject matter of a contract is or shall be as it is stated or promised to be. (2) To guarantee by an express covenant the

good title to and undisturbed possession of an estate.

warranty (1) In real property law, a covenant in a deed whereby the grantor binds himself and his heirs to secure to the grantee the estate conveyed to him and pledges, in the event of eviction of the grantee by PARAMOUNT TITLE, to recompense the grantee with other land of equivalent value (see section 283). (2) An assurance or undertaking, either express or implied, by the seller of property, that the property is or shall be as it is represented or promised to be (see sections 68, 69, 190). (3) In insurance law, a pledge or a stipulation on the part of the insured that the facts in relation to the person or thing insured or to the risk are as stated. The validity of the insurance contract depends upon the literal truth of such a pledge (see section 514).

waste An act or omission, causing injury to property, by a person in rightful possession, such as damage or destruction done or permitted to lands or houses by the tenant thereof, or to corporate assets by the corporation's management.

will (1) The legal declaration of a person's intentions as to the disposal of his estate after his death. (2) A written instrument, legally executed, by which a person makes a disposition of his property to take effect after his death (see section 527).

without prejudice Describing a judicial determination that in no way harms or cancels the legal rights or privileges of the parties concerned except as expressly stated. If a case is dismissed *without prejudice*, the plaintiff can bring suit again on the same cause of action.

without recourse Describing an endorsement of a negotiable instrument by which the endorser merely passes it on but accepts no liability to subsequent holders for its payment.

witness (1) A person who sees, hears or otherwise knows something and testifies to it. (2) A person who gives evidence under oath or affirmation, either orally or by deposition or affidavit (see section 85). (3) A person who affixes his name to an instrument executed by another in order to testify to the genuineness of the maker's signature (see section 530).

writ A written order issued by a court, commanding the person to whom it is addressed to do or not to do some act specified therein.

zoning The partition of a municipality into zones by ordinance; also, prescription of the purposes to which land and buildings in designated areas may be put and regulation of the structure and design of buildings (see section 277).

INDEX

Subjects are indexed by page numbers. When there are several references under a heading, the main entry is indicated by page numbers in *italic type*. Glossary entries are arranged alphabetically and are not included in this index. References to material that appears in charts are printed in **bold face type.**

advantages over litigation, 121
appeals from, 120–21
compulsory, 483
Architect(s), 335–37, 491, *497–98*
fee, 336
function, *335–37*
licensing, **492–93**
malpractice, 336
and purchase of development house,
339
Architect's certificate, 336
Architecture, *497–98*
Arkansas, 162
Armed forces, 52, 79, 102, 473,
692–95, 747
burial of members of, *691*
civilians, killing of, 168
social security, 522
unemployment insurance, 532
Arms:
right to bear and keep, *65*, **66–71**,
147–48, 164, 188
Arraignment, 136, *173–75*
Arrest(s), *173–75*, 347–48
citizen's, 79
false, 88, 348
and habeas corpus, 77
resisting, 146
Arson, *55*, *156–57*, **170–73**
Artificial insemination, 371
Artisan(s), *483–87*
customers' protection against, *485–86*
examination of, 484
legal denial of payment to, 487
license required, *483–84*, **492–93**
mechanic's lien, 486
obligation to customers, *484–85*
protection against customers, *486–87*
requirements, 484
Art objects, 585
Assassination, 148, **170–73**
Assault, *90–91*, **124–25**, *155–156*,
166–169, 597
aggravated, 156
criminal, by teacher, 380
indecent, 150
Assembly:
right to freedom of, *57–58*
unlawful, *147*
Assembly, state, *see* State(s)
Assent, in contracts, 201
Assessment of property, 350–51
reduction of, 351

special, 350
unequal, 351
Assets, liquidation of, 558
Assigned risk auto insurance, 293
Assignment for benefit of creditors, *555*
as act of bankruptcy, 557
Atomic Energy Commission, 35, 473
Attachment, writ of, 129, 553
Attorney:
in-fact, 488
at-law, 722
power of, 488
United States, 744
See also District attorney(s);
Lawyer(s); Prosecuting
attorney(s)
Attorney general, U.S., 744
and ban on discriminative job
practices, 454
Attractive nuisance, 105–6, 282–83, 345
Auction, public, of real property for
debt, 343–45
Automobile(s):
abandoned, 189
accidents, *see* Automobile accidents
buying and selling, *239*
payments still owed, *240–41*
chattel loan, 287
defective, recalled by manufacturer,
113, 245
equipment
mandatory in all states, 244
proscribed, 245
family, liability for, 377
financing, *239–40*
guests, obligation to, 106
homicide, 152, *263*
insurance, *see* Automobile insurance
"lemon," 245
loaned, 230, 280
mechanically safe, obligation to
maintain, *244–45*
new, replacement of parts, *245*
warranties on, *245*
operation of, *251–65*
owning, *239–50*
payments, on destroyed or stolen
car, *240*
periodic inspection, 245, **246–47**
registration, 188, *241–44*, **242–43**,
246–47
out-of-state, *244*
rented or leased, liability for, 230, *280*

824

Building code, 335
Building department, approval of new
    houses, 335
Building a house, *334–39*
  changes in specifications, 337–38
  contract, 337–39
  local codes, 335
Bulk transfer laws, 517
Burglary, 73, 151, *157*
  defense against, 101
  insurance, *584*, 588
Burial(s):
  benefits, social security, 527, 611
  cost of, 690–91
  and life insurance, 611, 620–21
  processions, 257
  provision for payment of, *657–58*
Business, *453–534*
  creditors, 517
  ethics, violation of, 192
  financial reports, 513
  forms of, 504
  goodwill, 516–17
  individual ownership, *504*
  lease, 516
  liability insurance, 594, 595
  life insurance, 621–22
  liquidation, 516
  partnership, *505–8*
  price of, 516
  records, *513–14*
  relationships, interference with,
    594–95
  sale of, *516–18*
  taxes, *514–15*
  termination of, *516*
  visitors, 349
  See also Corporation(s);
    Partnership(s)
Business records, 513–14
Buyer(s):
  legal remedies of, *224–26*, 245
  of merchandise, *111–13*
  real estate, rights and duties, *322–23*

California:
  nonoccupational disability benefits,
    531
  teachers' code of ethics, 502
Cameras, insurance for, 585
Canada, 585
  publishing in, 196
Canon law, 26, 404

Capital-gains tax basis, 669, *682–83*
Car, *see* Automobile(s)
Care, standard of, *103–5*, 273, 277, 349
Carpenters, 483
Carrier(s):
  common, responsibility for
    property, 233–35
  private, liability of, 233
Carson, Rachel, 711
Case(s), *see* Civil cases; Criminal
    cases; Lawsuits
Case law, 27
Casualty insurance, 576, *594–99*
  automobile, 283–90
Caveat emptor principle, 111, 227–28
Cemetery plots, *690*
Censorship, 55–57
Certificate(s):
  architects', 336
  birth, 37, **40–48**, 392
  death, **40–48**, *688–89*
    filing, *689*
    in life insurance claim, 624
  of deposit, *561*
  of eligibility, for VA loans, 533
  of fictitious business name, 505
  of incorporation, 509
  of occupancy, 324, 337, 339
  of reasonable doubt, 182
  of title, to car, 241, **242–43**
  withholding exemption, 514
Certified public accountant, 491,
    492–93, *499–500*
Champerty, 734, 740
Charge, in criminal case, *180–81*
Charge account(s), *551*
  account stated, 211
  right to privacy, 72
Charitable contributions, 203
Chattel loan, 37, 224, *240*, *547–48*
  on car, 240
  foreclosure, 554
  See also Security interest
Check(s), *538–42*
  cashier's, *540*
  certified, *540*
  clearance, *540*
  corporation, 539
  endorsement, *541–42*
    blank, 541
    in full, 541
  forged, 144, 542
  kinds, 539

834

Distribution, intestate, 352, 383,
696–703
District attorney(s), 39
District Courts, U.S., 30, **31**, 51–52, 171
District of Columbia, unemployment
insurance, 531
Disturbing the peace, 147, 166
"Diversity of citizenship," 30
Dividend(s), stock, 515, 563–64
See also Life insurance
Divorce, 34, 165, *403, 406–14*, **408–13**
action, 406–7, 414
alimony, 418
decrees, 402, 414, **415–16**
defense of condonation in, *417*
interlocutory, 414
and intestacy, 667
lawyers, 401–2, 406–14
and life insurance beneficiaries,
609–610
Mexican, 407
property settlement, 352, 414, 419
records, **40–48**
Divorce court, 406
Doctor(s), 491, **492–93**, *494–96*
in automobile accident, 266–67
fee, 495
liability insurance, 596
malpractice insurance, 494
and violation of medical ethics, 496
Documents, checklist of, 662–63
Domestic help, 452, 455, *474–75*
Domicile:
father's, as children's residence, 377
of married couple, 362
Door-to-door sales, 223
Double indemnity, 625, 635
Double jeopardy, 77
Dower, wife's right of, 352, **353–56**,
650–53
Draft-card cases, 139
Driver(s), of automobiles:
condition of, in automobile accident,
278–79
handicapped, 279
ill while driving, 263, 279
legal action against, after accident,
272
safety record, and automobile
insurance, 291
Driver education courses, **252–55**
insurance rate factor, 291–92
Driving:

drunken, 167, 263–64
with due care, *259–60*
examinations, 251, **252–55**
reckless, *260*
regulations, *256–59*
when ill, *263, 279*
Driving license(s), *251*, **252–55**, 262–64,
428–31
Drugs:
addiction to, **66–71**, 166, 205,
408–13, 627
sale of, 166, 216
Drunkenness, *see* Alcoholism
Dry cleaning, responsibility for
property, *230–31*
Due process, *73–74, 76–78, 172*, 188
Dues, union, 478
Duress, *63*, **408–13**, **440–47**
as defense in breach of contract, 215

Earthquakes, 79
Easement, in title, 321
Education, *see* Schools
Election(s), **63–64**
primary, all-white, 65
state, regulation of, *62–65*, **63–64**
Election, right of, 352, 649, **650–53**, 678
Electricians, 483, 486, **492–93**
Electricity, 582
Electronic listening devices, 65–72
Embalming, 691
Embezzlement, 160–61
Embracery, 146
Emergency vehicles, 275
Eminent domain, 34, 342–43
Employe(s), 453–83, **456–57**, **466–67**
accident caused by, 464
as agent of employer, 85–86, 463
and auto accident liability, *281*
federal, 454–55, *471–74*, 522
in unions, 474, 482
garnishment of wages, 130, **131–32**,
471, 553
group life insurance for, 604, 606
labor unions, 474–83
law of, *462*
legally striking, 480
rights and duties of, *464–70*
safety and working conditions,
459–60
social security, *521–28*
suit for wages, 458–59, 470–71
training of, 470

838

advantage of accused, 39
and basic rights of citizens, *52–54*
federal,
    and liens for unpaid taxes, 344, 471
    life insurance, 607–8
    sovereign immunity, 86, **448–50**
    and unemployment insurance, 521,
        531–32
    officials performing marriages,
        363–66
    power of condemnation by, 342
    protection of citizens' social welfare,
        521–22
    See also Civil Service
Grace period, 552, 628
Grandchildren:
    inheritance rights of, 667
    provision for, in will, 654
    support of, 398
Grandparents, support of, 398
Grants, government, for neighborhood
    law offices, 719
Group (health) insurance, *628–33*
    accidental death and dismemberment
        policies, 632–33
    claims, 633–34
    dental insurance, 632
    dependents covered, 632
    disability income, 632
        time limit on claims, 634
    dread disease, 633
    hospitalization, 628–29
    major medical, 630
    making claim, *633*
    nursing care, 629
    optional features, *629*
    payment of, 633–34
    physicians' attendance, 633
    psychiatric care, 630–32
    travel accident, 633
    types, 628–33
    See also Health insurance
Guarantees on condition of house
    for sale, 318
Guardian(s), *388–400*, 687
    ad litem, 373, 382, 388
    appointing, in will, *659–60*
    court appointment, of, 665
    and education of child, 377
    for incompetents, 398–400
    legal, when needed, *388*
    permission for junior driver, 251
    of person, 388, 399–400

of property, 388, 399–400, 660
public agencies as, 372
and wards, *388–89*
Guests:
    auto, liability for, **275–76**, *281–82,*
        286
    hotel, liability for property, 235–36
    house, liability for, 105–6, 348–49,
        591, 594
Guns, **66–71**, 148, 188
    See also Arms

Habeas corpus:
    right to, 77
    suspension of, 79
    writ of, application for, 182, 401
Hand, Judge Learned, 57
Hatch Act of 1939, 473
Health departments, 37
Health insurance, *625–28*
    benefit clause, 626
    claims, 636
    coverage for sickness or accident, 627
    disability under, 626
    exceptions, limitation and
        reductions on, 626–27
    grace period, 628
    insuring clause, 625–26
    private, *634*
    time limit on coverage, 627
    waiting period, 627
    See also Blue Cross; Blue Shield;
        Disability insurance; Group
        (health) insurance; Hospital
        insurance
Heirs, receipt of inheritance, *685–86*
Herbert, A. P., 104
Highways, 36, 241–44
Holmes, Oliver Wendell, Jr., 749
Holographic will, **643**
Home, *see* House(s)
Homeowner(s):
    defense of property, **66–71**
    deficiency judgment against, 340
    duties of, 164, *348–51*
    foreclosure, **341**, 342
    homestead rights, 344, 352
    and the law, *347–52*
    liability insurance, 116, 589–91
    rights of, *347–48*
        to redeem property, 342
    wife's, *351–52*
Homeowners insurance, 116, *580–91,*

841

double indemnity, 625, 635
duties of insured party, 597–98
employers', required, *461–62*
Federal Deposit Insurance
	Corporation, 545, 579
flight, 607
floaters,
	all-risk policy, *584–86*
	coverage, 585
	personal effects, 585–86
		exclusions, 586
	valued basis, 588
flood, 579
fraternal, *620–21*
government-administered, *578–80*
group, 465, *628–33*
homeowners, *580–93*
insurable interest of mortgagee, 593
loan, 579
major medical, *630*
malpractice, 596
by minors, 601
mortgage, rights and obligations,
	592–93
nature of, *575–80*
postal, *591–92*
premiums, 575, 576
property, *580–93*
	filing claim for, *586–87*
	on rented premises, 307–8
protection, start of, *576–77*
retirement, *617–18*, 620
	See also Accident insurance;
		Casualty insurance; Fire
		insurance; Health insurance;
		Liability insurance; Life
		insurance; Title; Unemploy-
		ment insurance
Insurance agent, 575–76
Insurance brokers, 293, *575–76*
Insurance claims adjuster, 267, 293–96,
	577–78
Intent, 83
	deliberate, 84
	to interfere with personal rights,
		87–93
	to interfere with property rights,
		94–98
	in torts, 85
Interest, *545–51*, **549–50**
	and amortization, 333
	on installment sales, 224
		rate, 240

limited, on FHA and VA mortgages,
	329, **331**
on loans, 545
rates and mortgage "points," 330
on savings accounts, 542, 544, 560–61
usurious, **549–50**, 551
Internal Revenue Code, 30, 61
Internal Revenue Service, 72, 514, 606,
	672, 673, 740
and estates, audit, 686
Keogh plans, 618, 620
International Consumer Credit
	Association, 72
Interstate commerce, workmen's
	compensation, 111
Inter vivos trust, 656
Intestacy, 383, 639, 640
	adopted child's inheritance, **394–95**,
		667
	distribution of estate, *665–66*,
	and divorced or separated husband
		and wife, *667*
		696–703
	meaning and dangers of, *664*
	testamentary pattern, 666
Intoxication, *see* Alcoholism
Inventory, of insured items, 587
Investment(s), *560–71*
	private, *562–64*
Investor(s), legal protection of, *568–70*,
	571–72
Invitees, obligation to, 106–7, 349
IOUs, 546
Italy, 58

Jefferson, Thomas, 722, 724
Jehovah's Witnesses, 74
Jewels, 584, 586
Job(s), *See* Employment; individual
		occupations and professions
Joint property, 352, 367–68, 671, 675
	bank accounts, 188, 539, 675
Judge(s):
	Anglo-American, freedom of, 39
	in civil case, 126–28
	contempt of court, 139–40
	in criminal case, charged by, 180
	exception to ruling of, 127
	immunity of, from libel or slander
		suits, 93
	impartiality, 38–39

law clerks for, 745
  responsibility of, 126
  role of, in juvenile cases, 385
  of state and local courts, 27
  trial, 34
Judgment, *128*
  attachment, writ of, *129*
  collecting amount of, 130
  debtor, 130
  by default, 268
  deficiency, 340, 344
  enforcement of, *129–30*
  garnishment, 130, **131–33**, 471
  money, 129
  notwithstanding verdict, 181
Judgment-proof individuals, 114
Judicial authority, offenses against,
    138–50
Judicial review, right of, 29–30
Jurisdiction, 122
Juror(s), challenges to, 177
Jury(ies), 79
  in divorce cases, 407
  grand, *175–77*
    authority of, 175
    citizen's right to, 55
    composition of, 175
    duty of, 175
    evidence received by, 175
    and felonies, 136
    and immunity from prosecution, 76
    indictment by, 176
  interference with, *146*
  size of, 78, 126
  sympathy to injured, 120
  trial by,
    in civil cases, 120, 126–28
    in criminal cases, 177–81
    in England, 26
    right to, *77–78*
  verdict, 181
Justice, obstruction of, *146*
Justice of the peace, **33**, *171*
Justinian I, Emperor, 26
Juvenile court, **33**, 163, 384–85,
    394–95, 432–39
Juvenile delinquent(s), 162–64, 383–86,
    432 39
  constitutional rights and treatment
    of, 163–64
  family courts and, 32
  wayward minor, 359, 384, *386–87*

See also Youthful offender(s)
Juvenile offenders, *see* Youthful
  offenders

Kennedy Library, 713
Kentucky, teachers' professional
    practices commission, 502
Keogh plans, 618, 620
Kidnapping, *156*, **170–73**
Kleptomania, 166
Korean War, 608

Labor-Management Relations Act of
    1947, 460–61, 478, 482
Labor practices, unfair, *460–61*
Labor unions, *475–83*
  agreements, 514
  closed shop, 477, 479
  collective bargaining, 476–77, 479, 483
  company, 460, 476, 479
  compulsory, 477
  craft, 475
  employers' recourse against, 479
  excessive fees banned, 478
  and government employes, 474
    482–83
  independent, 476
  industrial, 475
  joining, *477–79*
  management actions affecting, *479–80*
  recruitment by, 478
  right-to-work law, *453–55*, **456-57**
  role of, *475–77*
  strikes and lockouts, 480, 482–83
Laches, doctrine of, 123, 192
Lading,
  bill of, 220
  stated liability limit on, 235
Land, standards of care by owner, 105,
    349
Landlord(s):
  complaint, 310–11
  duties, 302–4, 307
  eviction by, 309–11
  failure to provide service, 307
  liability insurance, 595
  lien on tenant's property, 311
  obligation to make repairs, 307
  relations with tenant, 299–313
  rules and regulations, 305
  trespass by, 306
Landrum-Griffin Act of 1959, 479

social security for, 527–28
Release, insurance, 295, 578
Released time, 60
Religion:
  in adoption, 391
  discrimination outlawed in schools, 378
  established, 58
  freedom of, *58–62*
Religious property, 61–62
Rent:
  failure to pay, 309
  meaning of, 299–300
  strike, against landlord, 307
Rental agent, *300*
Rent control laws,
  local, 300
  and statutory tenant, 312
Repair, responsibility for property left, *230–31*
Replevin, 225
Repossession:
  of auto, 240–41
  of goods, 224, 225, 547–48, 553
Representatives, U.S., 27, 65, *93*
Reputation, interference with, *92–93*
Rescue, crime of, 141
Residential requirements:
  auto registration, **242–43**
  divorce, **408–13**
  marriage, **420–27**
  voting, **63–64**
Res ipsa loquitur doctrine, 107
Resisting arrest, 146
Restrictions, in title, 320–21
Retainer, 118, 724
Retirement:
  annuities, 620
  pension plans, 523, 618
  and social security coverage, 523–24
  tax sheltered plans (Keogh), 618
Retirement insurance, *617–20*
Revolution and sedition, 139
Revolutionaries, and rights of freedom of speech and press, 57
Rhode Island, nonoccupational disability benefits, 531
Rifles, **66–71**, 148
  See also Arms
Right(s):
  of accused, *76–78, 172*
  of assembly, *57–58*
  to bail, 173–74, 175

to bar public officials from property, 347
to bear arms, 65
of citizen, *51–78*
constitutional, *54–78*
of defendant, not to appear before grand jury, 176
to discipline children,
  of parents, *371*
  of schools and teachers, *379–80*
against double jeopardy, *77*
to due process of law, 76–78
to equal protection of the laws, *74–75*
to freedom of press, *54–57*
to freedom of religion, *58–62*
to freedom of speech, 54–57
to habeas corpus, *77*
to hold public office, *65*
as homeowner, *347–48*
of inheritance of family members, 667–69
interference with,
  intentional, *87–98*
  unintentional, *102–7*
to jury trial, *77–78*
of minor children, *382–83*
of minors, *370*
personal,
  interference with, *87–93, 103–7*
to property, 73–74, 83, *187–89,* 347–48
  interference with, *94–98,* 103–7
riparian, 187
against self-incrimination, *75–76*
of spouse, 367
squatter's, *95, 345,* **346**
states', 53
of stockholder, *512–13*
suspensions of, 78–79
of unborn children, *370*
of veterans, under GI Bill, *532*
to vote, *62–65*
widower's,
  of curtesy, 352, **353–56,** 649
  of election, 352, **650–53**
widow's,
  of dower, 352, **353–56**
  of election, 352, **650–53**
  of homestead, 352, **353–56**
to work, *453–55,* **456–57**
Right of way, property, 95–96, 321, 345–48, **346**
Riot, *147,* 582

855

distinguished from unlawful
assembly, 147
incitement to, 55, 147
conspiracy for, 139
Riparian rights, 187
Risk:
assumption of, *108*
and contributory negligence, 110
Road, conditions, and auto accidents,
277
Robbery, 151, *157*, **170–73**
armed, 159
insurance, *584*
Roman Catholic Church, 58
Roman law, 25–26

Safe-deposit box, 560
Safekeeping, responsibility,
lawyer's, for will copy, 662
for property left in, *232–33*
Safety, employe, laws, 459–60
Salaries, 462–64, 470–71
garnisheed, 130, **131–33**, 471
exemption from, 553
minimum, **466–67**
Sale(s), 218–28, *458–59*
bill of, 190
conditional agreement, 37, 224
contract for, 218, **124–25**
credit, *223–24*
door-to-door, *223*
installment, *223–24*
mail order, *223*
real property, *313–327*
Salesman, *487–91*
Satisfaction, of contract, 210–11
Savings account(s), *542–45*
inheritance of, 669
as investment, *560–61*
loan against, for auto, 239
Savings and loan associations, 544,
579
Schizophrenia, 167
School(s):
bus, 257
compulsory attendance, 377, **428–31**
discipline, 102, *379–80*
expulsion or suspension of child, 377
for handicapped, 378
parent-child relations and, 377–81
parochial, 60, 377, 378
public funds for transportation,
58–60

public, religious instruction in, 60
punishments allowed, 379
right to discipline child, *379–80*
separate but equal facilities, 74
School board:
discharge of teacher, 503
liability for student injury, *380–81*,
448–50
parent suit for disciplinary action,
379–80
Schoolbooks, 378
Search and seizure:
unlawful, 178, 181
unreasonable, 65
Search warrant, 72, 347
lack of, 91
Securities and Exchange Commission,
35, 512, 568–70
jurisdiction, 569–70
and rights of stockholders, 570
stock reports filed with, 570
supervision of exchanges, 570
Security(ies), *see* Bonds; Stocks
Security interest, 224, 547–48, 554, 558
Sedition, *139*
Self-defense:
defense to criminal charge, *170*
defense of privilege, *100–102*
Self-employment, *483–87*, *491–500*
federal income tax return and, 534
retirement plans (Keogh), 618–20
social security, 521, *523*
Self-incrimination, 176
right to protect self against, 75–76
Seller(s):
legal remedies of, *226–27*
as nonowner of goods sold, *221*
of real estate,
payments to, in house closing, 326
and purchase money mortgage, 330
rights and duties of, *322–23*
right to rescind contract, 226–27
Senate, U.S., 27
Senator(s), U.S., 65, 93
Sentence, in criminal case, *180–81*
Separation, *402–4*, **408–13**
agreement,
and divorce, 414
formal, 403
as private contract, 414
definition, *402*
Servicemen's Group Life Insurance, 608

856

859

breach of contract suit against,
304, 306, 307
relations with, *299–313*
liability insurance and, 307–8, 595
right to enjoyment of property,
306–8
statutory, 300, 312
at will, 299, 308, 311
Tennessee Valley Authority, 712
Tenure, 502, 503
Testamentary, letters, 679, **680–81**
Testator, 639, 655
Theft, 114, 161
insurance, 584
Therapist, physical, licensing, **492–93**
Thieves, judgment-proof, 114
Third parties, as agents, *490–91*
Threat, 163
Time deposit:
certificate, 561
rates controlled by Federal Reserve
Board, 561
Tires, warranties on, *248–50*
Title:
auto, **242–43**
to goods, 218–21
owner of, *218–19*
Title, real estate:
chain of, 319
encumbrances or defects in, 318,
319–21, 322
held by trustee, 340
insurance, 317, *321–22,* 324
fee-title, 322
mortgage policy, 322
owner's policy, 322
premium and, 322, 326
legally enforceable, 325
Tort(s), *83–98, 102–7*
abuse of process, malicious, 90
commission of, *117–24*
and crime, distinction between,
83–87, 135–36
defenses to, 98–102, 108–9
definition of, 83
intentional, 87–98
law of, *109–10*
lawsuits, 117–26, **124–25, 217,**
275–76
liability, *86–87*
of husband and wife, 368, **369**
of parent, 86, 87, 281, *374–77,*
375–76

of schools, **448–50**
malicious prosecution, 89
negligence, 83, 84, 87, *102–13,*
221–23, 348–49
in auto accidents, 251–60, 263–64,
277–79
responsibility,
for damages, 85
for persons who commit, *85–86*
of schools, *380–81,* **448–50**
trespass as, 147
Toy, injurious, responsibility for, 112
Trademarks, *193*
Trade names, *193*
Trade secrets, law of, *192–93*
Traffic:
court, 32, **33**
rules and regulations, *256–59*
violations,
charges and defense, 260, *261–64*
by minor, 385
Trailers, auto, *265*
Transcript, court, 128
Transit, responsibility for property in,
219–20, *233–35*
Transplants, organ, 689
Treason, 137, *138*
Treasury, Department of the, 35, 515
bills, interest on, *561–62*
Trespass:
criminal, 147
distinguished from burglary, 157
tort, 85, 95, **124–25,** *347–48*
by landlord, 306
Trespassers, property owners'
liability to, 105–7, 348–50
Trial(s), 76
as adversary proceedings, 38–39
in civil cases, 126–28
in criminal cases, *177–78*
motions, *181–83*
results and appeals, 181–82
rights of accused, 55, 76, 77, 136,
172
verdicts, 128, 181
See also Jury(ies)
Truancy, 377, 383
Trust(s):
accumulative, 657
charitable, 657
income from, 649
beneficiary of, 656, 686
inheritance, payment of, *686–87*

860